This publication is sponsored by the Association of Lifecasters International (A.L.I.). A.L.I is an international artists guild made up of approximately 1500 members worldwide. For more information, please see: www.lifecastng.org.

The Casting of Angels

The fine art of life casting

by

David E. Parvin, A.L.I.

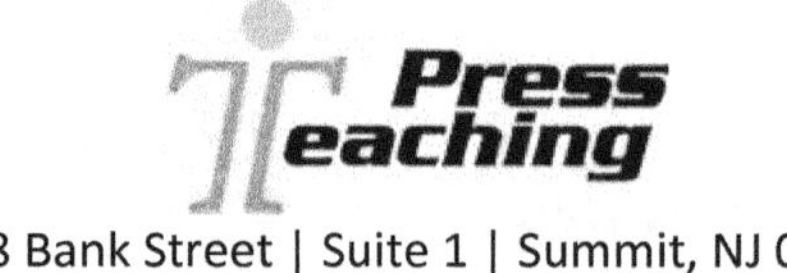

18 Bank Street | Suite 1 | Summit, NJ 07901
Telephone (908) 273-5600

Second Printing, May 2015

Library of Congress Control Number: 2015942122
ISBN 978-0-692-45473-2

Edited by Ed McCormick

Printed in the U.S.A.

Introduction

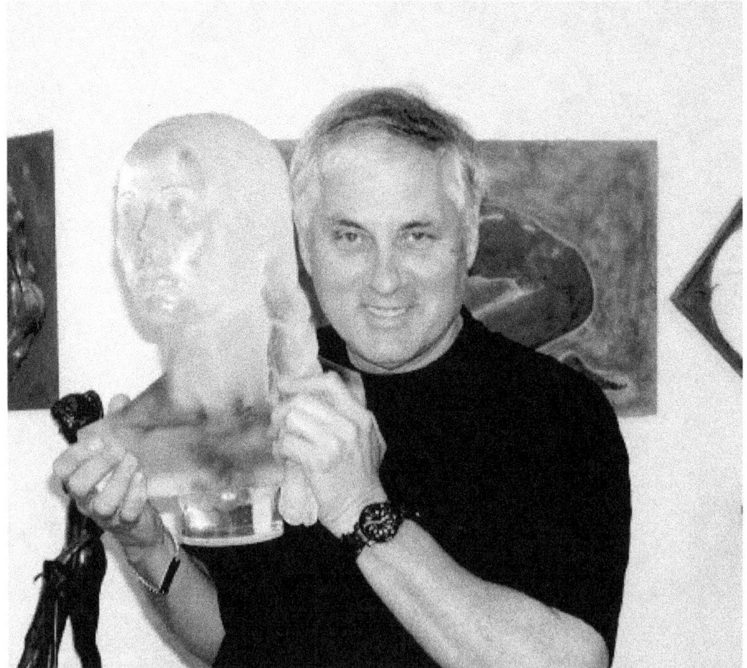

David E. Parvin in his studio in Denver, Colorado.

Pilot, sculptor, author and renown life casting artist, David E. Parvin passed away on October 25, 2014 at his home in Aurora Colorado. He was 71 years old. He was many things to many people, but above all, he was a great friend to those who knew him and admired this multi-talented man.

Dave, as he liked to be called, was born in the Midwest on February 23, 1943, raised in the Northwest and lived in Colorado for over 30 years. Although he attempted to sculpt before his third birthday, the road to becoming a professional sculptor had several detours: studying for the priesthood, earning a bachelor of science in natural science from Seattle University, flying helicopters for the Marines in Viet Nam, remaining married for thirty-five years, raising a son to manhood and becoming a grandfather.

He is a self-taught artist whose primary subject was the human form which he executed in a classical realist manner. Though principally known for his bronzes, he has also worked in wood, concrete, polyurethane, polyester, Forton MG, pewter, acrylic, glass and raku. Through his work, Dave became internationally recognized as a life casting expert and contributed many new techniques and materials to this art form. He was one of the artists to be honored with a lifetime membership in the Association of Lifecasters International (A.L.I.), and was one of only six to be certified as life casting instructors by the same institution.

Because Dave always felt an obligation to pass on his artistic experiences, he taught workshops on life casting, figurative sculpture and making a living as an artist. He has traveled by invitation as far as London, England and Australia to lecture.

He has written over sixty articles on various aspects of sculpting for a variety of art publications which we a pleased to present here in this volume of *The Casting of Angels.*

Contents

Life Casting.. 5

1. Life Casting, Fine Art of Cheating...6
2. Danger, Will Robinson..9
3. Standard Life Casting Compositions 13
4. The Perfect Model..16
5. Life Casting a Head in the Round Part 1 18
6. Life Casting a Head in the Round Part 2 23
7. A Little More Complicated Portrait Casting 28
8. Easily Eliminate Air Bubbles 32
9. Casting Perfect Ears..35
10. Don't Get Your Nose Out of Shape 40
11. Give Me A Hand 42
12. How to Cast a Dancers Foot...44
13. How to Patina a Life Casting..50
14. If it Looks Like a Duck 52
15. Life Casting Hair Part 1 56
16. Life Casting Hair Part 2 59
17. Making a Life Casting Mermaid Portrait 61
18. More Helpful Tricks in Life Casting..63
19. Photographs During Life Casting..65
20. Secondary Molds in Life Casting Part 1 68
21. Secondary Molds in Life Casting Part 2 72
22. Supporting the Model in Life Casting Part 1.......................................77
23. Supporting the Model in Life Casting Part 2.......................................81
24. When Two Heads are better than One 84

The Business of Art 86

1. Casting for Profit Part 1...88
2. Casting for Profit Part 2...90
3. Casting for Profit Part 3...93
4. Casting for Profit Part 4...96
5. Pricing for Beginners 99
6. The Good ,and the Bad ,and the Ugly 101

Mold Making.. 103

1. How to Make a Great Mold Part 1...104
2. How to Make a Great Mold Part 2...107
3. How to Make a Great Mold Part 3...110

1. How to Make a Secondary Mold 113
2. Solving a Mold Making Problem 118
3. Another Little Trick for Some Molds 120
4. Size Matters 122
5. Bas Relief on the Cheap 126

Materials 129

1. An Alternate to Using Plaster Bandages 130
2. More Uses for Cheesecloth 134
3. Another Use for Cheesecloth 137
4. How to Extend the Setting Time for Alginate 139
5. Forton MG Part 1 143
6. Making a Mold Using Alginate 146
7. Mixing Alginate 149
8. Mixing Forton MG 152
9. New Product, New Life Form 154
10. Putting MoldGel SILFREE To the Test 156
11. Testing FiberGel Alginate 158
12. Urethane and Acrylics 162
13. Test the Water Trap 165

Equipment 167

1. Acquiring a Pressure Chamber 168
2. Another Source for Vacuum Pumps 172
3. Making a Pressure Chamber 174
4. Making a Vacuum Chamber 176
5. Putting ArtMolds Pressure Chamber to the Test 178
6. Putting a Pressure and Vacuum Chamber to Use 184
7. The Revo Vacuum System 186
8. Using Vacuum and Pressure in Casting 189

Modeling 192

1. Making a 3-D Faerie Portrait 193
2. Faerie Portrait 197
3. Guy Louis XVI 198

Life Casting Instruction

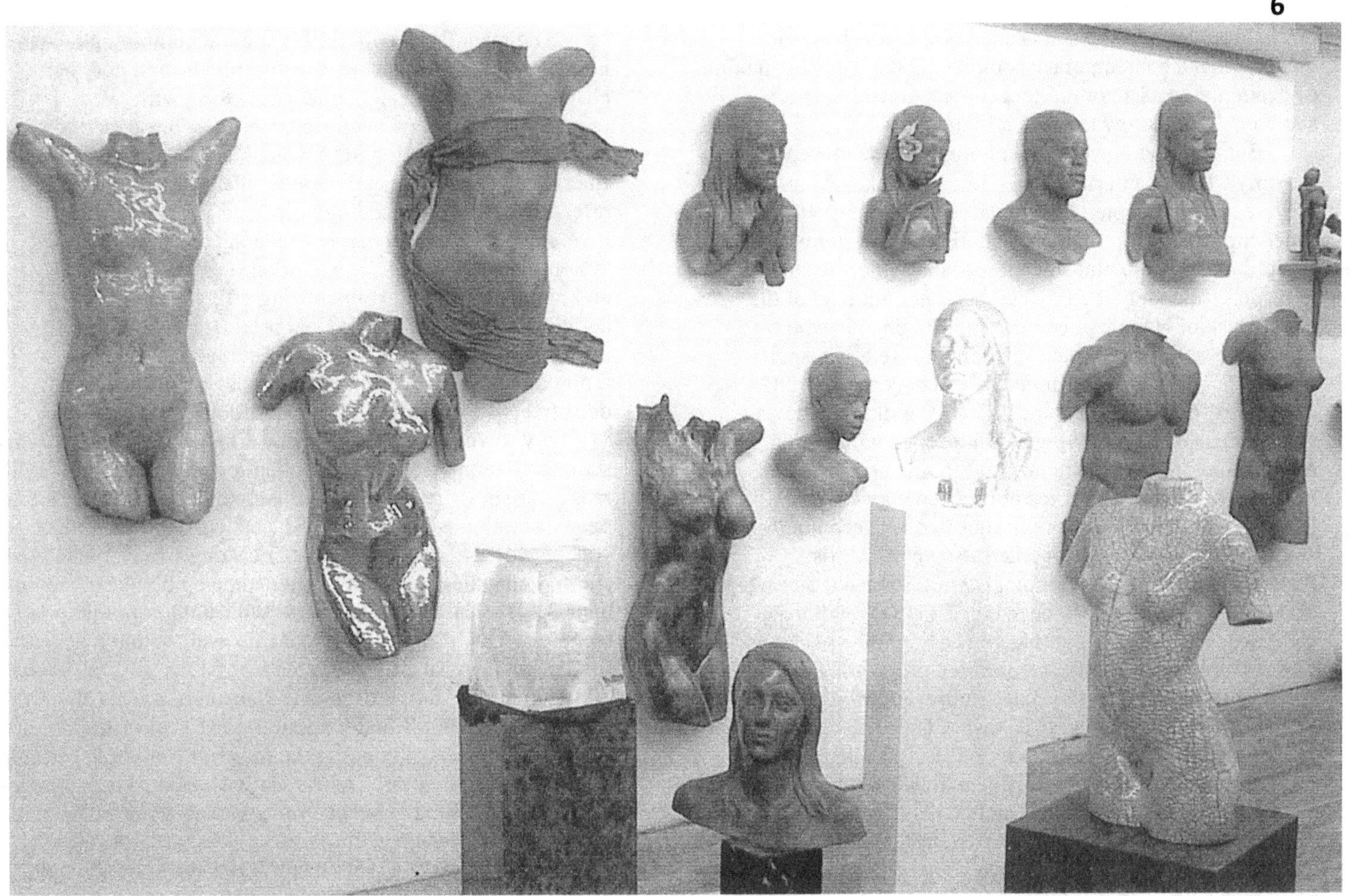
Life castings by Dave Parvin

Dave Parvin

Life Casting, Fine Art Or Cheating?

By Dave Parvin

Note: for this article, the word "sculptor" or any derivative of it such as "sculpting" or "sculpture" will refer to three dimensional art that is produce in the normally thought of way or the artist who produces it. "Life casting," simply "casting," or "caster," etc. will refer to molding directly from a person or to the artist.

"It's just a life cast..." How many times have I heard that? In fact, how many times have I said it myself' I suspect that there is no other sculptural technique that creates so much ambivalence. Anyone who sculpts the old fashioned way may feel that life casting is somehow, well cheating. After all, anybody can make a reasonable likeness by just pulling a mold off of something or someone. Most artists may have even tried it somewhere along the line. The results were about as dead as a corpse. But remember, when the first practical form of photography, daguerreotype was invented in the 1830"s painters looked upon it with equal disdain. The main complaint was that photography was not selective. A photographer was only able to capture what was actually there and was unable to add, delete, or change the image; it was felt that there was no creativity, no skill involved. Yet photography, which is every bit as much cheating as life casting, has gained acceptance as an art form. So what is so different, so disagreeable about something that could be call three-dimensional photography? Before I answer that, let's digress just a little, just a few thousand years.

Life casting has been around for a very long time. The Roman historian, Pliny the Elder, relates in his Natural History how one Lysistratus of Sicyonia made a plaster mold of a face and cast the positive in wax. In Malvina Hoffman's 1939 book, "Sculpture Inside and Out" she claims that "Molds were made from living subjects even as far back as 1300 B.C." She then gives detailed directions for casting masks from both living and dead subjects. It is hard to imagine that a contemporary book would describe the making of death masks as a normal procedure, something that a sculptor should know to make a living.

But until the invention of photography, a mask was the only way of capturing someone's exact likeness and it survived as an accepted art from at least as late as 1939. Since the most common mold material was plaster which had obvious detrimental side effects, the subject usually had to be dead to endure the process. Who has not read of the death mask of Napoleon or Lincoln? But anyone who thinks that any living caster, including myself, is responsible for inventing the techniques need only see an 1887 painting by Edouard Damon entitled Moulding. It shows an artist and assistant removing a mold from a model's leg. It reminds me of my own studio. And if anyone thinks that he/she is discovering new territory, get a copy of Carl Dames's Moulding and Casting subtitled Its Technique and Application for Moulage Workers, Sculptors, Artists, Physicians, Dentists, Criminologists, Craftsmen, Pattern Makers, Architectural Molders, etc. This book will make it very clear that almost anything you can imagine has been done before. But while the steps of the procedure have changed little, the materials have improved. Modern materials are an improvement in two ways. First of all, there is no reason ever to put plaster directly on skin. While there are some fast setting rubbers available which have the advantage of making reusable molds, they have some disadvantages in both safety and cost. The most suitable material for general use is alginate which is essentially powdered kelp. It is absolutely harmless to the skin, the detail is excellent, and it is relatively inexpensive. There are numerous brands available with different characteristics. I have tried every brand that I have come across and my favorite is Prosthetic Cream alginate. The second improvement is in the materials for the final positive. Any plaster will work, of course, but the only thing worse in terms of durability would be cast paper. An improvement would be any of the cast "stones" or Portland cement or hydrocal or fiberglass resin, etc. One can even pour wax directly into an alginate mold for casting into

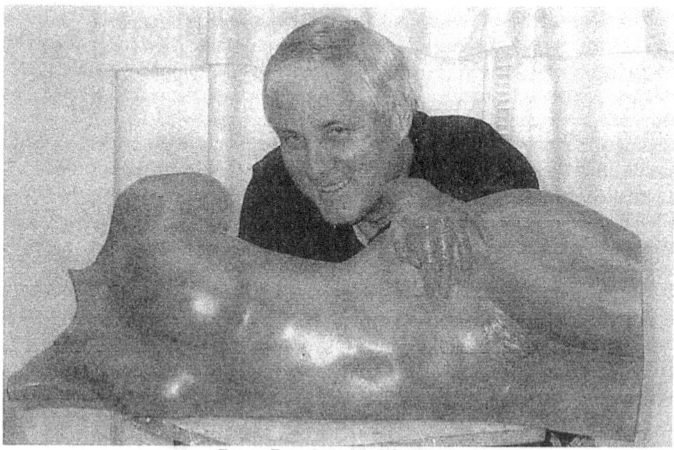

Dave Parvin with life cast

bronze. By far the most suitable material that I have used is Forton MG.

The manufacturer describes it as "...combining alpha hemihydrate gypsum cement with sophisticated polymer chemistry resulting in a permanent casting with remarkable variations in appearance." The basic matrix is three powders and a liquid to which you add chopped fiberglass for strength and various fillers for particular effects. For example, adding powdered limestone will give you a pure white marble appearance. Once the system is water soluble, it will accept water soluble dyes and pigments. The most interesting effect results from adding metal powders. The final product can be polished and/or patinated as if it were hot cast metal and looks remarkably like the real thing. It is easy to work with, odor free, very durable and not hazardous.

My own involvement with life casting began when sculptor Thomas Schomberg mentioned to me that a life mask can be very helpful for anatomical reference. I have been sculpting since childhood and casting for almost ten years and am well aware of casting's advantages and shortcomings; even I view it with some ambivalence. On one hand I feel that it is a technique with unique possibilities, a technique that every artist would do well to have at least a fundamental grasp of. Who could possibly see the work of either John de Andrea or Duane Hanson and even think that it-could be accomplished without a great deal of training and practice? The most famous piece of art in Denver is certainly de Andre's Linda at the Denver Art Museum. After all, great art is not just great realism nor great abstraction not great workmanship, it is great emotion.

So where, on the other hand, is the cheating? I would guess that most sculptors suspect that anyone whose primary work is casting probably can't sculpt and isn't willing to make the effort to learn how. I agree. I am always quick to point out that my primary work is my sculpture and not my castings. I admit that I don't want anyone to think that casting is all I can do because almost anyone can do it. I explain it this way. After one of my two or three day workshops and some practice, it isn't long before anyone should be able to make acceptable castings. In the same couple of days I could explain everything needed for one to be able to sculpt. But sculpting takes years of practice. It is analogous to photography versus drawing or painting.

But the question still remains about casting from life, why would anyone who is any sort of real sculptor ever want to try it? For reference. Don't most of us photograph our models in a particular pose so as to have something to refer to when the model isn't present? Well, why not do the same thing in three dimension? Some of the preparatory steps that I take when I begin a new sculpture is to cast at least the model's face and hands in the desired position. It is their very realness, their exactness that makes them so useful. In some ways, they are superior to the actual model. I can refer to them at any time and for as long as I need to. They can be turned in my hands and studied form all angles. I can even store them indefinitely and refer back to them if I enlarge the piece at a future date. The second issue is to make the casting an end in itself. Most people would treasure a bust of a loved one. But sculpting an accurate portrait takes time-enough time that the final product can require a significant financial investment. But I can cast a face including the neck and ears (in other words all of what is needed for recognition) and remain within most people's budget.

The actual impression takes only about fifteen minutes and the preparation and explanation require that the person be in my studio for only about an hour to an hour and a half. The process is reasonably pleasant but just involved enough that the subjects usually depart with a feeling of accomplishment for having "suffered for art" and been a partner in the creation of something. Unfortunately, the mask is not finished in the hour and half. It takes me about eight man-hours of work over a week's time before it's completed. One of the things that I do is to make a secondary mold in silicone rubber, partly because it improves the final product and partly because it allows for additional copies. It is not just the affordability that makes a mask so desirable; it is the realness. I have had people tell me that they had commissioned a bust of their child only to admit that they were disappointed with the results because it really didn't look like their child. Obviously, they chose the wrong sculptor. Portrait sculpting is not easy; you cannot be very far off and have it actually look like the subject. I like to say that around my studio, "parts is parts." And of course, I have cast the entire human body either as a whole or in pieces. The face is most important since we are recognized by our faces. The other parts that I most commonly cast are hands and feet of infants, clasping hands of couples, and torsos.

In order of difficulty, hands are the least difficult, followed by torsos, with faces being the most difficult part of the body to cast. Not only are faces very involved structures, but covering the face can induce claustrophobia, not to mention suffocation. I have not explained here step by step how to do a casting because it would be beyond the scope of this article. It is complicated enough and with just sufficient risk to the subject that it probably shouldn't be attempted at home without some instructions. I have developed some dummy heads so that one can practice prior to spreading goo on a living person.

I have been casting long enough that I do not ask whether life casting is fine art or cheating. To me it is just another art form, a different art form with its own limitations and advantages. But if great art causes great emotion, nothing is more satisfying to an artist than to arouse this emotion in even one person. I am often amazed at the reaction of parents to their children's castings. I have seen a mother cry over a hand, a face, or a body saying that she will always have her child at that age. The two things that are the essence of castings are realism and permanence. A photograph is real but will last only perhaps a hundred years. A video is real but may last only one generation. But a casting can capture a moment in time forever. A casting may survive until the sun goes supernova.

"Danger, Will Robinson!"

David E. Parvin, A.L.I.

The first rule of life casting should be the same as the first rule of medicine, "Do no harm." Yet some people continue to use materials and methods that carry risks. The risks could be either for the caster or the castee. This article will emphasize danger to the castee.

About twelve years ago, when I had only been life casting for about eight years and was relatively inexperienced, I had just finished casting the faces of the son and daughter of an emergency room physician. Wanting to get a little free advice from a safety expert, I asked the doctor if he had noticed anything in the process that was potentially risky. Probably more than anything else, I was just making small talk, something I am well known for. His answer surprised me. He said the the only thing he had seen that concerned him was that a person might faint with the mold still on his/her face. He went on to explain that fainting is often followed by vomiting and if a person were to vomit with his/her mouth covered, the person could aspirate, i.e. have vomit forced into his/her lungs resulting in serious injury or even death! I was stunned, instantly I realized that what I was doing could have more serious consequences than I had imagined and since then I have paid more attention to safety. In this article, I will cover what I have become aware of in over twenty years of life casting, starting with fainting.

At the time of the event described above, I had never seen anyone faint, but since then I have. While I didn't keep a log book, I suspect that I have seen it only seven or eight times. While a person is more likely to faint during a face casting than a torso or a hand, I do recall a person fainting during each of the latter two. The toro casting casualty was a young lady just graduating from college who had seen my work and thought a casting of herself would make a wonderful graduation present. Naturally, I agreed. We were just about finished, we had applied the alginate and constructed the mother mold of cheesecloth and fast setting plaster as in Photo #1 (though the photo is of a different person). It had taken less than 20 minutes to get to that point and in less than five minutes, the plaster would have setup enough that we could have removed the mold. The subject mumbled something about not feeling good and immediately, before I could respond, collapsed on the floor as if a sack of rocks, "THUD!" Once she was in a horizontal position, the blood returned to her head and she quickly revived. The casting was ruined but luckily and more importantly, despite having gone down in dramatic fashion, she wasn't sore, bruised, on injured in any way. She admitted to being hypoglycemic and that she hadn't eaten anything all day because **she didn't want to look fat!** We rescheduled for a couple of days later and she came in well fed and the casting went of without a hitch (or a stitch for that matter).

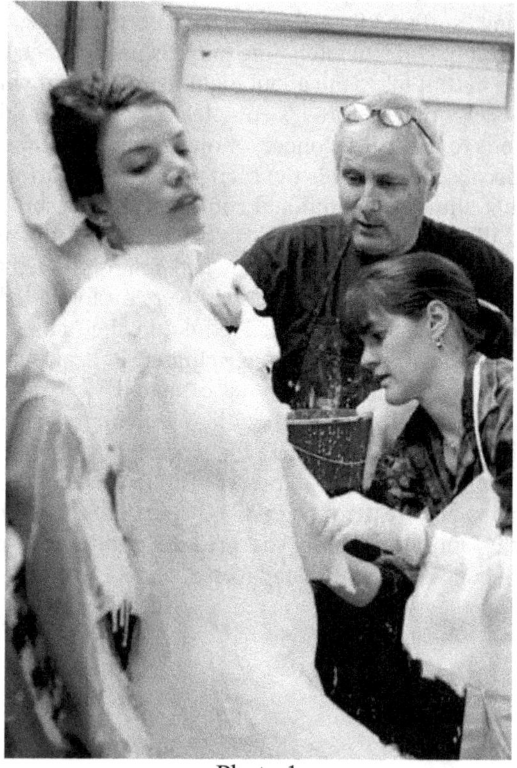

Photo 1

Having spent over ten years as a helicopter pilot for a hospital, I am pretty sure what would have happened if she had, say, hit her head when she had fallen and had knocked herself out. I would have called 911. This is the call that the paramedics would have been waiting for, the reason why they had become paramedics in the first place. There on the floor would have been an attractive young lady in distress covered only with goo that **they would get to clean off**. All they usually got were old people having heart attacks. I was certain that if I had gone afterwards to central dispatch, there on the radio counsel would have been a sign that read, "TO ANY CALLS FROM PARVIN STUDIO, ALL UNITS RESPOND." And if I had ever made another 911 call, my parking lot would have been full of ambulances, fire trucks, police cars, and maybe even a helicopter or two, all wanting to help!

Hand castings are so easy to do that one wouldn't imagine a person fainting. Photo #2 shows trusty and capable assistant, Jessica, with both hands in alginate to make them into a wall mounted business card holder Christmas present for her dad as in Photo #3. (Working at my studio is something like summer camp in that one is encouraged to make crafty items for mom and dad. Fortunately, no one has asked to make, shall we say, "more interesting castings" for boyfriends, at least not yet...) Amazingly, a woman with her hand in the goo actually fainted and went down for the count with another resounding

"THUD!" The reason was similar, she had eaten very little all day and had attended an office party where she had attempted to make up for lack of solid food with liquid nourishment. Fortunately, other than a bruised pride, she suffered no ill effects and also returned at a latter date for an event free casting.

The two examples I have given are not what the doctor was concerned about. While one could be injured from collapsing, vomiting with something on one's face could be far more serious. I suspect that I have seen someone faint while having a face casting done only about five or six times in over twenty years of life casting and with no ill effects. I can recall only once that someone actually collapsed. The other times, I realized the the person was becoming unresponsive and aborted the procedure. I have, however, at least once seen someone vomit after fainting just as the doctor warned. I guess the good news is that fainting has been such a rare occurrence. Usually, the person has fainted (or started to) just as the mold was almost completed. But the one who actually collapsed did so just as we applied the first bit of alginate to her forehead. We caught her or she would have been a limp puddle person on the floor. We revived her and started over without incident. However, something else did happen which I will come back to later. But first, I will explain how I try to prevent fainting which is possibly the reason I have seen it so rarely.

I always try to meet with a castee before the day that we actually spread the goo. Many times the life casting is a parent's idea and the child is somewhat suspicious. This first meeting allows me to put the subject at ease by explaining just what's going to happen. It also gives me a chance to see what I have to work with and plan the pose. It also gives me a chance to mention safety. Part of the explanation includes showing a short video of someone being cast, both face and body. I encourage the model to eat normally and during the casting not to lock booth knees. I stress to the model that at anytime he/she feels strange or weak, we will stop at once. Every few minutes during the actual casting, I ask how the model is doing. Communication is not a problem if the model's face isn't covered since we and just talk to each other. For a face, however, my instructions are to respond with a thumbs up for "O.K." and a thumbs down for "I want to stop!" I have gotten pretty good at appraising a model's status and if anything just doesn't seem right, even if the model has not requested to stop, we stop. I recall one face casting of a young lady during which she seemed to be a little unresponsive. We were just a few minutes from being finished when I said that we were stopping. Her mother, who was a nurse, wanted to finish. I said again that we were stopping and as I removed the mold, the girl fainted.

In recent articles, I explained how most of the time I position the model on an almost vertical padded board. If I decide to abort the casting, the first thing I do, if the face is covered, is remove the mold. Then my assistant and I lower the board into a horizontal position. Every time I have done this, the model has recovered within a few seconds with no ill effects. My advice is if something just doesn't seem right, quit immediately, there is no such thing as being too safe.

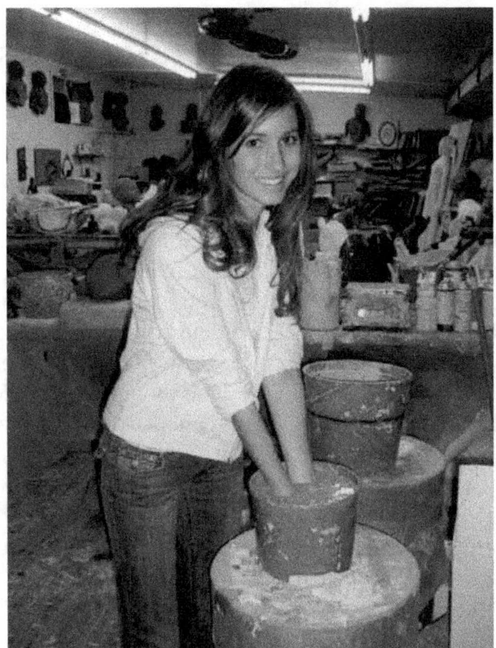

Photo 2

Along the same line as fainting is sleeping. It isn't hard to believe that if someone were lying down while being covered with warm goo that he or she might fall asleep. Probably the only danger would be to the mold because the model might wake up with a start and damage the it. However, I have seen a person actually fall asleep standing up and leaning back on a padded board. In this case, there is real danger of falling just as in fainting. If someone is so tired that he or she can not stay awake standing, then it is probably smart to reschedule for another day.

Once I had a reporter for a local newspaper come to my studio to write an article. Her college age daughter had volunteered to be the subject. The article was about casting her face though we also did a torso casting as well. Again, both went without a hitch or a stitch. I had requested that the reporter not explain the process in such detail or make it sound so simple that someone might attempt it from just the article without some instruction since one has to cover the model's face and one should know what he/she is doing. I had also asked that she let me proof read the finished article

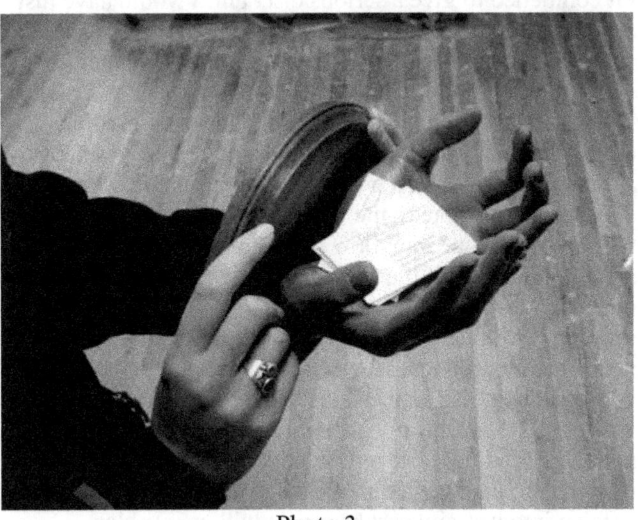

Photo 3

for errors which she promised to do. Poet Robert W. Service said in "The Cremation of Sam McGee," "A promise made is a debt unpaid..." Well, the reporter still owes me from what followed. First, her editor wanted the article more quickly than she anticipated and I did not get a chance to check it. Secondly, after making me sound like both a great artist and someone in line for the next Nobel Peace Prize for my humanitarianism, she did a great job of explaining the process until she said, "The next step, removing the mold, is critical and dangerous; the model can suffocate if not done properly." That particular newspaper was for the richest area in Denver. As you can imagine, even though the article was on the front page and was 99% excellent, I didn't get a single inquiry. That old adage that says that *publicity is only bad if it concerns children or small furry animals in a negative way* is true.

A mutual friend asked the reporter why she had said something so negative and she replied, "Dave wanted me to." Not only had I not wanted her to mention the that I might kill a subject, she was just flat wrong, removing the mold isn't dangerous. However, she did have a point that if proper attention isn't paid to the model's air passages, the model could suffocate. I can not even guess how many people, asking me about how a face casting is done have said, "So, what do you do, put straws up a person's nose?" To which I reply in my most condescending badly done French accent, "Only the most rank amateur would stick straws into someone's nose!" Straws are a really bad idea. Not only can the distort the shape of someone's nose, if bumped, can cause injury. If the alginate is just the right consistency, i.e. thin enough for application but thick enough to stay in place, it can be shaped around the nose without obstructing air flow. One of the reasons that I always work with an assistant is so that one of us is able pay close attention to assure that the model is able to breathe.

At my preliminary meeting with the model I always mention that the it is absolutely essential the he/she be able to breathe through his/her nose. If the model has a cold, we postpone the session. Recently I had a young man in my studio who said that he was never able to breathe through his nose. Now that was serious because he was a paying customer. Had this been a case of a friend or relative whom I felt compelled to give a serious discount, I would have just backed out of the deal and saved myself some time. But a full paying customer is another thing entirely. What I did was cast him with his lips parted enough for him to breathe. Actually, I have done this several times and the castings have turned out just fine. The only caution is an aesthetic and not a safety issue. You must be very careful when applying the alginate to the lower lip. If you force it into the mouth, the alginate may flow between the lip and the teeth, and it may look as if the subject has a wad of smokeless tobacco in there.

One last thing on noses. Earlier, I mentioned that the girl who collapsed just as we started applying the alginate had something else happen. As she fell foreword, my assistant, Melody, adroitly caught her not realizing that the model bumped her nose on Melody's collar bone. We revived her, gave her a non-diet soda to get some sugar and caffeine into her, and cast her again with no problem. However, when we removed the mold, she had a very noticeably bruised nose! We figured out what had happened and, fortunately, neither she nor her parents were upset and her bruise went away in a few days. I never expected to see a bruised nose again, but I was wrong.

This is another of those very rare occurrences, but I think every life caster should be aware of the possibility. Perhaps, on five occasions, I have seen someone's nose bruised without being bumped. It seems that the bridge of the nose isn't well padded and some people are so tender there that even the light weight of a mold can cause a bruise. Most of the ones I have seen have occurred to rather prominent noses. One was the really excellent sculptor, James Muir. He had asked me If I would make a casting of his face so that he could use it for reference. Sculpting from a cast is far better than looking at one's self in a mirror. Jim has a prominent though rather distinguished nose, the bridge of which was bruised in the process. But another whose nose became bruised was at the time the reigning Miss Colorado USA Teen and her nose definitely wasn't large. While I do not consider this to be a serious concern or very likely to happen, I probably would not cast someone's face within a few days of a beauty pageant, screen test, wedding, etc.

Before I move on from parts of the face, I know of someone who did something that I wouldn't touch with a ten foot pole. Believe it or not, he actually convinced his own children to let him cast their faces *with their eyes open*! He somehow got some of the drops that eye doctors use to numb eyes and used alginate. I suppose that it is possible that it might not be harmful, I really don't know and I never will.

Every bag of gypsum products made by US Gypsum such as plaster, hydrocal, hydrostone, cement, etc. has the following warning printed on it

"!WARNING!

When mixed with water, this material hardens and becomes very hot - sometimes quickly. DO NOT attempt to make a cast enclosing any part of the body using this material. Failure to follow these instructions can cause severe burns that may require surgical removal of affected tissue or amputation of limb..."

Amazingly, I still hear of people who apply gypsum products directly on skin. Even if gypsum products are not thick enough for the exothermic reaction to generate enough heat to be harmful, the possibility of chemical burns is still very real. Also, even a thin layer of plaster, etc. absorbs water and can seriously dry skin. Let me relate four stories, from the humorous to the tragic. During one of my workshops a retired dentist confessed that he had cast his own face right after he got out of dental school. He arranged what he needed on a table and sat down to do the job by braille, so to speak. He mixed the plaster and spread it over his face. He didn't realize that he had forgotten a step until he tried to remove the plaster, it was stuck fast. He had forgotten to use a release such a petroleum jelly. The plaster was stuck to all the hairs it touched. He had no choice but to pull the plaster off taking all his facial hair including the roots with it. He then poured some plaster into the mold. This plaster locked onto the roots and when he removed the positive impression from the mold the hairs came out too. So he ended up with a mask that contained all his facial hair. Said he, "It was the damnedest looking thing you ever saw!" Said I, "I'll bet it was."

Those old enough may remember that there used to be a television show called "911." There was a segment in which a high school age girl convinced her junior high age sister to let her cast her nude torso by spreading plaster over it. The older sister made the same mistake that the dentist above had done, no release. They finally called the fire department for help. The younger sister ended up in a bathtub while a crew of burly fireman chipped the plaster off her naked body. Though she wasn't seriously injured, she never forgave her sister.

There was a documentary on PBS that showed a South American artist making life castings of native peoples. He would talk some native into getting covered with plaster from head to toe. After the plaster had setup, the artist would break the plaster off. Then he would transport the pieces back to his studio, reassemble the puzzle, and fill it with plaster to get a reproduction of the native. As shown in the documentary, the plaster was applied in a heavy layer at least an inch thick. Jungles tend to be hot even without being packed in exothermic curing plaster. I was and still am amazed that the artist didn't kill some of his models.

A friend of mine named Todd Debrenceni is writing a text book for special effects. He relates the following as part of a section telling the reader to never apply plaster directly on skin. "The reality of the danger of direct application of plaster to skin was illustrated in January 2007, when a sixteen year-old girl suffered third-degree burns after encasing her hand in plaster as part of a school art project in Lincolnshire England. She subsequently had both thumbs and all but two fingers amputated. Be forewarned!"

The most commonly used material for life casting is alginate but <u>some</u> silicone rubbers can also be used. I say "some" because only a few specific ones are approved for skin contact. There are two kinds of silicone rubber, platinum cured and tin cured. All those approved for skin contact are platinum's, tin cured silicone rubbers are not approved. Some people are tempted to use non approved tin cured silicone rubber because it can be less expensive. One of the necessary characteristics needed for any life casting material is that it setup very quickly. While regular slow curing platinum and tin cured silicones are about the same price, it is much less expensive to accelerate tin cured silicones than platinums. The temptation is to use tin cured silicones with an accelerate though not approved for skin contact than use the more expensive fast setting platinum ones which are.

My concern is that anytime one uses something on a person's skin which is not only not approved but is expressly prohibited, one is not only putting the model at risk but also himself. If something went wrong and the model were injured, the artist would have a hard time convincing a jury of his innocence. Not only do I not want to hurt someone, but I would hate to see my artistic career come to an end by being sued out of existence. And any time even the possibility of spending time in the big house pops into my head, I imagine my roommate as a three hundred pound ax murderer named Bubba who makes me wear sun dresses...

In this article, I have been concerned with injury to the model. There is a whole another subject that I have not touched upon, the safety to ourselves of the materials and equipment that we regularly use. While this is a discussion for another time, there is one recent improvement that I will briefly mention. Since the most commonly used material for life casting is alginate which had always contained silica, the development of silica free alginate is significant. ArtMolds now has a line of SilFree MoldGel alginates that provide excellent reproductions and may very well help us avoid lung transplants. I'll cover this in more detail in the "discussion for another time."

Sculpture Journal February 2008

Standard Life Casting Compositions
#1 Praying Hands

By David E. Parvin, A.L.I.

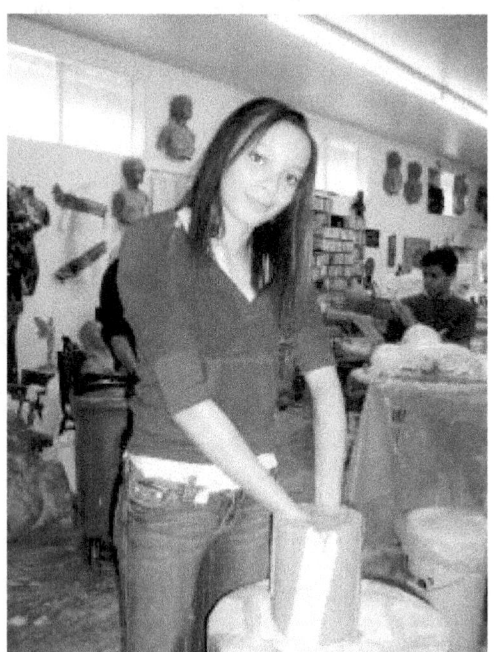

Photo #1

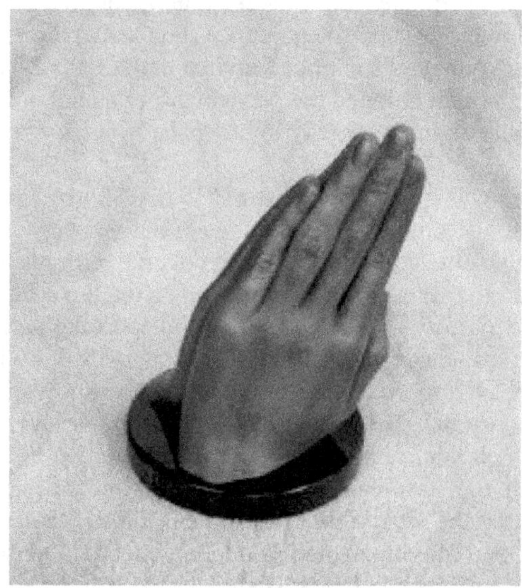

Photo #2

I often refer to life casting as being analogous to three dimensional photography but photographers have an advantage over life casters besides not getting so messy. Go to the photography section of any book store and you will find books that give examples of different poses for portrait, glamour, wedding, baby, fashion, etc. photography to help a photographer at least have an idea about where to start. Sounding and acting confident and knowledgeable reassures the client or model. It is always better to say, "Just turn your body slightly to the left, drop your chin a little, give me just a hint of a smile as if you have a secrete you know I would kill to learn but you're not going to tell me," than, "I haven't a clue of what to do." Regardless of whether the result is portrait, commercial, or fine art, positioning the person in a particular pose with the right props and lighting goes a long way in producing an acceptable photograph. But there are no books with similar information for life casters. Looking back at some of my early castings, most were pretty bad, While they looked like the subjects, they just weren't very artistic, almost the three dimensional equivalent of driver license mug shots. In the ensuing twenty years, however, I have learned some posses that are sure winners. This will be the first of a series of articles in which I share what I have learned, what works and, in some cases, what doesn't.

Whenever someone comes to me for a casting, I always spend some time getting to know the person. I want to determine if there is some specific aspect of the person that is so integral to him/her that it should be depicted in the life casting. I have cast hands holding all sorts of objects such as oar handles, baseballs, books, paint brushes, golf clubs, base ball bats, soccer balls, fly rod handles, and so on and on. Likewise, some people have wanted their hand(s) to mean something in sign language. Every year, 20 helpers and myself cast about 650 hands as part of a community kids' arts day. The castees take their cast hands home and remove them from the alginate themselves later. Since there is no way to see what one does with his/her fingers once they are submerged into the alginate, I have often wondered how many make the "one finger salute" to the disappointment of their parents. It is not only hands that can be individualized but also heads and torsos. The Smothers Brothers parodied the the old song The Streets of Loredo by singing, "I can tell by your outfit that you are a cowboy. Get yourself an outfit and you can be a cowboy too!"

A leotard makes one into a dancer or gymnast and a Speedo, a swimmer. Pointed ears and you become a Vulcan, werewolf, or faerie. The possibilities are endless. The castings that I will describe here can be done with just the hands or as part of a portrait bust and are appropriate for almost anyone, praying hands. It is beyond the scope of this article to explain in complete detail the processes required to make these two versions. I'm assuming that the reader has some knowledge of life casting but I have listed some previous articles in *Sculpture Journal* for additional information and clarification.

Praying hands is one of the most enduring subjects in both two and three dimensions. It seems that every catalogue of decorative nick knacks has an example. Whether the hands are young, old, or in between, they still strike a pleasing chord. Most parents really like their children's hands this way. Perhaps we enjoy seeing our children in a way we imagine them rather than the way they really are!

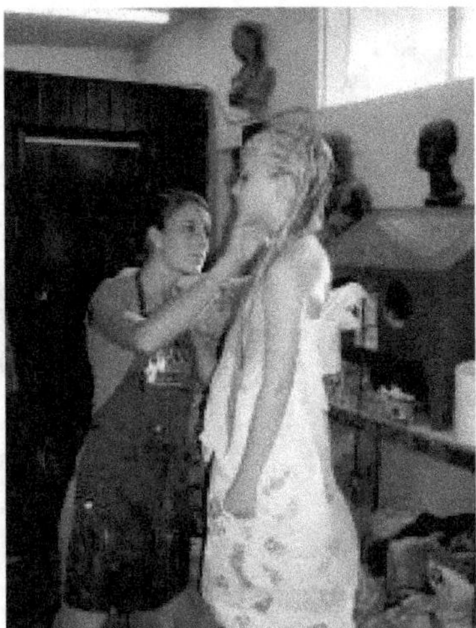
Photo #3

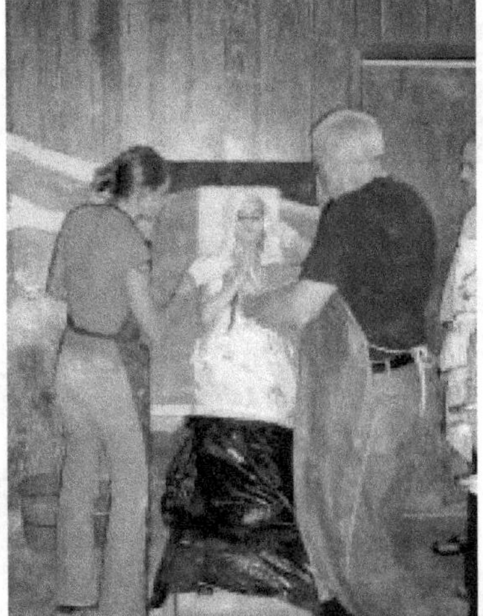
Photo #4

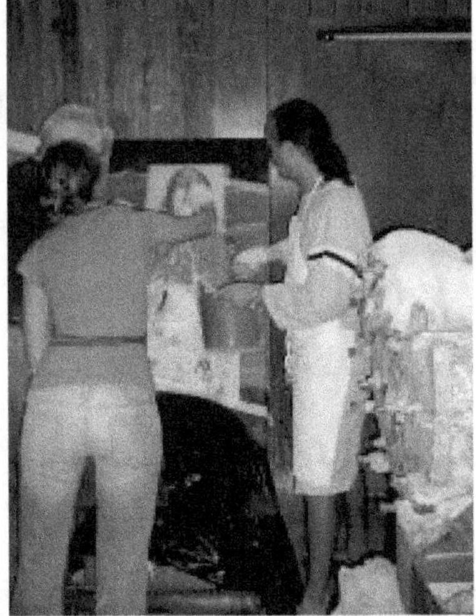
Photo #5

In photo #1, thirteen year old Laura has her hands in alginate. As soon as the alginate had setup, she removed her hands and I filled the void with Forton MG to which had been added copper powder. I could have used plaster or hydrocal and either left the hands white or painted on a faux patina (1). But the metallic Forton MG makes a better looking and longer

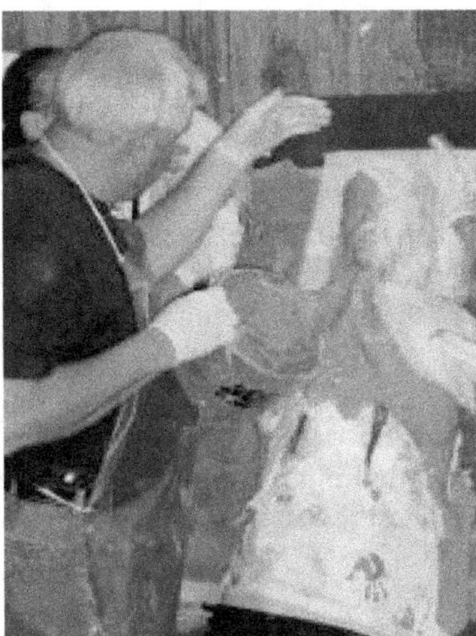
Photo #6

lasting product as in photo #2. One other trick I used was to de-air the Forton MG in a "Whip Mixer" which resulted in an almost bubble free casting (2).

In photo #3, one of my assistants, Kelsey, was finishing preparing our nine year old model, who is appropriately name Faith, for the portrait casting. The main thing that Kelsey had done was apply a thick hair conditioner, Cholesterol, to prevent the alginate from bonding to her hair (3).

In the next photo, #4, Kelsey and some old fat guy who often shows up in my photographs in my place, were applying the first layer of alginate. The important thing here is that the alginate be just the right viscosity so that it will stay in place. Two areas of concern are the fingers and under the forearms. If the alginate is too runny, it will simply run off, too thick and not only will it be difficult to apply but the alginate will not go on smoothly and will trap bubbles on the skin's surface. In photo #5, Faith's dad, Pat, had joined in the

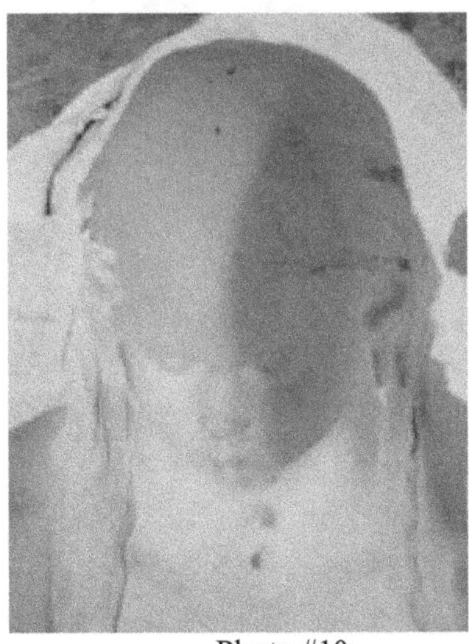
Photo #10

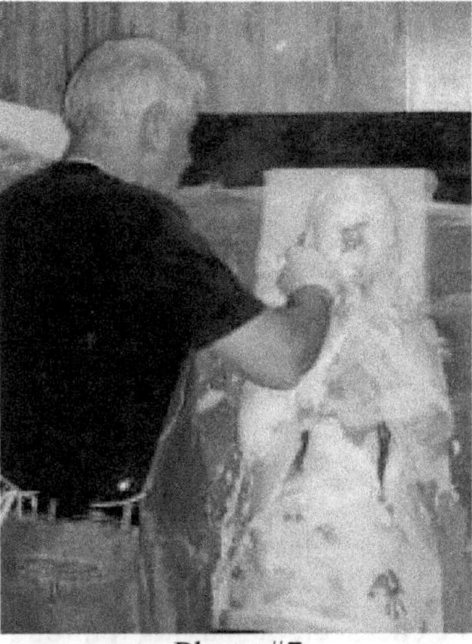
Photo #7

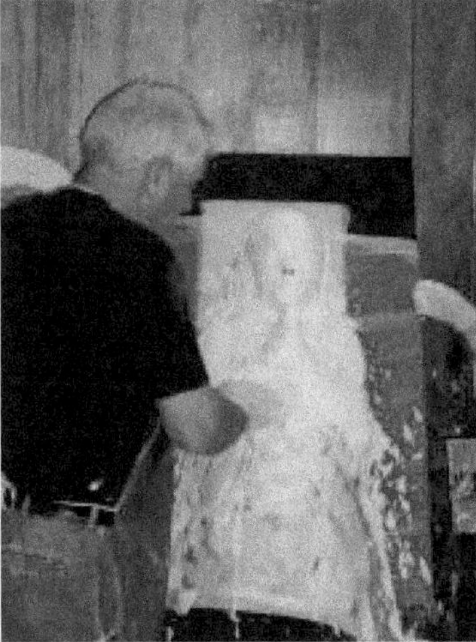
Photo #8

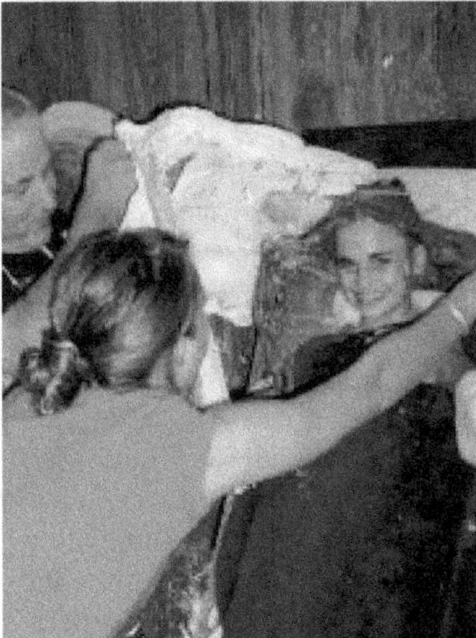
Photo #9

fun and was helping apply a second thin layer of alginate which was much more runny, about the same consistency as latex paint. Just as the first layer was starting to gel, we misted the surface with Algislo to assure bonding between the two alginates. Notice that the second layer is a different color than the first so that we can see exactly what has been covered.

In photos #6, the same old mystery guy was covering Faith with a layer of cheesecloth which stuck to the still wet outer layer of alginate. Those who have read my articles in past issues of Sculpture Journal may recall that I am absolutely convinced that plaster bandages are a far distant second to using cheesecloth and fast setting plaster which is easier, faster, cheaper, and produces less imperfections. (4.&5.) Next, fast setting plaster, Impression Dental Plaster, was pained on the cheesecloth soaking it through to the alginate (Photo #7). Afterwords, a second layer of cheesecloth and plaster was applied and the outer mold was finished. (Photo #8.)

Of the photographs taken during a casting and given to the model, the one of removing the mold is always my favorite. I remind the model to smile so that when she shows the photographs to her friends, future casting prospects, they will think, "It must not have been too bad, she's smiling." (Photo #9.) By the way, from the time I started mixing the alginate to when the mold was removed was about twenty minutes. The inside of the mold is shown in Photo #10. I like to include this shot as well because the face looks convex rather than concave.

My next step was to make a plaster impression from the mold shown in Photo #11. This could have been the final product. The next higher level of professionalism would have been to apply a faux finish. However, what I did was make a silicone rubber mold of the plaster and cast the final portrait in Forton MG with copper powder for an even better look. A rubber mold has some other advantages as well such as allowing one to make multiple copies. Photo #12 shows the plaster with several layers of rubber; not shown is the mother mold which was also made of Forton MG. (6.) The were three reasons I used copper powder rather than bronze powder. First, the copper results in a more bronze looking finish than bronze which, I feel, is too dark. Second, the copper reacts more intensely to patina solutions than the bronze. And third, copper powder just happens to be less expensive. To finish "Faith Praying," I applied a green patina to the hair and cloth, lightly went over the surface with 0000 grade steel wool, and took a cloth buffing wheel to the entire surface with Tripoli buffing compound. (Photo #13)

My goal is to make someone into a piece of art. Portrait photographers rarely produce something that has any value to anyone except the subject or the subject's family and friends. The measure of whether I have succeeded is if other people not connected to the castee respond favorably to it as in, "Wow, that's really neat piece of art, where can I get one?" That Is expected with torso castings and I routinely make limited editions of beautiful bodies. But I have displayed examples of portrait castings and had people purchase the samples rather than have themselves or their loved ones cast. This is especially been true of praying hands portraits.

1. "Real Beginnings for Faux Metal Finishes," *S.J.*, Sept. 2003, by Mark Fields.
2. "Putting Vacuum and Pressure Chambers to Practical Use," *S.J.*, Nov. 2003, by D.P.
3. "Techniques For Life Casting Hair," *S.J.*, Jul. 2006, by D.P.
4. "An Alternative to Using Plaster Bandages As the Supporting Mold For Alginate Life Casting," *S.J.*, Mar. 2004, by D.P.
5. "Another Use For Cheese Cloth in Life Casting," *S.J.*, Sept. 2005, by D.P.
6. "Secondary Molds in Life Casting," *S.J.*, Nov., and Dec. 2004, by D.P.

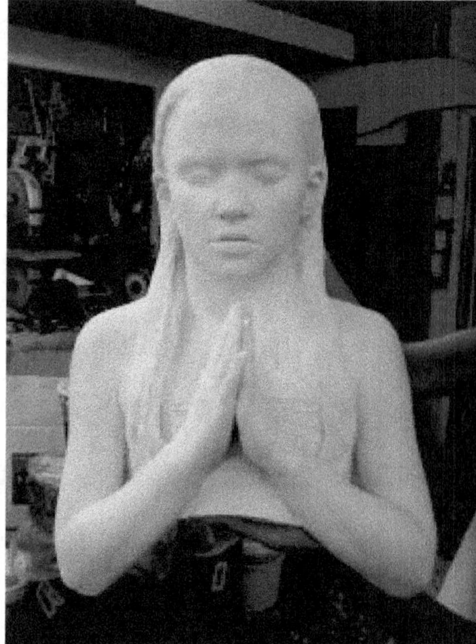

Photo #11

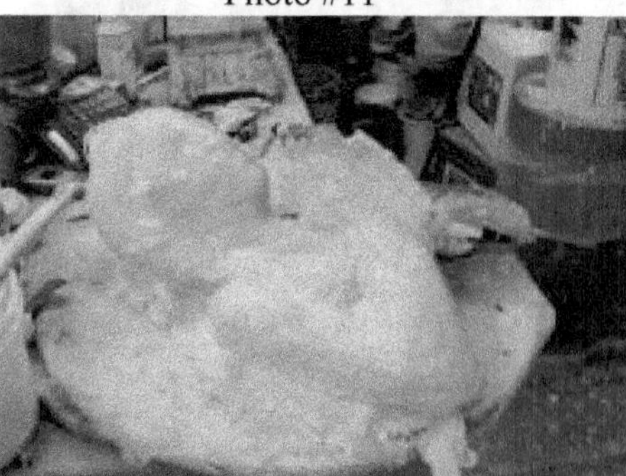

Photo #12

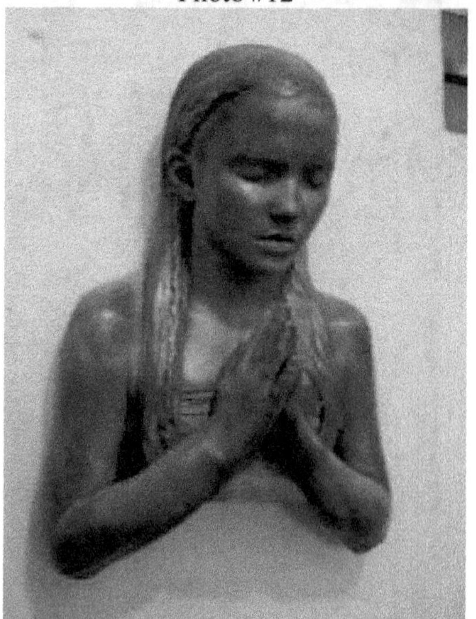

Photo #13

The Perfect Model

By David E. Parvin, A.L.I.

Recently, someone placed on the Forum section of the web site of the Association of Lifecasters International a link to a photograph and asked for "comments." The piece shown was a life casting of a female torso from the top of the neck to mid thighs. The casting appeared to have been made in standard gypsum material such as plaster, hydrocal, hydro-stone, etc. and had a painted-on metallic patina. The pose was straight with the weight evenly distributed on both legs. The left and right halves were symmetrical except that the right arm hung down the right side and the left arm crossed over the body with the left hand covering the genital area. The model had an athletic body which appeared to have been conditioned by a high endurance activity such as distance running.

In the October, 2007 issue of *SJ*, I wrote an article on critique titled "I Really Mean It, Please Give Me Your Honest Opinion." I explained that even though meaningful critique is so important for artistic growth, it can be elusive. True to form, a month after the request was posted, only one reply had been forthcoming. And also predictably, the reply was encouraging but offered nothing in the way of how to improve the work. Finally, I waded in and made three suggestions. The first was that the artist try using materials that produce a more professional look such as raku fired clay or perhaps resins or Forton MG combined with metal powders. The second was that posing the model with her weight on either leg would tilt the pelvis and along with lowering or raising either shoulder and turning the head to the side would establish a curve to the torso resulting in a more pleasing composition. The third was to use a model with a somewhat more softly conditioned look. I then referenced a series of four previous articles titled "How Do I Cast Thee For Profit, Let Me Count the Ways" which describe in much more detail how kick one's life castings up to a higher rung on the ladder of excellence. (These and other articles can now be found in the library section of the Association of Lifecasters International's web site, www.lifecasting.org).

In the article about critique mentioned above, I pointed out that most people really don't want critique but usually are looking for affirmation. However, I assumed in this case that the person really wanted meaningful advice. I would have much preferred to have talked in person. Unfortunately, we were separated by an ocean and practical communication is typing back and forth by email. I suspected that the artist had attempted to make something beautiful as possible; but it may very well have been that the stark stiffness of the piece was just what the artist wanted and my advice was not on the mark or even appreciated. At least I tried.

The first two suggestions were, I think, straight foreword and probably not taken as if I had been at all condescending. But the third was somewhat more delicate. I didn't want to come across as any number of television commercials which have irked me. One was a guy in a bazillion dollar sailboat who advised the viewer to contact American Fargo Lynch to chart a path that would assure the viewer a life of utter luxury in retirement. I always suspected that American Fargo Lynch would have suggested that all I would have to do is invest fifty or sixty thousand a month for thirty or forty years and I could have my own sailboat. Some life insurance ads have affected me the same way, "Contact New Washington Life to find out just how much life insurance you need to assure that your loved ones are secure if the unthinkable happens." I'm pretty sure that New Washington Life's idea of how much I need is considerably more than I think I need. I do not feel an obligation to leave enough money to wife, Emilie, so that she can buy a multimillion dollar condo in Hawaii and lounge around all day drinking margaritas with Bruce, the tennis pro/pool boy/masseur. For me to say, "Just use a perfect model," might be taken the same way. After all, for many, **a model at all** may be hard enough to come by.

But I can not over stress how important the perfect model is in life casting. With traditional sculpting, we can cheat. In other words, a model may be for just general reference. We can make the finished product what we imagine even if the result differs significantly from the model. But life casting shares the same limitation that photography has, "What is actually there is what you get."

There are two examples of photography that, I believe, have especially benefited from perfect models and without which would not have been so successful both aesthetically and financially. Take the annual Sports Illustrated Swimsuit Issue. Years ago when it first appeared, I was duly impressed. There weren't just pretty women almost barefoot all over, there were some of the world's top models almost barefoot all over. The second example is the work of photographer Howard Schatz. Anyone not familiar with Schatz, just Goggle him. I have a number of his books, the latest *H2O* is absolutely beautiful. I suggest purchasing it before it goes out of print and becomes more expensive as most of his earlier ones have. Part of the reason that I consider Schatz is the best current photographer of the human form that I am aware of, is that he doesn't compromise on his models, both male and female. Of course, he doesn't have to. He makes so much money that he can afford the very best. Schatz may even own a bazillion dollar sailboat and regularly send Mrs. Schatz off to the beach condo for a vacation complete with Bruce and he isn't even dead yet!

It isn't just beauty that a model must have because it isn't just beauty that we may be trying to capture. Photograph #1 is of a faerie portrait that I did. While my twelve year old model was certainly beautiful, it was her natural faerieness that drew me to her. The only change I made to her face was to add the pointed ears. Of the many hundreds of life castings that I have done, photograph #2 may be my most interesting portrait. A friend who owned a Native American talent agency told me that he had found the perfect face, "Looks like the Indian Head Nickel." I keep copy on my studio wall and visitors often comment on it. Other artists have requested copies for themselves and have used it for reference when sculpting Native American faces. (There is a tragic end to this story, the 100% Sioux whose face I cast was later convicted of murder and is now serving a life sentence.) We could be looking for an unusual characteristic, a certain ethnic look, a particular athletic conditioning, etc. Perfect can mean any number of things.

While I don't have the resources of Sports Illustrated or Howard Schatz, I have had the fortune to have worked with some absolutely wonderful models, even perfect ones. I described how I have found these models in an article that was published in *SJ* in September, 2004. That was so long ago that Jon the Exalted Benevolent Dictator, Keeper of the Secret Handshake, and Wearer of the Big Funny Hat at *SJ* (EBDKSHWBFH), decided to run it again as a public service in this issue. If I can find great models, so can anybody else.

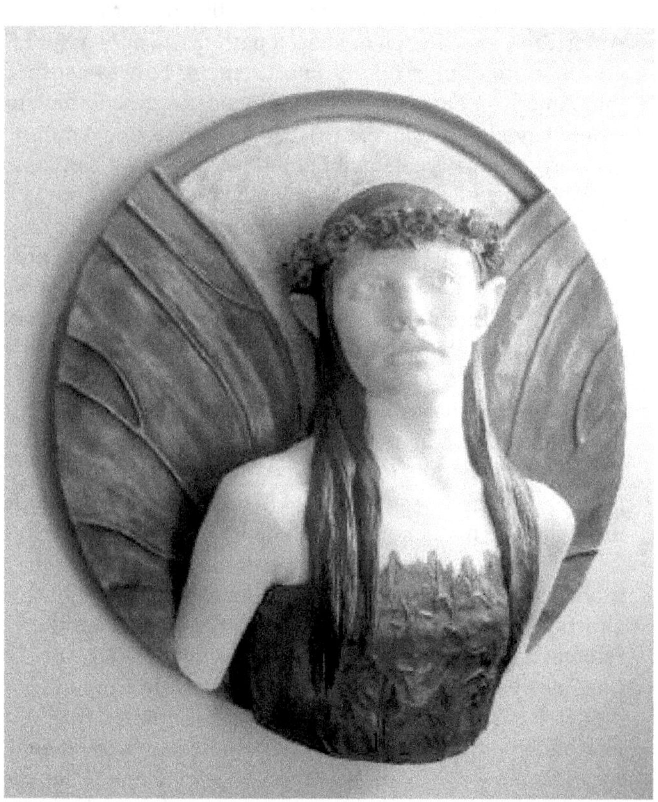

Photograph #1

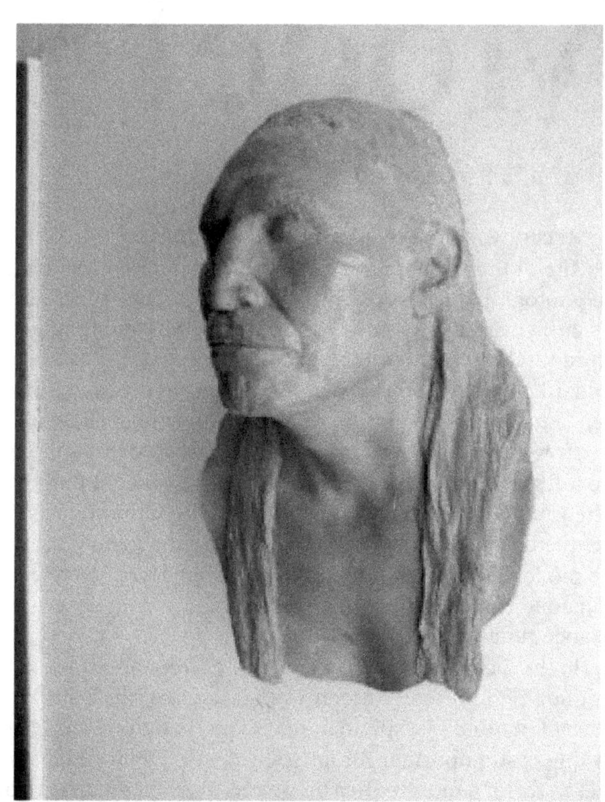

Photograph #2

Life Casting a Head in the Round

By David E. Parvin, A.L.I.

At the end of my article in last month's "Sculpture Journal" I had finished making an impression of a young lady's head in the round using alginate. In this article, I will finish making a free standing cold cast metallic bust attached to a base as in photograph #1.

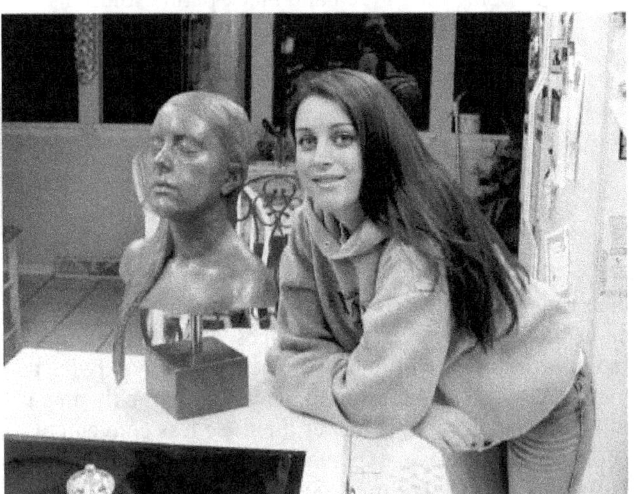

#1 Finished Head

The first step was to reassemble the two parts of the mold. I fitted the back half of the mother mold in place and then turned the completed mold upside down. (Photograph #2) I joined the two halves together securely by wrapping cheese cloth with Impression Dental Plaster making sure that the back half of the alginate fitted securely up against the mother mold. Because this part of the alginate was two layers thick, it stayed in position with minimum seam. If needed, Cholesterol can be coated on the inside of the mother mold to help the alginate stick to the back. Another trick is to use Super Glue along with a catalyst called "Insta Cure" which is available from hobby stores and which will bond alginate to plaster and even alginate to alginate.

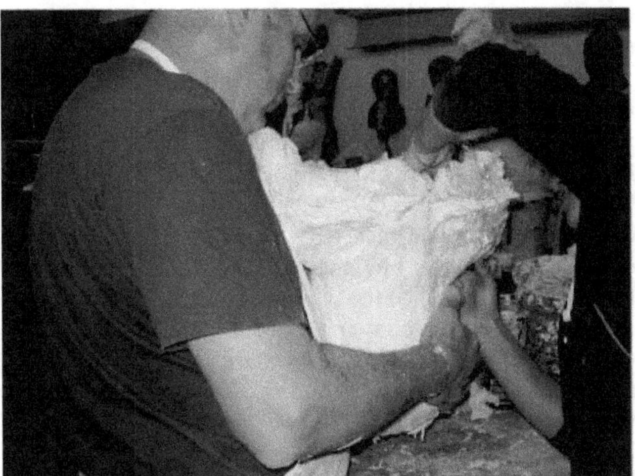

#2 Turning the mold upside down for assembly

I often emphasize that life casting has to be divided into two separate processes. In this respect, it is rather like photography in which taking the picture is one and working in the dark room or with a computer is the other. With life casting, the first is making the most perfect impression or mold that one can of the model. The second is what one does with that mold and where any number of artistic choices and opportunities lie. The simplest and most common solution would have been to fill the mold with plaster or something similar and, perhaps, apply a faux finish. What I did in this case was make a very believable "bronze" casting using the Forton MG casting system. I would need the following, all of which are available from suppliers listed in this magazine:

1. At least three pints, by volume, of blended metallic Forton MG powders.
2. At least 5 pints of blended plain Forton MG powder. (See below.)
3. At least 4 pints of the Forton MG liquid, VF-812.
4. Several 2 inch, inexpensive chip brushes.
5. A mixer attached to an electric drill.
6. An 8 inch piece of 3/4 inch copper pipe.
7. A 12 inch piece of 3/4 inch all thread.
8. Some rigid casting foam such as Polyfoarn R-8 from Polytec.

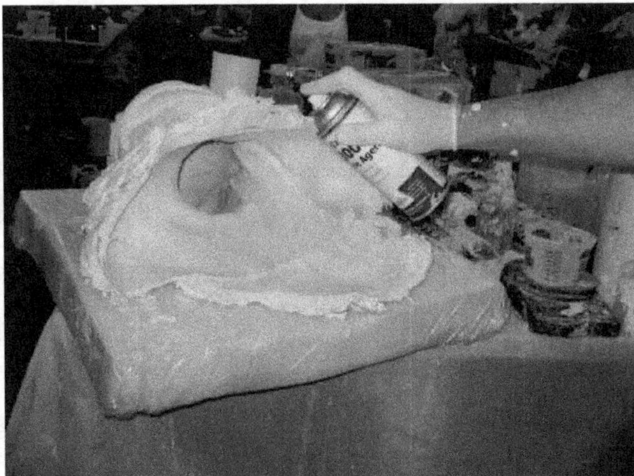

#3 Spraying in the first of two releases which act as barriers between the metallic Forton MG and the alginate.

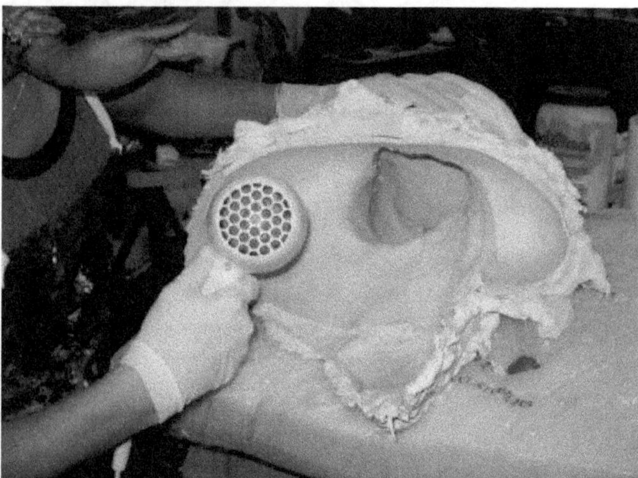
#4 Drying the releases

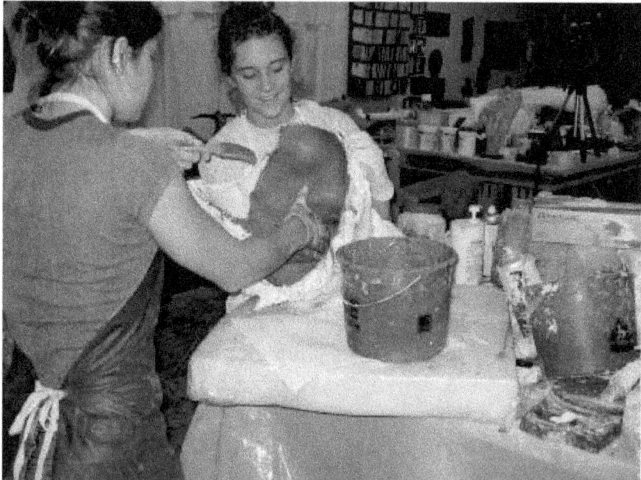
#5 Painting in the first layer of metallic Forton MG.

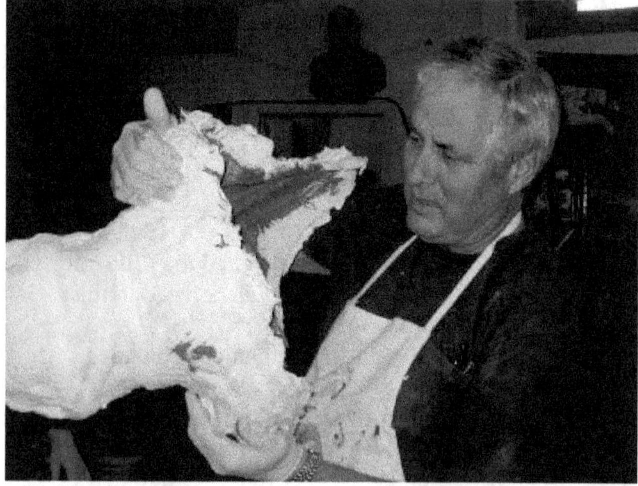
#6 Sloshing the second laver of metallic Forton MG around the inside of the mold

9. At least 8 ounces of "accelerant" made by dissolving 1 part aluminum sulfate into 10 parts of water. Aluminum sulfate is available from any place that sells garden supplies.
10. Several one-gallon, plastic buckets. 11. Several hands full of chopped fiberglass.

12. Some rubber gloves.
13. Some blue/green and black patina solutions.
14. 2 mold releases: Pol-Ease 2300 by Polytec and Synlube 531 by Synair.
15. Very fine, "0000," steel wool.
16. A cloth buffing wheel and a buffing compound such as "Tripoli."
17. A can of clear acrylic spray.
18. Some self-sticking felt or felt dots.

I should point out that I am aware of 4 other materials that are "copy cat" Forton MGs and may be substituted. But there are differences. They cost more ranging from just a little more expensive to over twice as much. Also, all of them set up much more quickly and as I will explain below, this makes their use less convenient. (For a more complete explanation of Forton MG, see "Mixing Forton MG Simplified," by yours truly in the July 2003.

When you purchase Forton MG, you get a liquid called VF812 and two powders, dry resin and hardener. A third powder, FGR-95 is purchased separately. Blending the Forton MG powders is a cinch. I use two clean 5-gallon buckets with lids, one for the plain and one for the metallic. I usually mix about half a bucket full. For the plain, I weigh out about 10,000 grams (22 pounds) of the FGR-95 and add 10% or 1000 grams (2 pounds and 3.2 ounces) of dry resin and 0.5% or 50 grams (1.75 ounces) of hardener. I use a 4-inch Jiffy Mixer attached to a heave duty electric drill for blending. For the metallic, blend as the plain but add twice the weight of metal powers as you did FGR-95. When ready to mix the VF-812 liquid and the blended powders, all you do is use twice as much of the powders, either plain or metallic by volume as you use the VF-812 liquid and mix.

Now, about metal powders, there are different kinds available such as copper, bronze, brass, aluminum, and others. I have found that copper powder in Forton MG results in a more realistic bronze look than bronze powder which makes a harder casting which doesn't respond to the standard blue/green patina solution as well as copper. I sometimes blend copper and bronze powders together for an in between look. I encourage you to experiment and determine your own preferences.

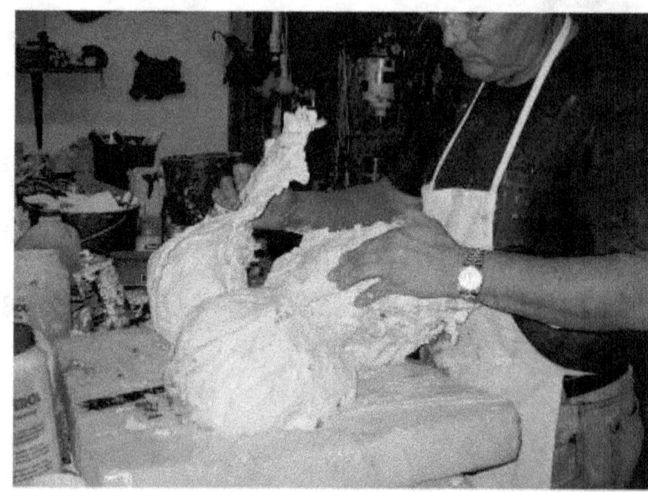
#7 Demolding the head

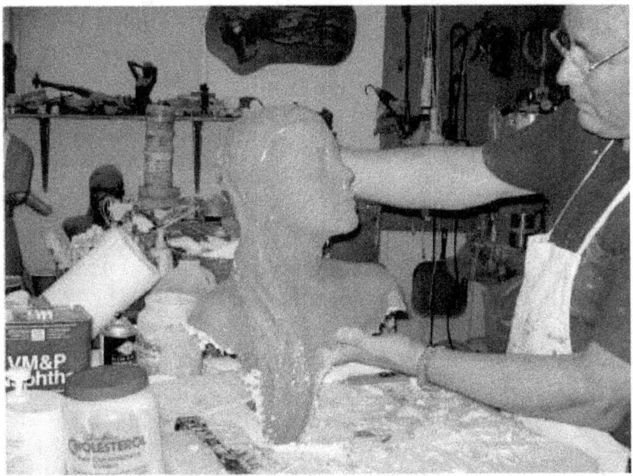

#8 The demolded head

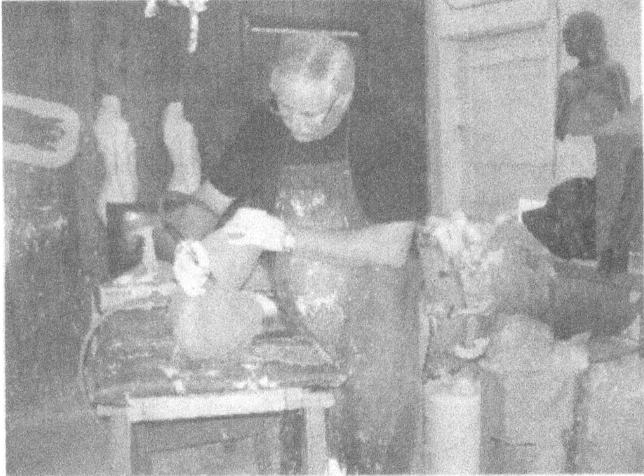

#9 Repairing the head with a pencil grinder

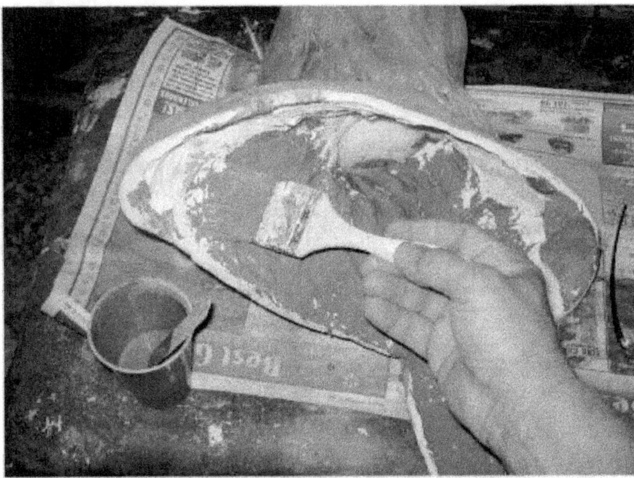

#10 Painting the inside of the head with metallic Forton MG

Now, back to the reassembled mold. This next step is not essential, but spraying light coats of two specific mold releases onto the alginate surface produces a cleaner casting when using Forton MG with metal powders. The first coat is Pol-Ease 2300 and the second is Synlube 531, which I dry with a hair drier for only about a minute. (See photographs #3 and #4.)

Next, measure a pint of VF-812 and dump it into a one-gallon plastic bucket. Using the same kind of pint container, scoop two pints of the metallic powder blend. With the electric drill and mixer, mix until smooth, which only takes about a minute. Dump half of the metallic wet mix into another bucket and set it aside. Add about a couple tablespoons of accelerant to the first bucket and mix for about 10 - 15 seconds. If the mixture becomes instantly thicker, you added too much accelerant and do not try to use it as it will probably set up before you can apply it into the mold. Assuming its consistency did not change, pour the mixture into the mold. While you can tip and rotate the mold so that the metallic solution coats the inside, you will have better luck if you use one of the 2 inch brushes to get an even, bubble free coating. Pay special attention to the ears. (See "Casting Perfect Ears" by this author, SJ, May 2004.) If you have large hands, as I do, having an assistant with small hands can be very helpful. (Photograph #5) Dump the unused half of the metallic mix back into the first bucket.

While the first coat is setting up, mix some plain Forton MG into the second bucket. A pint VF-812 and two pints of plain blend will probably be enough.

Just one coat of the metallic is sufficient if evenly applied. But to be certain that there are areas too thinly covered or not at all, I apply a second metallic coat. After about 10 minutes when the first coat will have set up to the point it no longer sticks to your finger when touched, mix in about half as much accelerant as used for the first coat in to the remaining metallic mixture and dump it into the head. Less accelerant is needed because the small amount that was in the unused part of the first batch will have been affecting the mix. As long as the Forton MG is liquid, you can coat the inside by tipping and turning the mold. (Photograph #6) But, as it thickens, you may have to use your gloved hand or one of the brushes to spread it evenly. Dump about a third of the new plain batch into the first bucket and stir. This will dilute what was left behind of the second coat keeping it from setting up and being wasted.

When the second metallic coat has set up, add another spoonful of accelerant to the first bucket along with a hand full of chopped fiberglass and stir. This mixture should be somewhat thicker, too thick to slosh around. Use a gloved hand and/or brush to apply. As soon as it has set up, repeat this step using the second 1/3 of the plain mix. To the remaining 1/3 add some accelerant but no fiberglass and use this last 1/3 to smooth off the inside surface. At this point the Forton MG should be about 1/4 of an inch (0.6 cm) thick which is plenty.

Earlier I said that the slow setting time of Forton MG is and advantage. It allows you to mix as much of the metallic or the plain mixes as required at one time. Then simply dump out what is needed for the next coat into a bucket; adding accelerant will make only this small amount set up. Repeat as necessary. With the much faster setting copy cats, you would have to measure and mix each batch separately which is more time consuming and tedious.

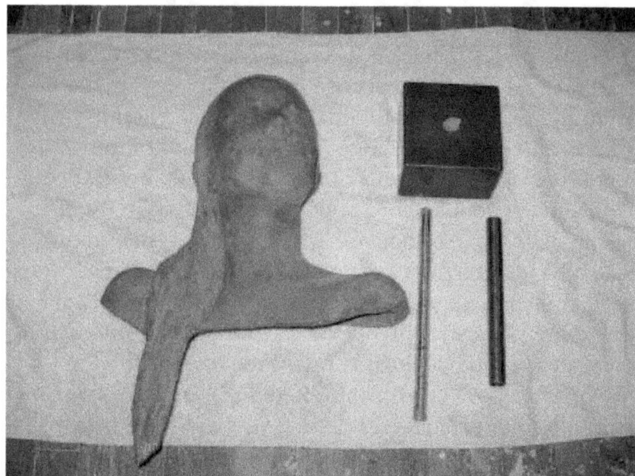

#11 The head, base and the all thread and copper pipe

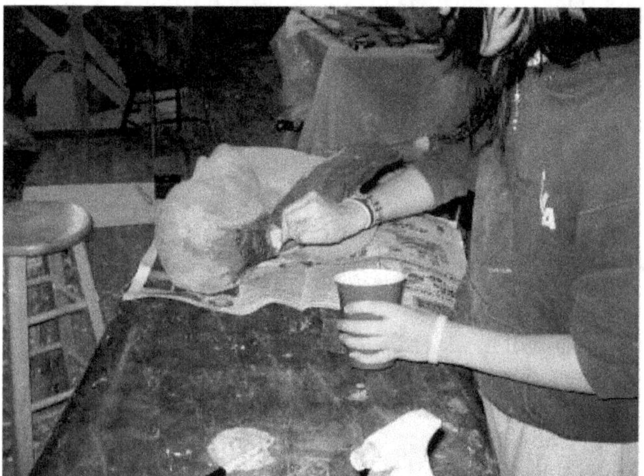

#12 Applying the patina solution

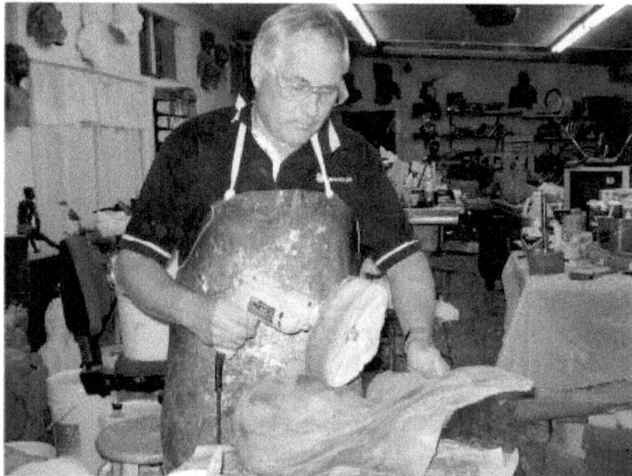

#13 Buffing

mix each batch separately which is more time consuming and tedious.

Wait about 2 hours before removing the mold. Pull back the alginate from the Forton MG at the edges of the mold. If the alginate separates cleanly and is not discolored, it's time. After you have cut through whatever you used to bind the front and back of the mother mold together, the back should come off easily (Photograph #7). Carefully peal off the rest of the plaster and alginate revealing the cast head (Photograph #8). Because of the moisture in the alginate, a very thin layer of the surface of the metallic Forton MG may not have set up completely. Try to touch only the hair and not the skin where any damage to the surface would be more noticeably. I always rinse off the outer surface of the head in a shower and let it dry for a couple of hours before preceding, at which point, the surface will have solidified.

You can always expect a little clean up to any casting such as bubbles in the alginate resulting in "outies" and bubbles in the Forton MG, "innies." The outies can be trimmed down using carving tools or an electric or air grinder (Photograph #9). Innies can be filled in by mixing a small amount of metallic Forton MG and applying as if putty. One of the really great things about For¯ton MG is that unlike plaster, it will bond to itself even after it has set up. With practice, you will be able to make repairs that are almost invisible.

Next turn the head upside down. Mix about 2 ounces (60 grams) of each of the 2 components of the casting foam and pour it into the head. The foam will expand almost 10 times. Add more as necessary until the head is filled to about the top of the neck. In order to make the inside of the shoulders, which may be visible when mounted, the same color as the outside, mix a few ounces of VF-812 with some of the metallic powder blend and paint the inside. Notice in photograph #10 in which I am doing this that the neck had been filled with foam.

All that was needed to complete the piece was a base, a way to attach the base to the head, and some final patina and buffing. Previously, to keep from purchasing expensive marble cubes for bases, I had made a mold of one such cube 6 by 6 by 6 inches (about 15 cms). To make the base for this project, I filled the mold about 2/3 full of metallic Forton MG. Of course any number of other things could have been used, depending on availability and budget. A Piece of 3/4 inch copper pipe looked like just the thing to attach the head to the base. The problem was that the 3/4-inch pipe is really 7/8 inch outside diameter. While 7/8 inch wood bits were readily available, a ceramic bit was needed to drill into the base and it seems that nobody makes a 7/8 inch ceramic bit.

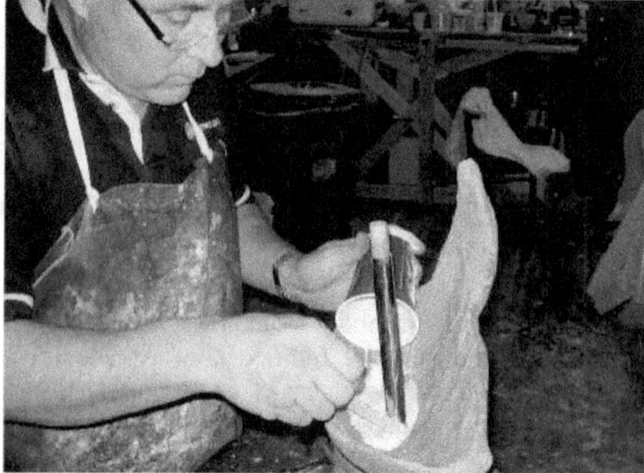

#14 Pouring in some plain Forton MG with fiberglass to secure the head to the connecting all thread and copper pipe.

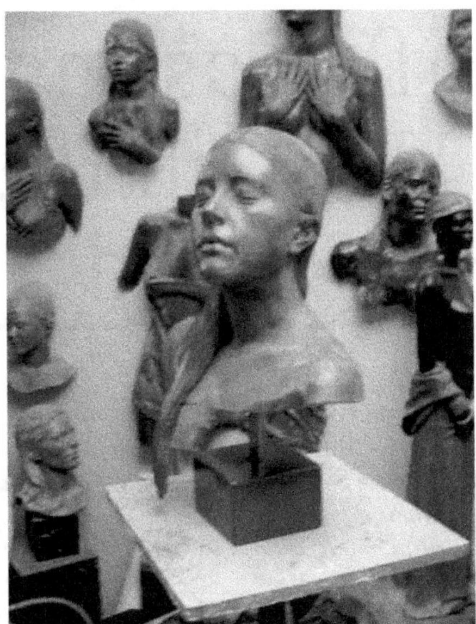

#15 The Finished head in the round

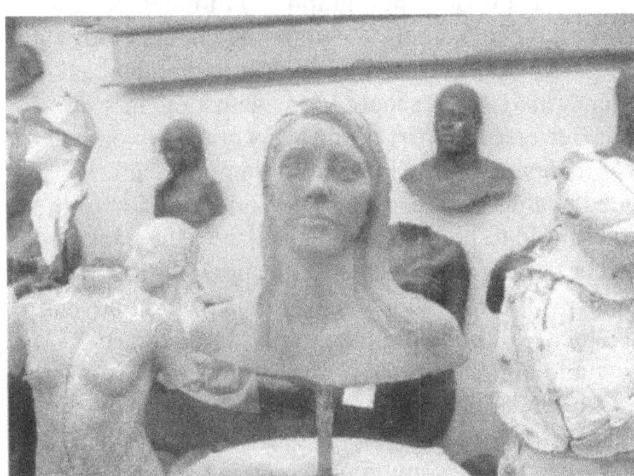

#16 A head that was cast in melted oil base clay and then significantly resculpted.

The solution was to drill 3/4-inch holes and use a piece of 3/4 inch all thread, 1 foot long, to connect the two parts. The 3/4 inch all thread just happens to fit inside 3/4 inch copper pipe which covered up the threads and made it look as if the head were attached by the copper pipe. Photograph #11 shows the parts ready for assembly.

Metallic Forton MG reacts more intensely to patina solutions the newer the casting is. Since I wanted the hair to be more green than the skin, the day after making the casting, I applied the patina solution to the hair. (Photograph #12). While still wet, I rubbed the hair with steel wool. The tiny pieces of steel wool, left on the hair, add an antique rusty color. It is best to allow the head to cure for at least three days before applying the patina solution to the skin parts. If the solution beads up, and doesn't want to evenly coat the surface, add a small amount of liquid detergent. As soon as the skin shows any sign of turning green, rinse off the surface and allow the head to dry. Using the finest steel wool, "0000", go over the entire head and remove excess green. It is best to do this outside as the dust contains chlorine and is not good for your lungs. Do not remove all the green nor try to actually polish the surface with the steel wool; rather use a cloth buffing wheel with the buffing compound. Do not over polish or you may remove the skin texture. To prevent the surface from slowly darkening over time, spray on either matte or glossy clear acrylic. Paste wax can be applied as well, if you desire. The base and the copper pipe were polished the same way except that a black patina solution was used.

To attach the head to the base I drilled 3/4-inch holes into the foam in the head and into the base and epoxyed the all thread into the head at the right angle. As soon as it was secure I slid over the all thread a piece of copper pipe, which had been cut so as to be just long enough, to go from the foam to the base covering up the all thread. Since the all thread was glued to the foam only it was necessary to attach it more securely to the head. This was done by turning the head upside down and pouring several cups of plain Forton MG with fiberglass over the foam and then spreading it from the pipe to the sides. Once secure, the bottom end of the all thread was glued into the base and a piece of self-sticking felt was attached to the bottom.

There are some other things that I could have done with the mold rather than directly cast the head in metallic Forton MG. For example as I said at the beginning of this article, I could have cast it in plaster and given it a faux finish. Or I could have cleaned up the plaster and made a secondary mold in silicone rubber and then cast the final piece in Forton MG or any number of resins from metallic to clear. If for some reason I wanted or needed to do major rework to the head, I could have cast it in melted oil based clay as shown in photograph #16. In this case I changed the expression, removed some small wrinkles making her look younger, opened the eyes, and completely reworked the hair. I then made a mold of the reworked head in silicone rubber and cast the final piece (not shown) in metallic Forton MG.

The special effects industry regularly casts entire heads as an intermediate step in making costume masks usually a skull-cap is fitted on the actor to cover up the hair. This simplifies the casting and allows for the use of skin safe silicone rubber, which clings to hair much more tenaciously than alginate. (See (How to Cast a Ballerina's Foot," by yours truly, SJ, Jan, 2005). The advantage of this rubber is that the mold can be used over and over and stored for years.

A head in the round might be a little intimidating for someone just starting life casting. But I would encourage giving it a try. It might take you to a whole new level.

David Parvin is a Colorado sculptor whose primary subject is the human form in a variety of materials. He also teaches life casting workshops held throughout the year. He may be reached at 303-321-1074.

Life Casting a Head in the Round

By David E. Parvin, A.L.I.

At the end of my article in last month's "Sculpture Journal" I had finished making an impression of a young lady's head in the round using alginate. In this article, I will finish making a free standing cold cast metallic bust attached to a base as in photograph #1.

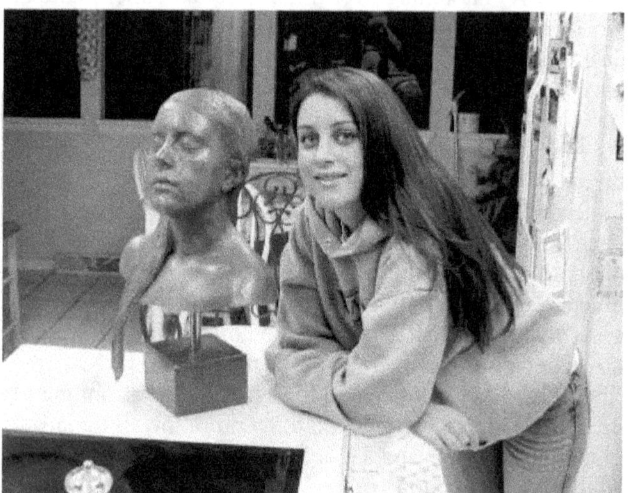

#1 Finished Head

The first step was to reassemble the two parts of the mold. I fitted the back half of the mother mold in place and then turned the completed mold upside down. (Photograph #2) I joined the two halves together securely by wrapping cheese cloth with Impression Dental Plaster making sure that the back half of the alginate fitted securely up against the mother mold. Because this part of the alginate was two layers thick, it stayed in position with minimum seam. If needed, Cholesterol can be coated on the inside of the mother mold to help the alginate stick to the back. Another trick is to use Super Glue along with a catalyst called "Insta Cure" which is available from hobby stores and which will bond alginate to plaster and even alginate to alginate.

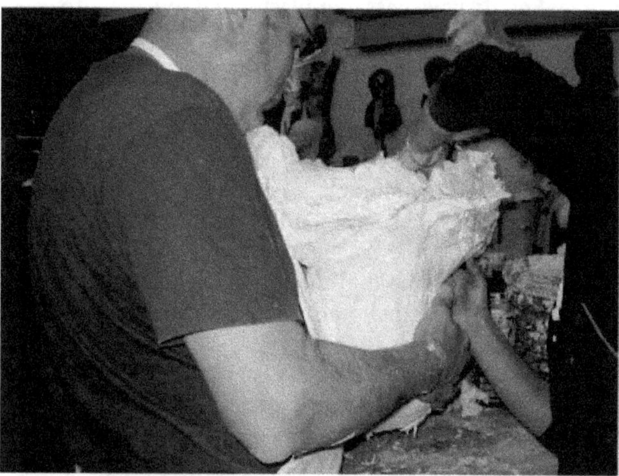

#2 Turning the mold upside down for assembly

I often emphasize that life casting has to be divided into two separate processes. In this respect, it is rather like photography in which taking the picture is one and working in the dark room or with a computer is the other. With life casting, the first is making the most perfect impression or mold that one can of the model. The second is what one does with that mold and where any number of artistic choices and opportunities lie. The simplest and most common solution would have been to fill the mold with plaster or something similar and, perhaps, apply a faux finish. What I did in this case was make a very believable "bronze" casting using the Forton MG casting system. I would need the following, all of which are available from suppliers listed in this magazine:

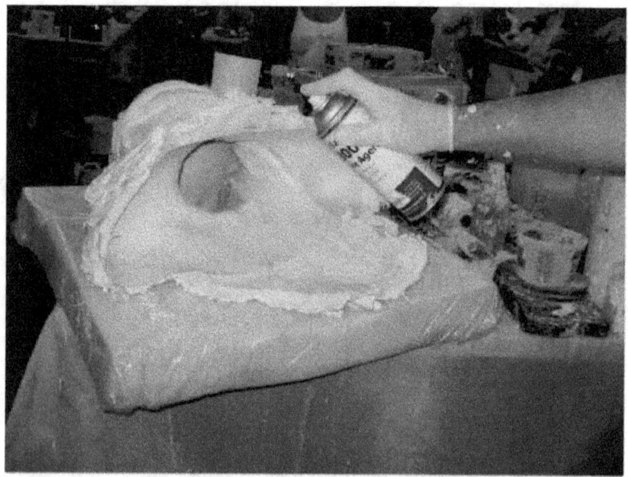

#3 Spraying in the first of two releases which act as barriers between the metallic Forton MG and the alginate.

1. At least three pints, by volume, of blended metallic Forton MG powders.
2. At least 5 pints of blended plain Forton MG powder. (See below.)
3. At least 4 pints of the Forton MG liquid, VF-812.
4. Several 2 inch, inexpensive chip brushes.
5. A mixer attached to an electric drill.
6. An 8 inch piece of 3/4 inch copper pipe.
7. A 12 inch piece of 3/4 inch all thread.
8. Some rigid casting foam such as Polyfoarn R-8 from Polytec.

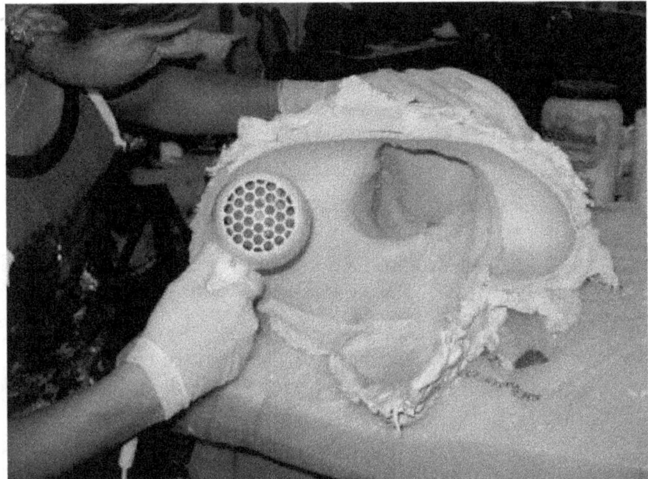
#4 Drying the releases

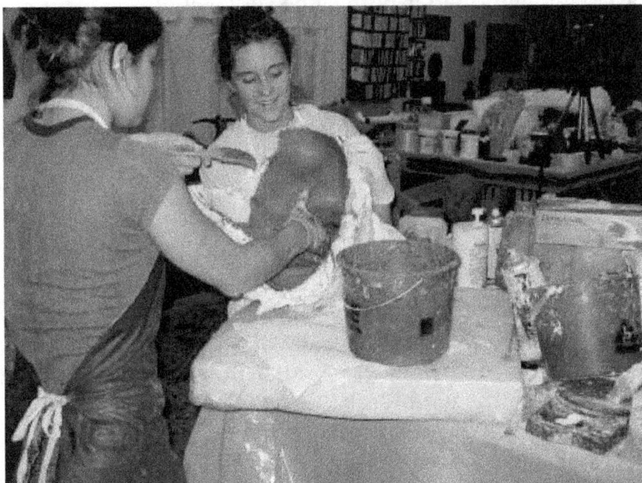
#5 Painting in the first layer of metallic Forton MG.

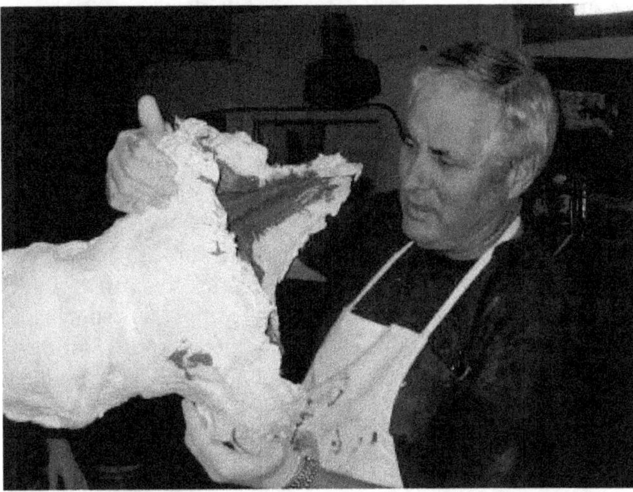
#6 Sloshing the second laver of metallic Forton MG around the inside of the mold

9. At least 8 ounces of "accelerant" made by dissolving 1 part aluminum sulfate into 10 parts of water. Aluminum sulfate is available from any place that sells garden supplies.
10. Several one-gallon, plastic buckets. 11. Several hands full of chopped fiberglass.
12. Some rubber gloves.
13. Some blue/green and black patina solutions.
14. 2 mold releases: Pol-Ease 2300 by Polytec and Synlube 531 by Synair.
15. Very fine, "0000," steel wool.
16. A cloth buffing wheel and a buffing compound such as "Tripoli."
17. A can of clear acrylic spray.
18. Some self-sticking felt or felt dots.

I should point out that I am aware of 4 other materials that are "copy cat" Forton MGs and may be substituted. But there are differences. They cost more ranging from just a little more expensive to over twice as much. Also, all of them set up much more quickly and as I will explain below, this makes their use less convenient. (For a more complete explanation of Forton MG, see "Mixing Forton MG Simplified," by yours truly in the July 2003.

When you purchase Forton MG, you get a liquid called VF812 and two powders, dry resin and hardener. A third powder, FGR-95 is purchased separately. Blending the Forton MG powders is a cinch. I use two clean 5-gallon buckets with lids, one for the plain and one for the metallic. I usually mix about half a bucket full. For the plain, I weigh out about 10,000 grams (22 pounds) of the FGR-95 and add 10% or 1000 grams (2 pounds and 3.2 ounces) of dry resin and 0.5% or 50 grams (1.75 ounces) of hardener. I use a 4-inch Jiffy Mixer attached to a heave duty electric drill for blending. For the metallic, blend as the plain but add twice the weight of metal powers as you did FGR-95. When ready to mix the VF-812 liquid and the blended powders, all you do is use twice as much of the powders, either plain or metallic by volume as you use the VF-812 liquid and mix.

Now, about metal powders, there are different kinds available such as copper, bronze, brass, aluminum, and others. I have found that copper powder in Forton MG results in a more realistic bronze look than bronze powder which makes a harder casting which doesn't respond to the standard blue/green patina solution as well as copper. I sometimes blend copper and bronze powders together for an in between look. I encourage you to experiment and determine your own preferences.

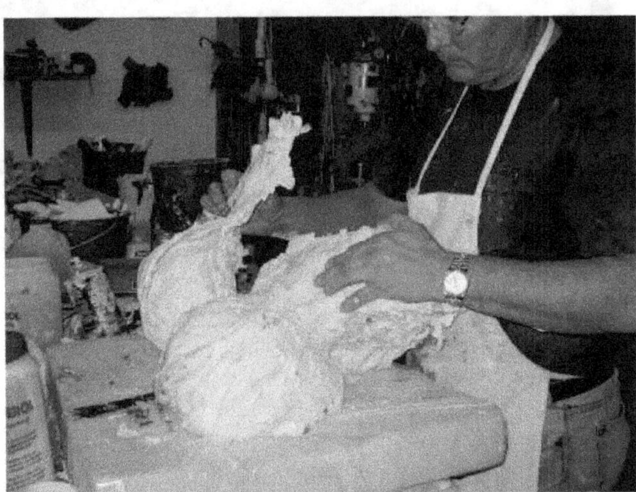
#7 Demolding the head

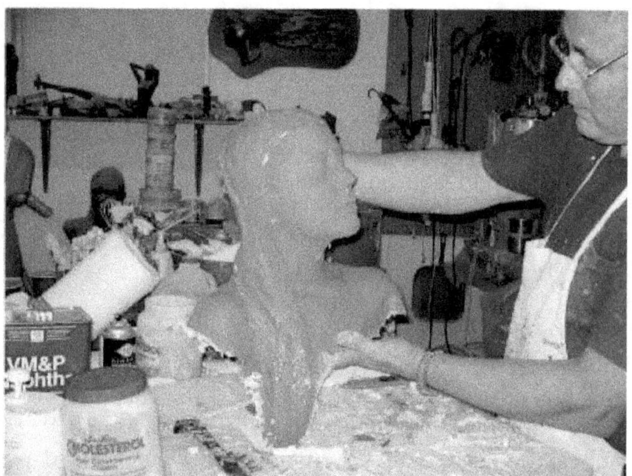
#8 The demolded head

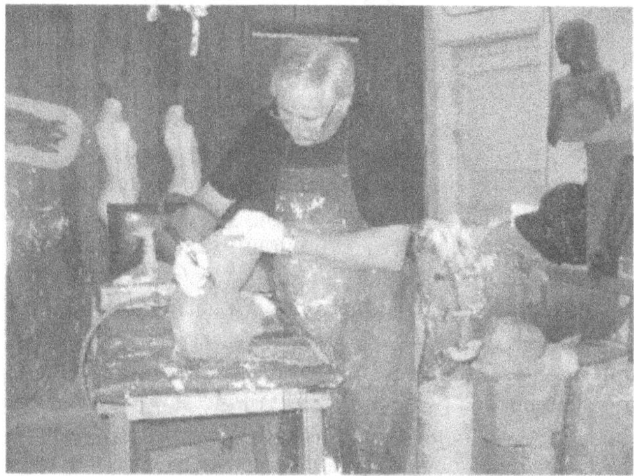
#9 Repairing the head with a pencil grinder

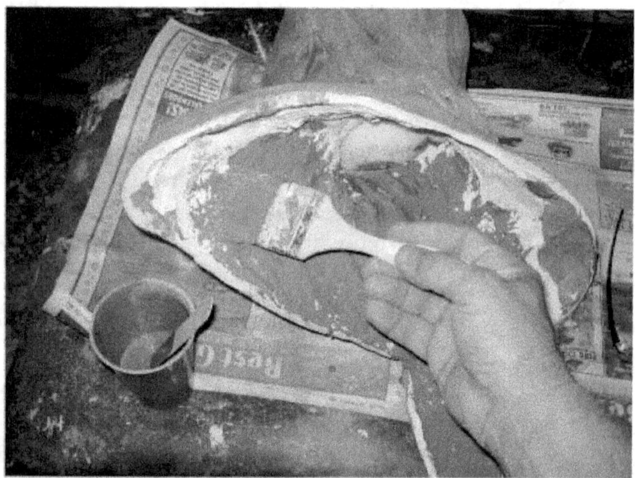
#10 Painting the inside of the head with metallic Forton MG

Now, back to the reassembled mold. This next step is not essential, but spraying light coats of two specific mold releases onto the alginate surface produces a cleaner casting when using Forton MG with metal powders. The first coat is Pol-Ease 2300 and the second is Synlube 531, which I dry with a hair drier for only about a minute. (See photographs #3 and #4.)

Next, measure a pint of VF-812 and dump it into a one-gallon plastic bucket. Using the same kind of pint container, scoop two pints of the metallic powder blend. With the electric drill and mixer, mix until smooth, which only takes about a minute. Dump half of the metallic wet mix into another bucket and set it aside. Add about a couple tablespoons of accelerant to the first bucket and mix for about 10 - 15 seconds. If the mixture becomes instantly thicker, you added too much accelerant and do not try to use it as it will probably set up before you can apply it into the mold. Assuming its consistency did not change, pour the mixture into the mold. While you can tip and rotate the mold so that the metallic solution coats the inside, you will have better luck if you use one of the 2 inch brushes to get an even, bubble free coating. Pay special attention to the ears. (See "Casting Perfect Ears" by this author, SJ, May 2004.) If you have large hands, as I do, having an assistant with small hands can be very helpful. (Photograph #5) Dump the unused half of the metallic mix back into the first bucket.

While the first coat is setting up, mix some plain Forton MG into the second bucket. A pint VF-812 and two pints of plain blend will probably be enough.

Just one coat of the metallic is sufficient if evenly applied. But to be certain that there are areas too thinly covered or not at all, I apply a second metallic coat. After about 10 minutes when the first coat will have set up to the point it no longer sticks to your finger when touched, mix in about half as much accelerant as used for the first coat in to the remaining metallic mixture and dump it into the head. Less accelerant is needed because the small amount that was in the unused part of the first batch will have been affecting the mix. As long as the Forton MG is liquid, you can coat the inside by tipping and turning the mold. (Photograph #6) But, as it thickens, you may have to use your gloved hand or one of the brushes to spread it evenly. Dump about a third of the new plain batch into the first bucket and stir. This will dilute what was left behind of the second coat keeping it from setting up and being wasted.

When the second metallic coat has set up, add another spoonful of accelerant to the first bucket along with a hand full of chopped fiberglass and stir. This mixture should be somewhat thicker, too thick to slosh around. Use a gloved hand and/or brush to apply. As soon as it has set up, repeat this step using the second 1/3 of the plain mix. To the remaining 1/3 add some accelerant but no fiberglass and use this last 1/3 to smooth off the inside surface. At this point the Forton MG should be about 1/4 of an inch (0.6 cm) thick which is plenty.

Earlier I said that the slow setting time of Forton MG is and advantage. It allows you to mix as much of the metallic or the plain mixes as required at one time. Then simply dump out what is needed for the next coat into a bucket; adding accelerant will make only this small amount set up. Repeat as necessary. With the much faster setting copy cats, you would have to measure and mix each batch separately which is more time consuming and tedious.

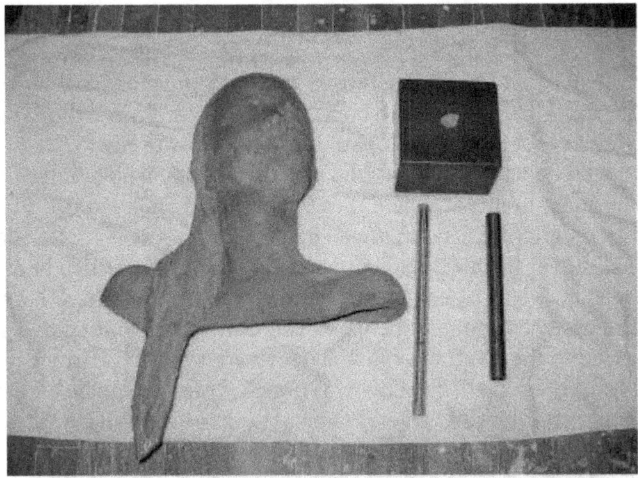

#11 The head, base and the all thread and copper pipe

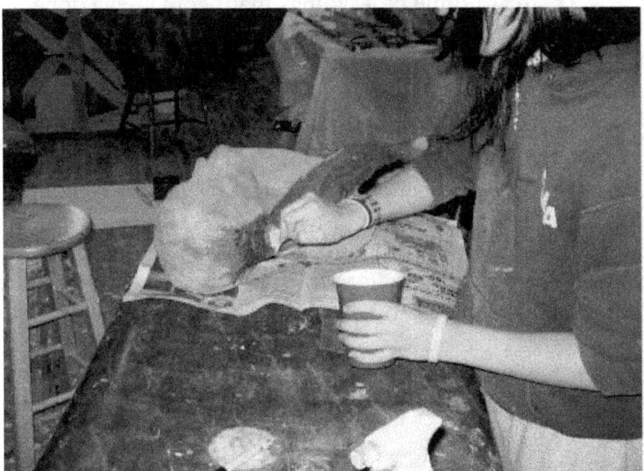

#12 Applying the patina solution

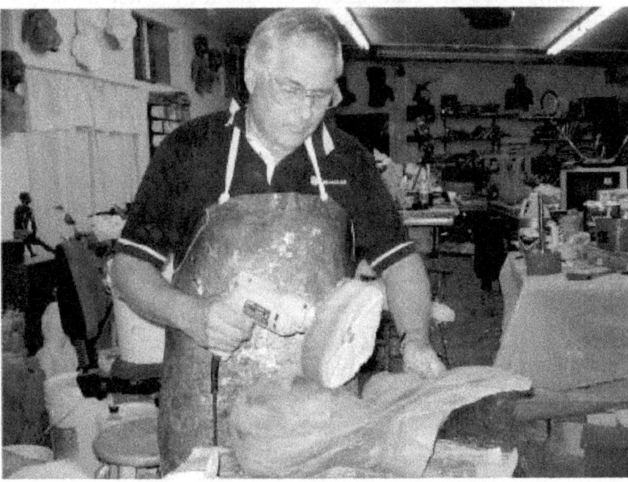

#13 Buffing

mix each batch separately which is more time consuming and tedious.

Wait about 2 hours before removing the mold. Pull back the alginate from the Forton MG at the edges of the mold. If the alginate separates cleanly and is not discolored, it's time. After you have cut through whatever you used to bind the front and back of the mother mold together, the back should come off easily (Photograph #7). Carefully peal off the rest of the plaster and alginate revealing the cast head (Photograph #8). Because of the moisture in the alginate, a very thin layer of the surface of the metallic Forton MG may not have set up completely. Try to touch only the hair and not the skin where any damage to the surface would be more noticeably. I always rinse off the outer surface of the head in a shower and let it dry for a couple of hours before preceding, at which point, the surface will have solidified.

You can always expect a little clean up to any casting such as bubbles in the alginate resulting in "outies" and bubbles in the Forton MG, "innies." The outies can be trimmed down using carving tools or an electric or air grinder (Photograph #9). Innies can be filled in by mixing a small amount of metallic Forton MG and applying as if putty. One of the really great things about For¨ton MG is that unlike plaster, it will bond to itself even after it has set up. With practice, you will be able to make repairs that are almost invisible.

Next turn the head upside down. Mix about 2 ounces (60 grams) of each of the 2 components of the casting foam and pour it into the head. The foam will expand almost 10 times. Add more as necessary until the head is filled to about the top of the neck. In order to make the inside of the shoulders, which may be visible when mounted, the same color as the outside, mix a few ounces of VF-812 with some of the metallic powder blend and paint the inside. Notice in photograph #10 in which I am doing this that the neck had been filled with foam.

All that was needed to complete the piece was a base, a way to attach the base to the head, and some final patina and buffing. Previously, to keep from purchasing expensive marble cubes for bases, I had made a mold of one such cube 6 by 6 by 6 inches (about 15 cms). To make the base for this project, I filled the mold about 2/3 full of metallic Forton MG. Of course any number of other things could have been used, depending on availability and budget. A Piece of 3/4 inch copper pipe looked like just the thing to attach the head to the base. The problem was that the 3/4-inch pipe is really 7/8 inch outside diameter. While 7/8 inch wood bits were readily available, a ceramic bit was needed to drill into the base and it seems that nobody makes a 7/8 inch ceramic bit.

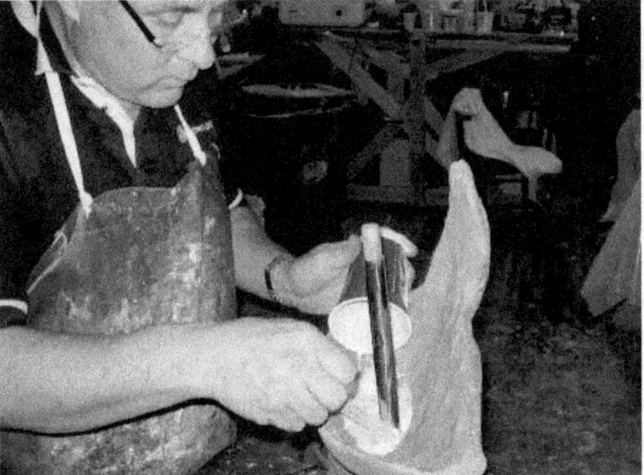

#14 Pouring in some plain Forton MG with fiberglass to secure the head to the connecting all thread and copper pipe.

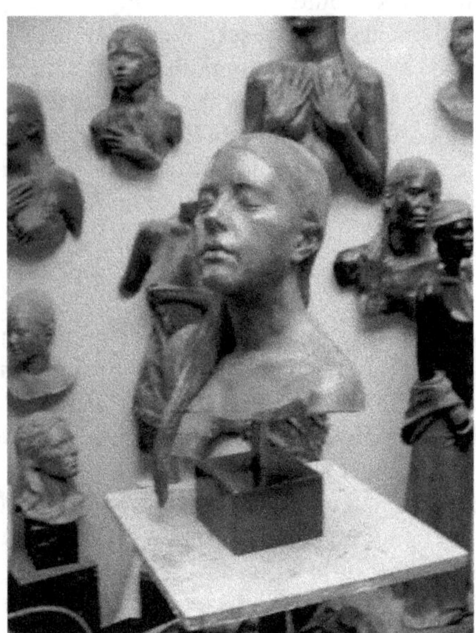

#15 The Finished head in the round

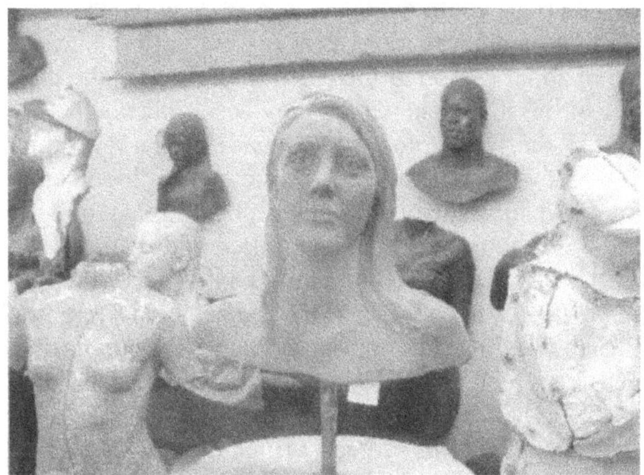

#16 A head that was cast in melted oil base clay and then significantly resculpted.

The solution was to drill 3/4-inch holes and use a piece of 3/4 inch all thread, 1 foot long, to connect the two parts. The 3/4 inch all thread just happens to fit inside 3/4 inch copper pipe which covered up the threads and made it look as if the head were attached by the copper pipe. Photograph #11 shows the parts ready for assembly.

Metallic Forton MG reacts more intensely to patina solutions the newer the casting is. Since I wanted the hair to be more green than the skin, the day after making the casting, I applied the patina solution to the hair. (Photograph #12). While still wet, I rubbed the hair with steel wool. The tiny pieces of steel wool, left on the hair, add an antique rusty color. It is best to allow the head to cure for at least three days before applying the patina solution to the skin parts. If the solution beads up, and doesn't want to evenly coat the surface, add a small amount of liquid detergent. As soon as the skin shows any sign of turning green, rinse off the surface and allow the head to dry. Using the finest steel wool, "0000", go over the entire head and remove excess green. It is best to do this outside as the dust contains chlorine and is not good for your lungs. Do not remove all the green nor try to actually polish the surface with the steel wool; rather use a cloth buffing wheel with the buffing compound. Do not over polish or you may remove the skin texture. To prevent the surface from slowly darkening over time, spray on either matte or glossy clear acrylic. Paste wax can be applied as well, if you desire. The base and the copper pipe were polished the same way except that a black patina solution was used.

To attach the head to the base I drilled 3/4-inch holes into the foam in the head and into the base and epoxyed the all thread into the head at the right angle. As soon as it was secure I slid over the all thread a piece of copper pipe, which had been cut so as to be just long enough, to go from the foam to the base covering up the all thread. Since the all thread was glued to the foam only it was necessary to attach it more securely to the head. This was done by turning the head upside down and pouring several cups of plain Forton MG with fiberglass over the foam and then spreading it from the pipe to the sides. Once secure, the bottom end of the all thread was glued into the base and a piece of self-sticking felt was attached to the bottom.

There are some other things that I could have done with the mold rather than directly cast the head in metallic Forton MG. For example as I said at the beginning of this article, I could have cast it in plaster and given it a faux finish. Or I could have cleaned up the plaster and made a secondary mold in silicone rubber and then cast the final piece in Forton MG or any number of resins from metallic to clear. If for some reason I wanted or needed to do major rework to the head, I could have cast it in melted oil based clay as shown in photograph #16. In this case I changed the expression, removed some small wrinkles making her look younger, opened the eyes, and completely reworked the hair. I then made a mold of the reworked head in silicone rubber and cast the final piece (not shown) in metallic Forton MG.

The special effects industry regularly casts entire heads as an intermediate step in making costume masks usually a skull-cap is fitted on the actor to cover up the hair. This simplifies the casting and allows for the use of skin safe silicone rubber, which clings to hair much more tenaciously than alginate. (See (How to Cast a Ballerina's Foot," by yours truly, SJ, Jan, 2005). The advantage of this rubber is that the mold can be used over and over and stored for years.

A head in the round might be a little intimidating for someone just starting life casting. But I would encourage giving it a try. It might take you to a whole new level.

David Parvin is a Colorado sculptor whose primary subject is the human form in a variety of materials. He also teaches life casting workshops held throughout the year. He may be reached at 303-321-1074.

A Little More Complicated Portrait Castings

By David E. Parvin, A.L.I.

Recently, I described casting praying hands. Whether just hands alone or as part of a portrait, praying hands is sure to please almost any client. In this article, I will offer two examples which are more complicated but will demonstrate what can be done with a little imagination.

Often I have been asked, "Which comes first, the idea or the model?" If a client comes to you wanting to be depicted in a certain way, you do the best you can with the hand you have been dealt. "Can you make me look like a kumquat?" "Why sure young lady." In fact, she might look more like a radish, but kumquat it is." After all, there's a mortgage to be paid and groceries to be bought. But if I am doing something for myself, usually the idea comes first and then I look for the right subject or model. But sometimes, as was in this first example, the model can be the inspiration. It began when an aspiring young ballerina, Caylie, and her mother, Sue, introduced themselves having recognized me from my involvement with Denver's dance community. I couldn't help but be impressed with how much Caylie looked like a faerie and I said so to Sue who told me I wasn't the first to have said that. I invited them to come by my studio even though I had no specific idea of what we might do other than something faerie-like. But before we met again, I got to thinking that Caylie would make a great faerie portrait. Of course, with the right modifications, **anybody** can be turned into a believable faerie. It's just that Caylie's naturally occurring *faerieness* inspired me to begin this project. Had she looked like a kumquat...

My idea was to start with a life casting and then turn her into a

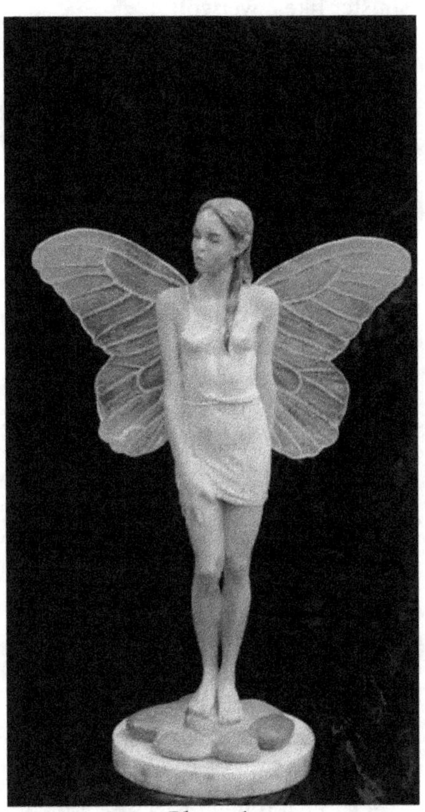

Photo 1

faerie. Of course, I could have sculpted Caylie in the more traditional method of having her sit for me while I shaped her likeness in wax or clay and then cast it in bronze or resin as in my piece, "Asrai" shown in photograph #1. But life casting is analogous to "three dimensional photography" and just as a photograph can be more real and personal than a painting or drawing, so can a life casting be when compared to a regular sculpture. Some may think that I was just following an easier path. But life casting is just another art form with its own advantages and disadvantages and while it may look easy, or at least easier than more traditional sculpting, doing it well does take some knowledge and practice. As in photography, anyone can take a snapshot, but not just anyone can be an Ansel Adams.

I was confident that Caylie at thirteen would have no problem being cast; usually a child eight or older will endure and even enjoy the process. But to put her at ease, I suggested that we first cast her foot en pointe, something all dancers are eager to do. Photo #2 shows an excited Caylie and her mom looking over her finished foot.

In photograph #3, my very able assistant, Audra, and I were in the final preparation of Caylie for casting. Her hair had been thoroughly coated with Cholesterol hair conditioner and a piece of cloth covered up her developing *assets*. The cloth had been fitted tightly so as to be invisible under whatever faerie garb we later decide to add. While her left ear was completely exposed, her right ear, not shown, protruded through her hair in a very faerie-like manner.

In photograph #4, the mold had just been removed and an excited Caylie had soft skin from the seaweed based alginate and well conditioned hair from the Cholesterol. Audra and I made a plaster cast from the mold which was completed by the time Caylie emerged from the shower, photograph #5. There are always at least some repairs that need to be made to the plaster cast such as trimming the back to lie flat and fixing any small imperfections. After which,I had a plaster cast of the human Caylie which was too nice to waste. I went ahead and made a rubber mold of the plaster and made a cold cast "bronze" copy for Caylie in Forton MG with copper powder, photo #6. At that point,I was ready to begin the really fun part, turning Caylie into a faerie.

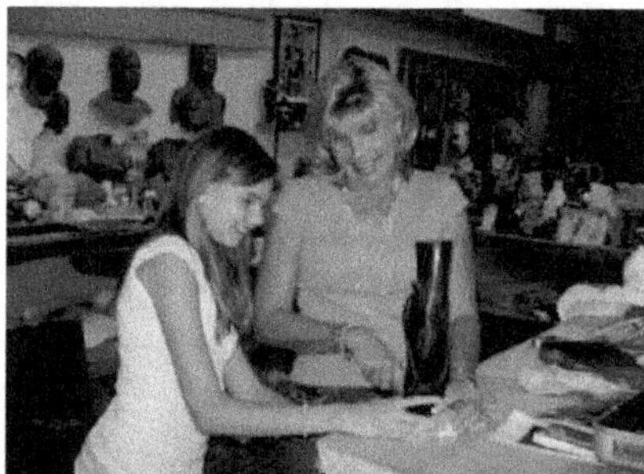
Photo 2

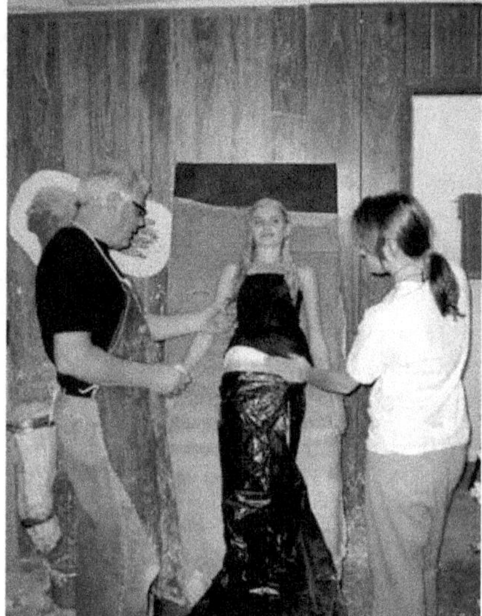
Photo 3

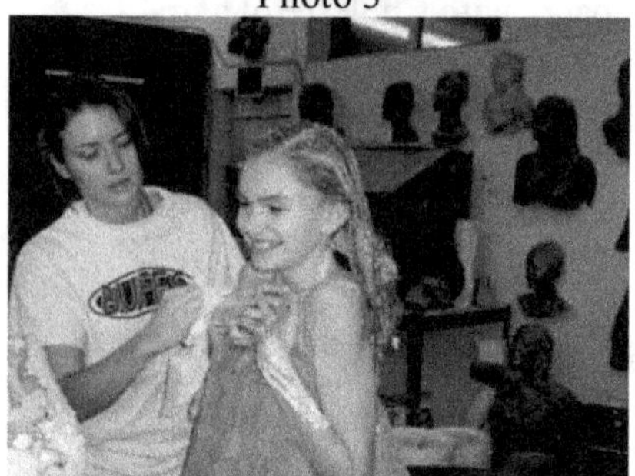
Photo 4

The first thing I did was to refresh myself on what a faerie should look like. Fortunately there is a helpful book with the encouraging title *How to Draw and Paint Fairies*.(1) Looking through the book, I realized that all I needed to do was give her pointed ears; open her eyes; and add some faerie accessories such as flowers, leaves, and wings.

Pointing the ears was a cinch. They were shaped in sculpting wax which adheres nicely to dry plaster. The great thing about pointing the ears was that there was no right or wrong, I just experimented until the ears looked right to me. My only real concern was to be sure not to make the ears so big that she looked

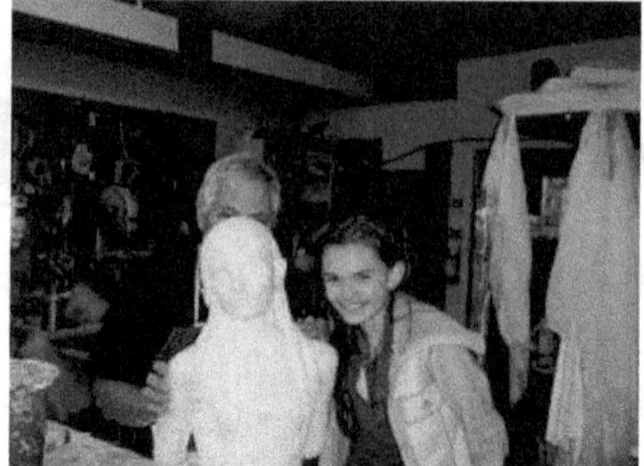
Photo 5

sinister like a werwolf.

I had Caylie return to the studio and sit for me so that I could get her eyes right. Unfortunately, opening the eyes is more complicated than just scraping part of the eyelids off. When a person opens her eyes, the tissue surrounding the eyes changes shape somewhat. So you have to add back as well as take away. This was also done with melted wax which was added on and then shaped as necessary. I used dental tools both for the carving the plaster and shaping the wax.

For her faerie outfit, we went to a craft store and purchased an assortment of artificial leaves and flowers. We glued the leaves flat on the body to make it look as if she were wearing a dress made of leaves. A garland of flowers would be added around her head at a later stage.

Since the finished faerie portrait would be a "relief" wall hanging, we attached the modified plaster casting to a 24 inch round piece of 3/4 inch fiberboard that would frame the work and provide a background for constructing the wings which were made in clay as was the molding along the outer edge. (Photograph #7) The next step was to make a mold of the new Caylie in silicone rubber; the first of three layers of which is shown in photograph #8. The outer or mother mold was made of Forton MG soaked in strips of cotton batting with scrim binder. Because of the undercuts on both sides of the face and shoulders, the rigid mother mold had to be constructed in four pieces in order to separate from the rubber layers.

I decided to cast the skin parts and the area above her head in white by using Forton MG with powdered limestone which when buffed would simulate white marble. Her dress,

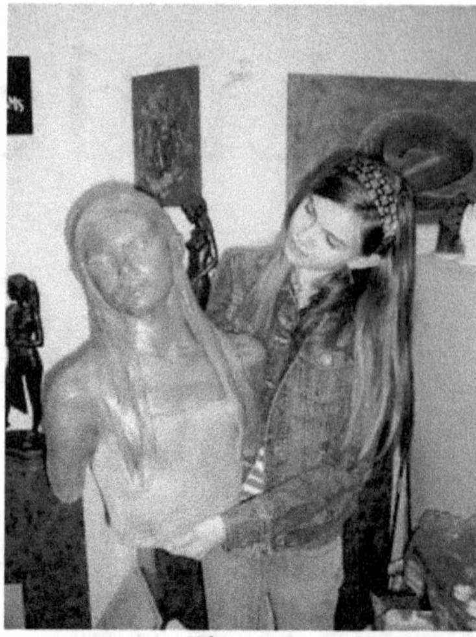
Photo 6

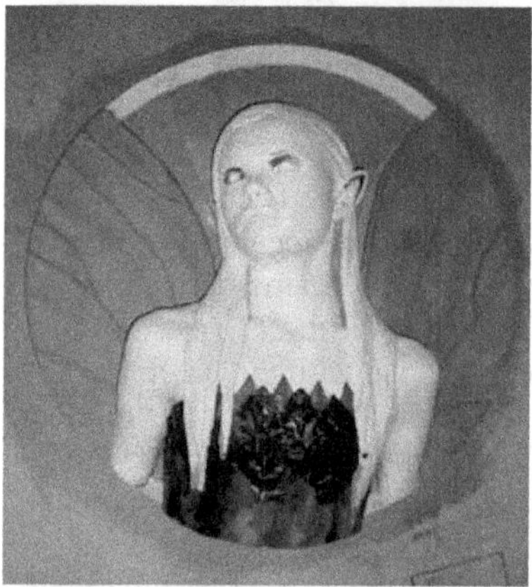
Photo 7

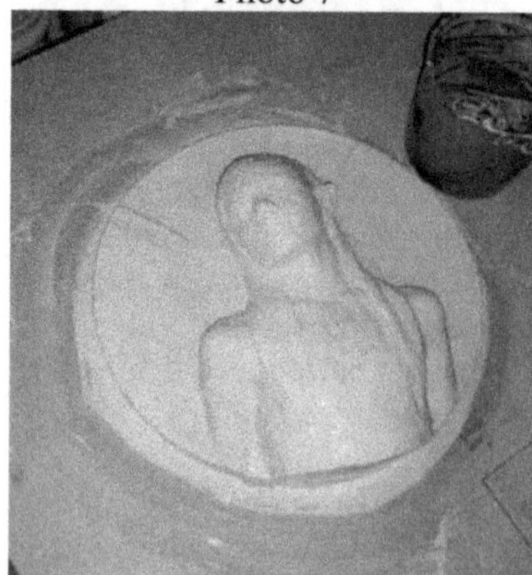
Photo 8

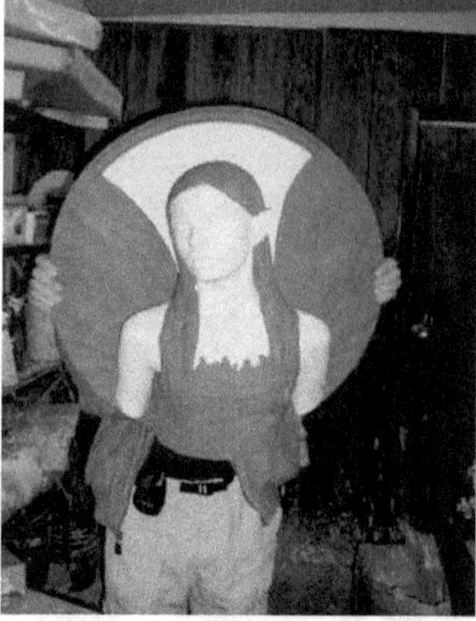
Photo 9

wings, hair, and the molding at the top were Forton MG to which copper powder had been added producing a very credible cold cast "bronze." Photograph #9 shows the casting fresh out of the mold. The hair was turned black with "Super Antique 40" and the leaves and wings became green by using a home made patina solution (2). The garland of flowers around her forehead was a string of artificial flowers that was coated with Forton MG with brass powder. A light blue wash was applied to the area above her so as to distinguish it from the flesh areas. Everything except the flowers was polished with soft cloth buffing wheels with either white or brown buffing compounds. The completed portrait is shown in photograph #10.

In my second example my model gets to become a mermaid. While the result is different, the process is essentially the same.

I once sculpted a small bronze statue of a adolescent mermaid trying on shells for the first time. (Photograph #11) Her left hand held a shell covering her left breast with another shell positioned in her right hand to cover her right breast. For this article, I wanted to tell the same story but there was a problem. While it is perfectly acceptable to sculpt a 1/4 life size adolescent mermaid with one breast exposed, a life casting is more like a photograph. Since it wouldn't have been proper to expose the model's breast that wasn't covered with a shell, I would need a model with hair long enough to preserve her modesty and reputation.

For the faerie portrait, the model looked so much like a faerie that she inspired the piece. But in this case, I had the mermaid idea first and then chose the model. It just so happened that I know a young lady, Laura, who met my criteria.

#1. She looked like a mermaid.
#2. She was the right age, 13.
#3. Her hair was long enough.
#4. She and her mother, Leslie, loved to visit my studio and play "let's make art history." I had already done several casts of her and she was excited to be part of the project, perfect.

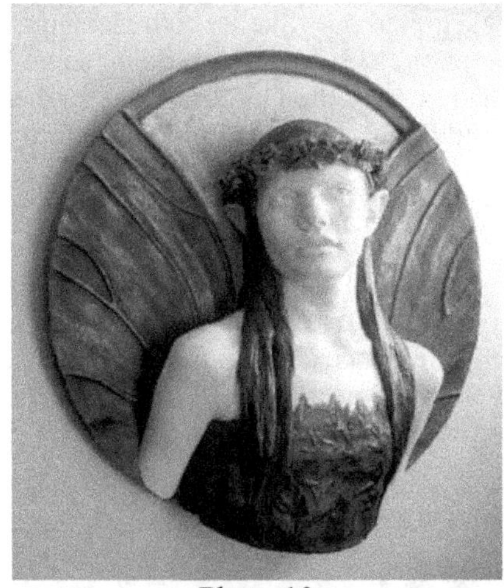

Photo 10

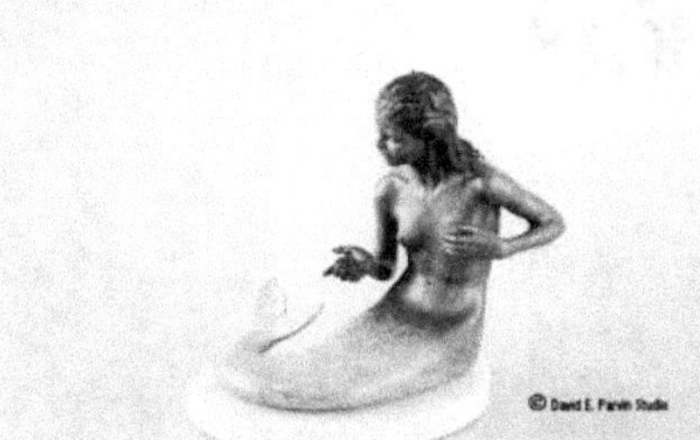

Photo 11

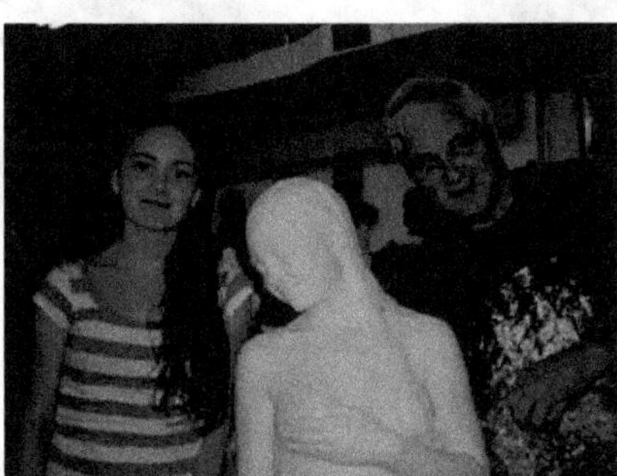

Photo 12

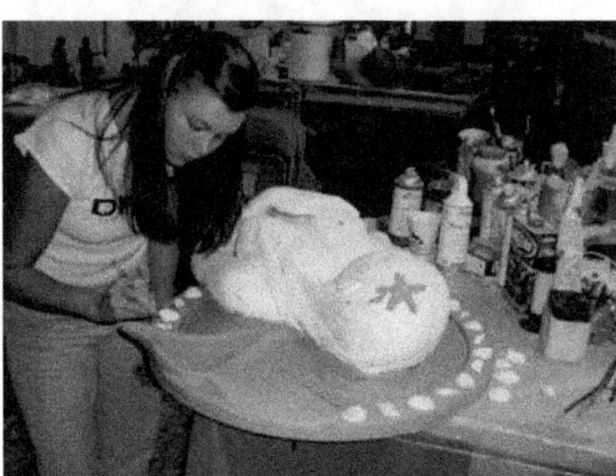

Photo 13

One of my assistants, Melissa, and I cast Laura in the same way as Caylie above resulting in a plaster positive. (See photograph #12.) After repairing a few minor imperfection, I attached the plaster cast to a 24 inch in diameter piece of fiberboard. I love the line from the old song "The Streets of Loredo" that goes, "I can tell by your outfit that you are a cowboy." So all that is needed to make someone into a cowboy, faerie, or mermaid is the right outfit. Add a few sea critters and a tail and presto, one mermaid. The sea critters are no problem; shells and starfish are available from any craft store. I would sculpt the tail in oil based clay. But first, I had to figure out something.

Just what does a mermaid's tail look like. Recently, I had read a hopeful sounding book titled *A Mermaid's Tale.* (2.) Unfortunately, It was "tale" and not "tail" and the book while well worth reading wasn't much help. Amazingly, no one has ever photographed a mermaid and the next best reference was paintings and drawings which offer lots of choices. There isn't even agreement as to how many tails. While most mermaids are depicted with one, some have two as if each leg became separate tails. Further confusion comes from the fact that mermaids are usually covered with scales on their lower half. Fish have scales but sea mammals don't. Scales or not, I have to think of mermaids as warm blooded mammals and not cold blooded fish. I have never seen a mermaid depicted with gills and have to assume that mermaids are air breathing. All this leads me to suspect that mermaids may have scales for some unknown reason, but are more likely to have tails that are mammalian. Unfortunately, there are three very different types of sea mammals: sea otters; whales, porpoises, and dolphins; and seals and sea lions. For my first mermaid, in photo #11, I chose a porpoise style tail and still think that it is the more attractive. So in this case, I decided to do the same. I'm safe unless someone actually takes a photograph of a mermaid and proves me wrong. I'll take my chances.

I intended this mermaid portrait to be a companion piece to the faerie portrait and I wanted both to be the same size. Since I was definitely short on space, I could only show the upper part of the top half of the mermaid. The tail, which I sculpted out of clay, would have to come up behind the head. I was unable to find the right size small starfish for Laura's hair, so I sculpted one. Shells, both clam and snail, were easier to come by and I added some around the edge of the fiberboard circle. In photo #13, Melissa, is doing some last minute tweaking before we made a mold of the modified Laura in the same way that we had done of the faerie, silicone rubber with a Forton MG mother mold. Forton MG was also used for the final portrait using various additives and dyes for the different parts. Photograph #14 shows me painting in the Forton MG. The finished portrait is in photograph #15.

With a little imagination, the possibilities are limitless, you might even come up with something that would have made old Ansel himself proud.

1. *How to Draw and Paint Fairies*, Linda Raverscroft, 2005, ISBN 08230 2383 4
2. A green patina solution can be made by adding one ounce (28 grams) of cupric chloride and six ounces (168 grams) of ammonium chloride to one half gallon (1.816 liters) of water.
3. *A Mermaid's Tail*, by Amanda Adams, Graystone Books, 2006, ISBN-13: 978-1-55365-117-8.

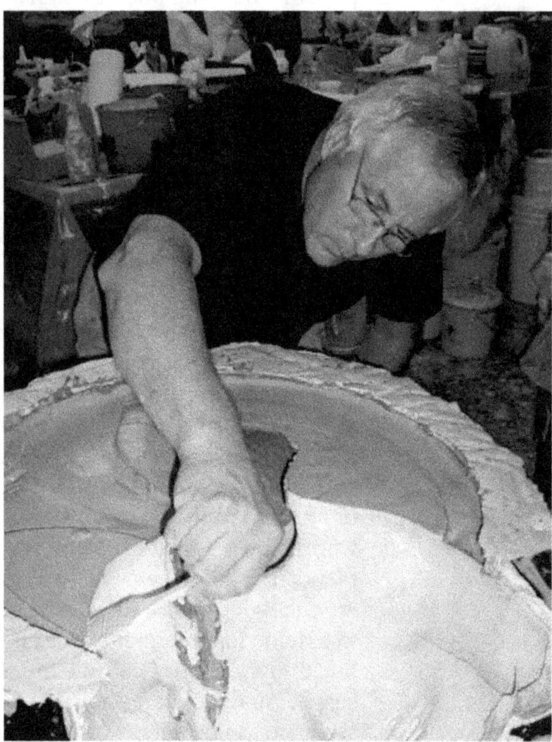
Photo 14

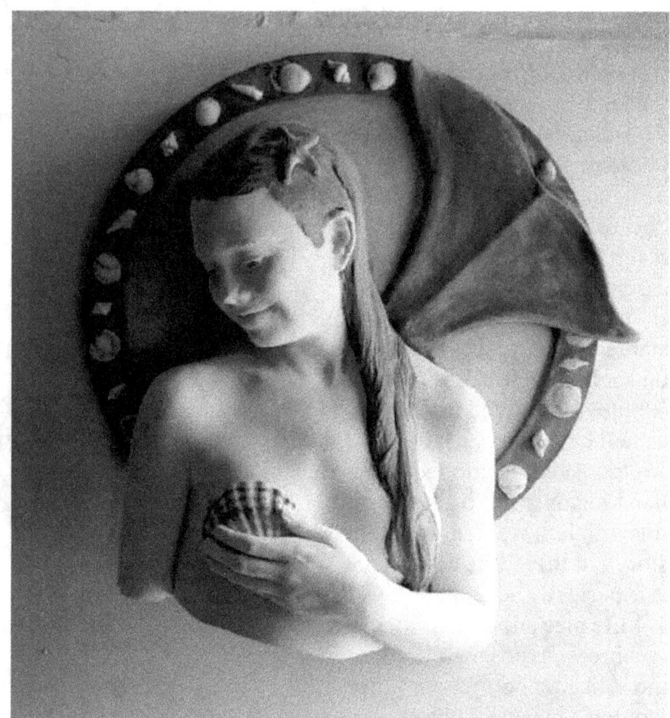
Photo 15

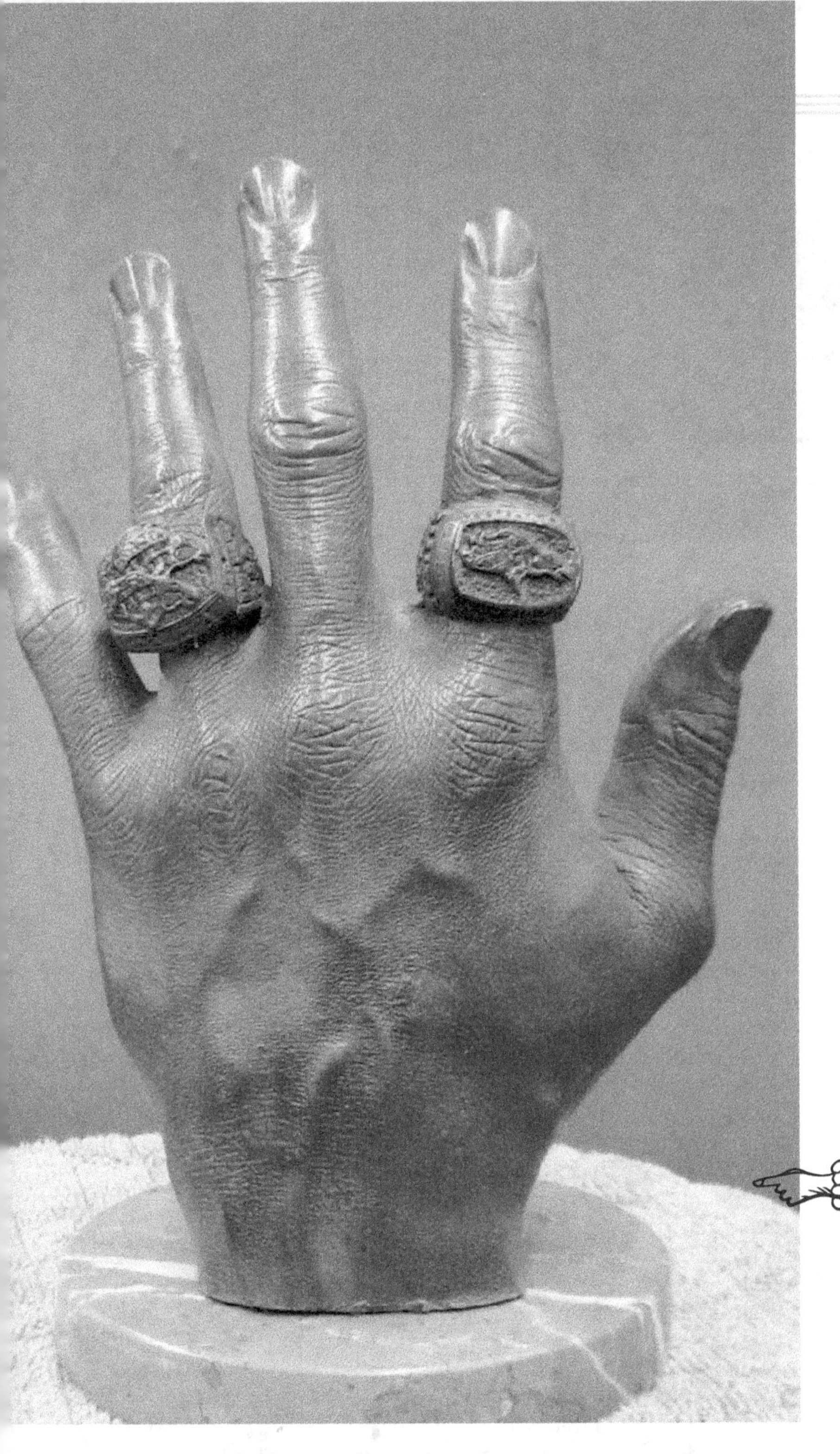

EASILY ELIMINATE Air Bubbles in HAND CASTING FINGERTIPS

By David E. Parvin, A.L.I.

Photo #1 shows a casting of the hand of Bronco great Rod Smith, complete with his two Super Bowl rings. Since the fingers were extended, the casting material (CM) was able to flow to the fingertips without a problem. But if the fingers are curled, air can be trapped in the fingertips, not allowing the CM to fill the mold and resulting in incomplete fills, or voids. Also, whenever components such as plaster and water are mixed, air bubbles are trapped in the CM, and they will tend to rise as long as the CM is in a liquid state. In both of these cases, curled fingertips are a perfect area for capturing these bubbles. Degassing (with a vacuum pump and chamber)the liquid CM helps with the second problem here, but not the first. Besides, not everyone has the capability of degassing.

While doing preliminary work on a future article on rotocasting I came up with a simple solution that requires no special equipment. It is so simple that plenty of other people must have thought of it as well; however, I have never read a reference to it anywhere. If you have already

One of the most commonly asked questions that I get and that also appears in the Forum section on the ALI website is how to eliminate air bubbles or voids in the fingertips of hand castings.

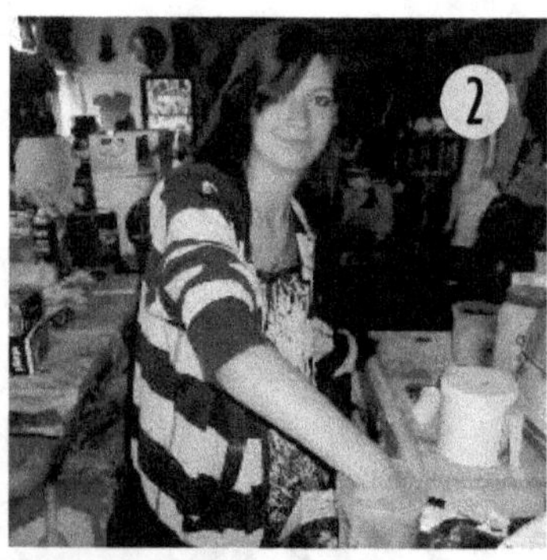

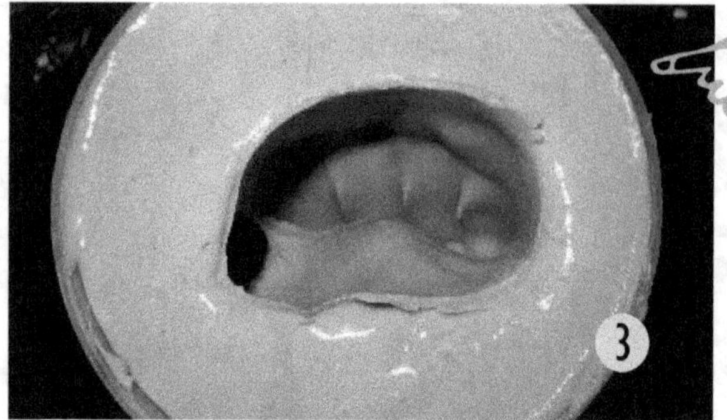

Very nice impression of Jay's hand with fingers curled downward.

This time the fingertips - including the fingernails - cast beautifully.

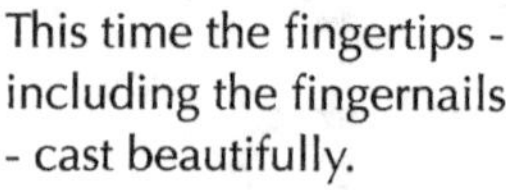

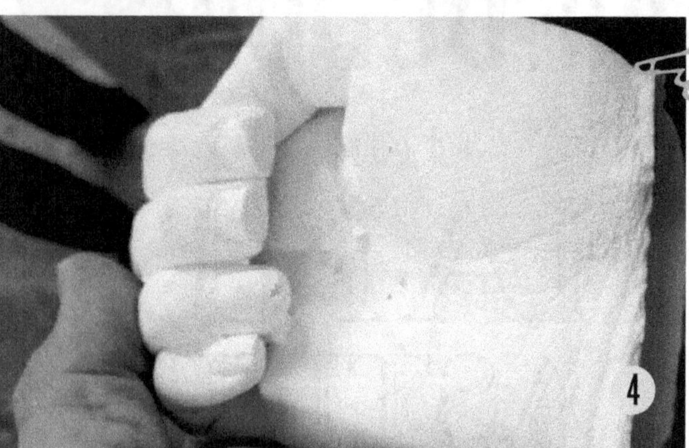

Even as carefully as I tried to fill the tips, it just didn't work.

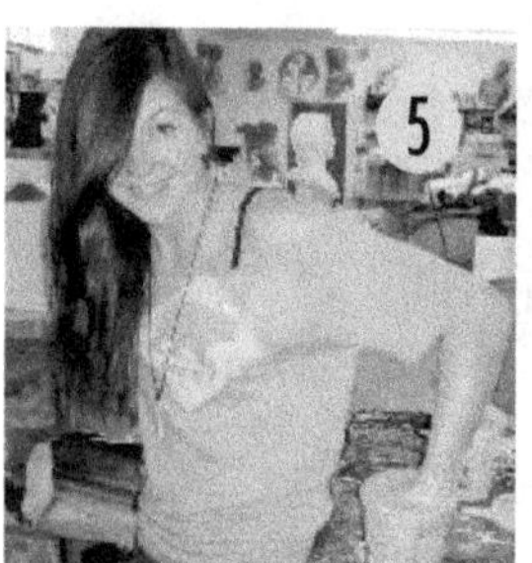

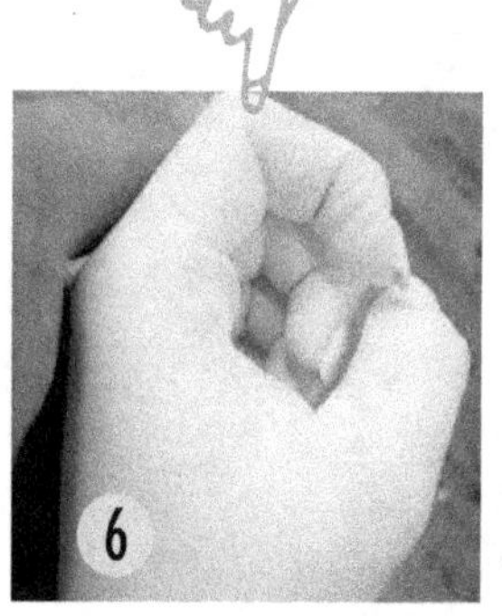

Cutting a groove arou
the inside lip will allo
the lid to fit secure

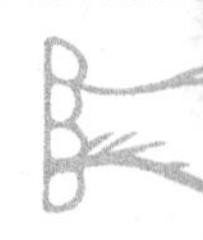

This arrow tells me
what side the fingers a
curled and what directi
to rotate the contain

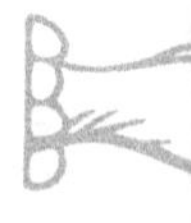

Rotate slowly in t
direction of the arro

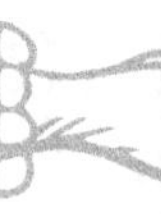

figured out how to do this, you are probably going to wonder what took me so long. However, if you haven't, you may just slap yourself in the forehead as if to say, "I could have had a V8!" But before I explain the solution, let me describe what normally goes wrong.

In photo #2, studio assistant Jay was getting her hand cast in MoldGel alginate impression material. As you can see in Photo #3, we achieved a very nice impression. Her fingers curl out of sight and back toward the viewer. The usual method life casters use to try to get the CM to flow to the fingertips is to fill the mold about half full and tip it almost horizontal with the fingertips at the bottom, hoping to allow the air in the fingertips to escape. You then can tip the mold as far as possible without letting the CM spill out, all the while tapping and shaking it. Repeat the process several times, each time bringing the mold closer to vertical until the mold is full. If the fingers are not too curled inward (toward the palm), this tipping method may suffice for you, but as you can see in Photo #4, the fingertips didn't cast, which is what often happens. So I tried it again, but this time I used my new method. I was using the hand of another assistant (Stevie) which I knew would be more challenging because of her longer finger nails. Photo #6 shows the results, which were successful. Here is how I did it. If you just read this, it might be a little hard to follow, but if you get a container (for example a glass) and pretend to follow along, it should make more sense.

Starting with a new mold - of assistant Alie's hand (Photo #7), I made sure that I used enough alginate to completely fill the container. In Photo #8, I trimmed off the excess MoldGel to make it level with the top of the container. In order to allow a lid to fit securely on the container, I cut a groove in the alginate around the inside lip (Photo #9). The arrow I drew on the container in Photo #10 served two important functions. First, it told me on which side of the container the fingers were curled. (Once you have added the casting material, it is difficult to know where the fingertips are located since you are no longer able to see into the mold.) The second function was to tell me in which direction to rotate the container to allow the air bubbles to escape the fingertips.

The next step was to pour in the CM which was done essentially the same way as before, (i.e., fill it about half full) only this time I put on the lid and rotated the mold with the lid toward myself and the fingertips and the arrow marking on the underside. Since the lid prevented spilling, I was able to go past horizontal, helping the bubbles to escape. I then rotated it in the reverse direction (turning it away from myself). This was the direction indicated by the arrow. I stopped rotating once there was no danger of spilling. I removed the lid and added more CM, repeated the procedure until the mold was full, and replaced the lid. Next came a very important step: rotating the container (in either direction) so that it was upside-down. At that point (since the CM had not started to set up) any bubbles left in the

ere I'm trimming the excess MoldGel away so
e alginate is level with the top of the container.

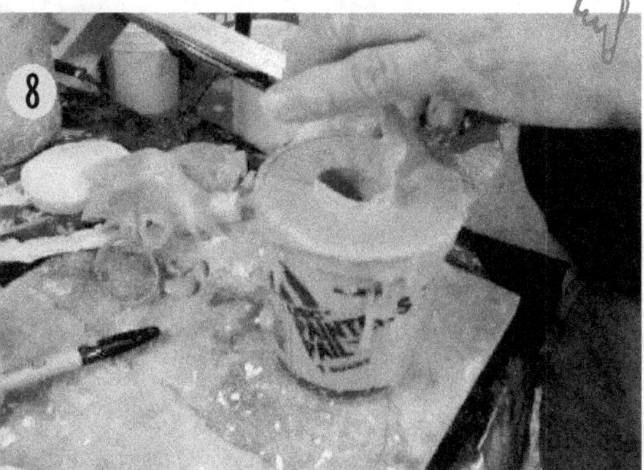

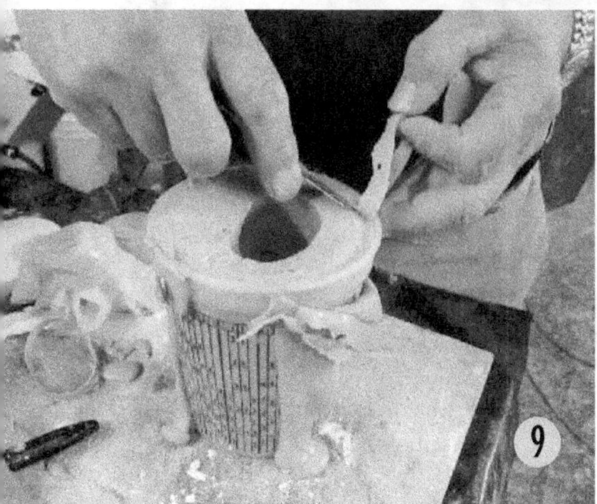

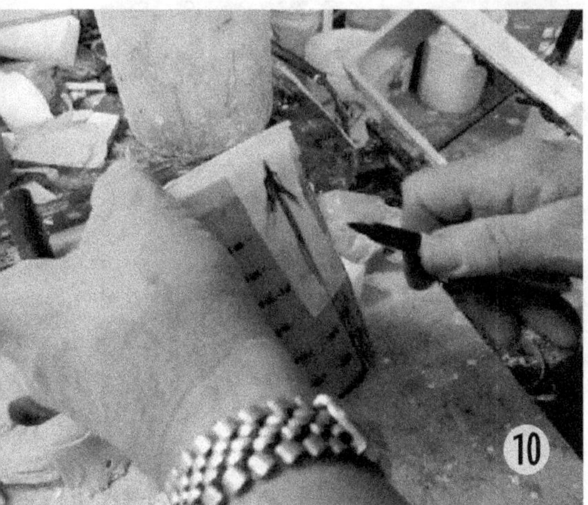

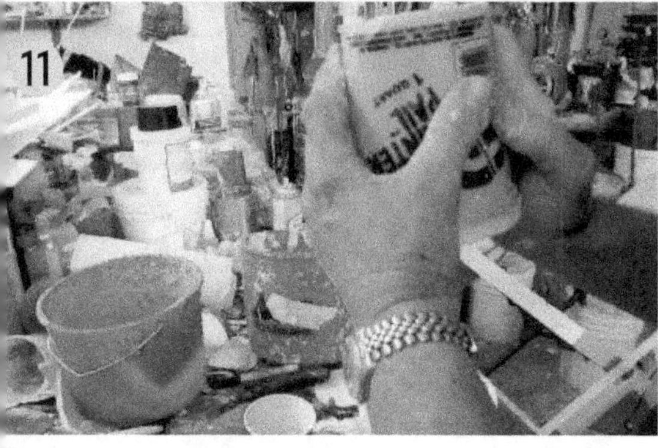

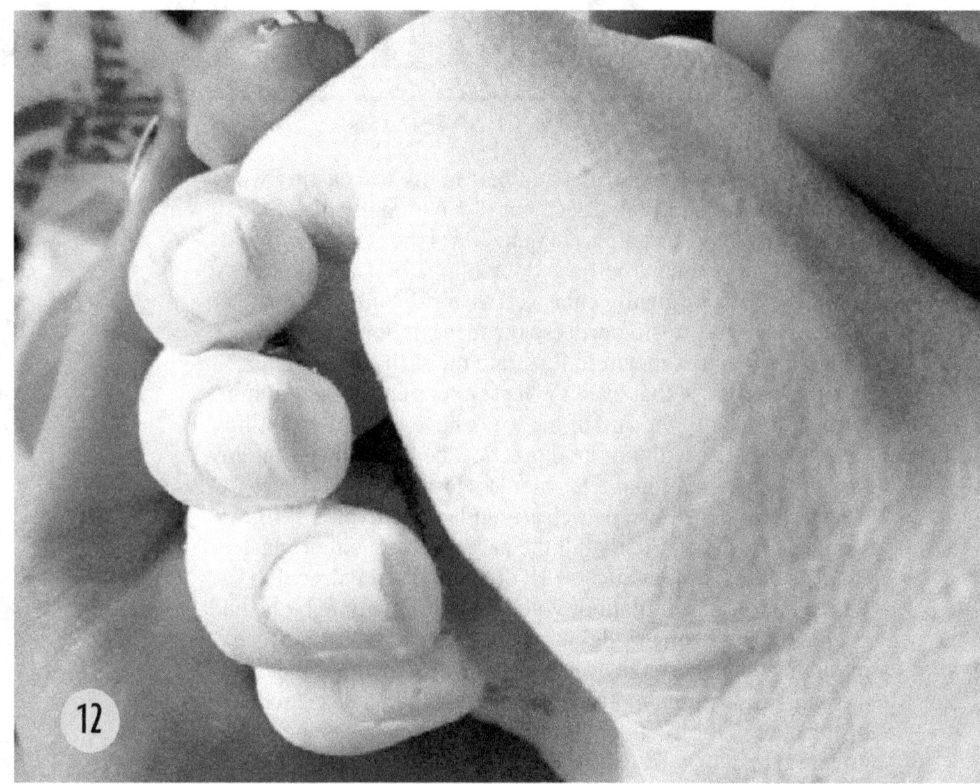

finger tips rose to the first joints beyond the knuckles. Finally, I slowly rotated the container in the direction of the arrow until the lid was on top and any bubbles traveled up the back of the hand and out the wrist. (Photo #11) As you can see in Photo #12, there are no fingertip bubbles.

This method should work well as long as you avoid other problems that can arise. For instance, it is important to mix the CM at the manufacturer's recommended water ratio to insure maximum strength, minimal imperfections, adequate flow ability, and expected working time.

There is another studio tip to consider. Also notice that in all the photos, there are almost none of those pesky little 'innie' bubbles on the surfaces of the castings. If you have the capability of degassing your CM, doing so can be very helpful. Although I have both vacuum chambers and a vacuum mixer (a Whip Mixer) I did not degas any CM shown in this article. While I encourage you (if you are a serious life caster) to acquire a method of degassing, I wanted to demonstrate that you can do very nice, almost bubble-free castings – if you use the following technique.

Imagine if you had just put some ice cubes in a glass to try to cool a drink. You would swirl the glass in small horizontal circles to move the liquid over the ice, right? You can use that same principle to move your CM to the surface of your casting, – in other words, you are trying to spin the liquid in the mold. After you have finished filling the mold as described above, take hold of your mold container so you can make rapid, small swirling motions with the container. Because of the higher density of the CM relative to the air bubbles, this circular motion will force the CM to the surface of the casting and significantly reduce small surface bubbles on the casting surface. It takes only five to ten seconds of swirling to accomplish your goal. I have found this to be a much better technique than using vibration. In fact, over-vibrating and/or tapping will often create more imperfections than they eliminate.

As I recall, most of the requests for the best method to reduce air bubbles in fingertips have concerned casting babies' hands. Sorry that I don't have any baby assistants, but child labor laws being what they are, I'm stuck with the ones I have. However, I think that you will find that this system works for all ages.

Casting Perfect Ears

By David E. Parvin A.L.I.

During the introduction part of my life casting work shops, I play a segment of a nationally distributed television program that shows the casting of hands, a pregnant belly, and the obligatory woman's chest complete with surgically enhanced assets. While it doesn't demonstrate the casting process for faces, it does show a collection of faces meant to illustrate the skill of the caster. But I can promise that even the least experienced person in my workshop will by the end of the week have more life casting knowledge and, with minimal practice, be better than that guy (and he was on national television!). How can I be so sure? There were four things that clearly indicated that his skills were rudimentary. Firstly, all the castings were either plaster (or something similar such as Hydro-Stone or Hydrocal) which had been left plain or with painted-on patina. None had been cast in a stronger, lighter, and much more professional medium such as bronze or Forton MG with metal powders and a chemically applied patina. Secondly, he had not opened any of the eyes. Thirdly, they all looked bald because he had covered the hair rather than cast it in all its glory; only bald people should be cast without hair. Lastly, none had a complete set of ears. While opened eyes are a matter of choice, nobody looks like him/herself without ears. (See photographs #1 and #2.)

In this article, I will explain how to cast perfect ears. Stay tuned, casting hair, opening eyes, and using the more professional materials and finishes will be the subjects of future articles.

Ears present one of the first speed bumps on the road to quality life castings. There are two problems: making perfect alginate molds of the ears and then getting the casting material to completely fill the void, stay in place, and be strong enough to survive demolding without breaking.

The biggest hindrance to molding ears is alginate that is too runny. Go back to Goldilocks, too runny and it all runs off, too thick means excessive surface flaws, the consistency must be just right. My preferred alginate is Fibergel E/FX made by ArtMolds. (For a complete evaluation of Fibergel FX, see "Testing a New Alginate..." in the May 2003 issue of Sculpture Journal.) I mix it at a ratio of 5 ounces (142 grams) of alginate to a pound (454 grams) of water. While some may think that this ratio is too thick and cause surface bubbles, I can assure you that it isn't and it won't.

One of several advantages of Fibergel is that I have found it to be more thixotropic, meaning that it stays in place better than other alginates of the same consistency. However, a very important point to remember is that you can not spread too thick layers of alginate on the model expecting the excess to run or drip off leaving just exactly the right thickness behind, the alginate tends to "avalanche" meaning when there is too much to resist the force of gravity, almost all of it slides off. Putting on only as much as will stay put requires some experience and a familiarity with the particular alginate one is using.

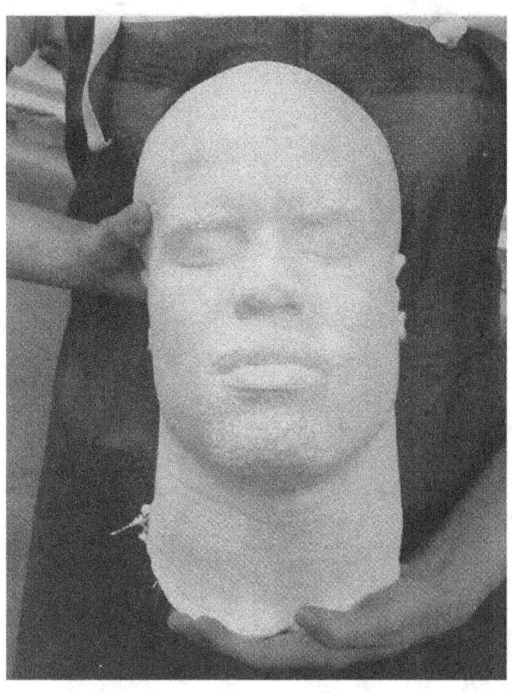

#1 Here is a simple plaster casting that only goes as far back as the front of the ears

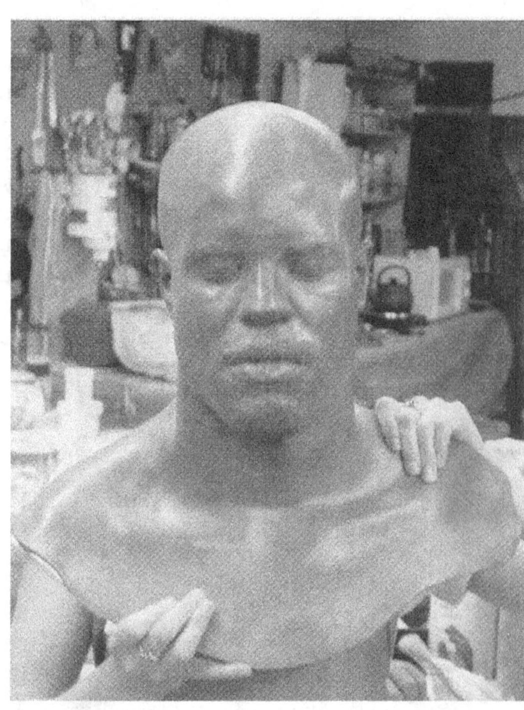

#2 This is the same face as in photo #1 except that it includes well behind the ears (Plus the shoulders) and is cast in Forton MG with metal powder. Even without knowing who the person is, it is obvious that this casting must look much more like the subject and is a more desirable portrait. By the way, this person looks bald because he is.

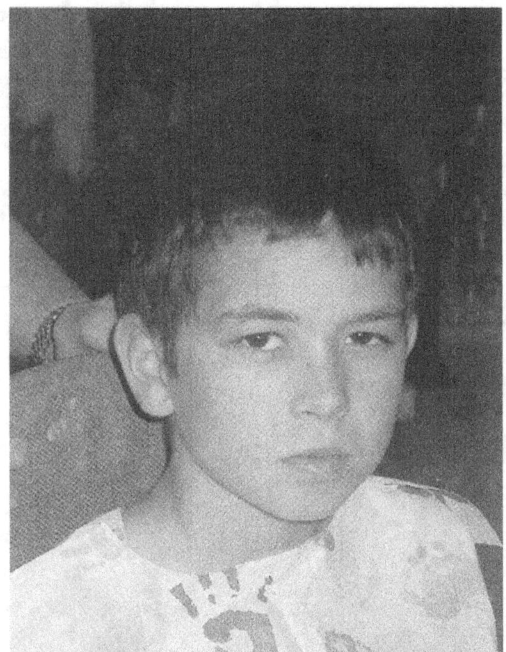

#3 This ear belongs to ten year old Mitchell illustrating a totally free standing structure. Compare this to Photo #4.

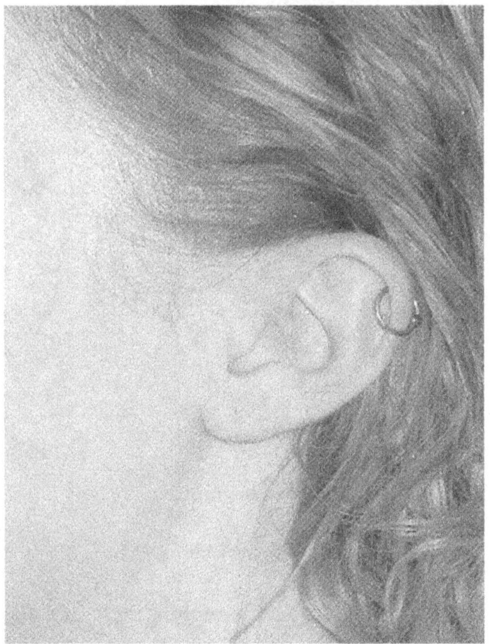

#4 Notice how Mitchell's older sister's, Melissa's ear is filled in the back by hair.

Let me digress here for just a minute and discuss mixing alginate. Many life casters mix alginate literally by feel, adding alginate to water and stirring by hand until it feels right. The problem with this method is that it takes too long to get to the perfect consistency leaving less time to apply the alginate and insure a flawless impression before it gels. I strongly encourage measuring the alginate and water and mechanically mixing with a paint or "Jiffy" mixer attached to an electric drill. Even the drill is important, it should have enough power and speed. For best results, it should draw at lease 4 to 5 amps and turn at a minimum of 2000 rpm's.

The exposed parts of the "cups" of the ears are not so much of a problem; alginate of the proper consistency will stay in place pretty well though it is important to carefully

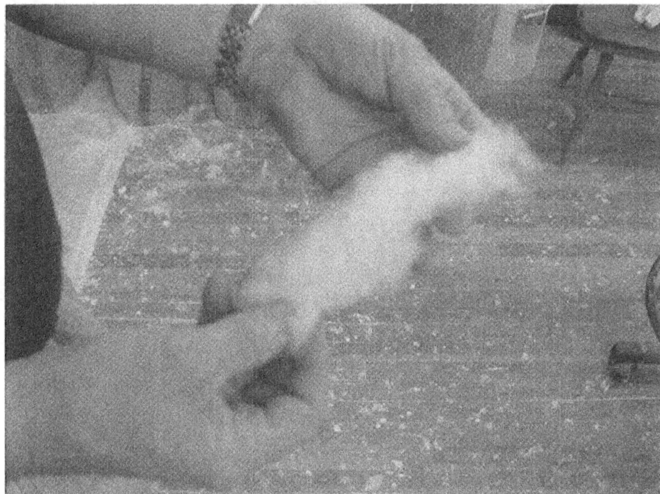

#5 How much polyfill is needed? The volume will be reduced when soaked in alginate.

push the alginate into the ears and check it several times as the alginate gets the back and the underneath of the ears that are most problematic. This is especially true if the subject has very short or no hair. Look at photograph #3 where the ear sticks out from the head completely exposed. Alginate may tend to run or drip off from behind and below the ears even if properly mixed. The answer is to help the alginate stay in place. After the alginate has been applied over the entire surface to be cast. I take a small amount of polyfill or

Long hair tends to fill in the space behind the ears so that the alginate does not have to. While this may not seem very significant, it really is.

synthetic pillow stuffing and dip it in what is left of the alginate. I use about enough to cover the palm of my hand so that soaked it is about 3 inches long and 3/4 of an inch wide. (See phonographs #5, #6 and #7.) I then place this alginate "sausage" behind and below the ear. Care must be taken to keep from pushing the ear outward making a classic Dumbo look. So that I can concentrate on the alginate application as a whole, I usually have someone else gently hold the alginate/polyfill in place with his/her fingertips until the alginate has set-up. While this only takes a couple of minutes, I instruct the alginate holder to stare at what he/she is doing. If one looks away, there is a good chance that he/she will allow the piece to slide out of place.

These soft cushion "sausages" behind the ears provide another advantage, they make it easier to remove the mold. Since the head curves inward right behind and below the ears, a tightly fitting, rigid outer or "mother" mold over the alginate can make the entire mold more difficult and uncomfortable to remove without this padding.

Long hair tends to fill in the space behind the ears so that the alginate does not have to. While this may not seem very significant, it really is. With long hair, it is as if the ears were flat structures on the side of the head and only need to be covered over rather than wrapped around in alginate.

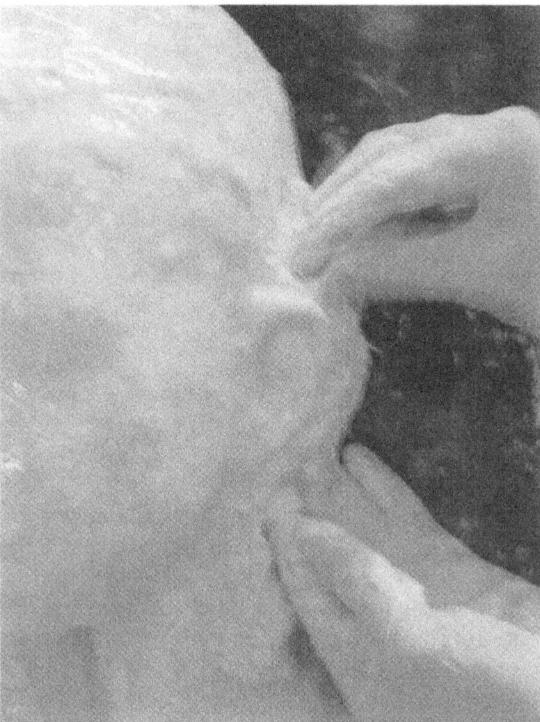
#6 Putting the polyfill/alginate "sausage" in place.

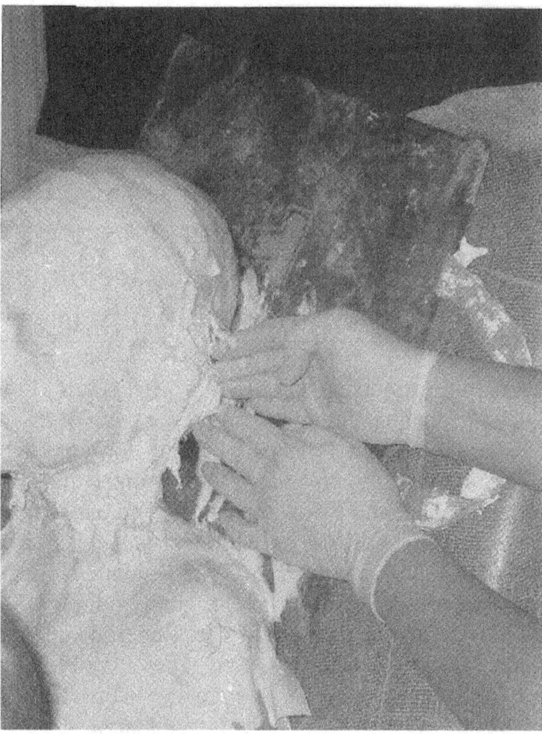
#7 Securing the "sausage" until the alginate sets up.

However, the area behind the earlobes and just below can still be a problem. I usually use a smaller amount of polyfill for this area as shown in photograph #8.

Let's assume that you have removed the mold and it appears that you have complete impressions of the ears. If your subject had long hair, you will have cast the ears and the hair and as you look into the mold you will be able to see pretty much all of the ears in negative. However, if the model had short or no hair, all you will see is about half of the ears. (Look at photograph #9.) I don't think that I had fully

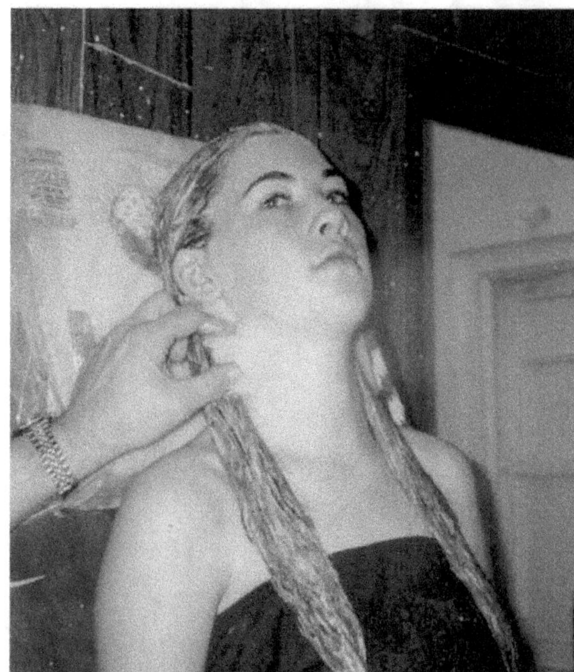
#8 with longer hair such as most females have, less polyfill will be needed. This ear and hair belongs to Ariana. (of course, the polyfill is not applied until the head has been covered with and the polyfill soaked in alginate.)

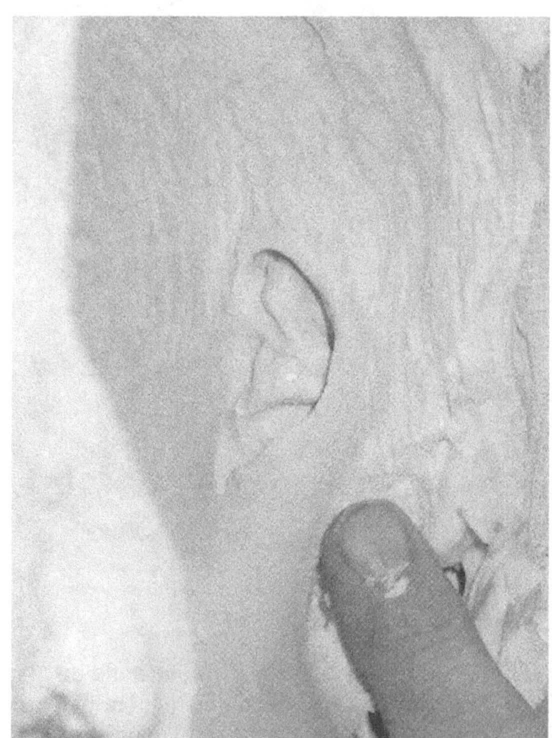
#9 Notice how with a boy's ear, only about half of the impression of the ear is visible in the mold. Anyone with longer hair, more of the ear would be exposed.

appreciated just how thin, about 1/8 inch, ears are until I saw this for the first time. At this point, no matter how or with what you fill the mold, you may have two problems. The first is simply getting the material into such a narrow space completely and without bubbles and then remaining in place until it sets up. Just forcing in the material with your fingertips doesn't work very well because some of it will likely run back

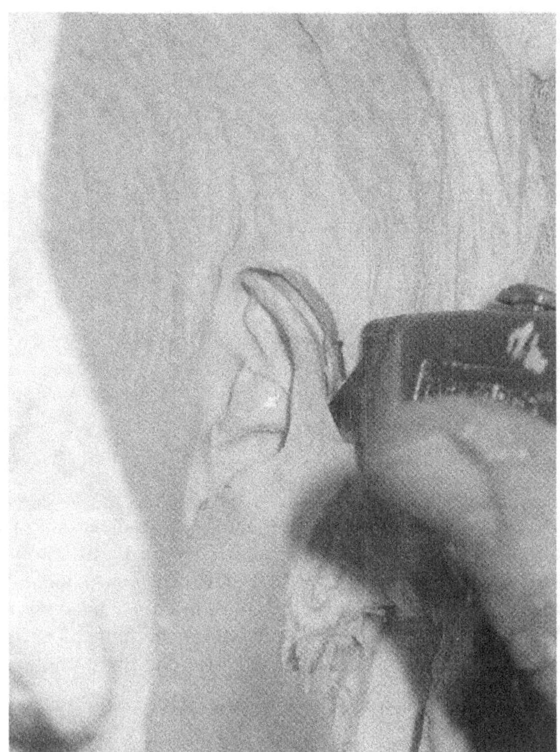

#10 Cutting some of the alginate away to open access to the ear cavity.

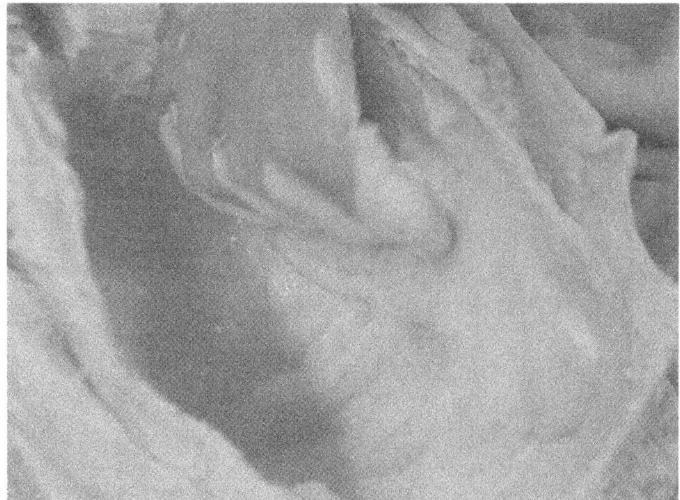

#11 Forcing plaster into the ear cavity of the alginate mold.

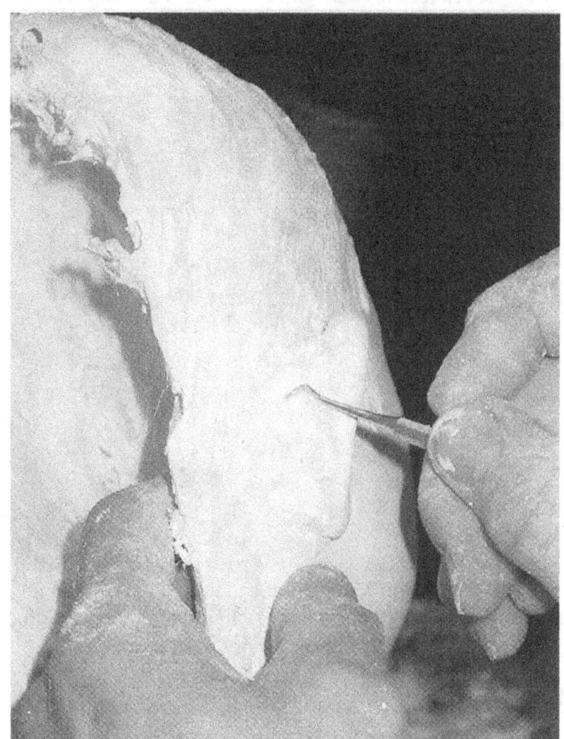

#12 Clearing some of the excess material from behind the ear

out. Even if you wait until the material has started to thicken up, it may be difficult to force it into such a thin area with fingertips that are wider than the space. And because the ears are so thin, even if you get them perfectly cast, definite care must be taken when removing the alginate. Even then the ears will always be the most fragile part of the cast, definite care must be taken when removing the alginate/. Even then the ears will always be the most fragile part of the mask and the most likely part to be damaged as the mask is admired and handled over the next, say, thousand years. There is a very simple solution.

All that is needed to provide more access for the material and strengthen the ears is to remove some of the mold material that filled in between the ears and the head. The space I am talking about is some of the same space that was filled with the polyfill/alginate sausages. You must use a very sharp blade such as a new utility knife or scalpel. The polyfill will resist cutting with a dull blade. Simply cut out most of this material without going beyond the ears. (Photograph #10) Remember, if hair has filled in part of this space, you may have to remove a little more alginate. Once opened up, there is enough room to push in the casting material with our fingertips. (Photograph #11) 1 have found that repeating this process as the material starts to set up usually results in the complete ear castings.

There is another way to get the casting material into the ear cavity that is only slightly more complicated but is very effective. You might be tempted to tip the mold on its side and fill the ear cavity, let it set up, tip it on its other side, fill up the second ear, and then apply your casting material of choice to the rest of the mold. Not a bad idea, one that may even work depending on the material. But there are two problems. The first is that some materials will not adhere to themselves well or at all if applied to some that has already set up. The second is that you are likely to get a noticeable seam where the older and newer materials meet. Just slightly change the procedure. Tip the model on its side and fill the first ear. Do not let it completely set up but just enough to stay in place. With some new material, paint over the exposed surface and the area around the first material. This will make the bond without a seam. Next tip the mold on the other side, fill the second ear and then apply the casting material to the rest of the mold. Add additional layers necessary for strength. (See photographs #13, #14 and #15.)

Caution, if you are using any standard gypsum product, additional layers should be applied before the previous layer completely sets up. As stated above, if one waits too long, the layers may not bond. In addition, since all gypsum products expand when they set up, the new layer may cause cracks in the first. But if the first layer is still somewhat "green," it will

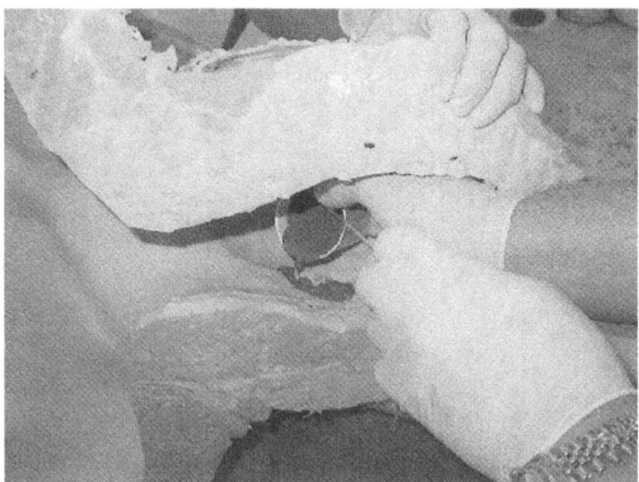

#13 Pouring Forton MG with metal powder into the first ear. Here the Forton MG is liquid enough that I can just pour it from a cup. (The very astute reader may recognize that this mold is not alginate. It is, in fact, a silicone rubber mold that was made from the original plaster positive.)

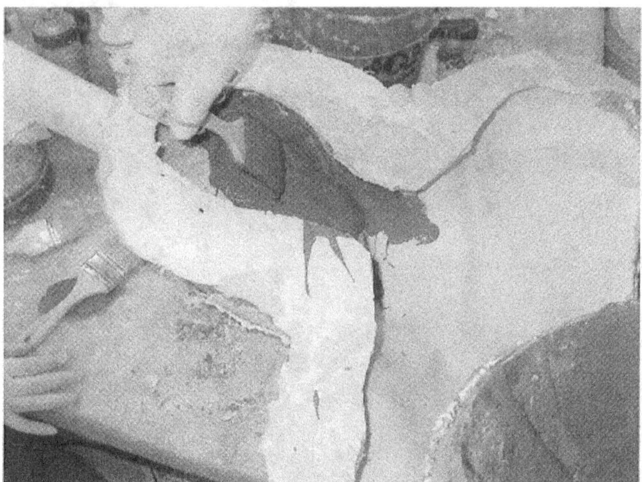

#14 Here the Forton MG has set up enough to remain in place (but not completely set up) and I am painting the area around this first ear with new Forton MG.

accommodate the expansion of subsequent layers. Don't break for lunch or go home for the night before applying all the layers. By the way, using Forton MG solves these problems, it neither expands or contracts and will bond to itself regardless of its age or state of curing.

Lets go back to where we have just demolded a set of perfectly cast ears. The obvious question at this point is that while the ears may look fine from the front and sides, won't they look odd from the back? The answer is "absolutely," but who cares? After all, if the mask is hung on a wall, the back of the ears are not visible anyway. Perfectly shaped ears that are strong enough to resist damage more than compensate for what you can't see. But if the casting is going to be displayed in such a way that the backs of the ears are visible, the extra material can be removed. (Photograph # 12) in this case, you will simply have to accept that the ears will be more fragile. It is far easier to do this than to repair ears that were only partially cast.

Remember, the world will always appreciate someone who can give a good ear...

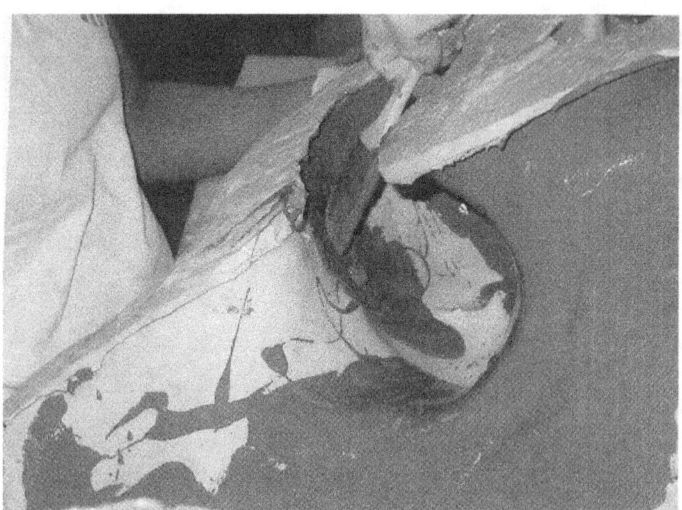

#15 I have tipped the mold so that the second ear is now on the bottom. Here the Forton MG had become just a little too thick to pour so I am forcing it in with a paint brush. As soon as the ear cavity is filled, I will paint the entire mold's surface with Forton MG. Additional layers of Forton MG without metal powders but with fiberglass fibers will be added for strength.

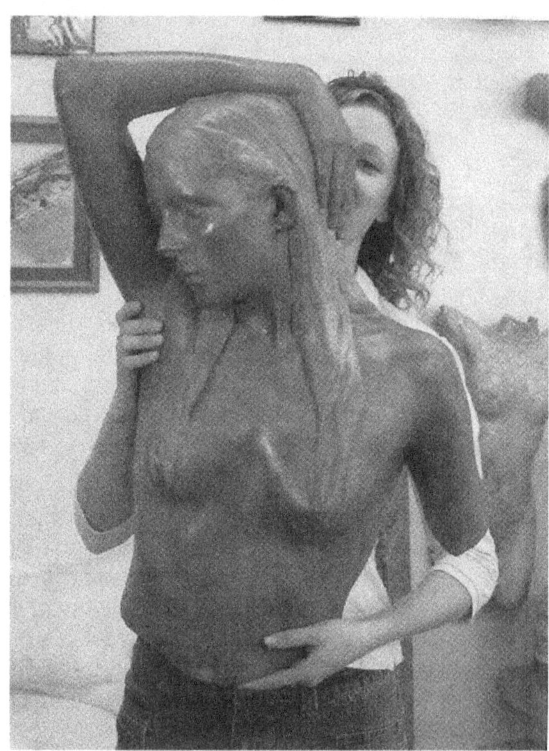

An example of a completed mask.

Photographs by Elliott Summons. Special thanks to the models who thought that they were coming by the studio just to get their faces cast and were delightfully surprised to model for this story. Who knows what great career may have been launched here.

David Parvin is a Colorado sculptor whose primary subject is the human form in a variety of material. He also teaches life casting workshops held throughout the year. He may be reached at 303-321-1074.

Don’t Get Your Nose All Bent Out of Shape!

By David E. Parvin, A.L.I.

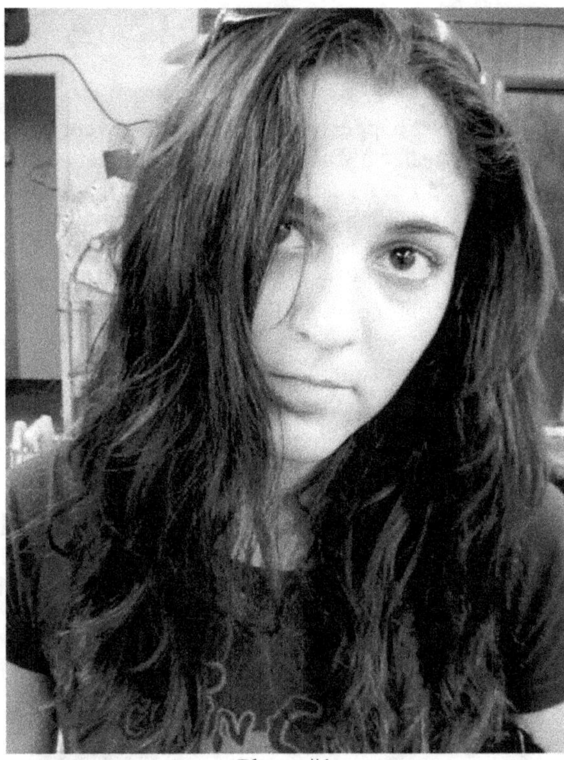

Photo #1

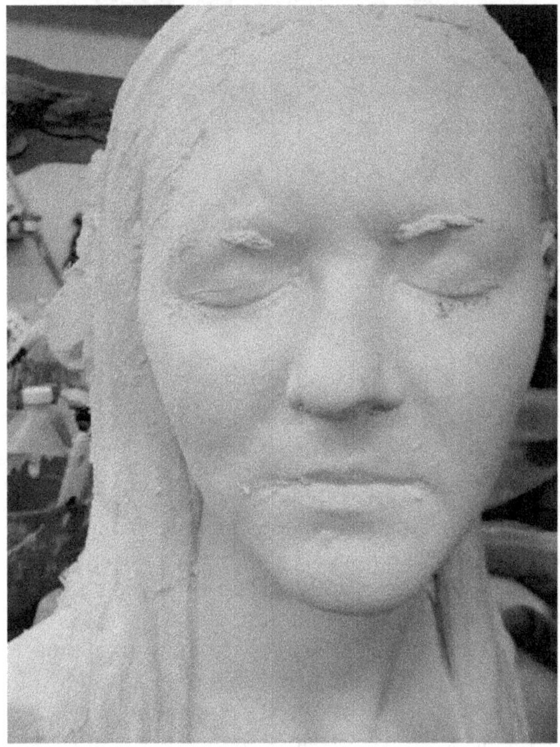

Photo #2

Anyone who watches TV has gotten used to the warnings that come with pharmaceutical ads. No, I’m not talking about the “if it lasts over four hours” one; warning heck, that’s surely got to result in more sales than the two people in bathtubs watching the sun go down! No, it’s the Lipitor commercials that warn against muscle aches being a sign of a rare but serious side effect. There are some rare but serious problems that can occur in life castings as well.

The first is what I call the “Bent Nose Syndrome” or BNS. Photo #1 is of Tiffany who is a very attractive young lady. But look at Photo #2. which is a plaster positive made from an alginate mold. Those who have read my articles over the years know that I never use plaster for a permanent casting. I correct what are usually small flaws in the plaster and then make a silicone secondary mold in which I cast Forton MG, polyurethane or polyester resin, or press water based clay for raku firing. However, this particular plaster mask has two problems that are so serious that it would be easier and faster to recast Tiffany than try to repair them.

Notice in Photo #2 that the nose is bent to her right which is not the case in real life. In over twenty years of life casting, I have seen BNS only three times. I learned early on that flaws in human anatomy are more noticeable in castings than in real life. Many a time I have thought that something about the casting wasn’t exactly right though I hadn’t noticed it in the model. But then found out the model really did have some small abnormality. But in this case, Tiffany’s real nose isn’t bent. I guess three times in over twenty years is a pretty minor problem, but I don’t like things happening that are out of my control and I at least want to understand the causes even if I can’t always be 100% the boss.

What I *think* happened in all three of these cases is that the models <u>moved slightly at a critical time.</u> If a model moves or shifts her/his position when the alginate is still liquid, it should just conform to the new shape. While the composition would be changed somewhat, the effect might be neutral, detrimental, or even an improvement. When I was a baby life caster, I would position the models head in a neutral straight on position. I think I was concerned that the model with no visual reference once the eyes were covered would have had difficulty maintaining a position with the head at an angle. Then one day I cast the face of a young lady about fifteen. I was so busy concentrating on the mechanics of the process that I failed to notice that she had shifted her head to the side and raised her chin slightly. When I made the plaster, I was amazed at how much the

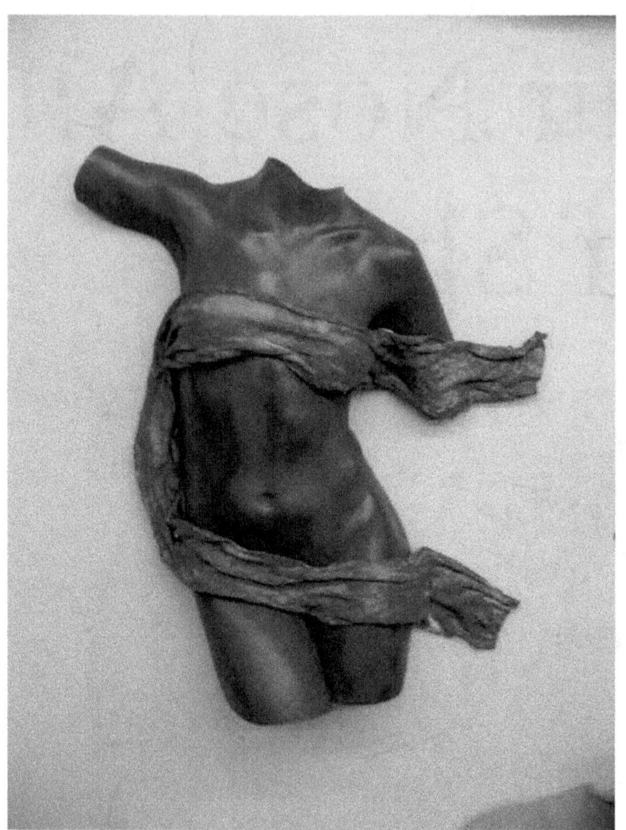

Photo #3

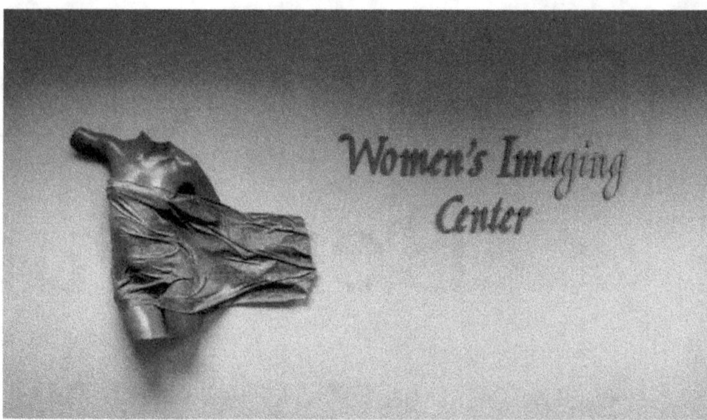

Photo #4

position had improved the casting as compared to others that I had done. Now I always start off with the head in an interesting position though the models do not always hold it.

If the models move after the alginate has setup, the alginate will wrinkle which will definitely show up in the positive. Whether or not it can be repaired is of course depends upon how much wrinkling is present which usually it occurs at the neck. However one of the worst examples I have ever seen happened while doing a front torso. The model kept leaning more an more to the side causing a large distortion at about naval height. My original plan had been to attach a removable band of cloth as in photo #3. What I ended up doing was trimming the wrinkles off the plaster to re-contour the torso and attach permanently a cloth similar to what is shown in Photo #4 which satisfied the customer.

I think that the bent nose results from the model turning her/his head slightly at just exactly the wrong time, just as the alginate is setting up. While anything can be corrected, the easiest thing to do in this case is just repeat the casting. Also, I doubt if there is much one can do to prevent a bent nose besides encouraging the model to try to maintain the selected position. After all, three in twenty years and hundreds of castings isn't too bad of a failure rate.

Above I said that there were two things wrong with photo #2. Notice how Tiffany is frowning. I try to remember to tell the models to close their eyes without frowning which definitely detracts from the beauty of the mask. Sometimes I forget and sometimes they frown anyway. Again, the solution is a recast.

Photo #5 illustrates the third and last rare problem I want to cover in this article. Notice how the lower lip is extended making it look as if she is using smokeless tobacco. What had happened was that her lips were open just a little and we pushed a small amount alginate between her lower lip and teeth as we applied the alginate. Alginate was first invented for making dental impressions and poses no health nor safety issues by being in one's mouth. However, a protruding lower lip does mess-up a portrait casting. It is possible to re-sculpt the lower lip which I have done when the model was not available for a recast. However, redoing the casting is a better solution if possible.

The problem with things that just happen is that they can go either way. Of the four examples in this article, three were detrimental and one was serendipitous. We can always fix the failures or at least hide them and then take credit we don't deserve for the successes. As I am writing this, I have something that is turning out better than I thought it would. Expect to see it in a future issue of *Sculpture Journal* with an explanation of where skill ended and luck took over.

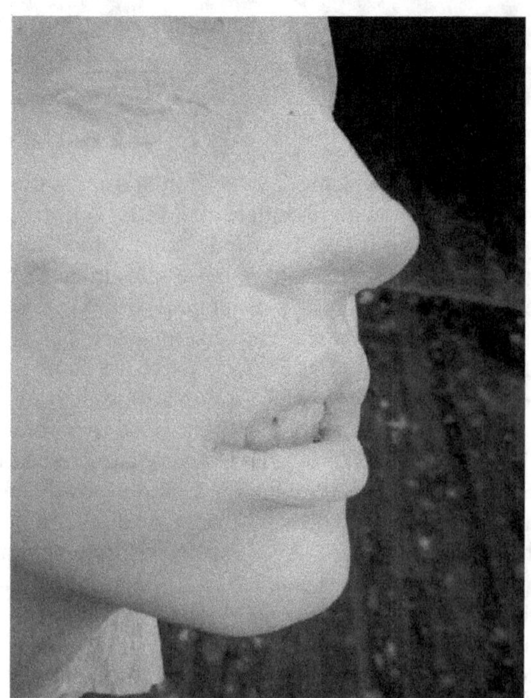

Photo #4

Give Me a Hand

By David E. Parvin, A.L.I.,

As I am starting to write this article, I'm feeling pretty smug. It just so happens that yesterday I reaffirmed my position as a world record holder. Yesterday 23 assistants and myself cast 661 hands in 5 hours for and average rate of one hand every 27.3 seconds. While not a personal best which was last year when we did 768 hands for a rate of one every 23.4. But conditions were far from ideal yesterday. As we were rounding the far turn, teeing off on the 18th hole, completing the last pit stop, it started to rain. The rain reduced the number of castees willing to stand in line. Nevertheless, 661 is almost certainly more than anyone else has ever done in the same time period. Yesterday's combined with the what we have done on the last Saturday in July for the previous fourteen years not only assures me the the most in five hours record but almost as surely gives me the record for the most hands cast in a lifetime. I have to humbly point out that I regularly do hand (and feet and face and torso) casting in my studio as well and have been doing so for over twenty years all of which count as well. Yes, I suspect that I hold a number of world records and my place in the Life Casting Hall of Fame is assured. What about my 23 assistants, well, this is the real world, the big leagues where they do almost all the work but I get all the credit.

I hope by this time any reader has realized that this guy Parvin is one conceited S.O.B. or he is leading up to a point. Well, the truth is "yes and yes." What we did yesterday was have a profitable day in a very weak art market. I would like to explain just how this happened in hopes that someone may benefit from my experience and do something similar.

It all began about fifteen years ago when I answered the phone, "This is Dave." The voice on the other end of the line replied, "Is this Dave Parvin the sculptor?" Right then I was pretty sure that I was going to like whatever came next because because the caller was impressed and respectful enough to call me "THE SCULPTOR." Besides, when someone calls you who already knows who you are it is going to be so much easier. After all, you lose a little of your bargaining power if you have to tell someone that you are indeed famous. The call was from the director of a local art center and she wanted to know if I would be willing to participate is a kids' art day by casting hands. Not only did she say the ten little magic words that open any door with ease, "We will pay you and your helpers and for all materials," but it just so happened that the particular suburb is the wealthiest in the Denver area. While one of "Dave's Laws" clearly displayed on my studio wall is, " We are not like Robin Hood, Robin Hood robbed from the rich, we rob

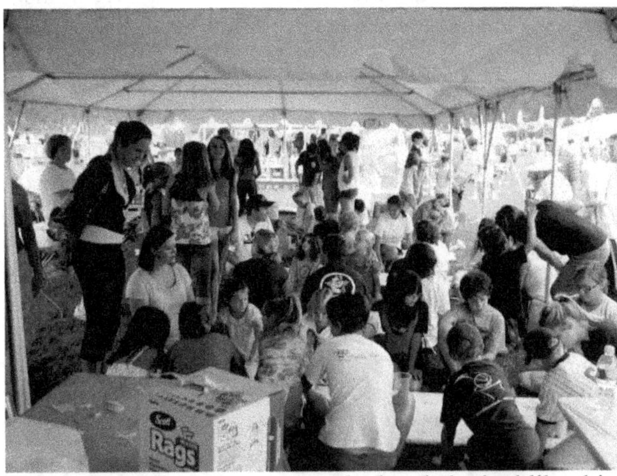

The 60 by 20 foot tent we cast the hands looked like this, full of people for five hours. In the foreground, young people either have their hands in alginate or are about to.

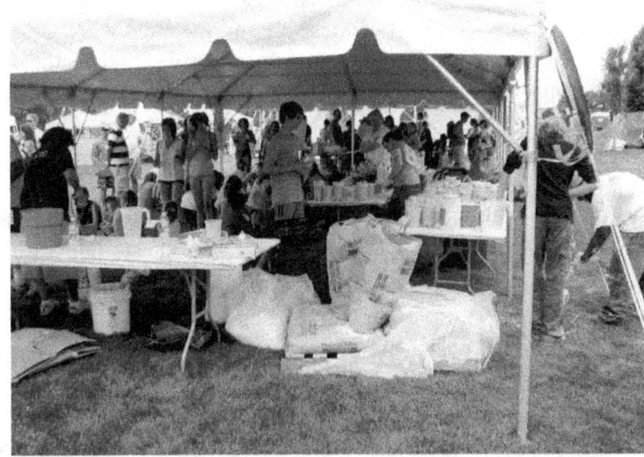

At the other end of the tent, the person on the left is one of four persons is mixing and pouring alginate. We used about 450 pounds of alginate.The two on the right are mixing and pouring white hydrocal. We used all of the eight bags of hydrocal shown.

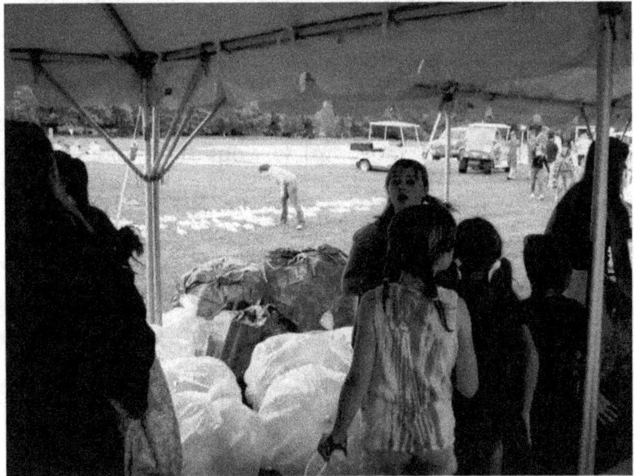

The kids are waiting in line holding the containers with their names and assigned numbers printed on the sides. The bags are full of two liter soft drink plastic bottles. Outside the tent are finished hands laid out by their numbers for easy identification.

from everybody," I have found the Robin had it right, there is just so much more you can rob from the rich. I accepted the offer.

That first year I showed up with two helpers and though I don't remember just how many hands we did, it couldn't have been very many. Even though the event was new and not very well attended we were not able cast every hand that wanted it. Nevertheless, we were invited back the following year with permission to bring additional helpers. I think I showed up that year with about five. It took about ten years for the kids' art day to reach it maximum size and for our numbers to grow to accommodate all who want a hand casting.

Whenever I look at something incredibly complicated such as and aircraft carrier, I always wonder how any one could possibly design something so complex. The truth is that if there were no boats, much less ships, it wold probably be impossible to start of with an aircraft carrier. But it all started with someone standing on a log and pushing himself across a small body of water with a pole. After a couple thousand years, someone tied two logs together and the first raft was invented. More time passed and the logs were hollowed, sales were added and so forth until step by step we ended up with a hundred thousand ton aircraft carrier with a crew of five thousand.

I am not saying that casting six or seven hundred hands is comparable to designing and constructing a mighty warship, but if I had been asks to do as many hands as we do now at from the git go, I couldn't have done it. By learning a little every year, the process just naturally evolved. Let me give you some examples. Having discovered that an ideal casting container was a two liter soft drink container it is just the right size and is also transparent and one can see if the child is touching the side which would result in a flat spot. So for the first few years, I went to the recycle drop off place at my local supermarket and picked up what I estimated I would need. I then cut the tops off by hand with a box cutter. But as the numbers grew year after year, it got to be a longer and longer process. We finally came up with a better solution. The city talks a soft drink bottler into donating all the new bottles we need. City workers pick the bottles up and slice off the tops with a band saw. Also, since a two liter container is larger than needed for the younger children, the city gets one quart deli containers from a local supermarket. The city even delivers the both sizes of the containers to the casting location and I am completely out of the loop.

Another example, the first couple of years, we not only cast the hands, but we also demolded them as well. Well, demolding takes far longer than casting. Not only do you have to wait until the white hydrocal has set up, but you have to very carefully remove the hand from the alginate or you will break off a finger or two or three, etc. Then you have the likelihood the child will break off a few fingers taking the hand home. I decided to print out a very detailed description on demolding and attach it to every hand while still in the alginate and the container. Now the child takes his/her hand home relatively protected by the plastic container which gives the hand time to be well set up. Also, several family members have an opportunity to get involved with the demolding. Lastly, on the back side of the direction, I have space to describe the David E. Parvin Studio and what services we offer.

It is not the purpose of this article to explain all the tricks and what is involved in casting a large number of hands. I only want to point out again that I have mentioned in some previous articles that sometimes an opportunity comes up that is somewhat outside what we normally do. The first time I did this project, it really looked like more of am inconvenience than anything else. But as the project has grown, so has my compensation. I am now VERY WELL PAID. Also, I get to provide some work for other people both skilled and unskilled. And don't forget that there are a whole bunch of rich folk who have casts of their children's hands on their mantles.

If anybody has an opportunity to do a similar project, please feel free contact me and I will provide a whole bunch more information about materials and equipment, how to find helper, how to divide the work between all the helpers, etc. But be creative and survive to sculpt another day.

How to Cast a Dancer's Foot On Point For Fun and Profit

by
David E. Parvin, A.L.I.

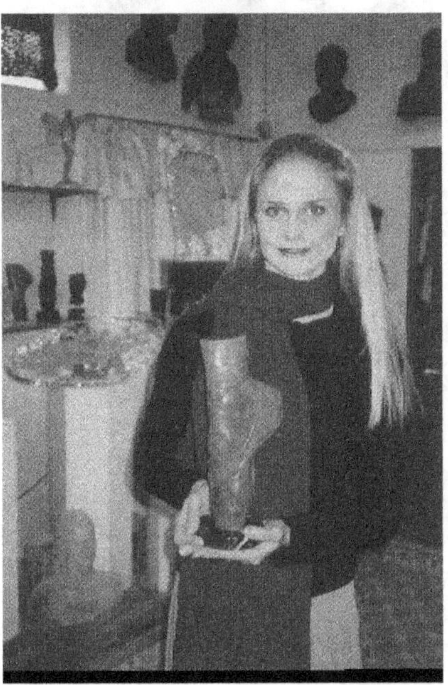

Chandra who is a principal dancer with the Colorado Ballet and her cast foot

One ofthe most popular life castings is of a ballerina's foot on point in a ballet slipper. For years I have used alginate with very good results. However, recently I have started using fast curing skin safe platinum cured thixotropic silicone rubber and have developed a better mousetrap. This article will explain a few tricks that will make this particular type of casting a cinch. But "fast curing skin safe platinum cured thixotropic silicone rubber" is just too long a name. I'm approaching the age when I probably shouldn't buy any green bananas and if I have to type out an eight word name too many times, well, I just might not be around to finish this article. I'll use FCSSPCTSR instead.

Though I have been aware of FCSSPCTSR's for years and have had some experience with them but still much prefer alginate for most life castings. For one thing these rubbers had been so expensive costing far more than alginate or regular silicone rubbers. Another problem has been that FCSSPCTSR's cling to hair much more tenaciously than alginate. A "face" casting for me usually comes down to mid chest and back behind the ears capturing the hair. It is simple enough to protect the hair with a release that prevents alginate from sticking to it while capturing the detail of the hair, especially if one uses the right type of alginate. Of course, there are products specially made to release hair from FCSSPCTSR's, but I have found that so much is required that detail is lost. Many in the motion picture special effects industry use FCSSPCSRs but usually cover the hair with a skull cap.

So what's different now. Well, for one thing, hair isn't going to be a problem since I have yet to meet a ballerina with a hairy ankle and foot. Also, now there are FCSSPCTSRs that are much more economical. When you consider that you can make a mold directly from the model that can be used over and over and stored for years, FCSSPCTSRs can be quite reasonable. The particular brand that I used in this article is called "LifeRITE" which is available form ArtMolds (artmolds.com or any of the suppliers who carry ArtMold products such as The Compleat Sculptor, Sculpture House, Ball Consulting, Walco Mfg. all of whom advertise in this magazine. There are also other brands available; Silicones, Inc. also found here is an excellent choice. I suspect that many readers have been confusing the acronym FCSSPCTSR for the common phrase, "For Charlies's Salve Same, Please Criticize Tenaciously" Sculpture Review." so to end the confusion, I'll use the brand name LifeRITE for the rest of this article.

The first step was to cast a circle of LifeRITE about 4 inches in diameter and $^{1}/2$ inch thick. This would be the base on which the dancer would place the toe shoe on to make an end plate for the mold to keep the final casting material from running out the bottom. A lid the right size made an excellent mold for this.

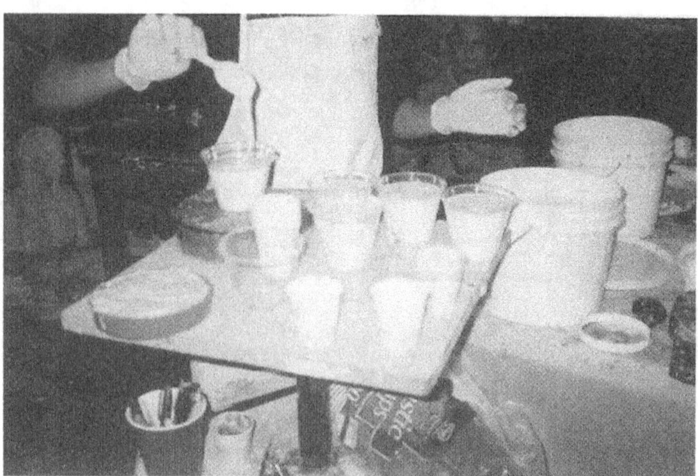
Photogaph 2, Lauren, my assistant measuring the LifeRITE

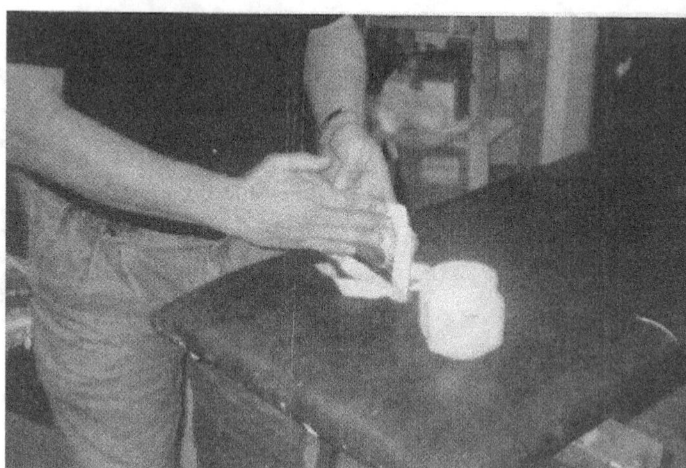
Photograph 3, Spreading petroleum jelly on the ballet slipper

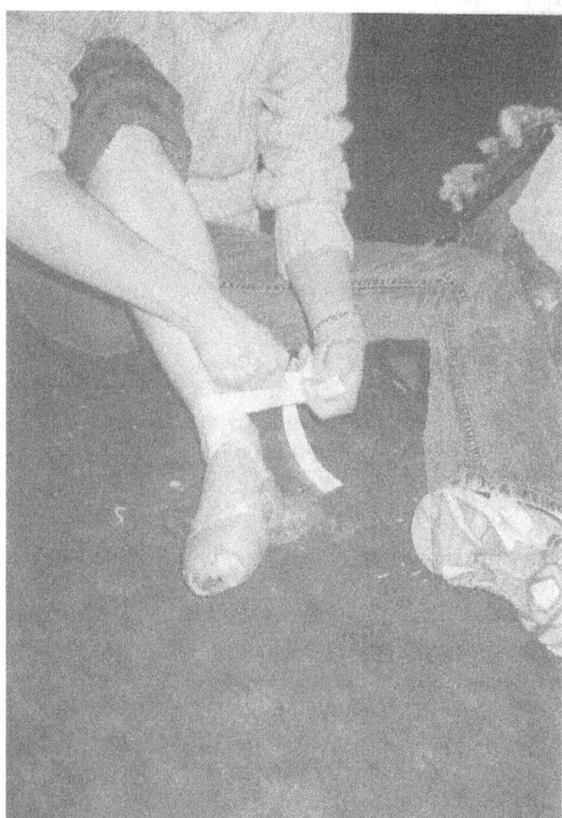
Photograph 4, Chandra tying the ribbons

LifeRITE (as are other brands) is a cinch to mix. There are two components, an "A" which is white and a "B" which is blue. The ratio is 100 parts A to 10 parts "B" by weight. For the base, I mixed 8 ounces of A and 8 ounces of B. I used a clear plastic disposable cup because I could see through the sides and bottom that the components were uniformly mixed. For stirring, I used a "giant craft stick" which is not to be confused with a tongue depressor even though they appear to be exactly the same. Remember, one is a medical devise and costs a lot while the other is available form any craft store for cheap. After about a minute of stirring, I poured the LifeRITE into the lid.

While the base was setting up, my assistant, Lauren, measured out eight, 8 ounce cups of LifeRITE along with 8 batches of the B (Photograph #2) since the B is 10% of the A, one might think that eight smaller cups of 8 ounce of catalyst would be just what is needed. But, alas, one would be wrong. Whenever one pours a liquid from a container, some of the liquid will be left behind. With small amounts, the percentage of left behind material can be significant. Fortunately silicone rubbers are not too critical; reducing the B component will only extend the curing time . But a fast cure is what we wanted for the dancer's comfort. The solution was to measure the 23 grams and pour it out. Weighing the cup again determined how much remained in the cup, in this case 4 grams. So Lauren weighted (4+23) or 27 grams of B in each of the 8 smaller cups. The 4 grams per cup were drained and collected later.

To the first two cups of A, I added two teaspoons of silicone oil as a thinner. This isn't essential but helps in capturing detail and preventing surface bubbles. Silicone oil has little or no (as far as I can tell) effect on the curing time and is available from same suppliers.

Silicone rubbers do not adhere but will tangle in the surface of anything that is porous such as a cloth slipper so a mold release was needed. But not just any release, some are not skin safe. Secondly platinum cured silicones are inhibited by sulfur, even very small amounts of sulfur which shows up in some surprising substances. If I had been doing this casting in alginate, plain old corn oil used in cooking would have worked just fine. It is hannless to skin but inhibits platinum cured silicones. Even aloe which is in many lotions contains sulfur. (Tin cured silicones are more inhibition resistant but are not skin safe.) Fortunately, petroleum jelly comes to the rescue. Dissolving 15 parts petroleum jelly into 100 parts naphtha makes a great all purpose, economical release. I painted the solution on the outside of the slipper soaking in into the cloth and leather sole. After a few minutes, the naphtha had evaporated leaving the PJ behind. As added insurance, I rubbed some PJ into the material as well. (Photograph #3) I did not apply any release to the ribbons until after the shoe was on the dancer. Chandra, had tied them (photograph #4) because the PJ would have made them difficult to tie.

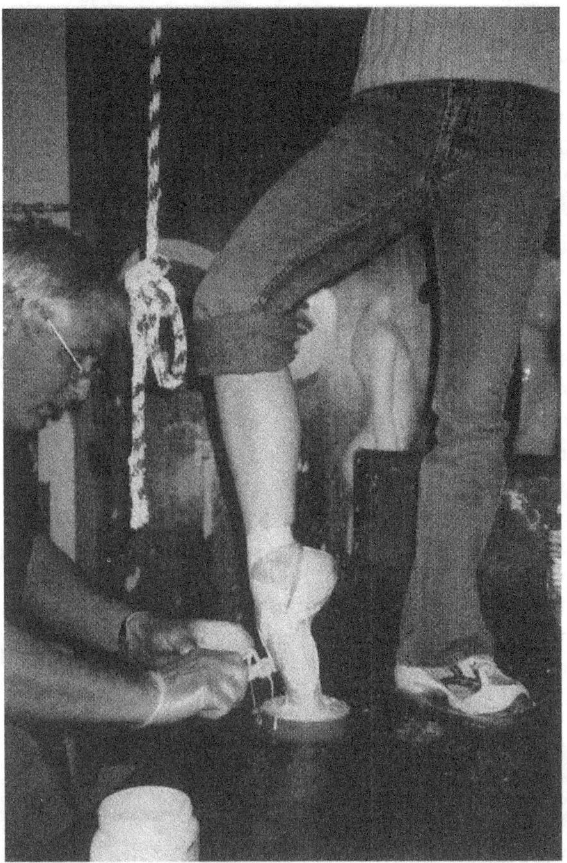
Photograph 5, Applying the first layer of LifeRITE

The next step was to apply the LifeRITE. As you can see in photograph #5, I had Chandra stand on a padded surface that was high enough for me to work comfortably. Though not visible in the photograph, the rope goes up to the ceiling, across to and down her left side allowing her to support herself with both arms. The idea was to build up the depth of the LifeRITE in layers until it was about 1/4 inch thick. At that thickness, no mother mold would be needed. But even though it is thixotropic, only a thin layer will stay in place. An assistant is essential to allow for the continuous application of the LifeRITE. It took about a minute to mix an 8 ounce batch using a craft stick. As soon as it was mixed, I began to apply it with the same stick. About two minutes later, I asked Lauren to start mixing the second batch. As I finished spreading on the first batch which covered the lower half of the intended area, Lauren handed me the second, and so on. By the time the second batch had been applied, the lower half was already set up and ready for another layer.

Now I am going to share a really neat trick, one of *Parvin 's Perfectly Pertinent Procedures for Pleasure and Profit.* Notice photograph #6. Beginning with the third cup, I applied a thicker layer of LifeRITE about an inch wide along the center of the back of the mold from top to bottom. As the ridge began to cure and thicken, I pushed 3, 1/2" finishing nails into the LifeRITE about every inch. If the rubber isn't cured enough and they slide down out of place, just wait a little while. Conversely, if the rubber has become too firm to accept the nails, add some more LifeRITE. Remember Goldilocks, not too hard, not too soft, but just right. As you apply the remaining rubber (photograph #7), be sure to cover the center of the nails so that they are embedded into the LifeRITE a good 1/2 inch. Do not cover the ends of the nails. (I realize that this nail trick may look like it's going nowhere; patience, Grasshoppers; there is more to it below.)

All silicone rubbers, but especially the platinum cured one can be accelerated with heat. A hair drier used as the batches are applied or at the end will significantly reduce the cure time. In this case, it took about 25 minutes to apply the LifeRITE and let it cure enough to remove the foot.

Once the rubber is no longer sticky, I pulled out the nails. (Photograph #8) I then made a cut down the center of the thick ridge. Notice in photograph #9 1 was using a scalpel blade # 12 that is shaped like a bird's beak with the cutting edge on the inside of the curve which allowed me to cut outward from the flesh.. I pushed two fingers between the

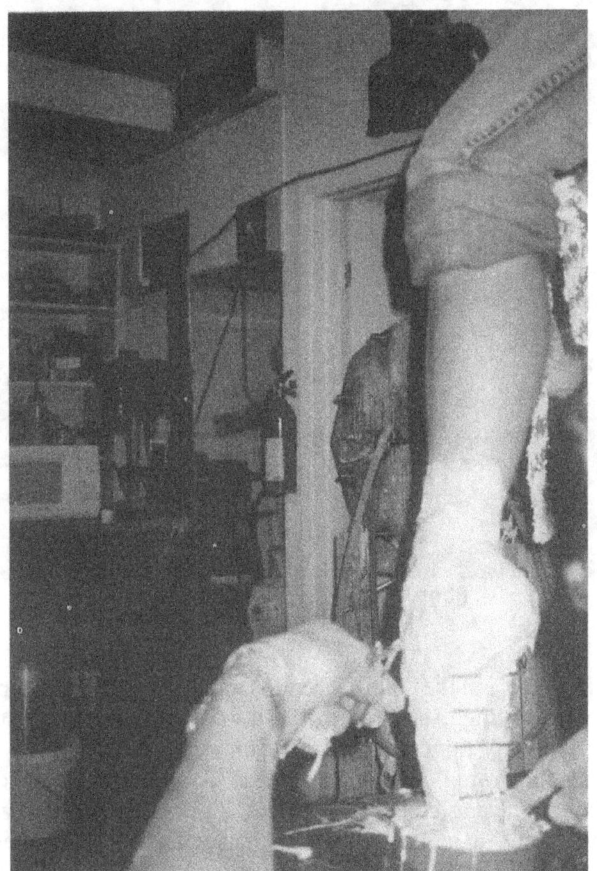
Photograph 6, Pushing the nails into the LifeRITE

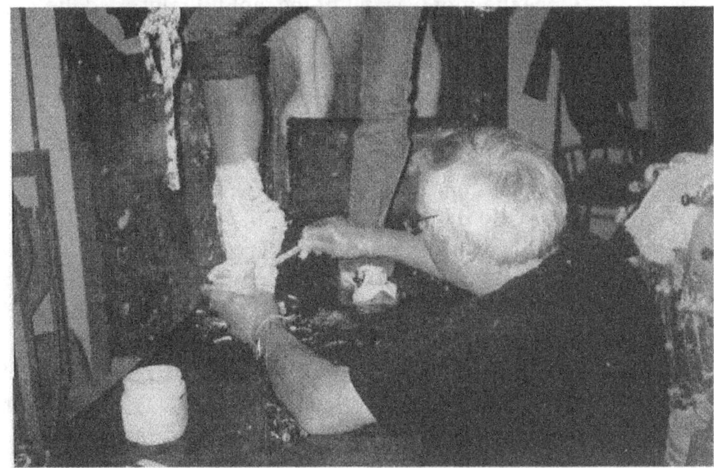
Photograph 7, Adding the last of the LifeRITE

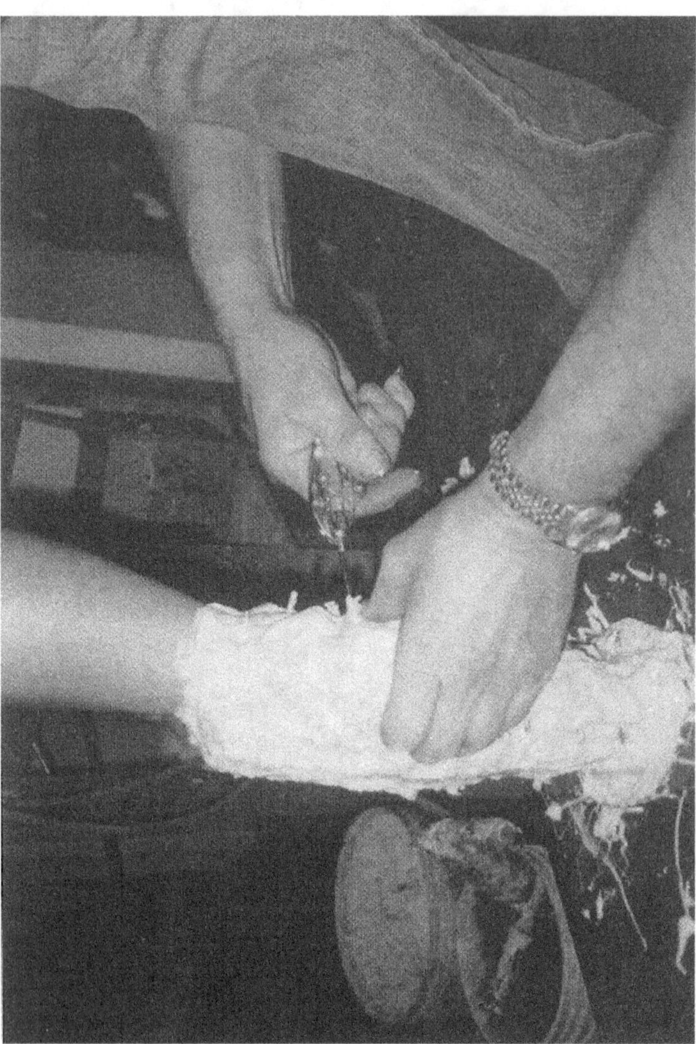

Photograph 8, Pulling out the nails

LifeRITE and the Achilles tendon and pulled out the rubber before cutting. As an extra precaution, I inserted a craft stick between my fingers. Be very carful, **it is extremely easy to nick the model!** Where the LifeRITE touched the leg and shoe, I made as straight a cut as possible so as to minimize the seam. But as I cut outward, I made a zig zag cut to help register the seam. It was only necessary to cut about half way down the sole to allow Chandra to pull her foot and shoe free.

Once the foot was out of the mold, I reinserted the nails (photograph #10 and using rubber bands around the ends of the nails, "stitched" up the seam as if preparing a turkey. The nails made the sides of the seam register exactly and the rubber bands held them tightly together. In photograph #11, I was looking into the mold for any thin spots where the light shines through which could be thickened easily by spreading on a little more LifeRITE. All that was left was to pour the final casting which I had decided would be a cold cast bronze using a particular urethane. Easyflo Clear Liquid Plastic made by Polytek, Inc. I could have used Forton MG with excellent results as well. (For a thorough understanding of Forton MG, see "Mixing Forton MG Simplified," "Sculpture Journal, July, 2003) The biggest advantage was that this urethane would set up and be demoldable in less time. The easiest way to determine how much urethane I needed was to weigh the mold empty and then fill it with water. Also any leaks would be apparent and could be stopped by more tightly securing the seam and /or smearing on more LifeRITE. It just so happens that one of the convenient miracles in the universe is that Urethane resins have almost exactly the same specific gravity as water. In this case, it took 1100 grams (2.4 pounds) of water and would require the same weight as resin.

Photograph #12 shows me pouring about an ounce of a 50/50 blend of copper and bronze poured into the mold. Tipping and shaking the mold caused a thin, even layer of the metal powders to coat the inside. Be sure to turn the mold upside down to dump out any excess powder. As I mixed the two components of the resin, stirred in a couple more ounces of metal powders for color. Easyflow Clear Liquid Plastic has a very short life of about three minutes which means one has to stir and pour quickly. Remember, this mold was strong enough to hold its shape without a mother mold. But to be sure that the weight of the urethane and metal powders didn't distort the mold, I cradled it in both my hands as Lauren gently poured in the resin. I continued to hold it for about five minutes until I was sure that it was solid.

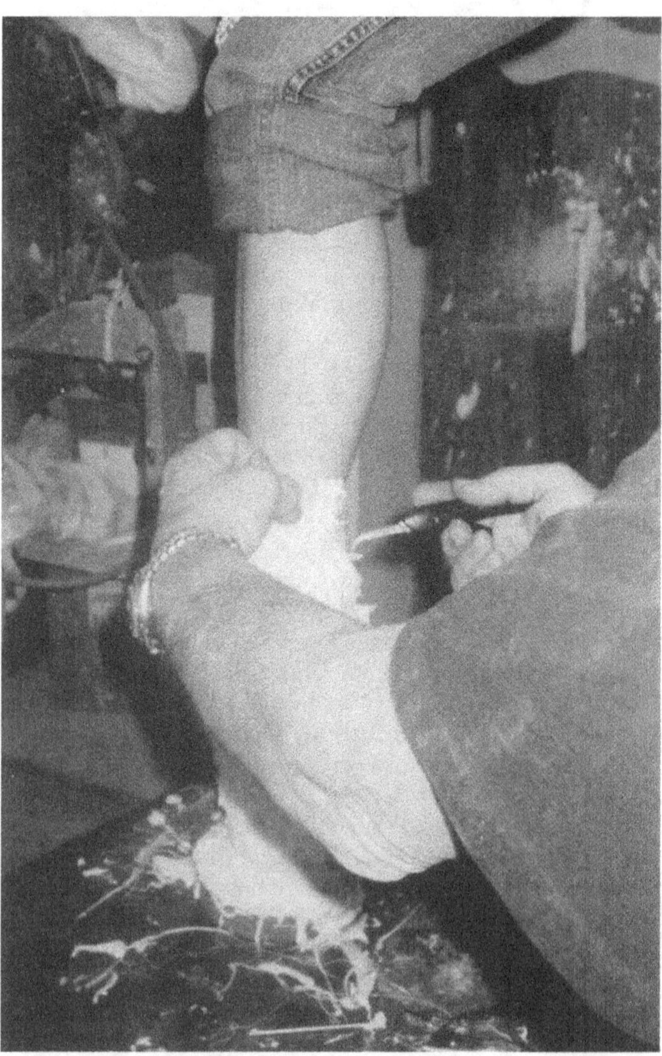

Photograph 9, Beginning to cut open the seam with a #12 scapel blade

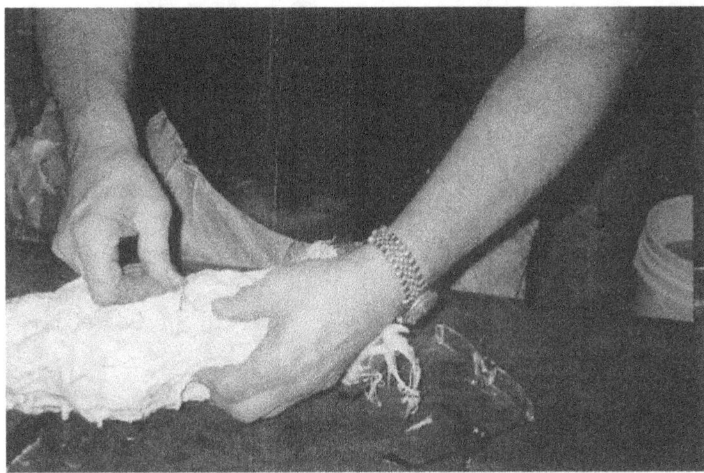

Photograph 10, Pushing the nails back in to assure alignment of the two sides of the seam

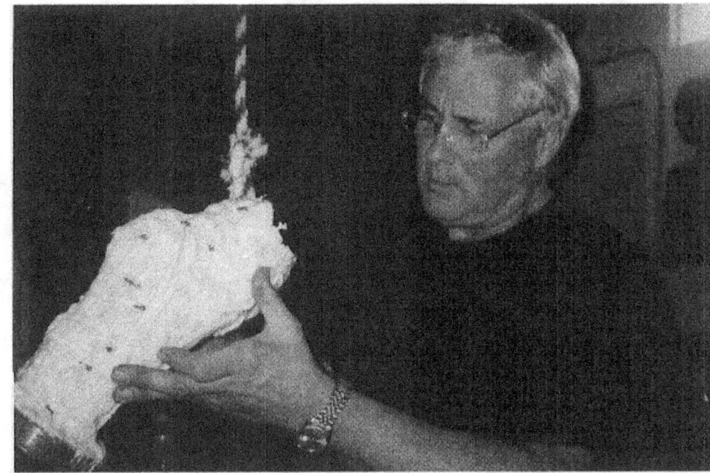

Photograph 11, Inspecting for thin spots in the LifeRITE

After 30 minutes I demolded it. It was almost flawless with only a couple of very small bubbles. I let it sit overnight, flattened the top on a belt grinder, painted it with a green patina solution, then dry buffed it with a cloth wheel and buffing compound, and attached it to a marble base. If I have to say so myself, it looked marvelous (photograph # 12). Photograph #14 shows a somewhat larger casting that was done almost the same way. But because of its size, it had to have a mother mold, was cast hollow, and was filled with a high density foam. Also a slower setting white urethane was used. The seam was done the same way with nails and was almost invisible. The detail was excellent with only a couple of minor flaws. All that was needed was a lamp shade and a 1953 Red Rider BB Gun and one could have a pretty darn good Christmas story.

The day I started this article began ominously. The sunrise was as bright red as the eyes of Satan. I could remember the voice of my saintly mother telling me that on such a morning, sailors take warning. I was standing in my studio next to a pile of clay that I was certain contained a masterpiece. But even after my second cup of black coffee tar, I couldn't jump start the muse. I was about to resign myself to the fact that today I wouldn't be taking a step toward even a footnote in art history when there was a knock at the door. "It's open," I yelled.

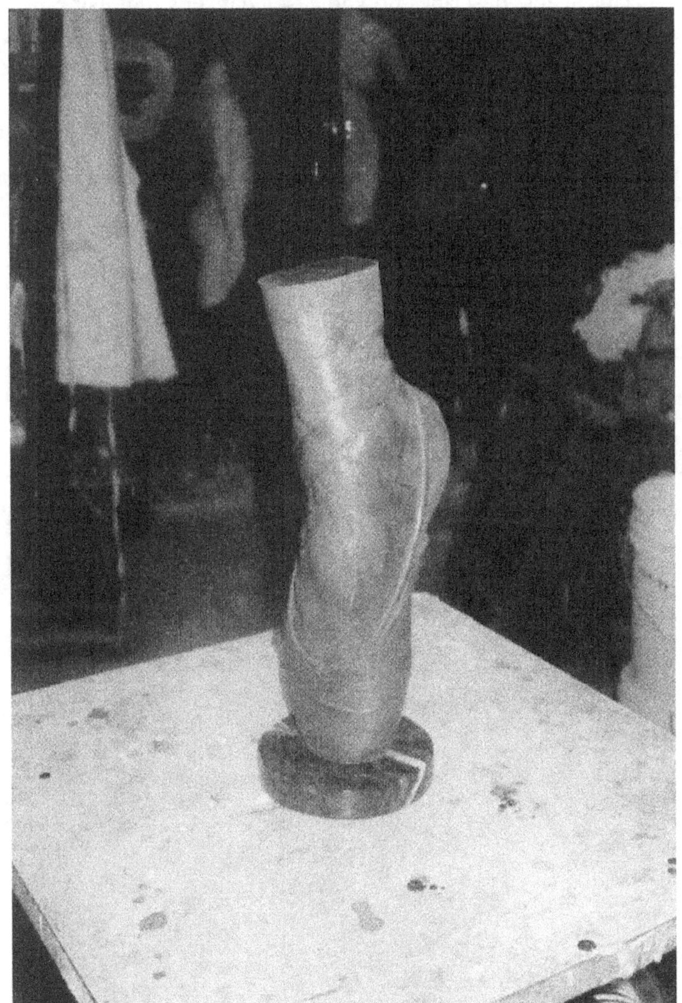

Photograph 13, Finished foot on a marble base

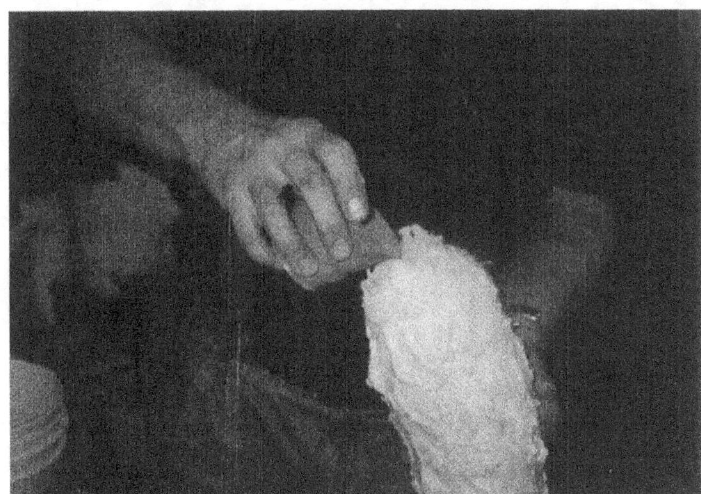

Photograph 12, Pouring in the metal powders

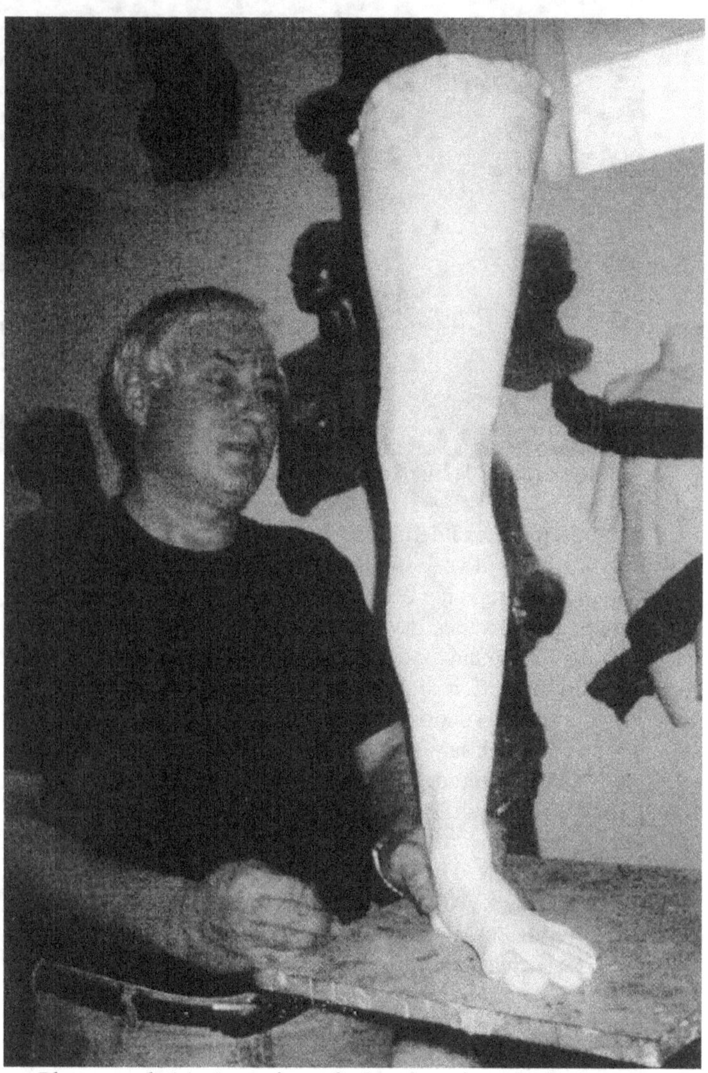

Photograph 14, A casting of a leg done in a similar way

This article describes how to cast a dancer's foot using fast setting skin safe thixotropic platinum cured silicone rubber. Another and perhaps easier way is to use alginate. I have described and demonstrated the alginate method in my DVD on casting hands and feet which is available through ArtMonds.

Sculpture Journal January 2005

"Mr. Parvin, my name is Gigget Mammiata and you are my last resort." Though I tried to concentrate on the statue hiding in the clay, I couldn't resist a voice that resonated softly as if from the cello of Yo Yo Ma to the melody and tempo of Mozart's Twenty-first Piano Concerto. Besides, anyone who had spent four years in a Catholic Seminary as I had would have instantly recognized "Mammiata" to be the plural of "boobs" in the accusative case. I looked up and remembered why I had left the seminary. Her dress was so tight that I could read clearly the raised letters spelling "Victoria's Secret" in two places. She had a face and body that reassured me that the human race wouldn't be dying out any time soon. She stood about 5 feet 9 and I was willing to bet the farm that she had to be about the same lying down.

I threw in the beginning of my new novel, "Dave Parvin, Sculptor and Private Eye" to see if anyone is still awake!

How to Patina a Life Casting Made of Forton MG with Metal Powder

By David E. Parvin, A.L.I.

One of the great things about Forton MG or FMG is that very credible cold cast bronzes can be achieved by adding metal powders and then getting the right patina. (For a more information on FMG, see "Mixing Forton MG Simplified," SJ, July 2003 by DEP.) While almost anything can be cast in FMG, it is especially useful for life castings. For this purpose, I prefer it to regular bronze because it is lighter, captures detail more precisely, is far less costly, can be used in one's home or studio, and doesn't shrink, expand, or distort. Resins, both polyester and polyurethane, have similar advantages, but FMG additionally is water soluble, odorless, and non toxic. Fortunately, the instructions for FMG include valuable information on applying patinas to FMG. but in this article, I am going to explain how easy it is to get a great patina on an FMG life casting. All that's needed are:

1. Steel wool, preferably 0000 or extra fine.
2. A floppy buffing wheel attached to an electric drill.
3. "Tripoli" buffing compound, preferably the water soluble kind.
4. Glossy clear acrylic spray.
5. Several 2'' cheap paint brushes.
6. One or more patina solutions.

In photograph #1, the alginate mold had just been removed from the model/subject, Ali. (It is just a coincidence that her name could stand for "Association of Life casters International.) At that point, I could have made a positive casting in metallic FMG directly in the alginate mold; however, I was planning on sculpting the eyes open and modifications are less obvious if a second mold is made for the final casting. I initially made a plaster positive. Since opening the eyes requires adding as well as taking material away and since I use wax for this purpose which will not stick

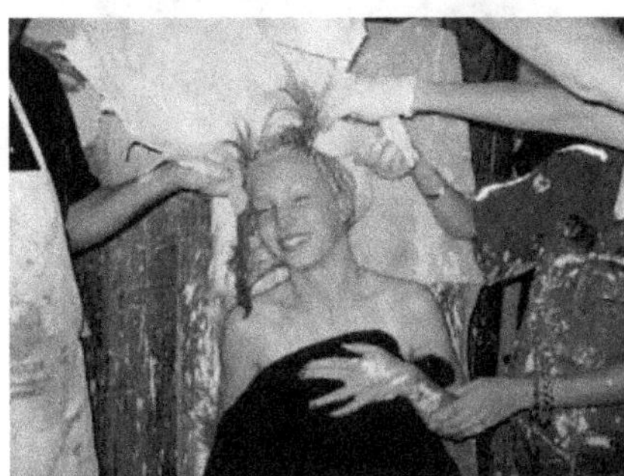

Photo 1: The alginate mold being removed from Ali

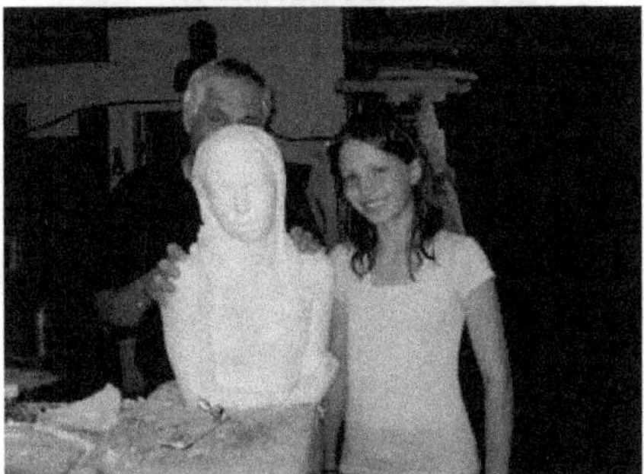

Photo 2: Ali in plaster.

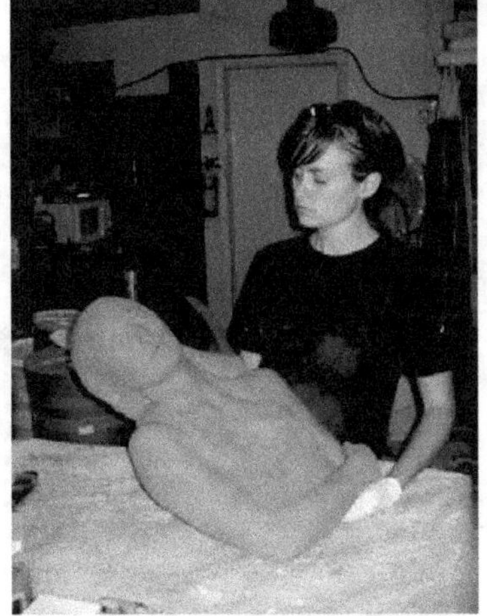

Photo 3: Ali in unpatinaed metallic Forton MG

to wet plaster, I allowed plaster Ali in photograph #2 to dry for a few days. After opening the eyes and correction a few small defects, I made a mold of plaster Ali in silicone rubber and cast her again, this time in FMG with copper powder, 500 RL, in the first two coats. Ali, held by assistant Audra in photograph #3 looked like pale chocolate (See "Secondary Molds in Life Casting, Part II, SJ, Nov. and Dec. 2004, by DEP.) She was then ready for patina.

A logical question to ask here is why use copper powder rather than bronze powder. There are a couple of reasons. The first is that I have found that copper powder in Forton MG produces a more convincing bronze look than bronze powder does which, in my opinion, is too dark. The second problem is that a copper casting accepts a patina, as described below, much more intensely. A third consideration is that bronze powder is about twice as expensive as copper powder.

There are two patina solutions that I generally use, green called "Verdigris" and "Super Antique 40" for black. Both may be purchased from several of the advertisers of sculpting supplies in the magazine. The best known patinaest in Colorado where I live, Pat Kipper, gave me a recipe for Verdigris many years ago which I will share in case anyone wants to become one step closer to self sufficient. Just add one ounce (28 grams) of cupric chloride and six ounces (168 grams) of ammonium chloride to one half gallon (1.8 liters) of water. Increasing the amount of cupric chloride will make the patina more blue.

The sooner after taking a FMG casting from a mold that one applies the Verdigris patina solution, the more intense the color will be. Usually, I like the hair and the cloth to have more color than the flesh and apply the solution to these areas the day the piece is cast. In photograph #4, another of my assistants, Kelsey, is applying the Verdigris. If one waits a day or two before this step, it's a good idea to buff the surface with steel wool to expose the metal in the FMG so that it will react better with the Verdigris. Leaving particles of the steel wool on the casting will cause them to react to the solution making an antique rusty effect that can be quite nice. Another way to get the same effect is to rub steel wool on the casting while it is still wet with Verdigris. It may take a while for the Verdigris to react with the copper, just be patient. Remember, the patina solutions are not paint, any color changes are the result of chemical reactions with the copper. If a patina solution doesn't want to wet the surface, i.e. tend to bead-up, there is probably some oil on the surface of the FMG, Adding a small amount of strong cleaner such a "Greased Lightning," to the solution will solve the problem. In photograph #5, Ali has "cured" for about 30 minutes and the solution has dried leaving the hair and cloth green. I had taken a "Q tip" and dabbed a little Super Antique 40 into the irises making them black. Super Antique 40 reacts intensely and almost instantly with copper FMG. It can also be used to darken hair, provide shading, or to just turn an entire casting black.

As for the skin, I generally prefer a more metallic color. If I need the life casting finished in just a few days I apply the Verdigris and as soon as it starts to turn green, rinse it off. Then I reapply the patina solution to the hair and cloth and let dry. A great way to dry something quickly is to put it into a car on a sunny day and let the green house effect go to work. If I am not in a hurry and can wait a couple of weeks, copper FMG will take a really nice bronze patina all by itself because of the moisture, pollution, etc. in the air. If I have time, that is my preferred method.

In photograph #6, I am using a 6'' buffing wheel attached to an electric drill. It is best to have a drill with variable speeds up to about 2500 R.P.M. and around 6 amps of power. It's a good idea to lightly go over the surface with steel wool to remove excess dried Verdigris prior to using the buffing wheel. I always use the steel wool outside so as not to breath the dust which contains chloride. With the drill, use water soluble Tripoli buffing compound which is also readily available. Be careful not to over polish especially if the FMG is no more than a few days old or you may polish off some

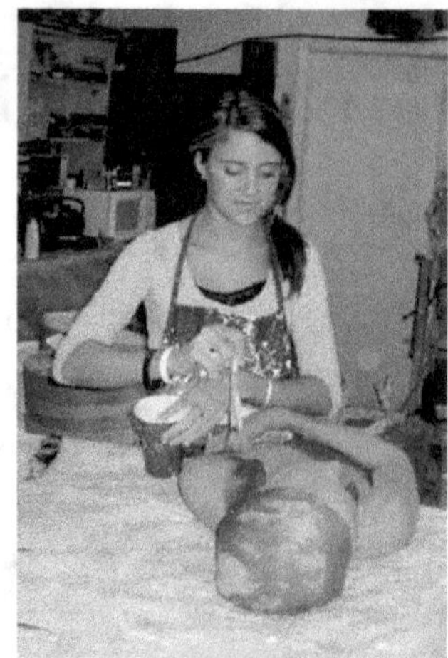

Photo 4: Applying the Verdigris patina solution

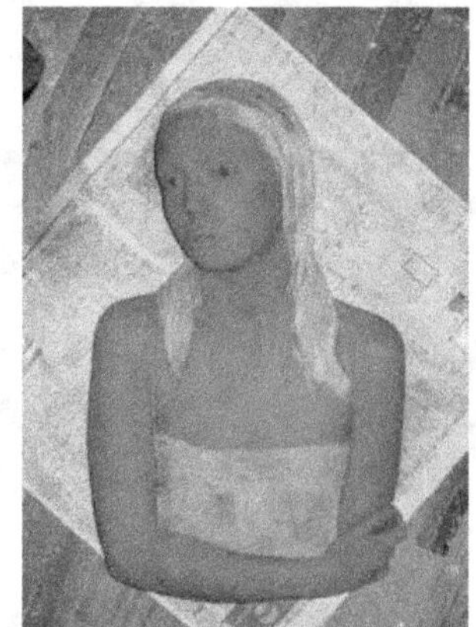

Photo 5: Ali's hair and cloth turned green

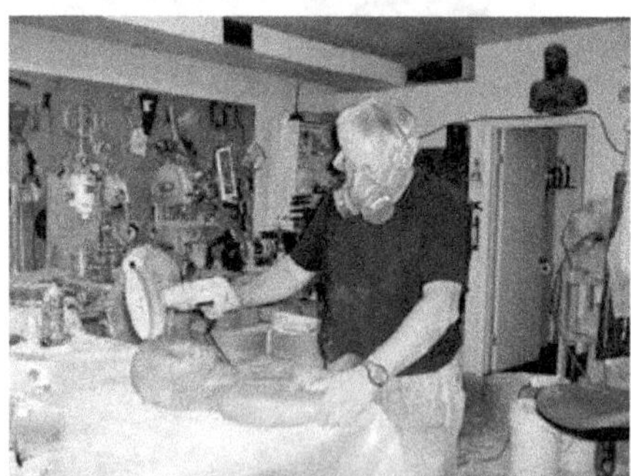

Photo 6: Buffing the entire surface

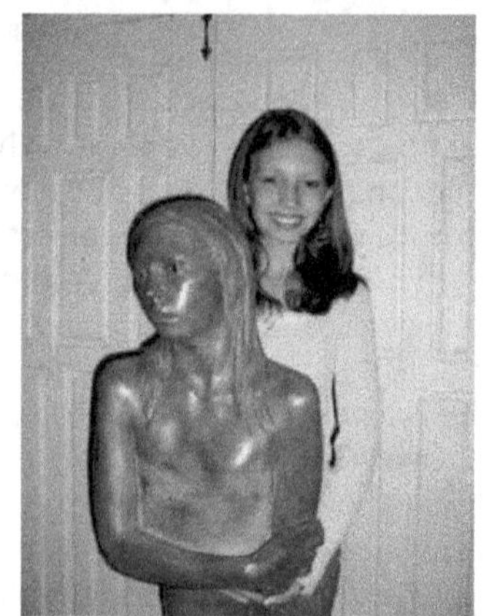

Photo 7: Ali and her finished casting

of the surface detail. Another caveat is to be careful not to catch the wheel on an edge of the casting or you may toss it half way across the room which may or may not damage it depending on weather it lands on the hard floor or a soft assistant.

The last step is to fix the color permanently by spraying on clear acrylic . If you don't do this, the copper will continue to react to whatever is in the air and the color will change over time. Be aware that the acrylic spray will mute or soften the green color made by the Verdigris. Often, I spray the skin and the hair but not the cloth allowing its color to change almost as if the patina there were "alive."

I would like to claim that I was the first to use Forton MG for life castings and I may have been, I did not get the idea to use it from anybody else and have been using it for somewhere around 20 years. However, any number of others may have made the same discovery. But the important thing to me is that a great deal of my work wouldn't have been possible without it. Certainly my life castings would have been less. Metallic FMG patinaed as described here definitely looks more professional than , say, plaster with a painted finish. Give it a try, I think you'll be surprised at how quickly you'll feel like an expert.

David Parvin is a Denver sculptor. He may be reached at 303-321-1074 if you would like to discuss art, fly fishing, flying, or grandchildren.

Sculpture Journal October 2006

If It Looks Like a Duck...

Or How to Cast a Complete Arm in the Round Without Distortior

By David E. Parvin, A.L.I.

Not long after I began experimenting with life casting in 1987, I tried something which seemed logical, but in fact didn't work. I had successfully cast some hands and feet by immersing them into containers filled with alginate. Obviously, I reasoned, I could simply get a taller container and cast a whole arm the same way.

But when I peeled off the alginate, the plaster fingers were flattened and reminded me of duck bills. I was baffled at first but then suspected that what was happening was that the weight of the alginate was causing it to compress, the effect of which would be greatest at the bottom of the column where the fingers were.

There are two common types of molds: block and skin, and each has advantages and disadvantages. What I am describing here is a block mold so-called because the object to be cast is simply surrounded by a "block" of some casting material such as alginate, rubber, plaster, etc.

The construction is simple, just construct a wall around the object and pour in the mold material and let it set up encasing it in a "block". The wall may also serve as a mother mold though if the molding material is thick enough then a mother mold may not even be required.

The "skin" in skin mold refers to a much thinner layer or "skin" of rubber or alginate which is painted on in layers on the object. Over the skin is constructed a conforming rigid mother mold which is necessary to hold the flexible mold material in shape. The main advantage of a block mold is its simplicity, saving time in construction. The disadvantage is that a block mold will require more of the molding materials which can be pricey.

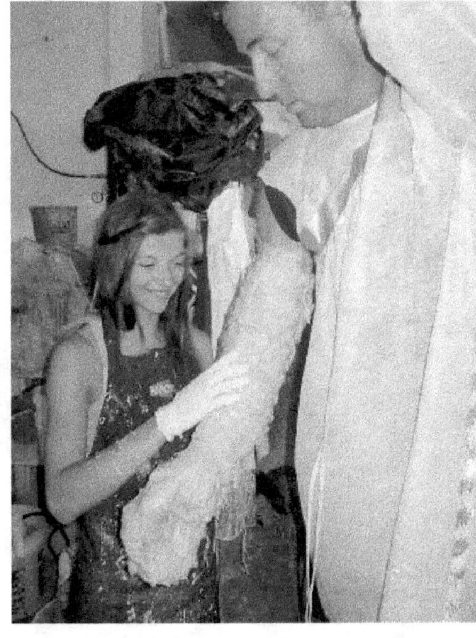

Photo 1. Life casting an arm using a skin mold was a flop.

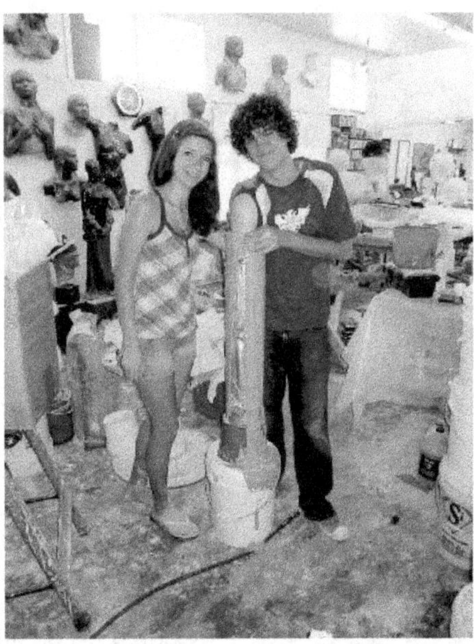

Photo 2. My assistant Jay's boyfriend, Alistair is cast in the block mold method for verification of duck beak problem.

Over the years, I have been able to cast decent entire arms and legs using skin molds. Because

> Squashed fingers can look a lot like baby duck bills.

less alginate is used in a skin versus a block mold, it doesn't want to compress under its own weight. But at the time I began this article I was discussing with a client a possible commission which would have required at least twenty pairs of arms, all forty of which would be unique. I decided to experiment to see if I could come up with an easy way to do so many castings.

Since I had not done a skin mold on a complete arm in some time, I decided to attempt one on a volunteer's arm to see how long it would take (photo 1) and if there were any unforeseen problems. In the photo to the left, my assistant Steve is covering volunteer Jeff's arm with two layers of alginate.

Over that we built a two part mother mold using fast setting den-

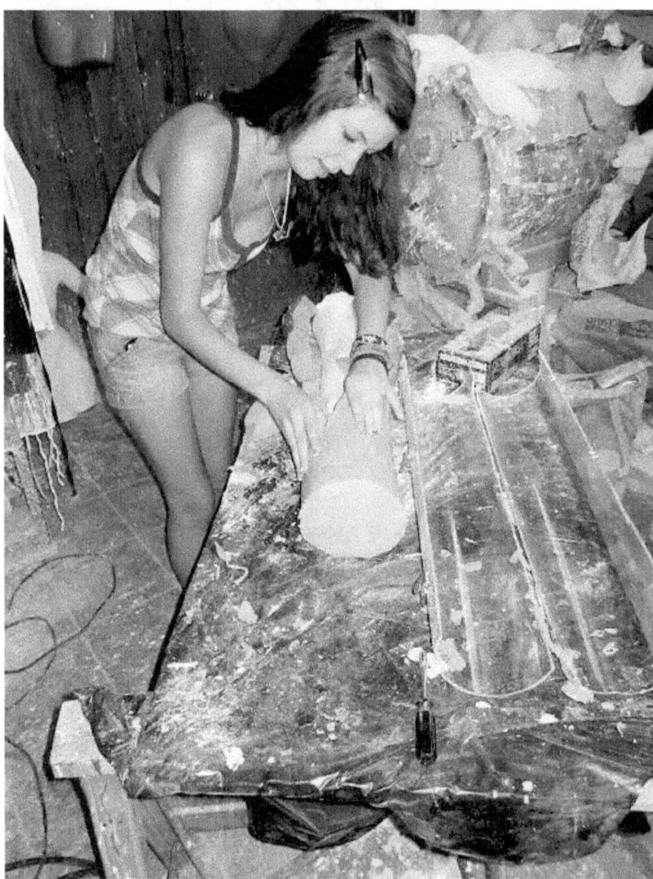

Photo 5. Jay is peeling off the alginate from the arm casting

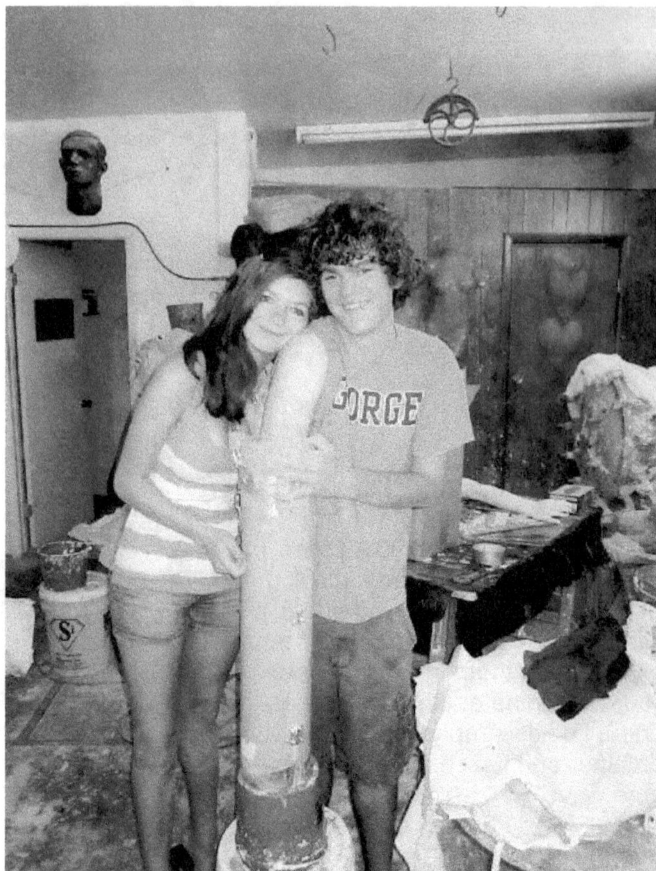

Photo 7. The tube is filled with alginate. With the expression on those two high schoolers' faces makes me suspect that the human race isn't dying out anytime in the immediate future

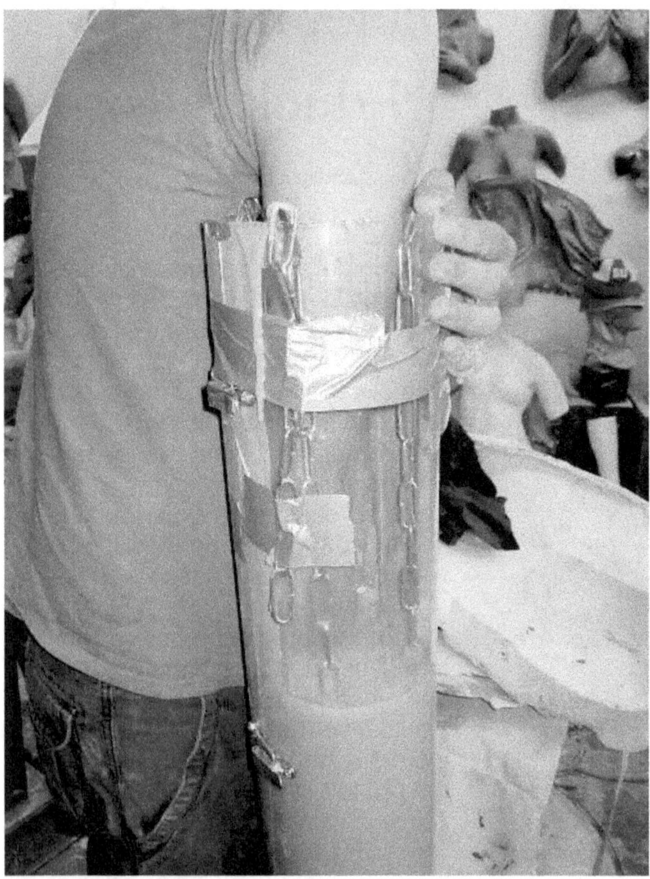

Photo 6. The mold now has three chains in it to support the alginate

tal plaster and cheese cloth. A method I much prefer over using plaster bandages. While it worked, Jeff had to patiently endure about thirty minutes of suffering for art.

Also the reason the mother mold had to be in two halves was because the alginate was not thick enough to allow Jeff to extract his hand without removing the mother mold and cutting a parting line in the alginate. No matter how carefully done, the parting line will show up in the casting and will have to be repaired. It worked but I got to thinking that if I could solve the duck bill problem with block molds I might be able to speed up the process benefiting both the *castees* and the *castors*.

The first thing was to construct a tube of six inch diameter clear Lucite. The length was long enough to include an arm of a six footer from the armpit to the fingertips. I cut it lengthwise on each side and attached the two halves back together with three hinges on one side and three latches on the other.

The bottom was plugged with a circle cut from a 2 -inch thick piece of Styrofoam insulation. The plug could be positioned in the tube depending upon the length of the arm being cast, saving alginate. We used some duct tape to seal the slits on the sides and around the bottom plug. We calculated the volume of the tube and estimated that it would take about twenty pounds of water and five pounds of alginate.

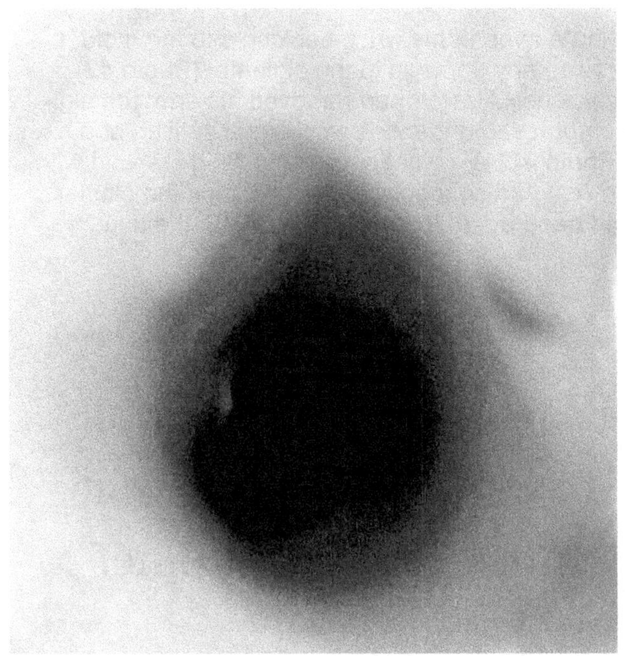

Photo 3. Peering down into the alginate mold, the alginate was not damaged when the arm was removed from it.

It had been years since I had tried to make a column block mold so I decided to do a test to be sure that I got the duck beak fingers which I remembered. So my assistant, Jay, talked her boyfriend Alastair into being the 'ginny pig'. We mixed two batches of ten pounds of water and two and a half pounds of FiberGel by ArtMolds which is my alginate of choice. (FiberGel by ArtMolds probably works better than any other alginate for this purpose because the fibers make it more tear resistant.)

We dumped one batch into the tube, had Alastair push his right arm into the alginate as far as he could, and then added the second batch. (Photo #2.) Because Alastair's arm was surrounded by a thick layer of soft alginate, he was able to remove it without tearing

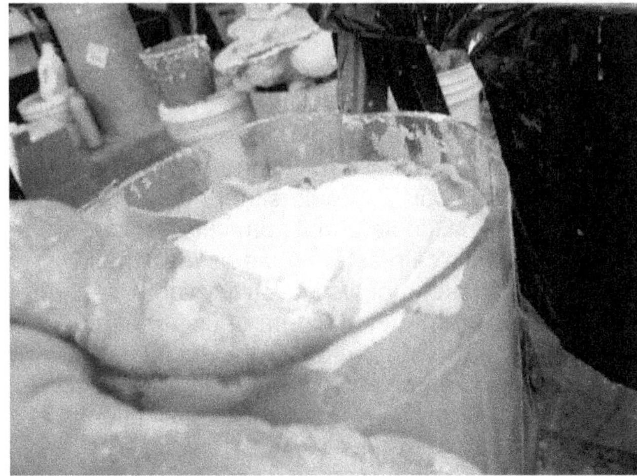

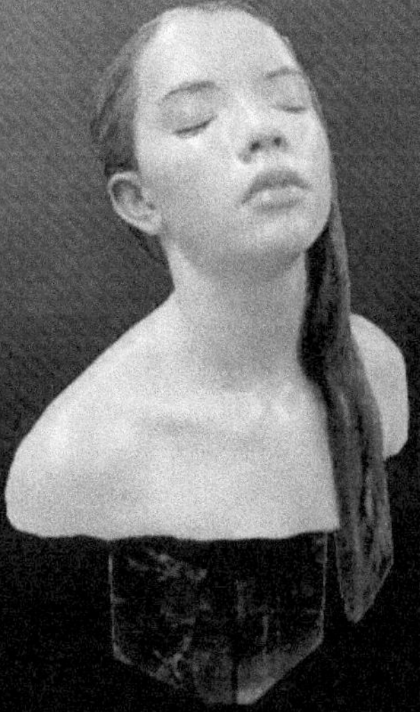

Photo 4. The Tube has been filled to the top, but settled about an inch after Alistair removed his arm. In fact when I poured in the plaster the alginate had risen back up slightly.

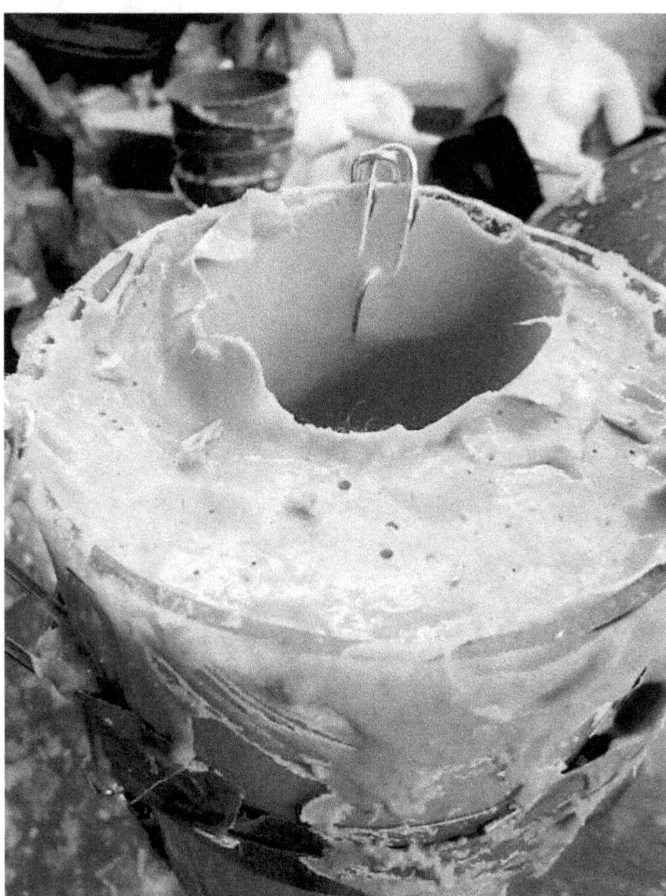

Photo 8. If you look at the edge of the tube where the alginate meets, it is almost level with the rim. Compare this with photo number 4 and you see that with the chains installed the alginate did not compress down into the tube mold even with the arm removed.

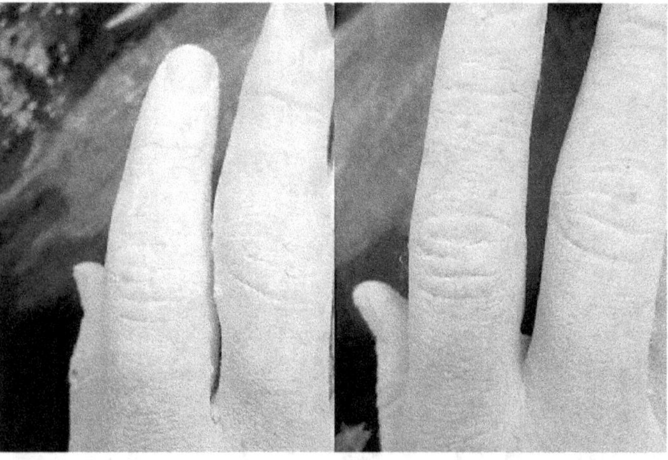

Photo 9. Note the distortion of fingers on the hand on the left. It is even more noticeable when viewed in person. Distorted fingers are the result of the weight of the alginate mold pressing down on and collapsing the cavities that the fingers occupied after the hanc is removed from the mold. This is a common occurrence when a hand casting goes beyond the wrist and up the fore arm as the weigh of the alginate builds the more of the arm that is captured in the mold. The hand on the right was cast in the mold using the supporting chains and show no distortion as the chains supported the alginate in the tube prevented its weight from collapsing the fingers.

the alginate even at his wrist. Looking into the mold, I couldn't see any damage to the alginate. (Photo #2). However, once Alastair had removed his arm, the alginate compressed under its own weight, settling about an inch. (Photo #3) We went ahead and filled the void with plaster. As I had suspected, when we took the plaster arm and hand out of the mold (Photo #9), the fingers

> Proving that chaining your block molds can prevent 'duck beak' syndrome.

were flattened.

What was needed was a way to lock the alginate in place so that it didn't slide down in the mold and compress. My first idea was to construct baffles inside the tube, and I may still try this. But it occurred to me that there was a simpler solution that just might work.

What I did was suspend three lengths of chain inside the tube from top to bottom. "Three" was a guess; just seemed like the right number. I suspected that the alginate would flow between the lengths of the chains and lock the alginate in place. (See photos 5 — 9.) As you can see from the last photos, the alginate did not compress and the fingers were that much the better.

I didn't try this system on a leg. Although I am confident it will work, I see three problems. The first is that the bottom of the mold will have to be large enough to contain the foot, making the construction of the tube more complex. The second is that because the foot will be more difficult to be extracted through the ankle void than a hand is through the wrist, it may be necessary to make a cut in the alginate from the heel up to about mid calf. The last problem is that there is such a difference in cross section between the ankle and the thigh that it will take a great deal of alginate to do a leg casting this way.

So legs, I would probably use a skin mold. If I needed to make multiple copies, I could either make the skin mold of the model in skin safe platinum cured silicone rubber or I could make a plaster, in the alginate mold and make a rubber skin mold from it. The type of rubber in this case; latex, urethane, platinum or tin cured silicone, is mostly just the preference of the sculptor though each has advantages and disadvantages. Deciding on the perfect rubber for a particular application is a discussion for another time. ❑

Dave Parvin is a Denver area sculptor who may be reached at parvinstudio@comcast.net but who much prefers to talk than type (720) 971-0824.

Techniques For Life Casting Hair

PART 1

BY DAVID E. PARVIN, A.L.I.

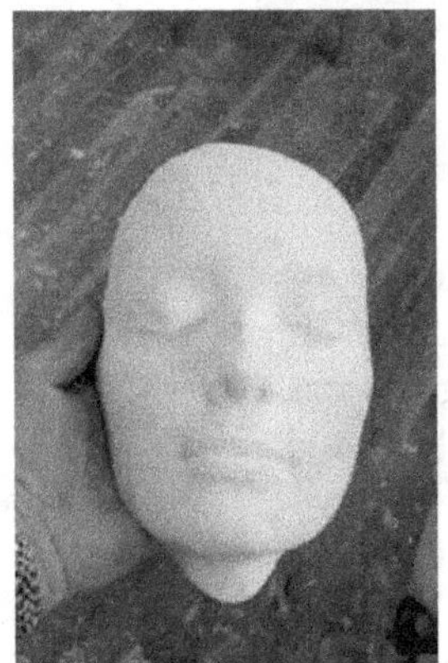

Photograph #1

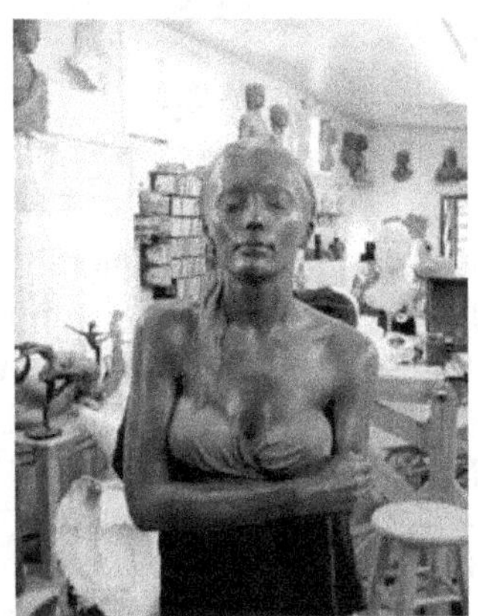

Photograph #2

Hair has always been important; so important that even in two biblical stories, hair was critical to the plots. Remember the brothers Esau and Jacob. Esau was a hairy man but Jacob was a smooth one. Jacob glued lamb's fur to his hands and convinced his poorly sighted father that he was his brother. Skip a few books, chapters, and verses, and one finds Samson whose strength was in his hair. Unfortunately, he fell for the wiles of Delilah who whispered, "Hey handsome want to come up for a good time and a haircut?" Not only are there many more references to hair in the Bible, but hair seems to show up just about everywhere. If it hadn't been for her long hair, Lady Godiva would have had to take the time to cover her assets before jumping on the horse. Don' t forget Repunsel and Goldilocks. Poetry is filled with hair,

"My hair is gray but not with years Nor grew it white in a single night As men's have grown from sudden fears."

And then there is music. Look no farther than old English folk songs:

`Black, black, black is the color of my true love's hair..., " "... *then a flash of phosphorus in her seaweed hair and I looked again and my mother wasn't there...,"* or

"She wept, she cried, she tore her hair, ah me what could I do... "

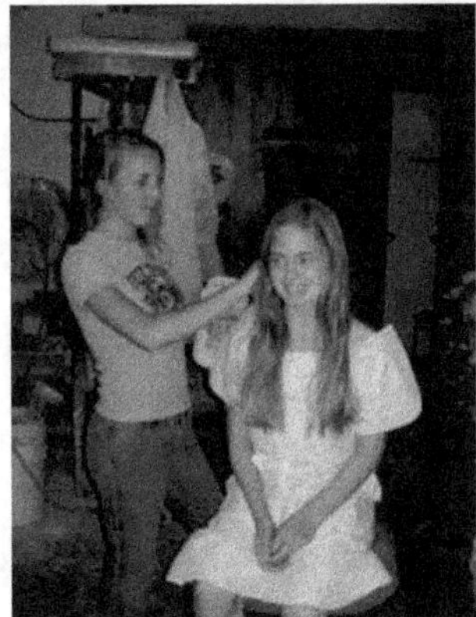

Photograph #3

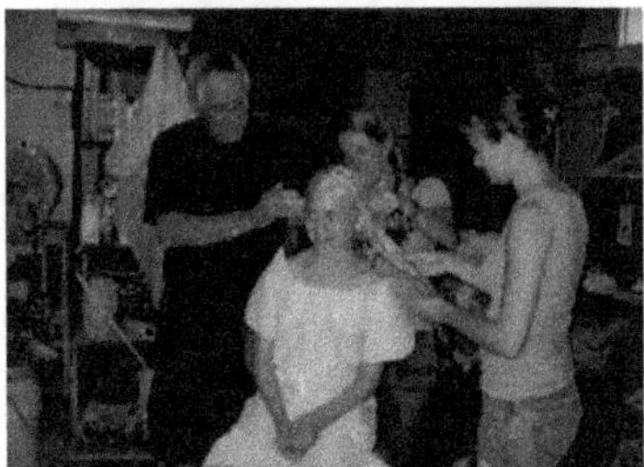

Photograph #4

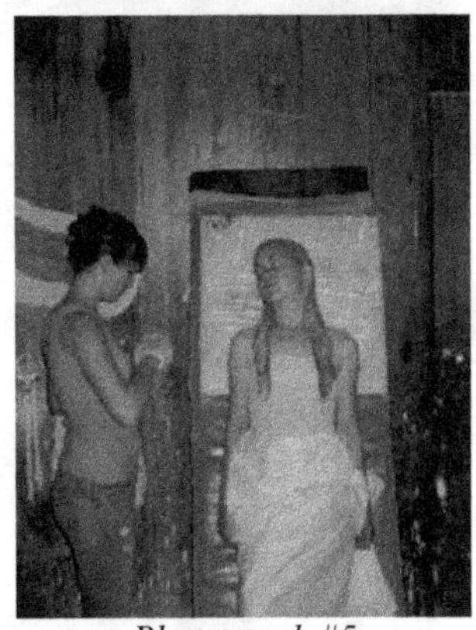

Photograph #5

In the sixties, there was a whole musical devoted just to hair in which some of the cast members stripped down buck naked to show off all the hair they were born with! Almost certainly, religion, history, art, poetry, music, theater, and civilization would not be the same without hair.

Amazingly, when I began life casting about twenty years ago, hair was something that just got in the way. It was usually tied back and covered; what stuck out was smeared with petroleum jelly or Crisco, neither of which washed out very easily. I don't remember exactly when, but it must have been at least 15 years ago that I got lucky. I was preparing a little girt of about eight for a face casting. As I was covering what little hair was visible with petroleum jelly, her mother who was a hair stylist, mentioned that she knew of something that might work better, a thick hair conditioner called "Cholesterol." The name seemed odd to me then and still does. Just imagine someone coming into a marketing meeting and announcing that he/she has just thought up the perfect name for their new hair conditioner, "Will Harden Your Arteries!" But I got some and tried it; it worked great and was easy to wash out. From that time on, I could promise that getting cast is like a stay in an expensive spa, including getting a seaweed wrap and the best hair conditioning ever.

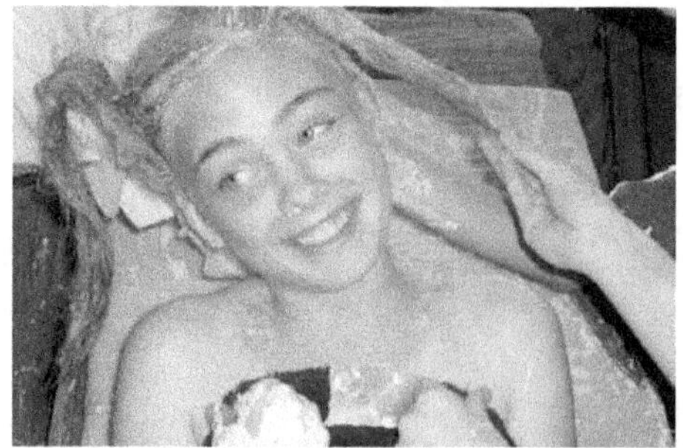
Photograph #6

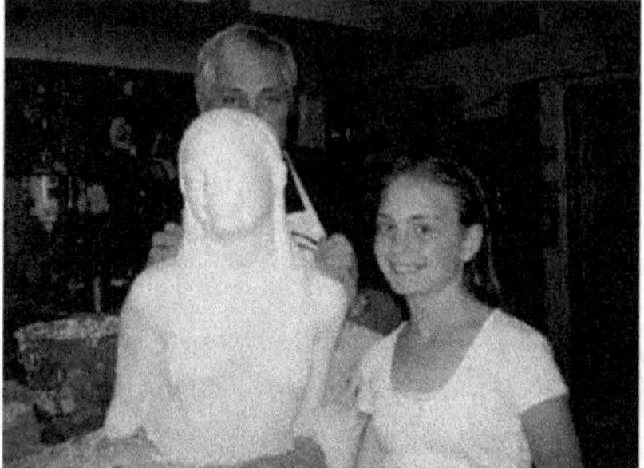
Photograph #7

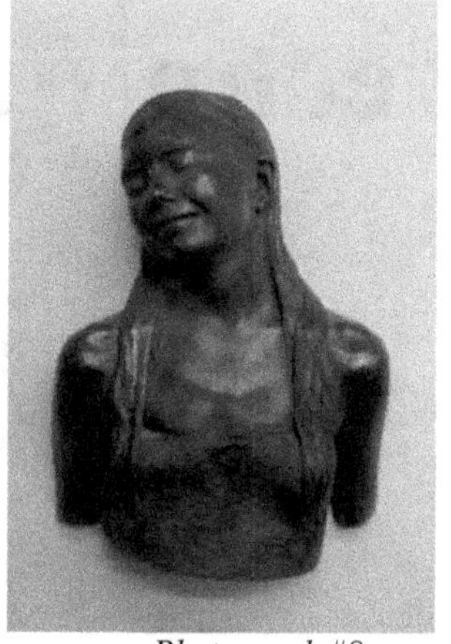
Photograph #8

Photograph #1 is of what often passes for a life casting of a face yet falls short because it doesn't include either the ears or hair. Photograph #2 is a more complete casting which looks a whole tot more like the subject partly because both ears and hair are included. (For casting cars, see SJ, "Casting Perfect Ears," May, 2004 by yours truly.) I have to be careful here and not say something that may not be the truth and make me sound even more arrogant than I really am. Remember who claimed that he had invented the internet and ended up loosing the big election? Being able to cast hair makes an incredible difference in life casting and he/she who solved the problem should certainty be remembered in the Life Casters' Hatt of Fame. But just because I was the first person I know of to figure out how a practical solution doesn't mean that I was the only or even the first. Even though I suspect that this was another original Parvin's perfectly pertinent procedures for pleasure and profit, I will only take credit for spreading the "good news" and not keeping it to myself.

Fortunately, casting hair turns out to be quite simple, all you need are the right product, a willing subject, and some instruction. Cholesterol should be available at any beauty supply store. ArtMolds, see advertisement in this issue, offers its own product for this purpose called "MoldEse," which is also an excellent choice. Caution, there are releases that are intended to prevent skin safe silicone rubber from sticking to hair. These will work but just as petroleum jetty and Crisco will be very difficult to wash o Lit.

Photograph #3 shows a willing subject, 13 year old Laura who has tong, thick, beautiful hair that is just made for casting. We have her apply the Cholesterol. While a plastic bag with a hole for the head will work, I purchase paper medical gowns which are very inexpensive and more comfortable cover-ups.

In photograph #4, another assistant, Audra, and myself are helping Morgan apply the Cholesterol. Don't just cover the hair; the trick is to work the Cholesterol completely through the hair right down to the scalp. You almost can't apply too much. It will take at least a pound for someone with as much hair as Laura's. Once applied, wait at least 15 minutes before starting the casting to allow the Cholesterol to dry out slightly stiffening the hair and enabling you to tweak it into the exact position desired. I usually use this time for any final preparations such as measuring the water and the alginate.

Photograph #5 shows Laura standing in position for the casting. Audra has just arranged her and is touching up some places that need a little more Cholesterol. The very last preparation will be to apply a little petroleum jelly to the eyebrows and eyelashes. The PJ will help define the eyebrows and will reduce the chance of putting out the eyebrows eyelashes. Cholesterol might sting the eyes slightly and this small amount of PJ is no problem to wash out. Note that Laura is now wearing a piece of

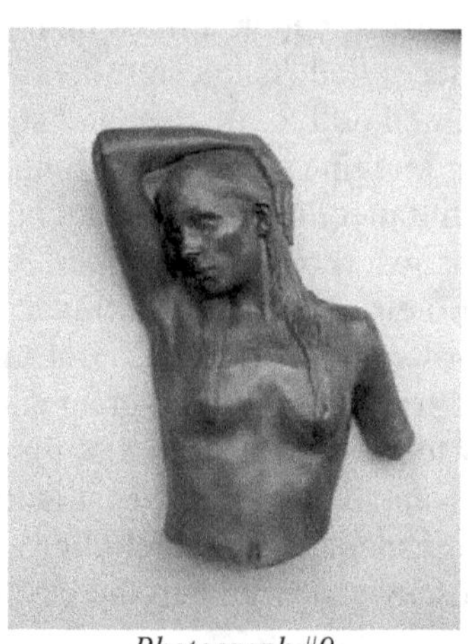
Photograph #9

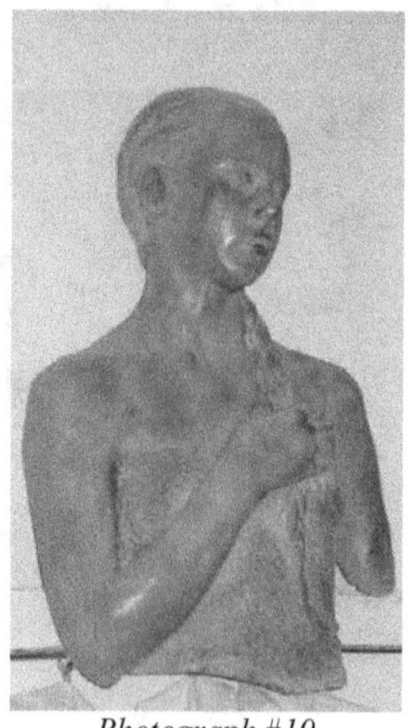
Photograph #10

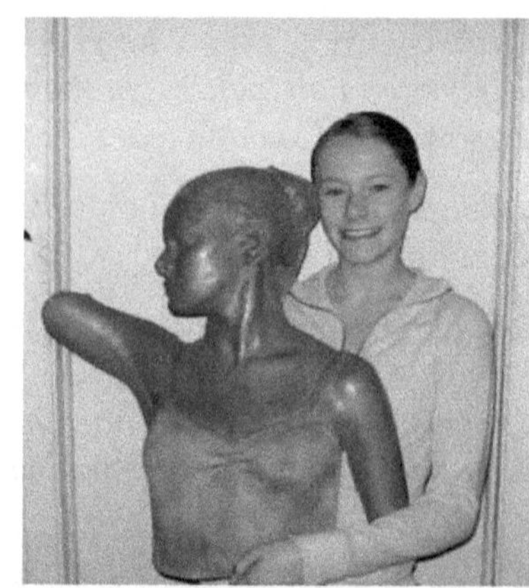
Photograph #11

lace which will add a very nice texture to the casting and make it look as if she was wearing something preserving her modesty and reputation!

In photograph #6, I have just lifted off the alginate mold. As it came free from the bottom, I had one of my assistants pull the hair loose from the mold. The hair will not be stuck into the alginate but will cling slightly because of the thick butter-like conditioner. Short hair comes free with no assistance. Note that Laura is smiling and in no discomfort at all.

While Laura was in the shower washing the conditioner out of her hair, I made a plaster positive from the alginate mold. In photograph #7, Laura has emerged from the shower no worse for the wear. If you have read my recent articles in SJ, (See esp. May 2006 for faces) then you are aware that I do not use plaster as a final casting material but will clean up this plaster positive and make a silicone rubber mold for the completed mask usually cast in Forton MG with metal powers. The completed casting is in photograph #8.

Casting hair does have some limitations. First of all, the hair will be matted down as if wet minimizing the styles that can be achieved. However, it is possible to shape enough texture into the conditioned hair so that the effect can still be very appealing. In any event, the results will be far better than covering up the hair. Short hair such as most men have and hair long enough to fall below the shoulders cast just fine. Hair length in between is the least advantageous. The problem is that if the hair will not reach and therefore touch and stick to the shoulders, the cast hair will just hang straight down and not be very interesting. It is possible for the model to wear a wig, even a cheap costume wig works quite well. Also, additional hair can be sculpted onto the casting.

Facial hair, beards and mustaches, cast very well this same way. However if the hair is short, I usually use petroleum jelly since it tastes better than the conditioner and will still easily wash out. If you are casting torsos, Cholesterol works for both pubic and armpit hair. Always let the model apply Cholesterol to her/his own pubic hair. Make sure that she/he applies a liberal coat; pulling out clumps of pubic hair is not conducive to friendship. Chest hair for the gorilla types can be a problem because matting down the hair will cause it to be very visible in the casting. If you do not want the hair to be part of the casting, it isn't necessary to shave or wax (ouch!) it off, trimming it back so that it isn't more than about a half inch (one centimeter) tong and using a very small amount of conditioner will solve the problem. Alginate doesn't stick to hair but it does tangle in hair that is long enough. Hair on arms and legs is usually short enough not to need any release at all.

Photographs #9 through #14 show examples of hair cast in different ways. #9 is what I call mermaid hair. White very appealing, the model must have hair long enough and be comfortable in this somewhat more revealing pose. The young lady in # 10 had her hair in a long braid. We did work a light coat of conditioner into the hair prior to braiding it and then applied some to the surface as well. The ballerina look in #11 was done the same way. #12 is different only in that the head was cast completely in the round with no difficulty.

Photographs #13 and #14 have hair that was sculpted. #13 is a face in the round. The subject had very fine blond hair that didn't cast with sufficient bulk to took right. I cast the head in oil based clay and sculpted on additional hair. For # 14, I cut the mask of a Native American model in half and sculpted the flowing hair complete with a wolf's face. Both of these were then remolded and cast in metallic Forton MG. Hair is really pretty easy to sculpt; I intend on describing the process in a future article.

There isn't enough space in this article or even in this entire magazine to cover the casting of hair in its almost infinite varieties. But if you have been avoiding hair, I hope I have given you enough information so that when you start your next casting you can say, "Walk right in, sit right down, daddy (or mommy, sister, brother, etc.), let your hair hang down."

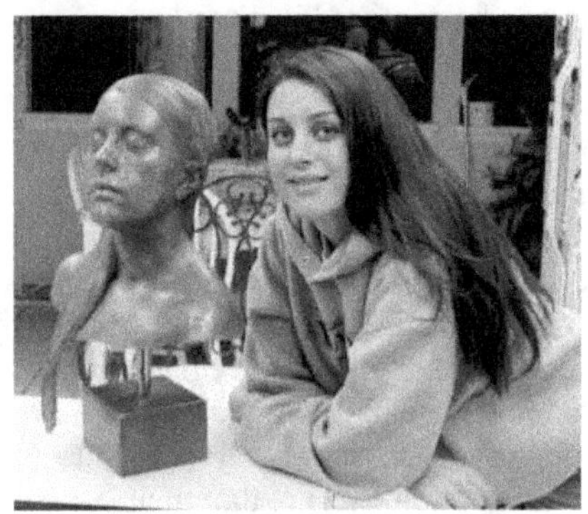

Photograph #12

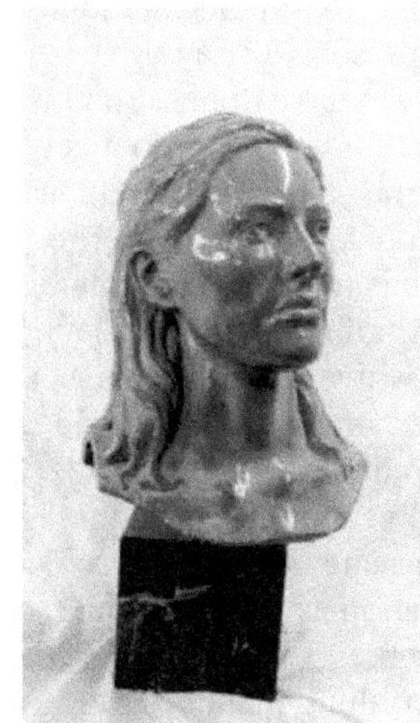

Photograph #13

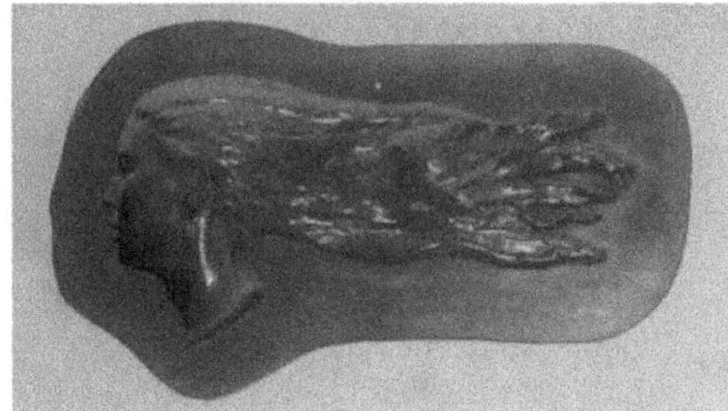

Photograph #14

Sculpting Hair in Life Casting,

Part 2

By David E. Parvin, A.L.I.

Last month, July 2006, I explained how easy it is to cast hair so that the finished mask becomes a much more recognizable portrait than without hair. But there are some limitations. For example, because the hair must be coated with a thick conditioner, it will have a "wet" look as if the person had just come from a pool or shower. The amount of detail that can be captured is directly proportional to the thickness or body of the hair. Photograph #1 shows a young lady whose hair was ideal for casting and required no enhancement. But what about when the subject has very thin hair or you just want to add hair for some special effect. For example, I have had women whose hair wasn't long enough request what I call mermaid hair as in photo #2, i.e. that their breasts be at least partially covered by their hair. A simple solution is to have the person wear a wig. It doesn't even have to be a good wig, a cheap costume wig will do nicely. (Photograph #3) But it's pretty easy to sculpt on additional hair. The procedure is to make an alginate impression of the model, cast a plaster positive, sculpt the hair on to the plaster, make a rubber mold of the repaired mask, and cast the improved version. I realize that is about the same degree of over simplification as explaining that to carve a horse from marble, just cut away everything that doesn't look like horse. I'll give you better directions but first let me explain a few things about hair, especially sculpted hair whether on life castings or more traditional sculptures.

The first and most important thing to understand is that in life, hair usually has volume and takes up space but has almost no weight. Imagine someone with long hair on a windy day; the hair can be blown straight out to the side without unbalancing the person. But hair made of bronze, marble, plaster, wood, Forton MG, etc. has both volume and weight. The same image sculpted has to be done just right or the piece will appear to be unbalanced. I said "usually has volume and... almost no weight" since if hair is compacted into a bun, braid, or, to some extent, a pony tail, it can seem to be more substantial and is easier to capture than loose hair. If the hair and its volume verses weight isn't quite clear, consider something similar, smoke and clouds. All three of these are no problem for a painter. Half way between a painting and a sculpture, a bas relief, works pretty well too. But a three dimensional, in the round sculpture is a little trickier to pull off and be convincing. There is a Latin phrase by Catullus that is a favorite of mine that **almost** fits here, "Sed mulier cupido quod dicit amanti in ventro et rapida scribere oportet aqua." For those who have forgotten their Latin, or more sadly, never learned Latin, "What a woman says to her lusty lover is best written on the wind or rapidly moving water."

I distinctly remember when I realized the second point I want to emphasize. I was in Scottsdale, AZ and was going from gallery to gallery enjoying the art. I came across a bronze pheasant taking flight as if escaping an enemy. The artist had meticulously sculpted in every detail of each feather. I have always been a fan of detail and accuracy and I am confident that I have seen far more work that was under finished than overworked. But in this case, the pheasant had no life whatsoever, it looked like a bronze stuffed bird; it just wasn't believable. At that moment I had an "ah ha" experience and understood something that I should have figured out much sooner, <u>sometimes it looks more real to sculpt (or paint) the way the eye sees it rather than the way it actually is.</u> Had the artist loosened up a little, he or she would have made a more believable pheasant in flight. Since then I have seen this same mistake

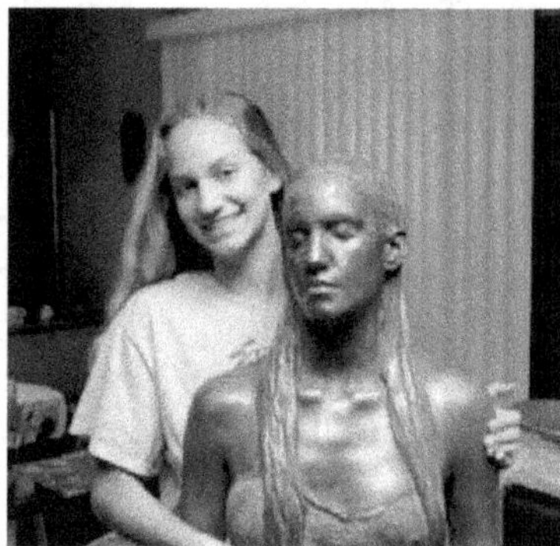

Photograph #1

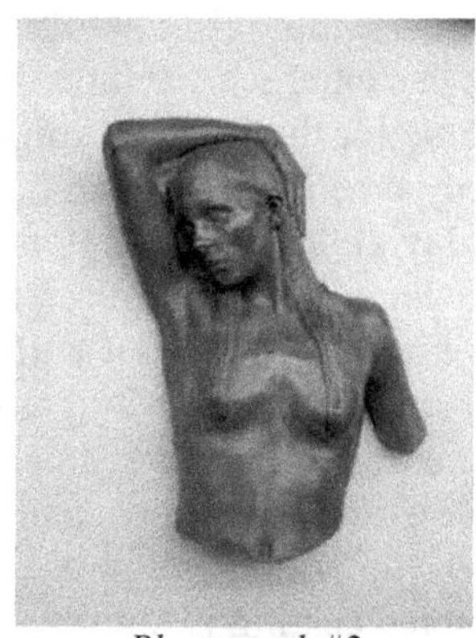

Photograph #2

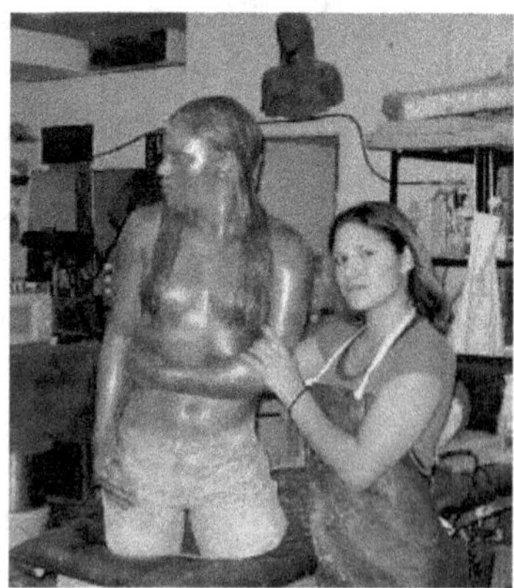

Photograph #3

Photo 1: Young lady with great hair for casting, required no additional sculpting.
Photo 2: Mermaid hair which covers enough of the breast to be respectable
Photo 3: An example of casting someone in a wig.

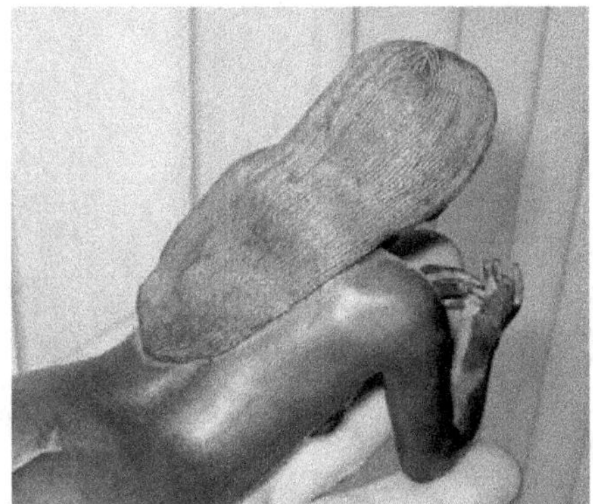
Photograph #4

over and over not only with feathers but also with fur on animals and hair on humans. Judy Collins was on the right track when she sang, "It's clouds illusions I recall..." It is the illusions of hair we want to capture.

Photograph #4 shows hair sculpted the wrong way, a heavy glob with lines indicating that it is supposed to be hair. I would like to be able to blame this on somebody else but, in fact, this was my very first bronze figure. If I skip foreword to something more recent, see the difference in photograph #5 which shows much more credible hair. This head began as a life casting of a young lady with very fine blond hair. Her hair was so fine in fact that the rough casting made her look like Tweedy Bird, i.e. almost bald. I sculpted on the additional hair.

There is another reason for keeping hair in the impressionistic range. Remember that anything in style will eventually be out of style. Jean Cocteau said, "Art produces ugly things that frequently become beautiful in time. Fashion, on the other hand, produces beautiful things that always become ugly in time." Generally, I try to make something that is not only beautiful now but will continue to be beautiful as long as possible into the future. The more exacting one is with hair, the more likely it is to depict a particular style and unless one is striving for historical accuracy, I have always felt that it is better to loosen up and generalize a little. Also, certain configurations are more timeless than others such as braids, pony tails, or just simply naturally flowing hair. There is a story told about a French woman who willed enough money so that the wig on a commemorative bust of herself be replaced periodically with one then in style so that she would always look her best.

In this article, I have tried to explain why sculpting hair whether on a life casting or a piece of more traditional sculpture, while not terribly difficult, does require one's attention to be credible. Next month I will go into some detail on just how to accomplish this as on the life size bronze figure in photo #6. I have been accused in this photo of using a really cool line like, "Been naked long?" But I can assure you that I was really saying, "Nice hair!

David Parvin is a Denver sculptor.
He may be reached at 303-321-1074 if you would like to discuss art, fly fishing, flying, or grandchildren.

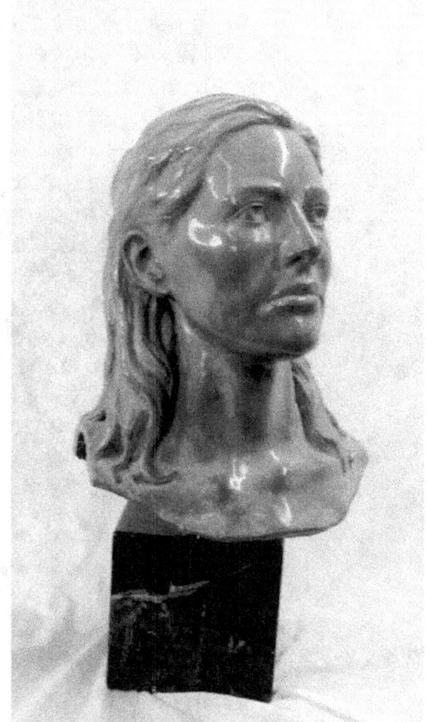
Photograph # 5

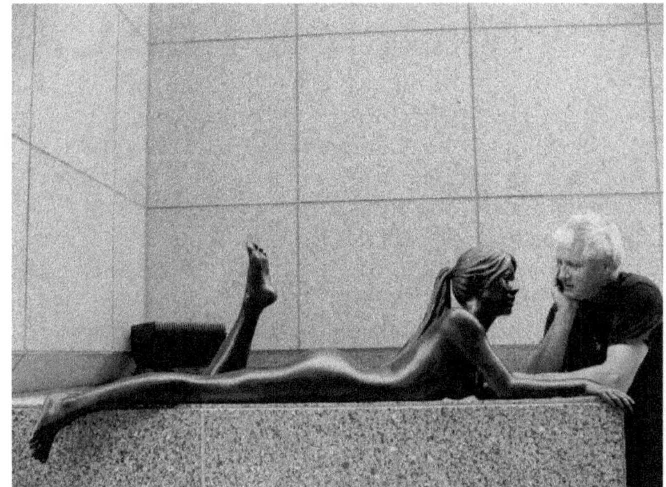
Photograph #6

Photograph #4: Really badly sculpted hair.
Photograph #5: Hair on a portrait bust that is completely sculpted on because the actual hair of the model was too short and fine to cast with any detail.
Photograph #6: Hair on a life size figure with sculpted hair,

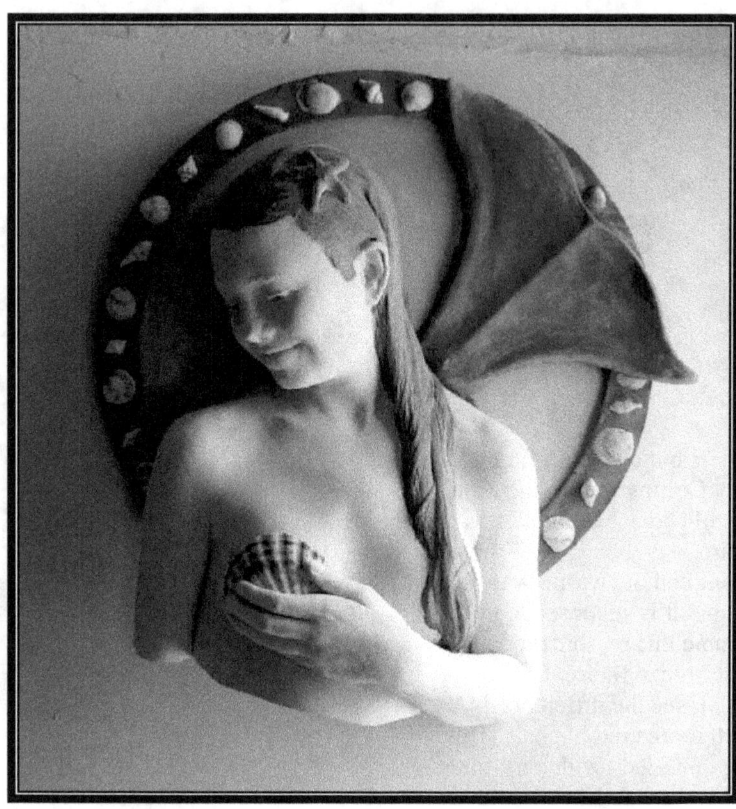

Making a Life Casting Mermaid Portrait

By David E. Parvin A.L.I.

In the Spring issue of *Faerie Magazine*, I described life casting a young lady and transforming her into a three dimensional faerie portrait. Here I'm going to do another transformation but this time my model gets to become a mermaid. While the result is different, the process is the same. I assume that most readers of course have stored their back issues in leather bindings for continual reviewing and to save them for posterity. Since there is no need to repeat myself, I can shorten this narrative. After all, saving a page of print will reduce the number of trees that have to be harvested for paper preserving some of the wild places for the fanciful creatures. For those who had not yet discovered the publication or didn't keep their Spring issues, a copy is available from the publisher with just a phone call.

The Concept

Once I sculpted a small bronze statue of a adolescent mermaid trying on shells for the first time. (Photograph #1) Her left hand held a shell covering her left breast with another shell positioned in her right hand to cover her right breast. For this article, I wanted to tell the same story but there was a problem. While it is perfectly acceptable to sculpt a 1/4 life size adolescent mermaid with one breast exposed, a life casting is more like a photograph. Since it wouldn't have been proper to expose the model's breast that wasn't covered with a shell, I would need a model with hair long enough to preserve her modesty and reputation.

Choosing the Model

In the faerie article, the model looked so much like a faerie that she inspired the piece. But in this case, I had the mermaid idea first and then chose the model. It just so happened that I knew a young lady, Laura, who met my criteria. #1. She looked like a mermaid. #2. She was the right age, 13. #3. Her hair was long enough. #4. She and her mother, Leslie, loved to visit my studio and play "let's make art history." I had already done several casts of her and she was excited to be part of the project, perfect.

Making a Life Casting

One of my assistants and I made an impression of Laura using a harmless molding material called alginate. Alginate was especially appropriate in this case since it main ingredient is made fro seaweed. A plaster positive cast of Laura was made from the alginate mold. (See photograph #2.)

Becoming a Mermaid

After repairing a few minor imperfections, I attached the plaster cast to a 24 inch in diameter piece of fiberboard. I love the line from the old song "The Streets of Loredo" that goes, "I can tell by your outfit that you are a cowboy." So all that is needed to make someone into a cowboy or a mermaid is the right outfit. Add a few sea critters and a tail and presto, one mermaid. The sea critters are no problem; shells and starfish are available from any craft store. I would sculpt the tail in oil based clay. But first, I had to figure out something.

Just what does a mermaid's tail look like? Recently, I had read a hopeful sounding book titled *A Mermaid's Tale*. (1.) Unfortunately, It was "tale" and not "tail" and the book while well worth reading wasn't much help. Amazingly, no one has ever photographed a mermaid and the next best reference had be paintings and drawings which offer lots of choices. There isn't even agreement as to how many tails.

While most mermaids are depicted with one, some have two as if each leg became a separate tail. Further confusion comes from the fact that mermaids are usually covered with scales on their lower half. Fish have scales but sea mammals don't. Scales or not, I have to think of mermaids as warm blooded mammals and not cold blooded fish. I have never seen a mermaid depicted with gills and have to assume that mermaids are air breathing. All this leads me to suspect that mermaids may have scales for some unknown reason, but are more likely to have tails that are mammalian. Unfortunately, there are three very different types of sea mammals: sea otters; whales, porpoises, and dolphins; and seals and sea lions. For my first mermaid, in photo #1, I chose a porpoise style tail and still think that it is the more attractive. So in this case, I decided to do the same. I'm safe unless someone actually takes a photograph of a mermaid and proves me wrong. I'll take my chances.

Since I intended this mermaid portrait to be a companion piece to the faerie portrait, I wanted both to be the same size. Since I was definitely short on space, I could only show the upper part of the top half of the mermaid. The tail, which I sculpted out of clay, would have to come up behind the head. I was unable to find the right size small starfish for Laura's hair, so I sculpted one. Shells, both clam and snail, were easier to come by and I added some around the edge of the fiberboard circle. In photo #3, one of my assistants, Melissa, is doing some last minute tweaking last before we made a mold of modified Laura.

<u>Casting the Final Portrait</u>

I made a mold of the modified Laura in silicone rubber which consisted of a soft inner layer of silicone rubber and a hard supporting outer layer called the "mother mold" made of Forton MG. The final portrait was cast in Forton MG using various additives and dyes for the different parts of the portrait. Photograph #4 shows me painting in the Forton MG. The finished portrait is in photograph #5.

1. *A Mermaid's Tail*, by Amanda Adams, Graystone Books, 2006, ISBN-13: 978-1-55365-117-8.

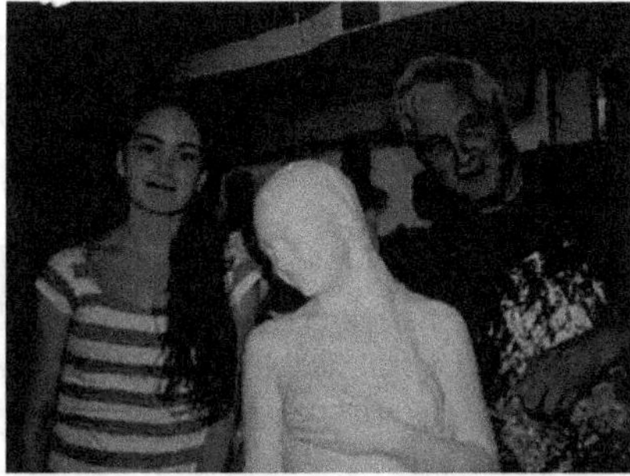

Photo #2

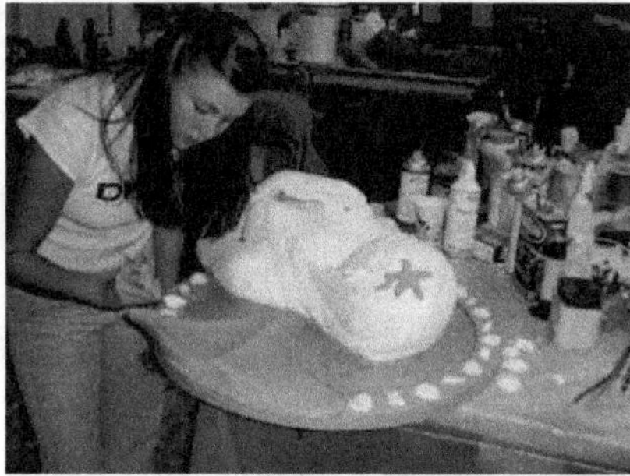

Photo#3

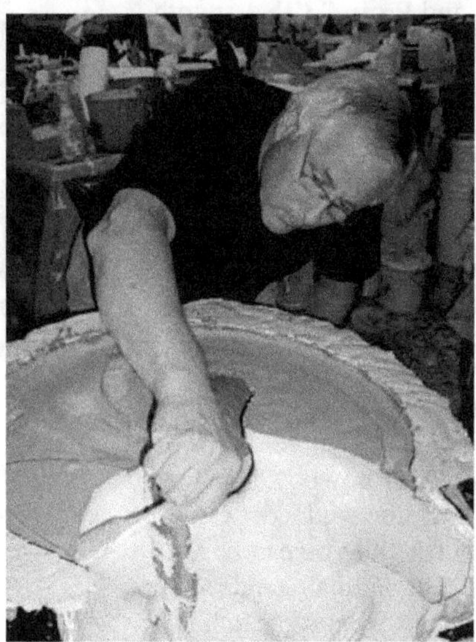

Photo #4

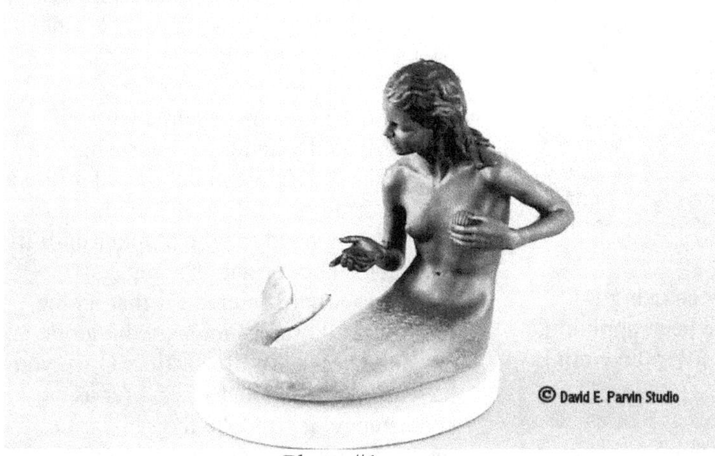

Photo #1

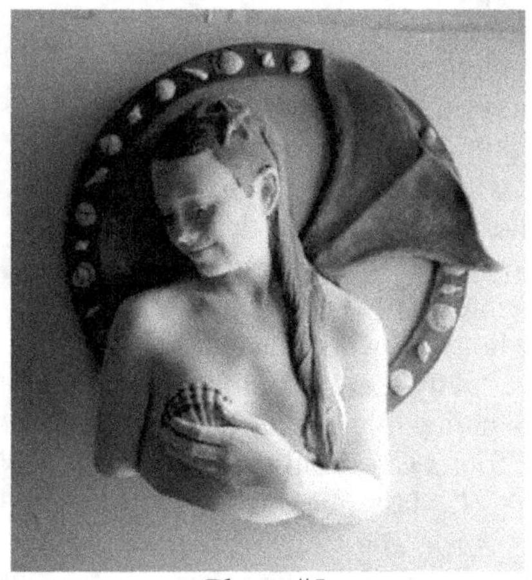

Photo #5

More Helpful Tricks in Life Casting

By David E. Parvin A.L.I.

I have no idea how many hundreds of life castings I have done in the last 20 years. One might think that by now I would have tried every possible variation and settled on the best techniques. That's almost right, I do use what I have found to be the most successful. But I keep discovering better ways both from my own experimentation and from other artists' suggestions. One of "Dave's Laws" framed on my studio wall is, "There's almost always a better way," and I really believe this and am always searching. In this article, I am going to share three new (at least to me) and better ones that I have recently added to my repertoire of "Parvin's Perfectly Pertinent Procedures for Pleasure and Profit." I'll start with the simplest. I will from time to time refer to things that I have written in previous articles. Just in case some readers can not locate every past issue of *Sculpture Journal,* an e-mail to jondavid@verison.net will get you the missing articles.

Often cloth is included in my life castings, sometimes for modesty or to help define something about the subject. Remember the line in the song "The Streets of Laredo," "I can tell by your outfit that you are a cowboy." To which the Smothers Brothers added, "Get yourself an outfit and you can be a cowboy too!" But alginate tends to cling to the fuzziness of whatever cloth is covering the model. The degree of clinging is proportional to the fuzziness of the cloth, minimal with spandex and aggressive with terry cloth. Whatever one uses as a release agent must be harmless to skin. But most commercial agents come with warnings to avoid skin contact. I have tried all kind of things over the years and up until recently had settled on plain old cooking oil applied from a spray bottle. It works reasonably well and is certainly skin safe. However, since it is my policy to give credit where do, my good friend Guy Louis XVI (see "Guy Louis XVI, Master of Ultra Realism," *SJ, April, 2004,* by yours truly) recently suggested fabric softener as an alternative. So far I have found that it is at least as good as cooking oil and since it isn't as slippery, it is easier to apply a layer of alginate to it. The

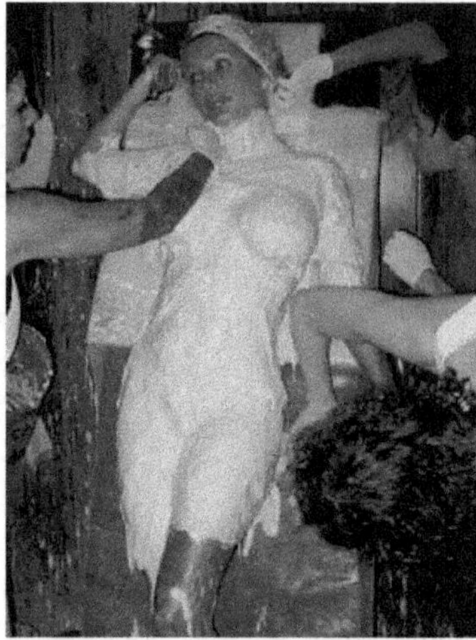

Photo #1

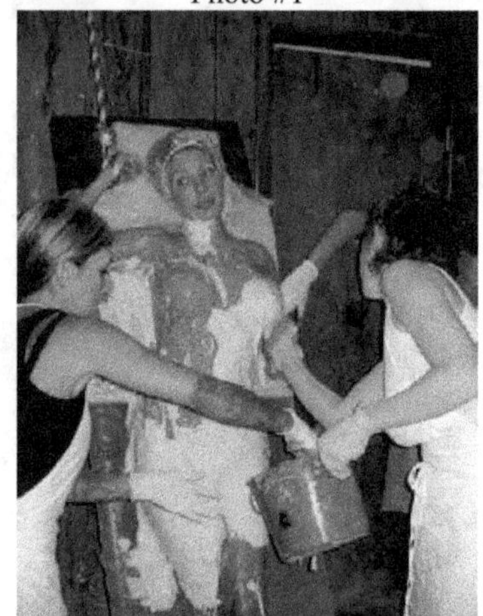

Photo #2

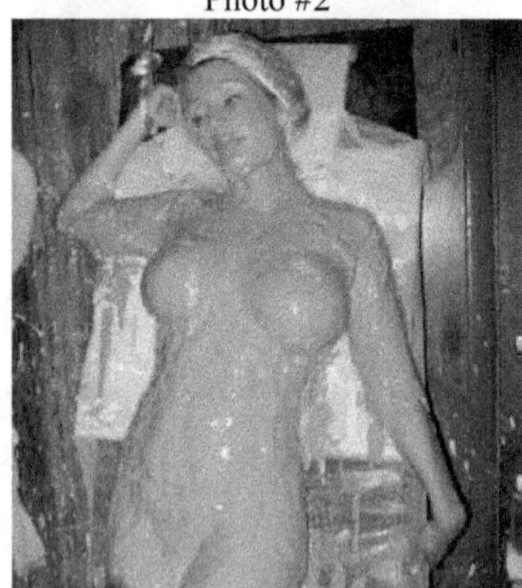

Photo #3

brand that I have been using is Downey and I have been applying it with a spray bottle after the cloth is on the model.

The second trick is just as simple, perhaps so simple that many of you have been doing it and I'm surprised and a little embarrassed that I didn't figure it out years ago. For casting a torso as in Photograph # 6, I use 8 pounds of water and 42 ounces of alginate (3632 and 1193 grams). The proportions are 5.25 ounces (149 grams) alginate per pound (454 grams) of water. Using my preferred alginate, FiberGel by ArtMolds, the mixture will be thick enough to stay in place almost without any dripping yet is not so thick that there is a problem with air bubbles. What I had always done was measure the water in one bucket and the alginate in another. When ready, the alginate was dumped into the water (never mix water into powder) and stirred with a paint mixer and an electric drill at at least 2400 R.P.M. until creamy with no lumps. That would take just a little over a minute. Then, sharing the same bucket, my assistant and I would spread the alginate over the model. Photograph #1 shows this step being done by three attendees in a recent workshop of mine. The only problem is that that amount of water and alginate is just about the limit that one can reasonably mix. Larger batches take longer to mix and the longer one mixes, the less time is available to apply the alginate before it sets up. A better method is to divide the alginate and water into two equal batches. I mix one half while an assistant mixes the other. With only half as much, the mixing only takes about 45 seconds. Each picks a side of the model and applies the alginate from his/her own bucket which is more convenient than sharing. This may not seem like much of a change, but try it, I am confident that it makes the application of the alginate easier and faster. My next trick takes up where this one ends.

But first, let me digress for a moment. There may be some who still mix alginate by hand, i.e. pour what looks like the right amount of water into a bucket or bowel and stir in the alginate mixing it by hand or with a mixer until it just seems about right. The biggest problem with this method is that it take too long and time is not something one has an excess of in life casting. Once you have determined what you prefer as a consistency, it will take the same ratio time after time. Just measure, combine, mix, and apply. Keep in mind that different brands of alginate will require different water/alginate ratios and occasionally batches of the same brand may vary slightly which with experience one can easily adjust for.

My last trick is a little more complicated but is more important than the first two. Before I describe trick #3, let me explain what I' m trying to improve. The alginate layer in a life casting has to do two things, make an impression of the subject and be able to bond to the supporting or mother mold. This second purpose is essential. If the supporting mold separates from the alginate, it will be very unlikely that the alginate can be positioned back into the mother mold without some distortion. Secondly, unless you are using FiberGel by ArtMolds, the chances that you will be able to remove the alginate from the model without tearing it are slim indeed. Prior to March 2003, the usual way to bond the two layers of the mold was to push some fuzzy material into alginate before it set up. The fuzz might have been cotton, doll's hair, mock wool, etc. Getting an adequate layer of alginate on the model and applying the fuzz before the alginate set up was sometimes a challenge especially with a larger and/or more complicated casting. Fortunately in March 2003, a product came out called AlgiSlo, also made by ArtMolds, that keeps the surface of the alginate sticky longer so that the application of the fuzz is a cinch. (See "How to Extend the Setting Time of Alginate, Testing a New Product," *SJ,* March 2003, by DP). AlgiSlo has a couple of other uses; one of which is to allow liquid alginate to bond to already set up alginate. Trick #3 uses this capability to make life casting easier and better. In photograph #1, the subject has been covered with alginate. As soon as this was done, the alginate was misted with AlgiSlo keeping the surface soft. The AlgiSlo is effective even if applied to completely set up alginate. Trick #3 is to mix a smaller batch of alginate and spread a thin layer of it over the first. I only use half as much water as I used for the first coat. In this case, 4 pounds of water were used. It is important that this second layer be somewhat more runny to make it much easier to apply. Instead of 5&1/4 ounces of alginate per pound of water, I use 4&1/2 ounces (128 grams). It will not run off because the second layer is so thin. I also use a different alginate, MoldGel Regular Set, primarily because it is a different color making it easy to see where it has been applied. Photograph #2 shows the

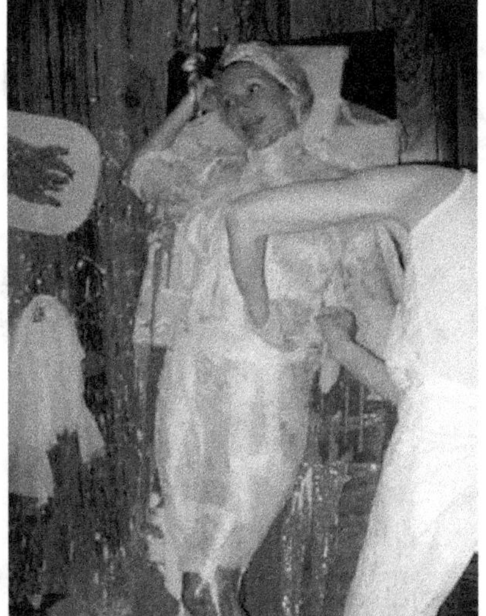

Photo #4

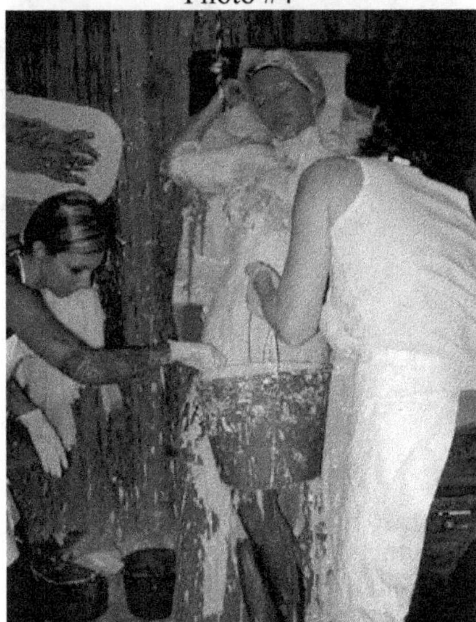

Photo #5

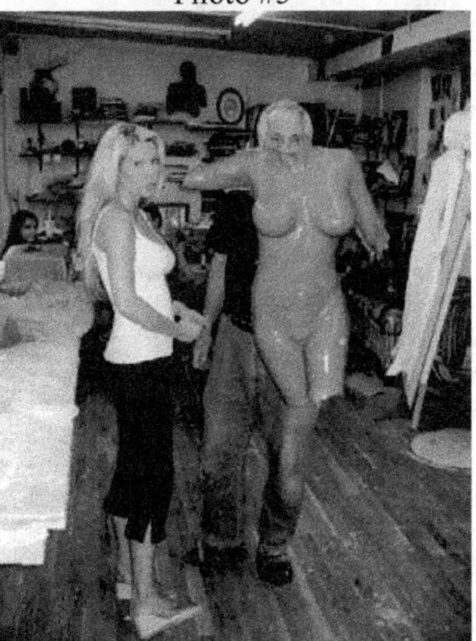

Photo #6

second layer being applied while in #3 the model is completely covered. You may be wondering why go to this extra trouble. The main reason is that this second thin layer of alginate will bond to the fuzz even better than if the fuzz is applied directly to the first layer of alginate. Another advantage is that this additional alginate layer gives one a chance to repair any problem areas that might have occurred with the first layer and possibly improve or even save the casting. This becomes especially important as one progresses to larger and/or more complicated castings.

In photo #4, the fuzz that bonded the alginate layers to the mother mold was being applied. What my workshop attendees were using wasn't rolled cotton or something similar but strips of cheese cloth. I encourage you to try this method which was thoroughly explained in "Another Use for Cheese Cloth...," *SJ,* Sept. 2005, and "More Uses for Cheese Cloth in Life Casting, *SJ,* Oct. 2005, both by DP.

Photo #5 shows the mother mold being constructed. Note, the mother mold was made using cheese cloth and fast setting plaster **and not plaster bandages**. I may not always know the best way but I am absolutely certain that plaster bandages are distant second choice for making mother molds. Fast setting plaster and cheese cloth is faster, less expensive, and causes less distortion than plaster bandages, period. (See "An Alternative to Using Plaster Bandages As the Supporting Mold for Alginate Life Casting," *SJ,* March 2004, by guess whom.)

If you have a trick that you're willing to share, please contact me at (303) 321-1074 or parvinstudio@comcast.net. Even if you do e-mail me, please include your phone number because I would rather talk than type. I promise to give you credit for any new idea that I find useful.

Photographs:
1. Subject covered with the first layer of alginate.
2. Starting to apply the second thinner layer of alginate.
3. The completed second layer of alginate.
4. The application of cheese cloth strips as a bonding agent.
5. The mother mold being constructed of cheese cloth and fast setting plaster.
6. About two hours after Photo #5 showing the casting in Forton MG with metal powder. All that was left to do was allow the casting to cure for a few days, apply a chemical patina, and buff.

Photographs During Life Castings

By David E. Parvin, A.L.I.

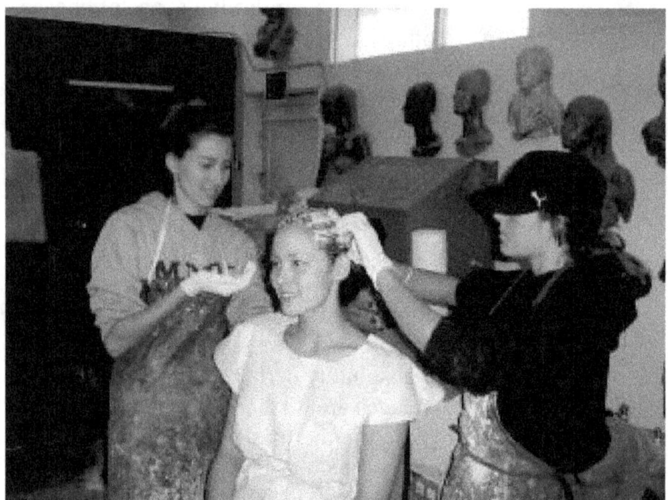

Photo 1

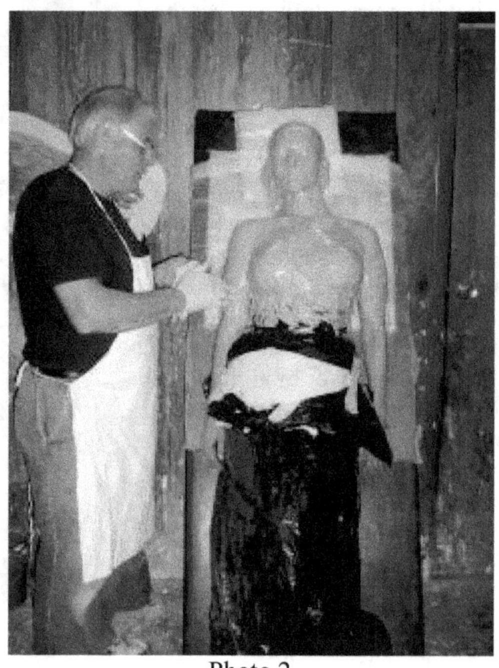

Photo 2

Last month, I wrote about having some inexpensive trinkets to give to visitors to one's studio. The idea was that taking something home might encourage a collector or potential collector to come back and actually acquire something. (Remember, people *buy* from fish mongers and used care salesmen but *acquire* art.) What I didn't mention is the most obvious giveaways of all, photographs.

I always tell anyone coming in for a life casting to bring a camera. Not only do I want the person to have a record of the historic event of getting immortalized, but I have an ulterior motive. I know that the castee will be excited enough that she/he will relate the experience to anybody in listening distance at least for the next few days. Just perhaps, some of those who hear the adventure will decide to be turned into a work of art as well. Nothing enhances a presentation better than visual aids and most do bring cameras. Surpassingly, some either forget or don't realize just how important a visual record will be to them, not to mention my future bank account, and actually show up sans camera. Not to worry, I always have one available.

Since the invention of the daguerreotype in the 1830s, photography has gotten progressive easier. At first, one had to prepare his/her own glass plates, make a multi minute exposure, develop the plates, and finally print the photograph. Around the turn of the 20th century, E. Kodak invented a camera that came with film already in it. After using up the film, you only had to send the camera with the film inside to Kodak and in a couple of weeks, you got your printed photographs along with the reloaded camera. As incredible a concept as that was, the drawback was that all the future Ansel Adams were without cameras part of the time. Then the always thinking E. Kodak decided that the average person could be trained to unload and reload a camera and from then on, one only needed to send the film in for processing and picture taking could continue uninterruptedly. While E. Kodak got very rich, better things like color and one hour photo finishing were on the horizon. Remember how just a few years ago, every strip mall had a one hour photo finishing establishment? Then digital photography changed everything and which got even simpler and faster. Now one can take photos and immediately transfer them to a computer. They can be edited and viewed on the computer, printed on the spot, emailed, or if you have the right equipment, projected onto a screen. Your client can relive the experience on the spot and then over and over later.

Usually the castee is accompanied by a family member (s) or friend (s) whom I ask to take some photos. Not only does this free me to concentrate on the casting but it also make the photographer feel as if he/she is part of the process. One of the really great things about digital cameras is that there is almost no limit on the number of photographs that one can take. In the old days of film, most tried to keep the number within a roll of film. Now there is no such

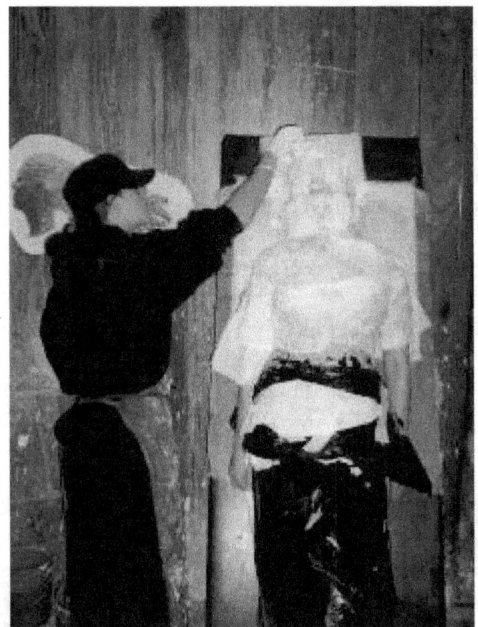
Photo 3

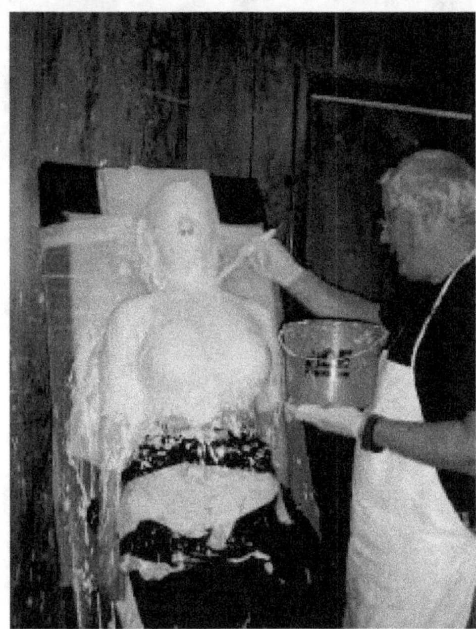
Photo 4

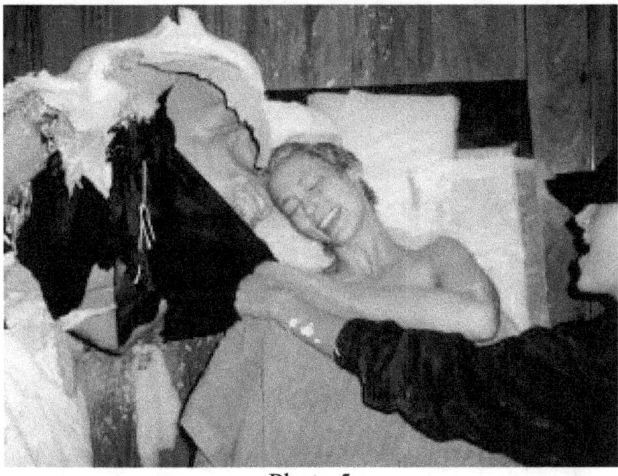
Photo 5

restraint. The card in my camera holds about a thousand photographs. I always tell the designated photographer to take all the photographs she/he wants. Many times the person takes far more photos than are necessary. What that tells me is that the photographer finds the life casting experience so interesting and exciting that there is a need to capture every little detail. Sometimes I end up with dozens when it really only takes as few as five to seven photos to tell the story. I am hoping that the castee will be saying "Look what I just did!" and show the photos to other people, potential customers. But since I don't want my potential customers to become bored, if the photos are on my camera, I edit out all but the best. The more I have to choose from, the better my chances are of getting really good shots. I may print up one of the photographs on the spot for the person to take with her/him but I do the editing and email the series of photos later the same day. It is important that the castee get the photos by email so that they can both easily be sent by me and shared by her/him.

The first seven photographs in this article are a good example of all that is needed to explain how a life casting is done and allow the model to brag about suffering for art:

Photo #1: Assistants Jessica and Kelsey applying Cholesterol hair conditioner. The castee is Jennifer Lamont who was Mrs. Colorado a few years ago.

Photo #2: The old fat guy who shows up in so many of my photographs having just applied the alginate.

Photo #3: Kelsey putting on the first layer of cheesecloth.

Photo #4: The old fat guy returns and is finishing putting fast setting plaster to two layers of cheesecloth.

Photo #5: Removing the mold. Please note that this step is usually makes the best photograph in the series.

Photo #6: The plaster positive made from the alginate mold. Also note that this is not the final product. What I do next is clean up any flaws in the plaster and make a secondary mold in silicone rubber which takes about twelve to thirteen hours of work spread out over several weeks. I then cast the finished portrait in Forton MG with copper powder for a realistic bronze look.

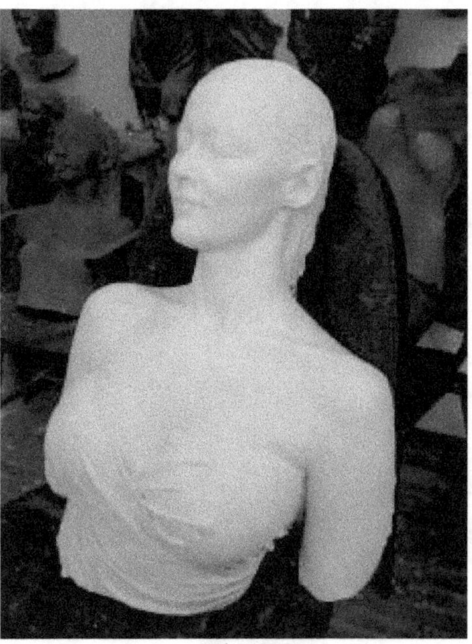
Photo 6

Photo #7: The finished product. I email this photo as well so that the castee a record of the the whole process.

Photo #8: This is a photograph that I like to take but somehow missed in the sequence above. This is a group shot. The subject in this photo is Tara Conner who was Miss U.S.A. in 2006. She is best known for almost loosing her title. However she was absolutely as nice as she could be when we cast her.

There is a photo that I have always wanted to take but just haven't had the right people and probably never will. I would like to do a group photo with all the people present including friends and family members but while the castee still has the mold on since can't see and has no idea what is happening. Everybody except the castee gets buck naked! When I imagine the castee getting the email with the photos and finding the *special one*, priceless...

Most people bring their own cameras which may be still or video or both. I know for a fact that most take far too many photographs because they often send me a disk titled "Jessica (or Eric, etc.) Gets Plastered." You would think that they would all know that I must have photos out the ying yang of people getting cast. However parents are so are certain that their son or daughter is so special that I will appreciate having dozens of photographs recording the event. What I do appreciate is the sentiment because it tells me that I have a satisfied client.

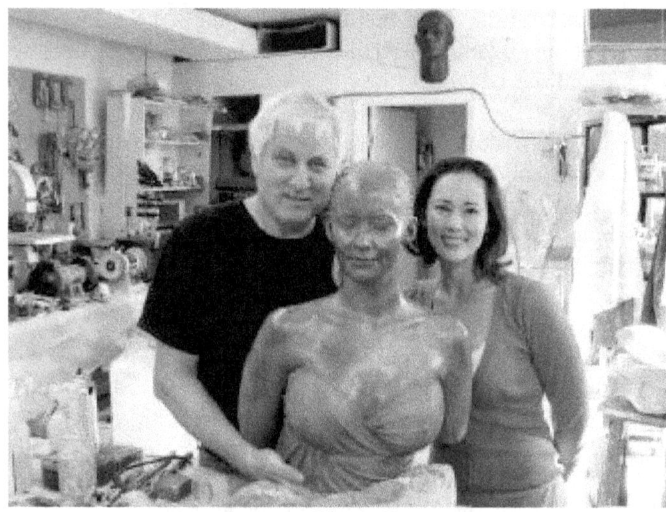

Photo 7

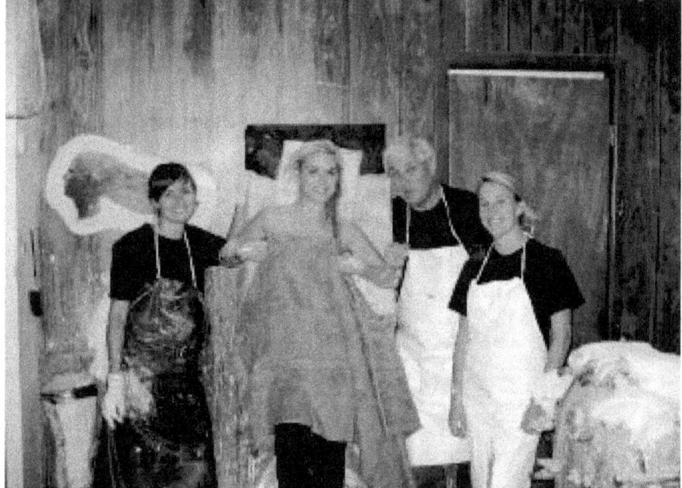

Photo 8

Secondary Molds in Life Casting, Part II

by
David E. Parvin, A.L.I.

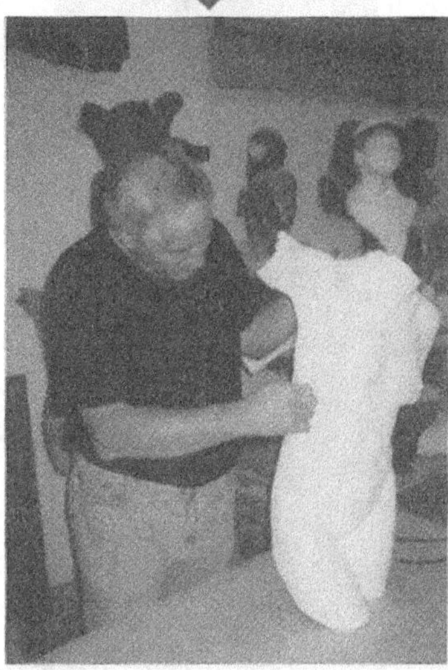

Plaster torso from an alginate mold

This is the first of a two-part article

In a previous article (Sculpture Journal, July 2004) I explained why and how to make secondary molds of life castings of infants' hands and feet. Here I am going to describe how to do the same thing except of a torso or body. While the technique is different, the "why" and some of the materials are the same. Now although this magazine is printed in the Northwest where they have more trees than they have any idea of what to do with, they (those North Westerners) want to keep it that way. If I go ahead and repeat what I said in the July article, this issue will have to be longer and longer and that means more paper from more cut down trees. Not only will I have angered a bunch of Oregon tree huggers, but may also be some link to global warming and the demise of the traditional family unit in America. So I can sleep at night, if you didn't have the foresight to memorize the July SJ. I am going to ask you to take it out from under your pillow and reread pages 12 through 24. To save even more paper, I will use abbreviations wherever I can. Notice "SJ" above for "Sculpture Journal." Please don't assume that I am referring to the Society of Jesus or the Jesuits. Jesuits never take the name of a month and almost never have pages 12 through 24. In the same way, I will henceforth call a secondary mold a S.M.; not ever to be confused with S&M even if you did as I did, graduate from a Jesuit university. In photograph #l, I am holding a plaster life casting of a torso which was made in an alginate mold. Most life casters use plaster, or some other gypsum material for the final product. It might be given a faux metallic patina or just left on natural. But for me, plaster is just an intermediate step, never the final product. In order to go beyond plaster, I will explain how to clean up flaws (there are always at least a few) and make a very simple but effective S.M. which will allow for multiple castings in materials that will let you in on Parvin's Perfectly Pertinent Procedures for Progressing Past Plaster for Pleasure and Profit.

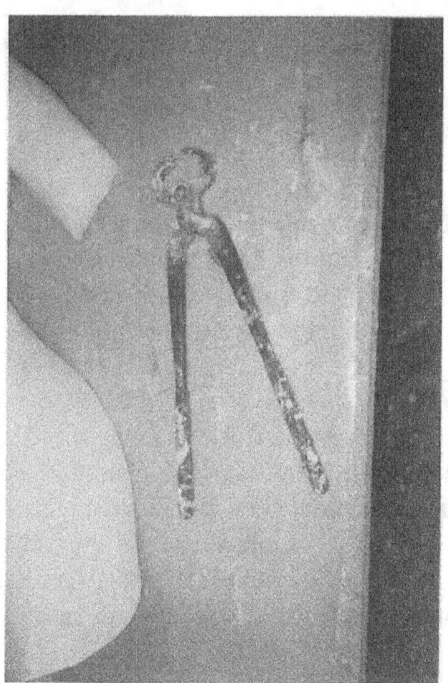

Horse hoof trimmer

By the way, if you are planning on making a S.M., I would suggest that you use plaster for the initial casting and not hydrocal or Hydro-Stone which are much harder, making trimming and repairing more difficult. I use Regular Dental Plaster but Number One Molding Plaster or Pottery Plaster are also good choices. All capture detail excellently yet are soft enough for easy working.

The next step, repairing any imperfections can take from as little as a half hour to several hours depending on how flawless the casting. The very first thing I do is trim the back edges of the torso so that it will hang flat against a wall. I try to do this and trim the ends of the arms and legs the same day that the plaster cast is made and still soft. There is a tool that can be very useful. It looks like an elongated pair of tile cutters. (Photograph #2) is actually used to trim horse hooves. This inexpensive tool is available at any horse tack supplier. I do the bulk of the trimming with it and finish off with a utility knife or box cutter. Remember, the casting mostly is just a series of tricks and the more you know, the easier it is.

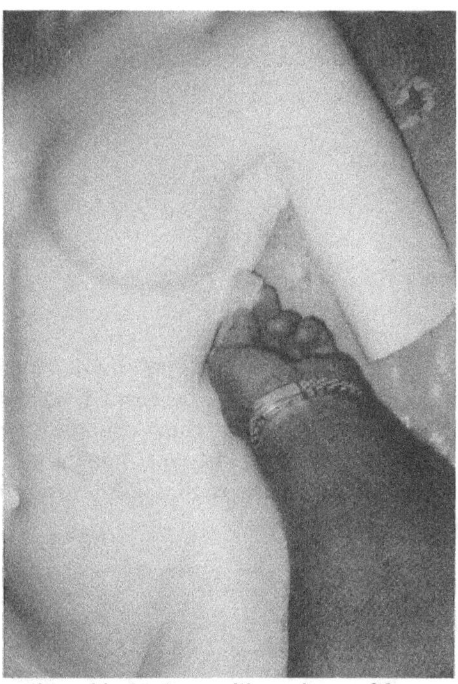

Reconstructing skin texture with a piece of foam and gesso

There are two basic kinds of imperfections in the plaster, innies and outies. Outies are caused by bubbles in the surface of the alginate which get filled with plaster. In other words, outies are bumps. They are easily trimmed back to the surface of the skin with a sharp tool. Be careful to cut or shave them rather than break them off or you may get an indentation that has to be filled, creating more work. Trim them down to the contour of the skin so that you can not feel any imperfections. Also, you can remove zits or other skin flaws that were on the subject; usually appreciated by him or her. I try to remove any outies larger than a small zit the same day that I cast the plaster. (I will explain below how to rebuild the skin texture below.)

The other type of flaws, innies are holes caused by bubbles in the surface of the plaster. These can be filled with plaster *as* long as the casting is still damp, but put the torso aside to cure and dry out for a few days. I then repair the innies by filling the holes with either sculpting wax or oil based clay. I prefer wax for very small repairs and clay for larger ones. As long as the plaster has dried out to the point that it no longer

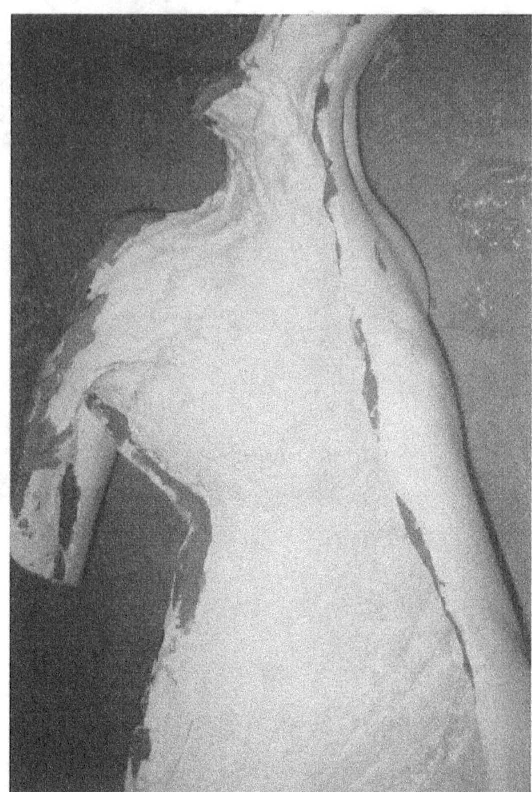

Backside of the casting showing clay used to thicken the edge

feels wet, both should stick to the plaster. The wax is dabbed into place with the tip of a pointed metal tool that has been heated with an alcohol lamp or burner. If the clay doesn't want to adhere, paint the plaster with a thin layer of melted wax and the clay will really grab on. If the melted wax will not adhere, the plaster hasn't dried out enough. Once you have filled an inny and shaped the surface to follow the contour of the plaster so that you can not feel any imperfections, you are ready to rebuild the skin surface.

Be aware that it isn't necessary to reconstruct the skin exactly. Pretty good will fool the eye and only you will know. Don't worry that the wax and clay repairs stand out like a sore thumb on the plaster because of their colors, the end product cast from the S.M. will be of a uniform color and the repairs should be invisible.

The first step is to construct any obvious feature in the skin such as the creases at the joints of the fingers. If the skin happens to be wrinkled, sculpt in as convincing wrinkles as you can. There are numerous techniques of reconstructing the fine details of skin, I'll describe two. For years, I took a small stylus and lightly dimpled the wax or clay to match the surrounding skin as closely as I could. While that worked, Guy Louise XVI (see SJ April, 2004) showed me a neat trick. Pour out a little gesso which is available from an art supply store. Take a small piece of something porous such as a sponge and put it into the gesso. Blot it several times and then dab it onto a repaired spot. Dabbing will leave little bumps on the repaired surface; the size of which will depend upon how thick the gesso is and the structure of the sponge.

In photograph #3, I am using a small piece of sponge-like material cut from a humidifier filter. The gesso dries in just a few minutes leaving the bumps that are quite skin like.

Filling in holes, trimming off pumps, and rebuilding skin texture are obvious repairs. But something that isn't so obvious is that the edges of the plaster casting should be at least 3/8" thick (or about 1 cm). As you will see below, this will allow you to build the rubber mold around the edges of the plaster which will in turn make it easy to have a uniformly thick edge on the final casting. If any part of the edge is too thin, thicken it with some clay (photograph #4).

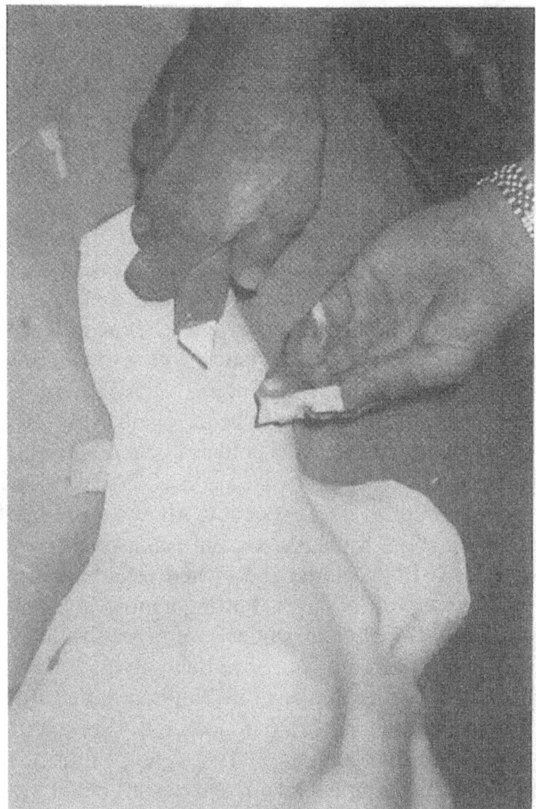

Cutting the rubber risers

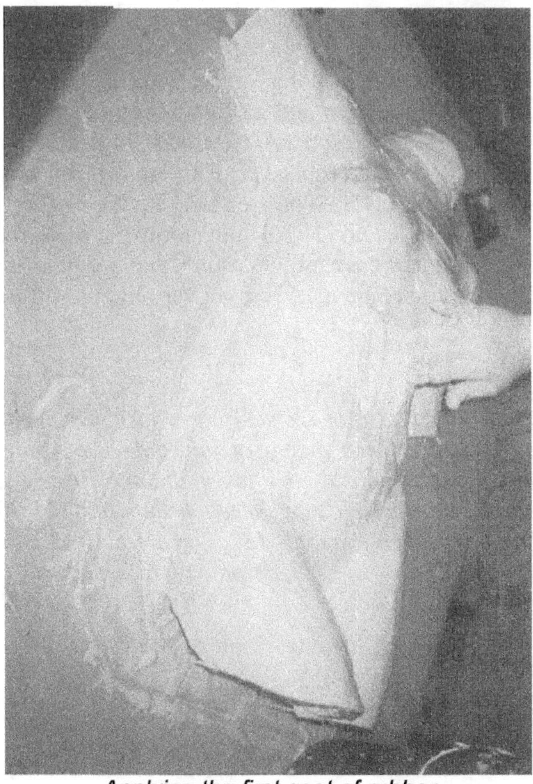

Applying the first coat of rubber

There are any number of types of brands of rubber available. I realize that choosing the best rubber for a particular application can be confusing. It is my intention to explain and simplify this subject in a future article.

In the July issue of SJ, I briefly mentioned the two most commonly used types of RTV rubbers, urethanes and silicones and that I much prefer silicones and why. For the purpose described in that article, I used a platinum cured silicone with a durometer of 15. The "platinum" was used primarily so that I would be able to cast urethane. The soft durometer allowed the mold to be easily removed from around the tiny fingers and toes. Since there aren't any fragile parts on this body and I have no plans of using clear urethane, a harder durometer tin cured silicone will do just fine and may even hold its shape more accurately than a soft rubber would. The biggest advantage to tin rather than platinum cured is that tin cured silicones are less likely to be inhibited by sulfur which is present in some clays and even in latex gloves. Since this will be a skin mold rather than a pour or block mold, it is imperative that the rubber have a thixotropic catalyst or a thixotropic additive. The rubber that I have used here is a tin cured silicone with a durometer of 25 called MoldRite 25 from ArtMolds with a thixotropic additive. (There are any number of types and brands of rubber available. I realize that choosing the best rubber for a particular application can be confusing. It is my intention to explain and simplify this subject in a future article).

One of the advantages of silicone rubbers is that almost nothing, including plaster, sticks to them and visaversa. It is not imperative that a mold release be used in this application. However, I have found that a solution of 15 parts petroleum jelly dissolved into 100 parts of naphtha and then painted over the plaster does allow the rubber to be removed even more easily. The naphtha evaporates almost immediately leaving a very thin coat of petroleum jelly without sacrificing detail.

In photograph #5, I am in the process of cutting four pieces of rubber about 2 X 1 X 'h inches. Into each one, I am cutting a notch about 1/4 inches wide and deep and then placing one of the rubber pieces under each of the four corners of the plaster. These rubber pieces lift the body just enough that the rubber that will cover it will also flow under the edges. The notches prevent the body from sliding off the rubber risers. As long as the rubber pieces are made out of the same type of silicone rubber (either tin or platinum cured) as the mold, the pieces will become permanently bonded to the mold rubber.

Follow the manufacturer's directions when mixing the rubber. Most use a ratio of 100 parts matrix to 10 parts catalyst though some are 50/50. Another advantage of

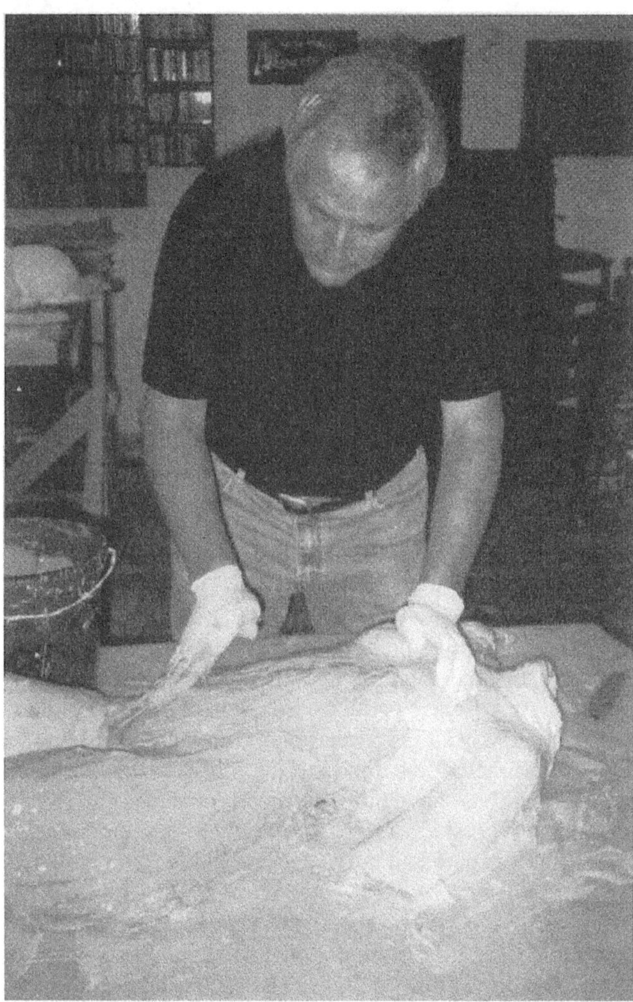

Applying the second layer of rubber, notice the color differential

silicone rubbers is that their mixing ratios are not nearly as critical as urethane rubbers. If, e.g., one accidentally uses 5 parts of catalyst rather than 10, it will cure, though at a slower rate. However, so that the rubber performs as advertised, accurate ratios should be observed. The catalyst may contain a thixotropic additive or you may have to add it yourself. It is generally very effective and about 1 part thixotropic additive is all that is needed. If you have the capability of de-airing the rubber, do it. (See "Using Vacuums and Pressure in Casting" in the August, 2003 issue of SJ) Of course, the amount of rubber needed depends mostly on the size of the object to be molded. For his torso, I used two layers of 5 pounds of rubber each. I much prefer two thin layers of rubber than one thick one because I have more confidence in getting a more uniform thickness to the rubber with two layers.

Applying the rubber is not difficult. The first thing I do is lift the body from one end and coat the bottom of the edges with rubber.

Then I set it back down fitting the edges into the grooves in the rubber blocks. I usually apply the rubber with a gloved hand rather than a chip brush. I do not just dab it on but spread it around sort of as if putting icing on a cake. If one is applying rubber to a clay model, care must be taken so as to not damage the soft surface of the clay. But since this torso is plaster, the rubber can be applied more aggressively. I want a uniformly thick layer about 1/8 inch thick. (See photograph #6) It is important that the rubber extend out from the edges of the body about one inch. Perhaps because I have de-aired it, I would apply a thinner first coat and use some of the standard tricks such as blowing air using the applied rubber. If you are using platinum cured silicone rubber, you can not use latex gloves because any of the rubber that comes in contact with the latex will not cure. Tin cured silicones do not have this problem. Vinyl gloves do not effect platinum.

If you care to smooth out the rubber, there are two ways to do it. The first is to take a chip brush, dip it into denatured alcohol, and gently rub the palm of your hand over the surface. The alcohol will not effect the curing time of the rubber. The alcohol may not completely prevent rubber from sticking to the brush or glove and you may have to clean with a paper towel periodically. The brush can be saved for the next coat by cleaning it with naphtha.

The curing time of the first layer depends upon the brand of rubber, the temperature, and whether an accelerator has been added. Often I allow the first coat to cure overnight and add the second and final coat the next morning. Unlike urethane rubbers, silicones will bond together even if one waits days, weeks, or months between coats. Since bubbles in the surface coat are to be avoided if at all possible, I rarely add an accelerator to the first coat to allow more time for careful application. Since the second coat isn't as critical, I usually do add an accelerator. A closed vehicle makes a wonderful greenhouse/ cover. Putting a mold in a vehicle on a sunny day will make the rubber cure in record time. And fossil fuels and trees aren't needed delaying global warming and the demise of the family unit! Platinum cured silicones are more responsive to heat than tin cured. If pressed for time, you could easily apply the first layer of rubber in the morning, the second after lunch, and construct the mother mold before the end of the day.

The second and final coat is applied in the same way as the first. The only differences are the addition of an accelerator and that a little bit of dye should be mixed into the rubber to change its color so that you can distinguish the old rubber from the new and insure an even second coat. (Photograph #7) Give special attention to high points and sharp edges where the rubber tends to run off. As soon as this second coat sets up, you are ready for the mother mold.

Next month David will tell more of his secrets about making quick and easy mother molds that are odorless, water soluble, non toxic, inexpensive, yet very light an strong.

David Parvin is a Colorado sculptor whose primary subject is the human form in a variety of materials. He also teaches life casting workshops held at his studio in Denver Colorado throughout the year He may be reached at 303-321-1074 for workshop dates. Now available is David's new DVD "Casting The Female Torso" in association with Life casters International.

Secondary Molds in Life Casting, Part II

by
David E. Parvin, A.L.I.

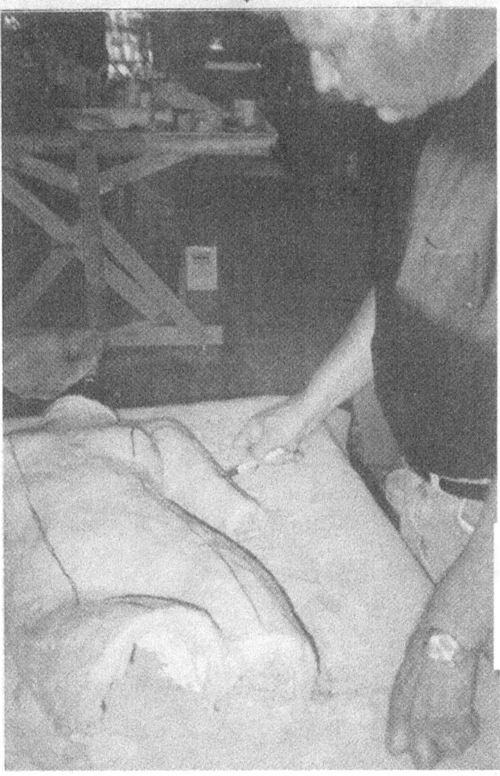

Photograph #1

Drawing the line to define the top edges of the side panels.

This is the second of a two-part article

Here is where I'm going to share another secret. I am going to tell you how to make quick and easy mother molds that are odorless, water soluble, non-toxic, inexpensive, yet very light and strong. In the beginning or once upon a time or at least 15 years ago, I was experimenting with different materials for making mother molds and I happened upon a great combination. I discovered that a particular kind of cloth dipped into Forton MG is all the above and can be used for almost any type of mother mold. The cloth is cotton batting and cotton batting with scrim binder. Only cotton batting with scrim binder will work for this purpose. The brand that I use, Heirloom, I can purchase from any number of cloth stores in my area and probably yours as well. But if you can not find it locally, ArtMolds carries it. Fiberglass cloth will work but is far more difficult to handle and it makes me itch. If you are not familiar with Forton MG, see "Mixing Forton MG simplified,"July, 2003 S.J.

The steps in making this mother mold that I am about to describe may not make any sense to you until you have seen the finished product. But if you will just read on, all should become clear. This mold will be made of three parts, left and right sides and a center section which will cradle the side panels holding them in place which will in turn hold the rubber so that it maintains its proper shape.

The first step is to take a marking pen and draw a line that will indicate how far in toward the center of the body that both the left and right sides of the rubber mold could be covered up with hard shells and the hard shells could still be removed. (See photograph #1.) Consider the undercuts. If there were no undercuts, you could cover the entire torso with a one-piece mother mold that would lift off the rubber. But because of the undercuts all around the torso, it should be obvious that the side panels must not be attached together.

Once you have determined the proper shape of the side panels, cut some strips of the cotton batting with scrim binder about four inches wide and in various lengths. The longest should cover the full length of the side panels as drawn. (Photograph #2) Take a flexible one gallon bucket and pour in to it three pounds of the Forton MG liquid, VF-812. If you have blended the powders that complete the Forton MG, simply scoop out twice the volume of the liquid; i.e. for every scoop of liquid, two scoops of blended powders. Stir with a paint mixer attached to an electric drill. Pour out about an inch of liquid into another flexible bucket. Add a couple of tablespoons of accelerant to the second bucket. The accelerant is just 10 parts of aluminum-sulfate mixed into 100 parts water and left to dissolve. The accelerant will cause the smaller amount to begin setting up in a few minutes while the rest will stay liquid for about an hour. (This is not the same as the rubber accelerant.) Dip one of the longer pieces of cloth into the second bucket and with a gloved hand thoroughly soak it in the Forton MG. (Photographs #3 and #4.)

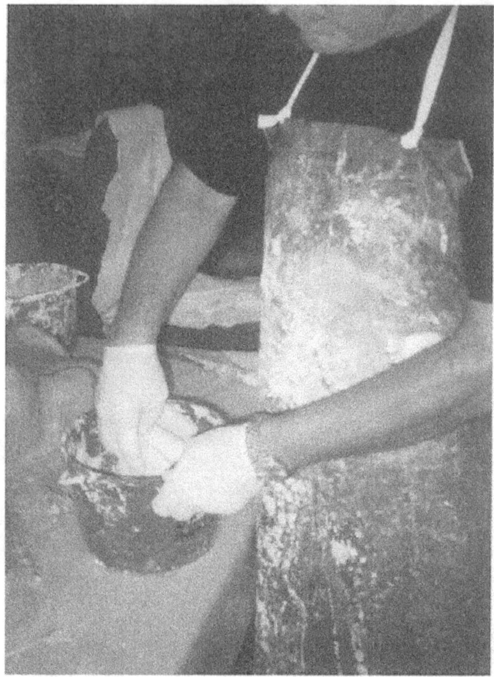

Photograph #3
Dipping the cotton batting into the Forton MG.

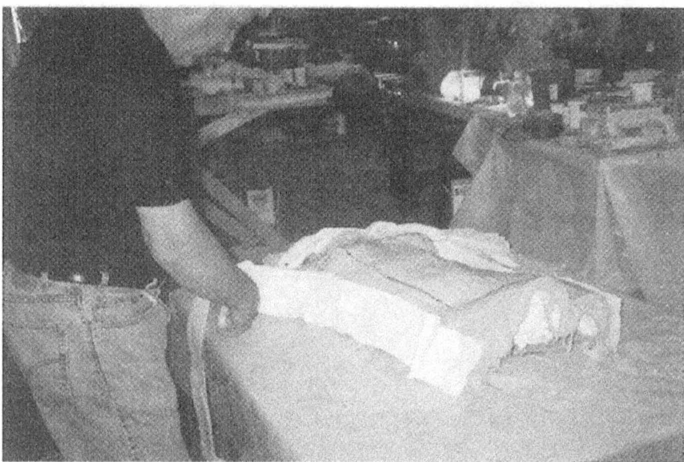

Photograph #2
Cutting the cotton batting.

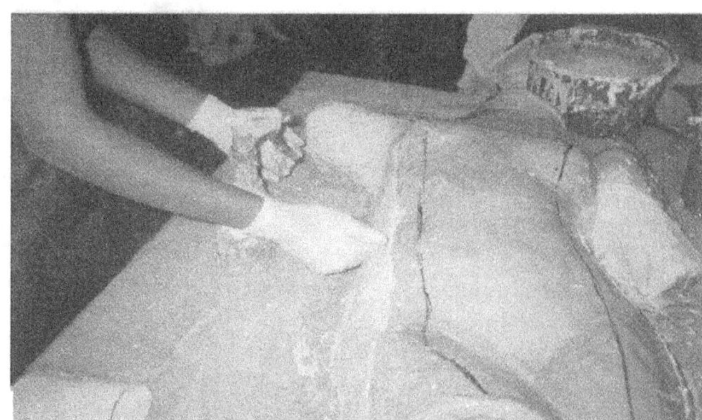

Photograph #4
Applying the first strips of the cotton batting and Forton MG for the side panels.

Spread it along either side of the body so that its bottom edge just touches where the inch of rubber extends away from the body. The soaked cloth should stay in place. Smooth out any air bubbles. If the cloth is too long, don't bother to trim it, just fold it back over itself. Repeat for the other side. Add more Forton MG and accelerant to the second bucket as necessary. Once you have the two side strips in place, if you have any extra Forton MG in the second bucket, add some more from the first bucket and stir. Diluting it will prevent it from setting up and being wasted. About this time, the first two strips should have begun to harden. Adding more Forton MG and accelerant to the second bucket as needed, dip more pieces of cloth into the Forton MG and cover the rubber up to the lines. The newer pieces of Forton MG soaked cloth will bond firmly to the first one as long as they overlap at least an inch. Use smaller pieces of soaked cloth to fill in any gaps in the side panels. (Photograph #5)

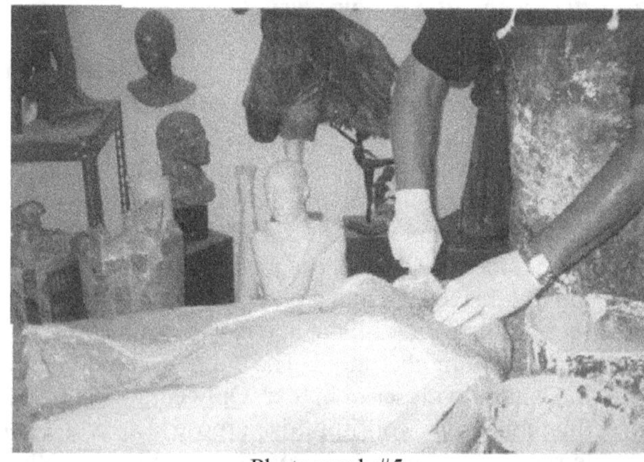

Photograph #5
Finishing the side panels.

Though the side panels are for the most part only one layer of cloth thick, they will be almost certainly strong enough. However, I will often take a strip of the cloth about 1-1/2 inches wide, soak it in the Forton MG, twist so that it becomes like a rope, and attach it to the bottom edge of the sides.

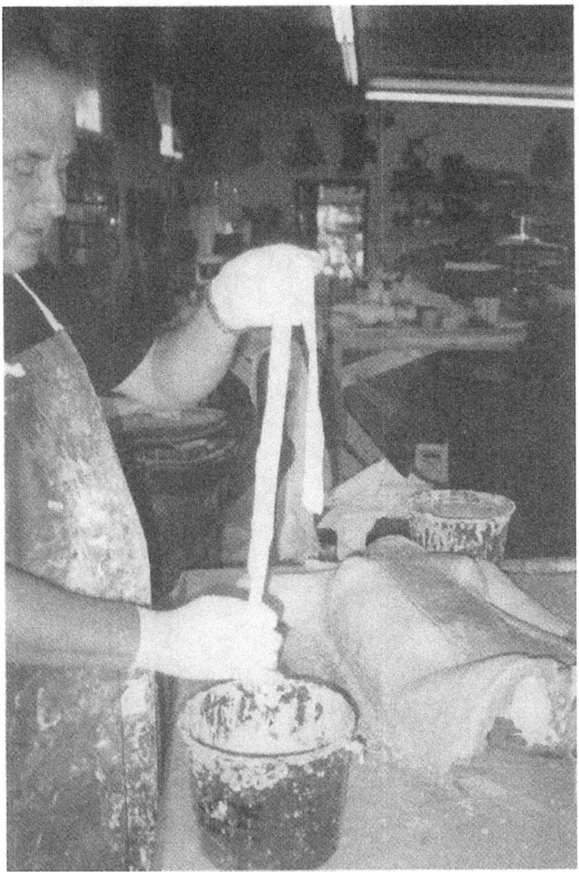
Photograph #6
Soaking a thin strip of cotton batting.

While rarely necessary, this does strengthen the side panels. (See photographs #6 and #7) Only two more steps to go.

What is now needed is a center section that will cradle the two sides and hold them in place when the mold is right side up and empty. The most important thing is that the center section not be attached to the sides. The easiest way I have been able to come up with is to cover the side panels with plastic food wrap. So that the plastic will stay in place, use a spray-on adhesive. (Photograph #8) Cover the side panels with plastic wrap and lay strips of Forton MG soaked batting over the center lengthwise. Be careful not to make the center section so wide that it wraps around into the undercuts locking it into pace. (Photograph #9 Since it is from the bottom or leg end of the mold that the center section will be lifted off, I strengthen the end by adding a second layer of cloth about four inches wide. Expect to run out of Forton MG before you finish the center section. I usually have to mix another pound of VF-812 with twice that volume in powders.

A real advantage to a mother mold made of cotton batting and Forton MG is weight. The total weight of the three parts of this mother mold in less than 13 pounds. A plaster mold would have been many times heavier. In most places, this mold is only bout 1/8" thick and yet is quite strong.

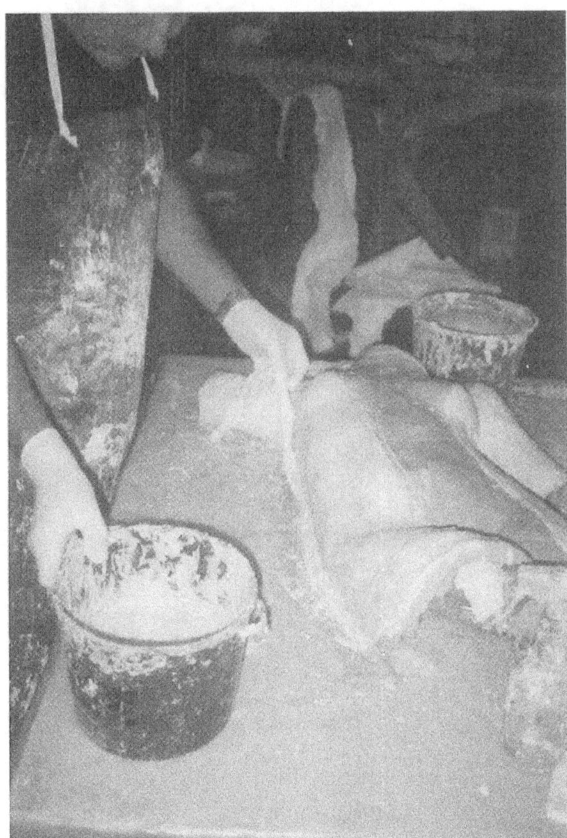
Photograph #7
Attaching a thin strip along the base of the side panel to strengthen it.

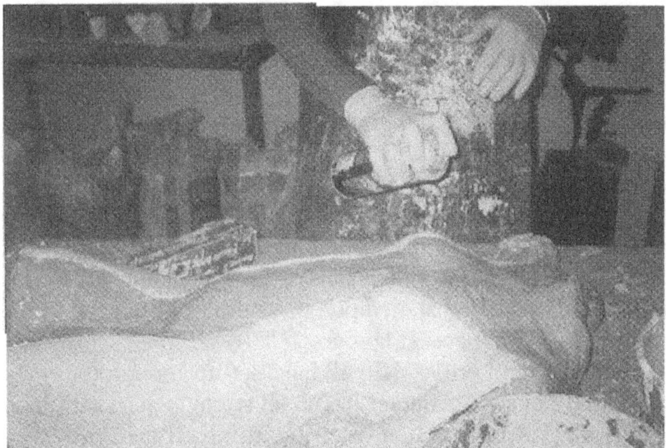
Photograph #8
Using the spray-on adhesive.

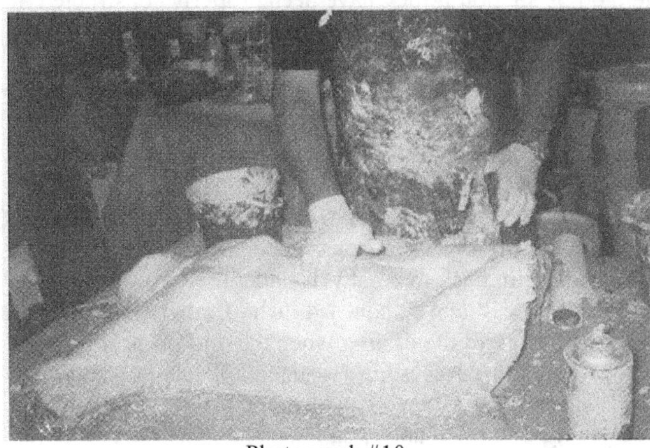
Photograph #10
Finishing the center panel.

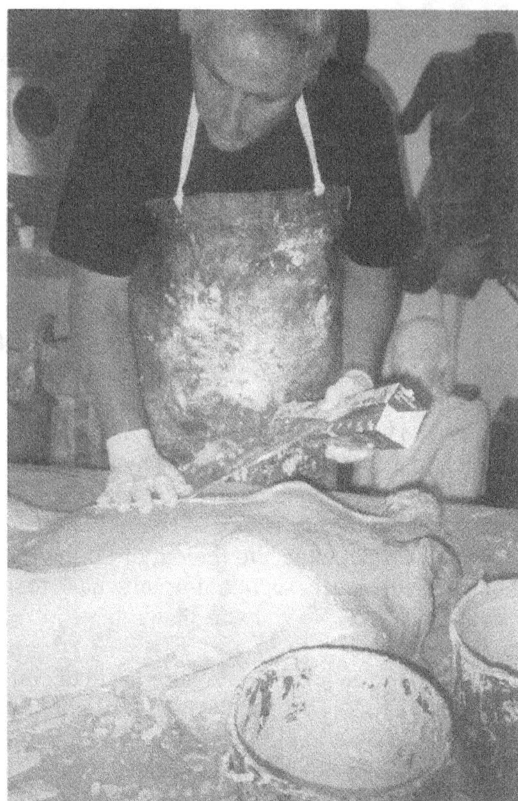

Photograph #9
Covering the side panels with plastic wrap.

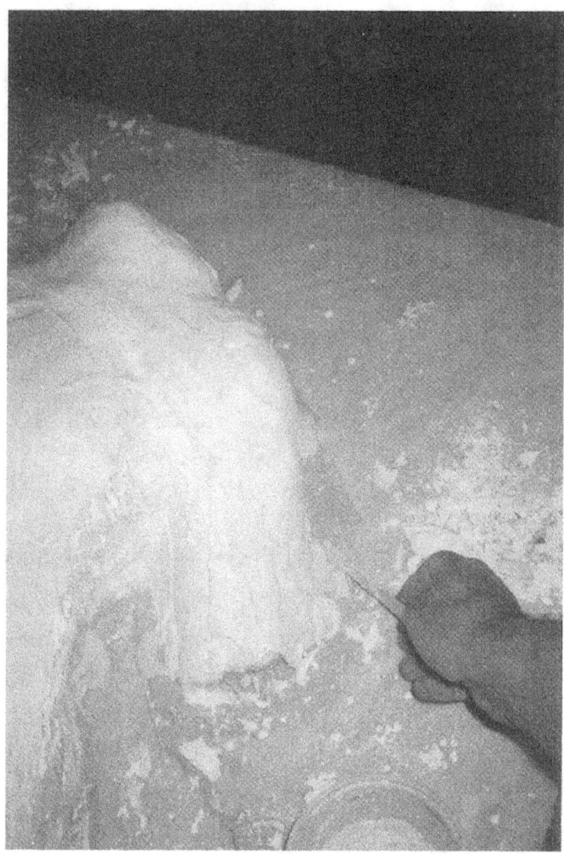

Photograph # 11
Putting on the rubber globs that will hold the edges of the rubber mold firmly in place to the mother mold.

The very last step is a very simple way of locking the rubber into place making the mold easier to use. Remember the rubber extending out about an inch from the edge of the mold? Mix up about 200 grams of rubber using about twice as much thixotropic additive and rubber accelerant as normal causing it to thicken up in 15 to 20 minutes. Put a gob about the size of a walnut every 10 inches or so on the rubber that is extending out from the sides. Make sure that they are pressed tip against the side panels of the mold. When the mold is right side up and empty, these globs will anchor the rubber firmly in place. (Photograph #10)

While the Forton MG will have set-up enough for demolding in a few hours, I like to let strengthen overnight. Demolding is just a matter of gently lifting off the center section followed by the side panels. (See photographs #11 and 12) The first time is the most difficult, the panels are held on by suction if they have been properly constructed. If you crack a panel, you can patch it with cotton batting and Forton MG. One the greatest advantages of Forton MG is that it will bond to itself even after it has completely cured. Once the suction has been broken and in all subsequent demoldings, the panels will come off much more easily. After removing the panels and putting them back together right side up, peal the rubber away from the plaster. With scissors, cut off any extraneous rubber around the edges. On the inside, trim back to what was under the edges of the plaster. This will leave about 1/4 inch of rubber that will define the edge of the casting when the mold is used.

While this process may seem complicated and a lot of work; it really isn't. Once you have the plaster repaired, everything described above can be done in less than three

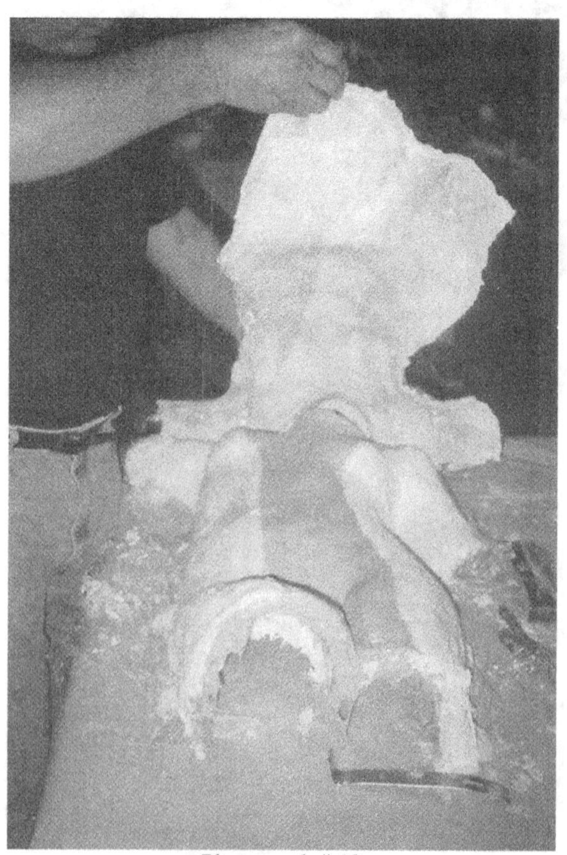

Photograph # 12
Lifting off the center section

hours of work spread over about two days' time. If necessary, it could be done starting at 8:00 am and be finished at 4:30pm.

In photograph #14, I have started painting in the first of several coats of Forton MG. This face coat contains metal powder which will produce a very realistic bronze look. (See photograph #15) In a future article, I will describe in detail how to use this type of mold for casting different types of materials including Forton MG, resins, wax, and clays for some very professional looking effects.

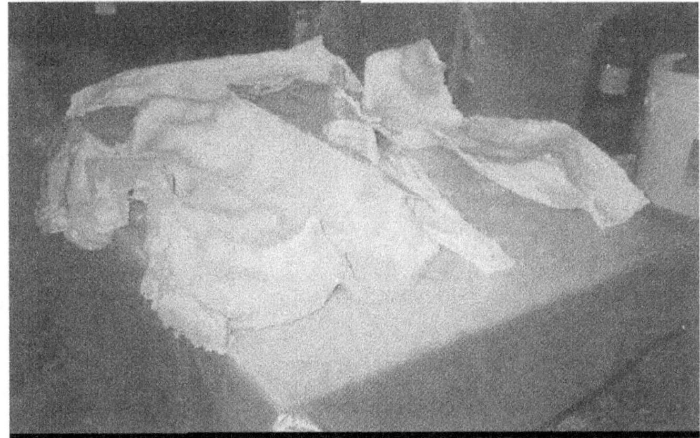

Photograph # 13
The four parts of the finished mold.

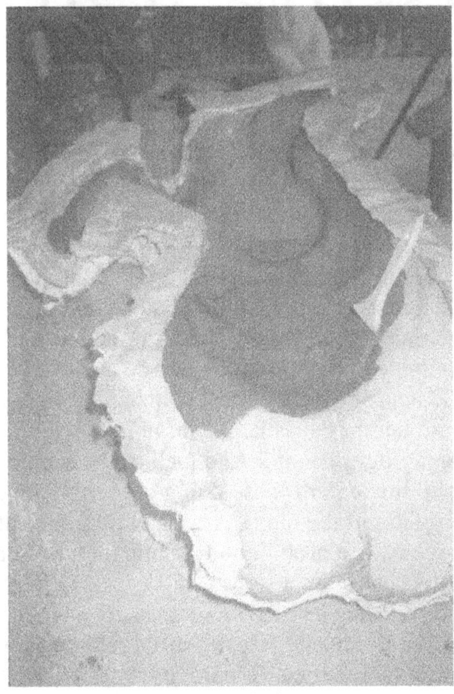

Photograph # 14
Painting into the mold a layer of metallic Forton MG.

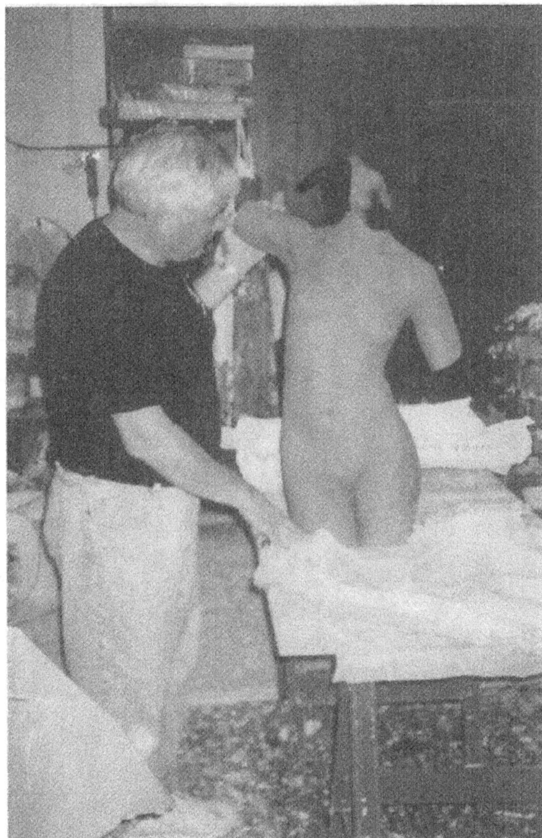

Photograph # 15
A casting from the mold in metallic Forton MG as it comes out of the SM. Once patined and buffed, it will look very much like bronze.

David Parvin is a Colorado sculptor whose primary subject is the human form in a variety of materials. He also teaches life casting workshops held throughout the year. He may be reached at 303-321-1074.

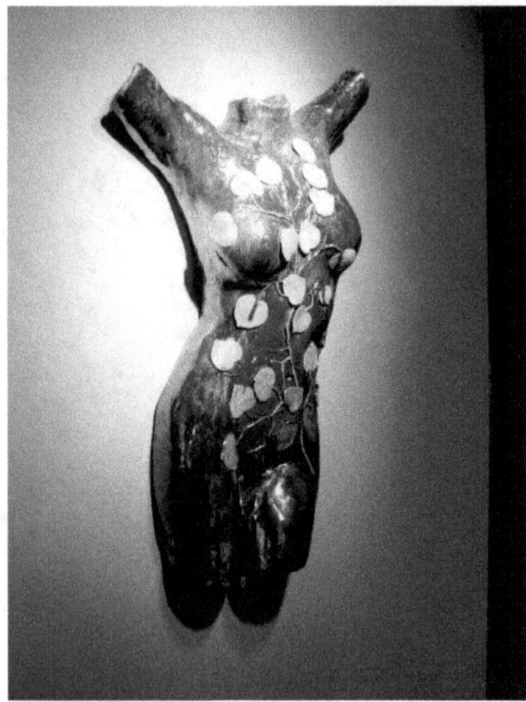
Photo #1

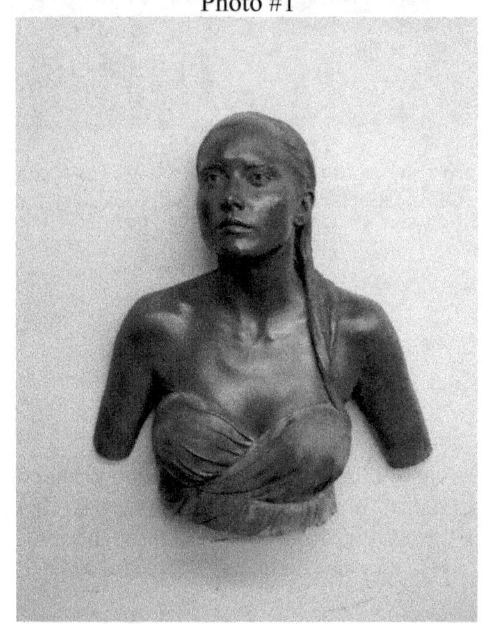
Photo 2

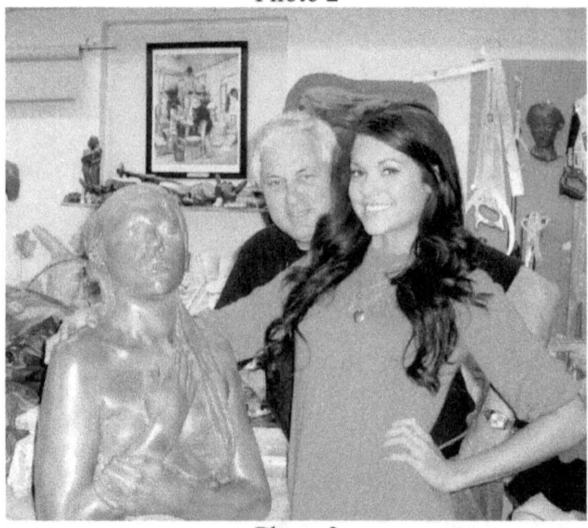
Photo 3

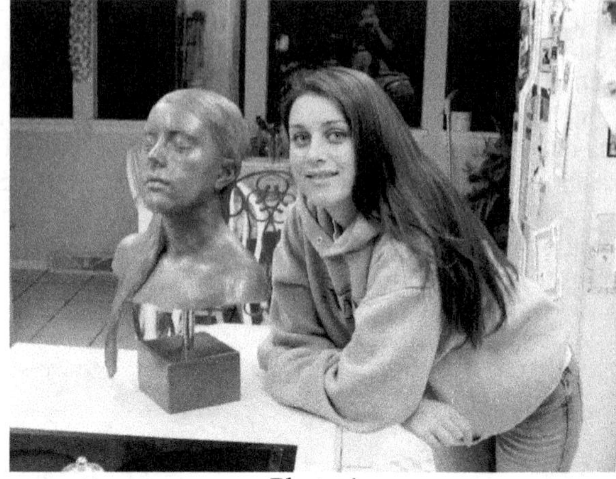
Photo 4

Supporting the Model in Life Casting, Part I

David E. Parvin, A.L.I.

When I began life casting 20 years ago, having had no instruction and being clueless, I tried to reinvent the wheel. I recall distinctly the first torso casting I attempted. I asked a young ice skater neighbor whom I had used as a model for several bronzes to don a leotard and be my first subject; perhaps "victim" is a better word. I applied alginate and constructed a mother mold. What I hadn't realized was that alginate tangles in the fuzz of cotton fabric and it was firmly attached to the leotard. I left the room so as not to embarrass (a word that appropriately almost contains "bare ass") her and she, with her mother's help, was able to wiggle out without damaging the mold. And luckily,I was able to carefully pull the leotard loose doing only minimal damage to the impression of the cloth. After painting in plaster I got what I thought was a pretty good casting, at least for a first try. I hung it proudly on a studio wall erroneously thinking that the main lessons learned were to select a leotard made of non fuzzy material and to use a mold release as well. I later realized that most models are only too willing to be cast oh natural making the process even simpler. But I digress. There was another and far more important lesson.

A few days after I made "Young Skater #1," a collector of mine who just happened to be an orthopedic surgeon, dropped by for a visit. I proudly asked, "What do you think?" he considered my latest contribution to art history for all of a second and a half and replied, "She is either four months pregnant or has a liver disease." I hadn't even noticed that her stomach protruded. The reason was because of the way I had positioned her, I had asked her to stand in the middle of the studio. The alginate is very light and didn't

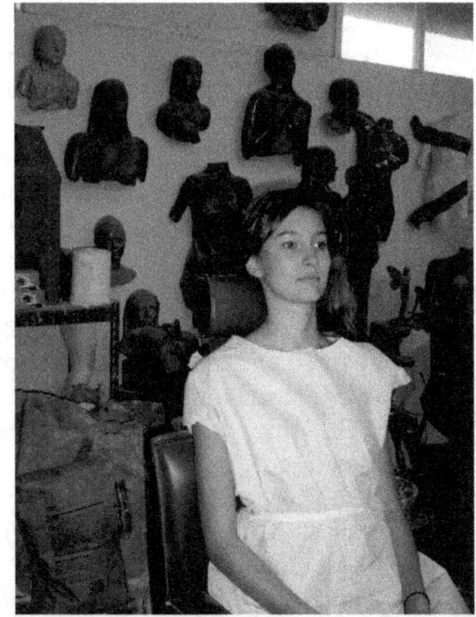
Photo 5

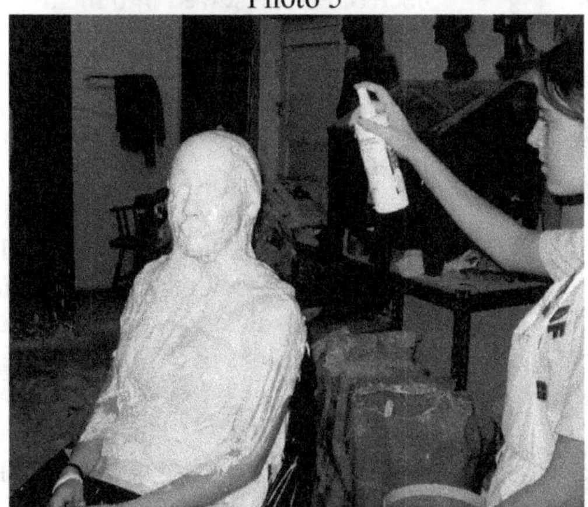
Photo 6

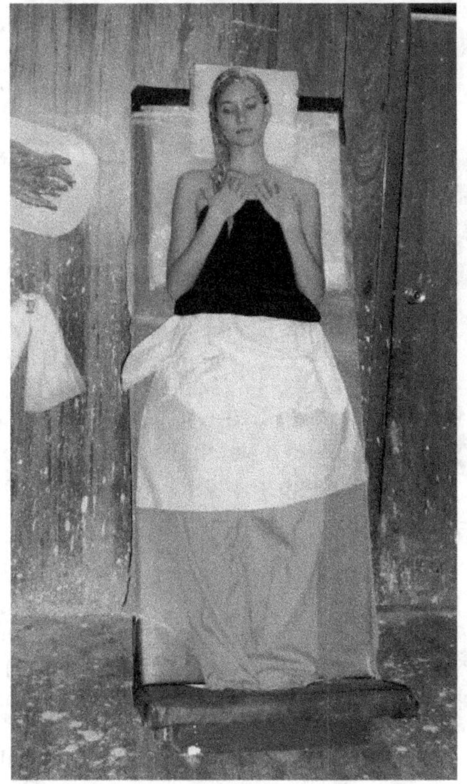
Photo 7

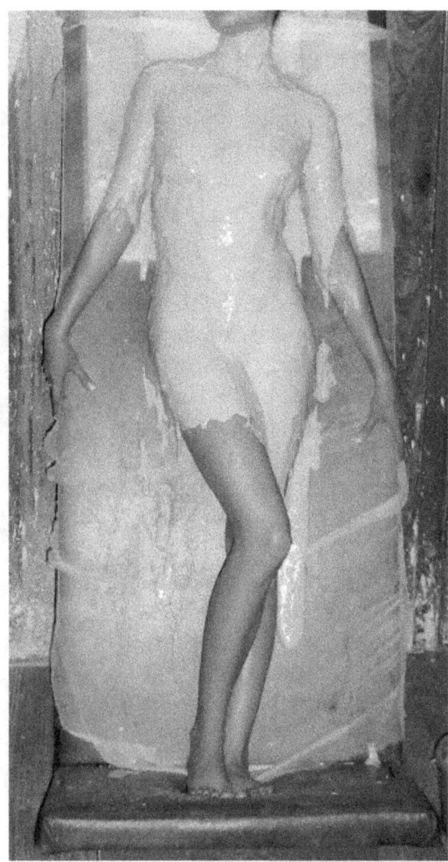
Photo 8

affect her stance. However, the weight of the mother mold was enough to cause her to extend her stomach and lean back to maintain her balance. The much more important lesson was that the model must be supported so that he/she can hold the desired position. Unfortunately, no one solution fits all.

My first thought was to have had the model lie down. But then I realized that there are two problems with this, both verified with later experimentations. The first is that if the model is female, her breasts flatten out unnaturally and unflatteringly. Also, less obvious is the fact the a lying down figure does not have the same spinal contour as a standing body. However, it is sometimes desirable and even necessary to have your model lie down; more about this later.

Heads don't come out any better than torsos if the model is lying down. The face is distorted compared to being vertical when cast. The extreme demonstration of the effects of gravity is to place a mirror horizontally and look down at yourself. You probably won't like what you see. But even face up, there is noticeable distortion. The effects of gravity are directly proportional to one's age, the older we are, the more saggy our skin. Also, if the model's hair is longer than a few inches, it will fall back and not hang down naturally.

When deciding how to support the model, there are several things to keep in mind. The first is the comfort of the model. Do not ask a model to do the impossible. Notice that in photograph #1 titled "Aspen," both arms are raised. Even though it took only between 20 and 25 minutes to make the mold, both of the model's arms went completely asleep. Had the arms not been supported, she could not have held them in place. Next is whether or not whatever body parts one is casting are accessible. For example, if a model is positioned too high, the casters may not be able to reach or even see where to apply the alginate. Too low can be a pain in the back.

Most of my castings are of three types. The first includes from the top of the head to below the breasts and far enough back to include the ears and hair as in photo # 2. Often one or both arms are part of the casting. (See photo #3.) The second is a torso which includes from the top of the neck to mid thigh as in photo #1. The third is a head in the round as in photo #4. (See Life Casting a Head in the Round Part I and II, *SJ*, February and March, 2005 by DP.) In this month's article, I will explain how I position the models for these. Next month, I will cover a number of different approaches.

The seemingly obvious way to cast a face would be to have the subject sit in a chair, preferably with an adjustable head support such as a barber's chair which not only supports the head, but also adjusts vertically and horizontally to position the model for comfort and ease of casting. In photograph #5, assistant Jessica, is situated in such a chair. If one plans on casting only the head down to the top of the shoulders, then this works just fine. I have found that the more of the model I include in the casting, the less suitable a chair is. A better solution just happens to be the same for torso casting as well. But before I describe it, there is one application in which sitting is the ideal position, a head in the round. In this case, I have the model sit but I remove the head support which would block access to the back of the head. (Photo #6)

For what I consider my normal castings as in photographs #1 through #3,I prefer to have the model stand while leaning back against a padded board which is "L" shaped so that the feet remain perpendicular to the back. Photograph #7 shows assistant, Jessica, in position. The casting board is tilted back about fifteen degrees, far enough for comfort but not so much as to cause distortion. Because she is standing, her face is at a convenient height. Notice the two foam pads behind her back and head. These are both for her comfort and for proper spinal alignment. Remember, a person's butt extends back further than

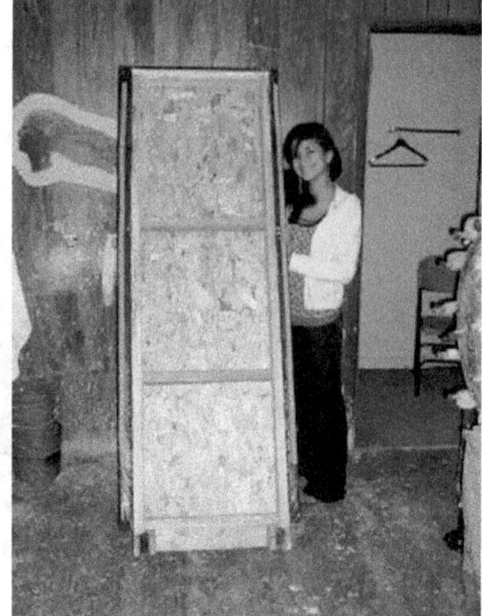
Photo 9

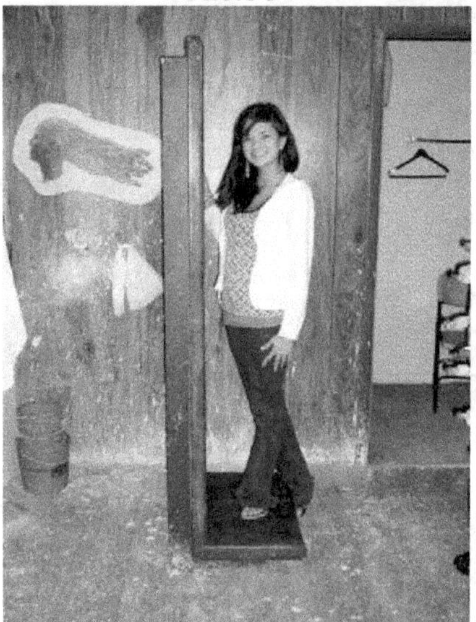
Photo 10

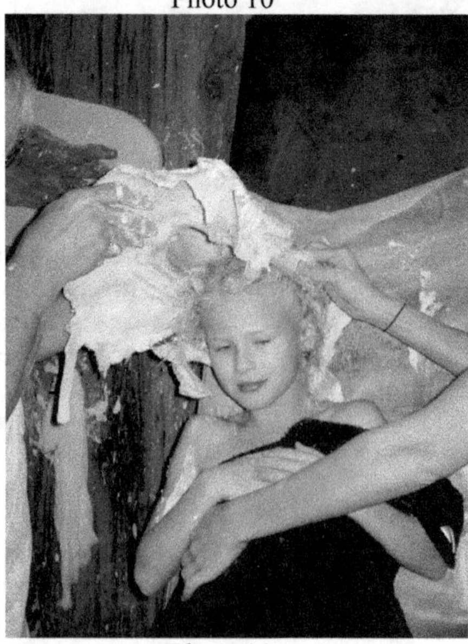
Photo 11

one's back. This especially true for females and leaning back without this additional support will make the stomach protrude foreword, much to the chagrin of the model. The additional support behind the head is for the model's comfort. Almost everybody needs this extra head support except for ballet dancers who, as a group I have found, have perfect posture. I have plastic covered pads prepared in both one and two feet squares and from one to four inches thick with two inches being the most used.

There are a couple of other things I want to point out in this photograph. The black cloth covering Jessica's "assets" is a non fuzzy stretch nylon that has had a piece of elastic sewed into the top. The cloth stretches sideways only and not up and down. Jessica is wearing a paper medical type gown which covered her while we worked "Cholesterol" hair conditioner into her hair. She is also wearing some old scrubs to keep alginate and plaster off of her pants. Behind Jessica is cheesecloth that is held in place by the hook side of velcro strips glued on the outside edges of the back of the backboard. (See below.) The cheesecloth serves two purposes. The first is to facilitate cleanup, the alginate and plaster drippings cling to the cheesecloth and are simply discarded later with the cheesecloth. The second is that alginate wraps around the model and also clings to the cheesecloth and helps keep the model in desired position. This same board works equally as well when casting a torso as in photo #8.

A casting backboard is very easy to construct as can be seen in photographs #9 and #10 along with five and a half foot tall assistant Amber for scale. All that is needed is a piece of 3/4 inch plywood or fiberboard supported by a 2X4 frame. The padding is just 2 inches of foam held in place with a nogahide covering. Be sure to make the 2x4 frame narrow enough to allow for attachment of the nogahide. The white strips down both sides of the back are the hook side of velcro for attaching the cheesecloth. The small dark rectangles at the at the bottom of each 2x4 support are rubber strips that wrap around the bottom so that the backboard will not slip when leaning against a wall. Pieces of bicycle inner tube about 8 inches long are ideal for this. For those who want more specific dimensions, the backboard shown is 76 inches tall and 25 inches wide. Since cheesecloth comes in one yard width, 25 inches is as wide as the backboard can be and still have the cheesecloth attach to the velcro strips on the back. The shelf extends extends out 16 inches. I have found that a casting board is very versatile and work even with small children and pregnant tummies and torsos. (Photos #11 and #12)

If some readers are wondering if we got Jessica all dressed up for photograph #7 just to take her picture, in fact we did cast her. Photograph #13 shows a Jessica not the worse for wear with a plaster duplicate of her face. This is not the final product. I will clean up some small imperfections in the plaster, make a silicone rubber mold of it, and cast her in metallic Forton MG which I will show in next month's issue of *Sculpture Journal*. Also, I will cover some more information on using a casting backboard and explain some other ways of supporting the models for different applications.

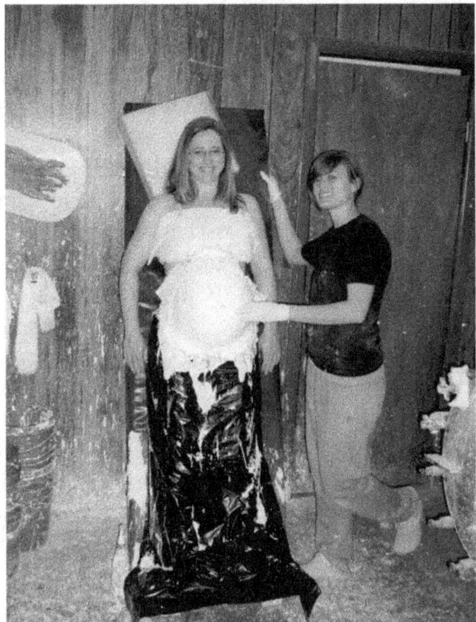

Photo 12

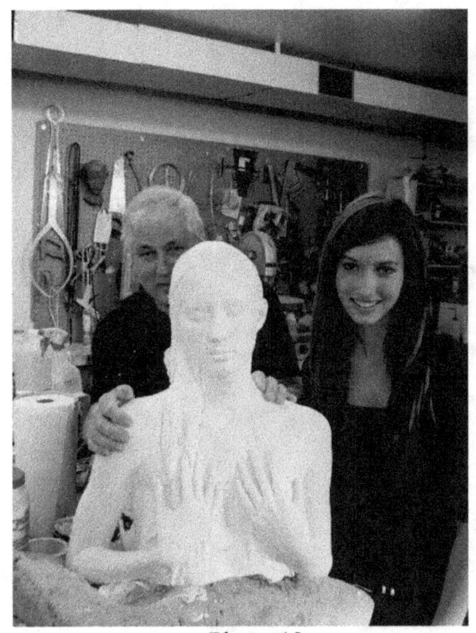

Photo 13

Supporting the Model in Life Casting, Part II

David E. Parvin, A.L.I.

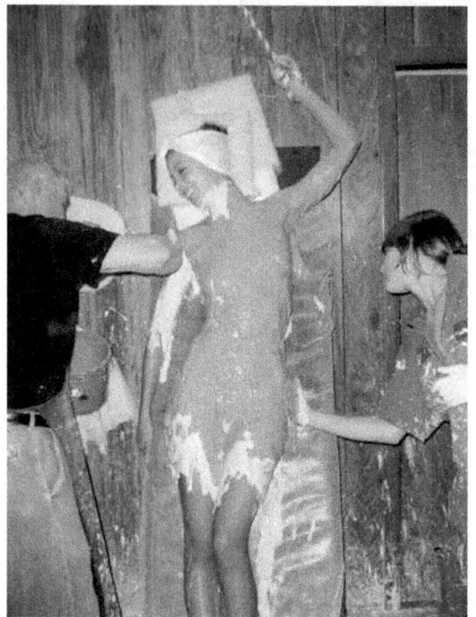
Photo 1

In lasts month's *Sculpture Journal*, I explained the advantages of positioning a model on an almost vertical padded board for support when making a life casting either face or torso. In this article, I will expand on the subject and cover some other methods.

One of the things I mentioned in passing last month was that if a model's arm (or arms) is raised while she is being cast, the arm or will almost certainly go to sleep. The model may insist that she (or he) can hold her arm in place without some support; but do not believe her, she can't. While it will only take about twenty to twenty-five minutes for an experienced casting team to make and remove the alginate mold, the model will loose feeling in and control of her arm and almost certainly distort the mold. Fortunately, providing support is simple. In photo #1, notice that the model's left arm is supported by a rope looped around her wrist. I realize that sometimes life casting starts looking like bondage and a few interesting photos to show friends and relatives is one of the perks the model gets from being cast. In order to keep the model comfortable while the completed mold is curing enough for removal, it is a good idea to remove the hand from the loop and bend the arm at the elbow for a few moments to restore circulation. (Photo #2)

If you are creative at all, you will probably eventually come up with a composition that requires that the model (s) be lying down; or at least makes it easier to do. I'll give you a couple of examples. Photo #3 is of nine year old twins. In the first attempt, I had them stand and lean against the padded board as explained in last month's article. Unfortunately, because of their age, they were unable to hold the position and I repositioned them lying down and successfully made the casting. But I have done older pairs who were able to stand up, e.g. photo #4. (See "When Two Head are Better than One, SJ, June 2004 by DP.)

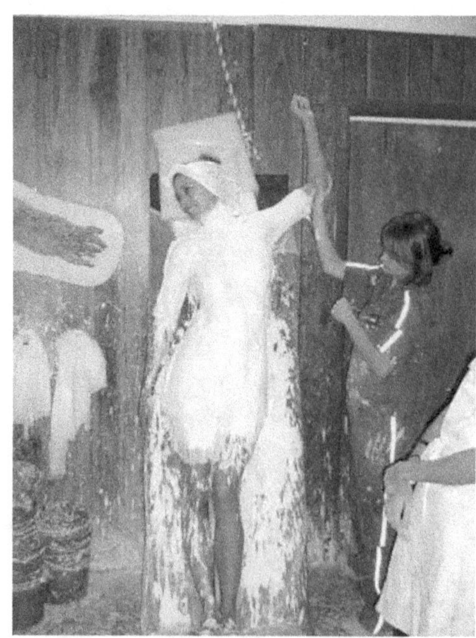
Photo 2

Photo #5 shows a Raku fired torso life casting of a young dancer. We were trying to make her look as if she were doing an arabesque. It would have been impossible for anyone much less a twelve year old to actually hold the position standing up long enough to do the casting. But lying down was a cinch.

The torso casting in photograph #6 could have been made with the model standing but I chose to have the model lie down because it made the casting easier to do. Normally, the breasts of a supine female body would be distorted and not look as if she had been standing. However, because, in this case, the right arm presses against and covers the breasts, the torso looks pretty much the same as if she had been standing. This simplified applying the alginate on the body as a whole and especially around the arms.

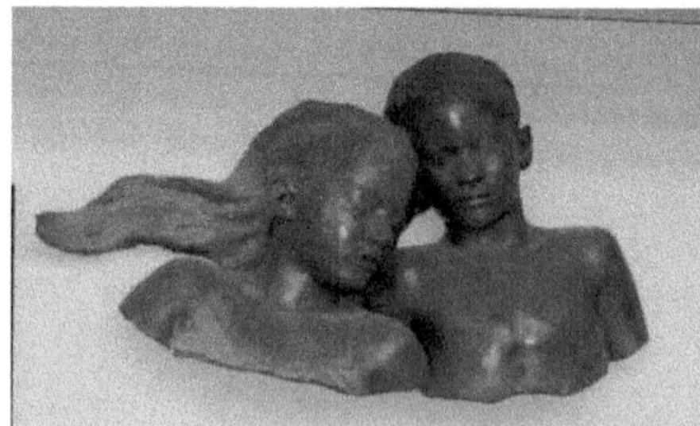
Photo 3

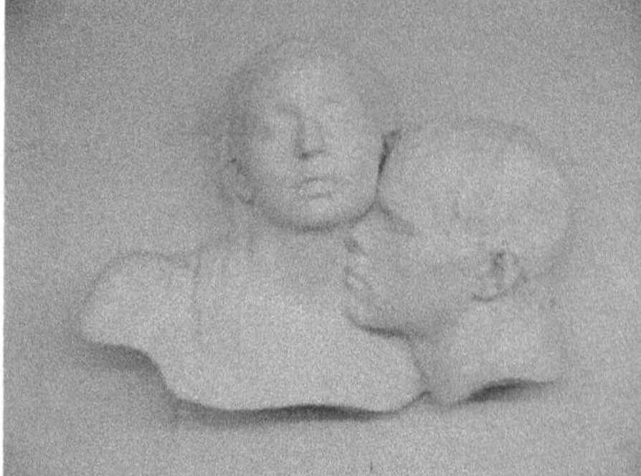
Photo 4

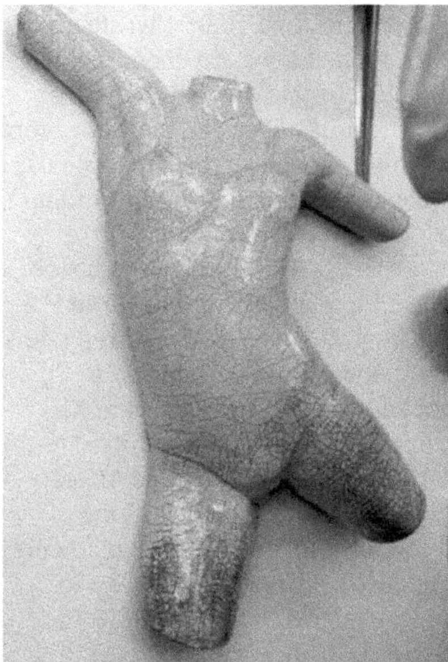
Photo 5

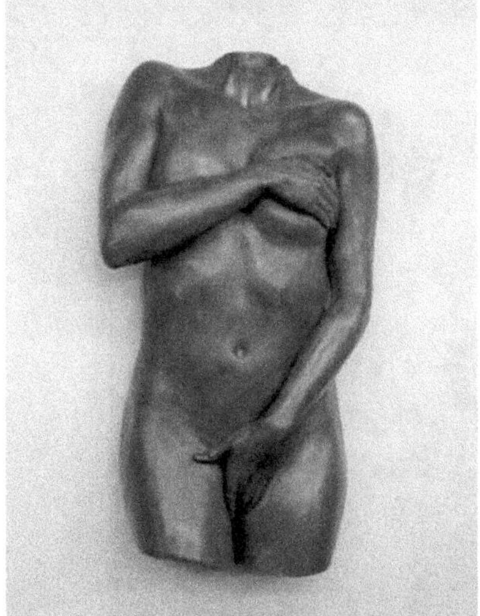
Photo 6

In the above examples, casting the model lying down was just a means to an end and not an end in itself. But in photos #7 and #8, the model was supposed to be lying down. This may look like a difficult casting but it really wasn't though there were a couple tricks required. First, it would have been a challenge to mix enough alginate to cover both the front and back of model and apply it before it set up. I divided the alginate into three batches and mixed one of them. Starting at the neck, I began to apply the first batch as an assistant simultaneously began mixing the second batch. By the time I had covered the first third of the torso, the second batch was mixed and I continued down the torso as the third batch was prepared. This way I was able to apply wet alginate to wet

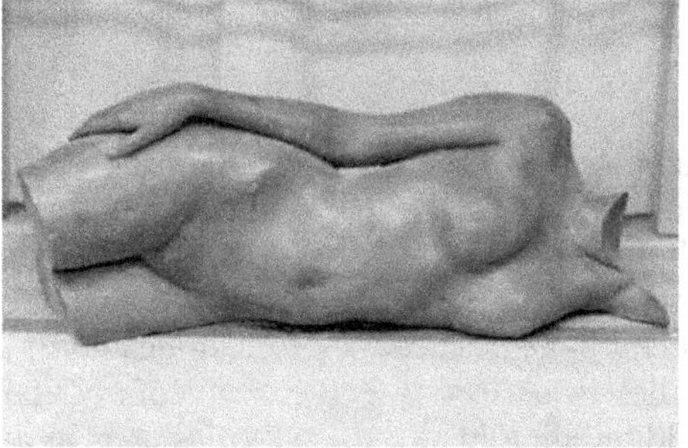
Photo 7

alginate for a seamless transition from neck to thighs. As I progressed along the body, I misted the outer surface of the alginate with AlgiSlo to keep it soft enough to bond to cotton which in turn attached to the mother mold. I constructed the mother mold using cheese cloth and Impression Dental Plaster rather than plaster bandages. (For an explanation of why this method is faster, easier, less expensive, and results in more perfect castings, see my article in the March, 2004 issue of *SJ* titled "An Alternative to Using Plaster Bandages As the Supporting Mold For Alginate Life Casting.") The completed mold was lifted off the model who easily slipped out the bottom without damaging the mold.

Last month, I showed the simple backboard that I use for casting a model in a close to vertical position. In fact, when appropriate, the board can be positioned well beyond almost vertical. If I lean it at shallow enough angle that I worry about it slipping, then I attach it to the wall with a rope and a large hook on its back and another on the wall. For the completely horizontal, a pair of sawhorses support it at a very convenient and comfortable height. (See Photo #9) Shown here is an example of something that I don't usually do, cast a female torso horizontally because of distortion of the breasts. However, in this case we were intentionally making a torso which would represent a sleeping figure.

If the position of the model (or models) is too extended for my regular board, I have another one that is four feet wide by six feet long which is also covered with foam and Nogahide. This larger board sits securely on the pair of sawhorses as well. In photo #10, we were using the

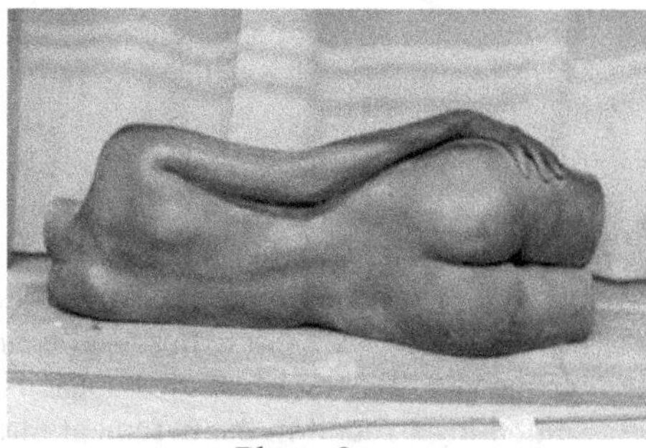
Photo 8

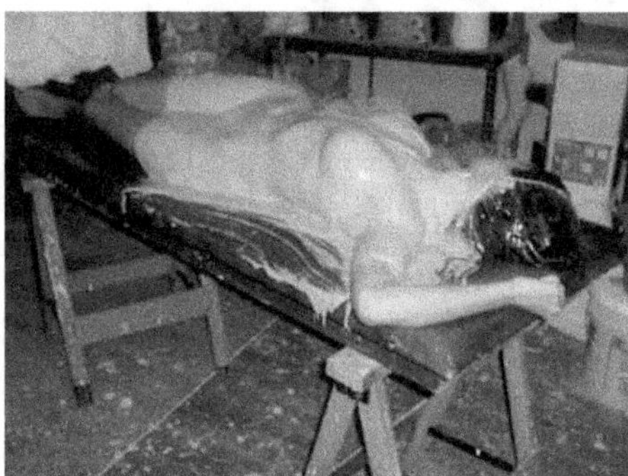
Photo 9

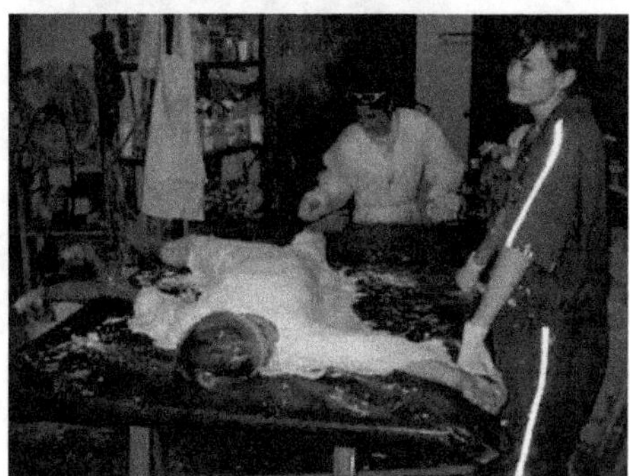
Photo 10

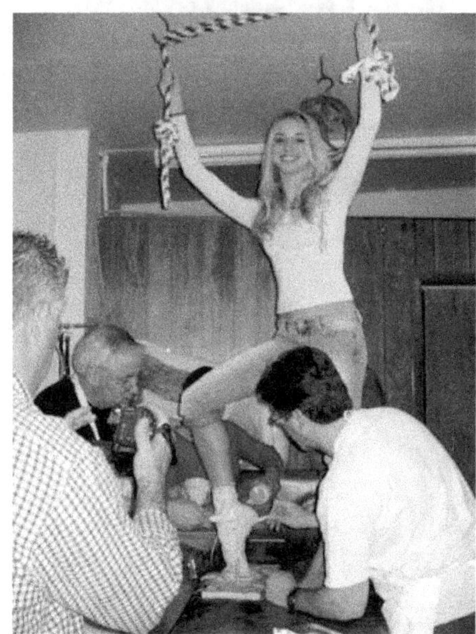
Photo 11

larger board so as to have enough space to position the model in an extended dance like pose.

I have had other occasions to use on of the padded boards on sawhorses. In photo #11, for example, we were casting a dancer's foot in a ballet slipper during a casting workshop. For stability, the model was holding on to a rope that had been hung over a couple of large hooks in the ceiling. Note that behind her head is an ancient pulley which also is attached to one of the hooks. The pulley is just something I found in the basement of the old building in which I have my studio and has no artistic use whatsoever; it just makes it look as if my studio might have just once been s butcher shop, or perhaps still is...

I have also used the padded boards as model stands when doing conventional sculpting, i.e. not life casting. When the model was posing for the statue in Photo #12, I used the narrower of my padded boards for her to lie on which she found to be quite comfortable.

Between December, 2005 and June, 2006 I wrote a series of four articles that explained how and encouraged people to learn more techniques so that they can separate themselves from the run of the mill life casters both for more personal fulfillment and also for monetary rewards. The use of padded boards as I have explained in this and last month's articles could help one progress to the next level.

At the end of last month's article, I showed a plaster cast of one of my assistants, Jessica. I explained that I never use plaster as in the finished casting. Since then, I repaired a few flaws in the plaster, partially opened her eyes, made a silicone rubber mold of the plaster, cast her in Forton MG with metal powder, and applied a green patina solution to the hair and cloth. In Photo #13, Jessica is holding the almost finished portrait. I say "almost" because the only thing remaining to do was buff it. Unfortunately, it needed to cure for a couple of days before buffing, time i didn't have to meet this article deadline. But at least, I hope, you get the idea.

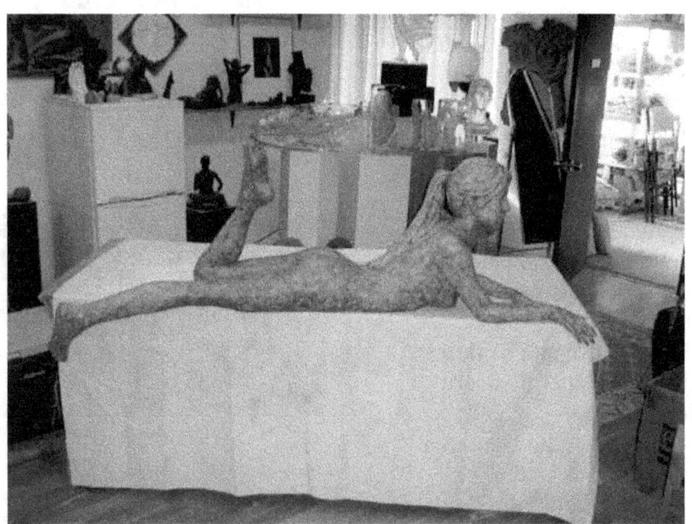
Photo 12

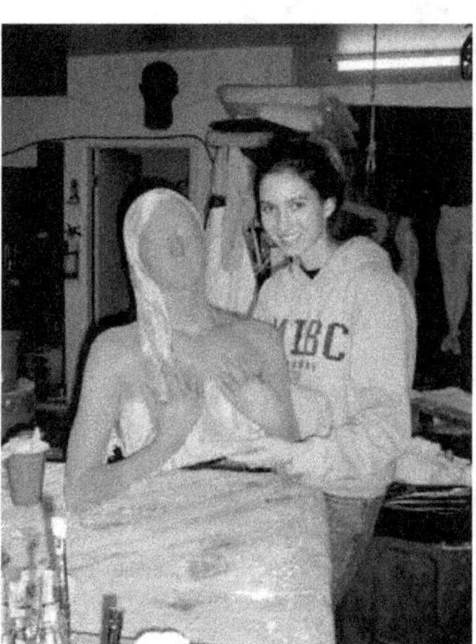
Photo 13

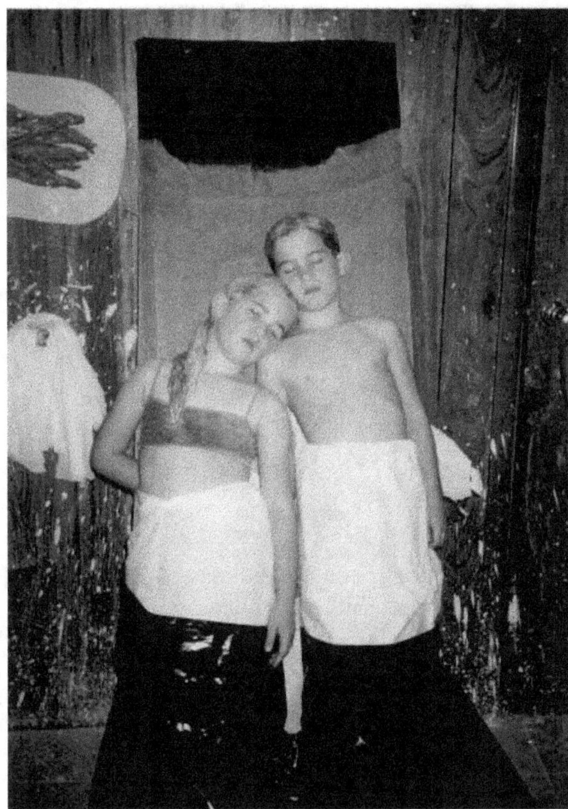
#1 Nine year old twins. They were too young to hold this pose

When Two Heads Are Better Than One

By David Parvin, A.L.I.

Even if you have been life casting for only a short period of time, you probably have been asked if it is possible to cast two people together, and if not, you will be. Fortunately, it is not only possible, it isn't that difficult. Both faces and bodies can be cast in pairs. Here I am going to discuss how to do faces. I will describe three different situations and then through in as an added bonus (no, not a set of steak knives) an example of how to combine three faces that were cast separately. I will save casting two bodies together for a future article and hopefully give any reader who might just possibly be on the fence about renewing her/his subscription a reason to remain in the fold. Amen.

Casting two together is not so much more difficult, it's just more complicated. The first thing is to figure out the composition to express whatever feeling you want the result to convey. In the following three examples, I had a brother sister, two lovers, and a mother and daughter, three very different expressions of love. Once you get the pose just right, you have to decide if the two can hold the pose while the impression is made. In the first case below, they couldn't and we had to find another solution. The second and third were no problem.

Before I get down to particulars, let me point out that I always work with an assistant, usually female. There are two reasons for the hired help. The first is that since most of my castings are of females (in various states of dress or undress). I follow the medical professions example and have another female present. The second is that as my castings have become more complex, i.e. covering more area. I really need a second pair of hands. But since two hands have exactly twice as may parts as one, the process is a whole lot easier with an extra assistant or two.

As far as the casting process goes, I suggest that you go about it the same way that you would for a single person. In other words, follow the same steps you are used to only for two. As you probably have already discovered the most critical step is supplying the alginate without suffocating the model. I leave the detail around the nose until the last. From that point on until the alginate has setup, my attention is put on keeping the nostrils clear. I rely on my assistant to look for and fix any other problems. When doing two, one of my assistants will concentrate on the person's nostril. The single biggest mistake that people do is mix the alginate so that it is too funny and it doesn't want to stay in place. My alginate of choice is Fibergel EFX made by ArtMolds. The mixing ratio is 5 ounces of Fibergel per pound of water. At this mixture, about a quarter inch layer will stay in place on a vertical surface with almost no dripping.

My first example involves nine year old twins, a boy and a girl. Normally I cast someone, either face or body standing and leaning against a padded board. While one might think that the logical position for the castee would

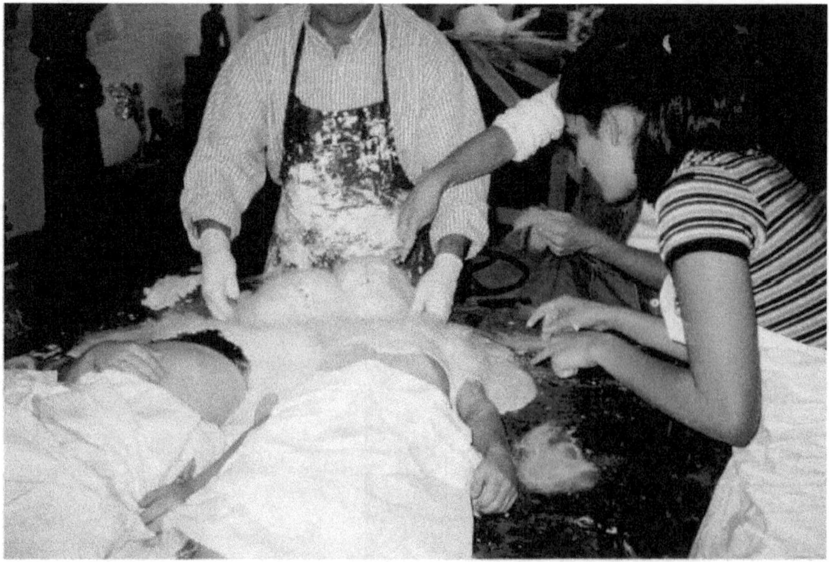
#2 The same twins lying down with the help of mom and dad and my assistant Lisa, the casting went off without a hitch.

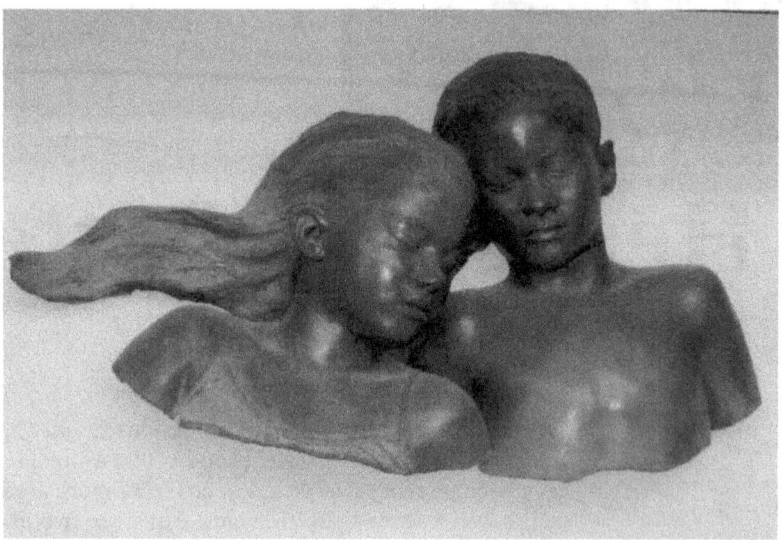
#3 The finished twins in metallic Forton MG

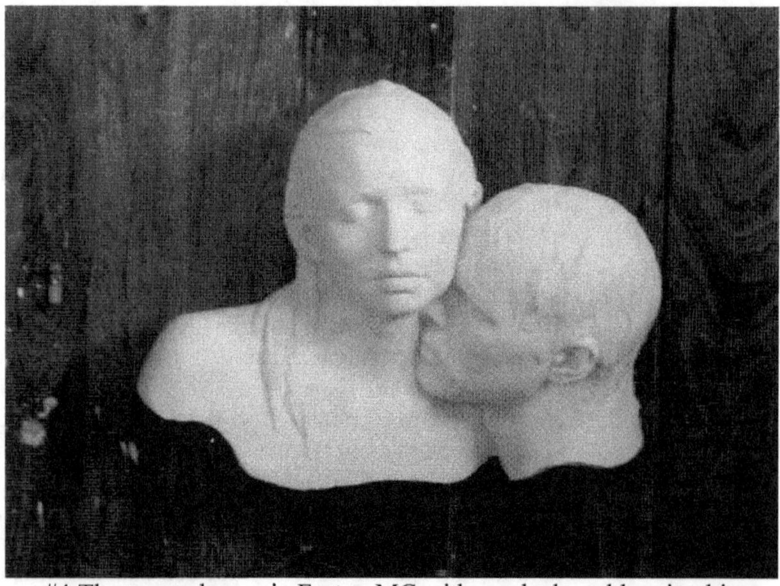
#4 The young lovers in Forton MG with crushed marble mixed in

be lying down, one would be wrong. If the person is lying down, the face is very much distorted and the older the person, the more distortion. If a woman's breasts are included, the effect is even more noticeable. In this case, I positioned the two kids' faces standing up but they just couldn't remain in place during the casting. Since we're talking nine years old, distortion was minimal. But because the girl's hair had to fall back rather than cascade down her chest, it is obvious that the children were lying down. Fortunately this composition of two innocent children asleep worked and they were easily able to hold the pose.

The second were a young couple in their last year of college. Casting this couple was the easiest of the three. We tried several poses and decided on the guy snuggling up to the girl in this position, the guy is the one seeming to say, "I love you so much..." If the faces had been reversed, then it would have been the girl doing the talking.

The last were a mother and her fourteen year old daughter. This was a little more difficult compositionally. After all, sleeping together wasn't quite right and neither was snuggling. What we came up with after trying several poses was to have the daughter rest her head on the mother's shoulder. As luck would have it, they had just returned form a Caribbean vacation and both had dread locks making their hair more interesting.

I should point out that 1 do not cast faces (except as a demonstration) in what is the usual method for most people where the final product is cast directly in the alginate mold. This finished product is likely made of plaster, hydrocal, or some similar material which is left in its original color or given a faux patina. While I do use the alginate mold to produce a plaster positive, for me it is only an intermediate step. After allowing the plaster cast to cure for a few days, 1 correct any flaws and then make a second mold in silicone rubber. I usually cast the final product in Forton MG with metal powders which is patinaed with different chemical solutions and finally mechanically buffed. The result is a much more professional product that resembles metal better than any faux finish can. In addition, the silicone mold allows me to produce additional copies if requested

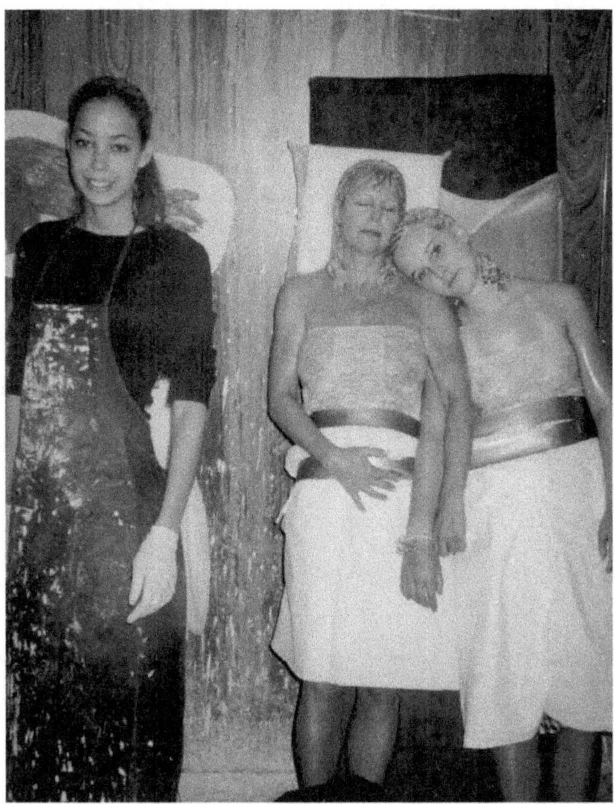

#5 Mother and daughter in position. Notice how helper Meijan is smiling because she is the gooer and not one of the gooes!

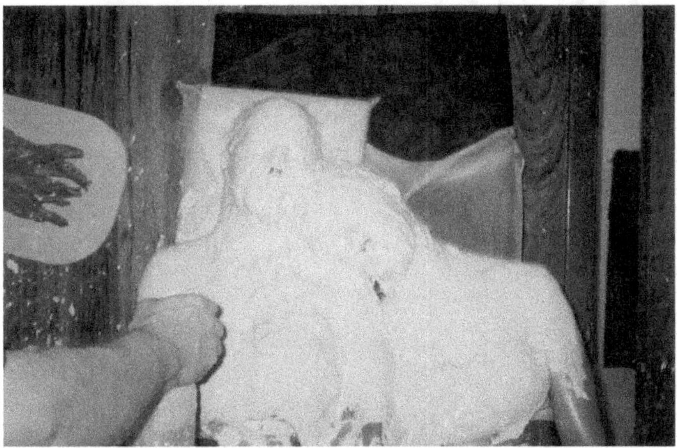

#6 Mother and daughter covered in Fibergel EFX

and lets me use other casting materials. Forton MG can also be mixed with aggregates and water soluble dyes to look like stone. I have also used polyurethane and polyester resins both colored and clear, wax, fiberglass, clay for Raku firing, and others. It is this system that allowed me to combine three faces. My last example, of a brother and two sisters, was pretty straight forward except that the mother mold got a little complicated as described below. The easy part was casting the three heads separately and arranging them. I had been instructed that the finished composition would have to fit into a specific area in the home. The size, shape, and location of this area pretty much dictated the positions of the faces. To provide a backdrop and supporting structure, I made the shape I wanted out of half inch thick clay spread out on a piece of MDFB. The faces were positioned and then attached by pressing clay around them. I covered three faces and the backdrop with two coats of silicone rubber. Because the heads protruded far enough that there were undercuts, the mother mold had to be made to come apart into seven pieces. After curing overnight,

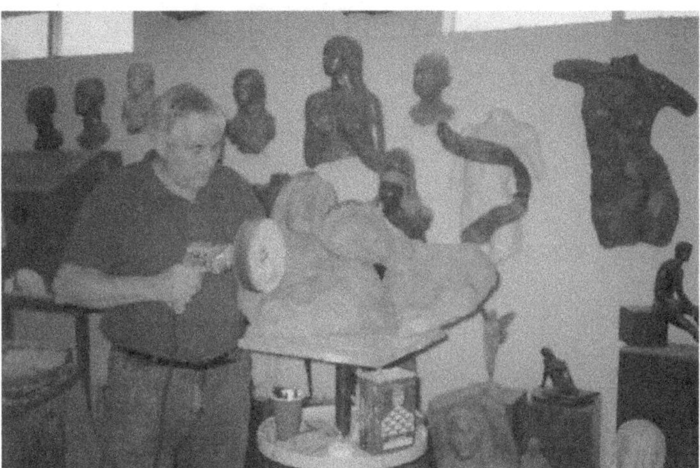

#7 Mother and daughter being buffed by the author

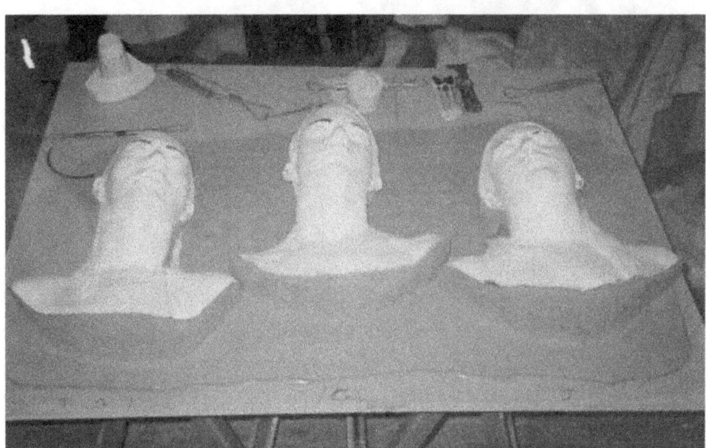

#8 The three heads in plaster arranged on a sheet of clay

the faces are demolded, the old was reassembled, and the final piece was cast in Forton MG with metal powders. After a few hours, the mold was removed, the patina solution was applied, and a little buffing completed the piece which 1 thought looked like a miniature Mt. Rushmore. (Sorry I do not have a picture of a finished mini Mt. Rushmore. I even "remember" taking such a photograph just before the father of the three took it away. But when I got the film back, no photograph. This getting old stuff is no fun).

If the opportunity knocks to cast a pair of heads together, give it a try. I suspect it will not only be a confidence builder, but it will also expand your product line and increase your income. As we say around the Parvin Studio, "Modo Fac" which is Latin for "Just Do It!"

David Parvin is a Colorado sculptor whose primary subject is the human form in a variety of materials. He also teaches life casting workshops held at his studio in Denver, Colorado throughout the year. He may be reached at 303-321-1074.

Business of Art

How Can I Cast Thee for Profit Let Me Count the Ways

by David E. Parvin, A.L.I.

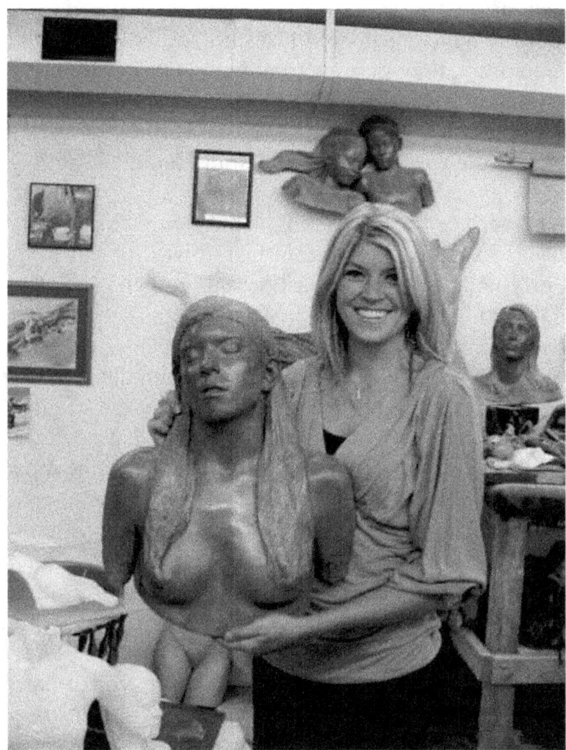

The `face" of a young woman with her hair just covering her breasts. Notice the casting of twin children over her head. At her left shoulder is a head in the round which has open eyes. All are in matallic Forton MG.

Perhaps you are someone who has done some life casting and found it so enjoyable that you would like to be able to justify doing a whole lot more but the reality is that most of us have only so much time and resources for hobbies. Of course, one could always do as Paul Gauguin did, desert one's family and sail to Tahiti and rather than paint the natives, spread alginate on them. A better course of action might be to turn the hobby into a profession which happens the instant that one starts getting paid to do it.

Of course, the same could be said for traditional sculpting as well. There must be any number of readers who would love to drop whatever it is that isn't all that satisfying but pays the bills and just make art. But life casting is especially seductive because it seems so easy. All one has to do is purchase a kit and cast a face, body, or a baby's hand and if one has followed the instructions carefully, the results will probably be reasonably successful. After all, even with a poorly done life casting of a face, the subject is recognizable. Compare that to what would likely result if someone with no practice or training were to try to draw, paint, or sculpt someone's face. Life casting is to sculpting as photography is to painting and while a snapshot is

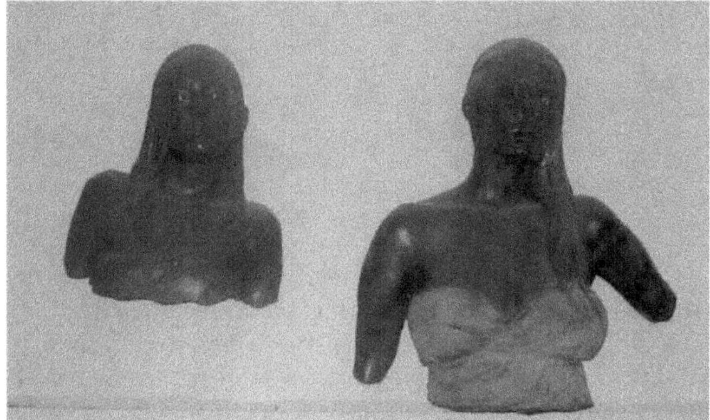

A young lady at 12 years old and again at 16. Cast in Forton MG with metal powders and a chemically applied patina

recognizable, it doesn't follow that the snap shooter is another Ansel Adams. And in the same way, while life casting can seem so deceptively easy, it isn't easy to do well.

As I will explain later, the better the end results, the greater the earning potential. For now, let's consider some ways that life casting can actually generate income.

Many people discover life casting by purchasing a kit available in most craft and art supply stores and casting a baby's hand and/or foot. Having successfully immortalized one's own child, the next step is to try friends', and finally move on to anyone who has an infant and a willingness to pay. But it isn't just the newly born that are fair game, any old hands will do. Here are some examples that I have done:

1. A parent holding his/her child's (children's) hand(s) or visa versa.

2. A whole family of hands either as a pyramid or a wreath. I once cast the hands of four generations of women from 17 to over 80.

3. I have cast hands holding all sorts of objects such as a baseball, crystal glove, paint brush, flowers, oar handle, wine glass, baseball bat, fishing rod, suturing tools in physician's hands, volley ball baseball, golf club, book, etc. One physician wanted his hand on someone's shoulder as if giving comfort.

4. One of the more standard castings is of an engaged couple's clasping hands.

5. And don't forget feet. While a newborn's foot is the most obvious, another very common request is a ballerina's foot in a toe shoe on pointe.

After hands and feet, the next logical challenge for a new life caster might be faces. Faces are especially important because we generally recognize and remember people by their faces. So adept are we at this that we can see someone from our distant past who has certainly changed with time and still recognize his/ her face. There even may be a particular part of the brain that is devoted just to faces.

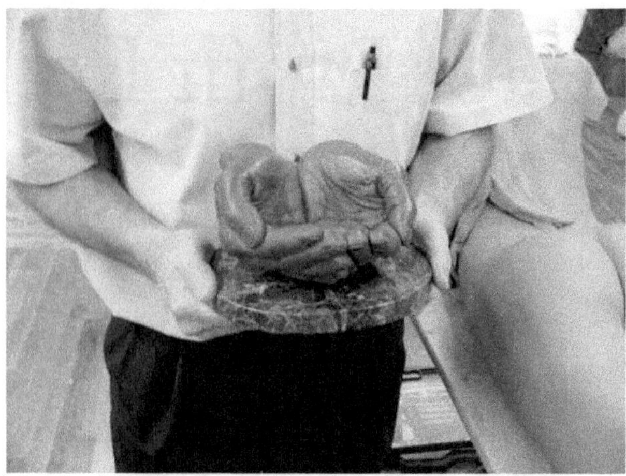

A pair of hands cast in polyurethane with metal powders and attached to a marble base

"60 Minutes" once aired a segment about some people who had received head injuries that prevented them from identifying faces even though otherwise they were normal. So severe were they disabled that they couldn't recognize their own reflections in mirrors!

Although I have cast the faces of children as young as five, the magic age seems to be eight. I have seen very few kids eight or older who wouldn't or couldn't get their faces cast. If possible, I like to capture someone's face at twelve or younger. Not only do you get them while they still look like children but you stand a very good chance of having the parents bring them back for another casting or two as they grow up. Let's all be thankful for repeat business.

I have done more face castings than any other type including:

1. Children.
2. A second or third casting as the child matures.
3. Two faces cast together such as twins, lovers, and mother and daughter.
4. Though children are more likely subjects, adults at any age who want a record of themselves for themselves or loved ones.

While any body part may be a candidate for casting, the last of the big three would be torsos. The most common torsos that I have cast are either the front or back of a body from neck to mid-thigh trimmed to hang on a wall as a bas relief. While I have found that women are more likely to want their bodies captured forever, people of either gender who are in their prime or who have gotten themselves in great physical condition are likely candidates. I can not even guess at how many women who are a "little older" have remarked after seeing some of my sample castings, "I wish I had done that when..." But I can tell you exactly how many men have said that, only two.

As I listed above for faces, hands and feet, here are some examples:

1. A front or back of a torso as described above. The castings may be either clothed or nude or both. While usually done for the person her/himself, may be for a significant other.
2. A common casting for me has been a dancer's torso in a leotard.
3. Usually, the front of the torso is cast and displayed on a wall as a has relief. However, sometimes the subject may want his/ her back cast instead or in addition.
4. A third possibility is a front and back together so that the result is a free standing piece in the round. A figure on its side including both front and back is a variation on this same theme.
5. More than once, I have cast two torsos together side by side. One particularly successful pair was a female front beside a male back.

While I have considered faces, torsos, and hands and feet separately, they may be combined in any number of ways. For example, when I cast a face, I usually include down to about mid-chest often with one or both arms. Sometimes the subject holds something in one or both hands.

Another use for life casting is providing anatomical references for other art work. In fact, it was for this purpose that I originally started life casting. Not only have I often found this to be beneficial in my work but have supplied castings to other artists for a price, of course.

There are any number of things that can determine if any of us will succeed. Some are completely out of our control such as inborn talent or a trust fund that pays the bills. But no matter what our circumstances, for the most part we are in control. To actually generate some significant income from life casting, two things are necessary: being able to do quality work and then knowing how to market it. One of my favorite quotes is by Moss Hart (by the way, I have no idea who Most Hart was or is; this may be the only thing he ever said!), "Writers, actors, and prostitutes have the same fundamental problem; competition from amateurs who are pretty good and who will work for free." Moss certainly could have included life caster. In my next article I will explain how to go beyond simple plaster castings that are "pretty good" to much more professional work using better materials and ideas. The four photographs in this article are a few examples. Marketing strategies will be covered later.

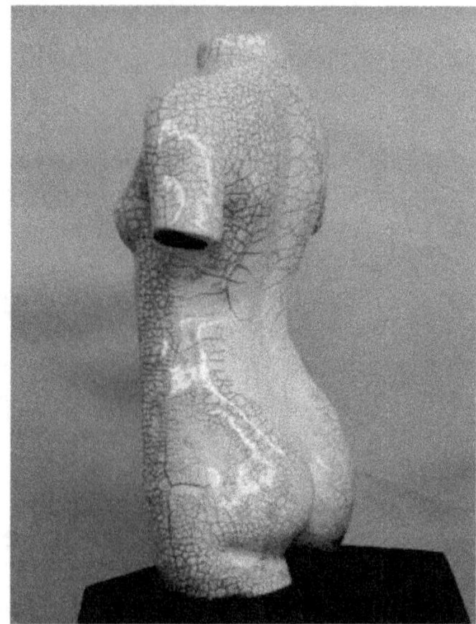

A free standing torso in the round which is raku fired with a white crackle glaze.

How Do I Cast Thee for Profit

Part II

David E. Parvin, A.L.I.

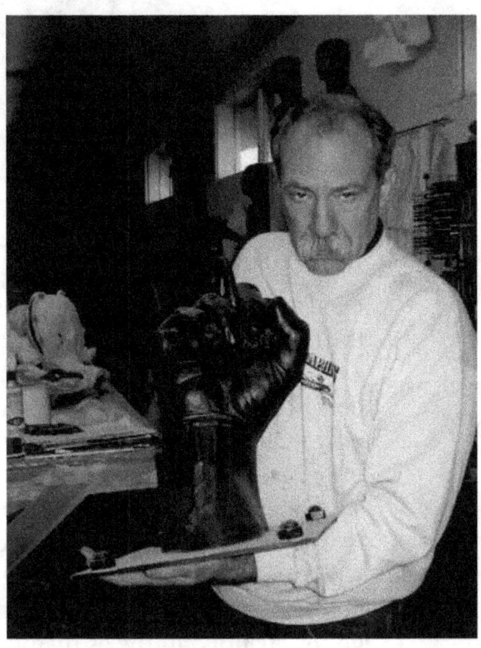

A bronze hand held by sculptor and friend Bill Hueg which I had size sculpted twice life size from a casting of a hand of the gentleman who ordered a number of copies as attaching points for awnings for a building. This is an example of using a life casting as a model rather

In the first in this series of articles, I explained that the three most common parts of the body that are cast for remuneration are hands/feet, faces, and torsos. (See "How do I cast Thee for Profit, Let Me Count the Ways: Sculpture Journal, December, 2005.) At the end of the article, I quoted Moss Hart who said, "Writers, actors, and prostitutes have the same problem, competition from amateurs who are pretty good and who will work for free." Certainly artist in general, sculptors in particular, and especially life casters have the same problem. The question is how to rise above the amateurs and command reasonable pay. I will describe two strategies which will be appropriate whether life casting for portraits or as stand alone pieces of art.

At the risk of sounding cynical, if you can become a **celebrity** artist, you're home free. What I mean by "celebrity" is simply that you are **famous**, you don't even have to be any good, just famous or even infamous will do. Art history has lots of examples of well known persons whose work commanded high prices far beyond what the work itself should have. If you just happen to have achieved fame from some legitimately honorable accomplishments such as a couple of Olympic gold medals or Nobel Prizes, then who could blame you for cashing in. That's exactly why paintings by Winston Churchill are worth more than those equally good paintings by almost any artist whom no one has ever heard of. Perhaps an easier plan would be to follow the Paris Hilton method. All you have to do is be born beautiful and stinking rich and then release a video of yourself engaging in some outrageously shocking activity and the public will love you. I have no doubt whatsoever that if Ms. Hilton decided to produce anything that could even remotely be called art, she and her, say, angles molded in clarified chicken fat would be featured in every vacuous publication and on similar television shows, Collectors would line up. Fortunately there is a more realistic and in some cases honorable path to follow. As Robert Frost said, "Some have relied on what they knew, others on being simply true, what worked for them might work for you."

I often have referred to life casting as three dimensional photography. What I mean by this is that just as anyone can snap a photo of something and capture its likeness very accurately without having to spend years practicing drawing and painting, so can one do the same thing three dimensionally without learning to sculpt. But there is also a historical similarity too. There was a time that photography was extremely difficult and only a few experts understood the process. Then in the first part of the twentieth century, Mr. Kodak came up with a process that allowed anyone to make photographs. In the same way, kits are now available that provide all the materials and instructions needed to make a life casting of any pan you want. But I often point out that it is very easy to make a simple life casting but it's not easy to do well. Just

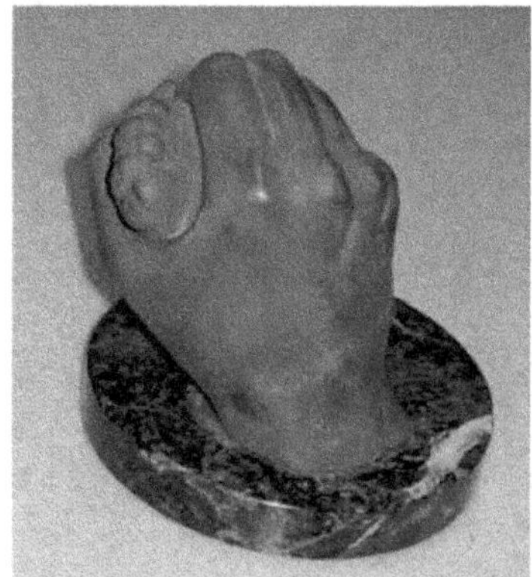

Mother's hand holding infant's foot. Metallic Forton MG on green marble base.

owning a camera doesn't make you an Ansel Adams and just purchasing a few kits isn't going to make one into an expert life caster.

Whether we are considering hands/feet, faces, or torsos, most of the "standard" life castings made from kits will be in white plaster or hydrocal. A notch up in quality is the application of a faux patina for a stone or metal finish. There are even some advanced kits that provide the materials for cold cast bronze such as using Forton MG. The next step is to stop using kits and purchase the materials in bulk. This is the critical junction, the time and place where one remains an amateur or becomes a pro. If you want to be able to charge a reasonable amount, your work should be better than what is likely done by someone with limited experience. After all, if it looks as if the average Joe Customer could have done it her/himself, then why would she/he be willing to pay you to do it? Here are some ways to separate yourself from the "...amateurs who are pretty good and who will work for free."

The strategies that I am going to explain apply to hand/feet, heads, and torsos and are intended for the new life caster. In this article, I will give some examples of

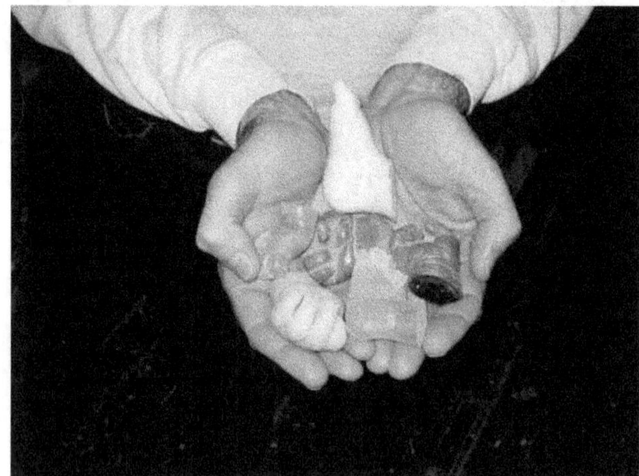

Infants' hands and feet in clear polyester resin, clear polyurethane resin, metallic Forton MG, metallic polyurethane resin, and clear polyester resin with crushed marble

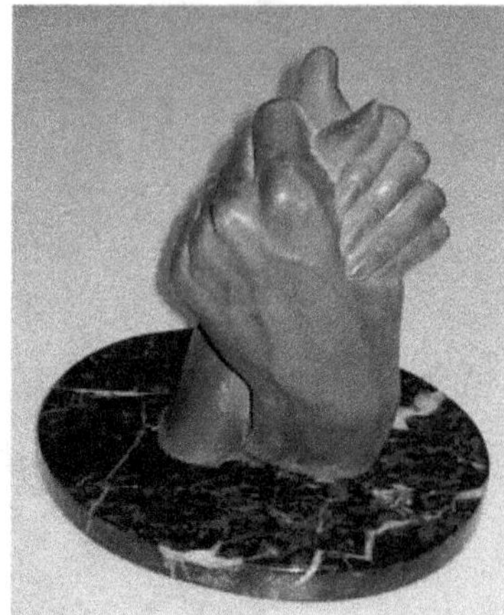

Engaged couple's hands. Metallic Forton MG with green marble base.

hand and feet done in more professional ways. Then in the next months, I will cover heads and torsos in detail.

1. Practice until your alginate impressions are consistently close to flawless, (While alginate isn't the only material that can be used to make life casting impressions, it is the most universally used.) There is a story told about a pottery teacher who divided a class into two sections. One was instructed to spend the semester working on only one pot but make it as perfect as possible. The other half was told to forget quality and just go for quantity, throw as many pots as possible. At the end of the semester, the most perfect pots had been made by the second group, "Repetitio mater studiorem est." "Repetition is the mother of learning." (When little tidbits of first year Latin some how pop up almost fifty years later, I'm sure old Father Riddlemoser ['Jumping Joe' to his students] probably smiles from on high.) The more flawless your impressions, not only will your work be more consistent, but you will not have to spend as much time correcting flaws.

2. As your skill improves as a result of #1, you will gain the confidence to attempt more complicated and innovative castings and ways of displaying them. One of the usual ways to display infants' hands and feet is to mount them in shadow boxes which can be easily constructed or just purchased from any craft store. I generally attach them to marble bases which, I feel enhances their appeal and value. The key thing is that you have the skill to provide whatever the customer wants.

3. Many times, I construct a secondary mold which allows me to make multiple copies which I can provide for an additional fee, of course. Another advantage is that if the rubber in the mold is properly de-aired, you will be able to cast under pressure for bubble free results. The secondary mold also makes it possible to utilize more materials as I explain below.

4. Use other more professional materials than just plaster or hydrocal. These include Forton MG, wax, and urethane and polyester resins. Forton MG and the resins allow for very effective cold cast bronze castings. Wax

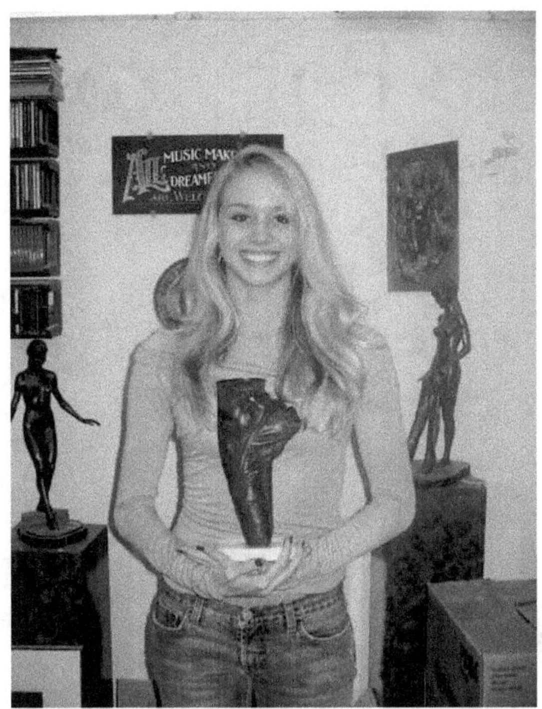

Dancer's foot on pointe in metallic Forton MG, black patina, on a white marble base. This is a very common request.

castings can be taken to a foundry and cast by lost wax into actual bronze. Forton MG and wax can be poured directly into alginate molds. Urethane resins are not compatible with the moisture in alginate unless an ingredient called "Watertrap" is used. Polyester resins will not work with alginate. However, all work just fine in silicone rubber molds. Remember, if you are using clear urethane, always use a platinum cured silicone rubber and not tin cured. One of the advantages of these other materials is that they are stronger than plaster and hydrocal and will allow more difficult castings to be removed from the molds without breakage

For more information, please take out your leather bound annual collections of Sculpture Journal and look up the following articles all by yours truly:

-"It's Very Clear, One Sculptor's Experiences With Urethane and Acrylic," January 2002.
-"Forton MG Simplified," July 2003.
-"Using Vacuums and Pressure in Casting," October 2003.
-"Making a Vacuum Chamber," September 2003.
-"Making a Pressure Chamber," October 2003.
-"Putting Vacuum and Pressure Chambers to Practical Use," November 2003.
-"Watertrap, Testing a New Product," December 2003.
-"How to Make a Secondary Mold," July 2004.
-"How to Cast a Dancer's Foot on Pointe...... January 2005.
-"More Uses For Cheese Cloth in Life Casting," September 2005.
-"A Great New Gadget," January 2006.

If you are tired of reading, what I have to say and would prefer to listen as I demonstrate, I have two instructional DVDs available. One is on casting the female torso and the other covers hands and fat. You may be able to find them locally or by contacting me directly at parvinstudio@comcast.net or (303) 321-1074. Either will do but I much prefer to talk than type. Earlier I quoted Robert Frost about some honorable ways to succeed. As noble as his words were, he went on to say in the same poem that, "it's better to go down dignified with boughten friendship at your side than none at all. Provide, provide," That has absolutely nothing whatsoever to do with casting around for fun and profit, it just seemed to me to be a good way to end the poem and also this article.

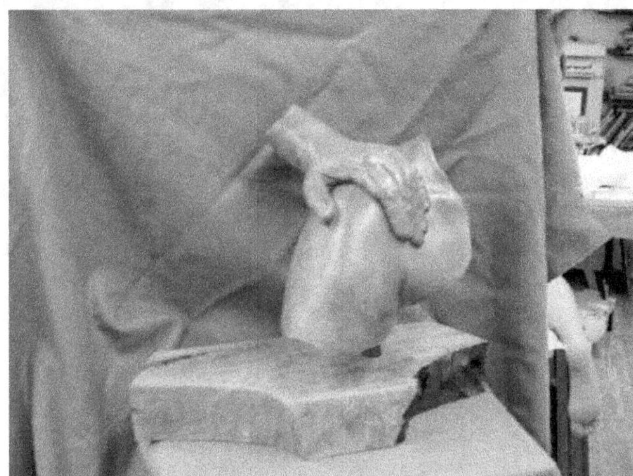

A physician's hand on someone's shoulder as if giving comfort. Metallic Forton MG on a wood bass I have cast all sorts of things in people's hands.

Dave Parvin is a sculpture living in Denver, CO. He has years of experience in life casting and holds workshops throughout the year. He may be reached at 303-321-1074

Sculpture Journal – February 2006

How Do I Cast Thee For Profit

Part III, Heads

By David E. Parvin, A.L.I.

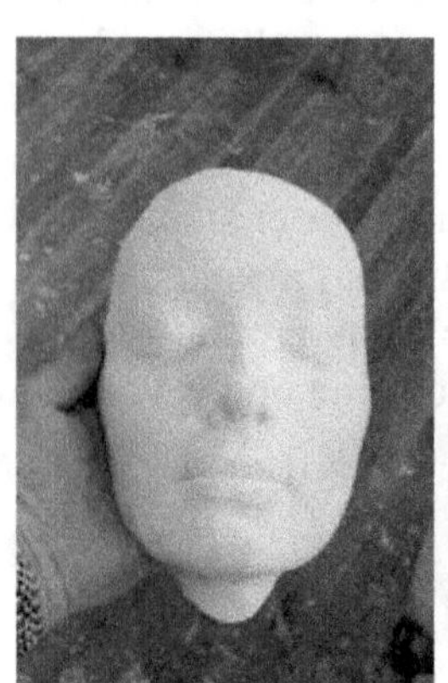
Photo 1

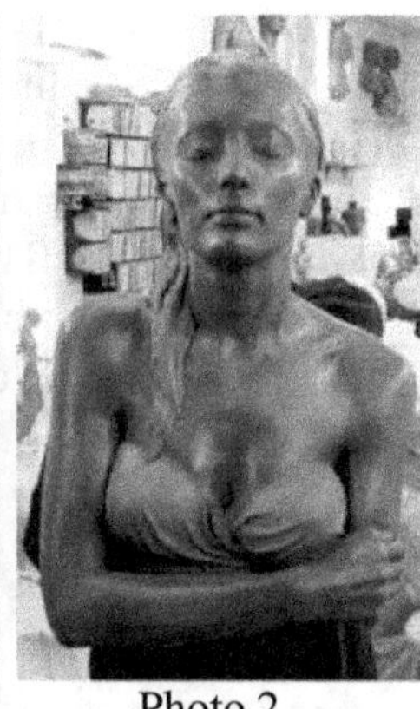
Photo 2

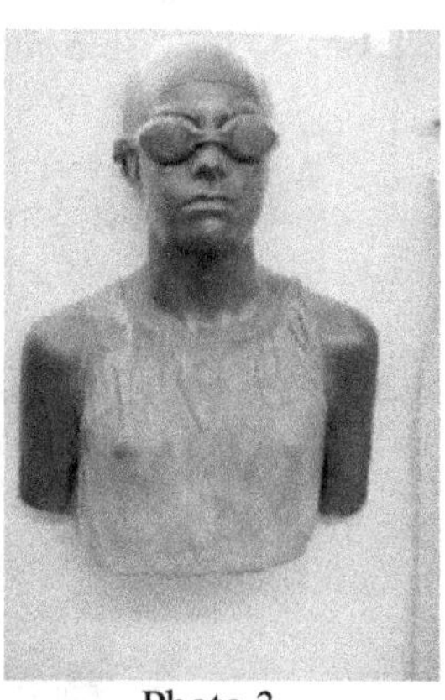
Photo 3

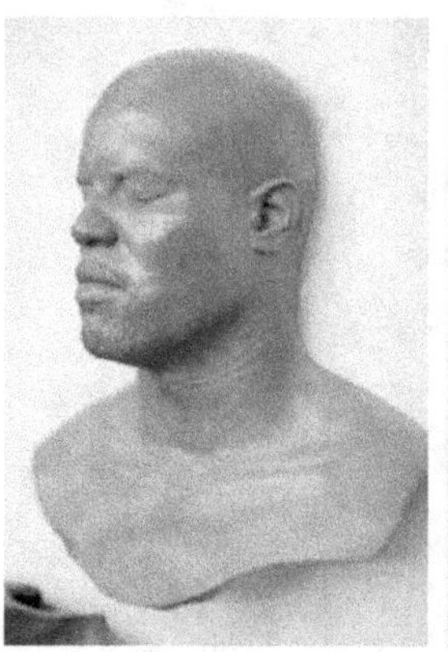
Photo 4

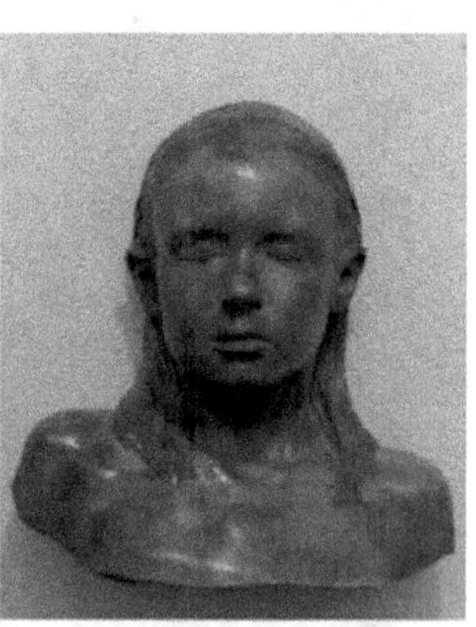
Photo 5

In this article, I will explain the differences between a very simple face casting and something much more professional, in other words, casting 101 verses casting 499. Of the three body parts (faces, torsos, and hands/feet) that I am covering in this series of articles, faces are definitely the most challenging. Faces have more detail, ins and outs, and different structures which require special care. In addition, the subject must be able to breathe to prevent him/her from becoming a victim. Also, claustrophobia is a possibility whenever the face is covered. Lastly, when a person has to be still for even ten to twenty minutes, there is a chance of fainting which is most likely during a face casting.

Some of the techniques that I will encourage the use of in this article I have covered in detail in previous articles in Sculpture Journal which are listed at the end. Some others will be covered in the future such as eyes and hair.

Several years ago, there was a guy featured on a nationally televised show as an "expert" life caster. His faces were no more than from slightly above the forehead down to just below the chin. None had any more than part of the ears and the hair was mostly covered. All were in plaster though some had been painted. I could have taught someone in a morning how to cast such simple faces, definitely casting 101.

A few years ago, I was commissioned to cast fifty faces for a community art project for a suburb of Denver. The person in charge wanted only what "Mr. Expert" above was doing; in other words, just the front about 1/3 of the head in plaster. I felt like saying, "You ignoramus, I'm Dave Parvin, master life caster; don't you realize that this is like asking W. A. Mozart to compose `Chop Sticks'?" But alas, when confronted with, "Here's what we want and here's the money," I decided that paying the rent and getting a few groceries was more important than my pride. From the time that I started a particular casting until I handed the finished "face" to the person was only about ten minutes. To do what I would much rather have done, what I will describe below, would have taken twelve to fifteen hours per face. But I still regret that the persons who volunteered to be part of the project ended up with masks that really didn't look like themselves. I did get paid, but I doubt if I would have done very many face castings since then, if that had been the extent of my ability. In this article, I will describe some ways to make face casting more professional, to turn your subjects into works of art, and improve your bottom line along the way.

1. Use secondary molds.

I never use plaster or any similar gypsum material as a final casting medium. (3) Usually my initial castings in the alginate molds are made in a soft, easy to work with plaster such as Regular Dental Plaster or #1 Molding Plaster. This allows me to correct any flaws and rework the piece as necessary such as opening the eyes and/or reshaping the hair. Once I am satisfied, I make a secondary mold using silicone rubber. Not only do I produce a far more professional portrait, but I have the ability to make extra copies if the client wants them. (1) Photograph #12 is a head that was cast in oil based clay rather than plaster. This was done to allow for extensive reworking. Not only were the eyes opened but the hair was completely resculpted, the expression was changed, her nose was slightly straightened, and some very fine wrinkles were removed. The end result was that she looked about ten years younger. Remember, life castings do tend to make one look

---

***Photo 1**: A life casting of a face that doesn't capture enough to show what the person really looks like. Material - plaster:*
***Photo 2**: The same face as in photo 1, but including hair, ears, and part of the upper- body. Material l- Forton MIG with metal powders and a chemically applied patina (FMG,, MP, CAP)*
***Photo 3**: A young swimmer with goggles, swim cap, and a bathing suit. Material- FMG,, MP, CAP.*
***Photo 4**: A male who is bald. This is how much 1 typically cast a male below the neck. Material - FMG,, MP, CAP.*
***Photo 5**: The face of a nine year old girl. For this age, I keep the casting very simple in order to make the process as short as possible. Material - FMG, MP, CAP.*

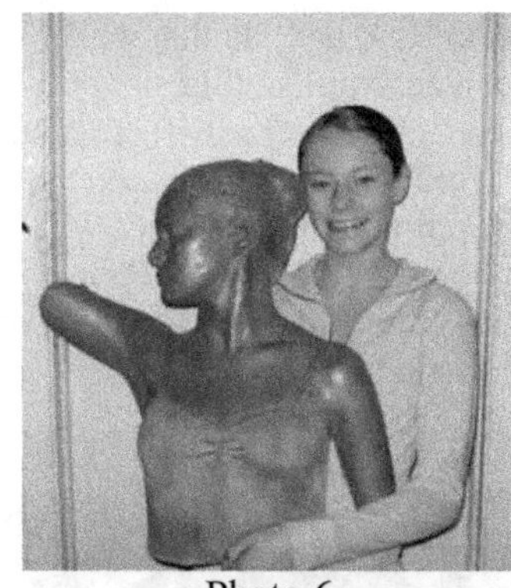
Photo 6

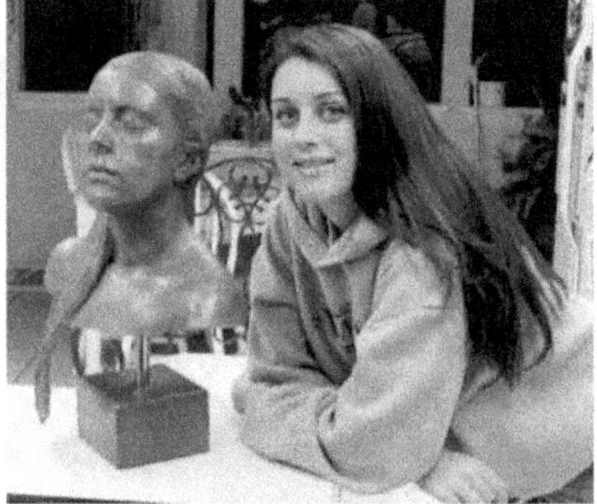
Photo 7

a little older, much like a driver's license photograph. Being able to enhance a casting can make for a more satisfied client.

2. More is better.

The number one important thing for any portrait, whether in two or three dimensions, is that the subject be recognizable. My contention is that in order to accomplish this, more than just the front of the face must be included. The problem is that if the casting includes only from the chin to the hairline, since the forehead isn't the widest part of the head, the casting looks like an egg small end up with eyes, nose, and a mouth! (See photograph #l.)

What I consider to be a face includes from the top of the head to at least most of the neck, and as far back as behind the ears. Hair is always included unless covered by something essential for the portrait such as a swim cap or the person is bald. (See photographs #2, #3, and #4.) For a male subject, I usually include the full width of the shoulders and down several more inches as in photograph #4. For females, I generally cast down below the breasts. Not only do females usually request this but it also allows for some creative and artistic ways of

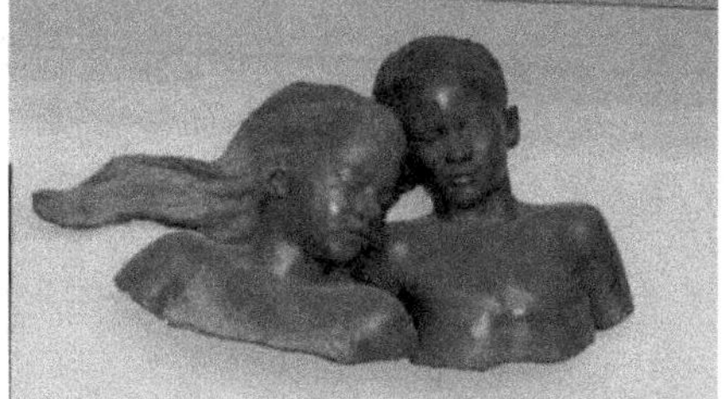
Photo 8

covering (or not) the breasts. Very often one or both arms are included. With small children, boys or girls, I usually keep the casting simple to shorten the casting process (photograph # 5).

3. Different materials.

In last month's SJ, I encouraged the use of different materials for hands and feet. While plain plaster, or some other gypsum product, is OK and faux or painted patinas are better (3), using other materials such as resins and especially Forton MG can produce much more professional results. There is one advantage to using paint-on finishes, they are very simple to do. The two disadvantages are that they can hide some of the surface or skin detail and since they only cover the surface, a chip or scratch will expose the plaster underneath. With resin or Forton MG, metal powders are through out at least the surface coat and no detail is lost. Also, the castings are more durable because the materials are much stronger and the color is in the material and not just on it. The additional strength and durability allows for castings that can be thinner and lighter. Forton MG can be cast directly in alginate molds and is almost as easy as plaster to use. (4) Resins by themselves are not compatible with the water in alginate and release C02 causing bubbles. The addition of "Watertrap" allows polyurethane to cast cleanly in alginate but is ineffective with polyester resin. (5)

While Forton MG is my usual first choice, I also use polyurethane and polyester resins. Photograph #7 is of a head in the round (8) in clear polyester resin and crushed limestone called "Pool Mix" which makes a pretty convincing cast marble. Photograph #10 shows ahead that was cast in clear polyurethane

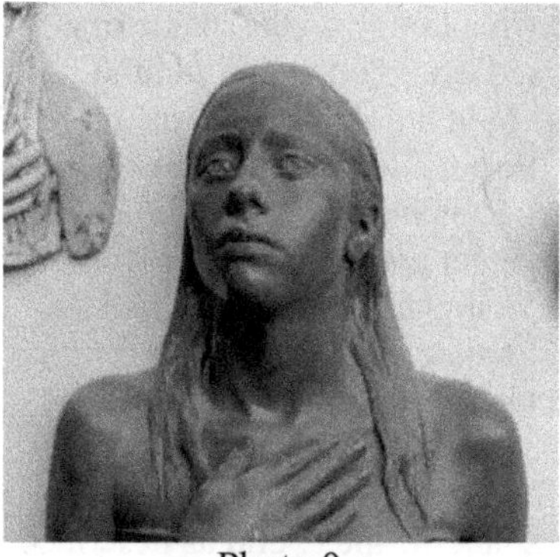
Photo 9

resin. In order to take advantage of the effect that a clear casting can produce, the back is flat. When seen from the back, the image reverses from a negative to a positive. (6)

Open The Eyes.

Some clients will tell you that closed eyes make a life casting look like a death mask. The solution is to open the eyes. (Photograph #9) Notice I didn't say "simply open the eyes." Opening the eyes in a realistic and accurate manner is probably the most difficult procedure in making a professional portrait casting. In my life casting workshops, I always give each person a casting of closed eyes and ask them to attempt to open one. Almost always the person, even some very experienced sculptors, have

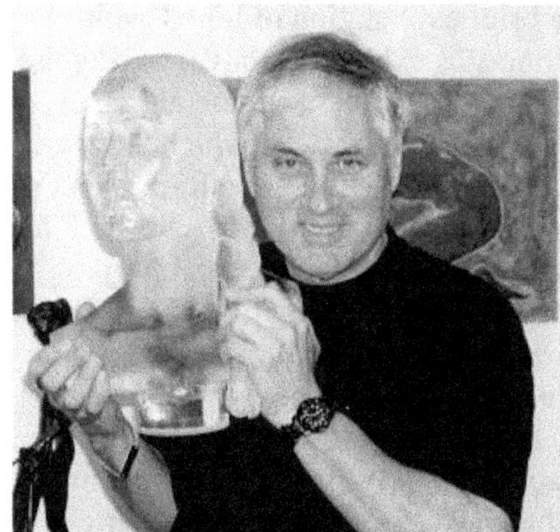
Photo 10

Photo 6*: Dancer with head turned sideways to show hair in traditional bun. Leotard and overall position also show that she is a dancer. Material - FMG, MP, CAP.*

Photo 7*: Head in the round. Material - FMG, MP, CAP.*

Photo 8*: Nine year old twins cast together. Material - FMG, MP, CAP.*

Photo 9*: Face with eyes open. Material - FMG, MP, CAP.*

Photo 10*: Free standing head. Material - clear urethane.*

drawn a line from the inside of a closed eyelid up and out in the approximate shape of an open eyelid to the outside corner of the closed eye. Then he or she will scrape off the upper eyelid. It doesn't work. In the first place, I had presented an impossible task. In order to accurately open an eye, the model must be present for reference; eyes differ considerably. Secondly, scraping off the eyelid as described above does not accurately open the eye. Thirdly, material must be added as well as taken away because the area around the eye changes slightly when the eye is opened.

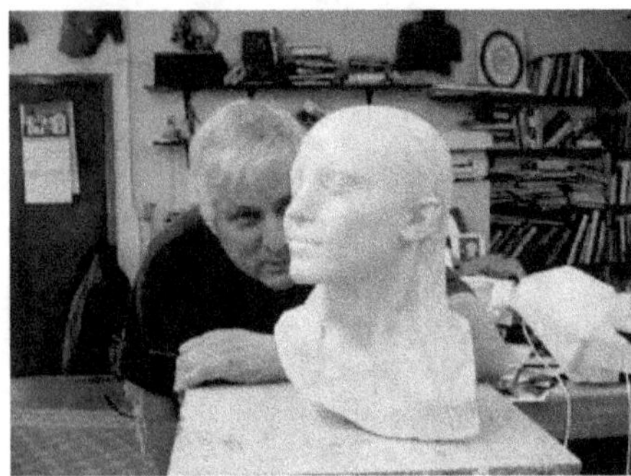

Photo 11

While it is beyond the scope of this article to provide adequate instructions for opening eyes, here is a brief explanation of how I do it. Since, as explained above, I make the original positive from the alginate mold in a soft plaster which is easy to work, I allow it to dry out for about a week so that wax or clay will stick to it. Then I have the model return to my studio and using him or her for reference, carve and fill in as necessary to accurately open one eye. This will take at least an hour. So as not to inconvenience the model more than necessary, I open the other eye after the model has left. While getting the first eve correct takes some practice, making the second a mirror image is just as challenging. I have yet to come across any really good instructions on opening the eyes of life castings. Since this is really sculpting and not casting, I would encourage anyone who wants to perfect the technique to study any of the better books for sculpting the head. (7) It is my intention, however to cover this subject in detail in a series of future articles.

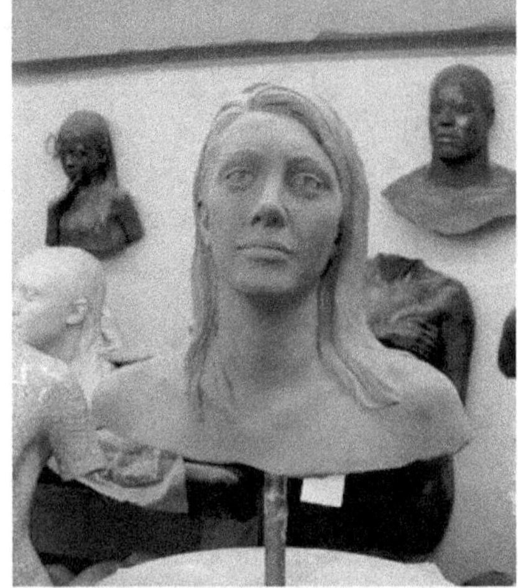

Photo 12

4. Be Creative.

Be open to something different. I usually ask my clients how they would like to be "captured in time forever." While most rely on my judgment, occasionally someone comes up with an interesting idea. Recently, a young girl, 13 years old, wanted to be cast as a ballet dancer. Wearing a leotard got us about half way there. But to really look right, she needed her hair in a bun. Since we were planning on making her into a wall hanging rather than in the round, her head would have to be turned almost completely to the side for the bun to be visible. She had hair well below her shoulders and, at first, I was reluctant to not include it hanging down. But she was right, the finished mask really looked good (Photograph #6) compliments of nine year old brother and sister twins (Photograph #8). Doing two at once is also more complicated and I recommend having at least two assistants. (9)

Photograph # 13 is of a profile of a Native American young lady with her hair flying behind her as if running. In her hair is a wolf. To make this, I cut a mask in half and sculpted in the hair and the wolf. This is an example of taking a life casting and turning it into a piece of art with possible appeal beyond just a portrait.

Most portrait photographs only have meaning to the subject and family. I tell my clients that I intend to make them into nieces of art. My goal is that when someone comes into his/her home and sees the casting, his first thought is, "Great artwork!" and not, "Is that you?" If you can accomplish this, not only will you get greater satisfaction but your work will be more marketable. My next article in this series will show some different and, I hope, exciting things that can be done with torso castings.

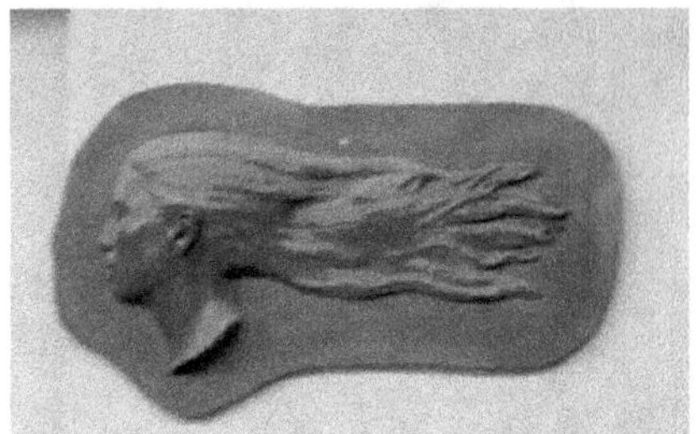

Photo 13

Information referenced here and except as noted are from previous editions of *Sculpture Journal* and written by yours truly:

1) "Secondary Molds in Life Casting," November and December 2004.
2) "Casting Perfect Ears," May 2004.
3) "Real Beginnings for Faux Metal Finishes" September 2003, Mark Fields.
4) "Mixing Forton MG Simplified," July 2003.
5) "Watertrap..." SJ, December 2003.
6) "It's Very Clear," SJ, January 2002.
7) I feel that Portrait Sculpting by Philippe and Charisse Farut, ISBN 9-9755065-0-1, is probably the best reference for opening eyes.
8) "Life Casting a Head in the Round, February and March 2005.
9) "When Two Heads Are Better Than One" June 2004

***Photo 11:** Head in the round with eyes open. Material - polyester resin with crushed limestone, makes a very effective fake marble.*
***Photo 12:** Head in the round in clay which had been considerably reworked. Finished portrait was in FMG, MP, CAP.*
***Photo 13**: Mask of Native American girl cut in half (the mask not the girl!) with sculpted hair and wolf. Material - FMG, MP, CAP.*

David Parvin is a Denver sculptor. He may be reached at 303-321-1074 if you would like to discuss art, fly fishing, flying, or grandchildren.

How Do I Cast Thee For Profit,

Part IV, Bodies

by David E. Parvin, A.L.I.

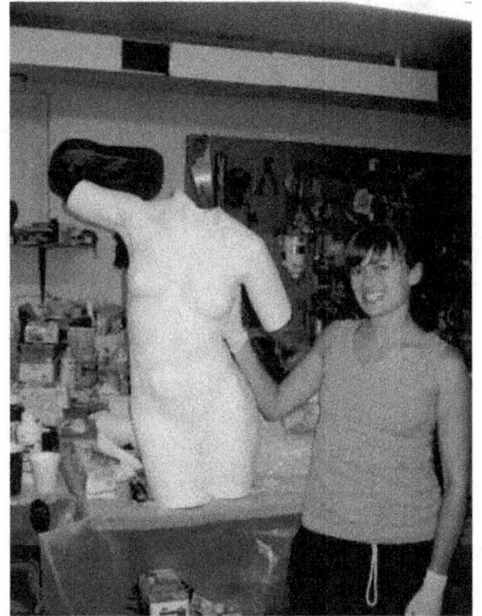
Photo 1

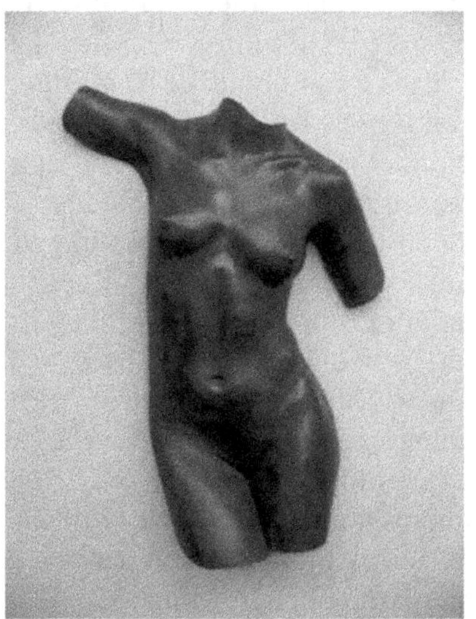
Photo 2

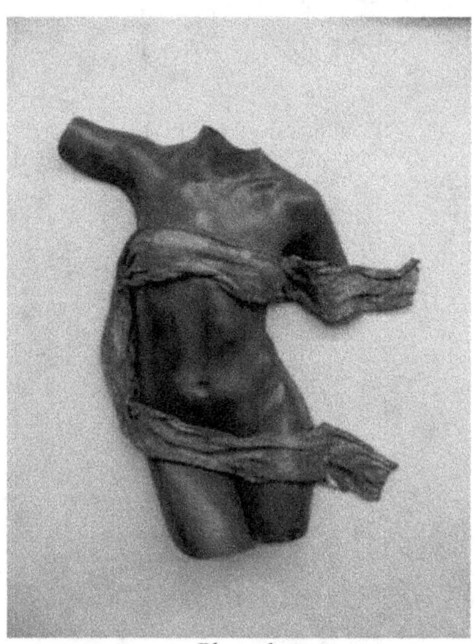
Photo 3

In three recent articles, I discussed casting faces, hands and feet and suggested that in order to distant yourself from the competition, go beyond the "normal" life castings by being more creative in your designs and taking advantage of materials that most life casters have not mastered; in other words, produce a better product. The same strategy can be applied to casting bodies as well. Anyone who has read my articles in this magazine over the last few years may remember that I am concerned about repeating myself and thereby consuming any more of our precious resources than is necessary. So in order to reduce the number of trees required to produce this issue, please review "How Do I Cast You for Profit, Part III, Heads" by yours truly in the May issue of *Sculpture Journal* in which I discussed this strategy in detail.

But bodies open up possibilities that faces, hands and feet are less likely to. This is true with other art disciplines as well. E.g., if one has an individual or family portrait done, even if the result is dynamite, it isn't very likely that anyone other than the subject(s) or family members would want to own it. There are exceptions, of course. In my recent article on faces, which I mentioned above, I showed a face casting of the current Miss Colorado, U.S.A. a copy of which I have had on display in a gallery to encourage people to get casting made of him/herself or a loved one. It just so happened that someone came by the gallery and just had to own my sample. At least to that one person, it wasn't just a portrait but a piece of art fulfilling someone's wishes for a price is something I am quite willing to do. Generally speaking, however, bodies have more potential for being of interest to others besides the model or the model's family, opening up additional marketing venues.

But whatever the intended use of the casting, the strategy for

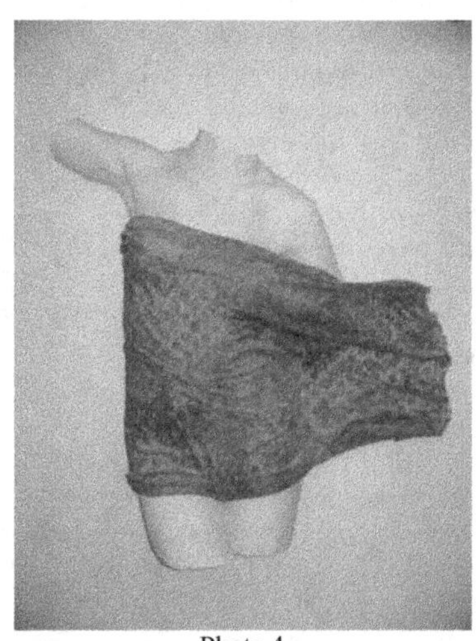
Photo 4

Photo 1: Plaster casting that was made in the alginate mold of the model. The few little imperfections were repaired with clay and/or wax (dark spots) and a silicone rubber secondary mold was made of it.
Photo 2: The same body but cast in the rubber mold in Forton MG (FMG) with copper powder (CP) and a chemically applied patina (CAP).
Photo 3: The same body with a detachable cloth which was dipped into FMG with MP and the same CAP. The cloth is held in place with velcro. This particulater style is, I have found, the most requested for portrait torso castings.
Photo 4: The FMG in this casting has powdered limestone (PL) instead of (CP) to give it the look of marble. The cloth which is also detachable is lace dipped into FMG, with CP and a CAP.

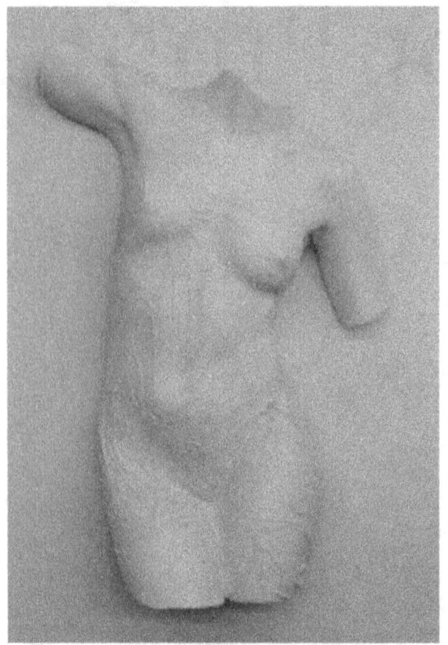
Photo 5

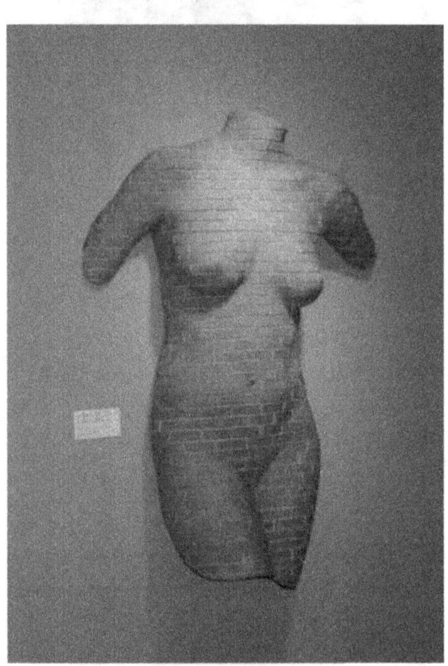
Photo 6

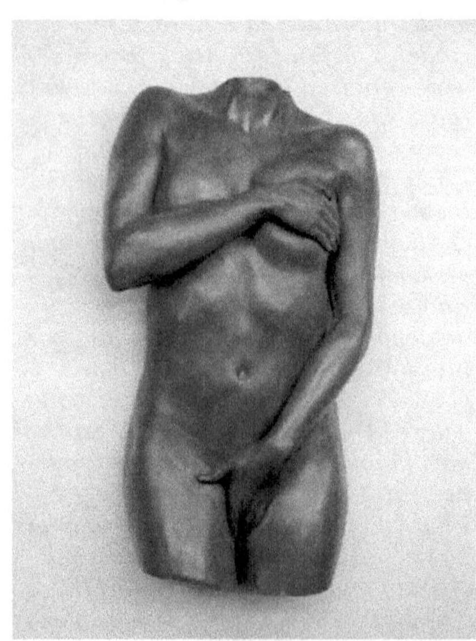
Photo 7

success is the same as for faces, hands and feet: be more creative both in designs and using different materials. The "standard" beyond which one should excel really isn't all that great. Actually there isn't just one "standard" but three. The first and least is a casting made of plaster bandages where the finished product is just the actual plaster bandages. In this case, there is no detail whatsoever, it looks like the outside of a medical cast. Even painting something on it, like one's "feelings" doesn't help much. Number two is hardly any better, using the plaster bandages as a mold for a positive impression using plaster or other doesn't help much. Number two is hardly any better, using the

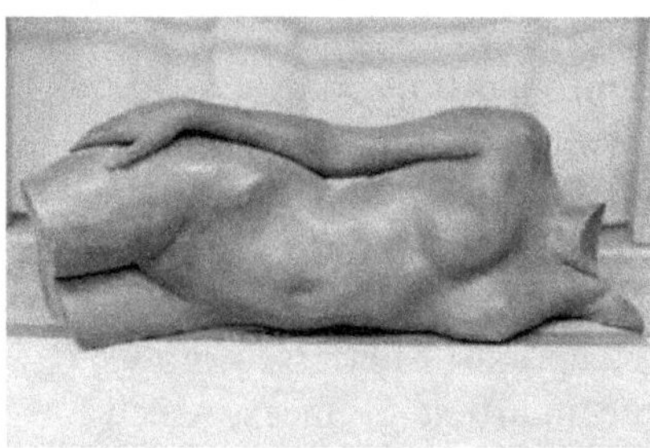
Photo 8

Photo 5: Also cast in FMG with PL. The effect of very thin cloth was achieved by covering the nude plaster torso with plastic from a dry cleaning bag and then another mold was made.
Photo 6: Made by cutting parallel lines in a plaster casting before making the silicone rubber mold. Cast in FMG with a red brick colored dye. The mortar between the bricks is just a painted gray acrylic. This piece is titled "Built Like... "
Photo 7: A little more complicated casting because of the arms and hands. FMG, CP and CAP.
Photo 8: Lying down torso in the round. Note the alginate mold of the model was made in one piece. Cast in FMG with CP and CAP.
Photo 9: Raku fired with flowers and white crackle glaze.
Photo 10: Raku fired with leopard spots and white crackle glaze.
Photo 11: Raku fired torso in the round as if a vase. Glaze is also white crackle.

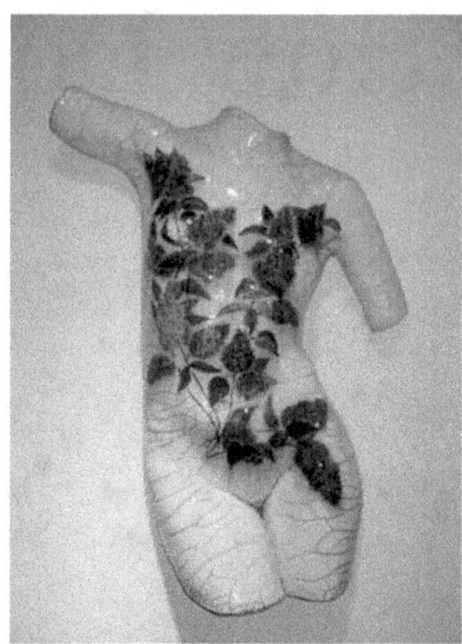
Photo 9

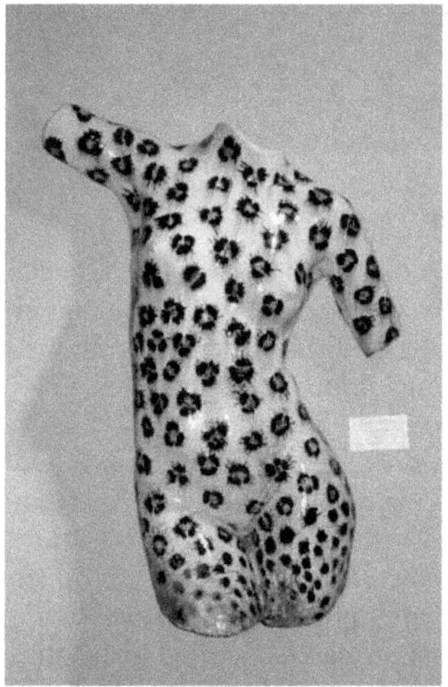
Photo 10

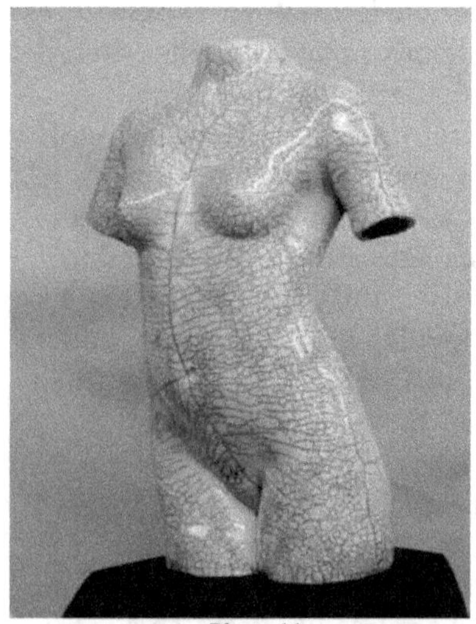
Photo 11

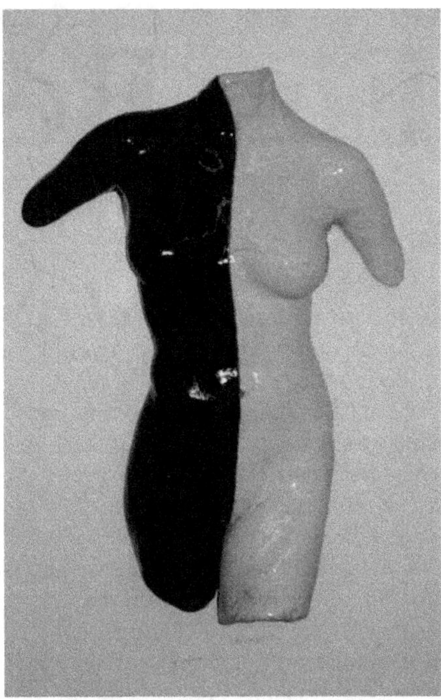

Photo 12: Raku fired with half black and half white crackle glazes.

plaster bandages as a mold for a positive impression using plaster or other gypsum material. All one gets is the basic shape but minimal detail. The third and best of these is a casting made from an alginate mold. Even if only made of plaster, hydrocal, etc., but skillfully done with minimal imperfections, the results can be quite satisfying. Adding a faux patina cranks it up another notch in quality and professionalism. But to really do it right, consider some alternative materials.

Photographs #1 through #5 and #9 and #10 are of the same torso and are intended to emphasize the possibilities that arise if one uses a secondary mold. Any of the plaster or Forton MG examples could have been cast in the alginate mold made of the model. However, since I wanted to use this torso in different ways and an alginate mold usually can be used only once, it was necessary to make a silicone rubber mold of the plaster casting. (See "Secondary Molds in Life Casting," SJ, November and December 2004, yours truly) Also, Raku firing require that the object be cast in pottery clay which will not dry out in an alginate mold. There are other materials that could have been used as well. For example, melted wax can be painted into either rubber or alginate molds and turned into bronze using the lost wax process. The disadvantages are high cost and weight. Also, some foundries might have a problem trying to cast a life-size torso in one piece and reconstructing skin texture where welded together is extremely difficult.

Photographs #9 through #12 are of torso's that were raku fired. In order to do these, the torso's were made by pressing clay into rubber molds. After letting it dry for a about a week, the clay was removed and fired. In some cases, a design was painted on. Next the torsos were covered with various glazing materials. After a second firing, they were placed while still cherry red from the kiln in a barrel containing combustible materials and covered with a lid engulfing the torsos with smoke as they cooled. I have many more examples of really interesting glazes but the black and white format of this publication doesn't do them justice. However, I hope that what I have shown here will inspire others to expand their horizons.

David Parvin is a Denver sculptor.
He may be reached at 303-321-1074 if you would like to discuss art, fly fishing, flying, or grandchildren.

Pricing For Beginners

by David E. Parvin, A.L.I.

One of the questions that I am most often asked is, "How should I price my work?" Obviously this is more often asked by a beginning artist since it is unlikely that an established one could have "made it" without having figured out a reasonable pricing strategy. If one takes a serious look at the art would, he or she might come to the conclusion that there must not be any real objective method to pricing when a blank canvas or a basketball enclosed within a Plexiglas box sells for the price of a luxury automobile. Fortunately there are tow simple methods that a new artist can determine a reasonable price until he or she becomes so famous that the sky is the limit.

The standard formula for a bronze piece is the foundry cost times four becomes the retail price. This, times four figure, is bro ken down as follows: one fourth for production, one fourth for the artist, and one half for the gallery. In other words, if it costs $1,000.00 to have the foundry cast it; the artist would get another $1,000.00 passing it along to a gallery for $2,000.00. The gallery in turn would sell it for $4,000.00.

I don't know how many times. I have heard an artist complain that a particular gallery "takes half my money." Remember, that money isn't the artist's; it's the gallery's. It is very expensive to run a quality gallery and few are making killings in today's art market. One of the galleries with which I deal had up until recently, rent of twenty-eight thousand dollars per month in a seasonal location with about six active months per year. Though the gallery now has a somewhat better deal, it still requires a commitment that I wouldn't want hanging over me. It is important to remember that we artists are the manufactures and we are paid the wholesale price unless we "get lucky" (see below).

The big returns come in as you sell additional pieces of the edition. The one fourth that you received for the first sale certainly doesn't repay you much for your time, materials, model fees, utilities, studio rent, etc. spent while sculpting the piece. However, after several sales, things start looking up. Once you have recouped your start-up costs for a particular creation, pretty much whatever money you receive minus the actual foundry cost is yours. If you have a competent foundry, almost all you will have to do is call up and order another copy of "Ontogeny Recapitulates Phylogeny" and inspect it when it's finished. Your one fourth for a few hours work can be pretty good wages.

But what about a one of a kind piece such as a commission? Now it is possible that you could receive a commission for a piece that would have an appeal to collectors other than the commissioner. If so, treat it as above. But let's say that the work is so specific that there is no likelihood of additional sales. I had a case once when a collector of mine handed me photographs of a dog and of a cat. He explained to me that his beloved pets had both died recently he wanted me to sculpt memorial plaques complete with sculpted has relief's of their likenesses in everlasting bronze, per omnia saecula saeculorem. Amen. What I did was estimate how many hours it would take me to sculpt the plaques and make the molds. I chose an hourly rate that made it at least worthwhile and told the collector that the cost would be so much plus the actual foundry expenses. If he had been a stranger I doubt if I would not have taken the commission since in the same time frame, I could have sculpted something that I could have sold over and over. But because of our previous relationship, I agreed. As it turns out, I now have another commission from this same collector for a life size figure that I am confident that will be a successful edition as well. It appears that my gamble will have paid off.

One of a kind pieces are what portrait artists do all the time. It doesn't matter if the artist is a photographer, a painter, or a sculptor. When he or she finishes a likeness of old Uncle Fred, it is highly unlikely that anyone outside of the family would be interested. In the same way a commission could be so site specific that it will not fit anywhere else. It is also possible that the person commissioning the work specifies that there only be one copy ever made. If I were asked for advise on to how to price it, I would tell the artist, add to any expenses enough so that he or she receives adequate compensation considering all the facts.

Sadly, I suspect that there are too many starving artists, but a better pricing strategy might bring some of them out of the darkness where there is the weeping'; and the gnashing of teeth and into the light where there is the joy of the master.

A few general thoughts on pricing:
1. The ultimate judge of correct pricing is the marketplace. It is essential that the work be appealing if it is to sell at a price derived by either of these two methods. Just because an artist has put in a significant number of hours and run up a big foundry bill doesn't assure that he or she hasn't just made a very expensive "boat anchor." On the other hand, if the pieces fly out of the galleries as quickly as they arrive, one might consider raising the prices.
2. In the real world, the value of a piece of art is based more on how well known the artist is than anything else.
3. It is important that if you sell work directly to collectors that your pieces are the same price as your galleries; do not under price the galleries or you may find yourself gallery-less. There was a time in my long lost youth that "getting lucky" had a very different meaning that now which is selling something for full price!
4. Pricing is very subjective since individual goals differ. On one end of the spectrum, a particular artist may only

want to be compensated enough so that he or she can continue to make art. In the middle is the artist who wants to make a living sufficient so that a normal life is possible. The other extreme would be an artist who wants to get fabulously rich and art is just the chosen path. Try to find a pricing policy that fulfills your personal needs.

5. Pricing isn't all that complicated; just try to take in more than you spend so that the margin will have made the project worthwhile.

I once had "T" shirts made with a silkscreen of one of my bronzes and the words "BE AN ATIS ST, MAKE $10 TO $15 DOLLARS A WEEK." I gave them to other artists and the twelve dozen of them didn't last long. Sadly, I suspect there are too many starving artists but a better pricing strategy might bring some of them out of the darkness where there is the weeping and the gnashing of teeth and into the light where there is the joy of the master. (Once in a while those four years I spent in a seminary has some value after all!)

David Parvin is a Colorado sculptor whose primary subject is the human form in a variety of materials. He also teaches lifecasting workshops held throughout the year. He may be reached at 303-321-1074.

Sculpture Journal Aug. 2005

The good The bad and The ugly

Pitfalls of Dealing with Galleries

By David E. Parvin A.L.I.

The title of this article could have been reversed to emphasize "bad" and "ugly,." But I do not consider galleries to be enemies or even necessary evils. Galleries serve a vital function in the strategy of connecting the art producers with the art collectors; in biological terms, not parasitic but symbiotic. But for the majority of artist/gallery interactions go smoothly and are mutually beneficial which definitely has been my experience. However, in the almost 25 years that I have been a serious, rather than a hobby artist, I have had my fair share of problems which I will relate in hopes of preventing similar occurrences for others.

My first negative experience happened with only the second gallery with which I showed and it was my first dealings with a gallery that was a significant distance from where I resided, about 500 miles. As a new sculptor, I probably would have shown with any gallery which condescended to display my work. After shipping off a small female nude about 15 inches long, I waited anxiously for a call saying it had sold and the check was in the mail. After a while of silence, I called and discovered that the gallery and my statue had disappeared. I was unable to find either or learn the circumstances.

There is an additional caveat if a gallery declares bankruptcy. One of the first things that can hapen is that a bank may confiscate any art in the gallery and sell it to recoup its losses even if the art had been on consignment and not the property of the gallery. I know that this doesn't seem possible and it certainly isn't fair, but as near as I can tell, it can happen especially if the artist doesn't have iron clad documention proving ownership. One gallery owner whom I queried on this subject said that it is best for the artist to retrieve his/her work before bankruptcy. Well that's pretty obvious because one might not know that a particular gallery is about to go under.

> I'm not negative towards galleries, I would have sold far less without them. Just remember that artists/gallery relationships are a two way street.

My second problem was with a gallery that continually gypped me out of part of my share of the sales. When I agreed to show with this gallery, the owner asked me if I would be willing to take 10% less without calling me for authorization if he had a particularly difficult customer who insisted on a deal. Naive as I was, I agreed. The good news was that the gallery consistently sold my work. The bad news was that all my checks were 10% short. Eventually I found out that my work always sold for more than the full list price. The gallery owner simply was cheating me.

I am not against galleries sometimes resorting to a deal to get a sale. I have been in sales myself over the years with a number of different products and know that some people will not buy without a discount. I have heard galleries brag that they will not discount, the price is the price, take it or leave it. But in the real world, it's pretty hard for a sales person to leave money on the table. Imagine a collector interested in a $10,000.00 acquisition that happens to have a 50/50 split., gallery to artist. The collector says that he will take the piece but the $10,000.00 must include any taxes and shipping which in this case would be $500.00. Even ifthe gallery absorbs the $500.00 it will still make $4,500.00 which would be lost once the prospect leaves without the deal. In the real world, which of the following is more likely to happen:
The salesperson politely declined the offer.

1. The salesperson politely declined the offer.
2. The salesperson laughs hysterically and yells, "Ever hear of Fat chance?"
3. The salesperson is so incensed that he/she challenges the customer to a dual to the death to repair the fabric of the space/time continuum that had been torn assunder the customer's insulting offer.
4. The offer is accepted and the $4,500.00 is used to pay the gallery lease and the college tuition for son #1 who is majoring in coeds and beer.

My third problem has been galleries which haven't told me that something has sold so that they can use or float my money as long as possible. More than once, I have paid a surprise visit to a gallery and noticed that something was not on display. The story is always the same, "Oh, it just sold yesterday!" Well, I wasn't born yesterday.

Along the same line, I have been informed of sales but still had to wait for my money. In one case, I was expecting a $12,500.00 check and April 15 was rapidly approaching. I had to find my tax payment elsewhere. In this case, eventually I did get the money plus 10% for the inconvenience which was an unusually good outcome.

While we are on payments, twice galleries have paid me checks that bounced. Both of these were in the $10,000.00 range. It will definitely get your attention when a week after you deposited a large check, some of which you may have already spent, you get a letter from your bank telling you that you are considerably poorer than you thought. In; both of these cases, thechecks cleared on the second try.

I have had the dubious distinction of being a well-stolen artist having had at least five pieces snatched from galleries. The truth is that small pieces are easy to grab, conceal and get out the door. In one case, three well-dressed women entered the gallery and while two distracted the salesperson, the third grabbed a bronze and ran. In another case, a window was broken when the gallery was closed, and one of my acrylic pieces was taken. No matter how careful a gallery is, theft can not be completely eliminated.

I have also had several pieces damaged by galleries. In one case, a glass display case collapsed. In another, someone used an improper cleaning solution and crazed the surface of two acrylics. Also several pieces have been dropped. Accidents will always happen, and just as for theft, that's why galleries would have insurance.

There are some things that one can do for protection. Obviously, choose a gallery carefully. If you are acquainted with any of the other artists represented, for sure contact him or her and ask about the good and the bad. Insist on a contract that spells out responsibilities, notification of sales, discounts if any and payment both percentage and time frame. Keep in close contact not not only for your protection but also because the better a gallery knows you, the more likely it is to represent you aggressively. As a courtesy, it is generally preferable to have an appointment when you stop by. However, an occasional surprise visit is probably a good idea to keep everybody honest. If you have reason for concern, you could have a friend drop in and report back to you. Remember, no one can force you to stay with a particular gallery. As an artist becomes more successful, he/she is in an increasingly advantageous position to control the situation.

As I said at the beginning of this article, I am not negative toward galleries. I would have sold far less without them. I encourage young artists to remember that gallery/artist relationships are a two way street and artists need to be as honest with their galleries as they expect the galleries to be with them.

Something happened in the last two decades that is having a negative impact on galleries. It used to be difficult for a collector to locate a particular artist which, of course, galleries were not eager to divulge. But now it is a snap because of the internet. Even if an artist doesn't have a website, as long as he/she has some success, his or her name will probably pop up in a number of places. This gives the collector a chance to make a deal in two different ways. One is to contact the artist and try to eliminate the middleman. A chance to make more than if the gallery closes the deal just might be pretty tempting to an artist who is struggling. One gallery recently told me that it dropped several artists for just this reason. The second is for a collector to locate another gallery who represents an artist and get into a bidding war. I've been told by several galleries that this happening more and more. While we artists can control the first situation aceing out any of our galleries, the second is a tougher problem especially in a world where most are used to shopping and comparing prices.

In a perfect world, art would be more like other commodities, galleries would buy outright from the artists. As soon as inventories got low, the galleries would reorder. It is largely the consignment system that contributes to the problems listed above. There wouldn't be any question about responsibility if the galleries had already paid for the work. While some artists have been able to demand purchase rather than consignment and a few galleries have insisted on owning what they stock (bless them) most artist's bankroll the galleries' inventories. How we ever got ourselves into this situation doesn't matter nearly as much as the fact that here we are. Alas, we artists somewhere along the line forgot the grandmothers' advice to her teenage granddaughter, "If he gets the milk for free, why would he ever buy the cow?"

David Parvin is a Colorado sculptor whose primary subject is the human form in a variety of materials. He also teaches life casting workshops held throughout the year. He may be reached at 303-321-1074.

Sculpture Journal June 2005

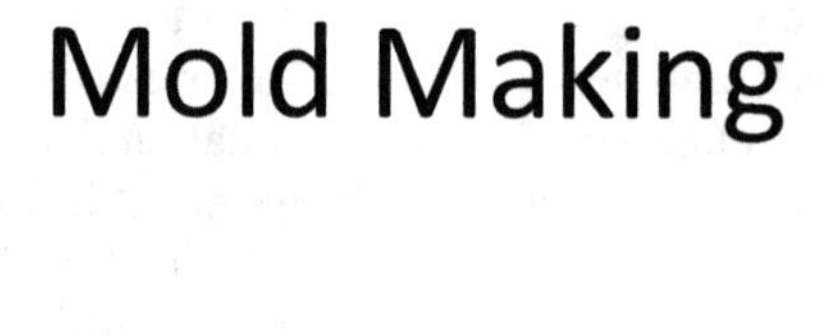

Mold Making

How to Make a Great Mold, Part 1

By David E. Parvin, A.L.I.

Have ten different mold makers each make a mold of the same object and you will get ten molds which vary in design, materials, and function. All might be satisfactory though you likely would be able to rate them from best to worst. This is the first of two articles in which, while I don't claim to have all the answers, I will explain how to make a really great mold.

The absolutely most important requirement for a mold is that it produces perfect reproductions capturing all detail without flaws or noticeable parting lines. There are other considerations such as durability and ease of opening and closing. In addition to filling these requirements, the mold that I will describe will allow one easily to make a new mold if the edition is so large that the first mold wears out.

Just so that we are all on the same page, let me define a few things even though most readers may already know them. First, the object of which the mold is made is not called the original, it is the *model*. Next, the names commonly used for the different types of molds may vary, overlap, or be ambiguous. The two most common types of molds used by sculptors are *block* and *skin*. The simplest of these to construct is the block mold; just surround the model with a box, cup, etc., which is called the *mother mold*, and pour in rubber. After the rubber has set up, remove the mother mold, cut open the rubber, take out the model, and the block mold is finished. Block molds are quick and simple to construct. But while they save time, they usually require more rubber and to some the cost of the rubber may be more important than the cost of labor. Also, the relatively thick rubber may make it difficult to remove delicate castings.

With a skin mold, the rubber is generally much thinner, more like "skin." This is achieved by painting the rubber on the model and constructing a tightly fitting mother mold over the rubber. Or another way is to construct the mother mold

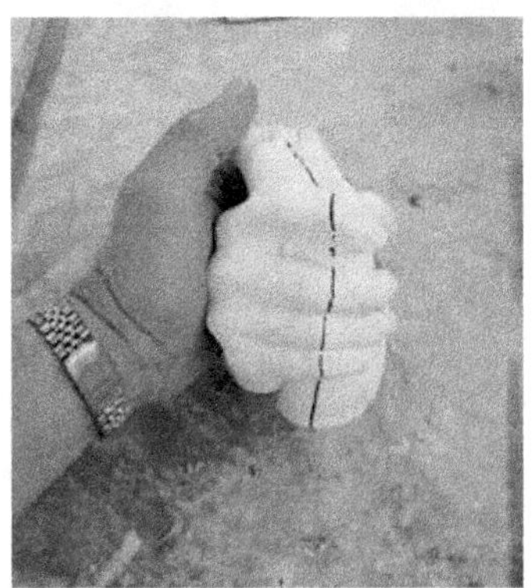

#1. The model, a mother's hand holding her baby's foot.

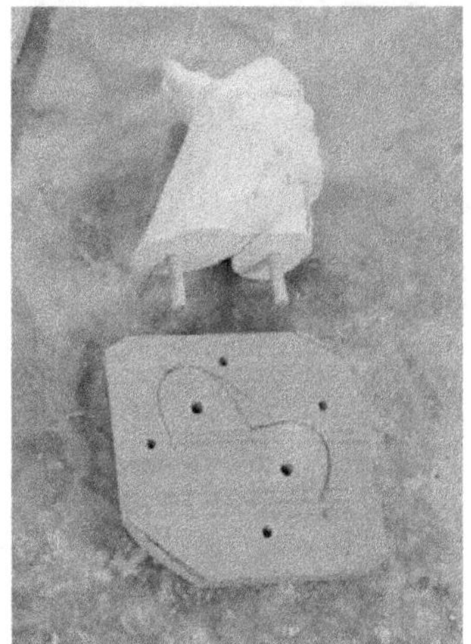

#2. The base with holes to fasten the model and the inserts.

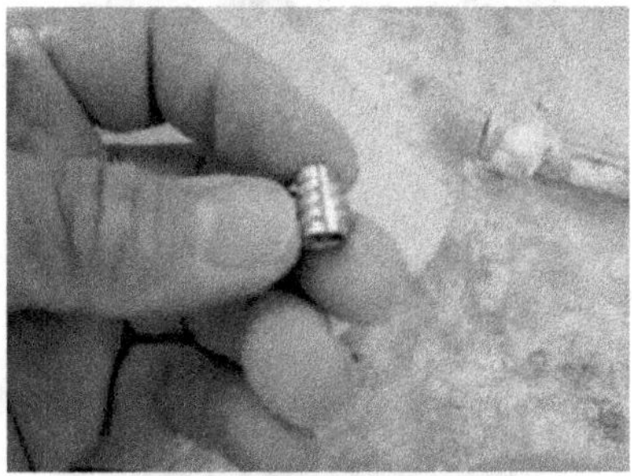

#3. A metal insert.

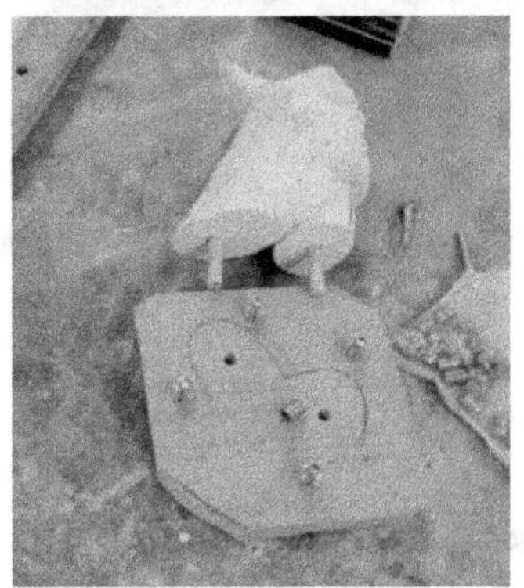

#4. The metal inserts attached to the base.

over the model leaving a narrow gap into which the rubber is poured. Here is where it can get confusing, a block mold is a pour mold while a skin mold may or may not be. Remember Logic 101:
If A = B and B may or may not = C, then

1. A = C.
2. A may or may not = C.
3. It's Tuesday.
4. All of the above.

(For more information on skin and block molds, see "How to Make a Secondary Mold," *SJ,* July 2004, "Secondary Molds in Life Casting, Part II", *SJ,* November and December, 2004, all by D.P. If you can not locate your leather bound archival copies of *Sculpture Journal,* contact Jon, the editor, who will happily e-mail the articles to you. Or, I will gladly do the same.)

In this article, I will describe how to make a really slick skin mold using the pour, not to be confused with "poor" or "pore," method. Since I generally write on life casting, I will mold a mother's hand holding her infant's foot. But, the model could have been anything. And while the hand and foot is relatively small, about 6" tall, I have used this type of mold for models up to several feet in height. For even larger models, life castings or not, I would probably paint on the rubber. It's going to seem that this process is pretty complicated with many little steps, and this is true. However, there are only six major steps:

1. Attaching the model to the base.
2. Covering the model with clay.
3. Building the mother mold.
4. Pouring in the rubber.
5. Finishing the mold.
6. Using the mold.

If as you read along something doesn't make any sense, I would suggest that you keep reading and a few steps later it may become clear.

Attaching the Mold to the Base

Photograph #1 shows the plaster model. Note the line drawn on the model which will serve as a guide to insure that when I cut open the mold, the seam will be where I have determined that it will be the least obvious.

Photograph #2 shows the base to which the model will be attached while the mold is constructed. I have drilled two 5/16" holes into the model and inserted dowels that are long enough to attach the model about 1/2" above the base. This spacing will allow for a small reservoir to be part of the mold to hold excess casting material. (If this doesn't make any sense, it will later.) The other four holes, which are 1/4" are for attaching what I am holding in photograph #3, a 1/4" threaded metal insert. While made for wood working, these inserts are really useful in mold making. In photograph #4, four inserts have been attached to the base by 1X1/2" bolts through the wood. Make sure that the bolts are long enough to reach the top of the inserts covering all the threads. To determine where the holes for the inserts should be, trace around the model and drill the holes at least 1/2" out from the edge of the model. Drill enough holes for at least two inserts for each section of the mother mold. Generally, two sections will suffice, however, very complicated shapes may require more.

In photograph #5, I have added clay "donuts" which are simply taking up the space that will be the reservoirs. While the reservoirs could be cut out of the rubber later, using the donuts is easier and they also prevent wobble when the model is attached as in photo #6. A little glue on the dowels is also helpful.

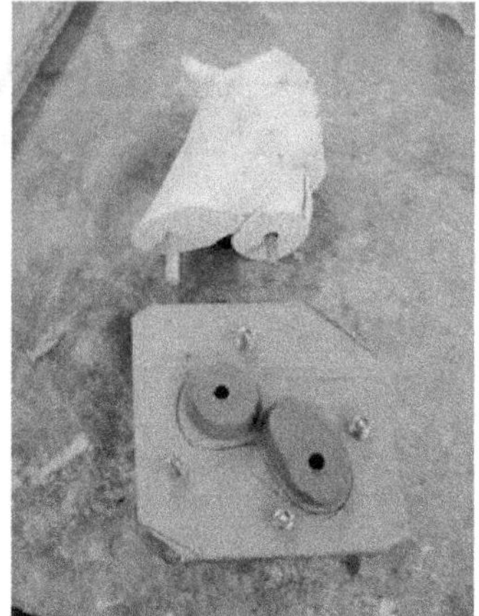
#5. The clay "donuts."

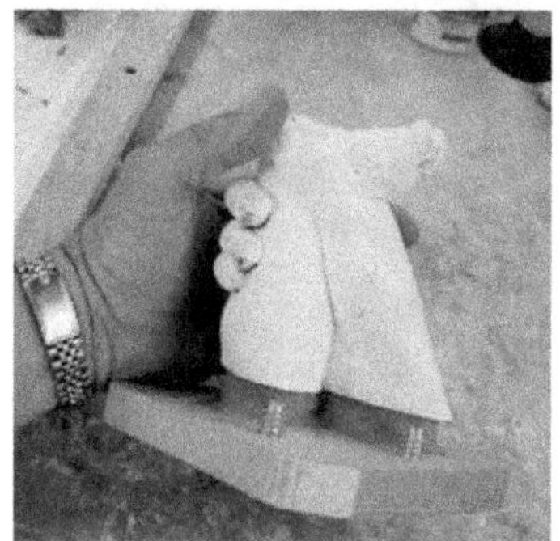
#6. The clay "donuts" in place between the base and the model.

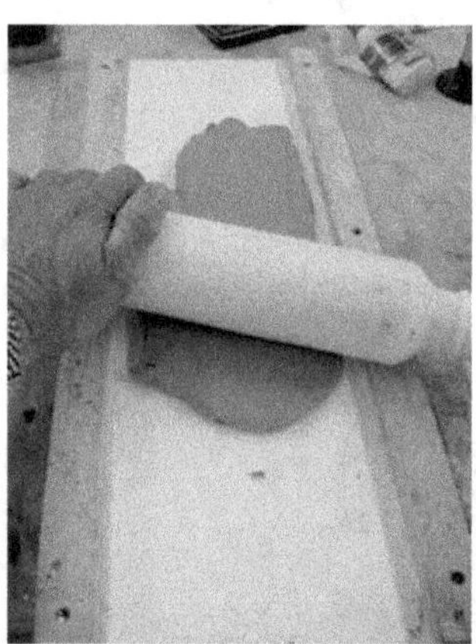
#7. Rolling out the clay.

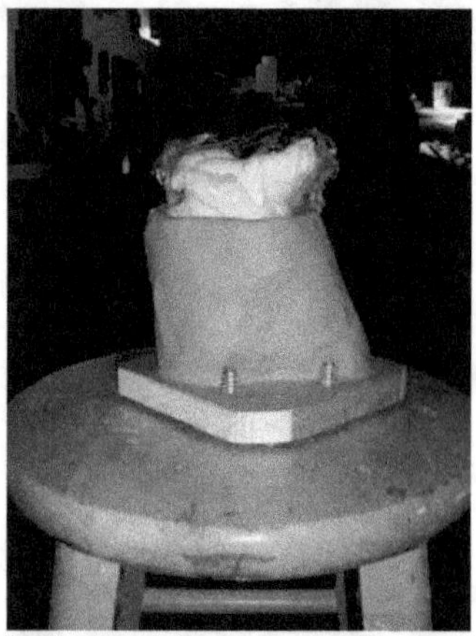
#8. The model protected with plastic wrap and partially covered in clay.

Covering the Model With Clay

In order to have uniformly thick rubber in the mold, the clay, obviously, should be a constant thickness. The easiest way to get uniformly thick clay is to use what I call "The Funky Method" named after a very fine ceramic and raku artist named Beth Funk who taught this to me. Attach a piece of 3/16" molding to each side of a board and use something round such as a piece of PVC pipe or a rolling pin as I am doing in photograph #7 to flatten the clay. There is no set rule as to how thick the clay (and therefore the rubber) has to be, anywhere from 1/8" to 1/2" will suffice. But I have found that it can be difficult to apply the clay without getting some thin places. Also, the model may shift slightly inside the mother mold when it's reattached after removing the clay. Therefore, I would suggest that one use clay at least 3/16" until she/he has made a few molds. For smaller models such as this one, I cut the clay into strips about two inches wide. Warming the clay will make the rolling, cutting, and applying easier. It is important that the clay doesn't stick to the model. So before applying the clay, cover the model with plastic wrap. See photograph #8. In this case, the model is plaster and shaping the clay around it isn't going to damage it. However, if the model is fragile, applying the clay must be done very carefully or, perhaps, a paint-on mold might be more appropriate. In photograph #9, the model has been completely covered.

Now it is time to give the clay covered model a "Mohawk." Because the rubber mold will have to be cut open somewhere to remove the model and the subsequent castings, every effort must be made to have the sides of the cut fit back together as perfectly as possible to minimize any seam on the castings. The clay must be made thick enough along where the intended cut is to go so that the rubber that replaces the clay will have enough depth so that when cut apart, the two cut surfaces will fit or key together exactly. Rubber 3/8" thick isn't enough. Also, the seam will have to be long enough to allow the mold to open sufficiently for the removal of the contents. And the Mohawk must also be wide enough to allow for making a zigzag cut without penetrating the sides. In photograph #10, I am fitting a strip of clay up one side and across the top of the clay covered model. This clay strip is about 1&1/2" thick and at least 1/2' wide. In photograph #11, eight things have been done since photograph #10. I will describe them in the chronological order.

The first was the attachment of the Mohawk by just filling the gap with clay and smoothing. Notice step

#2, the three clay bumps about four inches apart half way out on the Mohawk. These were made by adding pieces of clay and shaping as was step #3, the ridge on the outer edge of the Mohawk that goes the full length. The purpose of the bumps and the ridge was to insure that the Mohawk in which the seam will be cut fits exactly into the mother mold. Similar bumps and ridge were added to the other side of the Mohawk.

Since the mother mold must separate into two halves along the clay strip, the next step,#4, was to provide a barrier or shim so that first one side and then the other could be constructed without the two sticking together. Photograph #12 shows an ideal material to accomplish this, a printer's plate which is made of very thin metal, so thin that it can be cut easily with scissors. These plates are a by product of the printing process and usually can be gotten from any printing shop just for the asking. The shim as shown was made in two parts, the straight piece on the left side and the curved one on the right coming up over the top. Shaping the pieces of the shim is very simple. Just put the printer's plate behind the clay and trace it from the lower right corner up over the top to the end of the Mohawk. Cut along the line and fit the shaped printer's plate along the center of the Mohawk. Trim the shim until the fit is pretty close. Cut the shim from the plate so that it is about two inches wide. Press the shim about 1/4" into the center of the clay Mohawk as in photograph #11 which should anchor it securely. Be careful, you can easily cut yourself with the printer's plate material. Repeat for the vertical shim on the left side. Where the two pieces of metal meet and overlap slightly at the upper left corner, they can be joined with epoxy, super glue, etc. A paper clip is a simple way to hold them until the glue dries.

What I have done up to this point is made it possible for the two sides of the mother mold to be constructed separately so that they will come apart. I have also assured that the rubber part of the mold will fit precisely into the mother mold. What we now must do is assure that the two halves of the mother mold

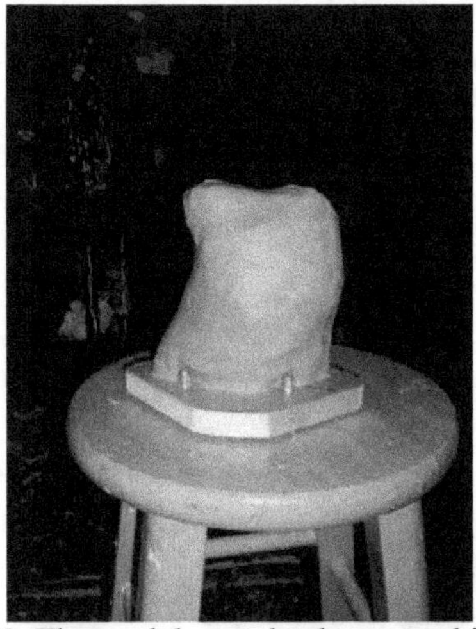

#9. The model completely covered in clay.

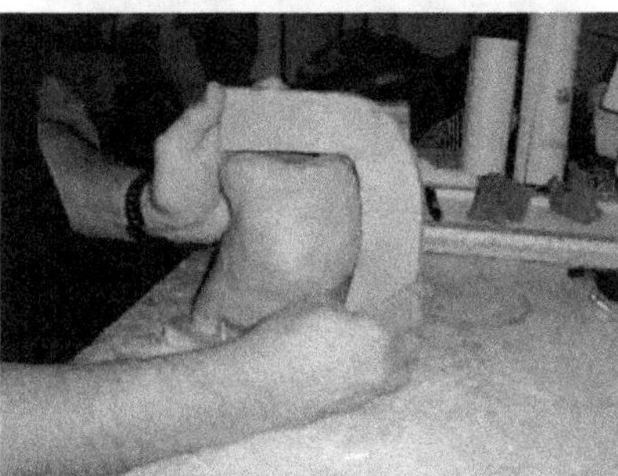

#10. The clay that when attached will be the Mohawk or the place for the seam in the rubber.

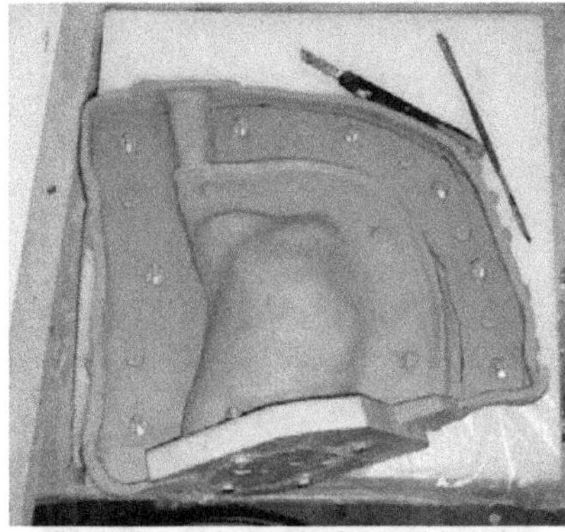

#11. One side ready for making the mother mold.

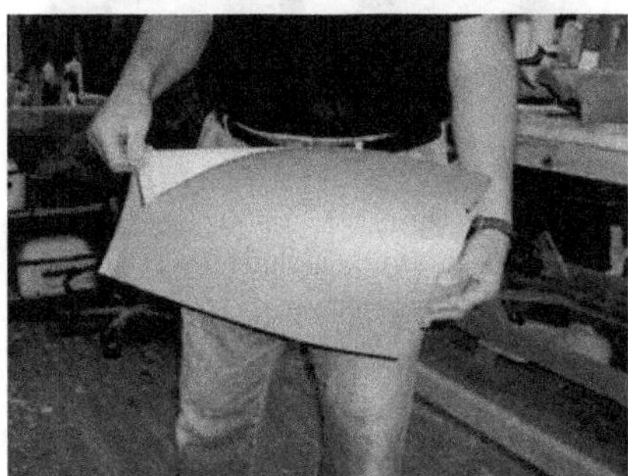

#12. A printer's plate that makes excellent shims.

lock precisely in place. In step #5, some more threaded metal inserts were glued along the centerline of the shim. Notice that the ones along the Mohawk are closer together than the ones on the left side. This is because the rubber will only be cut apart at the Mohawk and the fit must be more precise there. Notice also that the holes in the metal inserts have been plugged with clay. This to prevent the mother mold material from getting inside and clogging the threads. The bumps, step #6, between the inserts are self sticking clear plastic dots made by 3M and can be purchased anywhere that picture framing materials are sold. Their purpose is to align the two parts of the mother mold so that the bolts can be inserted easily to fasten the two sided together.

Once the mother mold is finished and the clay has been removed, we will need a way to pour in the rubber. Notice the clay extending from the top of the Mohawk to the outer edge of the shim; this will be a built in funnel for the rubber. Half will be in each side of the mother mold. This funnel needs be only about an inch in diameter.

The eighth and last thing shown in photograph #11 is the narrow piece of clay that goes all around the shim. This is just a wall about 1/2" tall which will contain the liquid material for the mother mold.

While I have only covered two of the six major steps in making a really great mold, we are over half way through, the rest is both easier and simpler. As I have mentioned earlier, if you are a little confused, patience, Grasshopper, it will all become clear in next months article.

David Parvin is a Denver sculptor. He may be reached at 303-321-1074 if you would like to discuss art, fly fishing, flying, or grandchildren.

Great Mold Part II

David E. Parvin, A.L.I.

When I began writing on this subject, I thought that it would take two articles. But as it turns out, it will take three. It isn't that it is so difficult but rather that there are many small steps that need to be explained. While this may seem unnecessarily complicated and lengthy, the resulting flawless castings will make it all worthwhile. In "Great Mold Part I," *SJ*, Nov. 2006, I explained attaching the model to the base, covering the model with clay, and was almost finished with building the mother mold. In this article, I will complete the mother mold. Next month, I will pour in the rubber, finish the mold, and put the mold to use.

Building the Mother Mold

At the end of last month's article, I was almost ready to spread on what would become one side of the mother mold. The only thing remaining was to apply a mold release. A great release is a solution of 15 parts by weight of petroleum jelly to 100 parts naphtha. The petroleum jelly doesn't dissolve very quickly and I would suggest mixing the two at least a day before needed. Applied with a soft paint brush, the naphtha will quickie dissolve leaving a thin, even layer of petroleum jelly. This will not only facilitate separating this first side of the mother mold from the clay and shim but will also smooth out the clay. I learned of this release solution from Michael Sisbarro who is another contributing writer to *Sculpture Journal* and have found it to be an excellent all around release agent and I always keep some made up.

The next thing was to decide on a material for the mother mold and there are lots of choices such as plaster, FGR-95 Hydrocal, polyester and polyurethane resins, fiber glass, epoxy, and Forton MG. I prefer the latter because Forton MG is easy to use, odorless, water soluble, inexpensive, and very strong allowing for thin molds that are light in weight. (For more information on Forton MG, see my article, "Mixing Forton MG Simplified," *SJ,* July 2003.) But applying the material over the clay is done approximately the same way regardless of which is used. Since all of these materials are liquid, all are applied in layers. But Forton MG is especially ideal for layered applications. Other materials require you to mix a batch, apply it, let it thicken, then mix another batch and repeat until you have a sufficient thickness. Forton MG is so much easier because you can mix the entire amount that you think you will need, dump just enough for one layer into a separate container, add an accelerant which will cause just the separated amount to set up quickly, apply, and then repeat with the next layer. The accelerant is a solution of 10 parts aluminum sulfate to 100 parts water. Aluminum sulfate is a fertilizer available anywhere that sells gardening supplies, and, compared to many of the products that we artists use, is cheap. A tablespoon of accelerant to a pint of Forton MG will cause it to solidify in about 10 minutes. The amount of isn't critical, just be aware that the more you use, the faster the reaction. In photograph #13, I am painting a coat of plain Forton MG over the clay and the metal shim. Next, not shown, two thin coats containing chopped fiberglass fibers were added. In photograph #14 assistant Morgan is finishing up with a final layer of plain Forton MG to give the outside of the mold a smooth finish. As soon as the last layer of Forton MG has set up, give it about 30 minutes, it is time to repeat the process for the other side.

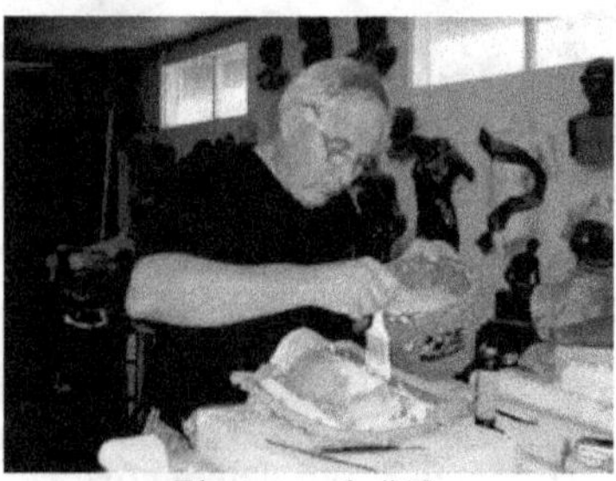
Photograph #13

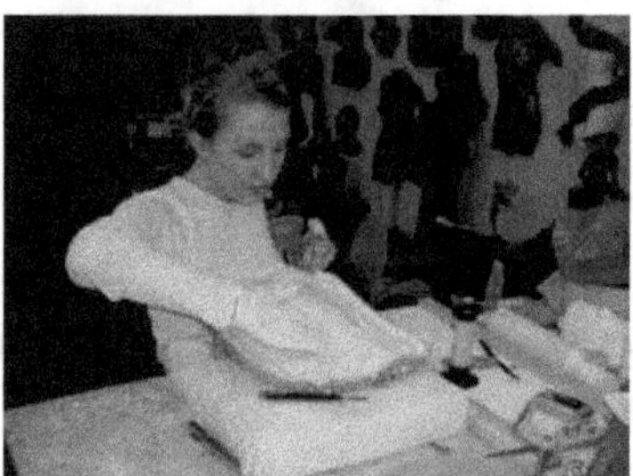
Photograph #14

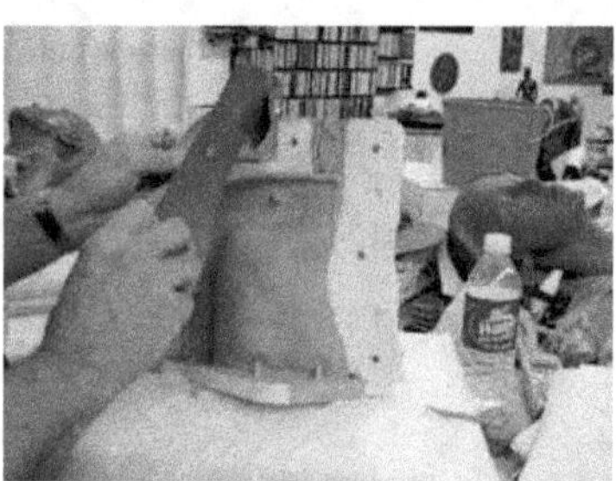
Photograph #15

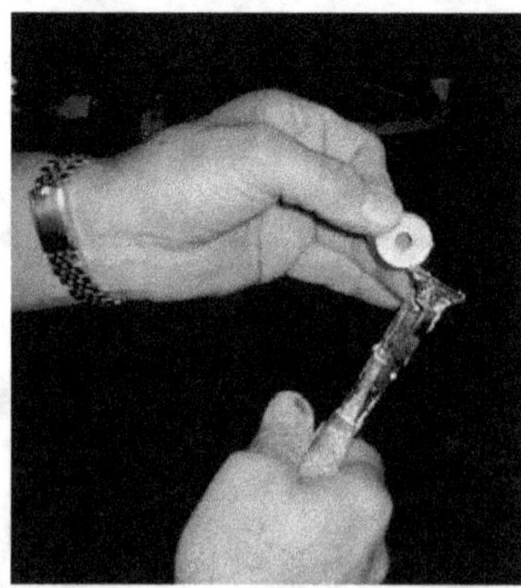
Photograph #16

The thickness of the mother mold will depend on what it is made of. With most of the materials mentioned above, including Forton MG but not plaster, no more than 1/4 inch (about 1/2 cm.) is sufficient. Be sure to bury the threaded metal inserts up to their tops. Don't worry if the tops get covered, the clay that was pushed into the ends should keep the threads clean.

In photograph #15, I am removing the metal shim. Notice the ends of the threaded metal inserts and the small indentations from the plastic "feet." These indentations will assure that the two sides of the mold align perfectly so that the bolts will fit easily and properly into the inserts. Also notice that the clay dam that had surrounded the metal shim to contain the liquid Forton MG has been removed and will have to be reinstalled for the same purpose for side number two.

The next step is a small thing and optional but it makes taking the mold apart and assembling it more convenient. I'm going to imbed fender washers into the second side of the mold which will help distribute the pressure of the tightened bolts to the Forton MG and also prevent the washers from falling off whenever the mold is disassembled. In photograph #16, I am crimping or roughing up the edges of a washer with a pair of side cutters so that the Forton MG will more securely anchor it in place. In photograph # 17, I have taken the bolts that will hold the two sides of the mother mold and stood them vertically, heads down. With a drop of super glue, I am attaching the washers to the bolts. (Keep reading, this will make sense in a minute.)

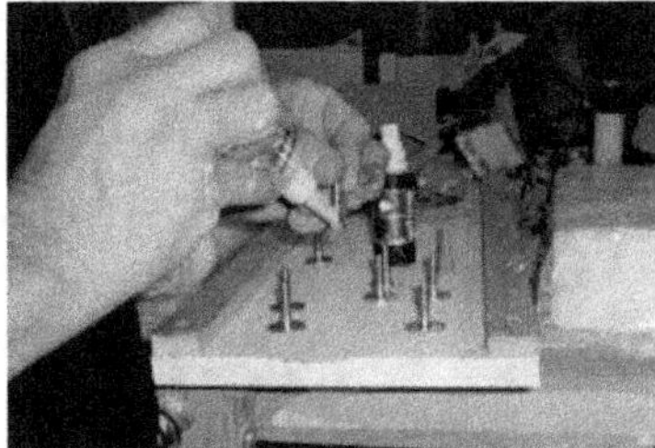
Photograph #17

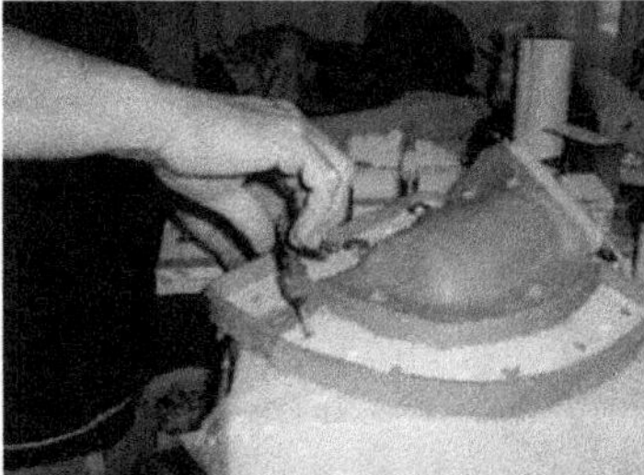
Photograph #18

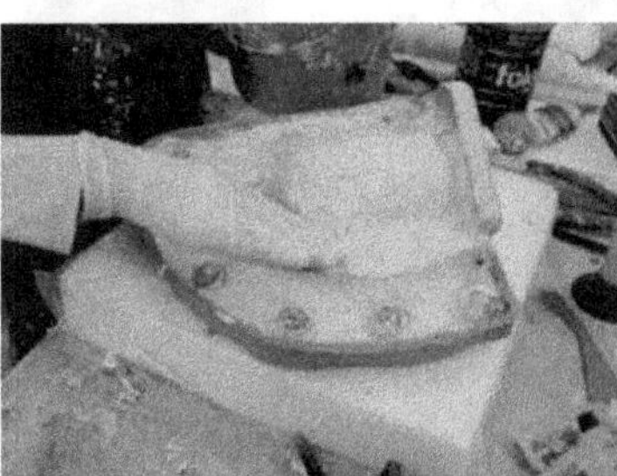
Photograph #19

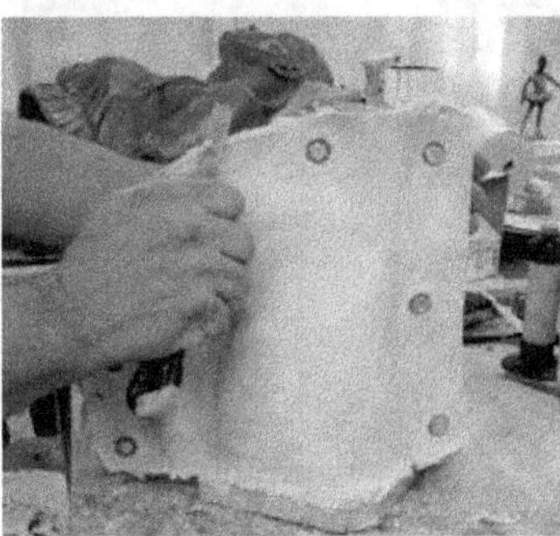
Photograph #20

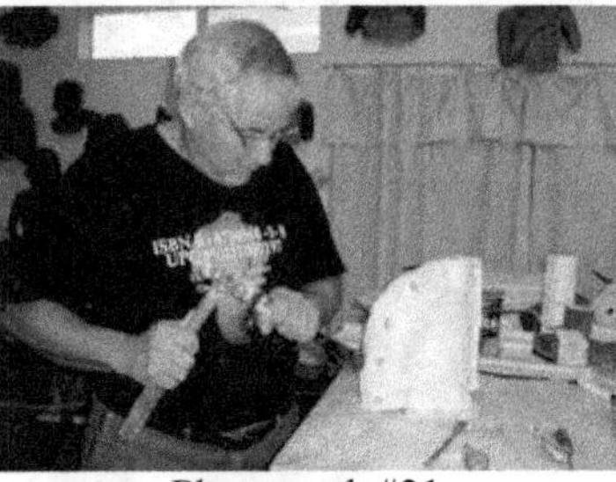
Photograph #21

There are five things to note in photograph #18. First, notice that two of the bolts and washers have been inserted into the threaded inserts. The washers were screwed down only within about 1/4 inch (1/2 cm) of the first side of the mother mold where they stay suspended in place because of the glue. This will allow for the subsequent Forton MG to go under the washers as well as over their edges to anchor them in place and prevent them from falling off every time the mold is taken apart. Next, if some Forton MG did manage to get inside and clog up the treads of any of the inserts, a 1/4X20 tap, as I am demonstrating, will clean out any Forton MG and/or clay. In order to position the washers at the right height, the bolts may need to extend beyond the outside edge of the metal inserts which may have been covered with a layer of Forton MG. Screwing in a bolt or a tap should break right through as long as the Forton MG is thin. If, however, you inadvertently covered an insert with a thick layer of Forton MG, drill through the center of the insert out through the Forton MG with a 13/64 inch drill bit prior to inserting a bolt or tap. Do not use a 1/4 inch bit since it would destroy the threads.

Third, the clay that is next to the tap in my hand will be the entry channel for the rubber once both sides of the mother mold are completed and the clay has been removed. Add more clay here so that this side looks as it did for the first side in photograph #11 in last month's article. The eventual channel should be no less than 3/4 inch (2 cms) in diameter.

Fourth, as you can see, I have rebuilt the clay dam that goes around the outside of the mold. Just as for side one, the dam will contain the liquid Forton MG as the layers are applied.

One of the really great properties of Forton MG is that, unlike other gypsum products, new material added to old (set up) bonds beautifully. But, since it is essential that the new side of the mother mold not stick to the first, a release is necessary. I applied the naphtha nd petroleum jelly solution as explained above. However, as added insurance, I spread a little more petroleum jelly on the Forton MG.

In photograph #19, one of my assistants is spreading on the second layer of Forton MG which, as will the third layer, contains shredded fiberglass. The first layer was plain Forton MG to assure a smooth surface on the inside of the mother mold. The fourth and final layer also will be plain for a smooth outside surface. If you look carefully, you can see that the heads of the bolts have been surrounded with small rings of clay. These rings make it easy to bury the washers without locking in the bolts. Once the Forton MG has set up, the clay can be easily scraped out exposing the sides of the bolt heads for easy fitting of a socket or nut driver. Also important is that the two threaded metal inserts that were bolted to the wood base are being completely covered.

Photograph #20 shows the completed second side of the mother mold. I had just removed the clay dam and was trimming any rough edges with a box cutter. Another reason I like Forton MG is that on the same day that it is cast, it can be easily worked with a knife. Let it cure for a couple of days, however, and it is so hard that one would need a grinder, file, or belt sander.

Once the bolts have been removed (don't forget the four through the wooden base), with just a little gentle encouragement, the two sides of the mother mold should separate as in photographs #21 and #22. It is important that the model remain in a fixed position relative to the base and mother mold to insure that the rubber will be the desired thickness so do not disconnect the model from the base. Please notice that I am wearing a "T" shirt that advertises the ISBN number of my instructional video on casting the female torso; not quite subliminal but shameless none the less.

Removing the clay shouldn't be difficult. If a little scraping is necessary, use something that will not scratch the inside of the mother mold since the Forton MG is still new. A plastic spoon works well. Collect the removed clay; its weight will provide away of estimating how much rubber is required. More on this below. The easiest way to get the last of the clay out is to use a brush with hot water and detergent. In photograph #23, my assistant, Audra, is using some 220 grit sandpaper to make the inside of the clean mother mold even smoother. (Audra has a rather board look on her face as if reassuring herself that she is still better off than working in fast food. The other possibility is that she is ignoring fellow sculptor Eliott Summons who is behind her watching her through a glass ball.)

Before reattaching the sides of the mother mold to the base and each other, coat both the model and the insides of the each half of the mother mold with the naphtha and petroleum jelly or some other mold release of your choice. A mold release is **essential** if urethane rubber is used since urethane rubbers bond to almost anything. For silicones, a release isn't an absolute requirement but will allow the mold to be more easily disassembled after the rubber has cured. More on rubbers later. To insure that the rubber doesn't leak out the seams of the mother mold, spread a little additional petroleum jelly on the inside of the flanges and where the mother mold touches the base.

Photograph #24 shows the mother mold after the clay was removed and one side has been reattached to the base. In the next photograph, #25, I have positioned the other half of the mother mold, secured it to the base with two bolts, and am bolting the two halves together. The next step will be to pour in the rubber. But first there are two questions that need answered, which rubber and how much. Those questions along with the final simple (I promise) steps in finishing up I'll cover next month.

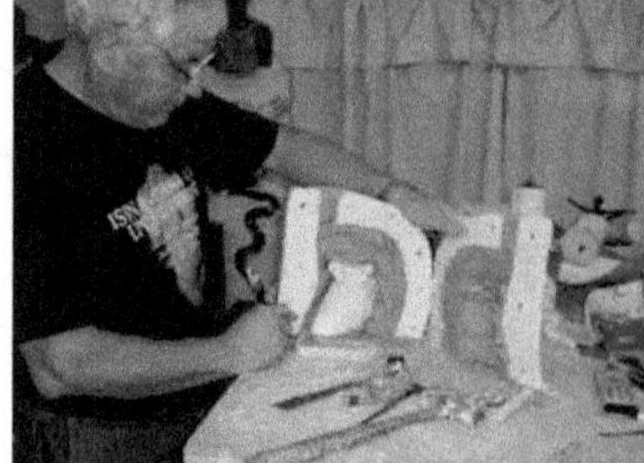

Photograph #22

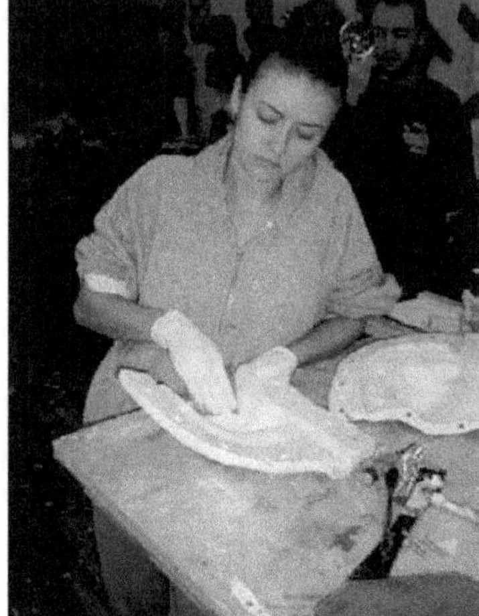

Photograph #23

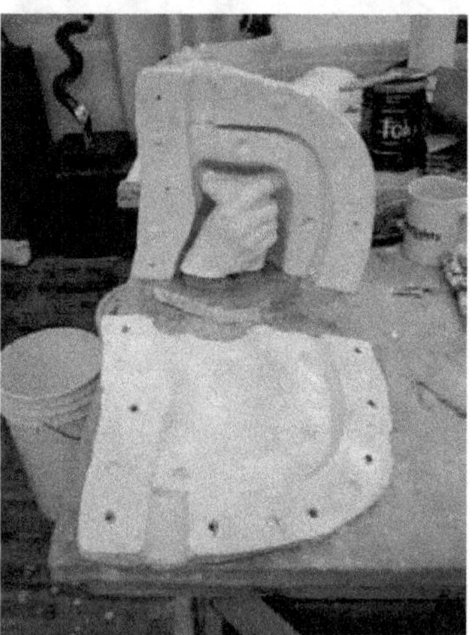

Photograph #24

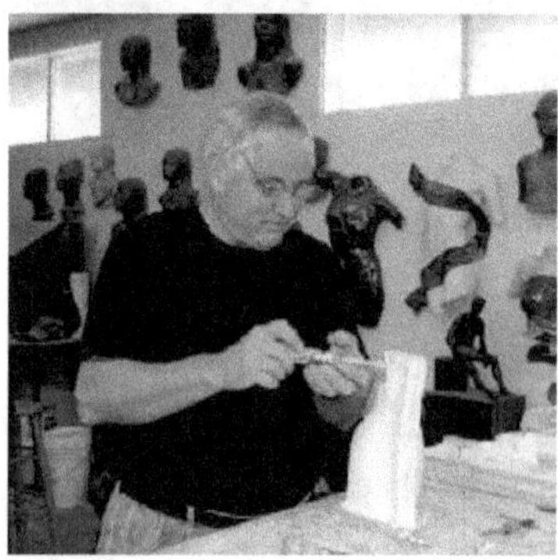

Photograph #25

David Parvin is a Denver sculptor. He may be reached at 303-321-1074 if you would like to discuss art, fly fishing, flying, or grandchildren.

Great Mold Part III

David E. Parvin, A.L.I.

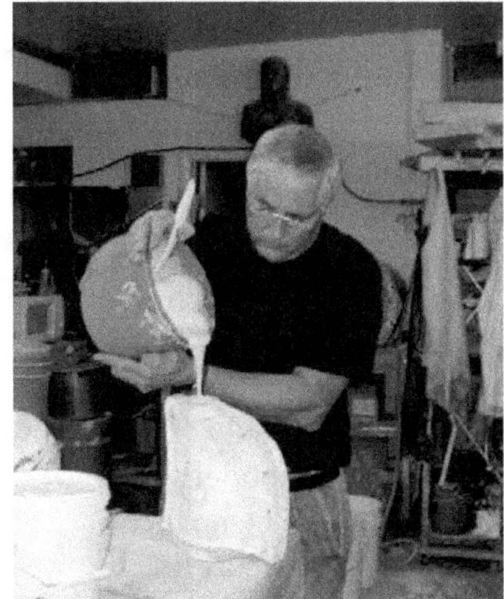

Photograph #26

At the end of last month's article, I was ready to pour in the rubber and finish a really great mold. My next step was to determine how much rubber would be required and then choose which rubber to use.

Pouring in the Rubber

What I needed to do was to fill the space with rubber that had been occupied by clay. In other words, if I had known the volume of the clay, all I would have needed was an equal volume of rubber. It just so happens that the specific gravity of most types of rubber is very close to that of water or one cubic centimeter weighs one gram. But rather than playing Archimedes and placing the clay in water and measuring its displacement or filling the mold with water, there was an easier way. I used "Dave's Law" that states, "The amount of rubber required to fill the space between a mother mold and a model is approximately equal to 70% of the clay by weight." In this case, the clay weighed 1,680 grams so about 1176 of rubber was estimated. This was only a close guess because the model had been wrapped in plastic preventing the clay from fitting snugly and filling every nook and cranny. In fact, I came out a little short, the actual amount of rubber needed was 1215 grams or two pounds and eleven ounces. I just mixed and added a little more. Since rubber is not inexpensive, having a pretty good idea of the amount needed helps prevent mixing too much and wasting it.

As to which rubber, there are two types most used by mold makers, silicones and urethanes. I much prefer silicones and have discussed why in detail in a previous article (See "How to Make a Secondary Mold," *SJ*, July 2004.). In this case, I preferred a rubber with a low viscosity so that it would pour in and around the model filling the void completely. Since the model had significant hollows and undercuts, the rubber needed to have a low durometer meaning that it would be soft enough to separate first from the model and then from the castings pulling out of tight areas without tearing. A durometer of 8 to 15 is considered low and a low viscosity would be 15,000 to 20,000 centipoise. For more information on the properties of silicone rubbers, (see "How to Select and Buy Silicone Rubbers," *SJ*, May 2005, by Michael J. Sisbarro.). The rubber I selected was a tin cured silicone with a durometer of eight and a viscosity of about 15,000 centipoise.

I mixed the rubber according to the directions specified by the manufacturer. I then de-aired the rubber with a vacuum chamber. Photograph #26 shows me pouring the mixed components of the rubber into the mother mold. Once I was sure that there were no leaks, I placed the mold into a pressure chamber, set the pressure at 50 p.s.i., and let it cure overnight.

O.K., some readers are probably saying, "Oh great, I don't have either a vacuum or pressure chamber!" Don't despair, it is possible to make an acceptable mold without either one. But using one or both absolutely will result in longer lasting molds with fewer flaws. For a complete discussion on both vacuums and pressure in casting, see the following *Sculpture Journal* articles by yours truly:

"Using Vacuums and Pressure in Casting," August 2003

"Making a Vacuum Chamber," September 2003

"Making a Pressure Chamber," October 2003

"Putting Vacuum and Pressure Chambers to Practical Use," November 2003.

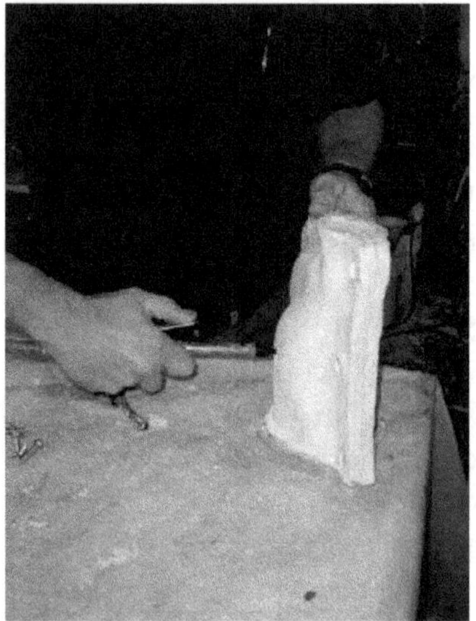
Photograph #27

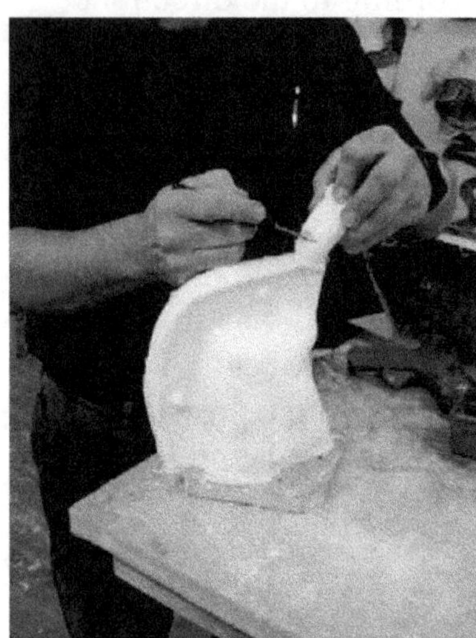
Photograph #28

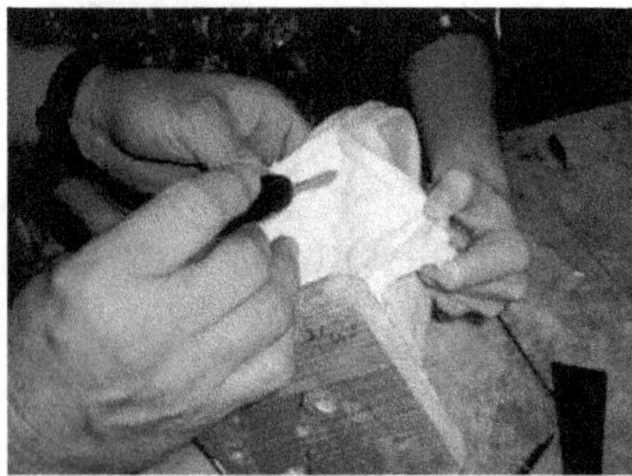
Photograph #29

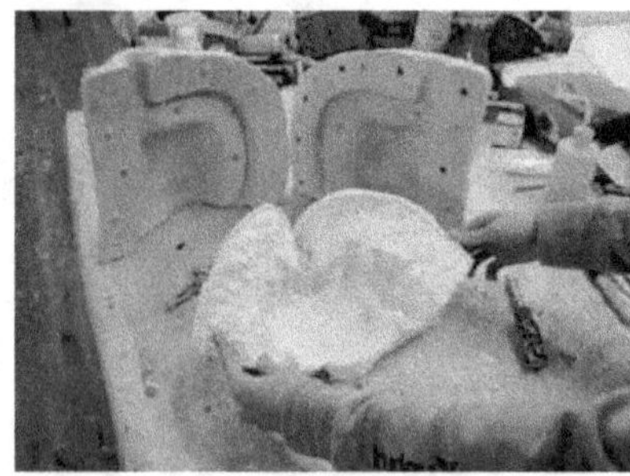
Photograph #30

Finishing the Mold

In order to remove the mother mold and expose the now setup rubber, I first unscrewed all the bolts. Since I had used a silicone rubber, it was very unlikely that the mother mold and the rubber would be stuck together except by suction. Gently inserting a sharp wedge or pry bar into the seam would probably have been sufficient. However, photograph #27 shows a simple but very effective trick. I had drilled a small hole, about 1/8" or 1/3 cm., through the Forton MG in the middle of each side of the mother mold. One who has never done this might worry about drilling through the rubber. The fact is that it is much easier to drill through Forton MG than rubber. As long as only slight pressure is applied to the drill, you will fell the bit break through and then stop, barely nicking the rubber. Then blowing air into the hole and between the rubber and Forton MG will separate the two easily.

In photograph #28, I was cutting off most of the rubber that filled the pour spout. This really wasn't necessary since this particular rubber structure wasn't actually in the way or doing any harm. But to leave it dangling there just didn't seem like a proper thing to do in Colorado; maybe in California ... Where was Sigmund Freud when I needed him?

The only thing remaining was to remove the plaster model, the need for the reproduction of which started this epic journey. All it takes are two hands to spread the seam apart as a third hand wields something very sharp, preferably a scalpel as in photograph #29. Make a zigzag cut so that the rubber keys back together until very close to the model. For the last 1/4" or 2/3 cm., make the parting cut as straight as possible so that parting line on will be minimized. Remember to follow the black line that was drawn on the model (photo #1) so that the parting line will be where you had determined that it would be the least conspicuous. Proceed slowly and carefully so as not to cut your assistant, yourself, or through the sides of the Mohawk. Don't make the parting line any longer than necessary, cut only far enough to extract the model. Photograph #30 shows the rubber spread apart like a butterfly shrimp after the model had been removed.

Using the Mold

To reproduce the model with this mold was just a matter of deciding what material to use, mixing it, filling the mold, letting it cure as necessary, and extracting the reproduction. Almost anything that will go from liquid to solid such as plaster, hydrocal, hydrostone, concrete, polyurethane and polyester resins, epoxy, wax, Jell-O, chocolate, Forton MG, etc. would have worked fine. The only thing that I can think of that I could not have used was optically clear polyurethane resin which requires a platinum cured silicone rather

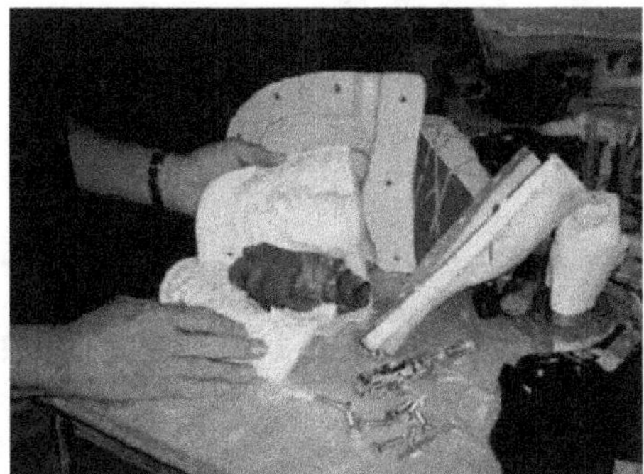

Photograph #31

than a tin cured one. Photograph #31 shows the first reproduction made in this mold which was cast in Forton MG with copper powder. This casting came easily out of the mold with **no flaws**. There were no bubbles either innies our outies and no voids. The parting line was almost invisible and disappeared with just a little rubbing with my thumb. The finished product complete with marble base is in photograph #32.

I could have made a mold of the hand and foot used in this three part article a much easier way by just building a box around it and filling it with rubber as I described in detail in the above mentioned article in *SJ* July 2004. But a mold made the simpler way will have much thicker rubber, at least in places, and if the sculpture is delicate, it might be difficult to impossible to remove the castings without breaking them. The rubber in the mold I have described here is much thinner and allows for more delicate and/or complicated castings. Since the mold comes apart and goes back together so easily, it is a pleasure to use especially important for larger editions. The most important thing that any mold can do is accurately reproduce the model with the absolute minimum of flaws in order to preserve the integrity of the sculptor's work. And because correcting flaws is tedious and time consuming, extra time spent in making the best mold possible can save time

and money. There is one more advantage, if the mold is used so many times or is stored so long that the rubber deteriorates, just reattach the mother mold around the model and pour in new rubber and you're back in business with a new mold.

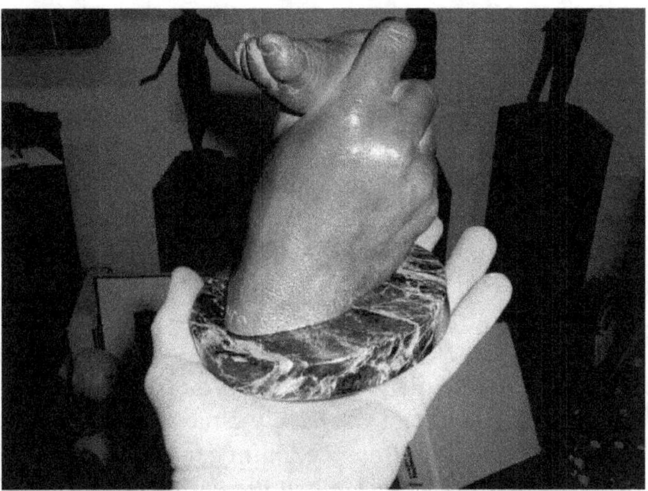

Photograph #32

David Parvin is a Denver sculptor. He may be reached at 303-321-1074
if you would like to discuss art, fly fishing, flying, or grandchildren.

How to Make a Secondary Mold

by David E. Parvin, A.L.I.

Weather one is trying to derive income from life casting or just wants to produce the highest quality products possible, being able to make secondary molds is an essential technique. In this, the first of several articles, I will describe how to make the simplest type of molds, block or pour molds in this case of infants' hands and feet. In the following articles, I will explain how to make molds of faces, bodies, and multiple hands.

You may be asking why not just cast the infants hands and feet over and over until you have enough copies for the parents, grandparents, "and his sisters and his cousins and his aunts." (Sorry, Gilbert and Sullivan just pops out sometimes.) You could, except that for even experienced casters, multiple perfect impressions of wiggly babies' hands and feet can be problematic. But while allowing one to cast additional copies is the most obvious advantage of secondary molds, there are several others. The first is that different materials can be used giving the client a variety. Some of the different materials can not be cast in alginate molds. Also, if the customer realizes later that he/she left out old, great, rich uncle Bob who just happens to be making a new will and might generously remember the little tyke with the proper memory jogging gift, you can supply it?

The last advantage may not be quite as obvious, but you will probably get more perfect castings from the secondary molds. Let us say that your hand and foot had been cast in plaster or something similar. Often there are imperfections, usually bubbles either in the plaster (innies) or in the alginate (outies) or tips of fingers that are missing due to trapped air in the mold.

Outies are the easiest to repair since you just trim them off and texture the surface to blend in. Innies and fingertips are more difficult because you have to add material. It does take some practice before one can sculpt the last digit of a finger and not have the mother notice. Even if plaster is wet enough for new plaster to be added to old, there can be a color difference. Paint can cover up a multitude of imperfections but can also cover up some detail such as fingerprints. I have found that the easiest way to make repairs is using wax or clay. You must wait a few days so that the plaster will have dried enough that the clay or wax will stick. But of course, wax and clay are different colors than the plaster and paint will not help here. But if you remold after making repairs, what ever material you use to cast will all be the same color and the repairs would be hardly noticeable if at all.

Note: one material that does stick to itself wonderfully is Forton MG both plain and with metal powders. Forton MG can be cast directly in an alginate mold but of course, the mold will most likely be usable only once.

After repairing any imperfections in the plaster hand and foot, attach them to bases made of wood, plywood, or MDFB. Using a 1/4 inch drill bit, drill a hole into the plasters and into the bases. Attach the pieces to the bases with a 1/4 inch piece of dowel that is long enough to suspend the pieces about 1/2 inch above the base. This 1/2 inch space is very important as you will see below.

The cured rubber molds will have to be cut or opened on one side to remove the castings. There will be seams in the castings where the cuts are made but they should be almost invisible if properly done. The best place to cut open the foot mold is along the back of the heel. For a hand, along the outside edge down to the tip of the little finger. To help in cutting the molds in the right places, I make heavy black lines in permanent ink to indicate where to cut.

The next step is to attach the pieces to the bases with the pieces of dowel and hot glue.

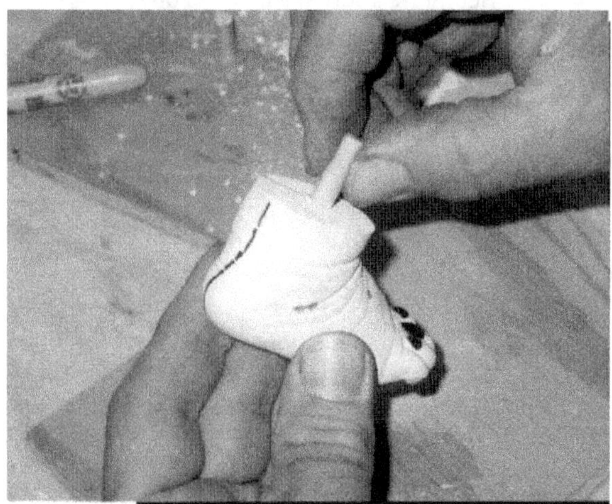

Putting the dowel into the plaster foot
Notice the black line

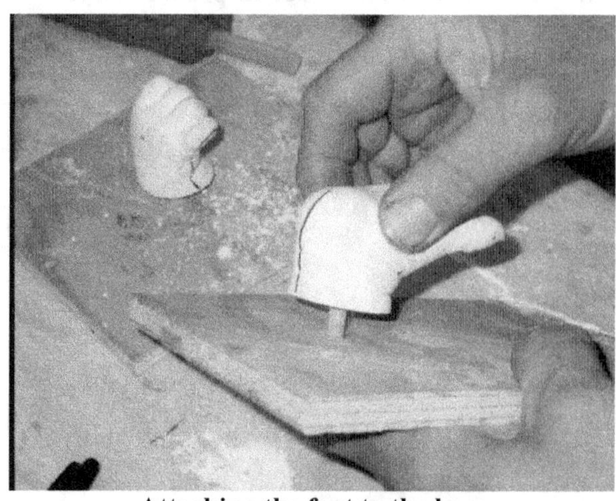

Attaching the foot to the base

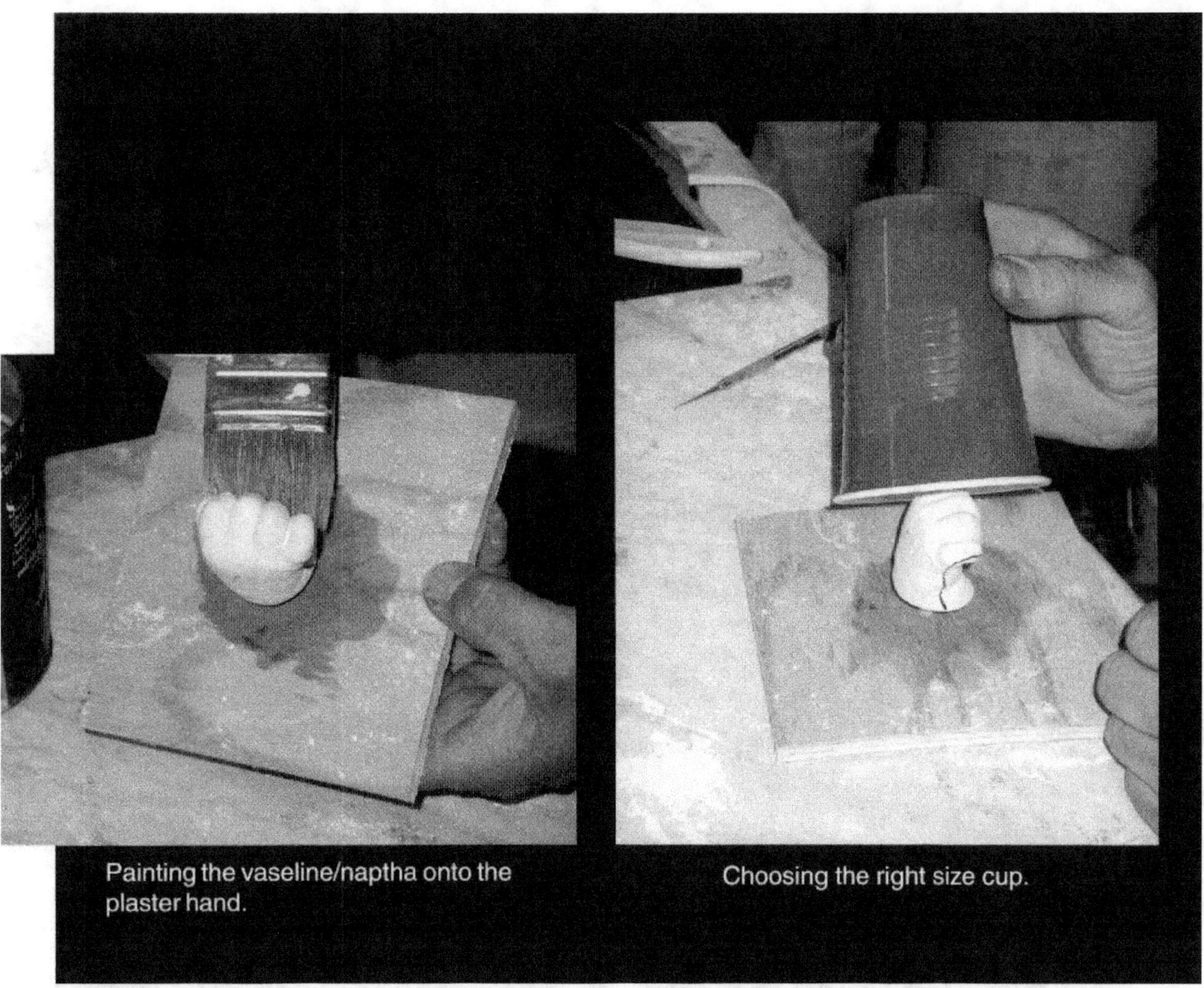

Painting the vaseline/naptha onto the plaster hand.

Choosing the right size cup.

The mother or outer mold for the hand is just an inverted plastic cup with the bottom removed. The cup should provide 1/2 inch of clearance when centered over the hand. However, when the cup is glued into position, it should be 1/4 inch from the thumb side and 3/4 inch from the opposite side where the incision will be made. As I will explain, the right type of rubber will not require a mold release. However, I paint the plaster with a solution of 15 parts Vaseline and 10 parts naptha by weight. I also paint the base around the dowel out to just inside where the cup will cover. Doing this will allow the mold to be more easily dissembled but is not absolutely necessary.

Next put the cup in position and glue it in place with a hot glue gun. Note: I did not paint the naphtha and Vaseline outside the edge of the cup because it might have kept the glue from attaching to the base. Also, liquid rubber tends to run out of even the smallest opening. Therefore, glue around the edge of the cup several times until you are absolutely positive that there is no possible way that the rubber could leak out. Then do it all over again and just maybe it won't leak! This mold is now ready for the rubber.

For the foot, a cup is not a practical mother mold because if you use a cup that is '/2 inch beyond the toes and the heel, it will extend an inch out from the sides. Not only will this take too much rubber adding to the cost, the mold will be so stiff that it will be difficult to spread it open to remove the castings. I simply build a box around the foot using the cardboard from a milk or orange juice carton. The box should surround the foot with a '/2 inch of clearance along the sides, 1/4 inch at the toes, and 3/4 inch at the heel where the incision will be made. A mother mold will not be needed because the rubber will be rigid enough by itself and the mold may be held tightly closed with several rubber bands. Now for the rubber.

The type of rubber one chooses is very important and one has many choices. I will try to keep the selection simple. The two most commonly used rubbers are urethanes and silicones. The disadvantages of urethane are that the components must be measured precisely, the components must be mixed evenly and exactly, it tends to stick to the object being molded and to the casting especially if the final casting material is urethane, and the mold has a shorter life that one made in silicone. The only advantage is that urethanes are about half the price of silicones. However, this is really a false advantage because the few dollars saved on small molds will be lost many times over fixing

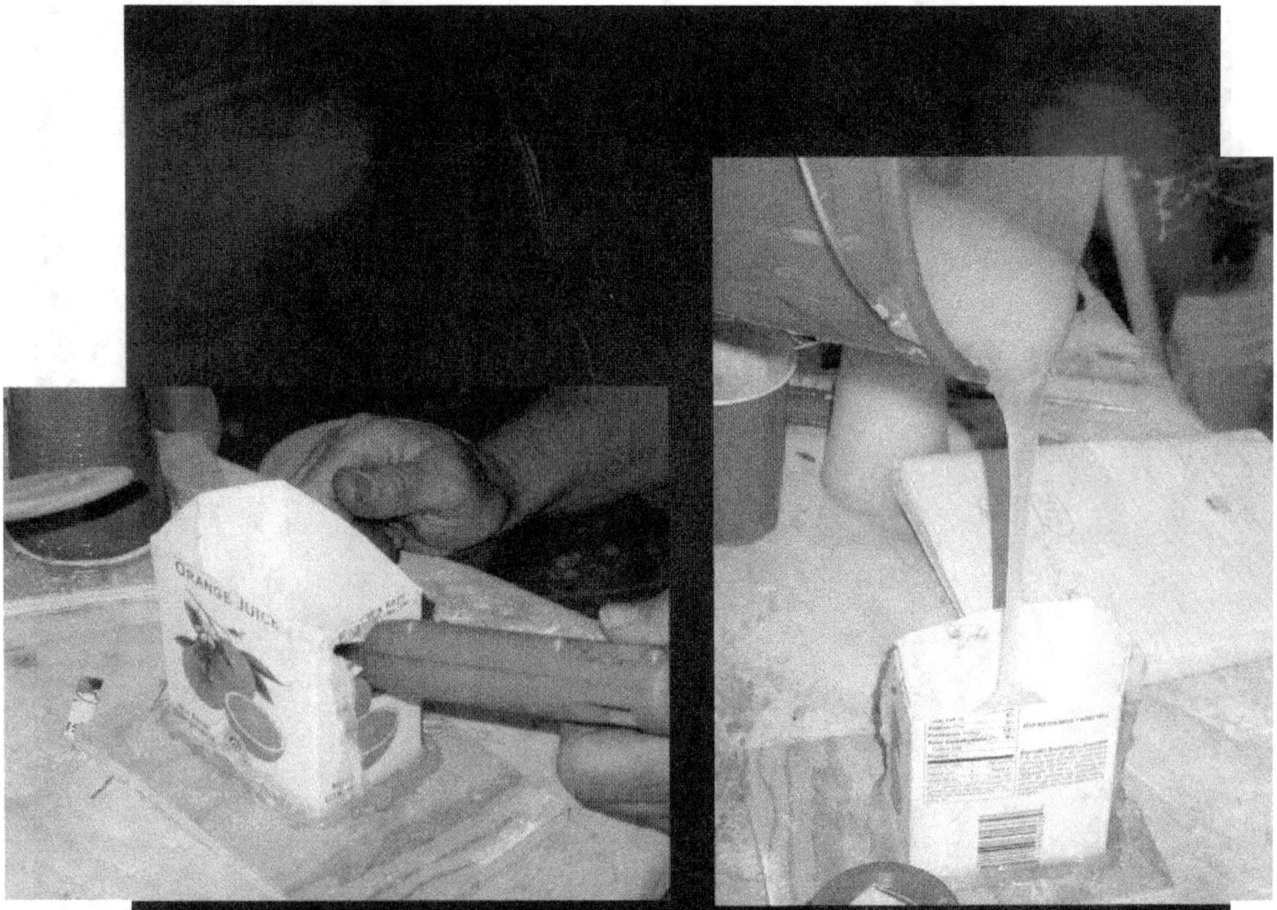

Constructing a box around the foot.

Pouring in the rubber.

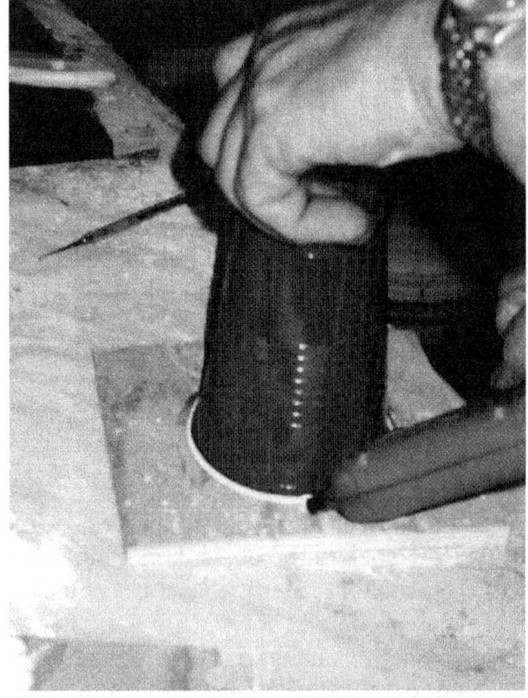

Attaching the cup to the base with a hot glue gun:

imperfections and problems caused by using urethane rubber. As for silicone rubber, there are two types, tin cured and platinum cured. The "tins" are a little easier to use because they are not as sensitive to contaminants that can cause inhibition. However, "platinums" are more durable, have no shrinkage whatsoever, and will cure very quickly if exposed to heat. The only time that you must use a "platinum" is if you cast clear urethane which will not set-up in a "tin" mold. Follow the directions and you should have no problems with either.

I would suggest that whatever rubber you choose, choose one that is soft, i.e. has a low durometer of 15 or less: You will be much more likely to be able to remove the little hands and feet from soft rubber molds are less likely to leave visible imperfections in the castings.

In this case, I choose a translucent platinum silicone rubber with a durometer oft 5. The platinum was to allow for some clear urethane castings. The translucence would make it easier to follow the base line when cutting open the molds.

The next step was to figure out how much rubber was needed. I computed the volume of the molds to the top of the hand and foot. I did not

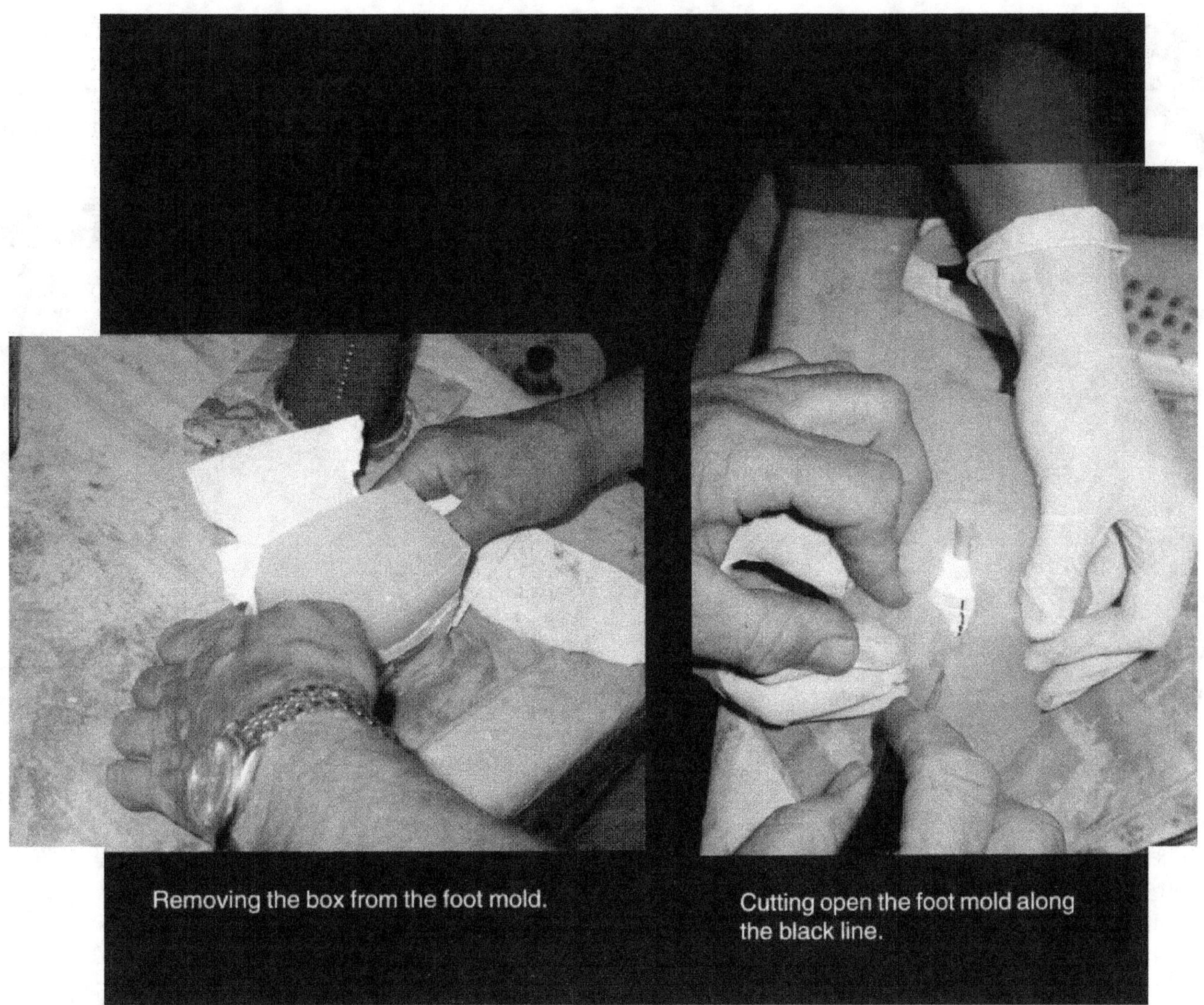
Removing the box from the foot mold.

Cutting open the foot mold along the black line.

subtract anything for the volume taken up by the hand and foot figuring that that would allow for enough rubber to cover both sufficiently. The simplest way to calculate the amount of rubber needed would have been to weigh how much water it would have taken to till the molds to about 1/4 inch above the hand and foot. Rubber and water have almost exactly the same specific gravity and so many grams of water would have required the same number of grams of rubber. However, I didn't want to take a chance on tilling the mold with water. The volume of a box is just the width times the weight times the length. The volume of a column is Pi times the square of the radius times the height. Since a cup is not rally a column, I just used what I guessed to be an average of the radius. In this case, I came up with 835 cubic centimeters for both. This meant that 835 grams of rubber would have been required and they were.

Following the directions for the rubber, I measured out 835 grams of matrix and catalyst. Most silicone rubbers are mixed at 10 parts catalyst to 100 parts matrix by weight. However, another common ratio is 50/50. Just follow whatever is recommended. You want to take some care when mixing. Make sure that you scrape the sides and bottom several times. Often the catalyst changes the color of the mixture and a uniform color means that the rubber has been thoroughly mixed. In this case, both the matrix and the catalyst were translucent and neutral. Since there was no way to tell by looking when had mixed it properly, I just mixed it a little longer than I would have otherwise done and it set up perfectly. Once mixed just pour it carefully in to the molds unless...

If you have the capability of de-airing the rubber, do so. I not only have a vacuum chamber but also possess a number of pressure vessels. So I was able to de-air the rubber prior to pouring it into the molds and allow the rubber to cure under 50 p.s.i. of pressure. Note: these steps are not necessary but will result in more perfect and longer lasting molds. (For a complete discussion on this subject, see "Using Vacuums and Pressure in Casting," "Making a Vacuum Chamber," "Making a Pressure Chamber," and "Putting Vacuum and Pressure Chambers to Practical Use: by yours truly, "Sculpture Journal," August, September, October and November 2003.

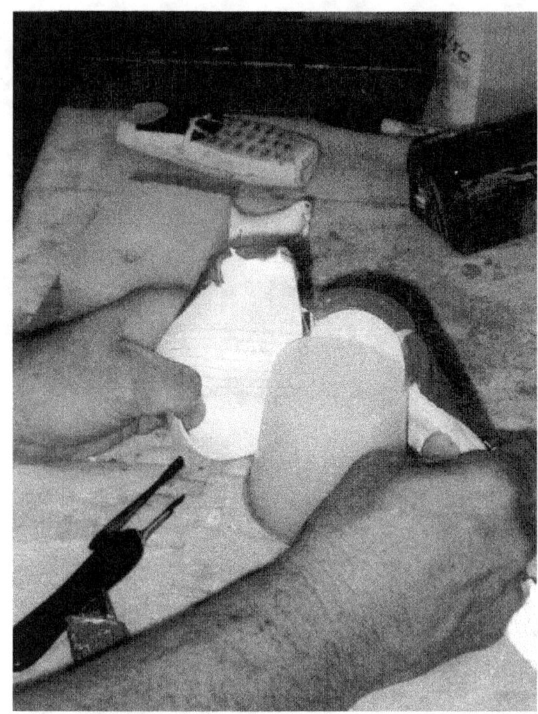

Removing the cup from the hand mold Notice the enlarged hole on top of the foot mold.

Once the rubber has cured for the recommended time in the directions, cut off the cup and the box. Using a very sharp blade such as a scalpel, cut open the molds along the black lines. The incisions should only have to go to the bottom of the heel and the tip of the little finger. Zigzag the cut near the surface for registration. But where the rubber touches the plaster on the black line, make the cut as straight as possible so as to minimize any indication of the seam in the castings. Enlarge the hole around the dowels to become a reservoir for extra material. Some materials shrink when they set up and without the reservoir you may lose part of the wrist and ankle.

Spread open the molds and pull out the plasters. If they come out easily without breaking off any toes and fingers, you should be able to cast any material in the mold; including plaster, hydrocal, Forton MG, etc. However, if the fingers or toes do break off, you will probably want to use something stronger such as polyurethane or polyester resins.

When you fill the molds, use your best technique to minimize bubbles such as tipping, shaking, vibrating, etc. Again, if you have the capability, de-air and pressurize. Once the material has cured, remove your copies. You will probably find that some material has solidified in the enlarged opening/reservoir. A few seconds with a belt sander will remove this. All that remains would be any buffing or patina depending on the material.

I realize that this process may seem rather complicated, but it isn't. The time required to make these molds and cast the first copies, excluding the cure times, took no more than an hour. It took far longer to write this article.

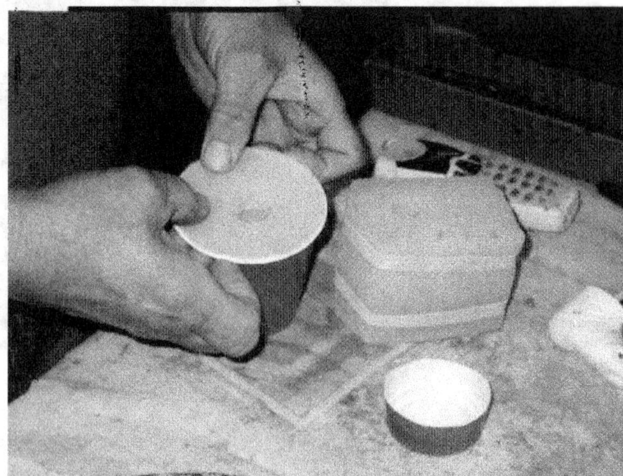

Fitting the hand mold into a new cup which has had its bottom removed. Notice rubber bands around the foot mold.

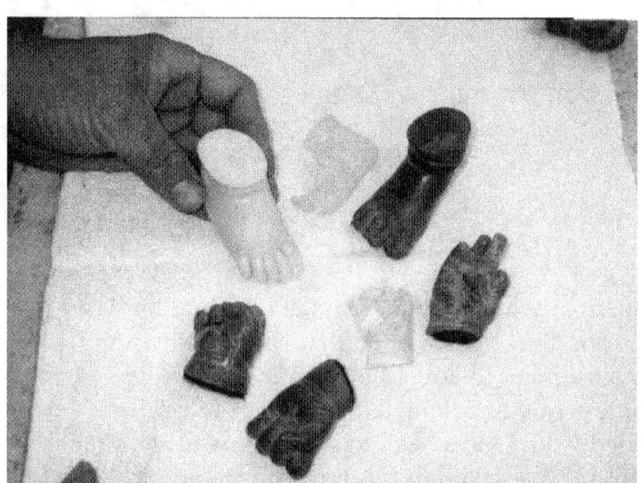

Baby feet and hands cast in different materials. Forton MG with metal powders, polyurethane resin with metal powders, POLYURETHANE a clear polyester resin and polyester with crushed marble.

David E. Parvin is a Colorado sculptor whose primary subject is the human form in a variety of materials He also teaches life casting workshops held at his studio in Denver, Colorado throughout the year. For inquires regarding his schedule of workshops he may be reached at 303-321-1074.

Sculpture Journal July 2004

Solving a Mold Making Problem

By David E. Parvin, A.L.I.

I love a good mystery; it could be in a book, play, movie, or in my studio. Granted, the sculpting mysteries rarely involve dead bodies or large amounts of missing valuables; but are more of the "how in the world am I going to do that" variety. Recently such an problem presented itself. But let's start at the beginning.

Several years ago I was asked if I could make something that could be an appropriate trophy for a lady named Dawn Denzer in honor of the work she had done for raising money to fight Parkinson's disease. For many years, Mrs. Denzer had been the social editor for the Rocky Mountain News, but unfortunately, had just previously been diagnosed with Parkinson's disease. I had known her from many a social function and felt I owed her for mentioning my name often in her column. I suggested that a cast of her hand holding something especially meaningful to her would be appropriate and my idea was accepted. I went to visit Dawn who was deteriorating in an assisted living facility. When I asked her what she wanted in her hand, she replied, "A Champaign glass, remember the good times..." Making the trophy was a piece of cake. I simply had her hold a champaign glass and submerge her hand into a container of alginate. The void made by hand was filled with Forton MG with copper powder. Since I had de-aired the Forton MG with a vacuum mixer, the impression was bubble free. After applying a vertigreen patina solution and buffing, the glass and hand were attached to a marble base (photo #1). I thought I had come to the end of the story, but I hadn't.

Recently, someone from the Colorado Neurological Society told me that they had decided to make an annual Dawn Denzer Award which would be presented to a particularly significant supporter. I was asked if it would be possible to duplicate Dawn's casting for the award. "Piece of cake," I replied and thought until I remembered the she had passed away recently. Had she still be with us, I could have just cast her hand again holding a glass. As I described above, a life casting of a hand holding something is very easy to do. I have done hands holding a golf club, oar handles, baseballs, a bat, a book, a fishing rod, etc. For a duplicate, all one has to do is mold the hand and the object together. Of course, the object will be duplicated in the same material as the hand. No one wanted a Forton MG Champaign glass. So in this case, I could make a mold of the original hand and champaign glass, extract them, place another Champaign glass into the mold and pour in metallic Forton MG which would become fingers around the stem. Still seemed doable until I realized that the Champaign glass was a problem. Since I would be making a mold of a rigid hand, the duplicate glass would have to be exactly like the original in order to fit. Unfortunately, I could not find any like the original. The fingers would have to be repositioned to fit a different glass; no easy task since the original cast of the hand was very rigid Forton MG.

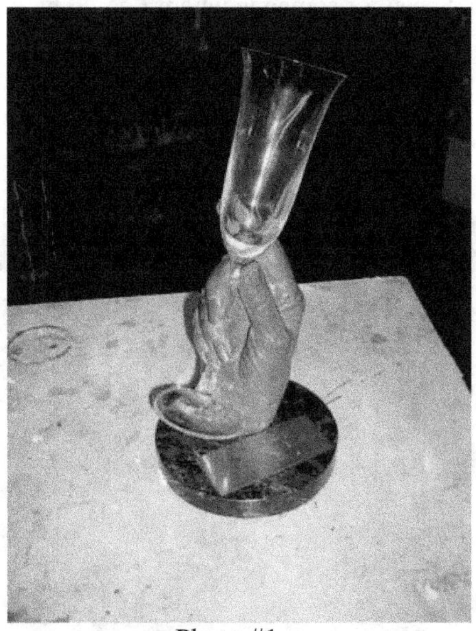

Photo #1

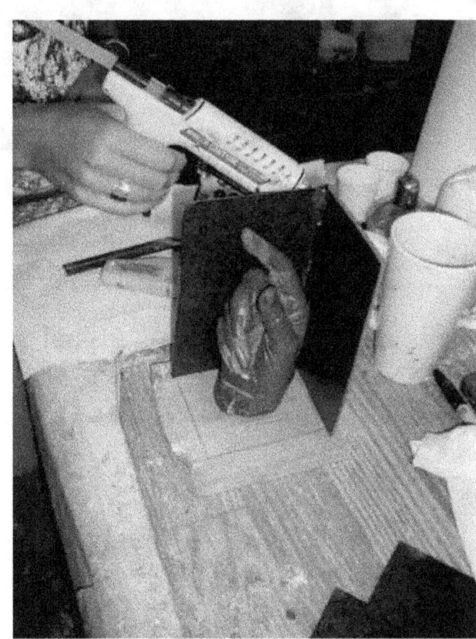

Photo #2

The solution was to make a replica of the hand in a softer material. I broke the stem of the Champaign glass so that I could remove it. Next I constructed a masonite box around the hand (photo #2) and made a block mold using a very soft tin cured silicone rubber (11 durometer). After removing the original Forton MG hand, I cast a duplicate hand in urethane rubber (photo #3). Anyone who has read my articles over the last few years might remember that I much prefer silicones over urethanes, at least as far as rubbers are concerned. The only time that I use urethanes is if I want something cast in rubber using a silicone mold. Urethanes will not bond to silicones and visa versa. However, the new, flexible hand had a problem, the surface was sticky and would rub off with only casual contact causing a slight loss of detail. My rubbers expert, Michael Sisbarro, told me that for some reason, urethane rubbers with durometers less than 40 have a tendency to suffer surface inhibition when cast in tin cured silicone rubber. Because Dawn had been, let's just say, a little older with some definite character in her hands, I thought that a minimal loss of detail might not be noticeable and it wasn't. I fitted a new glass in the hand and made another block mold.

In order to make the hand grasp the new glass firmly, I had pushed pieces of wire, straightened out paper clips, into the thumb and several of the fingers. This allowed me to bend the fingers into new positions and have them remain in place. After the new mold had cured overnight, I made a zig zag incision, removed the glass and rubber hand, replaced the Champaign glass (Photo #4), closed the mold around the glass, and poured in Forton MG with copper powder. To prevent bubbles, I had vacuum mixed the Forton MG and allowed it to set up under 50 p.s.i. pressure. The end result, which was deemed acceptable, is shown in photo #5.

It would have been nice if this project had been for someone whom I could have charged big bucks. But I didn't feel right about charging anything to a non profit which is trying to rid the world of a crippling disease, especially a disease to which I have no assurance that I am immuned. I guess solving the problem has to be payment enough. And, after all, I'm still living the good times.

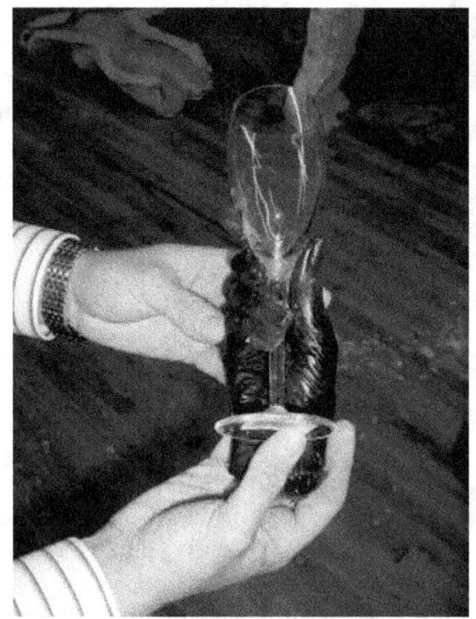

Photo #3

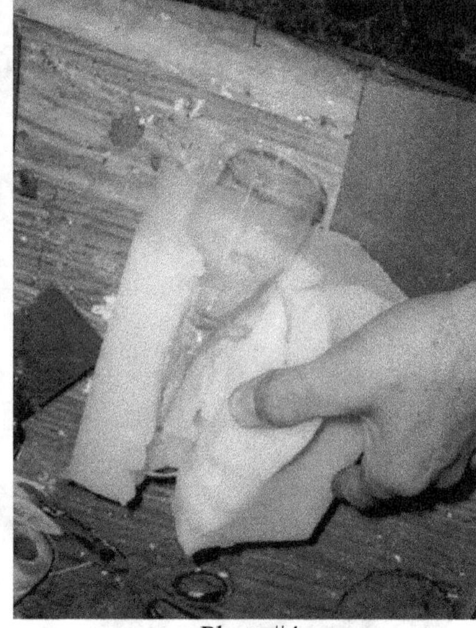

Photo#4

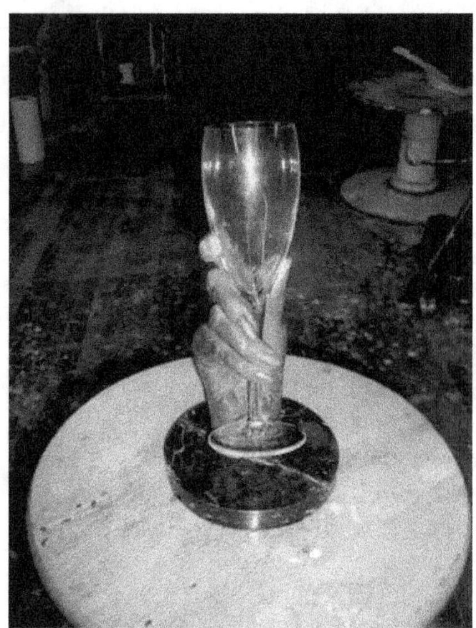

Photo#5

If you have questions or a trick that you're willing to share, please contact me at 303-321-1074 or parvinstudio@comcast.net. Even if you do email me, please include your phone number because I would rather talk than type. I promise to give credit for any new idea that I find useful.

Another Little Trick for Some Molds

By David E. Parvin, A.L.I.

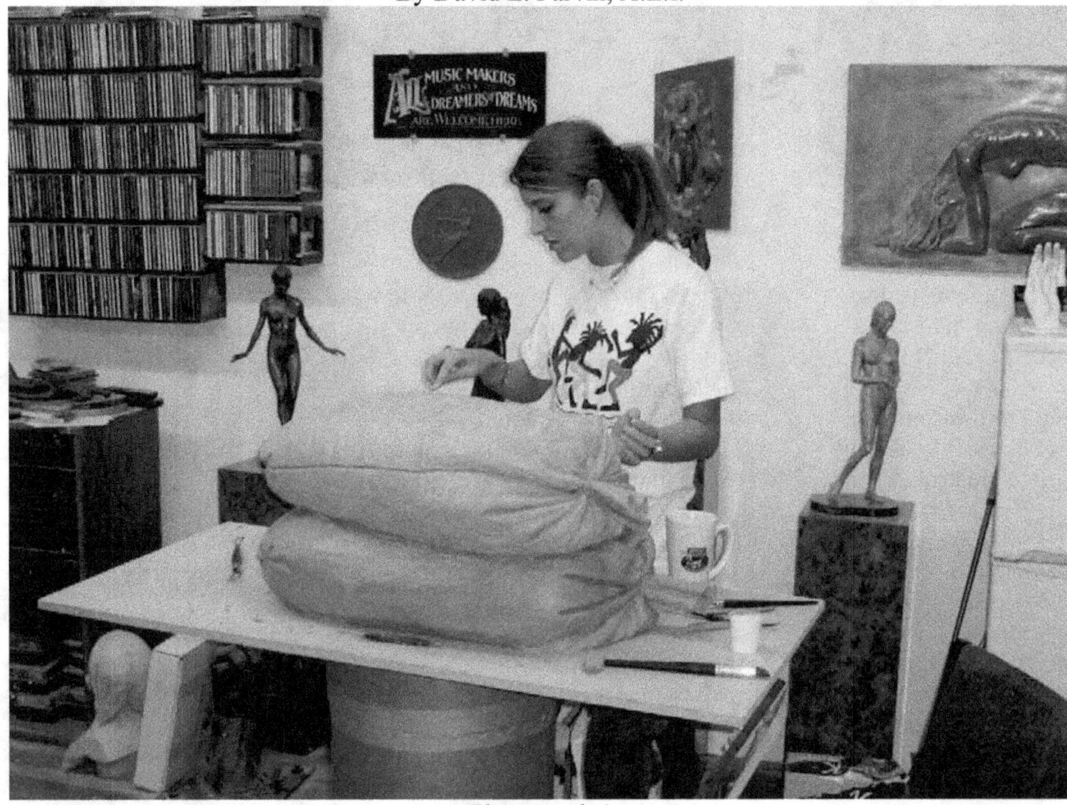

Photograph 1

Rule #11 on my studio wall under "Dave's Laws" is, "There is almost always a better way." While "better" might be an equally effective method or process but faster and/or cheaper, what is much more important to me is a method or process with more perfect results or allows me to do something that had been beyond my capabilities. Something that I had not been satisfied with was a way of securing the rubber inner layer of a mold to the supporting or "mother" mold.
In photograph #1, one of my assistants, Kelsey, is finishing the texture on two sandbags, which we had sculpted one and a half times life size, as part of a veterans' tribute garden for the City of Westminster, Colorado. The next step would be to make a one piece rubber mold of the two sandbags. Being one piece would allow the foundry to produce a single wax of both sand bags. Even if the foundry decided to cut the wax into smaller pieces for casting, I was hoping that the bronze pieces would likely fit back together more precisely than if the mold had been made in sections. But with such a large mold, the rubber might not remain securely in place against the mother mold especially if the mold were tipped and rotated when the wax was painted in unless the rubber were attached to the mother mold. There are any number of ways to lock the rubber to the mother mold. The most common is to use pill trays as molds for neat and uniform rubber keys. These are especially effective if the keys are attached by their smallest side causing them to lock into the mother mold. (See photographs #2 and #3.) These keys can be used anywhere such as on the sides or around the opening of the mold. However, they can be difficult to lock into place.

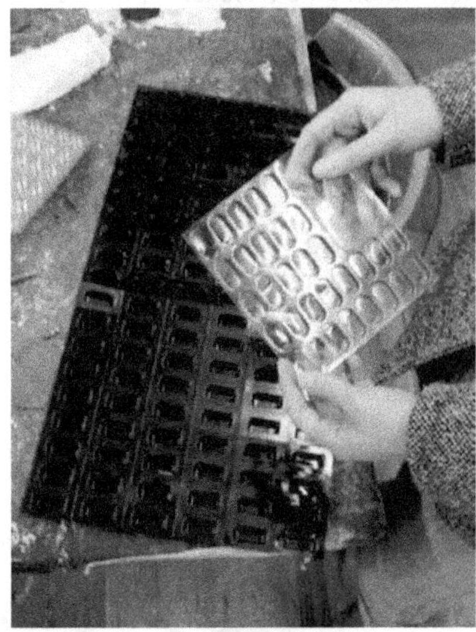

Photograph 2

As I considered the problem and it's solution, a number of things occurred to me. First, the device would have to be made of rubber with good elongation. Also, its base would have to be wide enough to allow for a firm bonding to the rubber mold. And coming out from the base, it would need to start out narrow and widen so that it would lock into the mother mold. Since it is easier to pull something into place than push it, a narrow part would have to extend trough a hole in the mother mold far enough to be grabbed onto and pulled. So I got a piece of clay and shaped something that seemed to fit the bill. What I came up with is in photograph #4. It was only then that I realized that I had reinvented the baby bottle nipple

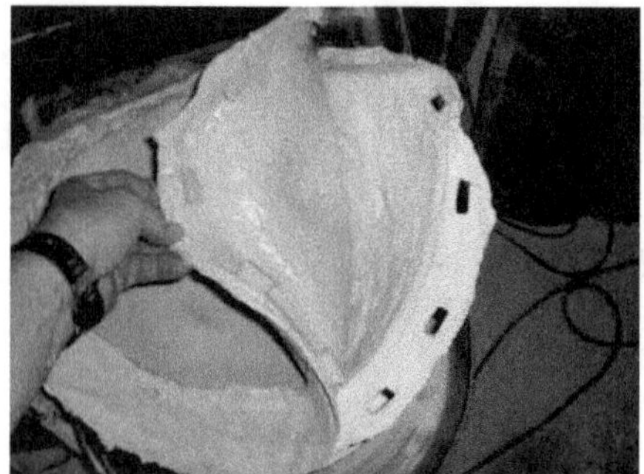
Photograph 3

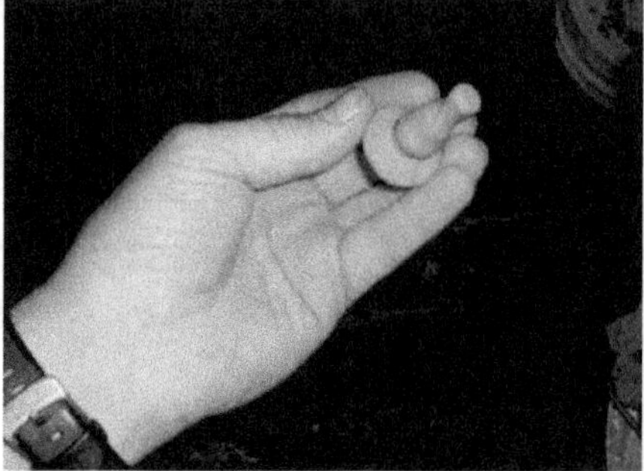
Photograph 4

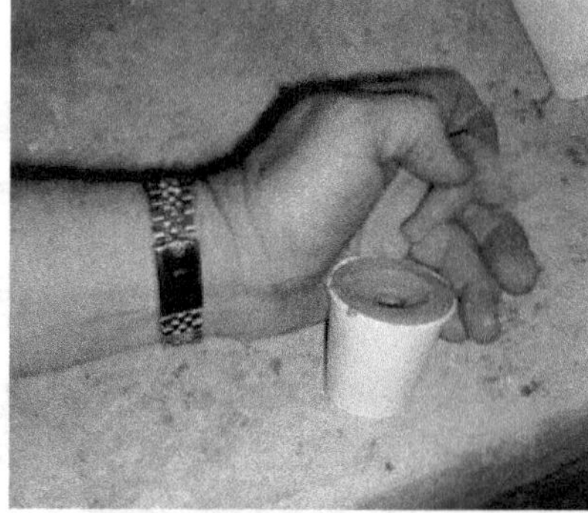
Photograph 5

or perhaps come up with a design for a very stable bowling pin that could transform bowling into a sport more like hockey or soccer, i.e. one with very low scores.

The next thing I did was make a copy in silicone rubber. All I did was fill a small cup with alginate and press in the clay model. As soon as the alginate had set up, I extracted the clay and an poured in the rubber, a tin cured silicone with a durometer of eight. In photograph #5, I am holding the prototype fastener and the alginate mold. I could have used this mold at least several more times, but since the alginate would have soon deteriorated, I made some molds in more durable materials, plaster, polyurethane resin, urethane rubber, and Forton MG . These molds were made the same way as I had made the alginate mold except that the rubber fastener was put into cups of the other materials which all worked about equally well. All casting were cured under a pressure of 50 p.s.i. While not absolutely necessary, pressure casting does eliminate bubbles.

In photograph #6 we had applied four layers of thixotropic tin cured silicone rubber and placed the fasteners where I felt they would be most needed on the sides and around what would be the opening for the mold. The fasteners were held in place until the rubber set up with hat pins which are barely visible in the photograph.

One of the real advantages of silicone rubbers is that they really bond together. I could make a supply of fasteners and even after a year, they would still bond perfectly to uncured rubber. Urethane rubbers are not as forgiving to work with though I could have used urethane rubber in this article.

The finished mold is in photograph #7. The mother mold was made using Forton MG and cotton batting with scrim binder. This method allows for a mold of even this size to be only about 1/4 inch thick and there for relatively light. (For a more thorough description of this process, see "Secondary Molds in Life Casting Part II," *Sculpture Journal*, Nov. and Dec. 2004 by yours truly.) I simply built the mother mold around the bulb part of the fasteners. Notice that the ends of the fasteners protrude out from the mother mold.

If you are still awake, you may be wondering, "Why bother?" Well, we took the mold apart, removed the clay sand bags , and reassembled the mold. The fasteners positioned the rubber perfectly into the mother mold and assured that the rubber stayed securely against the sides. The really slick thing was how easy it was to poke the end of the fastener through its hole in the mother mold and pull it into place. (Photograph #8.) It was easier and more effective than any other method I had used in the past.

I can't keep calling my little innovation "the fastener," I need a name for it. Perhaps I should call it "the Parvin." I have been trying to come up with something that Parvin could stand for. The "Pa" could be "perfectly awesome," but the "rvin" is giving me trouble. But in any event, I am so proud of it that I would be happy to send a sample Parvin to anyone who wants one along with a simple mold for making as many as he/she wants. The only charge would be for shipping; the fastener and mold along with any handling would be free. Call me if you want one. (303)321-1074.

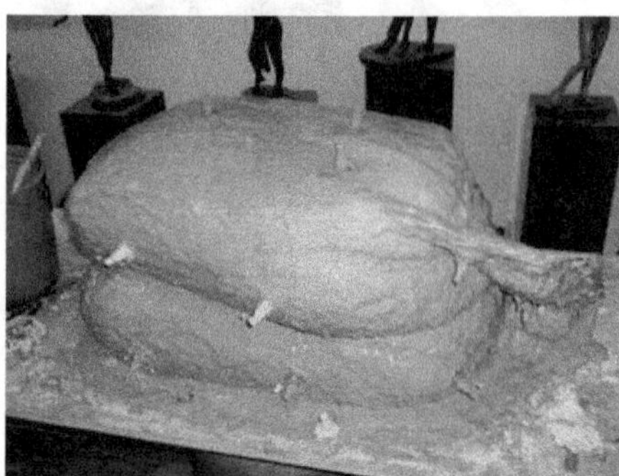
Photograph 6

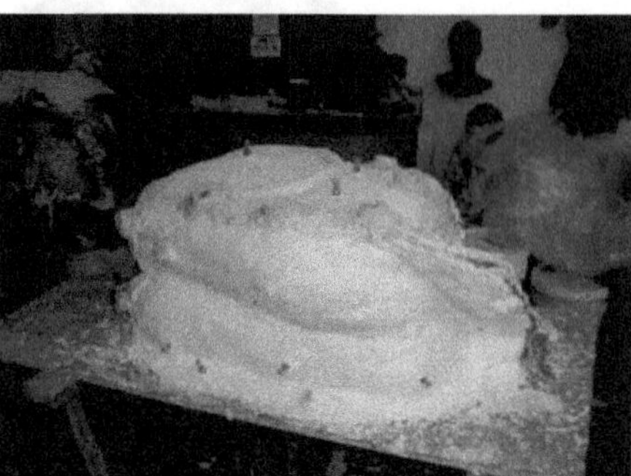
Photograph 7

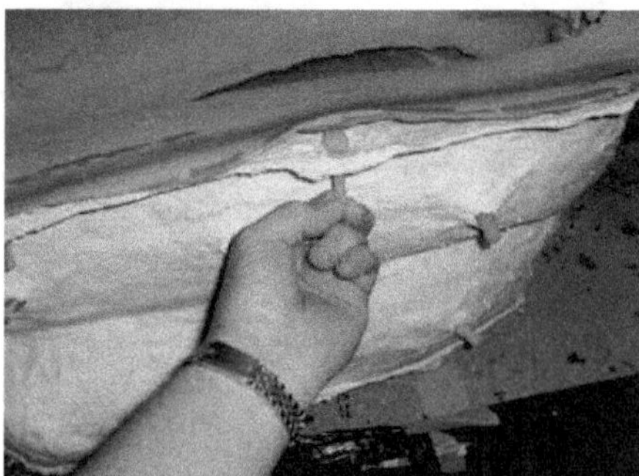
Photograph 8

If you have questions or a trick that you're willing to share please contact me at 303-321-1074 or parvinstudio@comcast.net. Even if you do email me, please include your phone number because I would rather talk than type. I promise to give you credit for any new idea that I find useful.

Size Matters

By David E. Parvin, A.L.I.

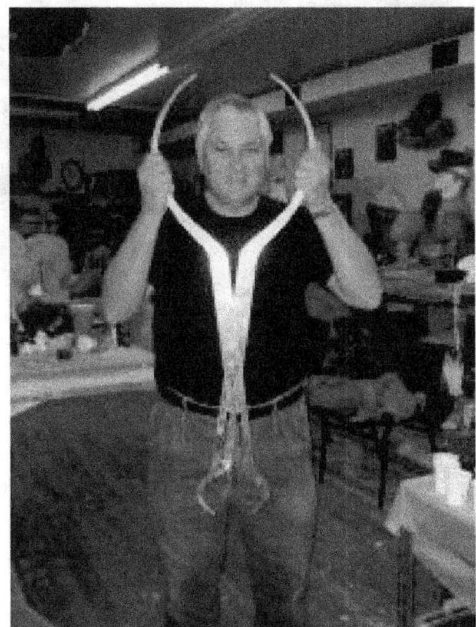

Photo #1. Now this is a pair of calipers, Mate!

As far back as I can recall, often I have needed to change the size of something I had sculpted, sometimes enlarging and sometimes reducing. In my youth, I just made it over in a new size using nothing more than a ruler to approximate the new dimensions. Later, I learned of and used some of the mechanical devices that had been developed as aids. More recently, I have taken advantage of the new technologies that are making both enlarging and reducing so much simpler. In this article, I am going to briefly cover both the old and the new ways and hopefully encourage any readers who have always hoped that one size fits all to expand or contract their creations.

If I were to daydream about my next commission, I would be more likely to imagine the client saying, "Great work, the twelve inch maquette is just what I want, now go ahead and make it thirty feet tall!" than, "... only now make it two inches tall." I suspect that most sculptors are more interested in and already more familiar with enlarging than reducing. Fortunately, the process is the same except that large pieces are milled out of foam and small ones are grown in resin or wax or milled in wax. More about that later. First, let's briefly look back in history.

If you are lucky enough to own or have access to one or both historic sculpting books, *Sculpture Inside and Out*, by Malvina Hoffman or *The Materials and Methods of Sculpture* by Jack C. Rich, you can readily read how complicated and time consuming it used to be to change the size of a piece of sculpture. The first was written just prior to World War II and the second just after. New technology has changed everything. The difference between what sculptors had to do then as compared to now is comparable to navigation in the same time frame. Pressing the "where am I" button on a GPS receiver versus taking celestial readings with a sextant followed by thirty minutes of longhand calculations is loosely analogous to enlarging and/or reduction then verses now.

Methods for enlarging using mechanical devices have been in use since at least the renaissance. Simple calipers, also called proportional dividers, allow one to take a measurement with one end and provide what the proportional measurement should be on the other end. The pair that I am holding in Photo #1 may have been the last of that size ever made. It was a gift several years ago from Bruner Barrie of Sculpture House. At the time, Bruner explained that he had had this particular pair in stock for some time with no prospects in sight because everybody seemed to be taking advantage of the new technologies. I think he felt that I am the only sculptor he knows ancient enough to know how to use calipers; probably a good call on his part since I also own sextant. In any event, it is a well known fact that you can tell a lot about a man by the size of his calipers.

Another helpful device was a pair of frames built to different scales allowing one to measure a locus on one piece and determine where the same locus should be on a piece of a different size.

The most sophisticated device was called a pointing machine or a pantograph. The concept is quite simple. Two turntables are connected so that they maintain alignment when turned. An arm is attached by a universal joint out from the turntables on a line through their centers. Protruding from the arm are two styluses that are the same distance apart as the centers of the turntables. The scale of enlargement (or reduction) is determined by the ratio of the distance between the styluses or turntables and the overall length of the arm. Some models of these were very precisely made, elaborate, and expensive. Malvina Hoffman shows several examples in her book. One of the foundries in my area had a large example which was still in use about fifteen years ago. Bruner Barrie of Sculpture House told me that he carried one for years in his catalogue but discontinued it about 20 years ago because people found it very difficult to adjust correctly. Also, it was relatively expensive and took up a lot of space.

About 20 years ago, I decided to build my own pointing device. After some trial and error, I came up with a design that was simple enough for me to construct. My innovation was to use fixed styluses, in other words, they did not move forming the ends of a parallelogram. This greatly simplifying the construction made adjustment easier. Though I was not able to reach every point on the model with this design, I could transpose enough points that enlarging (and reducing) was still very easy to do accurately. In the past, I had many artists look at it and want their own Parvin Pantograph. Three actually took some photographs and measurements and build them. One even went into the enlargement business and helped support himself until he was able to do so from the sales of his own sculpture. I have used my device many times including enlarging from 1/4 to full life size on three different occasions. It works just as well for reducing. I still use it sometimes. Photo #2 shows fellow sculptor Elliot Summons enlarging a face to 1 1/2 life size. Though we could have used the newer method that I will describe below, it took only about a day's work to finish the face. But now that there are simpler ways to enlarge or reduce and the pantograph for the most part has gone the way of the sextant. (I am hanging on to my sextant as well. If we have a total energy failure, I will still be able to point up or down and figure out approximate where I am.)

The first time I wanted to reduce accurately something I had sculpted was about twenty years ago. I had been asked to design and sculpt a medallion which would include a bas relief a dancing figure for an annual ballet competition sponsored by the Denver Ballet Guild. I made a 10 inch model first in order to get design just right. (Photo #3) The figure wasn't particularly difficult to sculpt but the letters would have been much more time consuming had I not taken a shortcut by using plastic ones. Gluing them in place was so much easier and faster than sculpting perfectly matching ones. I then sculpted the small version shown cast in bronze microscope under a magnification of 10 power and tiny tools made for eye surgery, time consuming but not too difficult. I decided that sculpting tiny perfect letters would have been just too time consuming and I elected to leave them off. This last year, I repeated the process to test the technology and even the letters turned out perfectly.

Since most sculptors are probably more interested in enlarging than reducing, I'll say a few things about enlarging before reducing. Photo #5 shows a one foot high maquette for a 1&1/2 life size piece titled "Grieving Friends" to be the centerpiece for a Veterans' Tribute Garden" for Westminster, CO. I was awarded the commission which will include six more figures. Realizing that this project would be more than one sculptor could do in the time allowed, I brought in two accomplished sculptors as partners, Bill Hueg and Elliot Summons. In this case, the maquette was made as a rough sketch only and we sculpted a much more accurate and detailed 1/3 life size larger maquette. (Photo #6) This larger size was shipped off to a company that scanned it and carved out 1&1/2 version in foam. (Photo #7) We specified that the foam be 1/4 inch undersize so that a layer of clay could be applied so that we could recapture the desired surface detail and texture. (Photo #8) Once the large figures were finished in clay over foam, they were molded and cast in bronze in the traditional manner. Six foot plus Bill Hueg is shown for scale with the completed, except for patina, "Grieving Friends" in Photo #9. Now let's reduce something.

Reducing is almost the same process. The first thing is to scan whatever it is to be reduced. If the smaller piece is large enough, it could be milled out of foam just as in enlarging. However, if smaller, then the piece will probably be either constructed in wax using a thermojet 3-D printer or grown in light sensitive urethane resin. If very small, then it is milled with a miniature 5 axis milling machine.

Something happened about a year and a half ago that got me interested in again doing the ballet medallion mentioned above as an experiment. 3-D scanners had been so expensive that they were out of the range of most sculptors, probably costing as much as a luxury automobile. But then the company Next Engine came out with a table top 3-D scanner for less the $3,000.00. (www.nextengine.com) I bought one. Photo #10 shows computer literate Elliot Summons with my new pride and joy. Elliot scanned the original 10 inch medallion complete with the letters. He added more words to the back and also a ring around the edge. The data was emailed to a rapid prototyping company who grew me the new medallion in Photo #11. It was a simple matter to make a mold of the new medallion and cast some samples in metallic urethane and some in wax for bronze.

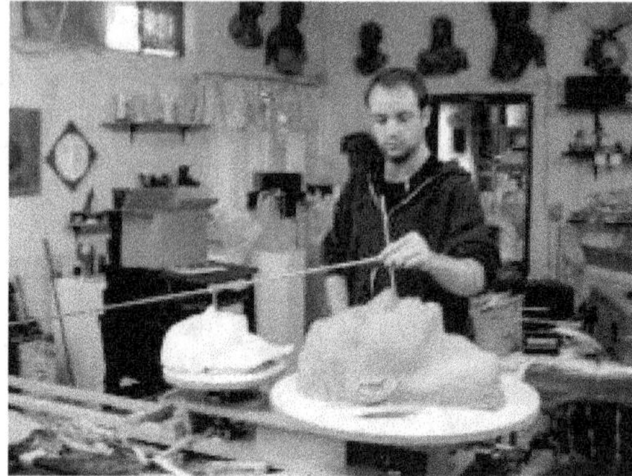

Photo#2. Elliot using my home made pointing machine.

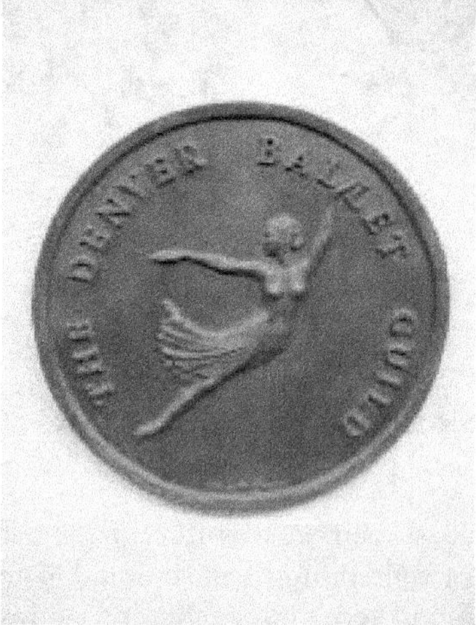

Photo #3. The 10" model for a 2 1/4" medallion. Here in metallic Forton MG.

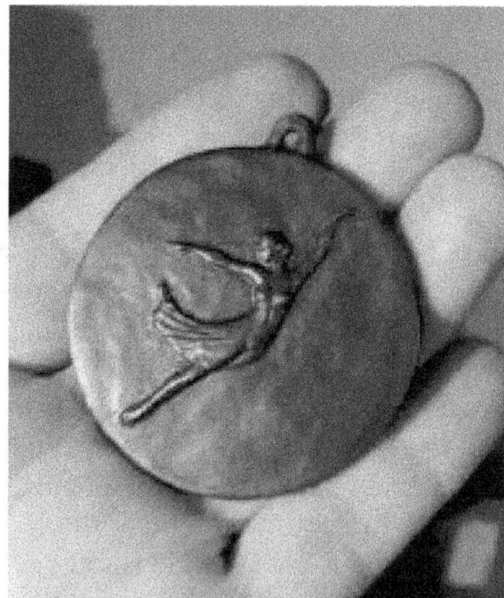

Photo #4. The hand sculpted small medallion in bronze.

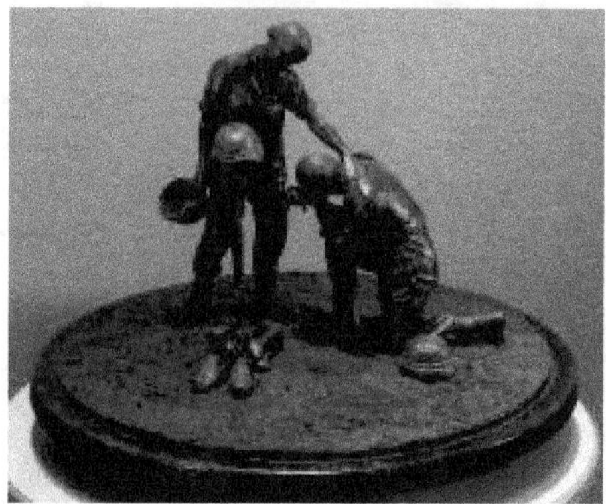

Photo #5. The 12" maquette for "Grieving Friends."

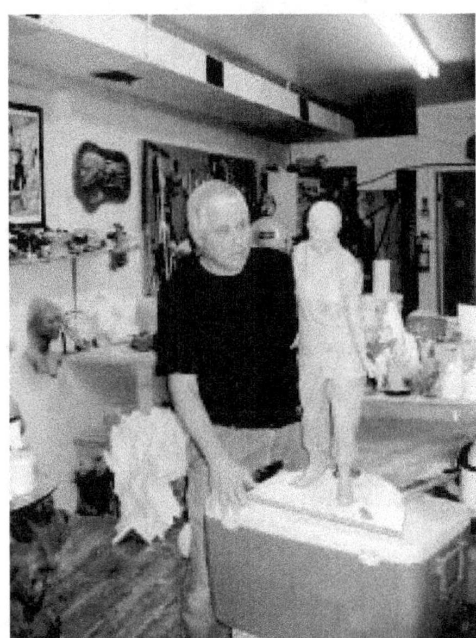
Photo #6. The 3' maquette

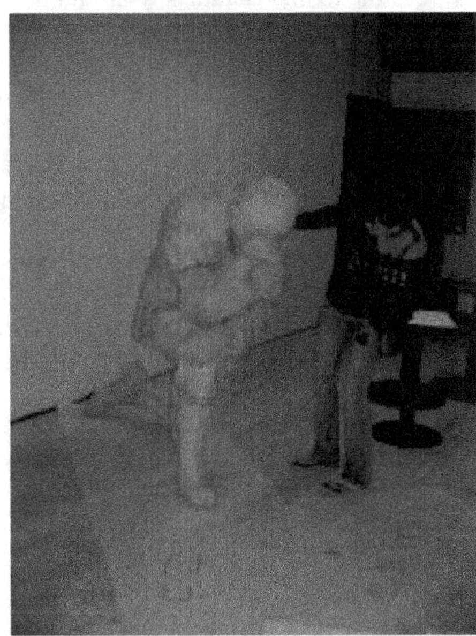
Photo #7. The male figure milled out of foam.

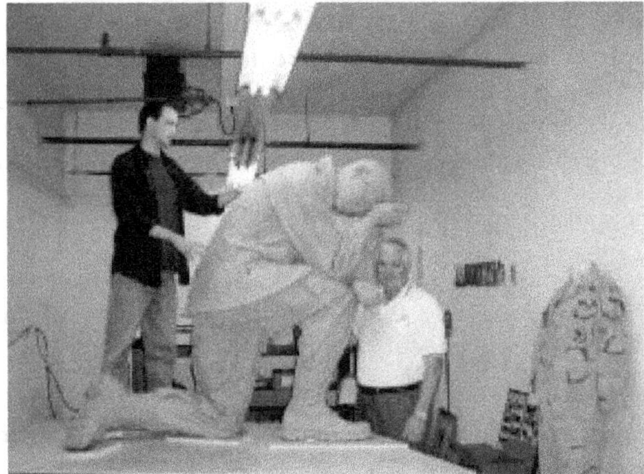
Photo #8. Elliot and self with the male figure covered in clay and detailed.

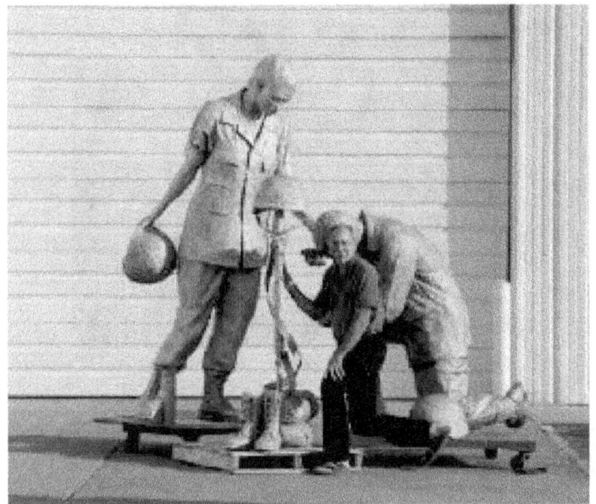
Photo #9. Bill Hues and the completed, except for patina, "Grieving Friends."

The ladies at the Denver Ballet Guild decided that it would be so special if I would make even smaller version one inch, the size of a quarter, which they could wear as charms. To accomplish this, another method was used. I had Elliot rework the data without the letters and make the charm proportionally slightly thicker. The revised data was fed into a miniature 5 axes milling machine which was designed for making intricate jewelry. What I got was a quarter size prototype carved out of very hard wax. I then roughed up the surface around the figure and scooped out the edges. Next I molded the charm in silicone rubber, cast some waxes under pressure to eliminate bubbles, and had the waxes cast in sterling silver by a jeweler. Two examples are in Photo #12; both are sterling silver but one has been plated in 18 carat gold.

What got me interested in writing this article is what I am going to in Photo #4 using a binocular describe next. Since reducing the medallion to 2 1/4 inches and 1 inch (5.72 and 2.54 cms) worked so well, I wanted to try something in the round. In Photo #13, assistant Jessica is behind three versions of a small statue of mine titled "Brooke." Jessica is there for scale, a purpose she fulfills somewhat better than a ruler or Bill in Photo #9. "Brooke" as I producer her is the 10 inch (24.5 cms) white version on the left. I had Eliott scan her and then I had her grown in photosensitive resin 1/2 size and 1/2 again. Since length reduced arithmetically but volume reduces by the cube, 1/2 becomes 1/8 by volume and 1/4 become 1/64. The smallest is really quite small, 2.5 inches (6.15 cms) but the detail is remarkable good. (Photo #14.)

While I have always enjoyed sculpting directly on a small scale, I have found the work tedious. Being able to construct a model at a more convenient size and then have it reduced accurately is a tremendous advantage. In addition, the door opens into more possibilities. For example, I could take a portrait head, scan it, and have it cast in miniature so that it could become a piece of jewelry. On the other hand, Bill, Elliot, and myself intend on offering "Grieving Friends" in a tabletop size. We have already sculpted the maquette which is too small and both the three foot and nine foot versions which are too large. Using the rubber molds for the nine foot figures, we are casting the pieces in forton MG partially to preserve them if something happened to the molds. But we will scan each piece, assemble them in a

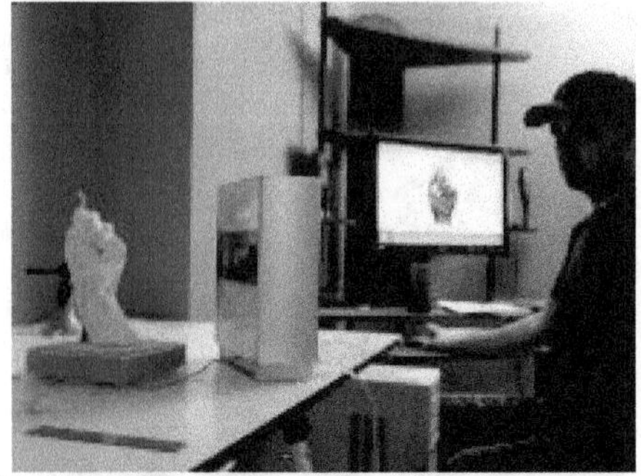
Photo #10 Eliott Summons using the tabletop 3-D scanner

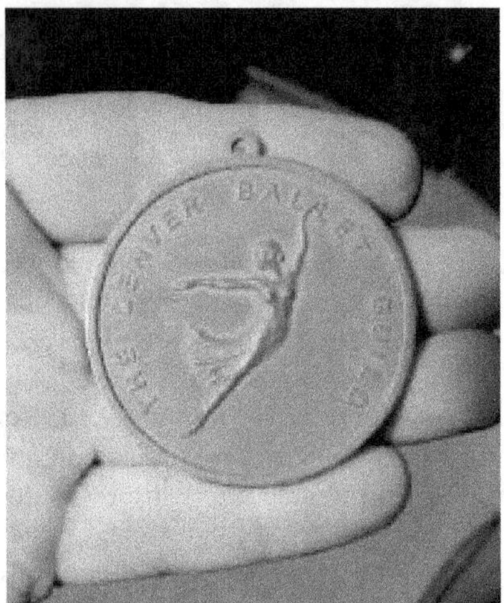
Photo #11. The medallion redone using the new technology. Notice the letters and the boarder. Shown here cast in resin with copper powder.

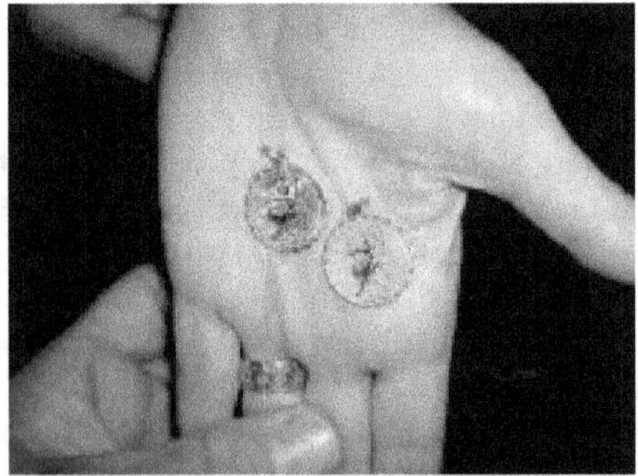
Photo #12. The quarter size charms in silver

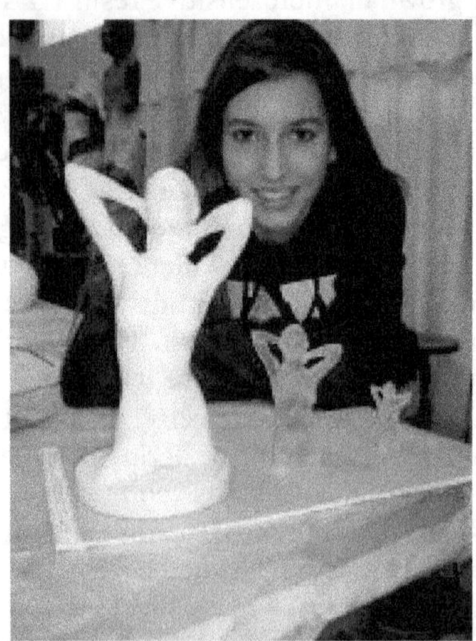
Photo #13. Jessica and the two smaller "Brookes" which were grown in photosensitive resin.

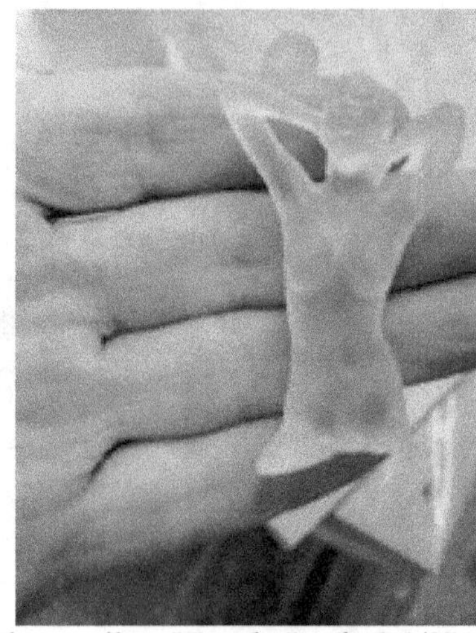
Photo #14. The smallest "Brooke" only 2 1/2" tall. The detail is remarkable.

computer, and have have the tabletop versions grown as perfect replicas.

It is now possible to make statues without knowing how to sculpt in the traditional way. One can dress (or undress) a model, put him or her in the correct pose, scan, and have the statue made large or small in the methods I have described. We artist are way behind industry which has used similar technology for years. The Boeing 777 was the first aircraft made without constructing a nonfunctioning mockup. Most products are now developed this same way. Part of"Grieving Friends' is a rifle stuck into a sandbag with its bayonet. As an experiment, Eliott constructed the bayonet image on his computer, no physical model in clay or wax or anything else ever existed. The computer data allowed the milling machine to construct a perfect 1 1/2 life size bayonet.

There will always be people who feel that any new technology is cheating and besides being immoral will cause the destruction of "real" artists. The same thing was said about photography in its early years. Buy almost 180 years later, painters are still here. I have no doubt whatsoever that had our materials and techniques been available to Michelangelo, Rodin, French, St.Gaudens, etc., etc., and etc., they would have embraced them. But just as it would have been unethical for an early photographer to pass of a photograph as a painting, we have an obligation to be honest with our collectors and not claim to have produced something by a method we actually didn't use.

Speaking of collectors, if you become proficient at changing the size of your work, the next time a collector asks, "Exactly what size is that piece?" You can answer, "What size would you like it to be?"

Note: Two of the very best companies for both reducing and enlarging, Daniels Engraving and Cyber FX, are regular are regular advertisers in Sculpture Journal.

Bibliography

Hoffman, Malvina, *Sculpture Inside and Out*, W. W. Norton and Company, 1939.
Rich, Jack R., *The Materials and Methods of Sculpture*, Oxford University Press

Sculpture Journal

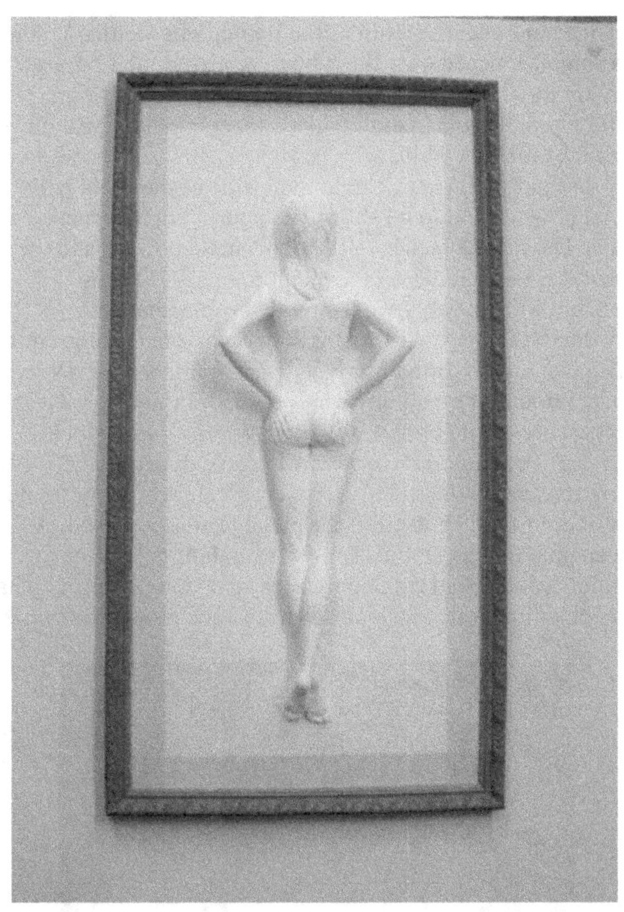

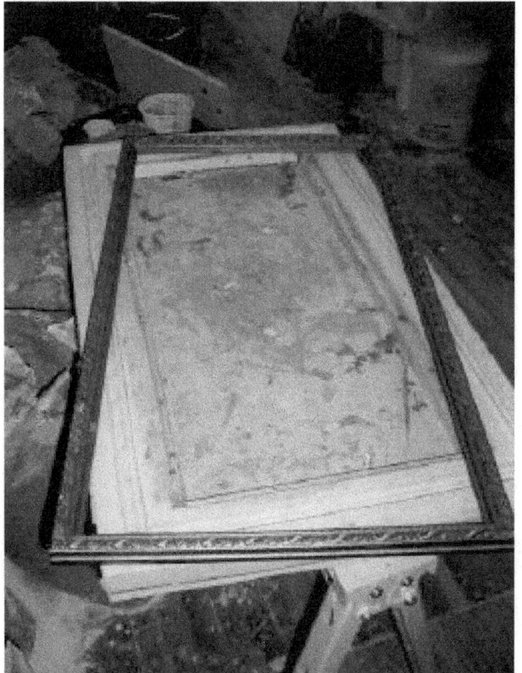

Photo 1

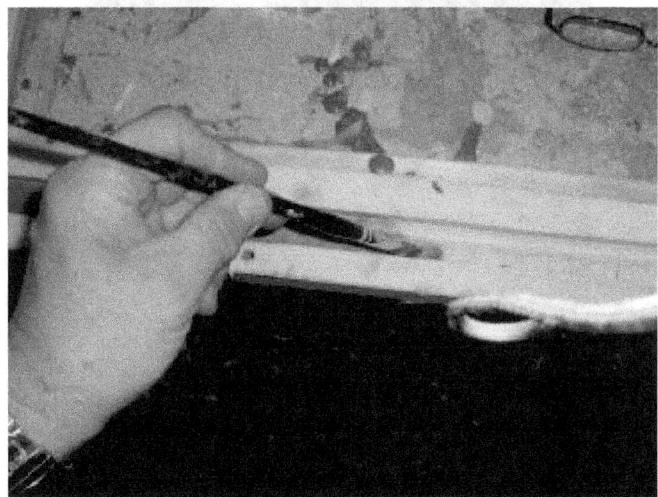

Photo 2

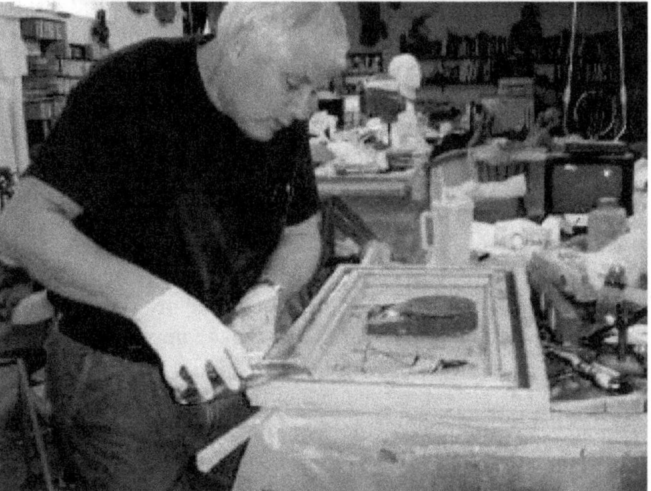

Photo 3

Bas Relief on the Cheap

By David E. Parvin, A.L.I.

Unless you are so well established that you a immune to a downturn, you have to be aware of and affected by the current softness in the art market. I suspect that the only beneficiaries are collectors; it has to be a buyers' market. Those of us who create, manufacture, or sell art are carrying on the best we can in lean times. We sculptors have an especially difficult path to follow because of the high "development" cost in bringing a new piece to market. Consider the painter who only has to purchase a canvas, some paint, and a frame and in some relatively short amount of time has something that might be turned into cold hard cash. We sculptors also have to purchase raw materials, but our creations often take far more hours to shape and we are still a long way and many dollars short of a return on investment. After all, it can be several months from, "I'm done," until the other people have finished molding and casting and we can expect to enrich some collector's life and the collector ours. So I got to thinking about adding to my portfolio without having to take out a loan or sell a relative for medical research.

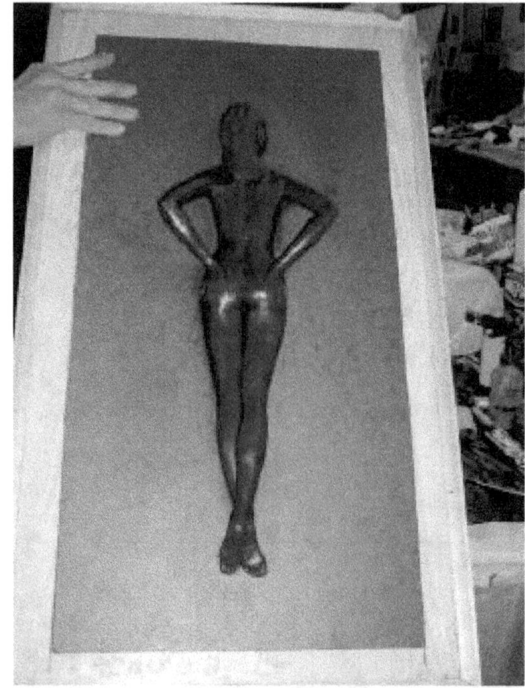

Photo 4

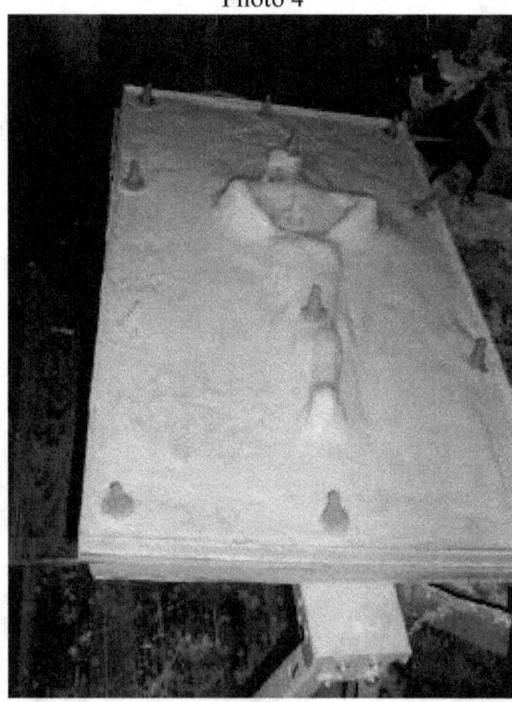

Photo 5

I decided to make a bas relief mostly because there was an idea I had been itching to tackle and this gave me an excuse to get to it. Besides, someone once told me that people have more wall space than table tops. While this would not be my first bas relief, it would be my first with a frame. A trip to my closest framer gave me new respect for painters. Frames are not cheap and I would need at least thirty of them. It seemed to me that if I ordered one just the right size, I could make a mold of it and cast as many as I need. So that I what I did. Photo #1 shows the custom made frame and the mold I made of it. The mold was a simple block mold made by placing the frame on its back, constructing a wall about an inch outside and another wall about an inch inside of it and filling the space inside, outside, and over the front of the frame. After letting it cure overnight, I turned over the rubber, removed the frame, and I had my mold. By keeping the inside wall, i could fit the mold around it and maintain its rectangular shape without making a mother mold.

In Photo #2, I am dusting the inside of the mold with metal powder. Photo #3 shows me pouring in polyurethane resin. The resin attaches itself to the metal powder and the result is a very credible fake metal frame. While any urethane will probably work, my favorite with metal powders id Easyflow Clear by PolyTec. Because it doesn't change color to white or gray as most urethanes do, a very small amount of metal powder is needed. I initially tried copper, brass, and bronze powders. While all three looked just fine, I preferred the brass. Add some dyes and the variations are endless. I also tried polyester resin but found that it didn't attach itself to the metal powders as well. An acceptable finish can be achieved by painting, however. While less expensive, the polyester takes longer to set up has a much stronger odor which seems to stick around forever.

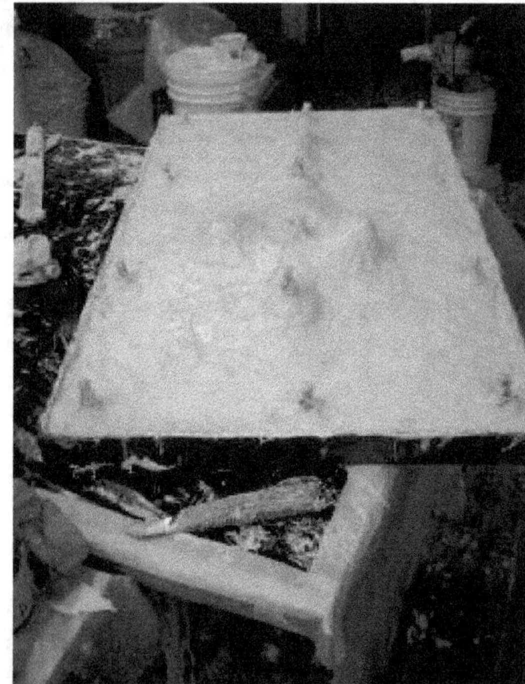

Photo 6

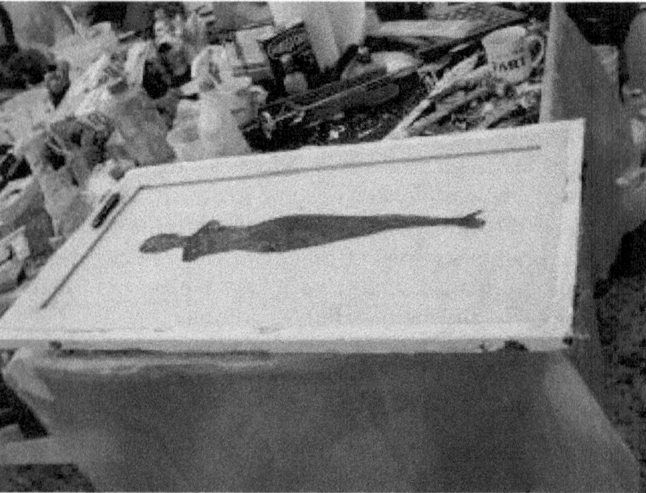

Photo 7

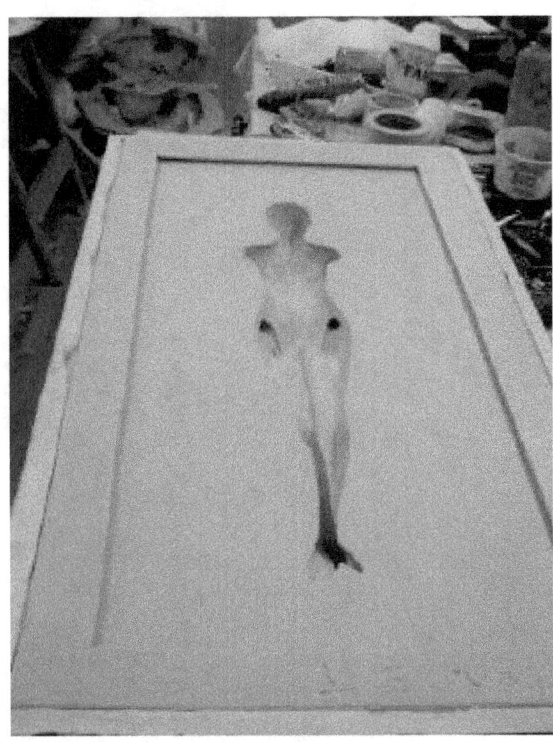
Photo 8

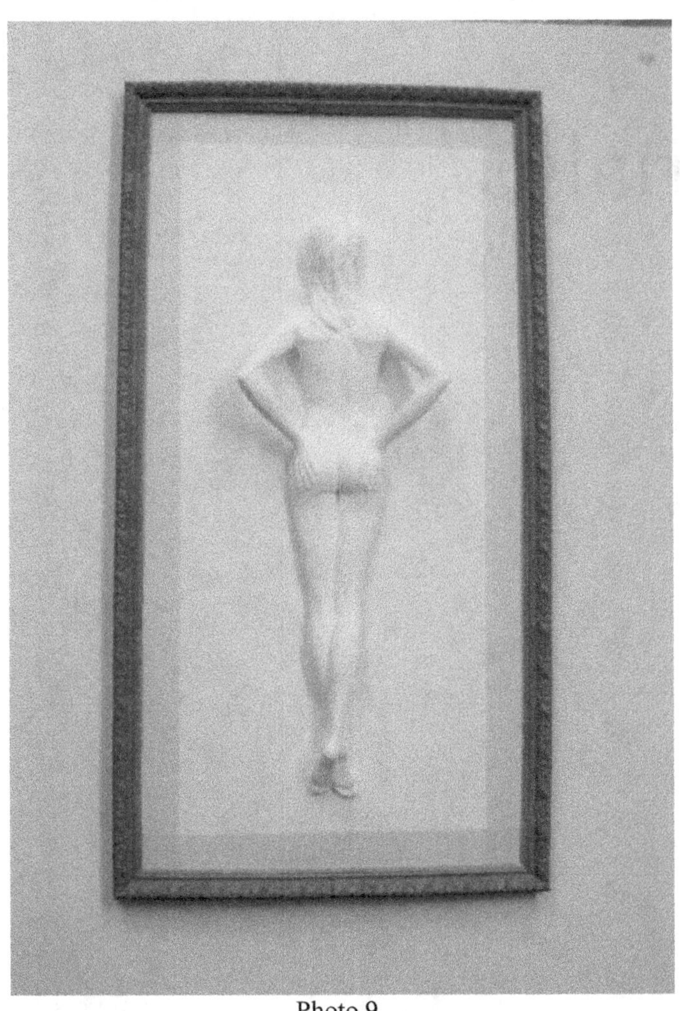
Photo 9

As I was playing frame maker, I was sculpting the bas relief which is the bare backside of a female figure sort of like a nude Irish dancer floating in space. Photo #4 shows the completed wax sculpture attached to a piece of Masonite. (I always sculpt smaller figures in wax because I feel I can get better detail than I can in clay.) In Photo #5, I have covered the figure and the piece of Masonite in the same kind tin cured silicone rubber that I used for the frame's mold. The "nipples" are rubber extensions that will hold the mother mold securely in place. (These were explained in an article I wrote in *SJ* in 2007 titled, "Another Little Trick For Some Molds.") Photo #6 shows the mother mold made of Forton MG held in place by said nipples.

After letting the rubber cure overnight, I removed the Masonite leaving the wax figure in the rubber. (Photo #7.) The completed mold sans wax figure is shown in Photo #8. If you are wondering how I got the arms of the mold, I had to cut the mold from the shoulders along the inside of the arms to the wrists.

The last photo shows the finished bas relief inside a fake metal frame. The relief itself was cast in PolyTec Easyflow 120 which is specially designed for rotocasting. The Rotocasting properties allow for one to rock the mold as if panning for gold and produce in several layers a bubble free casting front surface, a uniform thickness, and a professional looking smooth back.

I realize that my explanation here is a little abbreviated. But the purpose of this article was to get myself and perhaps some others to thinking about how to keep going in lean times. After all, what I have done is make a new piece completely in my own studio for just my labor and the cost of about ten pounds each of silicone rubber and polyurethane resin. Since I finished her today and wrote this tonight, its too early to see whether I have art fame or art shame. But to quote a Scottish folk song, "At least I tried!"

Sculpture Journal December 2008

Materials

An Alternative to Using Plaster Bandages As the Supporting Mold For Alginate Life Casting

By David E. Parvin, A.L.I.

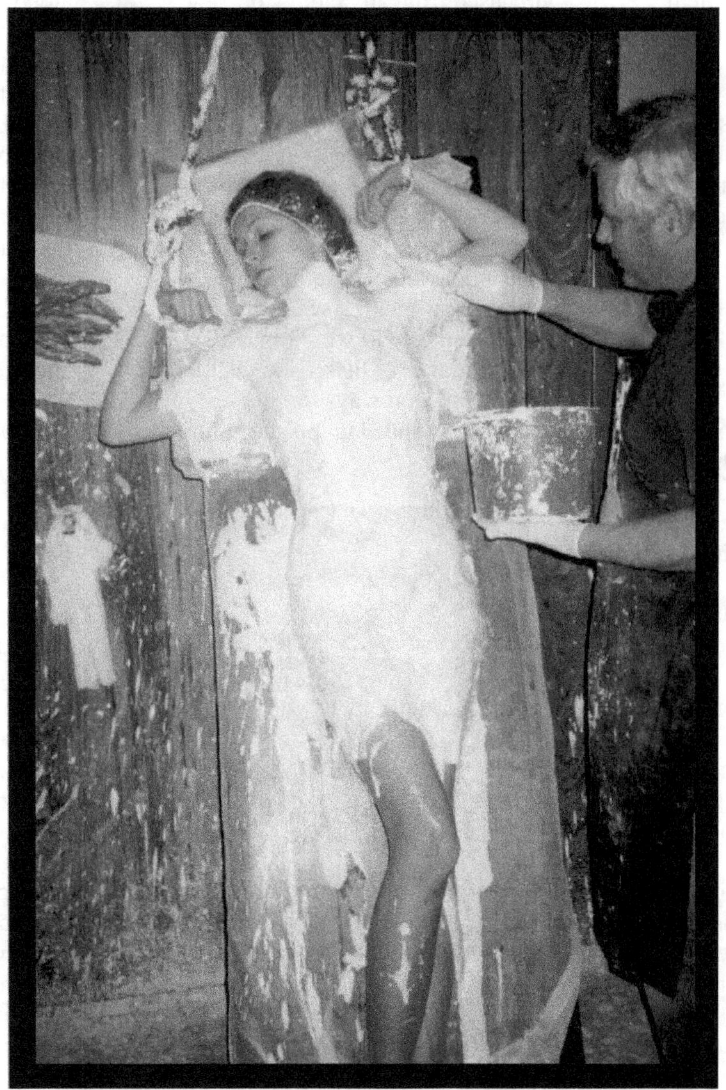

Photographs by Andy Hall

The author painting thin plaster into cotton which is stuck into the alginate of this torso casting.

I do not encourage anyone to be self taught. I can speak with some authority because I have been almost entirely self taught. I could have saved so much time by not reinventing the wheel over and over. This was especially true when my wheel was inferior to someone else's on my studio wall is, "There is almost always a better way." And I am always looking for a better way. (There are other helpful hints on my wall such as, "We are not like Robin Hood. Robin Hood robbed from the rich, we rob from everybody!" But I will save them for future articles.) However, sometimes one gets lucky and comes up with something that is better. What follows is one of these.

As far as I know, every other life caster that I have ever met uses plaster bandages as supporting or "mother" mold for alginate or silicone impressions. While it is true that plaster bandages are relatively simple to use and almost everybody has been taught to use them, there are some disadvantages including greater expense, slower application, and induced flaws in the end product'

1. One has to purchase the bandages and while not especially expensive are more costly than what I am proposing.

2. The application of plaster bandages is a very slow process. Ideally, one person wets the bandages and another applies them to the model. As slow as that is, applying the bandages solo is much worse. There is a faster way.

3. Generally one embeds some sort of fuzzy material, such as cotton, into the alginate to bond the alginate to the mother mold. The plaster in the bandages must soak through the fuzz. The bandages are not all that "juicy" and some clumps of fuzz may not get throughly soaked leaving air spaces that can result in bumps or "outties" in the positive casting, incomplete soaking of the fuzz may also weaken the adhesion of the two layers. (For an improved way to apply the fuzz, see "How to Extend the Setting Time of Alginate and Testing a New Product" Sculpture Journal, May 2003.

4. The fourth and last disadvantage is by far the most important. Applying plaster bandages can easily cause dimples in the casting. Here is what happens. The bandages must be spread on with at least a little pressure to conform to the alginate without air pockets or bubbles. The first layer is not the problem. If one depresses the alginate and the flesh beneath it, the flesh, alginate, and wet bandage will likely return to the proper contour. But if the bandage has partially setup, and deformation likely will remain. This is a common occurrence when a second layer of bandages is applied for additional strength. I have been told by some life casters that a certain amount of dimples is expected. Also, I suspect that some new life casters may not even notice the dimples because a not quite perfect life casting can still be quite impressive. But one's idea of perfect or even acceptable changes as one's skills improve. There is a way to get more perfect results. Simply stated, any solution for more flawless castings while saving time and money is to make your own bandage substitute using cheesecloth and a very fast setting plaster and applying them with no pressure. Only a few things are needed.

1. Cheesecloth. May be purchased from any cloth store. Comes in boxes of 100 yards though it may be purchased in lessor amounts. It comes folded twice to make four layers.

2. Fast setting plaster. I use impression Dental Plaster with is made by U.S. Gypsum and has a setup time of 3.5 to 5 minutes. If this is not available, Laboratory Dental Plaster with a setup time of 6 to 9 minutes will work almost as well. If neither of these is available, there are several ways to significantly speed up plaster. More on this later.

"I suspect that anyone who has used plaster in any significant amount is aware of at least three ways of accelerating the setting time."

3. A bucket for mixing. I use flexible 1 or 2-1/2 gallon buckets depending upon the size of the casting.

4. A 3" brush for faces and/or a 4" one for bodies. I use the cheapest throw-a-way ones I can find.

My life casting process is pretty much the same as anyone else's until the construction of the mother mold. In other words, a layer of alginate is applied over the area to be cast and some fuzz is embedded into the alginate. (If anyone is still embedding the fuzz prior to the alginate setting up, please review the above mentioned article, "How to Extend the Setting Time..." for a much simpler way.) Rather than wetting plaster bandages and applying them over the alginate, begin by using a paint brush and quickly wet the entire surface with fast setting plaster that has been mixed to about the consistency of cream. All you want to do is soak the fuzz down to the alginate, you are not trying to cover the alginate with a layer of plaster. Since "about the consistency of cream" is a little vague, I'll make it easy for you. The recommended mixing ratio for any of the dental plasters is 70 parts water to 100 parts plaster by weight. I suggest using 70 parts water to 70 parts plaster for a 1 to 1 ratio. Different plasters have slightly different recommended ratios but 1 to 1 should work with any plaster. The normal will make the plaster too thick. The normal would make the plaster too thick to soak through the fuzz and the layer of cheesecloth (see below); and if using IDP, it would set-up far too quickly. Soaking all the fuzz with a brush is very quick taking a minute max even for a torso from the top of the neck to mid thighs.

While the next step is easier and faster for two people to do, it can be done solo. I have my assistant place a piece of cheese cloth over the alginate-fuzz plaster and I paint it with additional plaster making sure that it is soaked through. The essential thing here is that only the tip of the brush is touching the mold and there should be no distortion or dimpling. The plaster impregnated cheesecloth pieces will adhere to the alginate very well even on vertical or overhanging surfaces. Some helpful pointers: the cheesecloth comes folded so that it is four layers thick. Do not unfold it. Use pieces about 18 inches long though I generally cut a few pieces about 12 and 6 inches long for covering smaller areas. I always go from the top down and the outside edges in. There is no need to overlap the pieces of cheesecloth more than an inch. Do one piece of cheesecloth at a time; paint the plaster on a piece of cheesecloth before putting another piece on the casting. The temptation will be to put on all the cheesecloth and then start applying the plaster. Even the thin cream

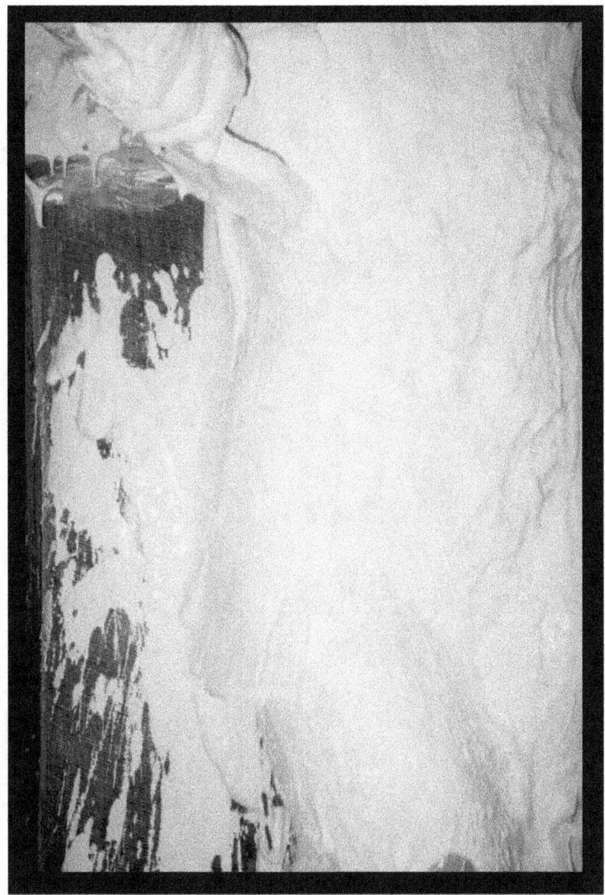

Painting plaster onto a piece of cheesecloth as a substitute for plaster bandages

like plaster will begin to thicken in just a few minutes. Once the plaster becomes too thick to soak through the cheesecloth, adding some water may buy you some time, but not but not much. When casting a torso or larger, I usually have to mix a second batch. If you mix the second batch in the same bucket in which there remains a small amount of the first plaster, the second will setup even more quickly so that mixing additional plaster only adds a few minutes to the process.

One layer of cheesecloth is usually sufficient. However, if I am concerned that some protruding part of the mold, e.g. the breasts, might collapse when the mold is placed "face down" on a foam pad, I will cover just that area with a second layer. Once can also stir into the plaster some fibers such as chopped fiberglass and paint it over the cheesecloth layer. If I want to stiffen the entire mold without adding the weight of another layer, I often take a piece of cheesecloth about three feet long and dip it into the plaster. I then twist it into a roll and place it along the outer edge of the mold. I repeat this until I have encircled the entire mold. Applying the cheesecloth and plaster should only take 4 to 5 minutes. The outer mold is sufficiently strong when it is warm to the touch. Removing the mold off the model, casting a positive, and demolding should be the same as if made from plaster bandages.

Some people may get the bright idea of dipping the pieces of cheesecloth in the bucket of plaster and spreading them on with their fingers exactly as if they were bandages. But I can assure you that they will stay in place better and will produce far less dimpling if applied as I have described.

If you do not live in a large metropolitan area, congratulate yourself for not living in a large metropolitan area, but you may have trouble finding a fast setting plaster such as impression Dental Plaster or Laboratory Dental Plaster. While you may order them from a dental supplier, they will cost four or five times as much as they would have if purchase from a U.S. Gypsum dealer. To find the closest dealer who carries these, go to www.gypsumsolutions.com

Let's suppose that neither IDP or LDP are available to you, what are your options? First of all, understand that all you need is a plaster that sets-up very quickly but does not get so strong that the outer mold is difficult to remove. Forget "Plaster of Paris" which can be purchased at your local hardware but is of such low quality that it's all but useless. (I once did a demonstration using Plaster of Paris and had to wait over an hour for the mother mold to set-up enough to remove it. I was running dangerously low on jokes and tap dance tunes!) Also don't consider Hydrocal or Hydro-Stone; both are too strong. US Gypsum Company manufactures at least 29 different plaster and gypsum cements for artistic and industrial applications. For specifications on any U.S. Gypsum product, go the web site mentioned above. My first alternative choice would be Regular Dental Plaster which sets up in 19 to 22 minutes. My next choices would be equally Pottery Plaster, # 1 Pottery Plaster, or Molding Plaster which set-up in 27 to 37 minutes. The above plasters are relatively soft allowing for easy removal of the mother old. All that is needed is a way of speeding up the slower ones.

I suspect that anyone who has used plaster in any significant amount is aware of at least three ways of accelerating the setting time; mixing with warmer water, adding table salt, and adding powered old plaster. So that I not lead anyone astray, I experimented with these, plus two other methods and spoke with a US Gypsum Company's technical assistance expert at 1-800-487-4431. I used Regular Dental Plaster with 70 degrees F (21 degrees C) water. I also mixed the samples to a much thinner consistency than normal, i.e. like cream as mentioned earlier by using a 1 to 1 ratio of plaster to water. The control sample was slightly thicker in 10 minutes, was too thick to use in 18 minutes, and was strong enough to demold in 24 minutes.

After establishing the baseline with the control sample, I mixed a batch using 100 degrees F water. Much to my surprise, the warmer water batch took <u>longer</u> to set-up. Since this was contra intuitive, I repeated the experiment and got the same result. Mr. Technical Expert explained that warmer water will reduce the setting time but only if the water and the plaster are within 10 degrees F. Otherwise, the temperature difference "shocks" the plaster and increases the setting time. Warm water is readily available, but heating pots of plaster might be a little inconvenient. There must be a more practical way

The second thing I tried was adding table salt. I used 3% of the weight of the plaster (or water, since they weighed the same). The salt did reduce the setting time but Mr. Technical Expert said the salt weakens the plaster and should not be used as an accelerant.

I even tried adding a solution of aluminum sulfate and water which accelerates Forton MG wonderfully. It doesn't work with plaster at all.

My next step was to mix a small amount of plaster in water (too little to setup) and let it cure for about 15 minutes. I then added more plaster to make the 1 to 1 ratio. This batch was slightly thicker in 3 minutes, too thick to apply in six minutes and strong enough to demold in 10 minutes. This is certainly doable. All one would have to do is make a water/plaster mix before starting a life casting and then use the mixture instead of plain water to mix the plaster.

The fastest method that I tried was to add crushed plaster to the mix. I took a piece of dried plaster that was as several weeks old and pulverized it with a hammer. Then I sifted it through a kitchen colander producing a fine powder. I added this reconstituted plaster to the next sample at a ratio of 5% old to new. I mixed the plasters into an equal amount of water by weight. The mixture was noticeably thickening up ill 2 minutes, w as too thick to apply at three minutes, and ready to demold at 8 minutes. This compared to 10, 18 and 24 minutes with the control sample.

Mr. Technical expert told me that shat I had done by pulverizing old plaster is produce *terra alba,* which is Latin for "white earth." He recommended this method for accelerating plaster. (Having spent four years of my youth studying for the priesthood, I have great respect for things with Latin names.) It seems my 5% was overkill, 1% is supposed to produce maximum acceleration. I was given one caveat (another Latin Word!) When using terra alba, it must be fresh. Apparently the crystals' surface smooths over with exposure to the moisture in the air and the terra alba becomes less potent. Keeping it in an airtight container helps. Also smashing it again breaks open the crystals and restores its effectiveness. While terra alba is not difficult to make, U.S. Gypsum sells it by the bag full.

One additional trick I was told is that the longer and more thoroughly you mix plaster, the faster it will set-up. I did not do any experiments with varied mixing time, but I have no reason to doubt the Mr. Expert.

If this seems unnecessarily complicated and difficult, it really isn't. I would encourage you to get some Impression or Laboratory Dental plaster and some cheesecloth and give it a try. I have shown this method to at least several hundred people in my workshops, most of whom have had some experience in life casting. I have yet to have anyone say that he/she would rather go back to plaster bandages The only negative feed back has been problems in getting fast setting plasters in their hometowns If after going to the web site, you cannot find a practical source, you may have to resort to accelerating slower plaster. While it will taken little experimenting. I am confident that it will be well worth your time.

David Parvin is a Colorado sculptor whose primary subject is the human form in a variety of materials he may be reached at: 303-321-1074

More Uses for Cheesecloth in Life Casting

by David E. Parvin, A.L.I.

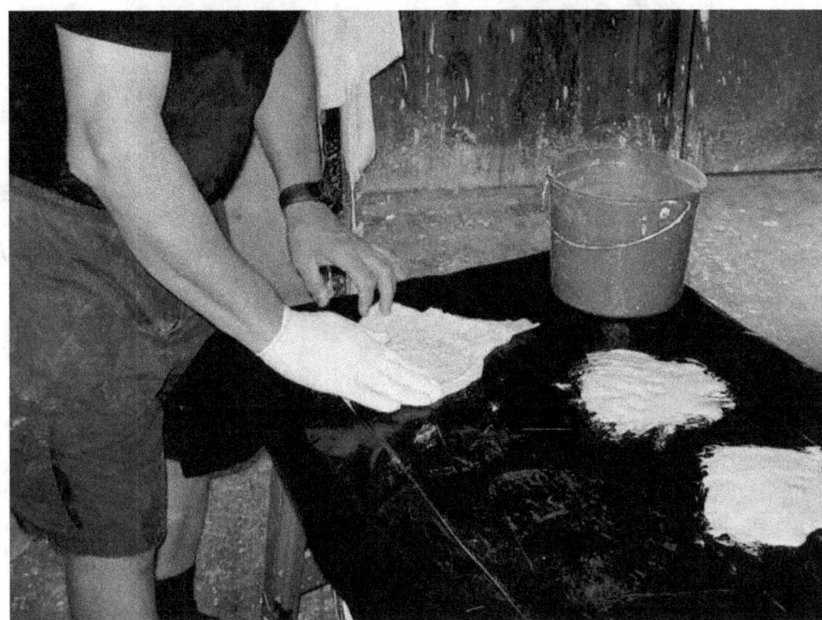

Photo l. Spreading alginate over apiece of cheese cloth prior to covering one of the alginate `pancakes. "

In the March 2004 issue of Sculpture Journal, I explained that cheese cloth along with fast setting plaster have definite advantages over the more common plaster bandages for making mother molds in life casting. The only time that I would recommend plaster bandages is if someone is interested in doing just one casting. The easiest way to achieve this is to purchase a kit which will have everything needed and will almost certainly provide plaster bandages for the mother mold since they are easy both to supply and explain how to use. However, if one wants to become a serious life caster, using cheese cloth and fast setting plaster will save time and money and consistently result in more perfect castings. Last month, August 2005, I described how cheese cloth can be used to bond the alginate layer to the mother mold instead of using rolled medical cotton. While cotton usually will do the job nicely, I rely on cheese cloth for difficult and or complex castings. In this article, I will explain how to use cheese cloth to strengthen alginate itself. In fact, the alginate can be so tear resistant that one can do some castings that one might have thought could have only been achieved with fast setting platinum-cured skin safe silicone rubber but without the rubber's disadvantages such as high cost and the tendency to pull out hairs.

To determine for yourself just how tear resistant alginate can be, mix up a small batch of say one pound of water and five ounces of alginate. Take about a third of your batch and spread it out on a flat surface as if it were a pancake. Besides, it makes another pancake. Cut a piece of cheese cloth just large enough to cover one of the pancakes. Spread about half of the remaining alginate over the cheese cloth. Turn it over and repeat with the other side. (See photo # 1) Lift up the alginate covered cheese cloth and cover one of the pancakes being careful to work out any air bubbles between the layers. Allow the alginate to set up. Pick up the plain alginate and see how easily you can tear it. (Photo #2) Next try the alginate with the cheese cloth. You may be able to tear it but only with considerable effort. (Photo #3)

A few hints before I describe some applications. The tear resistance of plain alginate depends upon the formulization. The strongest that I have come across is FiberGel by ArtMolds which has fibers blended into it allowing it to be very soft and flexible yet extremely strong. (See "Testing a New Alginate...," Sculpture Journal, May 2002, by yours truly.) While any good quality alginate may work for most applications, none have the tear strength you can get by adding cheese cloth.

Remember, one alginate has setup, new or still wet alginate will not bond to it unless it is treated. If possible, the cheese cloth covered layer should be spread over the first layer before the first layer has set up. But if one is running out of time (I always set a timer and keep an eye on it so I know just how much time I have), one can mist the surface of the first layer with Algislo, also by ArtMolds. This will keep the surface ungelled for a few more minutes giving more time to apply the second layer. And even if the first layer has set up, misting it with Algislo will soften the surface enough so that the second layer will bond.

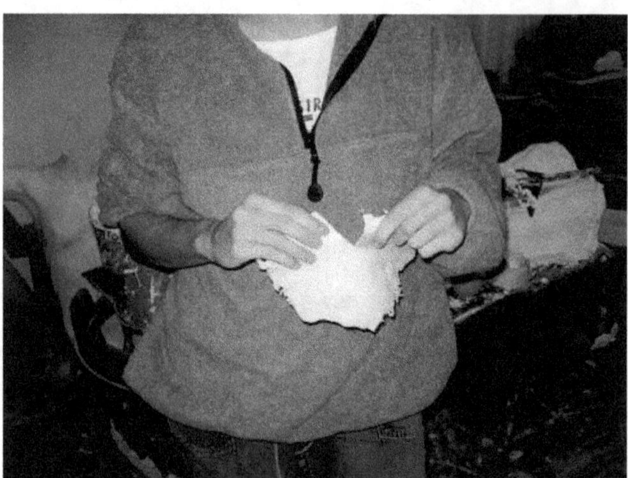
Photo 2. Able bodied assistant, Audra, tearing the plain alginate `pancake. "

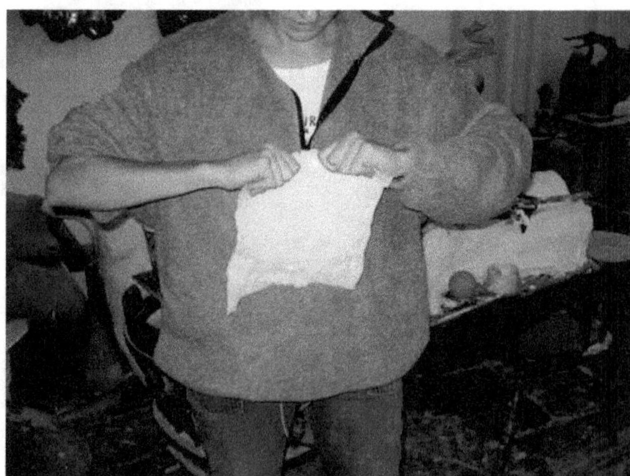
Photo 3. Audra trying without success to tear the alginate covered cheese cloth reinforced `pancake. "

Remember, once alginate has set up, new or still wet alginate will not bond to it unless it is treated.

Okay, so you can make very strong alginate, so what? Upon discovering that lightning is electricity, Ben Franklin asked himself how knowing this could be of any use to man kind. He then invented the lightning rod saving countless lives and property. Tear resistant alginate probably isn't going to be quite as beneficial to mankind, but it can be useful. I'll give several examples.

The easiest life casting to do is a hand. All one has to do is select a container somewhat larger than the hand, pour in some alginate, stick in a hand until the alginate sets up, pull out the hand, pour in whatever you want the hand to be made of, let it harden, and remove the alginate. Myself and nineteen assistants recently cast 651 hands in less than six hours just this way. Now supposing one wanted to cast more than just the hand up to the wrist. Sounds simple enough, just get a taller container. The problem is that there is a limit to how high up the arm you can cast before something unexpected happens. The cast forgers become flattened out and look like duck beaks. The first time this happened to me, I was baffled. I finally figured out that if the column of alginate is tall enough, its own weight compresses the alginate at the bottom causing the fingers to be squashed. The obvious solution is to make a thin, lightweight mold.

If you have used fast setting platinum cured skin safe silicone rubber, FSPCSSR, you know that an arm can be covered up to at least the elbow and the FSPCSSR removed as if it were a glove, i.e., without cutting a seam. The FSPCSSR mold may even be rigid enough to hold its shape without a mother mold. Filling the mold with plaster, Forton MG, etc. will give you a seamless casting of the hand and arm. The disadvantages are the expense of the FSPCSSR and its tendency to pull out hairs. In my experience, using enough releasing agent to eliminate the "waxing" effect results in an unacceptable loss of detail. The same kind of mold can be made with alginate and cheese cloth. Just coat the arm and hand with alginate and then apply a second layer made of alginate covered cheesecloth. Using a piece that is long enough, start at the elbow and either wrap it down around the arm and hand or apply it straight down the arm, around the hand and back up the other side. You may have to try this several times to get the knack of it. This mold will come off the model in one piece without tearing with a little gentle pulling. Unless the model is extremely hairy, there should be no discomfort.

The easiest way to support the mold for filling is to suspend it from the open end. Someone can simply hold it while another person pours in the casting material. But this requires that the mold be held until the material sets up. What I have done is cut three pieces of string about eight feet long. To each end, six in all, I have tied large fish hooks. I drape the strings at their midpoints over a ceiling hook so that the fish hooks hang about four feet above the floor. I attach the hooks around the open end of the mold and suspend it at a convenient height indefinitely. It is a good idea to crimp down the barbs on the fish hooks for easy removal from the mold. (Or, for that matter, for easy removal from yourself if you get careless!) This method should allow for distortion free and seamless castings. (Photo #5)

If you think that it's necessary, you can build a mother mold in plaster around the suspended alginate and cheesecloth. Just paint several layers of fast setting plaster over the alginate. You may even gently, so as not to distort it, wrap the alginate with a layer of cheesecloth and paint very wet plaster into it.

In the Feb. and Mar., 2005 issues of Sculpture Journal, I write two articles on casting a head in the round. While the process as described generally works just fine, I have since started applying a piece of alginate covered cheesecloth from the temple on each side of the head rearward to just short of the center of the back of the head. Do not overlap the pieces in the back or it will make cutting the seam more difficult. The rest of the process is the same as in the articles. The result is that spreading apart the mold in the back to get

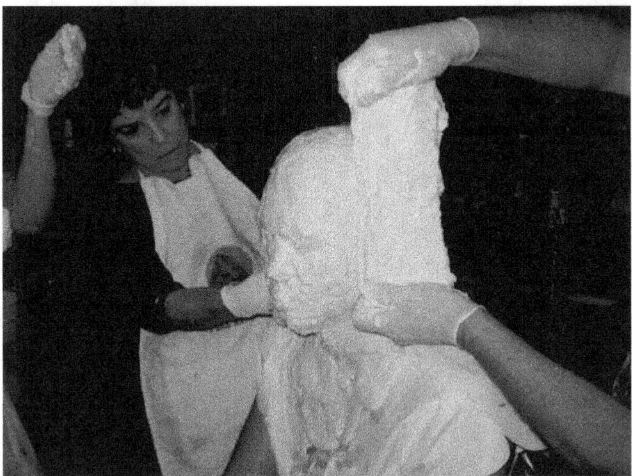

Photo 5. Applying a piece of alginate covered cheese cloth to the temple when casting a head in the round.

the model's head out is far less likely to tear the alginate and assures that- the mold will close back-up precisely aligned.

A third use is to help alginate to stay in place. For example, if you were casting arms crossed in front of a person's chest, you may find that the alginate tends to drip or run off the bottom sides (undercut areas) of the arms. (Properly mixed alginate, i.e., not too runny is essential here.) Applying alginate covered cheesecloth over and under the arms can be very helpful.

While cotton usually will do the job nicely, I rely on cheese cloth for difficult and or complex castings.

By the way, you may be thinking as I did, why not just eliminate the first layer of alginate and just apply the alginate covered cheesecloth directly to the skin much as some life casters use plaster bandages instead of alginate. But just as plaster bandages are terrible for capturing detail, the alginate covered cheesecloth applied directly to the model results in too many surface bubbles.

Using alginate covered cheesecloth is a technique which I have found to be very useful. I am certain that I will find additional applications in the future. Remember, one of the differences between a good life caster and a great one is that the great one knows more tricks. Good luck!

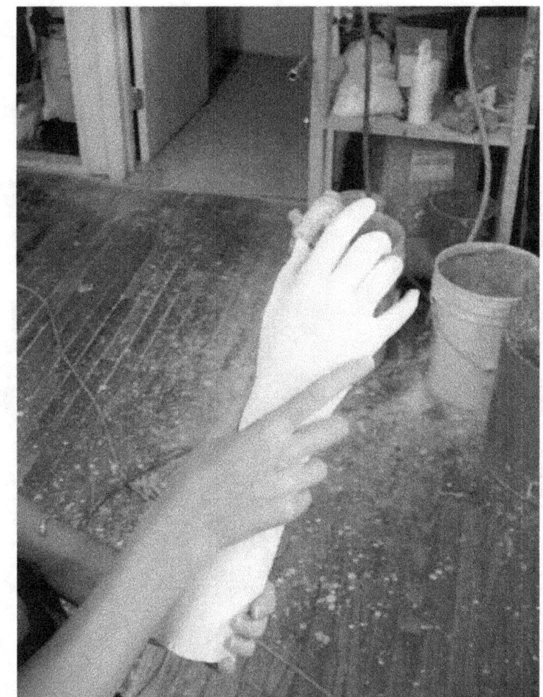

Photo 4. A seamless and distortion free plaster hand and arm.

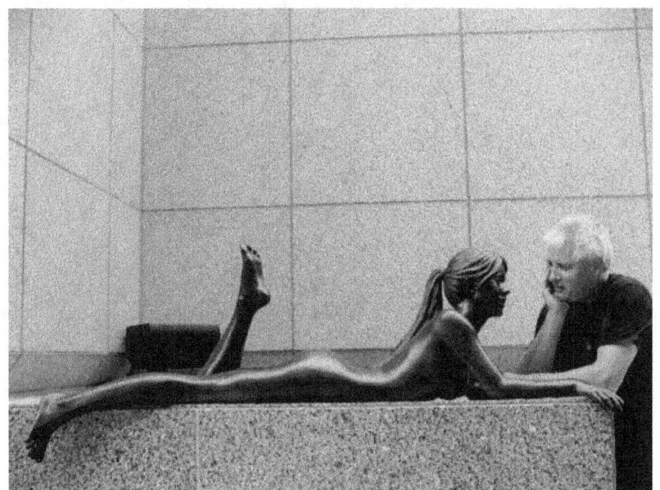

Dave Parvin face-to-face with his recent commissioned bronze sculpture in downtown Denver, Colorado

David Parvin is a sculpture living in Denver CO. He has years of experience in life casting and holds workshops throughout the year. He may be reached at 303-321-1074

Sculpture Journal October 2005

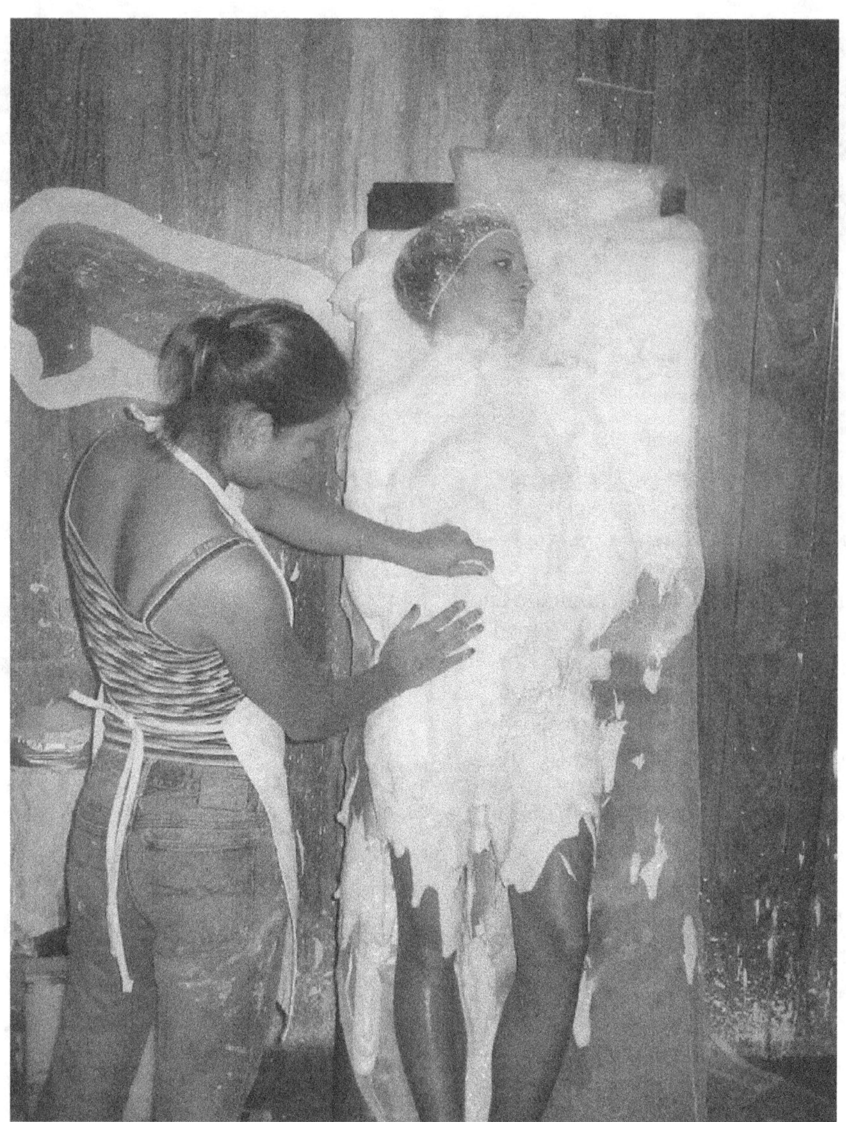

Another Use For Cheesecloth in Life Casting

By David E. Parvin, A.L.I.

One of the keys of being able to accomplish more complicated and flawless life castings is knowing the right tricks. In this article, I'm going to share one of mine. But first, some may recall that in the past I have always tried to be sensitive to the trees in Oregon. You see, up until just recently, *.Sculpture Journal* was published in Oregon and every month Oregonian firs, pines, and cascaras had to be sacrificed at the: "Altar of Disseminating Knowledge through Pulpification" in order for this publication to go forth and enlighten the darkness of ignorance. Whenever I could, rather than retell something I had already covered in a previous article, I referenced the article; saving so very many trees. I was conscientious, almost to a fault, even though Oregon seemed to have more trees than the entire Mid-west and one would hardly have been missed. But alas, it appears that not everyone shared my concern and Oregon has apparently run out of trees forcing Jon White to move his magazine to Southern California where a tree is a rare sight indeed. Well I hope everyone now understands, because if a rain forest can't fill this magazine appetite for trees, how in the world can a desert? When they say, "California is the land of fruits and nuts," they aren't referring to trees. Now if you will just take down from the mantel your leather bound collection of 2004 Sculpture Journals, open to page 4 of the March issue, and read "An Alternative to Using Plaster Bandages as the Supporting Mold For Alginate Life Casting I will not have to repeat myself except for a very brief summation. In that article, I explained that using cheese cloth and fast setting plaster rather than plaster bandages can save time, money and result in far more perfect life castings. These advantages thoroughly demonstrated in my DVD "Casting the Female Torso." In this article, I will share another use for cheese cloth that may expand your life casting horizons.

Sometimes cheese cloth can be used more effectively to bond the alginate to the mother mold rather than some more commonly used material. Just incase the reader is new to life casting let me explain the importance of this step. The impression of the person consists of two main components, the alginate layer on the skin and a rigid mother mold that allows the alginate to hold its shape when removed from the mold. Unfortunately, the two components do not stick together without a little help. And if not bonded together, the mother mold will came off by itself leaving, the alginate behind still on the model. At that point, the life caster would have two problems, getting the alginate off without tearing it and then seating it back into the mother mold perfectly positioned. Using **FiberGel** by **ArtMolds** with its higher tear resistance helps, but the real solution is to bond the two layers together so that they remain joined and aligned.

For the last almost two decades, I have tried numerous different materials and for the last few years had settled on rolls of medical cotton. Not only does the cotton generally work very well, but its application is easy to teach and learn. Just cut the cotton into four to five inch squares and separate them into two halves exposing the more loosely packed centers. After the alginate has been applied to the model and just prior to its setting up, press the cotton squares into the alginate and pull them away leaving a layer of cotton embedded into the alginate. Repeat until all the surface of the alginate has been covered. As soon as the alginate has set up, the cotton and the layers will have become one. This is true whether one uses plaster bandages or the better method with cheese cloth and fast setting plaster as explained in the above mentioned article.

> ...Sometimes cheese cloth can be used more effectively to bond the alginate to the mother mold rather than some more commonly used materials.

One problem with applying the cotton in this way is that you will be trying to accomplish two things at once, covering the model with a perfect layer of alginate and attaching the cotton. The alginate may gel before you can get all the cotton in place. There are better ways. Simply mist the surface of the alginate with **Algislo**, also by **ArtMolds**, which, if applied before the alginate sets up, will keep the surface soft for several additional minutes giving more time to complete this step. An added advantage is that if you discover an area where the alginate is two thin a second layer of alginate will bond to the first, if misted with **Algislo** possibly saving a casting. I have been using and teaching these methods for several years and will continue to do so. (See "How to Extend the Setting Time of Alginate & Testing a New Product," Sculpture Journal, March 2003.) But there is an Alternative which I also use and I will now describe.

The reason that I developed this other method is that I was occasionally having a minor problem in that the "positive" castings in plaster, **Forton MG**, hydrocal, etc. made shallow indentations. One of my assistants, a very savvy young lady named Kelly Rooney (I mention her name because she recently moved to California to pursue a career in Make-up and special effects and you may soon see her name in some motion picture credits. Good luck Kelly!) noticed that these imperfections most often occurred on the shoulders. What we deduced was that the firmness and rounded shape of the shoulders created suction holding the alginate and mother mold in place. When the mold was removed, the suction would hold the alginate against the skin and the mother mold might very slightly separate from the alginate before the alginate came loose from the skin, the alginate wouldn't seat itself exactly back into position. When the "positives" were cast the places of separation were minor but still visible.

What was needed was something that would still be simple to use and yet more securely bond the alginate and the mother mold. Pieces of cheese cloth do nicely. Cheese cloth comes in strips about six inches wide and four layers thick. Do not unfold the layers. Cut into lengths of three to ten inches and cover the alginate very much the same way you would with cotton. Just put the strips in place and gently tap it into the surface of the alginate. (See photo #1 where the above mentioned and soon to be famous Kelly is doing just that.) Make sure that the cheese cloth follows the contours of the alginate layer without bridging over hollow places or pulling on the alginate. In the first case, the mother mold will not be able to fill any air spaces between the alginate and the cheese cloth. In the second, the cheese cloth can pull against the alginate causing a line in the "positive" casting. Using fairly short pieces of cheese cloth helps prevent both of these problems. Be careful not to overlap the cheese cloth pieces more than about a half inch. Having a supply of cheese cloth pieces in various lengths will help in applying it without excessive overlapping. It is important that the plaster in the mother mold saturate through the cheese cloth right down to the surface of the alginate to prevent air spaces which are more likely to occur if the cheese cloth is applied to thickly. Soaking through the cheese cloth is also more easily done with fast setting plaster applied with a paint brush than with plaster bandages. As soon as the cheese cloth has been soaked with plaster is as if a layer of plaster bandages had been applied and the mother mold is about half way constructed. I then apply another layer of cheese cloth and plaster for added strength. As soon as the plaster gets warm the mold is ready to remove. The time from mixing the alginate to removing the mold from a torso as shown in the photo should take from twenty to thirty minutes.

For smaller and simpler castings I will still use the cotton method. As the molds become larger and more complex I will use cheese cloth in places that require extra strengthening. In the casting in the photo notice that both arms are included causing a complex surface with ins and outs and overhangs. Consequently, I decided to use cheese cloth on the entire surface.

In a future article I will describe how cheese cloth can be used to strengthen alginate so that a totally seamless mold of an arm can be made, or a head or torso, can be cast in the round more perfectly and with less effort than one might imagine.

Sculpture Journal- September 2005

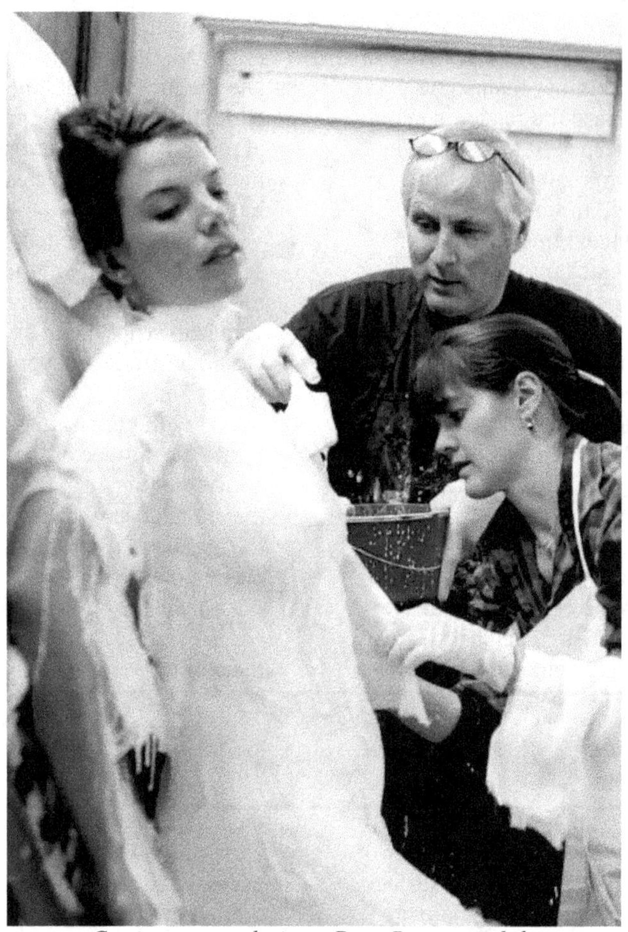

Casting a torso during a Dave Parvin workshop

How To Extend The Setting Time of Alginate

Testing a New Product

by Dave Parvin

The setting time of alginate must follow the Goldilocks Syndrome. Too quick and one can not get the job done. Too slow and the subject becomes the victim. It has to be just right. There are dental alginates that set-up in as little as a minute. Great for infants' hands but far too fast for faces, bodies, or more complex hand casting. Most of the alginates that are formulated for artists that I have used have a setting time of about five minutes, enough time for a simple casting. But as my life-casting has become more and more complex, I have found that a few more minutes working time is essential.

Here is the problem. Imagine that you are casting a face. If a face to you is just from the top of the head down to part of the neck and back to part or all of the ears, then five minutes is plenty of time to mix the alginate, apply it, and embed some sort of fuzzy material such as cotton or mock wool before it sets up. But a face to me means from the top of the head down to at least mid chest and back well behind the ears and including the shoulders and often one or both arms and bands; five minutes just isn't enough time.

The alginate that I prefer is Moldgel SloSet which is formulated for about eight minutes setting time. (More about this alginate later). But even if eight minutes were always adequate, there is another reason for any serious life caster to be prepared to slow down the setting time. I have been made privy to alginates's dirty little secret. Apparently, it is extremely difficult to precisely control the setting time. My source who has 40 years of experience in formulating and

There are four ways to extend the setting time of any alginates: varing the water temperature, varying the water to alginate ratio, adding the standard powdered retarder, and the best way using a new liquid retarder, "Algislo."

manufacturing alginates tells me that all manufacturers struggle with this. This partially results from problems in blending the ingredients. Also, the relative humidity present in the air while the alginate is being manufactured has an effect; the more humidity, the faster the setting. Thinking that you have five or eight minutes to work and finding that you have only three or six minutes can seriously mess with your schedule unless you are prepared.

There are four ways to extend the setting time of any alginates: varying the water temperature, varying the water to alginate ratio, adding the standard powdered retarder, and the best way using a new liquid retarder, "Algislo."

The setting time of alginate is inversely proportional to the temperature of the water. The colder the water, the longer the setting time. Conversely, warmer results in faster. Aside from the possible intended affect of raising goose bumps and puckering nipples, cold alginate can shrink other parts and nobody wants to be called "Tiny." But the biggest disadvantage is uncomfortable for the subject.

Another factor is the alginate/water ratio; more water means a thinner, more runny mixture and a longer setting time. This sounds like the answer, however, this is the least desirable approach. Alginate should be about the consistency of oatmeal but without' lumps; thick enough that it will remain in place from 1/8 or 1/4 of an inch thick on a vertical surface. Too thin and it will simply run off. Too much water will also weaken the impression.

The third solution is almost the answer. There is a retarding agent widely available that is in a fine white crystal form that looks like table salt but isn't. The first time I ordered some of this it came without any directions. I called the manufacture. Even though the technical representative was supposed to be the expert, he didn't seem to be real sure of the amount required for the several extra minutes that I needed to cast the front half of a torso. He suggested that I use about an ounce per pound of alginate. After 30 minutes, the alginate was just as liquid as when it had been applied. Another phone cal l and I realized that the expert was clue less (perhaps this explains why this particular manufacturer is no longer in business). Fortunately the model was a good sport and after getting her cleaned up, we tried again using a much smaller amount which worked. If you try this method, be sure to follow the directions exactly since a little goes a long way. But remember that I said that this "solution is almost the answer." The problem is that often soft spots can occur in the mold. I had been directed to add the crystals to the alginate powder. It seemed to me that a more logical method would have been to add the crystals to the water so I tried it but with the same result. Some experimentation convinced me that the crystals do not dissolve quickly enough to allow for a uniform distribution throughout the mixture and were heavily concentrated, there will be soft areas of ungelled alginate.

Now we get to the fourth solution and the part where "they lived happily ever after." There is a new product that solves the problem; it is a liquid called "Algislo" made by ArtMolds. When I first got some of it, I experimented by mixing 5 ounces of ArtMolds Regular Set alginate to 16 ounces of water at 21 degree C. (70 degree F.). In the next batch, I substituted ½ ounce of Algislo for 1/2 ounce of water: then 1 ounce for 1 ounce, etc. (Note: I did not just add the Algislo without reducing the water or the extra liquid would have changed the viscosity of the mixture). The results are shown in the following table on the chart.

Chart

Alginate	Water	Algislo	Setting Time
5 oz	16 oz	0	3 min. + 00 sec.
5 oz	15 1/2 oz	1/2 oz	4 min + 05 sec
5 oz	15 oz	1 oz	4 min +45 sec
5 oz	14 1/2 oz	1 1/2 oz	5 min + 40 sec
5 oz	14 oz	2 oz	7 min + 10 sec
5 oz	13 1/2 oz	2 1/2 oz	9 min + 00 sec

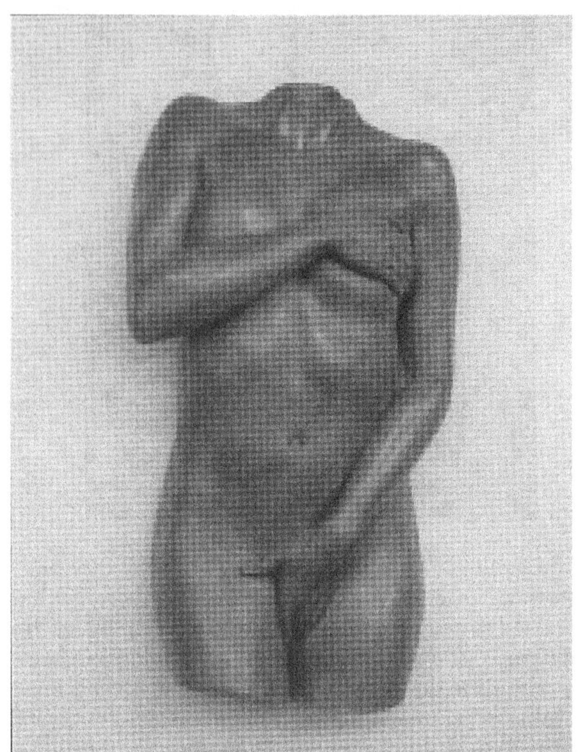

"'`Modesty," the ins and outs around both arms and hands require special attention

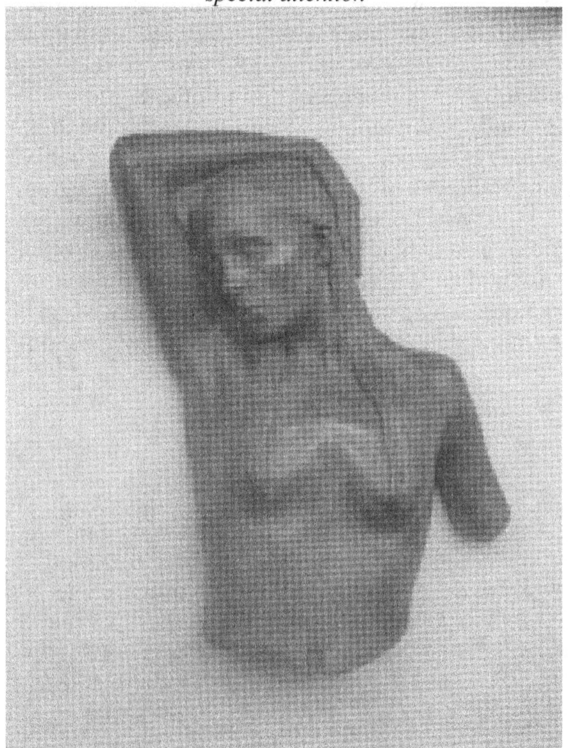

"Nina" the area covered, the complete right arm, and the hair add to the complexity of this moderately difficult portrait casting.

I used to paint on the bonding agent with a brush; now I use a spray bottle. Not only is it much faster, but it will not damage the still liquid alginate as a brush would.

The really exciting thing to me was that! I got no soft spots either in the test samples or in actual castings. I suspect that this is because Algislo being a liquid blends uniformly into the water and the water/alginate mixture. While I intend to live apply ever after, I do have a caution. One can not take a fast setting dental alginate and simply add enough retarder to produce an adequate eight minute alginate. Specifically, additional alginic acid must be blended into maintain the desired characteristics or the alginate may only set up to about the consistency of a soft boiled egg, too fragile for a durable impression. The better manufacturers reformulate for the desired setting times. If you are using high quality alginate, you can easily get up to an additional 3 or 4 minutes working time without any problems.

There is another way to get longer working times using Algislo. But before I explain it, I would like to digress for a moment. As I said above, when casting a face or a body there are two steps that must be accomplished prior to the alginate's setting LIP. The desired area must be coated with alginate and then something fuzzy such as cotton, mock wool, etc. must be embedded into the alginate which will in turn bond the outer mold to the alginate. If one runs out of time, why not just mix a new batch, apply it over the first, and continue? While this does not change the setting time, the result is the same since one would have twice as long to accomplish the first two steps. This works as long as the first layer of alginate has not gelled. Unfortunately, one of alginate's snore peculiar characteristics is that new will not bond to old once the old has set up unless a bonding agent is used.

The setting time of alginate is inversely proportional to the temperature of the water. The colder the water, the longer the setting time. Conversely, warmer results in faster.

Once upon a time many years ago, I discovered that a solution of baking soda and water makes an effective though not the best bonding agent. Prior to discovering 8 minute MoldGel and when I was still using 5 minute alginates, I had pretty good results with this method. But there are two disadvantages, two layers takes more material than one and adds another step taking more time resulting in more discomfort for the subject. However, this can be used to build a thick layer of alginate when needed for a particularly difficult mold. Also, if after applying the alginate, you discover that there are places where the alginate is too thin or where the fuzz wasn't embedded, they can be repaired this way. As it turns out, after testing both, I am convinced that Algislo will bond alginate layers more securely than baking soda.

While experimenting for this article, I discovered a technique that I am finding to be very helpful. Using a spray bottle, misting a thin application of Algislo to a layer of alginate just before the alginate sets up will allow all but the surface to gel. You then have several additional minutes to embed the fuzz. Anyone who has some experience with life casting will probably see the advantage of this. Using this method, one can concentrate on a more perfect application of alginate without being rushed to get the fuzz in place. The torso in the accompanying photograph titled "Modesty" is an example of how useful this can be. The problem is that the ins and outs and undercuts involved with the two arms make it very difficult to apply the alginate and embed the fuzz in one layer. What I would have done in the past was apply the alginate and carefully tweak it so that the application was as perfect as possible as it gelled. Then I would have painted on baking soda/water, applied a second layer of alginate; and added the fuzz. Now what I do is just before the alginate sets up spray on the Algislo and apply the fuzz eliminating time and alginate. I am finding this works so well that I am using this system with all but the simplest of castings.

Another advantage of Algislo is that even if you are too slow in its application and the alginate has gelled, Algislo will soften the surface allowing you to embed the fuzz. Baking soda will not do this.

Note: I used to paint on the bonding agent with a brush; now I use a -spray bottle. Not only is it much faster, but it will not damage the still liquid alginate as a brush would.

One last point that I would like to make is that all alginates are not alike. I have had people in my lifecasting workshops proudly produce some alginates that they had purchased "over the Internet at a bargain price. Well, I'm always looking for a bargain too so I have suggested mixing up a sample and testing it. While there may very well be some bargains out there that I have not found, what 1 have seen so far is that you get what you pay for. The usual problem is the sot t boiled egg consistency mentioned above without even adding any retarding agent. I can only assume that the low price is the result of skimping on materials. The two alginates that I currently use almost exclusive now are ArtMolds Regular Set and SlowSet. The regular set will gel in as little as three minutes with very warm water. I use it when I need speed such as for infant's hands. The SlowSet's 8 minutes is ideal for more complex castings. Stick with quality and your castings and your frustrations will be the better for it.

About the author

Art Review has called him "...the premier life casting expert in Colorado, maybe in all the West." Dave Parvin was honored by being one of the first artists given life membership in the almost four-year old Association of Lifecasters International. Though principally known for his classical, figurative bronzes, Dave has also worked in wood, pewter, cast marble, urethane, concrete, polyester resin, raku, glass, and most recently acrylic. About sixteen years ago, Dave became interested in life casting. He has become recognized as one of the innovators in life casting having developed many new techniques.

Dave enjoys sharing his experience and expertise and routinely offers workshops in life casting, art marketing, and sculpting.

Presently showing in seven galleries from California to Indiana, Dave has a long list of commissions, juried show participation, and media recognition. He may be reached at parvinstudio@attbi.com. However, he would much prefer to talk than type and would prefer to be called at 303-321-1074.

Sculpture Journal - March 2003

Forton MG Demystified, Part 1

By David E. Parvin, A.L.I.

Recently I have become aware that there are people who are reluctant to use Forton MG (FMG) because they have the impression that it is complicated and expensive. I would like to dispel both of these concerns and encourage people to take advantage of one of the most useful materials available for sculptors.

While FMG does cost somewhat more than just plaster, hydrocal, hydrostone, or any other gypsum product alone, all are inferior to FMG which was developed for outdoor applications and is far more durable especially when exposed to weather. FMG can be blended with metal powders to make amazingly credible cold cast metal pieces. FMG will bond to itself even when completely cured allowing for repairs and alterations. FMG is far stronger and allows for thinner, lighter life casts, bas reliefs, mother molds, etc. FMG really should be compared to resins or metal, both of which are far more expensive. And unlike resins,

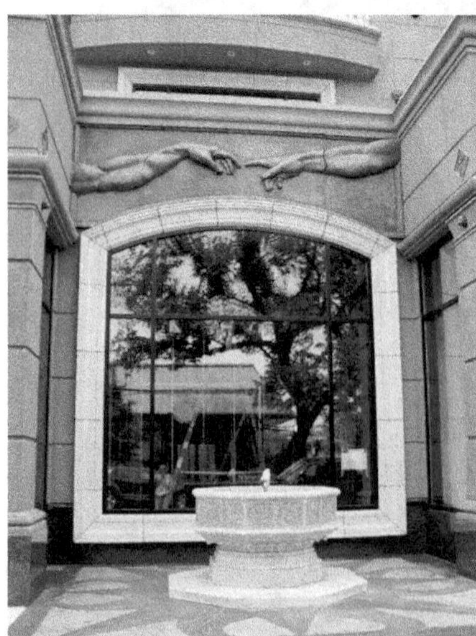

Hands 16 feet across in Forton MG with metal power. This has been in place for about seven years and looks the same as when installed.

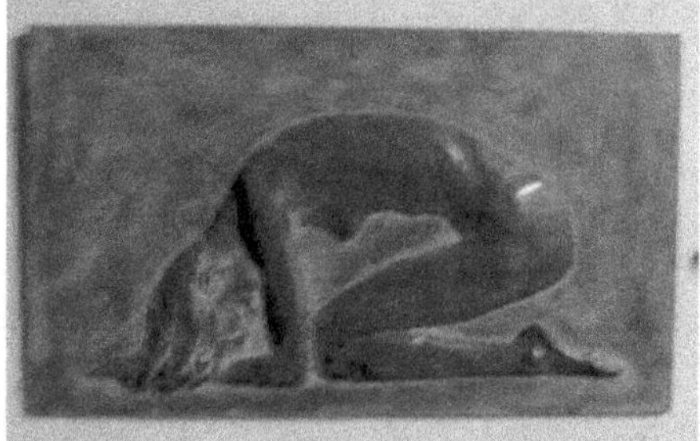

This was my first application of Forton MG. I was amazed with how much it looked like real bronze.

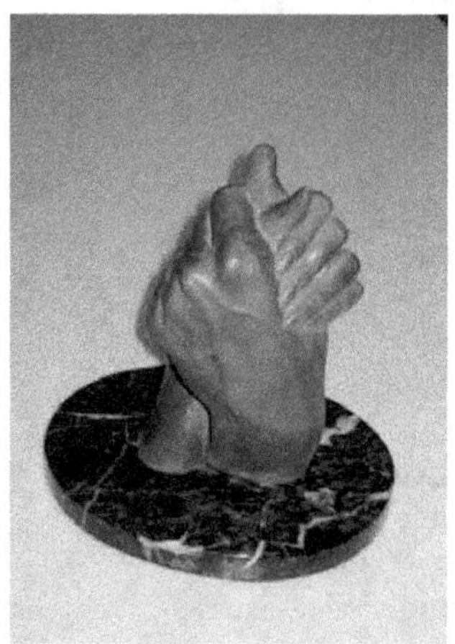

Hands of newlyweds

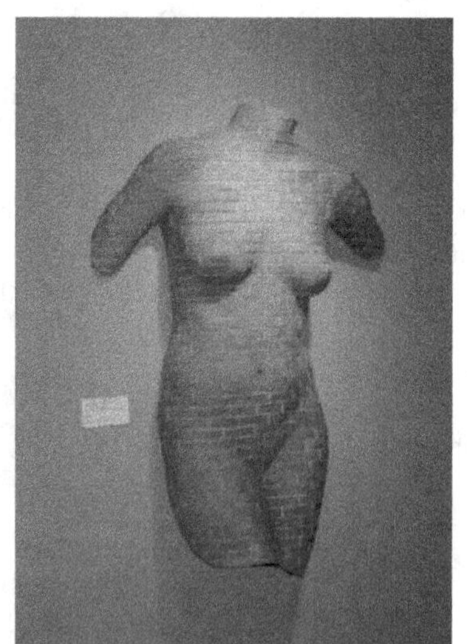

Life cast torso titled "Built Like..." in Forton MG with a brick colored dye

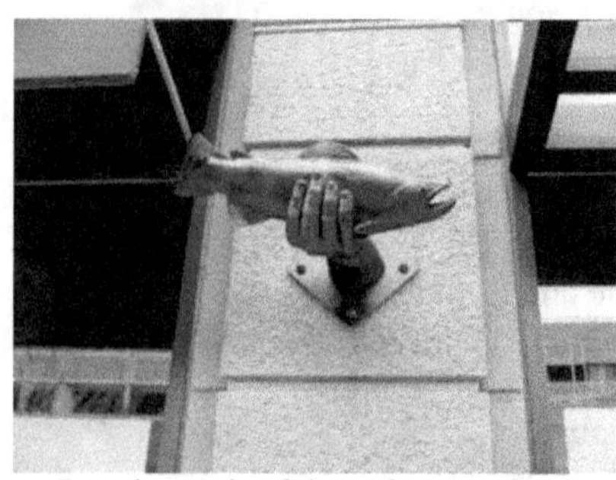

I made a pair of these for a seafood restaurant. The fish is about two feet across

FMG is odorless, non toxic, and water soluble. And unlike any other casting material, FMG neither expands nor shrinks making it ideal for accurate life castings. Considering its advantages, I consider FMG to be bargain. There are some FMG copycats available, five that I can think of. I have personally tested them all and the truth is that they are pretty much the same as FMG with three things. Four of the five come with the three solid ingredients pre blended. (See below.) The fifth consists of two liquids which are mixed together for activation. Pre blending may at first seem like a significant convenience, however, as I will explain, blending is a piece of cake and pre blending comes with a penalty, a higher price. In some cases, the copycats are multi-times more expensive.

The ingredients for plain FMG are an acrylic based liquid, VF-812, and three powders: FGR-95 Hydrocal, a resin, and a hardener. For at least the first ten years I used FMG, I keep the ingredients separate and using a table I had made, weighed out the ingredients for whatever size batch I needed. I had done this so long that it was second nature. However, I saw that people in my workshops often found the weighing of the ingredients to be confusing. Hiram Ball of Ball Consulting which makes FMG kept telling me to blend batches of the solids for the various mixes I was likely to use. Then to mix, one would only have to pour out whatever amount of VF-812 one thinks she/he would need and then scoop out twice that volume of solids. In other, no weighing, just for each scoop of VF-812, add two scoops of the blended solids. This is true whether using plain FMG or with additives such as metal powders.

I purchase FMG in the five gallon kit size which consists of five gallons of VF-812, ten pounds of resin, and six ounces of hardener. The FGR-95 is purchased separately in either fifty or one hundred pound bags. If one had a container large enough and a mixer powerful enough, you could mix a hundred pound bag of FGR-95 and the ten pounds of resin and the six ounces of

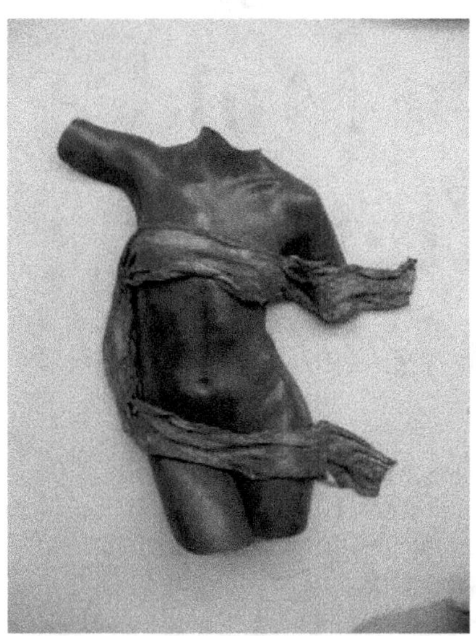
This is a very standard life casting with metal powders. The cloth was dipped in FMG and is detachable from the casting

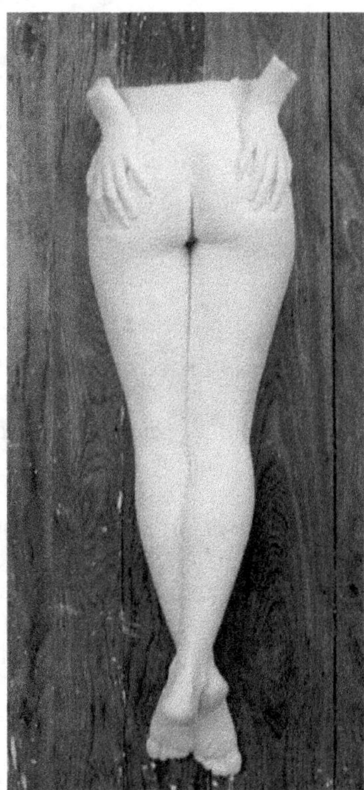
This this life casting has powdered limestone or Athletic Field Marker to enhance the white color

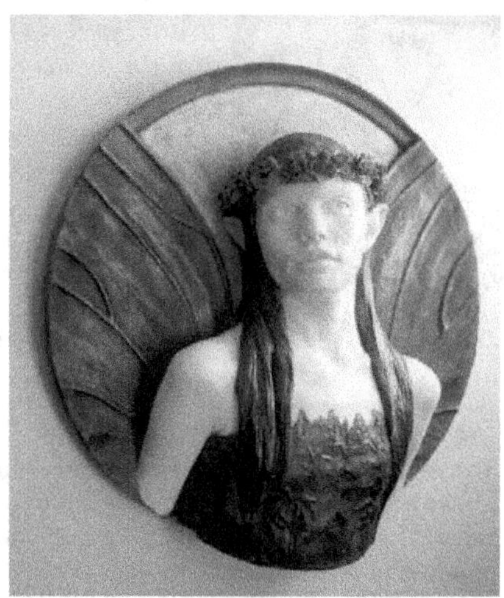
This faerie portrait is a combination of metallic, white, and dyed FMG. For an explanation of how I did this, see "A Little More Complicated Portrait Castings" in the April 2008 issue of "Scupture Journal

hardener. But it is much easier and more uniform to blend in small amounts. The proportions of powders for plain FMG are some quantity of FGR-95, one tenth as much resin, and one half of one percent of the FGR-95 for the hardener. Let me make that more clear. I take a five or fifteen gallon bucket and dump into it ten liters of FGR-95 or about twelve pounds. (It is much easier to work in metric since ten percent of ten liters is one liter and ten percent of twelve pounds is one point two pounds and most scales aren't calibrated in tenths or hundredths of pounds.) I then add one liter of the resin. I calculate the hardener the following simple way. One percent of the FGR-95 in this case would be one hundred grams, cut it in half for the correct amount which here is fifty grams. I then use a five inch Jiffy Mixer and mix thoroughly repeating the measuring and mixing until I have an almost full bucket.

For FMG with metal powders, the procedure is almost exactly the same except that to each layer, I add one and a half as much metal powder as FGR-95. In the above example, I would have added fifteen liters of metal powder to each layer. Since FMG powders are white and the metal powders are, well, metallic, I just mix until I have a uniform color.

There is one other mixture that I use. While plain FMG is slightly gray in color when it first sets up, it turns almost pure white as it cures. But if I really want something to be perfectly white, I add either powdered or crushed limestone which can be purchased from building suppliers as Athletic Field Marker and Pool Mix.

All gypsum products including FMG have greater compressive than flexural strength. This is why rebar is used in concrete. Fiberglass either chopped or in sheets is the rebar of choice for FMG. However, if I am making mother molds in life casting, I use a particular kind of cloth which is more flexible than fiberglass and conforms to the contours better. The last ingredient is a solution of aluminum sulfate and water (1:10) which is used as an accelerant for controlling the setting time of the FMG.

In the twenty years or so that I have been using FMG. I have used it in almost every way imaginable. I would have produced a much smaller body of work without it. In Part II, I will explain how simply and inexpensively one can produce life casting, mother molds, bas reliefs, solid castings, and more.

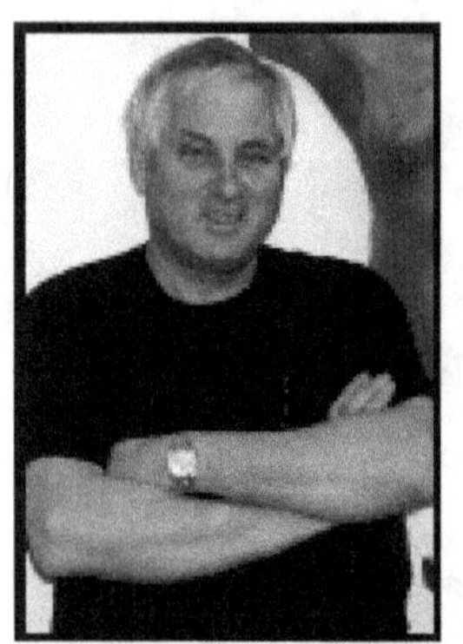

Dave Parvin is best ***known for his realistic figurative*** *sculptures form miniatures to monumental in bronze, pewter, acrylic, and Forton MG. In addition, he is one of only 5 sculptors to have been designated as a Certified Lft casting Instructor by the Association of* ***lifecasters international.*** *He routinely offers workshops in lifecastinq mold making, art marketing, and realistic sculpting. He may be reached at* parvinstudio@comcast.net *but prefers talking to typing at 303-321-1074.*

Making a Mold Using Alginate

Why Alginate?

By David E. Parvin, A.L.I.

About 20 years ago, life-casters on the cutting edge began experimenting with alginate for directly molding the human form. Up until that time, most had used plaster. Plaster has at least two disadvantages. Esthetically, its ability of capturing detail is minimal. But more importantly, applied directly to skin, plaster can be hazardous to the subject's health. Alginate, whose principal ingredient alginic acid is extracted from seaweed, has long been used by dentists to make impressions of teeth (see the following article for more information on the history of alginate). Able to capture the finest detail while being harmless to both the castor and the castee, alginate has become the standard mold material for life casting. But taxidermists may find alginate a very useful substance for mold making as well.

Compared to other flexible mold materials such as the various types of rubber compounds, alginate has definite advantages. One is cost.

Compared to other flexible mold materials such as the various types of rubber compounds, alginate has definite advantages. One is cost. For example, most quality silicone rubbers cost around $10 per pound. But a pound o£ alginate mixed with water is 1/3 to 1/4 that. Secondly, alginate is completely nontoxic to skin contact and has no harmful fumes; it's even odorless. It's also a cinch to mix. While silicone rubbers are not temperamental, most urethanes are. Critical' care must be taken in measuring and in thoroughly mixing to prevent soft spots that never cure. Certainly there are optimum alginate/water ratios for particular applications, but it mixes easily and as long as it's wet, it will set-up. Because it's water soluble, clean up is a piece of cake. Alginate doesn't stick to anything though it will tangle in hair, feathers, fuzzy cloth, etc. unless coated with a release (more about this later). Perhaps its greatest advantage is that its setting time varies from as little as a minute to 8 or 9 minutes allowing for something to be very quickly molded. O.K., so what's the bad news? The only negative is that it's fragile and generally an alginate mold can only be used once or at best only a few times and will quickly dry out and cannot be stored for future use.

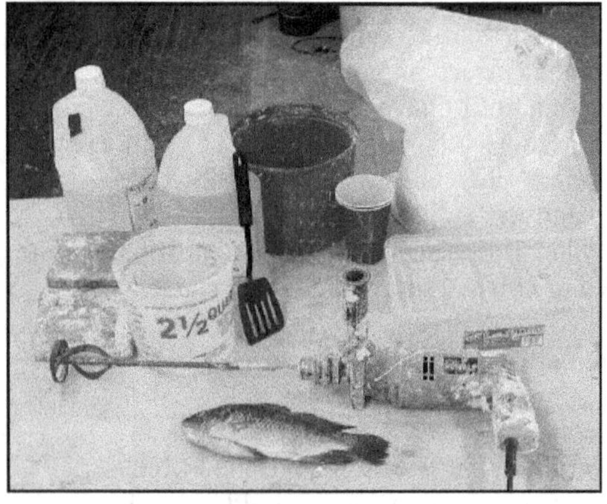

Assemble everythingyou will need before starting the project.

MAKING A MOLD

Anyone who has ever made a rubber mold will have no difficulty in making an alginate mold. But even someone who have never made a mold should have no difficulty if he/she simply follows the steps below: Make sure that you have everything that you will need such as some alginate. Alginates differ in consistencies, setting times, strength, etc. depending on the brand. My personal favorites are Moldgel Regular Set and Slow Set made by Artmolds, Inc. (I explain why later in this article). The amount needed is dependent, of course, on the size of the mold, but a couple of pounds will be sufficient for most small molds. Next you will need something for an outer or "mother" mold such as a Tupperware container or a milk carton. A scale accurate to a half-ounce or so and several small plastic containers will suffice for measuring and mixing. Some sort of a mixer such as one used for paint and attached to an electric drill; or even a whisk will do for small batches using up to a couple of pounds of water. Parts of thin plastic pill trays, while not essential, will make two halves of a mold fit together more precisely. Any number of things could be used for the final casting of the positive such as plaster, hydrocal, urethane resin, etc. The last and most important thing needed is something to cast. For this article we'll use a fish.

I estimated how much mixed alginate it would take to fill the plastic food storage container (hereafter known as the "mother mold") to a depth of about 1 inch by putting the empty mother mold on the scale and weighing how much water it took to get the 1 inch. (Note: mixing the alginate into the water hardly increases the volume). In this case, 2 pounds of water was just about right. I poured 2 pounds of cold tap water into one of the mixing containers. (Another note: the gelling time of alginate is inversely proportional to the water temperature. Since I wasn't concerned about comfort for the dead fish, cold water provided several more minutes working time than warm or hot water would have). The consistency you want for the mixed alginate is about that of thick pancake batter. While water/alginate ratios vary with different brands, 5 ounces of alginate per pound of water is probably going to be pretty dose in most cases. I weighed 10 ounces of Moldgel Regular Set Alginate into another container.

I dumped the alginate into the water and mixed with the electric mixer for about one minute. Remember to always mix powders to liquids and not the other way round or all you will get is gooey lumps. I then poured the mixed alginate into the mother mold and leveled it with my fingers. I placed the fish on its side and gently pushed it half way into the alginate. Since the fish and the alginate mixture have about the same specific gravity, the fish showed no tendency to sink or float up. I took several pieces of the plastic pill tray and pushed them into the alginate. These will act as keys to ensure the mold halves will fit align precisely when casting. These did tend to float up so I held them in place for just a couple of minutes until the alginate gelled. I then pulled out the plastic pieces.

By just looking, I estimated that it would take about twice as much mixed alginate to fill the mother mold to the top as I had mixed for the first layer. I measured 4 pounds of water and 20 ounces of alginate, mixed them, and poured them into the mother mold filling it almost to the brim. I took the lid to the mother mold and, turning it upside down, pressed it in the mother mold until it touched the alginate. This last step probably wasn't necessary but it did make a sixth side to the mother mold.

After about three minutes the alginate had gelled. I waited several more minutes to allow the top layer to gain additional strength and then took the mold apart. The top just lifted off. It can be a problem to get the alginate out of the mother mold because it is held in by suction. The best solution is to drill a small hole in the bottom of the mother mold and blow in compressed air. Once I had the "brick" of alginate in my hand, I gently pulled the top from the bottom; they separated easily and cleanly. I removed the fish and rinsed out the mold with water.

CASTING THE FISH

Now All I had to do was fit the two parts of the inner mold together, slip them into the outer mold and I would have a void the size and shape of the fish with excellent surface detail that's just waiting to be filled with some permanent material. There is only one problem - there is no way into the void since the fish was completely surrounded by the alginate solution. In order to provide an inlet, I took a 3/8-inch drill bit and made a hole into the topside of the inner mold at the highest point of the fish void. The size of this hole is determined by the viscosity of the casting material. Since I was planning to use a urethane resin which pours as easily as water, the hole could be quite small. The location of the hole is at the highest point to prevent trapping air, causing voids in the final casting. For some irregular shapes, it might be necessary to drill one or more small holes to vent air which otherwise could be trapped. I then cut a larger hole in the lid so that I would be able to pour the resin into the opening in the alginate. Now I was ready to go back to the first of this paragraph and proceed.

One of the advantages to Moldgel brand alginates is that they are formulated to be compatible with fast set urethane resins allowing for a light, strong casting with excellent detail and minimal bubbles. The resin that I selected was Easyflo 60 Liquid Plastic made by Polytec. I chose this particular resin from others I keep in stock because it sets up in just a few minutes, so quickly in fact that it doesn't have time to react with the moisture in the alginate, which would cause bubbling. To estimate the amount of material needed to fill the void, I weighed the reassembled mold, filled it with water, and

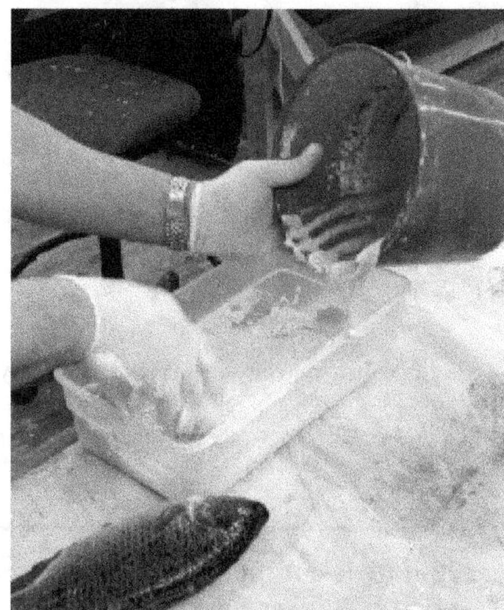
Pour the mixed alginate into the mother mold and smooth it out with your fingers.

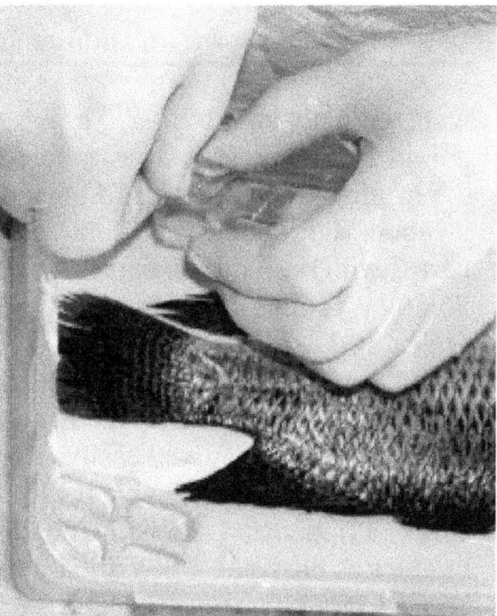
Plastic pill tray pressed into the alginate makes good alignment keys.

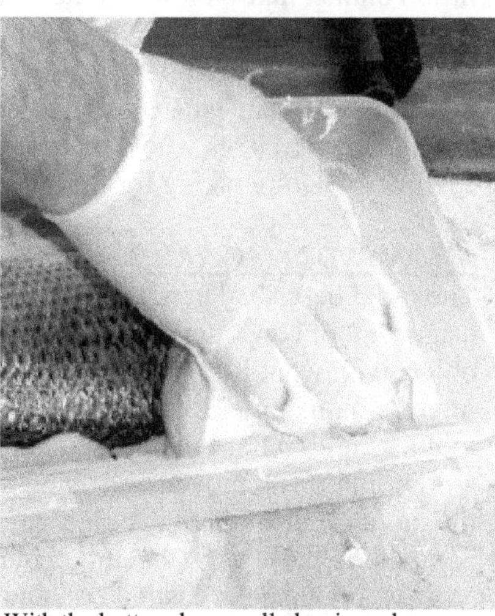
With the bottom layer gelled, mix and pour a top layer, nearly filling the mother mold.

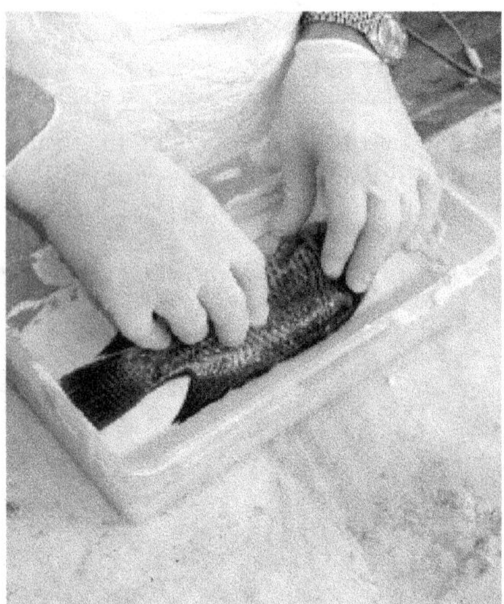
Place the fish onto the alginate bed and gently push it halfway into the alginate.

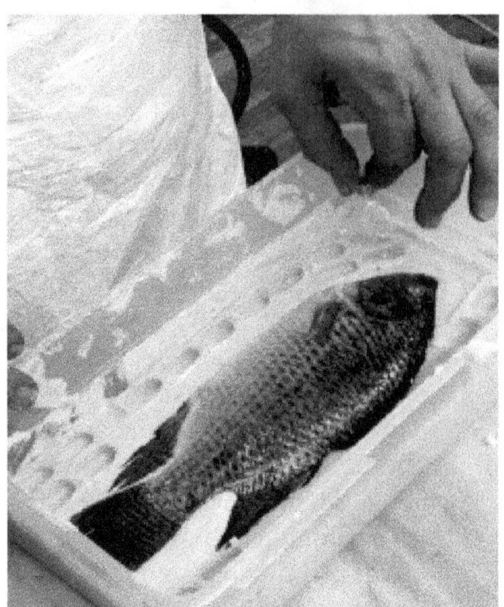
When the alginate gels, pull out the plastic pill tray keys.

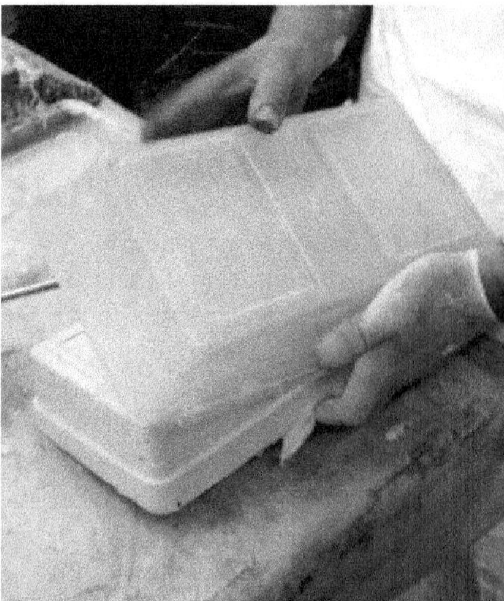
Waiting several minutes after the alginate gelled, the mold could then be removed.

Alginate is completely nontoxic to skin contact and has no harmful fumes; it's even odorless. It's also a cinch to mix. While silicone rubbers are not temperamental, most urethanes are.

weighed it again; it took 600 grams of water. At this point, I dumped out the water, disassembled the mold, and dried out the inside with a hair dryer. I guessed that 650 grams would be about right. Since Easyflo 60 consists of a part A and a part B with ratio of 100 parts A to 90 parts B by weight (or 50/50 by volume), I weighed out 342 grams of A and 308 grams of B.

Mixing and pouring is a no brainer. I just dumped them together and stirred for about 30 seconds. The two parts were so runny that they mixed easily. The same runnyness allowed filling of the mold through a relatively small hole. While filling, I tipped and shook the mold to eliminate as many bubbles as possible. Once filled, I set the mold aside for about 15 minutes. Easyflo 60 sets up in about five minutes but very thin structures, such as the tail fin because it has so little volume, takes a few minutes longer.

The last steps were to take the mold apart and remove my brand new plastic fish and do some very minor clean up of the minimal seam where the two alginate parts of the mold joined together. This whole process took less than 45 minutes even with picture taking for this article.

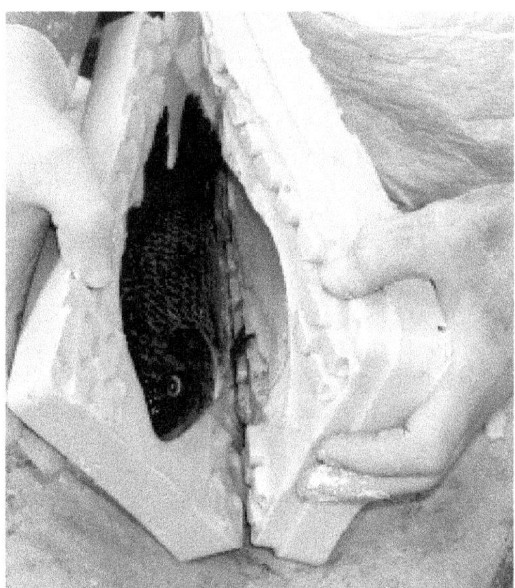
Once free of the mother mold, gently pull the top from the bottom to separate the mold halves.

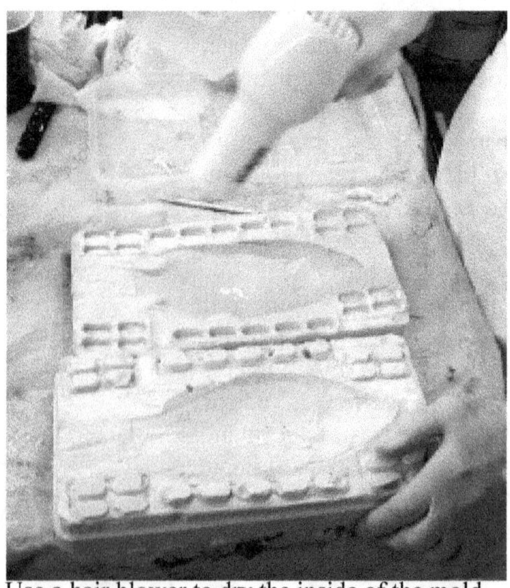
Use a hair blower to dry the inside of the mold.

A FEW ADDITIONAL THOUGHTS

The mold described here is a "block" or "pour" mold. A more usual way of constructing this type of mold is to surround the object with what is to become the mother mold and pour the impression material into the void between the object and the mother mold. After the impression material has set up, the mother mold is removed and using a scalpel or Exacto Knife the mold is cut so that the object can be removed. Put the two parts of the mold back together, pour in the casting material, let it set up, take the casting out, and you have duplicated your original object.

A second type of mold is a "skin" mold, so named

because the impression material is painted over the object making a "skin". The mother mold is formed over the skin. Larger molds are almost always constructed this way. Alginate make excellent skin molds as well, but their construction is a subject for a future article.

While alginate doesn't stick to much of anything, it will become entangled with anything fuzzy such as feathers or fur. While any number of things can be used as a release such as petroleum jelly or cooking oil, the most convenient thing that I have found is a thick but inexpensive hair condition with a terrible marketing name, Cholesterol. Its advantage is that it is water-soluble and washes out of most anything easily. It is also a great hand cream and may be purchased at any beauty supply store.

Be aware that all alginates are not equal. I am sure that I have used in excess of ten different brands over the years and they have ranged from excellent to terrible. I have had students in my workshops proudly present some bargain alginates that they found on the Internet, which upon testing proved to be wholly inadequate. Usually the problem is that the bargain alginates set up to about the consistency of a soft-boiled egg resulting in a mold that is too fragile and cannot capture detail. While there are a number of very good alginates available, the two I prefer are Moldgel Regular Set and Moldgel Slow Set. The only difference between the two is the setting times. White both meet the much higher demands required for serious lifecasting, perhaps their greatest advantage for molds as described in this article it that they are formulated to allow casting in urethane resins, not all alginates are.

One of the little tricks that I discovered on my own some years ago is that the tear strength of alginate can be significantly increased by mixing in a small amount of fibers. This allows for the casting of more intricate shapes. At first I was cutting up cotton to make my own fibers. Fortunately Ball Consulting (see below) found a source of I/ 8th inch nylon fibers that work just fine without sacrificing any detail.

The source of the materials mentioned in this article are: Moldgels, manufactured by Artmolds Inc. at 908273-5401 or info@artmolds.com. Artmolds is the major supplier for life casting materials. Ball Consulting, Inc is a major supplier of sculpting materials including Moldgel alginates, the nylon fibers, plastic pill trays, and Polytec resins. Ball can be reached at 800-225-2673. For those of you lucky enough to live in Colorado as I do, a source for all the above is Sculpture Depot in Loveland at 970-663-5190.

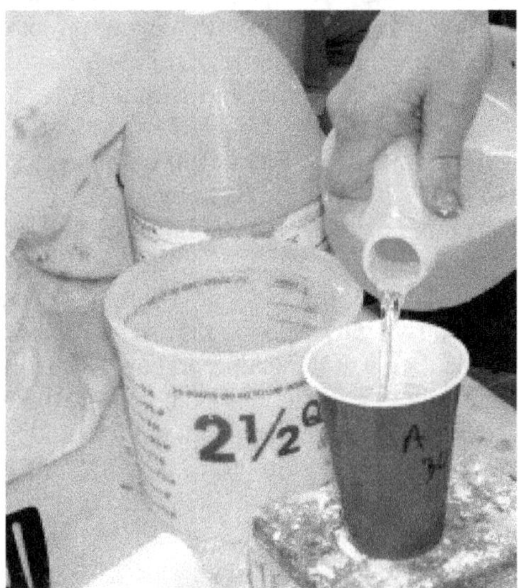

Mix your favorite casting material according to directions

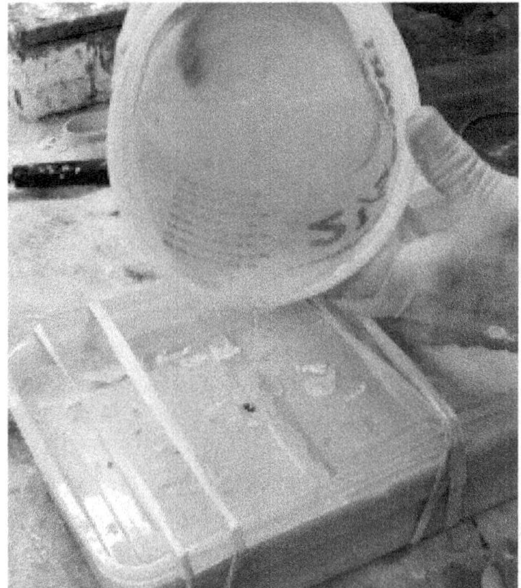

Fill the fish mold through the pour hole in the hole

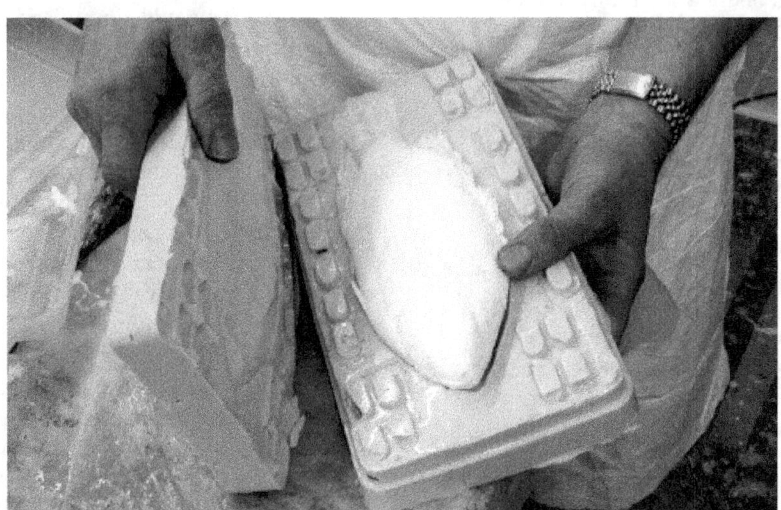

Once extra time has allowed thin areas to set up properly, separate the mold halves and remove your plastic fish.

Some Thoughts on Mixing Alginate

By David E. Parvin, A.L.I.

Recently, there was some discussion on mixing alginate on the Association of Lifecasters International "Forum." I just assumed that since "great minds think alike" or that great minds would have for the most part come up with similar solutions to the same problem. I was wrong. I will come back to that later after I have discussed some thoughts about alginate in general and described a surefire mixing method.

The Basics

Alginate comes to us in powder form which is mixed with water to a consistency similar to pancake batter. The viscosity or "runniness" of the mixture is controlled by the alginate/water ratio. The desired viscosity depends on how we are using the alginate. For example, if we are making a "skin" mold (in which the alginate is spread over the model), the alginate needs to have a higher viscosity than if making a "block" or "pour" mold (in which the part to be cast is either submerged into a container of alginate or the alginate is poured into a container surrounding the part). For best casting results, it is essential that the alginate/water ratio be just right for the particular application. I call this the Goldilocks Principal, too wet and it's too runny, too dry and it's too stiff, somewhere in-between and it's just right.

But the alginate/water ratio also effects several other things. Less alginate or more water slows the setting time of the alginate along with a low viscosity. A far better way to increase the setting time is to use "Algislo" by EnvironMolds or just purchase a slow set alginate. (See "How to Extend the Setting Time of Alginate, Testing a New Product," Sculpture Journal, March 2003, by yours truly. Using less alginate than what is recommended by the manufacture will reduce the strength of the alginate and can make it more like a soft boiled egg than rubber. Too little water or too much alginate will make something that feels like bread dough, too thick to apply or even submerge something into it. Below I will describe just what Goldilocks would have liked.

The temperature of the water is very important. The setting times claimed by the manufacture are for the recommended alginate/water ratio at a water temperature of 80 degrees F. (27 degrees C). 80 degrees sounds pretty warm but that is about the water temperature of most swimming pools which feels pretty cool when you first get in. If you are tempted to use water cooler than 80 F. to extend the setting time, your model may demand victim pay as additional compensation. Again, using Algislo is a better solution. Warmer than 80 degrees will significantly reduce the setting time and if you are not anticipating it could prevent you from completing the casting.

I have seen this next thing happen only once but have heard of it several other times; the alginate fails to setup. Alginate not kept in an airtight container especially in a humid climate can loose its potency with time. However, a more likely culprit is the water. Iron in water can prevent the gelling process. In my case, the water had come from a well and even a day later, the mixture looked like cottage cheese curds in water. The solution is simple, if you have any reason to question the water, make a small test batch first and if there is a problem, use bottled drinking or distilled water.

Something that I have always found curious is that mixed volume of alginate plus water is no greater than the water was by itself. The reason that that seems strange is that the volume of the alginate is, depending on the alginate, between half and all the volume of the water. In other words, if you needed a gallon by volume of mixed alginate, one might expect the he/she would start with less than a gallon of water and adding the alginate would increase the volume of the water. It doesn't. If you need a gallon of mixed alginate, you need to start with a gallon of water.

I always think of the amount of alginate needed for a particular casting in terms of the volume of the water and not the amount of alginate. Since a pint (volume) of water weighs a pound (weight) as in " a pint's a pound the world around," I calculate what I need to prepare by the number of pints but then talk in pounds. For example, the torso of a normal size female should take about eight pounds of water. My preferred alginate for skin molds is ArtMolds "Fibergel" by EnvironMolds which takes five ounces/pound (312 grams /liter). It makes more sense in my mind to say I'll need eight pounds (1.8 liters) of water, which is constant, than forty ounces (1.3 kilos) of alginate, which could vary considerably with different alginates.

I wish I could simply and absolutely state that the alginate/water ratio is in all cases such and such, period. Not only does it vary depending upon the application, but also by the brand. In addition, individual batches from the same manufacture may ever differ slightly. As a general rule, the ratio will be around 4.5 to 5 ounces of alginate per pound of water (281 -- 312 grams per liter) for a skin mold. For a block mold you can reduce the alginate by 10%, more or less, to make the mixture pore more easily if you want. The alginate that I have used with the least alginate to water ratio is MoldGel by EnvironMolds. It only take 3 ounces per pound (187 grams per liter). If you are comparing the cost of different alginates, the actual cost isn't the price per pound but the price of the amount needed. What looks inexpensive may in fact not be the good deal it first appears. I think that this is the third time that I have mentioned Goldylocks in this article. But here is where the "just right" is really important. If it takes 5 ounces of alginate per pound of water, 5.5 will be too thick, and 4.5 will be too runny.

Often the directions for mixing alginate may state the ratio by volume only. The reason for this is that not everybody has a scale and the manufacturer wants everyone to use the alginate and not just people who own scales. The bad news is that the alginate in power form may not have a uniform density. The weight of the alginate scooped out of the top of a container may weigh something different than what is scooped from the bottom. It probably matters little if you are mixing for a pour mold where Goldylocks isn't as picky. But the alginate water/ratio for a skin mold is more critical. An experienced caster can recognize too runny or too thick and quickly add more water or alginate. The problem is that even slow set alginates gel in six or seven minutes and there isn't a lot of time to waste trying to tweak the mixture. The good news is that you can now purchase very accurate scales for very little money. Harbor Freight has a twelve pound scale accurate to within two grams for about thirty bucks and often on sale for about twenty. Weighing the alginate and water will assure consistency and save time.

<u>The Correct Mixture</u>

Photograph #1 shows a model's torso covered with a "skin" of alginate. Notice that the torso is completely covered with a smooth layer of alginate but it is not dripping or running. The thickness should be from 1/8th to 1/4 inch (0.3 to 0.6 cm.). I suspect that the biggest mistake that I have seen new life casters make is to mix the alginate for a skin mold so that it is too runny. The assumption is that the runnier it is the less bubbles you will get on the surface. But the problem is that it will not stay in place and just runs off the model. If you move the alginate over the model's skin as if "putting icing on a cake," don't just slop it on, you have almost no bubbles on the skin surface, no drips, no runs, no errors.

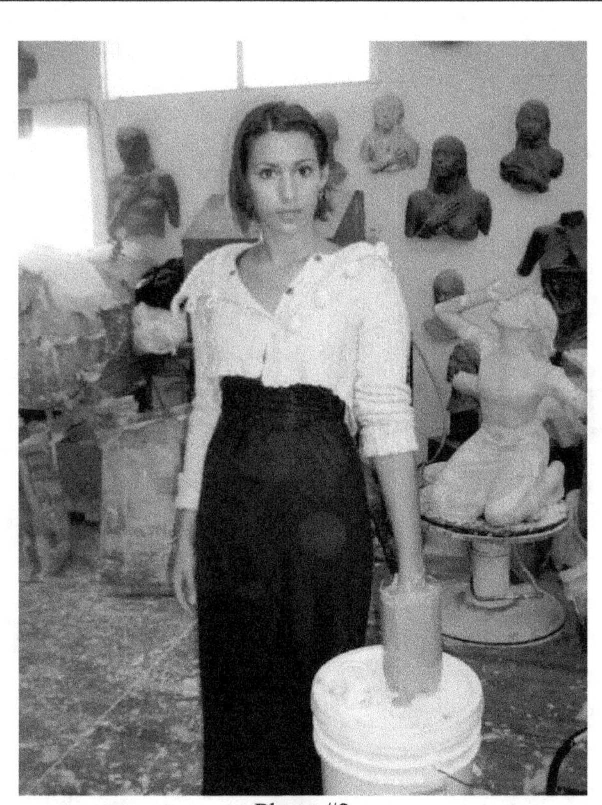

Photo #2

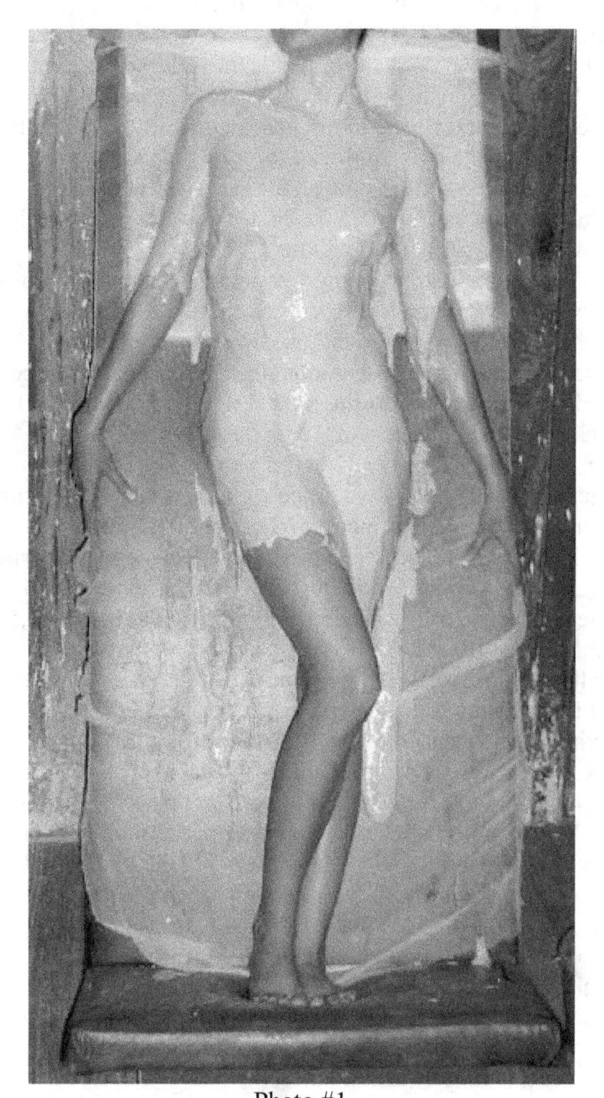

Photo #1

In photograph #2, she has her hand in a two liter plastic soda bottle full of alginate. The viscosity in this case is far less critical. The alginate/water need only be mixed so that it is thick enough to set up somewhat stronger than a soft boiled egg yet not so thick that you can not pour it into the bottle. It might also seem that the runnier you mix the alginate, the less bubbles you will get on the surface of the skin. But in fact, if the alginate is runny enough for the bubbles to easily rise, they will come up as stick to the skin especially if the surface has a horizontal component. The If you use about 10% less alginate than you would have used for a skin mold, you should be about right.

<u>Making it Simple</u>

If you are still with me, you must be thinking that this is way too complicated! It really isn't and now I am going to make it very simple. I purchase alginates in larger quantities, usually fifty pounds at a time. The first thing I do is make a quick test so I know exactly how to mix the new batch. I put four ounces (114 grams) of 80 degree F. water into a small cup. I measure out the correct amount of alginate as per the manufacturer's recommendations. I set a timer and dump the alginate into the water. I stir with a "giant craft stick" until smooth and creamy, thirty seconds to a minute. (A "giant craft stick" looks like a tongue depressor but costs about one cent rather than a dollar.) If the thickness doesn't seem right, I add a little alginate or water until it does at which time I reweigh it. Holding one of my hands vertically, I spread the alginate over the palm and wait for it to gel and note the time. I write the setting time and the mixing ratio on the container such as 7 min., 5 oz./lb. I know the proper ratio and what the setting time will be .

To mix the alginate/water for an actual casting is a piece of cake. I have found it is easier to mix two four pound batches than one eight pound one. My favorite mixing containers are the red one gallon plastic buckets from Ace Hardware which are just the right size and very durable. I take four clean buckets and weigh out four pounds (1.8 liters) of 85 degree F (29 C) water into two of them. The water will cool slightly when the alginate is added. Into the other two I weigh 20 ounces (568 grams) of alginate.

For very small amounts of alginate, i.e. a one pound of water batch, a whisk works just fine. But for more than that, I use an electric drill with a speed range of 0 to at least 2,500 R.P.M. rated for at least seven amps. I would not use cordless drills because they probably don't have the speed and I don't want to chance the battery dying in the middle of mixing. Attached to the drill is a 2 1/2 to 3 inch "Jiffy Mixer" or a lower cost paint mixer available at any building supply, paint, or hardware store. To contain any splashing, I put the one gallon bucket into a larger one. I start off at a slow speed until all the powder is wet and then increase to full speed while moving the mixer all around the bucket. The four pound batch should take no more than one minute to become creamy smooth and lump free. If mixing two batches, I have an assistant mix the second one either simultaneously or right after the first, either way works just fine. I always have a spare drill and mixer handy even if I am only planning on using one.

Several times above, I mentioned using "Algislo" to retard the setting time. You do not want to just add it to the water because doing so would change the alginate/water ratio. I normally add an ounce of "Algislo" per pound of water. I scoop out about an ounce of water per pound and then add the same volume back in of "Algislo."

I would like to tell you that I have never screwed up my measurements and had a batch that obviously wasn't right. But that would be a lie and I would hate to waste a lie on something so trivial. I always have some water and alginate close by if needed. When you have been mixing alginate for over 20 years as I have, you get so that you can eyeball adjustments pretty well. But I tell the newbies in my workshops that if they even suspect that something isn't right and can't figure it out immediately, stop and start over. Even with slow set alginate, one doesn't have much time to waste and trying to use alginate which is too thick or too thin will probably result in failure. Even if you get the mixture finally correct, you may have lost too much time to get it on the model.

There is an old argument about how to combine a liquid and a powder. Do you mix the liquid into the powder or visa versa. One of my old girlfriends in college, Patty the home ec. major, would have insisted that you always add the powder to the liquid. If you pour the power into the liquid fairly slowly stirring all the while, the liquid will gradually thicken. But if you try to slowly pour liquid into a powder while stirring, you will just get a big glob until you get enough water in to completely wet the powder. Patty was right. However, if you have the right amount of water and powder, you can just combine them any way you want and start mixing. It really doesn't make any difference. And very experienced life casters can probably mix alginate in a swimming pool with a toothpick.

What I have described is what I have found to be the easiest way for me to mix alginate which is also the easiest way that I have seen for a newbie to do it as well. Over the years, when I have told attendees to my workshops to just combine and mix from plasters to alginate until it looks right, I have looked up and seen a room full of lost puppy dog eyes. They were so relieved when I gave them some numbers to use. By the way, for myself, I do mix some things like plasters by feel, but I always carefully measure alginate.

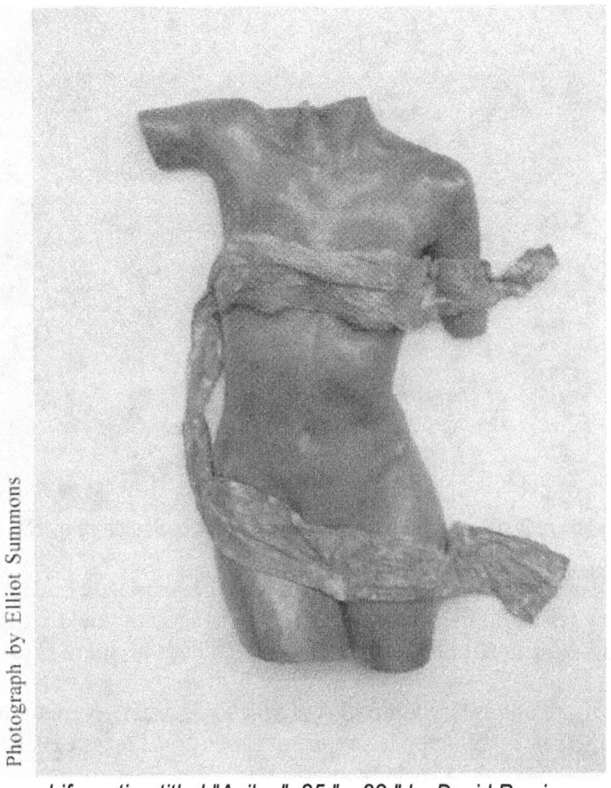

Lifecasting titled "Anika ", 25 " x 32 " by David Parvin

Mixing Forton MG Simplified

by David E. Parvin

My discovery of Forton MG has been very important to my artistic career. At that time over 13 years ago, I was about to give up on achieving a realistic marble look for a particular bas relief since several different attempts had ben unsatisfactory. It was suggested that I try Forton MG with "Pool Mix" (crushed limestone) added. It worked beautifully. Since then, I have used it in many applications. For example, with the right cloth it can be used to make very thin and light yet remarkably strong mother molds. But the most important use to me has been to add metal powders to produce cold casts that look amazingly like hot cast metal. To date, my largest piece has been a bas relief 16 x 5 feet and my smallest use was a medallion about the size of a quarter. It can be painted or poured into molds. It is nontoxic and odor free.
It neither shrinks or expands. It mixes easily and is forgiving if the recommended ratios of materials are not followed exactly. It sets up in any kind of molds including alginate. Since it is water soluble until it sets up, cleanup is a snap. Though not intended for constant water contact as in a fountain, it was designed for outside applications and holds up well to the elements. The setting time can be controlled from just a few minutes to an hour.

So what's the bad news? Well for me there isn't any but I have found that some people new to it have found it confusing to mix. I have been mixing it so long that weighing out one liquid and three different powders and then using different proportions if metal powders are used is a cinch. But Hiram P. Ball, Jr. of Ball Consulting, Ltd. recently has greatly simplified the process. When he first explained it to me, I couldn't see the purpose since I wasn't having any problems in the first place. However, after giving it a try, I have to humbly admit that he is absolutely on target.

The secret is to use pre-blended ingredients which can either be purchased or blended oneself. My suggestion is if you are new
to Forton MG, purchase the pre-blended. Later you have a little experience, blend it yourself and save. Once you have the pre-blended dry materials, mixing with the liquid couldn't be simpler. All you do is mix one part liquid to two parts powder either by weight or volume. What I have been doing is using two, one pint plastic cups, one for the liquid and one for the powders. (The size of the containers would of course depend upon the amount needed). I simply fill one container with the liquid and scoop out two containers of the pre-blended powders, and mix. If that weren't simple enough, the same 1 to 2 ratio works for metal powder mixtures as well. My assistants have been delighted with this simplified method. I should point out for the reader who has never used Forton MG that the ingredients are a liquid called VF-812 which looks and smells like white latex paint (which it isn't), a dry resin, and FGR 95 hydrocal. If purchased pre-blended, the FGR-95 and the resin come in the same container and separately with the right amount of VF-812. If not pre-blended, a "kit" consists of a container of VF-812 and a box of resin. The FGR-95 is purchased separately. I purchase 5 gallons of VF-812, 10 pounds of resin, and 100 pound bags of FGR-95.

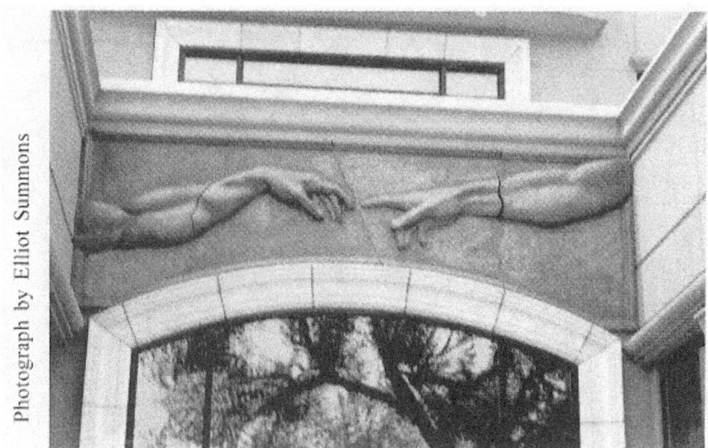

Bas relief, 16'x 5', for building at 2nd and Columine, Denver, Colorado. Sculpture by David Parvin and Eliot Summons

Do-it-yourself pre-blending is also a no-brainer. All you do is get a clean plastic bucket that can be sealed. For every 10 pounds of FGR-95 add 1 pound of dry resin and mechanically stir. To get a metal powder dry blend just add I and'/ pounds of metal powder for every pound of FGR-95 and stir until a uniform color. That's all there is to it. You can increase the metal powder ration up to
2 pounds per pound of FGR-95 for a more intense metallic look if you so desire. Any metal powders such as brass, copper, or bronze can be used individually or together, 50/50 copper and bronze mixture is an excellent choice.

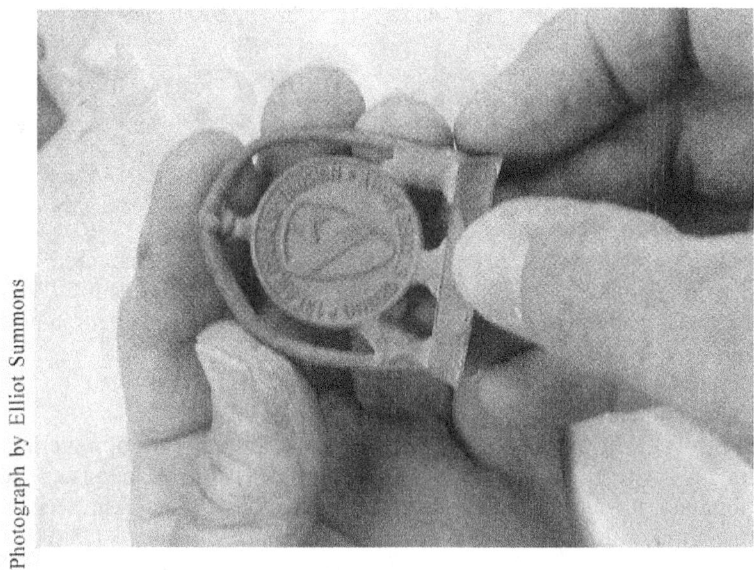

Cast of a Vietnam era medallion. 1 1/8 " in diameter. All in Forton MG with metal powders.

For more information, contact Ball Consulting by any means listed in the Ball Consulting advertising in this magazine. Or call me at 303-321-1074 since I have used tons of the stuff.

New Product, Life Form

By David E. Parvin, A.L.I.

I get excited about any new product that promises to be an improvement. Dave's Law #11 on my studio wall is, "There is almost always a better way." Or as fellow contributor to *Sculpture Journal*, rubber expert, and good friend Mike Sisbarro points out, "If I have been doing something the same way for a long time, I'm probably doing it wrong because someone has likely come up with a better way." Recently I got really excited! Another good friend, Todd Debreceni, who is an expert in makeup and special effects both professionally and academically, recently returned from an international conference in London with something that sounded too good to be true, a new fast curing skin safe platinum cured thixotropic silicone rubber called Life Form. So what about Life Form is so important and that if Julie Andrews had been present, we would have substituted "fastcuringskinsafeplatinumcuredsiliconerubberLifeForm" for "supercalifraglisticexpealidoscious" and danced around singing? Before I explain, let me digress.

The two most used life casting materials are, of course, alginate and fast curing skin safe platinum cured thixotropic silicone rubber. (At my age I have to make every second count since I am running out of seconds. A nine word name no matter how descriptive, just is too long. If I have to type it out over and over again, I just might be around to finishing this article. So in order to save time both for myself and for any of you readers who just might be getting a little long in the tooth, I will use the abbreviation for generic FCSSPCTSR and Life Form when referring to this new FCSSPCTSR in particular.) Alginate and FCSSPCTSR each has its advantages and disadvantages. Alginate is less expensive and easier to apply. FCSSPCTSR is much stronger and produces a mold that can be used over and over again. (For a more information, see "How to Cast a Dancers Foot For Fun and Profit," *Sculpture Journal*, January 2005, by DP.) I confess that I am an alginate man through and through. I am a registered member of the Alginate Party and always vote right down party lines. FCSSPCTSRs have a particular disadvantage that has limited my use in the past, a disadvantage that Life Form has, to my amazement, eliminated.

The disadvantage that every other FCSSPCTSR that I had used in the past is that they all <u>stick tenaciously to hair</u>. Hair isn't much of a problem for alginate. (See "Techniques For Life Casting Hair," *Sculpture Journal*, July 2006, by DP.) In my opinion, using FCSSPCTSR on any parts of the body requires that the victim shave all hair off or cover the hair with a barrier such as a skull cap or a thick layer of releasing agent. There are a number of releasing agents made for this purpose, but I have found that if applied in a sufficient quantity to be effective, the skin texture is lost. So when Todd Debreceni told me that Life Form doesn't stick to hair, though my socks started rolling up and down, I didn't believe him.

Unfortunately, Life Form is a British product and not available in the U.S. yet. Fortunately, I have met its distributor, Justin Neill, and was even a guest in his home a few years ago. I emailed him and arranged for a sample. (See contact information at the end of this article.) Not to worry,Justin is in the process of setting up a US distributor.

Life Form consists of two components, Part A and Part B, which are use in equal amounts. Both A and B are thick, rather like putty. They are the same blue color and have no odor. Photo #1 shows 10 grams of each in a plastic up. Notice that the components have no tendency to run. I mixed them together and spread them on my arm with no release agent. (Photo #2.) The life form set up to the point that it could not be spread in about two minutes. I left it on my arm for about five minutes to be certain that it was well cured. While I do not have especially hairy arms, I had just done this experiment with another FCSSPCTSR, the removal of which even with a release agent was very uncomfortable. I am confident that if I had removed it quickly, all the hairs would have come off with the rubber as if having been waxed. Amazingly, I say again *amazingly*, the Life form came off with barely a tug on the hairs. Since Todd is somewhat more hairy than I (not necessarily a sign greater masculinity), We spread some Life Form on his arm as well with the same results.

Before proceeding to a more thorough test, I emailed Justin with four suggestions. First, make the two components different colors so that one can easily tell when they are thoroughly mixed. Second, slow the setting time slightly because two minutes isn't much time to mix and apply. Third, thin it down a little so that it's easier to apply without capturing bubbles on the surface touching the skin yet still thick enough to stay in place. And four, find a US distributor. Justin replied that all four of my suggestions were already in the works. It's always a comfort to know how great minds think alike...

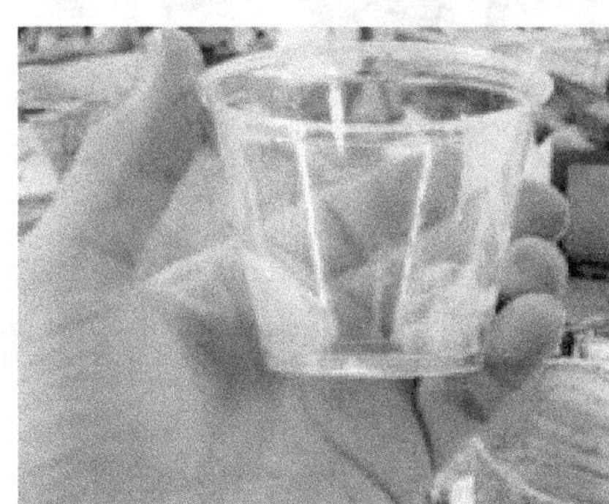

Photo 1

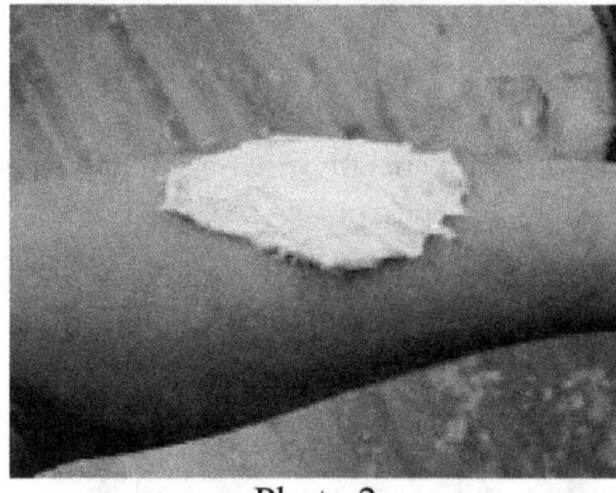

Photo 2

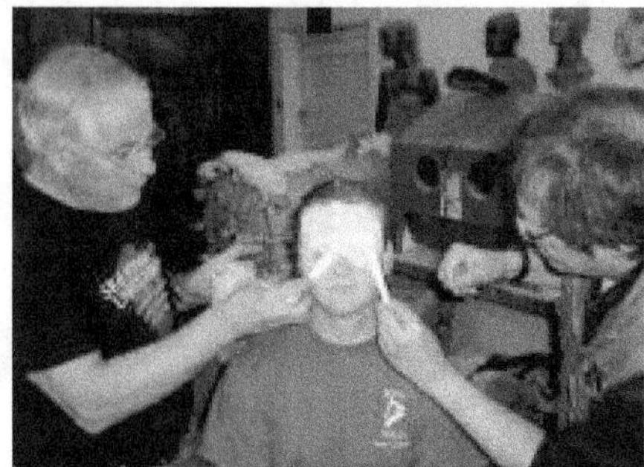
Photo 3

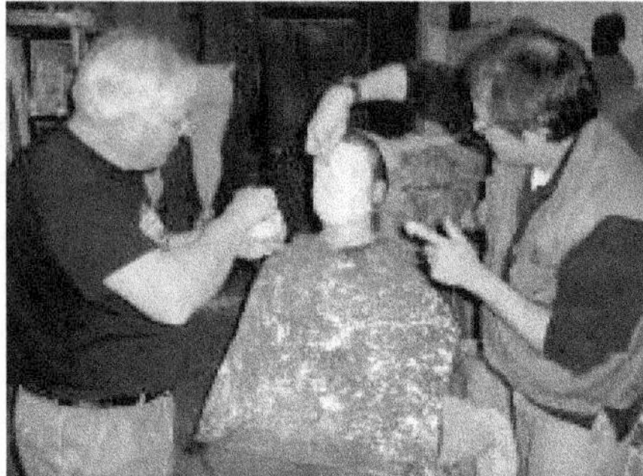
Photo 4

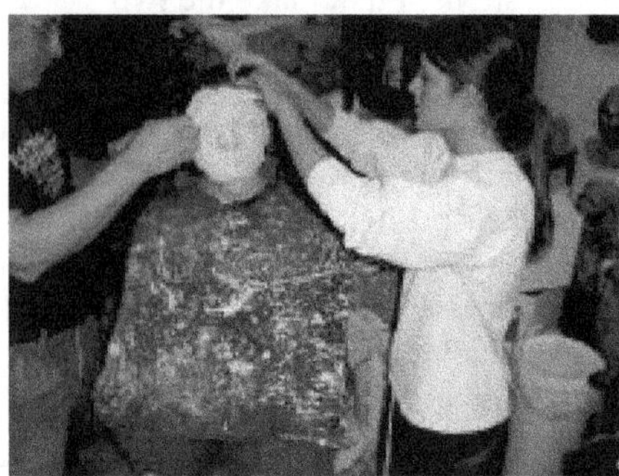
Photo 5

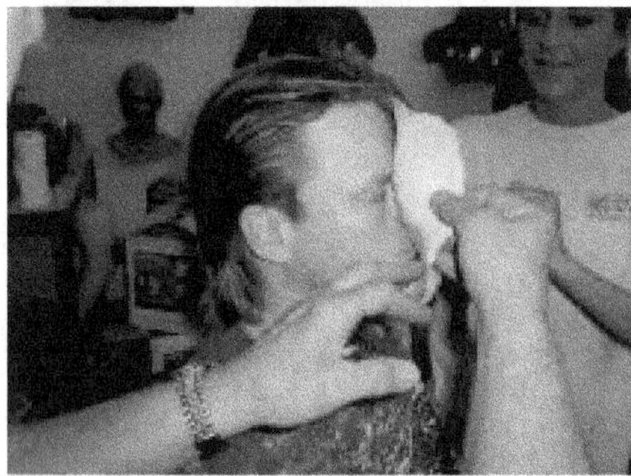
Photo 6

It seams to me that the special effect folks (E/FX), who already use FCSSPCTSR on a regular basis will be especially interested in Life Form. So Todd and I decided use it in a test casting appropriate to what he and his compatriots normally would do. One of his students, Ron Root volunteered to be the model.

All FCSSPCTSRs set up so quickly that one can not mix enough to cover much of an area without setting up before one gets it all on. The solution is to measure out several small batches, mix one and while it is being applied, mix another, and so on. It is essential that the application start at one end, edge, or side and proceed in one direction over the model so that rubber is always being applied wet to wet. If allowed to set up, there will be a seam where uncured rubber meets cured. In this case we went from Ron's forehead down his face. Normally for E/FX, a skull cap would be applied to the model; however, we wanted to have the Life Form actually touch Ron's hair.

We measured out four 3 ounce batches (85 grams) of 1/2 A and 1/2B but did not stir them. In order to reduce the viscosity, we added 10 percent silicone oil. Prior, we had made test batches using up to 30 percent with no apparent degradation of the Life Form. In Photos #3 and 4, Todd, the hairy one, and I are applying the Life Form. Out of view, assistant Kelsey is mixing the next batch as we proceeded down Ron's face. In Photo #5, Kelsey and I are removing the Life Form from the edges. In Photo #6, the Life Form has come off the eye lashes and brows easily and with no discomfort. We had applied a small amount of petroleum jelly to the lashes and eye brows but it probably hadn't been necessary. In Photo #7, the hair that was touching the life Form is sliding out with no discomfort visible on Ron's face. As shown in Photo #8, the Life Form had minimal flaws. We did not construct a mother mold which would have held the rubber's correct shape, but we were only curious about how well the Life Form would perform.

In the last two photographs, I had taken a glob of Life Form an applied it to my left sideburn without any release agent. Again, it came off easily without any discomfort which was fortunate because if my sideburn had been ripped out, I would have looked like a lopsided Elvis.

In the past, I had thought of FCSSPCTSRs of being useful in very specific situations such as casting a ballerina's foot. Ballerinas are not known for being particularly hairy. But even though I will continue to be a member of the Alginate Party, I will probably cross party lines in favor of Life Form much more often than I would have with other FCSSPCTSRs. I am looking forward to when Life Form is more available and I can put it to a more thorough test.

Justin Neill can be reached at justin@mouldlife.co.uk.

Todd Debreceni is a Denver area educator, author, and professional makeup/special effects artist. He has a new book by Focus Press titled *Special Makeup Effects For Stage and Screen*. His email is tdebreceni@gmail.com.

Dave Parvin has done so much good shit that there isn't room to list it!

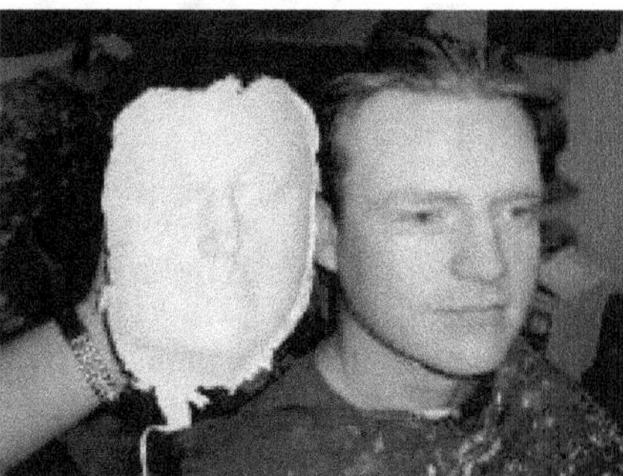
Photo 7

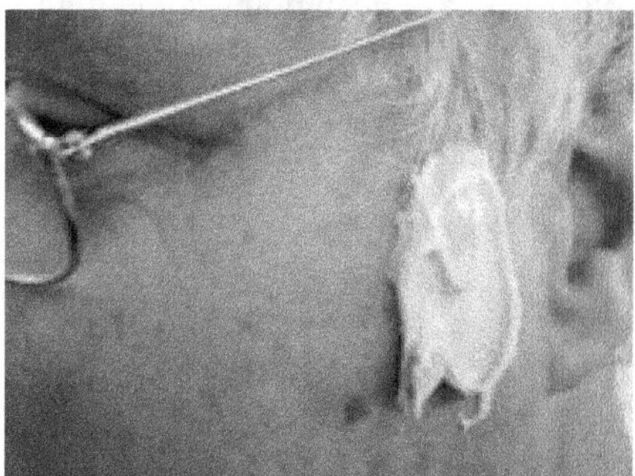
Photo 8

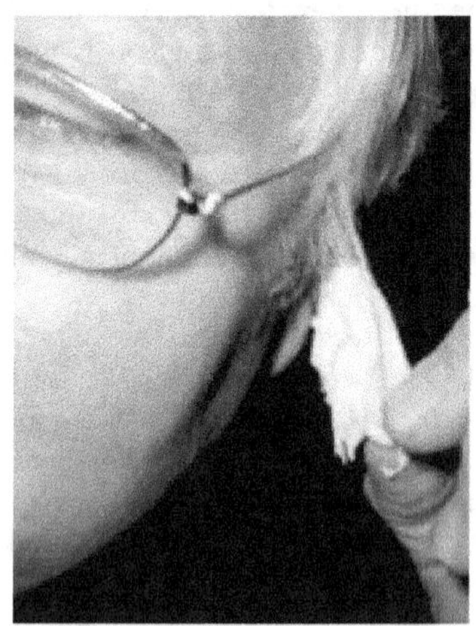
Photo 9

Putting MoldGel SILFREE to the Test, Part One

By David E. Parvin, A.L.I.

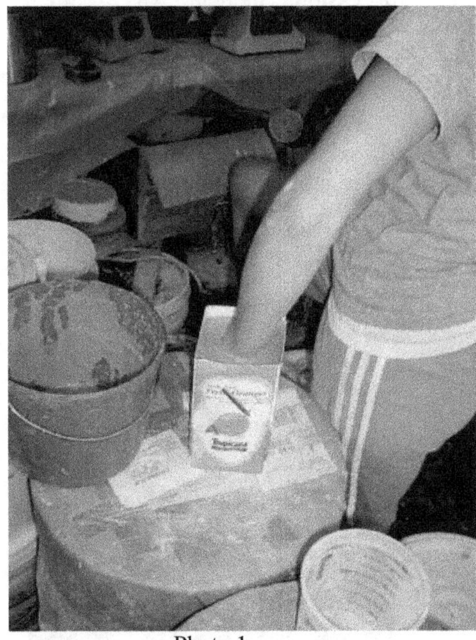

Photo 1

One of the really great things about having been sculpting for over half a century and life casting for a fifth of a century is that occasionally you are sent something new asking only for your evaluation. About the only thing better to play with than new stuff is free new stuff. So when Ed McCormick of ArtMolds called some months ago and said that he was sending me a sample of a prototype of "MoldGel SILFREE" which he promised would be the first really new alginate in sixty years, my socks started rolling up and down. Ed said that after considerable research and experimentation his company has come up with an organic replacement for the silica that until now had been an ingredient in all alginates. While heavy and or prolonged exposure to silica can be very unhealthy, the risks associated with the occasional exposure for most life casters is probably minimal as long as basic precautions are taken; but "minimal" is not the same as **none**. And some of us very active life casters' exposures are more than occasional. I got to thinking how embarrassed I would have been last year if, say, right in the middle of casting Miss USA, Tara Conner of later notoriety, I had suddenly fallen over dead from silicosis. Not only would my assistants, Audra and Morgan, had to step on and over my carcass as they finished with Tara, but they would have had to explain to Donald Trump that his copy of Tara's casting was only half an original "Parvin" since I would not have lived long enough to sign the finished work no doubt greatly reduced its value on a future edition of Antiques Roadshow.

I was impressed with the first prototype sample and reported so back to Ed McCormick. During this time, Ed was refining the formula and the manufacturing process, a never ending quest, and sent me prototype number two. I played, we talked, and just recently I got some of what is very close to the final product which should be available by time this article arrives in your mail.

When you open a container of MoldGel SILFREE, you will notice that it has both a pleasing light blue color and a pleasant peppermint bouquet (sounds so much better than smell or odor) yet it looks pretty much like any other alginate. But when you feel it, it seems to be somewhat courser and less dusty. The first thing I did was mix some small samples using 100 grams of water at 80 degrees F (27 degrees C.) but varying the amounts of MoldGel SILFREE to determine the proper ratio and the setting time. For casting hands and/or feet in a container, ArtMolds recommended a mixing ratio of one part MoldGel SILFREE to three parts water. By checking the weight of the one and three parts, I determined that this ratio by weight was about two and a half ounces MoldGel SILFREE per pound of water (71 grams per 454 grams). I mixed a larger batch and cast a hand of assistant Audra. (Photo #1)

Before continue with the testing, let me explain something. Manufacturers want their products to be as simple as possible to use, and rightly so. This is why ArtMolds recommends measuring by volume rather than by weight. After all, anyone can come up with a cup but may not own a scale suitable for weighing accurately within a few grams. If one is measuring liquids, weight and volume directly correlate. "A pint's a pound the world around" is true for water and close for beer. While the specific gravity of other liquids may be considerably different, once one has determined the volume for a specific weight of any liquid, the right sized scoop will always provide the desired weight. But powders are different because they may at times be fluffy or compacted or something in between. Hence, the weight of a pint of a particular powder may vary. Fortunately, for casting hands by filling a container with an alginate/ water mixture, using one scoop of Aljasafe for every three scoops of water will give pretty consistent consistencies.

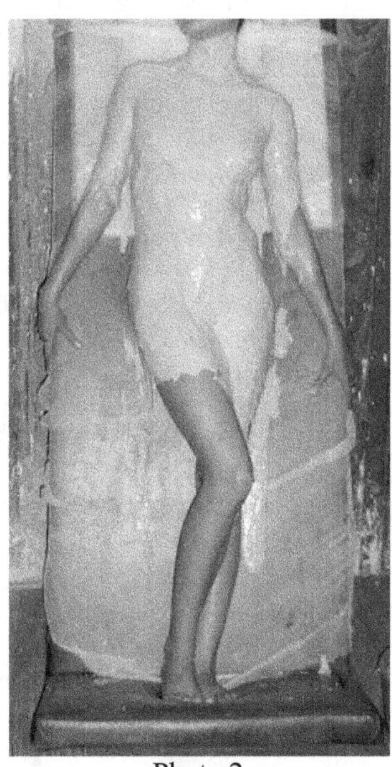

Photo 2

However, for other applications in which the alginate must stay in place on vertical surfaces, the consistency of the alginate must be just right. In my version of "Goldielocks and the Three Bears," the three bears had decided to become life casting experts. After purchasing and viewing my dvd titled "Casting the Female Torso," subscribing to *Sculpture Journal*, and joining the Association of Life Casters International, they were ready to give it a try. Following my advise in "One Artist's Successful Approach To Finding Perfect Models," *SJ*, September 2004, they got Goldielocks to get barefoot all over and be their first subject. But alas, they hadn't paid attention to the dvd in which I state that water/alginate ration must be fairly precise. In their first try, the solution was **too runny** and it all dripped off. In the second, it was **too thick** and they were unable to apply it smoothly and evenly. Fortunately, Mamma Bear suggested that they review my dvd and they weighed the third batch and it was **just right**. What a great story, my two little grandsons just love it!

When you want alginate to stay in place on a vertical surface, such as bodies or faces, it is important that you determine the proper ratio and use it every time. There was a time in my early days of life casting that I would continue to add alginate as I mixed until it seemed right. The problem was that it took too long. Even most slow setting alginates jell in five to seven minutes which isn't much time especially if you are attempting a difficult casting. A much better way is to weigh out the correct ratio of alginate to water and mix with a high speed drill. The correct ratio varies somewhat with different brands and it can take some experimentation to determine what is just right.

So exactly what is "just right?" Referring back to the three bears, in the first case, there was too little alginate or too much water and the solution all ran off Goldie. In the second, there was too much alginate or too little water making it impossible to spread it on Goldie uniformly and without trapping air bubbles. But the third was the correct ratio and even Baby Bear could spread it on Goldie without trapping bubbles on her skin and it would stay put at a thickness of three sixteenths to one quarter inch (about 0.2 to 0.25 cms); i.e., **just right**.

For the other kind of mold used in life casting where a body part such as a hand is simply inserted into a container of alginate, the correct ratio is actually counter intuitive. One might very well think that in this case, the runniest mixture that will still jell would be desirable. After all, wouldn't that allow any air bubbles to rise to the surface leaving behind a flawless mold? Well, one might thing so but one would be wrong. If the solution is runny enough for bubbles to rise, they get trapped by the undersides any horizontal areas on whatever body part one is casting. These bubbles result in "outies" in the final product. In this case, thin enough to wet the skin completely but thick enough that any air bubbles do not rise is **just right**.

Getting back to MoldGel SILFREE, while the recommended ratio of one to three works for casting in a container, I would prefer a thicker solution of about using 3 1/2 ounces of MoldGel Silfree per pound of water (100 grams per 454 grams). For faces and bodies, I found 4 ounces of MoldGel SILFREE per pound of water (114 grams per 454 grams) to work very well. At these ratios, it takes less MoldGel SILFREE than any other alginates I have used, about 20 to 25% less, making it more economical.

But MoldGel SILFREE is very different than other alginates in several ways. As soon as you start mixing it, you will notice that that it just seems more <u>organic</u>. This is because it is. Rather than use a mineral, silica, as a filler, it uses "food grade ingredients." Also, any other alginates that I have used have almost no transition state, they are liquid and then in just a few seconds are solid. MoldGel SILFREE jells over about a full minute's time. I found this to be very helpful. When I noticed that it was firming up, I knew that it was time to apply the cotton or cheese cloth to bind the alginate to the plaster layer. The next difference is that once the MoldGel SILFREE has set up, it isn't initially as tough as other alginates. But by the time the mother mold is finished it will have firmed up considerably.

O.K., so MoldGel SILFREE is more economical, safer both for the user and the environment, and is just somewhat different, the real question is, can one produce the highest quality castings? In photograph #2, my assistant Audra and I had covered a volunteer with a layer of MoldGel SILFREE Sloset. Notice that it is staying in place without an significant dripping. The alginate remained in a workable state for about 5 1/2 minutes when it began to jell over about a minute. Audra and I did not have to change our normal casting procedure at all. Photograph #3 shows the plaster positive made from the MoldGel SILFREE impression. The detail was excellent and there were only a few small "outies" that were not the fault of the alginate.

ArtMolds plans on making SILFREE in at least three versions, fast, regular, and slow. I will be experimenting with all of these and will provide further details in next month's *SJ*. Let's see: safer, more economical, and excellent quality, seems like progress to me.

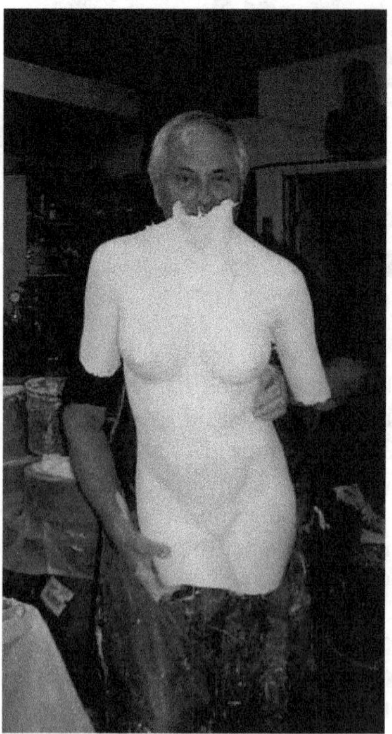

Photo 3

Testing a New Alginate or FiberGel E F/X Grade Alginate, *Fame or Shame*

by David E. Parvin, A.L.I.

With so many alginates on the market, is there room for another? Almost certainly not unless there is something that definitely separates it from the rest. Ed McCormick of ArtMolds is convinced that his new FiberGel E F/X Grade alginate may just have what it takes and has filed for a patent.

A Little Background

During World War II, the U.S. Navy began using alginate for dental impressions in place of agar which was only available from Japan. Alginate quickly spread to the rest of the dental profession. L(For a detailed history of alginate, see "Alginate Life Casters' Gold" by Ed McCormick, "Art Casting Journal" September 2001) The name of the first artist to recognize alginate as an ideal material for life casting has been lost to history but it is easy to imagine the scene. He or she was probably a dentist who, when removing a cast of some poor victim's incisors to molars, suddenly realized that this alginate stuff just might be able to cast some more interesting parts than teeth!

Life casting had begun.

The biggest problem with using dental alginates to cast any part bigger than a mouth is that they set up too quickly. Eventually, alginate became available that had setting times of 5 to 8 minutes which allowed for more elaborate castings. These were and are essentially dental alginates slowed down. Most of these alginates are still produced by dental firms as line extensions. And so it has gone up until now. ArtMolds may be the only company that manufactures alginates exclusively for life casting.

The problem is that just slowing down the setting time doesn't produce the optimum life casting material. (See "How to Extend the Setting Time of Alginate" by yours truly in the March, 2003 issue of Sculpture Journal.) Along with some other features, the ideal life casting alginate also must be just the right compromise between two of its opposing characteristics, strength (tear resistance) and durometer (hardness/softness). Alginate can be manufactured to be very strong but it will also be very hard. Make it soft and it will also be fragile. If very soft, the alginate will easily tear, particularly with thin structures. On the other hand, a very strong alginate can be so inflexible that it will tear rather than pull free from tight places. One of the more common problems occurs when c

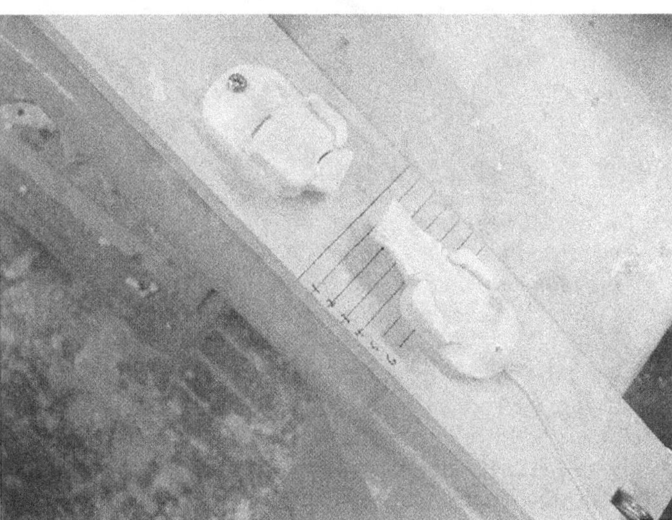

Stretching a sample for strength

casting a face. The impressions of the inside of the ears can tear loose. If the alginate is too hard, it can be difficult to remove the mold from the subject or vise versa. Also, the greater the likelihood of pulling out hair. Life casting is not suppose to also be a bikini wax! Up until now, all alginate shave been compromises. In other words, manufactures have tried to make alginate as strong as possible without being too hard. The better brands have done this very well and there are some excellent alginates available that serious life casters, myself included, have used for years with great results. But ArtMolds's Ed McCormick has a new approach. Ed believes that he has discovered a way to increase strength while maintaining an optimum softness by adding just the right amount of special, proprietary fibers. He claims that in addition the fibers do not in any was impede detail but actually improve the consistency so that the alginate will better stay in place on the subject without running off. Let's see.

Devising a Testing Procedure

When Ed asked me to take a look at his pride and joy and give him my honest opinion, I had to devise a method to determine if his patent pending fibers really do increase the strength. I could have just poured out puddles of several different alginates, let them set up, and pulled them apart to determine relative tear resistance. But that would have been too subjective. I needed a way to actually measure the strength.

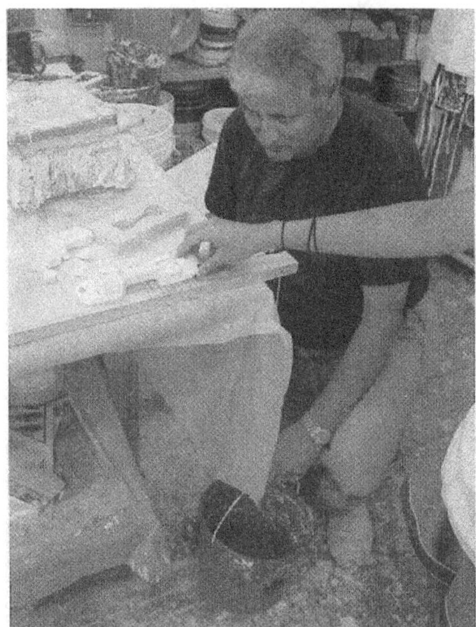

The author beginning to test a sample of alginate for strength and elongation. The assistant's hand is positioned to keep the end of the alginate and its cradle from hitting the author in the face when the sample breaks.

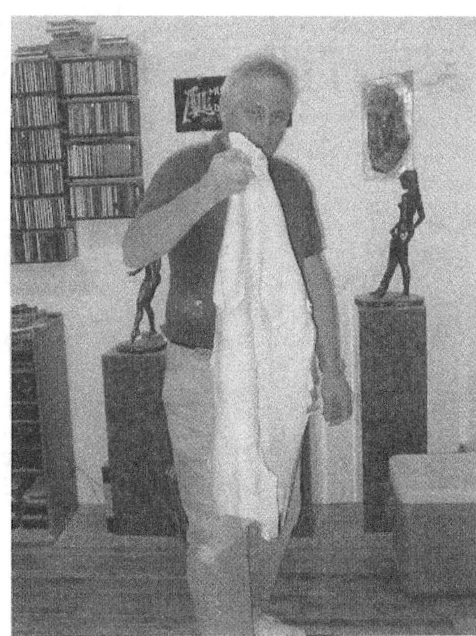

The author holding up one of the E FIX body impressions by one end without it tearing. This was impossible with the other brand of alginate.

What I did was sculpt a 5 inch long "dog bone" with a center that is 1/2 inch wide by 1/2 inch thick. I made a mold of this in silicone rubber allowing me to cast exact duplicates in alginate. The hardest part was figuring out a way to grasp the ends without damaging the alginate. My solution was to cast two cradles in urethane that precisely conform to the ends of the alginate specimens. One of the cradles was fastened to a flat board with a pulley at one end. I tied a string to the other cradle and passed the string over the pulley. A hook was tied to the end of the string to attach an empty bucket. (If you are completely lost, see the photograph and I think this will all make sense.)

To test the alginate, all I needed to do was cast an alginate specimen, slip it into the cradles, pour water into the bucket stretching the specimen until fracture, and weigh the bucket to see how much weight was required. To assure consistency, all the samples were mixed at a ratio of 5 ounces of alginate to one pound of water. The waster was 80 degree F. To eliminate bubbles and insure a uniform density, the specimens were put into a pressure chamber and allowed to set up at 50 p.s.i. Testing was done after 20 minutes of cure time. Since I was curious as to how far the specimen would stretch before failure, I marked the board at one centimeter intervals. While I don't have any illusions that my method would meet A. S.T.M. American Standards for Testing Materials, scrutiny, I am confident that it is accurate enough for the purposes of this article.

First Impressions

When I opened the container, it was immediately obvious that FiberGel E F/X Grade at least looks and feels different.

Any other alginate that I had ever used looked and felt pretty much like flour. Of course, alginates come in different

First Impressions

When I opened the container, it was immediately obvious that FiberGel E F/X Grade at least looks and feels different.

Any other alginate that I had ever used looked and felt pretty much like flour. Of course, alginates come in different colors but the color is uniform throughout. But not with E F/X. While the basic material is a neutral color, there are obvious specks of red.

Closer inspection reveals that these red specks are very small pieces of fiber. Rubbing it between your forgers reveals additional colorless fibers.

My first thought was that there is no way this concoction of alginate of fibers would mix into the creamy smoothness that I am used to. But it does. Ed McCormick had also sent me a sample that is exactly the same but without the fibers; it looked and felt like any other alginate. I mixed a small batch of each and cast the palms of my hands. They felt almost the same except that the E F/X had more body. In other words, mixed with the same ratio of water, the E F/X is more thixothropic which means that it tends to stay in place without dipping or running off better than the same mixture without the fibers. When removed from my hands, the detail looked identical. As near as I could tell, Ed's promise of better adhesion without sacrificing details true.

Another characteristic of E F/X is its fragrance with smells to me like citrus. It is pleasant without being overwhelming.

Test Results

I tested both the FiberGel E F/X Grade and the same alginate without the fibers several times to assure consistency and accuracy. Simply states, the secrete fibers increased the tear

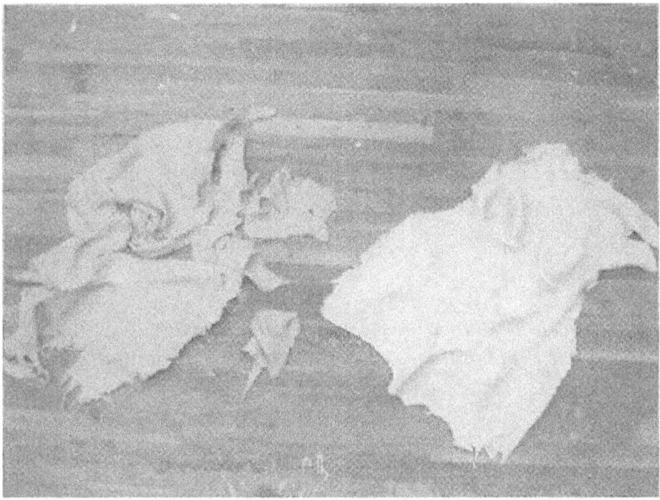

The E FIX and control alginate body impressions after removing them from the model and lifting them by one end.

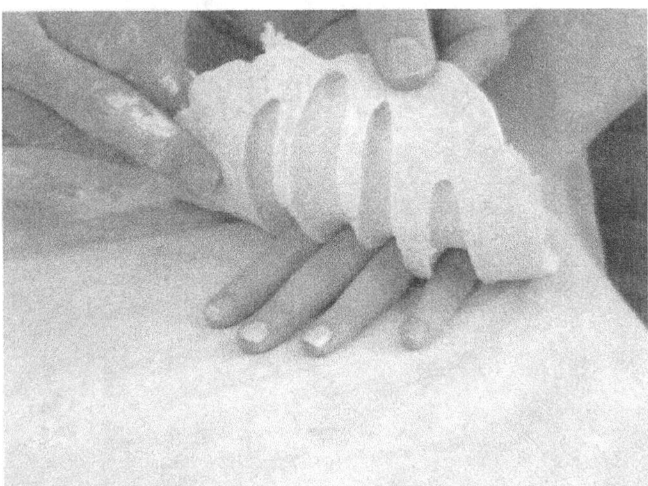

Pealing an E FIX mold off of a hand without tearing the thin alginate between the fingers.

strength 16%. The elongation for both types was the same, over 4 centimeters. Since all I had done was demonstrate that the E F/X is stronger than it would be without the fibers, I hadn't really compared it to any other product. I decided to test another brand which I happened to have on hand. I will only say that this particular brand is one of the most respected and used among serious life casters. I have used it myself and recommended it often. Its tear strength tested at only 61.5% of the E F/X. Its elongation was less than half. In terms of soft, stretchy, yet tear resistant, FiberGel E F/X Grade Alginate is clearly superior.

Out of the Lab, and into the Real World

I decided to determine if E F/X's attributes are of any real advantage. I had one of my assistants place a hand palm down on a flat surface with her fingers slightly apart. I mixed up a few ounces of e F/X and spread it between and over the fingers. After letting it set up, I lifted off the alginate. The thin material between the fingers came out without tearing. Next I tried an even more real world application, casting bodies. I made two impressions of a standing front female torso from the top of the neck to the mid thighs. For each, I mixed 8 pounds of water and 40 ounces of E F/X. In my experience, this amount of material can be mixed using a high speed drill with a j iffy mixer in a minute flat. The E F/X took just slightly longer, about a minute and 15 seconds to achieve a uniformly smooth consistency. I spread on the E F/X, paying special attention to undercuts such as armpits and under breasts. It went on smoothly and stayed in place from 1/8" to 1/4" with very little running. I did not complete the molds, that is, I did not construct supporting mother molds. I was more interested in seeing if I could peel off the alginate ein one piece without tearing it. I could. Even though the alginate weighed 10-1 /2 pounds, I could lift it by one end without its pulling itself apart. Holding it up to a light, the thickness was uniform.

For one of these I used 80 degree F. water and the E F/X set up in 6 minutes on a warm body. For the other I used 90 degrees water and the setting time as 5 minutes.

By way of comparison, I performed the same test using another alginate. I couldn't even peal it off the model without serious tearing. When I attempted to hold it up by one end, it simply tore apart. The difference was remarkable. (Seethe accompanying photographs.)

If alginate isn't blended thoroughly in the manufacturing process, soft spots can occur. The result of this effect will be un-gelled alginate remaining on the model's and a corresponding flaw in the casting. In both of the above tests, the E F/X came off cleanly. Close inspection of the impression confirmed no soft spots. And except for a very few small ones, the surface was bubble free.

About Mixing Ratios

For years, I mixed alginates too thin. I had the mistaken idea that thinner meant less bubbles. What it really meant was that a lot ran off the subject and was wasted. I finally figured out that it could be considerably thicker than I had been using and still be bubble free at the surface. Most quality alginates require about 5 ounces of alginate to 1 pound of water for the mixture that I prefer. However, the ratio can vary consider-ably depending on how much alginic acid (the costly ingredient) that a manufacturer uses. Many "bargain" alginates may require more alginate to the pound of water-reducing the bargain.

It seemed to me that during the above tests on the bodies, the mixture was just about right. But for comparison, I mixed three small samples using 4.5, 5, and 5.5 ounces of E F/X per pound of water. While all three were workable, the first was just a little too runny and tended to drip while the last was just a little too thick resulting in a few small surface bubbles. 5 ounces to a pound of water is right on. However, a 4.5 or even a 4.0 mix would work in a container and the 5.5 would be helpful for serious undercuts.

Delayed Shrinkage

Ed McCormick had told me that in his experiments E F/X seemed to retain moisture and delay shrinkage of the mold.

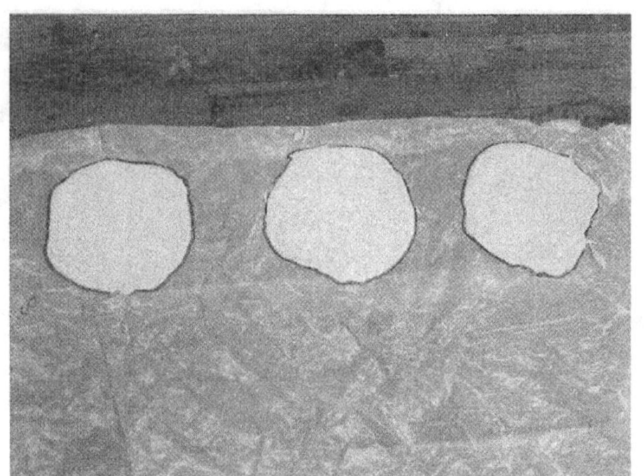

The three `pancakes " of alginate at the beginning of the 26 hour dry out.

This would then allow one to delay casting in the mold without distortion if necessary. I have to admit that I was skeptical of this claim but came up with two test. The first was to mix a sample of E F/X and two other alginates up. I traced around their circumferences and let them dry out for about 26 hours. The second was to cast the same face twice using e F/X and another alginate. These were finished molds including plaster mother molds and were also allowed to dry out for abut 26 hours. (The 26 hours just fit my schedule and had no other significance).

When I examined the "pancakes," it was obvious that all three had shrunk inside their original circumferences and that the E F/X was closest to its original size. Careful measurements determined that the other two had shrunk 8.0% and 6.2% while the E F/X was only 3.5% smaller. In addition, the E F/X was flat while the other two's edges were noticeably curled up. Both of the face molds showed shrinkage but the control sample had a definite split while the E F/X was intact. While I wouldn't recommend that someone wait 26 hours to use a mod, it was obvious that E F/X will delay shrinkage and allow one more time to complete a project.

What's in a Name?

E F/X sounds like a science fiction as in the "e F/X Files" or the "Creature from E F/X" and in fact there is a connection. ArtMolds says that it is "specifically formulated for high-demand, high-production, high-end E F/X (special effects) work." Of course it is also available to the rest of us.

Cost

At this time, the final cost of E F/X has not been set. Because of the added materials and the additional blending required to produce a uniformly consistent distribution of fibers, it will cost a little more that other premium grade alginates. While we all like a bargain, I have always tried to distinguish between the cost of materials and the actual cost of producing the end product. Better materials may reduce the overall cost of production by saving time and or problems or allow for a product that would have otherwise been impossible.

Where to get it

ArtMolds has distributors throughout the U.S. and Canada or can be ordered directly. For details, email them at: info@artmolds.com

Dave Parvin enjoys sharing his experience and expertise and routinely offers workshops. He can be reached at parvinstudio@comcast.net or 303-321-1074.

Sculpture Journal – May 2003
www.artcastingjournal.com

It's Very Clear, One Sculptor's Experiences With Urethane and Acrylic

By David E. Parvin

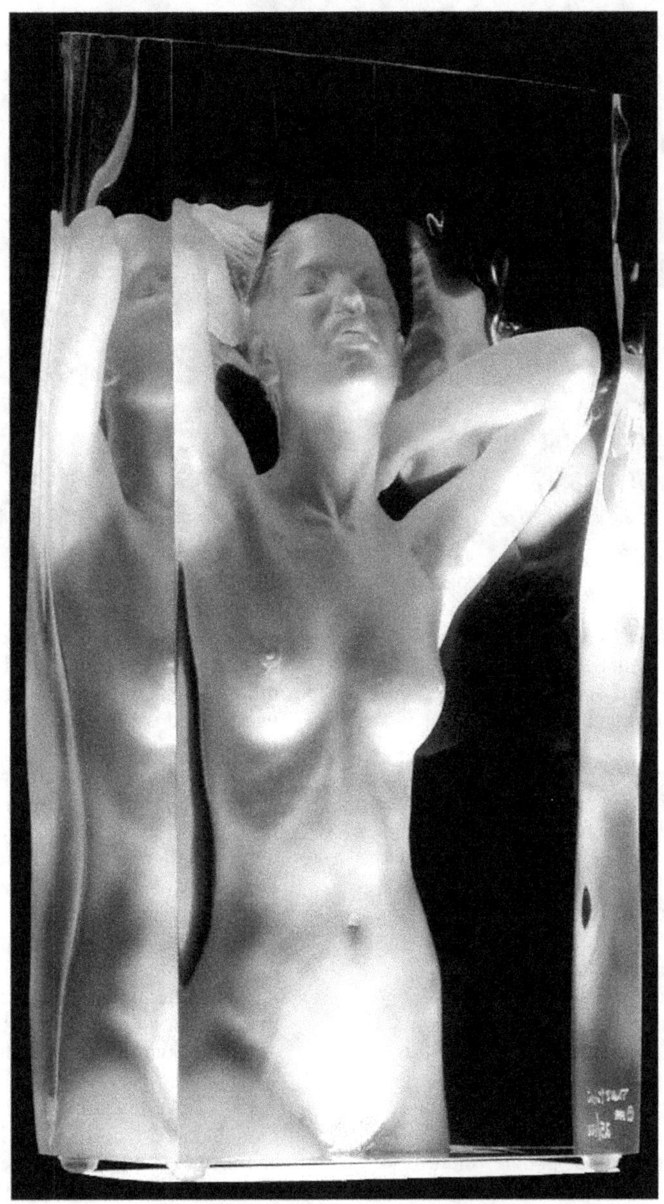

Sculpture by David Parvin, titled "Britton"

I can not recall just when I first saw the clear acrylic sculptures of Frederick Hart and Michael Wilkinson but it must have been not long after I made the decision to become a serious sculptor myself in 1981. What I do remember is being very much taken with the ethereal quality of the acrylics. I imagined my own name etched into some icy blocks of mystical sensuality, except for two roadblocks. Number one, there was no local source for casting acrylics and I was dubious about having something produced where I would not be close enough to be involved. Secondly, considering the prices of the above artists' work, I assumed that the production cost must have been astronomical. Even some superficial research convinced me that casting acrylics was beyond my capabilities. Could there be another solution?

The quest for the holy clear began simply enough. While at my Denver area source for materials, Western Sculpting

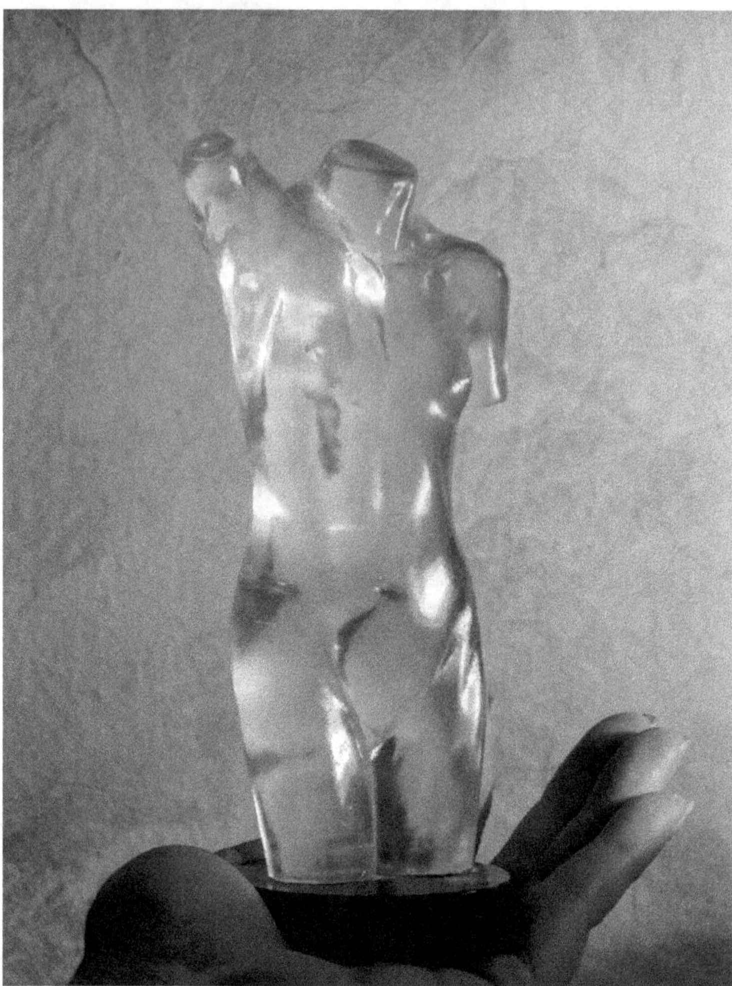

Sculpture by David Parvin, title "Victor"

Supplies, I saw a sample of clear urethane. Eureka, it looked like just what I needed. What's more, I was assured that it was a no brainer to cast, just mix the two components and pour into a rubber mold and the trinity of clear casters would be Hart, Wilkinson, and Parvin. Amen!

The first thing I did was sculpt a small torso which I optimistically titled "The Victor" anticipating my assured triumph. I constructed a rubber mold and poured in the urethane. The unexpected result was the first of many, the urethane did not set up and all I had for my "best laid schemes" was a pile of goo. Discussions with the supplier and manufacturer assured me that the most likely problem was that the silicone rubber mold probably contained formaldehyde which inhibits urethane. The solution was to heat the mold to 175 degrees Fahrenheit for 18 hours to drive out the culprit. There were two problems. The first was to convince my skeptical wife that using the kitchen stove for this purpose was somehow in her long term best interest. The second was that it didn't work and I became the owner of a second glob of goo. Back to the phone.

It was becoming obvious to me that the people whom I would have expected to know the answers didn't. The supplier and the manufacturer of both the urethane and the rubber were at a loss. I kept searching and finally got lucky. I discovered Terry McGinnis at BJB Enterprises a supplier of polyurethane and related products. Terry was the first person I had been able to find who was an authority on urethane. If I had not found him, the quest might have ended in failure with only two globs of goo.

What I found out was that there are two types of silicone rubbers, tin cured and platinum cured. I had been using the tin which is just fine for almost all applications except clear urethanes much prefer the platinum. The good news is that platinum only sounds more expensive, in truth, they are just equally expensive as tins. The bad news is that my supplier didn't have any platinum cured silicone rubber in stock and it was several weeks before I had a new mold ready to try again. It worked, the urethane cured just fine except that "The Victor's" surface was rough and covered with small raised lines. Back to Terry who informed me that the lines are called "worm tracks." He then asked the size of my creation. When I informed him that it was small, about 6x2x1 inches, he remarked that in the clear urethane world, that was a rather large casting. The surface roughness and the worm tracks were a result of shrinkage. What I needed was a slower setting urethane with less shrinkage. After my new material arrived, I tried again. Sure enough, the surface was just fine. In fact, it was so smooth that I could clearly see that "Victor #4" was full of bubbles. So far I had two globs of goo, some worm tracks, and a collection of bubbles. The quest was about to get much more interesting.

At this point, I contemplated the mysteries of life. I thought back to college and how I had sat through two years of chemistry (you know, rhymes with mystery) and a year of physics wondering all the while of what possible use these subjects would be. It was a comfort to realize that perhaps there is a purpose after all.

There are three sources for bubbles: air trapped in the mold, air captured in the solution due to agitation, and air dissolved in solution. (A fourth would be gases produced as a by-product of a chemical reaction which is not applicable here). The first of these is the easiest to control. Major problem areas in a mold are vented to allow the air to escape. Smaller areas can usually be accommodated by carefully tipping the mold during filling. Agitation from mixing or pouring into the mold produces the bubbles that are visible. If the solution has a long enough working time or "pot life" at least the largest of these will rise to the surface and escape. Very careful mixing and pouring into the mold helps prevent these bubbles. The dissolved air presents a bigger challenge. Fortunately, as we shall see, the solution to this problem completely eliminates the remaining bubbles from the first two as well.

One of the characteristics of liquids is that they are capable of dissolving other substances including gases. This takes place on a molecular level and often the dissolved substance is totally invisible. Much of what is known about this phenomenon is attributed to Jacques-Alexandre-Cesar Charles (1746-1823) who being French was especially interested in hot air. What J.A.C. Charles would have told us is that the amount of gas that can be held in solution increases with pressure and decreases with temperature. Releasing the pressure from a container of carbonated drink causes fizzing, the bends results from nitrogen bubbles forming from rapid decompression, and bubbles will appear on the sides of a cold glass of water warming to room temperature. The setting up of urethane is an exothermic reaction. What had happened to my last "Victor" was that as it warmed up, bubbles formed which could not rise and escape because of the simultaneous thickening of the solution. Had I de-aired the urethane with a vacuum chamber, any existing bubbles would have enlarged (Boyle's law) and joining with air coming out of solution escaped the mixture leaving little or no air to form bubbles. And/or if I had cast the piece under pressure, the air would have stayed in solution. It is curious that reducing pressure and increasing pressure produce the same result.

I have noticed that there is some confusion about using vacuums as a casting tool. The general idea is that if you have a mold in a vacuum chamber, the casting material will be able to completely fill every nook and cranny. This is true with molten metals but not with most anything else. De-air the urethane in the vacuum chamber and then bring it back to atmospheric pressure, the urethane will have less air in the solution than it can hold. If you pour it into the mold in a de-aired state, no bubbles will form as the solution heats up. Also, any small bubbles that might be trapped in the urethane as it is poured into the mold should dissolve and disappear.

Pressure works in the same way only better. Casting under a pressure of only 50psi will not only insure that no bubbles form as the urethane heats up and will dissolve any bubbles trapped by agitation but will also force the urethane into every nook and cranny.

I was able to construct both for a total investment of less than $400.00. Both have served me well and are still used at least weekly. In addition, I have acquired another six pressure vessels including one large enough to climb into.

I was confident that the next "Victor" would be bubbles free, and it was. However, it was covered with little bumps as if she had the chicken pox. What I hadn't taken into account was that the rubber in the mold had not been de-aired and when pressurized, the tiny bubbles in the rubber collapsed causing dents in the rubber surface. I constructed a new mold only this time I de-aired the rubber prior to application and cured the mold under pressure. Since then, I have always de-aired rubber for any application and cured it under pressure when feasible. De-airing and/or pressure curing increases the rubber's density and extends the life of the mold in addition to reducing the number of bubbles on the mold's surface.

Back to the quest, I cast my first "Victor" that set up, had a smooth surface, and was bubble free. What I wanted next was a more highly polished surface. I tried several buffing compounds and quickly discovered that polyurethane is easy to melt if aggressively attacked. I was able to do only a fair job of polishing, not the end result that I wanted. In frustration, I abandoned the quest and pursued other interests.

Several years later, I was shooting the bull with my sculpture supplier and the conversation got around to polishing clear urethane. It was suggested that I try buffing compounds made for automobile finishes which are polyurethane paints. This rekindled my interest and I sculpted a new piece titled "Britton" with five flat surfaces and the figure hollowed out as a negative in the back surface. The paint polishing compounds work very well though it is extremely tedious. A piece no larger than "Britton" can take 15 to 20 hours to polish.

There were other problems. For example, some clear urethanes have a slight yellowishness. This can be compensated for by adding a drop of blue dye to the mixture. Careful, two drops in even four or five pounds of material will turn the casting blue. A continual concern is contamination which shows up as spots. I always work in a clean area and carefully filter the solution.

Loveland, CO, Mitch Meisner of Meisner Acrylic Casting approached me about producing my pieces in acrylic. I was skeptical for the reason stated earlier but decided to let him do one as an experiment. It is more expensive though not excessively so, the cost is comparable to casting a similar size figure in bronze.

I have no plans to try to cast acrylics myself. Mitch and I have discussed and compared the two materials. According to him, to be successful, one would need a definite knowledge of polymer science and some very expensive equipment. The learning curve is very long. He recalls that it took him over five years to get a decent casting and another three for a great one. From what I went through, I have no reason to doubt this.

There are some advantages to clear urethane compared to acrylic. For example, urethane can be cast in silicon rubber molds which can be very flexible allowing for more intricate forms than can be attained with acrylics which require a stiffer mold material. Urethanes are more receptive to dyes. But the greatest advantage for me is the ability to cast in my own studio. I have enjoyed the quest and will continue to experiment with and cast in urethanes. But for the production of editions of "Britton," "Emergence," Dancing With the West Wind," and others, I will leave it to the foundry.

David E. Parvin Studio 6857 Leetsdale Drive
Denver, CO 80224-1522
(303) 321-1074

Sculpture Journal – January 2002

Watertrap, Testing a New Product or the Continued Search for the Holy Grail

By David E. Parvin, A.L.I.

There are a number of problems that I have not been able to solve. I'm not talking about discovering the meaning of life or the composition of Dark matter; I'm referring to some things that I have tried as a sculptor to do but just haven't had the success that I want. When I have no challenges remaining, when I know everything and can do anything, I will have found the Holy Grail. Of course, I will always be grail-less. But every once in a while, I get one step closer. Using Watertrap allows me one such step.

Anyone who has done any significant casting of urethane knows that urethane and moisture are not compatible. The isocyanate in the urethane reacts with water to produce carbon dioxide. Rubber molds work just fine as long as they are dry. But attempting to cast urethane in an alginate mold is a different story; mixed alginate is about 75% water. The amount of C02 produced is inversely proportional to the setting time of urethane. Very fast setting urethanes generate far less gas than slow ones and come closer to casting acceptably. But in my experience, even the fastest setting ones still have too much surface distortion.

Recently, I was talking with Arnold Goldman of Monster Makers and the conversation came around to incompatibility of urethane and alginate, a completely logical direction for just about any conversation to take right after, How about them Denver Broncos. Arnold claimed to offer a product called Watertrap that eliminates the problem. I was skeptical but open minded enough to accept a free sample for evaluation. (One of the benefits that comes from writing articles is that people think you must be an expert and give you free things to try, alleluia!)

To test Watertrap, I mixed eight pounds of water and two pounds and two ounces of Artmolds' Fibergel; the ratio is four and three quarters ounces of alginate per pound of water. I made alginate molds of both hands of one of my assistances, Lauryn Harrow. (Those of you who are particularly well read on current events will recognize her name as one of the eight finalists to be the next new face and body for the 2004 Sports Illustrated Swimsuit Issue. One of the benefits that comes from writing articles is that even drop dead beautiful women think you must be an expert and are willing to work for you, alleluia!). Using Polytek's very slow pot life Easyflo 60, I poured about one hundred grams of part A in each of two plastic cups and equal volumes of part B. In a fifth cup I measured the same volume of Watertrap. Lauryn and I then mixed in A and B and at the same time the other A and B along with the Watertrap. I then poured both batches into the two alginate molds. The results were striking. The surface of the hand cast in the plain urethane looked like the surface of a golf ball and skin detail such as fingerprints was missing. The hand with Watertrap was almost perfect with clean fingerprints. Notice the photographs of Lauryn's hands. (By the way, if you would like to see more than just Lauryn's hands, see the Sept. 29 2003 issue of Sports Illustrated).

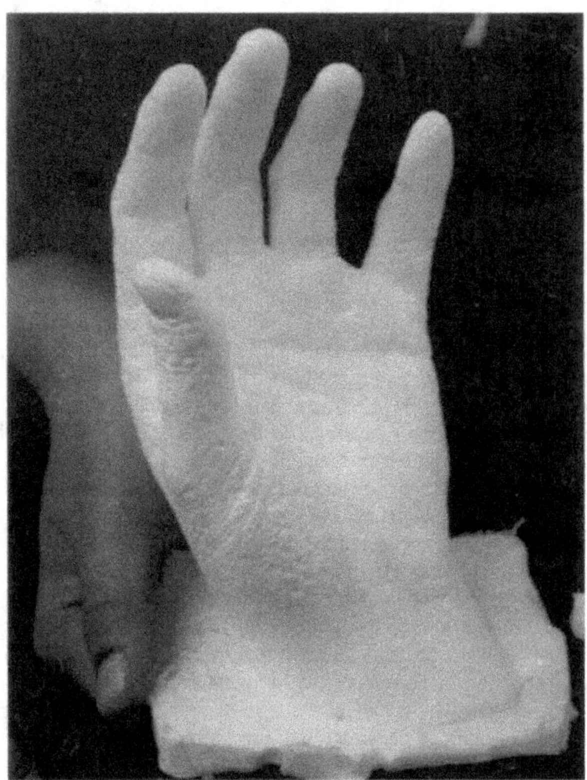
Lauryn's hand cast in urethane without Watertrap showing the rough surface.

Let me point out a few observations: 1. Easyflo 60s components are very runny and mix together easily. Watertrap is a fine powder and requires some additional stirring in order to dissolve it smoothly into the urethane. I would suggest that one mix it into either the part A or B before mixing the two components since very fast setting urethanes leave little time for delays. Adding the

Watertrap only very slightly thickens the urethane mixture.

2. Anytime a powder is stirred into a liquid, some additional air bubbles will also be mixed into the liquid. With that in mind, I would suggest that the Watertrap be mixed into the part A which is thinner and more runny than the part B and from which the trapped bubbles can more easily rise to the surface and escape if allowed to sit for a few minutes before mixing with the B. If you have the capability, de-airing the part A and Watertrap solution will provide for an even more bubble free casting.

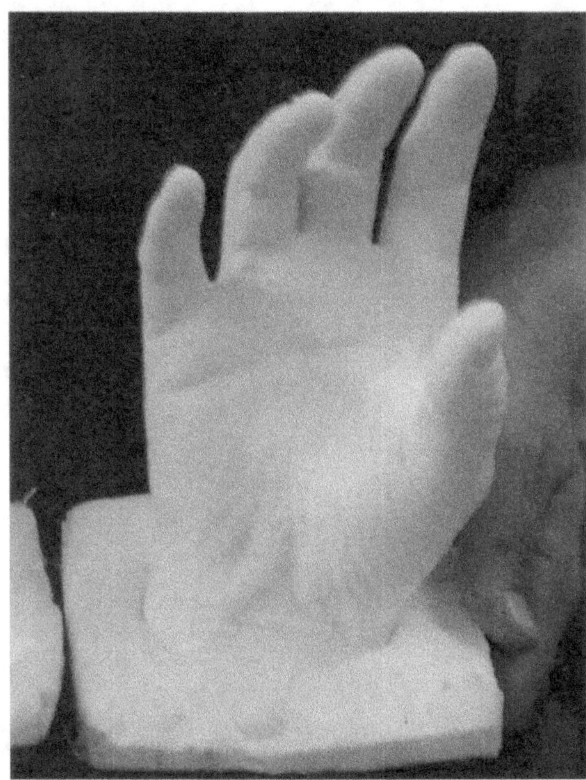

Lanryn's hand cast in urethane with Watertrap showing excellent detail.

3. Adding the Watertrap does not noticeably increase the volume of the mixture.

4. Watertrap being white does lighten the color of the mixed urethane but has almost no effect on its color once it has solidified.

5. The Watertrap batch had a very slightly longer setting time, about ten seconds more. Using a surface reading thermometer, I noticed that the temperature of the Watertrap batch was about ten degrees F cooler than the plain urethane at any point in time as they set up.

6. Note that I had not made any attempt to eliminate moisture from the inside surface of the molds. Further experiments demonstrated that using a hair dryer to dry the inside of the mold makes for even more perfect castings.

7. Just to cover all bases, I mixed a batch of urethane, Watertrap, and copper powder and got a very metallic looking hand.

8. While I had no way of testing to be certain, the Watertrap did not appear to have any effect upon the strength or hardness of the urethane.

9. I also tried mixing Watertrap into polyester resin and pouring it into an alginate mold. It didn't work; all I got was goo.

10. Apparently Watertrap has such affinity for water that it can bind with moisture in the air and can loose some of its effectiveness. Even if it has been kept in a tightly closed container, it may still absorb some moisture. I discovered that spreading it out on a pan and drying it at about 200 degrees F in an oven for a few minutes restored it to its most effective state.

Watertrap may be purchased from:

The Monster Makers
7305 Detroit Ave.
Cleveland, OH 44102
(216) 651-7739
monstermakerssales@monstermakers.com

As I said above, when I first heard of Watertrap, I was very skeptical, but it really does work. It is great to be one step closer to the Holy Grail, one step closer to perfection.

Photographs by: Elliot Summons

David Parvin is a Colorado sculptor whose primary subject is the human form in a variety of material. He may be reached at. 303-321-1074.

Equipment

ACQUIRING a pressure CHAMBER

By
David E. Parvin, A.L.I.

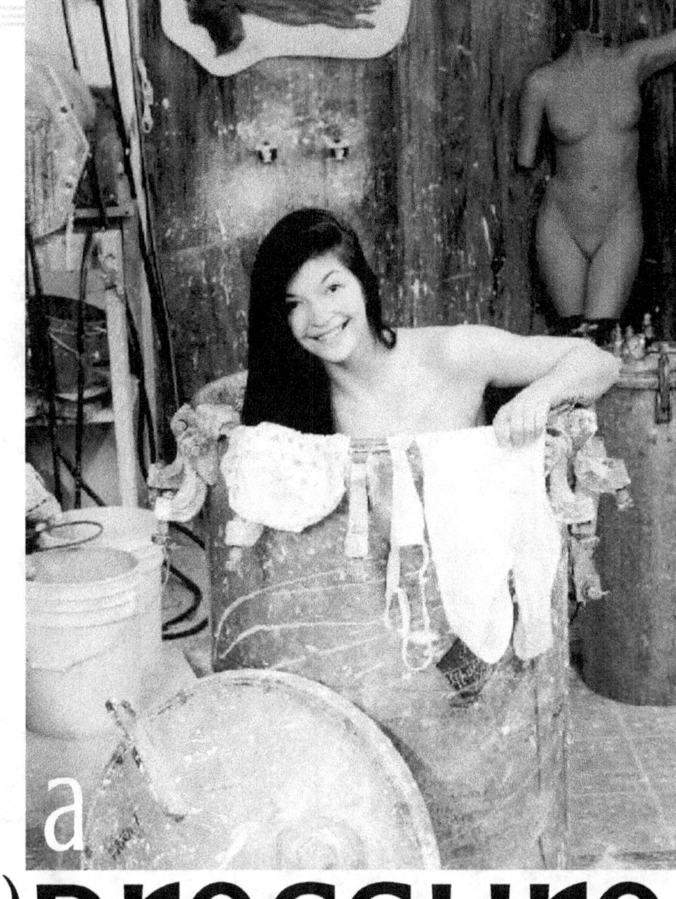

RIGHT| Stevie demonstrates the size of my largest pressure pot.

This is the third in a series of four articles about constructing and using both vacuum and pressure chambers to achieve bubble-free castings with greater detail. The first article explained the "why" and the second told how to acquire a low cost yet very functional vacuum vessel. This one will describe how to acquire or assemble a similar pressure chamber. In next month's "Artmolds Journal," I will show how to use both of these to achieve some results that would be impossible without them.

In last month's article, I described an inexpensive yet very functional vacuum chamber. The great news is that a pressure chamber, tank, vessel, or pot is also simple to come by. Our friends in the painting industry have done most of the work for us by providing pressure paint tanks in all kinds of sizes that need only minor modifications plus a pressure source for our purposes.

Pressure paint tanks (PPTs), are designed to hold a specific size container of paint, such as one, five, or fifty-five gallons. The painter puts the appropriate container of paint into the PPT, seals the lid, and applies pressure to force the paint out through a hose and spray gun. The author has acquired eight PPTs from one to fifty-five gallons over the years, only two of which are the same size and design. Notice in Photo #1, one of my studio assistants, Stevie, is demonstrating the size of my largest PPT and paying a tribute to the old TV sitcom "Petticoat Junction." On the right side of the photograph is a fifteen gallon PPT standing upright, and partially visible on the left is a tank lying horizontally. This one is about eighteen by fifteen inches (about 21 gallons) and was custom made for me. Though my PPTs range from one to fifty-five gallons, the size I use find most useful is two and a half gallons (of which I have two). The inside volume is about nine inches wide and ten inches deep. These are available nationwide through Harbor Freight, and ArtMolds offers a similar one. If purchased from Harbor Freight, some modification is necessary for our application. ArtMolds does the modification for you.

Disclaimer: no naughty bits were exposed in the writing of this article. To protect Stevie's "pure as the driven snow reputation" and just in case her dad, priest, or boyfriend happens to read this article, she was actually completely dressed inside the PPT.

I mentioned that I have eight PPTs, all different, except for two. All had to be modified since they were designed for spraying paint and not for pressurizing artwork. So the modifications were slightly different, but if one understands what changes are required it shouldn't be a problem to modify any PPTs one acquires in the future. I am going to use the PPT available from Harbor Freight for my explanation.

I have two of these in my studio, and though they appear to be identical (except one is gray and the other is black), they had slight differences. So to be sure that I am up to date with what is currently available I went to my closest Harbor Freight. Photograph #2 shows one of these assembled for its designed use. The parts from the top down are: a handle, a

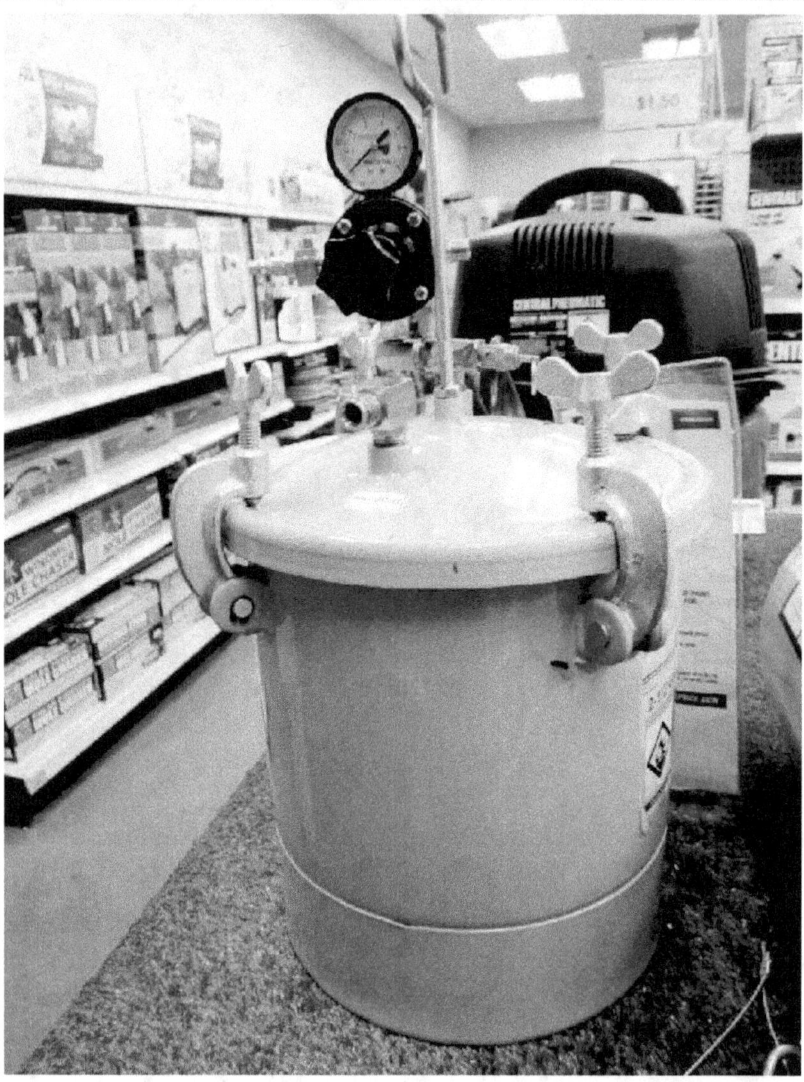

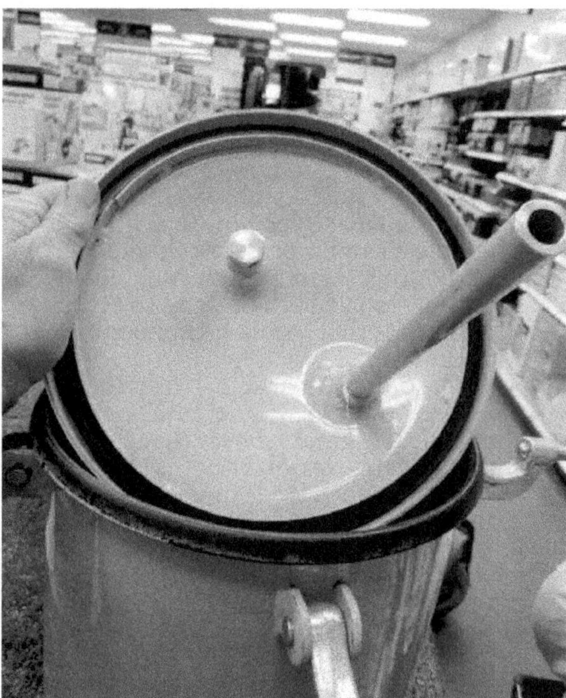

ABOVE | An assembled pressure paint tank (PPT).

RIGHT | The fluid tube.

pressure gauge, a regulator, a horizontal manifold to which the regulator is attached on top and a pressure relief valve on one end, the lid on which is a threaded elbow, and the pressure tank.

The first step to modifying the PPT is to remove the top. Inside is a fluid tube which extends almost to the bottom of the tank through which paint under pressure comes out of the tank to the spray gun. This tube would just be in the way for our use. To remove, just unscrew it. See photos #3 and #4. In my two older but similar PPTs this tube was attached permanently and I had to cut it off to remove it. Because this pipe was the path for the paint to escape from the tank, there remains a hole in the lid that would prevent pressurization. Threaded into this hole is an elbow on the outside of the lid that is the attaching point for a hose to carry the paint to the spray gun, photo #5. My first thought was to remove the external elbow and install a plug. Unfortunately, the elbow was attached so firmly that I couldn't get it loose. I took the easy way out and screwed a cap onto the outside threads plugging the hole.

At this point I had a functional pressure vessel. I could have connected an air hose to the regulator and pressurized the PPT and it would have remained pressurized as long as the pressurized hose remained connected. There are two problems with this. Let me explain the simplest one first. It would be convenient if the hose could be detached and the vessel would hold its pressure so the hose would be available for other uses but the intake coupling could leak. To solve this, all that is needed is an on/off valve between the male intake coupling and the regulator and the problem is solved.

While the second problem is also easily resolved, it is a little more complicated to explain. The regulator looks like something we need; if for nothing else, it could make spouses, children, and visitors respect us more for mastering what is obviously a complicated piece of machinery. But this regulator was designed to regulate the amount of paint coming out of the tank by adjusting the amount of air coming into the tank. It does not restrict the incoming air to a set pressure or it would be of more value (see below). In other words, the pressure inside the tank will eventually equal the pressure in the intake line. All the regulator does is allow one to control the rate of

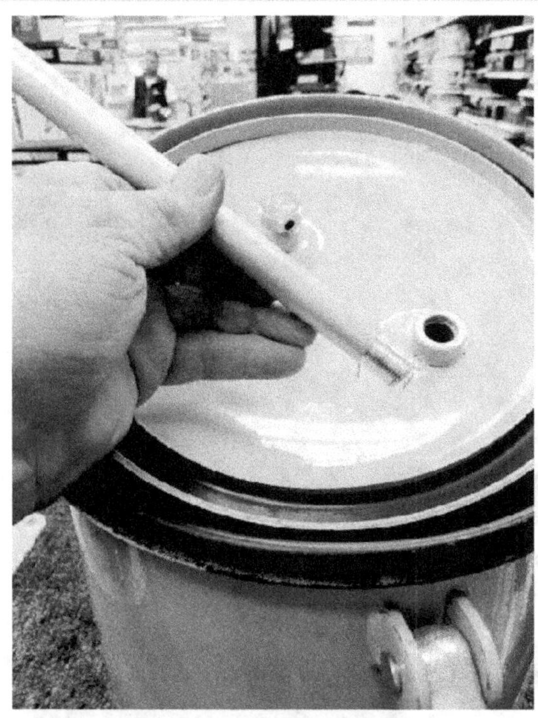

pressurization. The same control can be had by modulating the on/off valve, so the regulator is superfluous. I also found that it was just enough to interfere with the twisting of the thumb screws that secure the lid and just plain in the way. As you can see in photograph #6, I removed the regulator, attached the pressure gauge on top of the manifold where the regulator had been, and attached the on/off valve and air intake male pneumatic coupling. I have been using this modified PPT for about ten years.

But wouldn't you know that the design of the new Harbor Freight PPTs has been changed just enough to require a slightly different a modification to accomplish the second step above. If you compare the intake manifolds in the new PPT in Photo #5 and the old PPT in Photo #6, you will see that pressure gauge attaches on top of the manifold, which is where the regulator had been. But on the new PPT in photo #5, the regulator is connected on one end of the manifold. To modify the new PPT requires a "T" fitting between the on /off valve and the manifold. Photo #7 shows the components needed for this and Photo #8 shows them assembled, which would attach on the end of the manifold in place of the on/off valve in Photo #6.

There is one more slight modification which didn't occur to me until I had been using PPTs for some time. Notice in Photo #3 that there is a hex shaped structure above and to the left of the fluid pipe. This is something new on these PPTs which were not on the ones I have owned for years. Its purpose is to diffuse the intake air from blowing straight down into the tank. I discovered that if I placed a mold directly under the intake, the incoming stream of air could blow some of the casting liquid out of the mold. So I made my own fix by installing an elbow on the intake as shown in Photo #9. I am mentioning this just in case you acquire a PPT which doesn't have this.

Be aware that there is one real safety concern when using these tanks. I do not mean to be condescending but we do have Murphy's Law and the Darwin Awards. The

Be aware that there is one real safety concern when using these tanks.

TOP LEFT | The fluid tube removed.

BOTTOM LEFT | Intake manifold on the new PPT

BELOW | Intake manifold on the old PPT

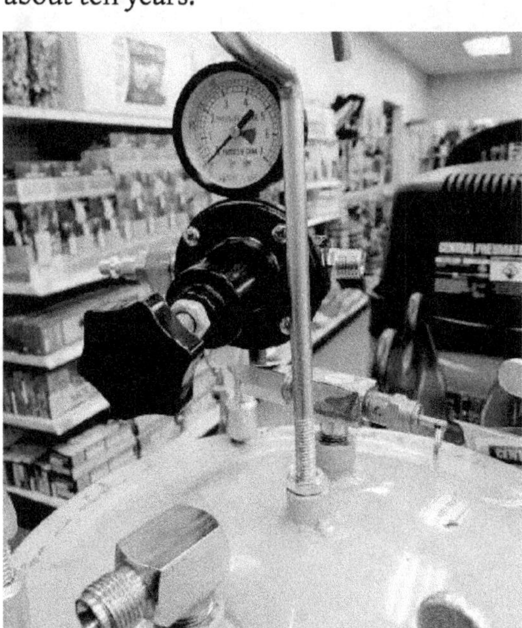

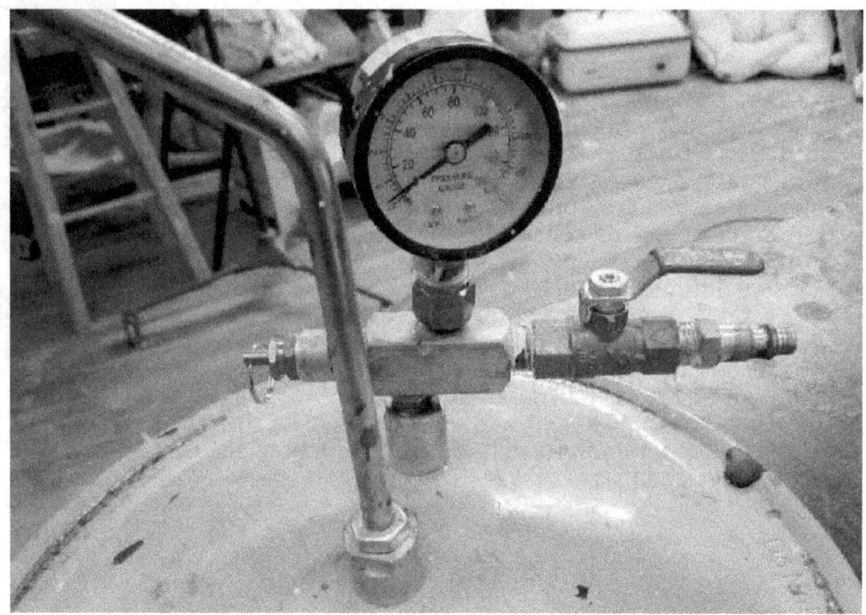

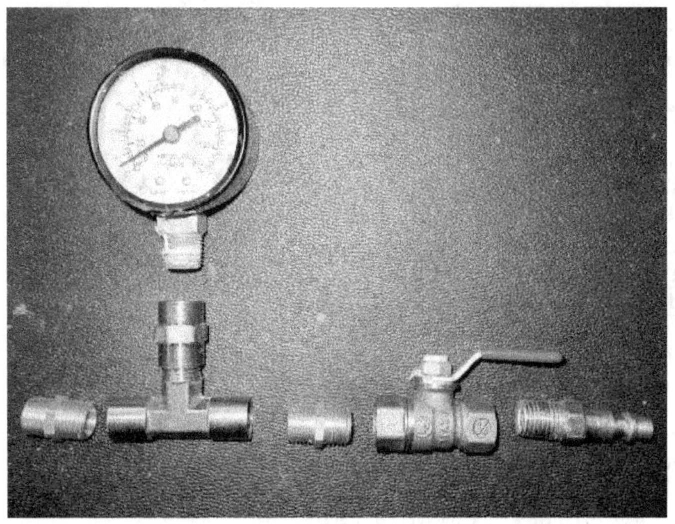

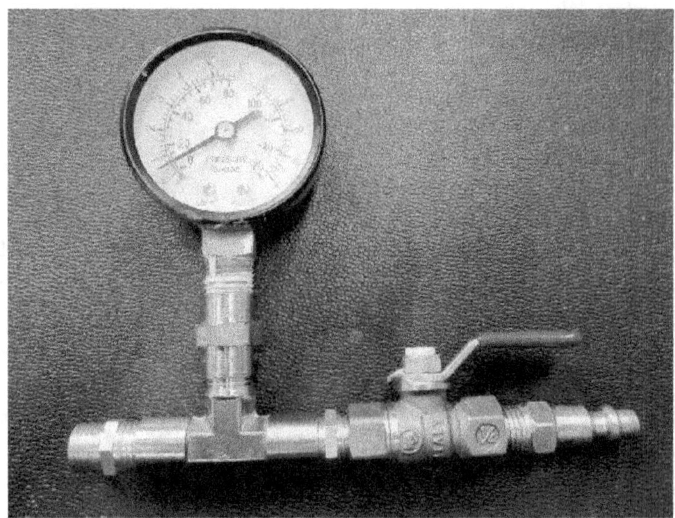

ABOVE | Components needed to convert the PPT to a usable pressure pot. | Assembled components.

problem and danger is that some PPTs are designed for 50 psi while some will take as much as 110 psi. Most compressors will put out over 100 psi. It is very easy to get distracted when filling a PPT, and over pressurization is a real possibility. It is, therefore, important that the safety valve be retained. Sometimes the valves leak and one might be tempted to remove a leaky one and plug the hole. But one would be smarter and safer to replace it with a new one. I am concerned enough that one of my assistants not blow him or herself up that I have installed a pressure regulator set at 50 psi branching off my compressor. This allows me to have a "safe" line on my work bench and still retain 110 psi available for tools and the higher pressure tanks at another location. Of course, I could have adjusted the outflow regulator on my compressor to 50 psi but I was concerned that switching from high to low to high, etc. was an accident waiting to happen.

For anyone just starting to think about the advantages of pressurizing, my suggesting is that you start by ordering a PPT from ArtMolds or get one from your local Harbor Freight. Then if you find you could use something larger check with a painting equipment dealer. But if you keep your eyes open and be patient, I suspect that you will find any number of used but functional ones. At this time, I have eight vessels from one gallon to fifty gallons. Only three were purchased new, one used, and four were actually given to me.

Some of you may be wondering why a pressure tank can't be used as a vacuum chamber, eliminating the need for two different vessels. The answer to this - along with a great deal more information - will be revealed in the fourth and final article in this series, in the next issue. In the meantime, please don't hesitate to contact me either through "ArtMolds Journal" or directly.

Dave Parvin is a Colorado sculptor whose primary subject is the human form in a variety of materials. He may be reached at: (720) 971-0824 or parvinstudio@comcast.net.

BELOW | Installed elbow on the intake.

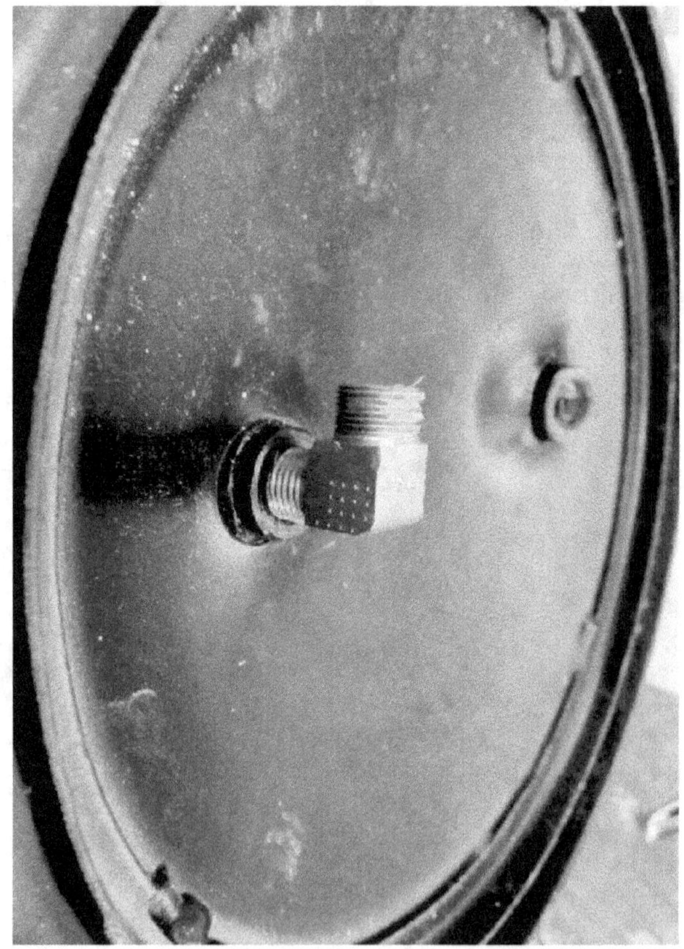

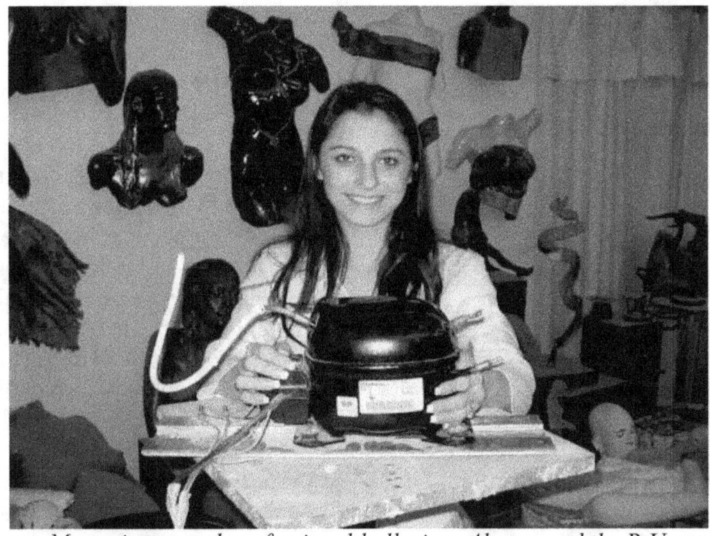
My assistant and professional ballerina, Alyssa, and the R U.

Another Source For Vacuum Pumps

Or a great idea from a stupid mistake

By David E. Parvin, A.L.I.

I could claim that I was up to my neck in creativity producing what would at east get a whole chapter in Sister Wendy's next book, *The Greatest Art In America,* when I was overcome by a tsunami of inspiration. But alas, old George and I agree that one shouldn't tell a lie. The truth is that while I was hard at work on something that will probably get no more than a footnote in Sister Wendy's next book, I got thirsty. (I just love it when something great starts out because of something as trivial a getting thirsty.) So I walked over to my little office-size refrigerator to get a can of my favorite thirst quencher, fizzy water. Apparently someone had consumed the last can without restocking the refrigerator and even though I am the only one at my studio who drinks this swill, I was sure that someone else was at fault. At that point, I could have walked away and broken the chain of events that was drawing me in to do something stupid. But instead I thought, "Not to worry, you have plenty of warm cans of fizzy water, all you need to do is pour one over ice." I opened the freezer door only to find that the ice cube trays were held fast in frost. Instantly I saw the solution, defrost the refrigerator. I had come to a critical fork in the road. One road sign said, "Just turn off the refrigerator and be patient and in time you will get your ice and your cold fizzy water." The other sign said, "Be a man, get something sharp and show that frost who's boss!"

I'm embarrassed to admit that I had been at this same fork in the road two times previously in my life and on both of those occasions I had taken the same manly path with the same "Oh damn" results. This time I grabbed a putty knife and started removing frost.

I could have used a screwdriver but I can assure you from past experiences that the results would have been the same, a loud hissing sound of whatever has replaced freon escapes to the ozone layer. I'm a slow learner.

O.K., you're probably wondering if this story is going anywhere that could possibly be of any value to other artists and if not, will it ever have an end. The answers are yes and yes. As I was unplugging my now worthless refrigerator, it occurred to me that the guts of a refrigerator is a compressor. Compressing a gas causes it to heat up. Releasing the pressure causes it to expand and cool down. All a refrigerator, freezer, or air conditioner does is put this process to use. The important thing here is that if a compressor blows out air from one end, it sucks air in the other. While it didn't seem very likely to me that the silent running little unit from my small refrigerator could possibly blow out enough air to be of much benefit, making a vacuum in a small chamber requires the removal of very little air. I just might have stumbled on to something!

I removed the working parts of the refrigerator (Photograph #1), henceforth to be called RU for refrigerator unit, plugged it in and it blew air out one side and sucked air in the other. As I expected, it didn't move very much air. Just for the fun of it, I tied a rubber glove onto the outflow side and let it run until the glove exploded; it took three minutes (Photograph #2). It took my studio compressor less than ten seconds to do the same thing; however, it must be remembered that the compressor has a tank that is a reservoir of compressed air. If I had emptied the tank and had the compressor fill the glove, it would have taken somewhat longer. I then attached the air side of the RU to a small pressure chamber which is nine inches by nine inches (Photograph #3). This is the same pressure chamber that I explained how to make from a paint pot in "Making a Pressure Chamber," SJ, Oct. 2003.) It took the refrigerator unit two minutes to fill it to twenty-five p.s.i. and three more minutes to get twenty-eight p.s.i. which was as much pressure as I could get. As I expected, my discovery isn't much of a compressor. My regular compressor will put out

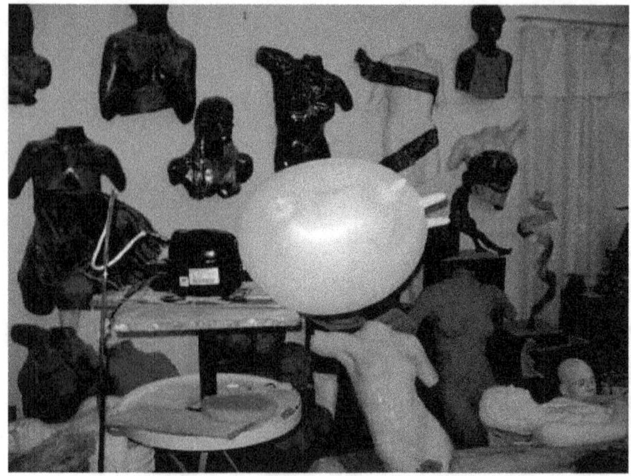
The RU blowing up a rubber glove

110 p.s.i. I usually use just fifty p.s.i. and I can pressurize this same pot in just a few seconds.

While at first glance it would seem that the RU is too slow and doesn't put out enough pressure, however, it might still be of use at a lower altitude. I work in the "Mile High City," the actual output might be as much as 33 p.s.i. But even 28 p.s.i. could be enough for some uses though it wouldn't be sufficient for running air powered tools. (For a thorough explanation of the advantages see "Using Vacuum and Pressure in Casting" and "Putting Vacuum and Pressure Chambers to Practical Use," SJ, August and November 2003.) Also, one could use the RU to fill a portable air "bottle" and have the 28 to 33 p.s.i. instantly available.

As a vacuum source, the RU definitely shows more promise. To see how much vacuum I could pull, I tested the RU with a vacuum meter and was able to get 23 inches of mercury which is as much as I can get from my Whip Mixer at my altitude. Keep in mind that a new Whip Mixer is in the one thousand dollar range. But for a better test of the RU, I attached it to my home made pressure chamber which is about 11 inches tall and 11 inches in diameter. (Photograph # 4 My September 2003 article explained how I constructed this chamber.) I was able to get 10 inches of mercury in 90 seconds, 15 inches in 3 minutes, and 20 inches in 7 minutes. The maximum vacuum I was able to achieve was 20.5 inches. Using my vacuum pump, I was able to get 21 inches in about 30 seconds. (I suspect that my seal on the vacuum chamber's lid was leaking slightly and prevented getting

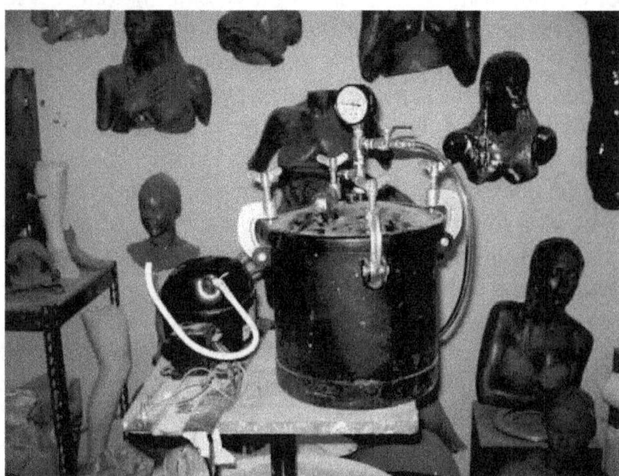
The RU attached to a pressure chamber

closer to 23 inches.) While the RU is slower than a vacuum pump, it is fast enough to de-air anything except the fastest setting materials.

There are a couple of questions that I have not covered. 1. Does the RU need the coolant, which escaped, for lubrication - and will running it empty, destroy it? 2. Are RUs made for larger or normal size refrigerators and freezers have larger capacities and be more useful? Fortunately there was a name on the RU, Embraco. A quick search on the internet got me a phone number, (770) 814-8004. What I found out is that the coolant does lubricate the RU and it was suggested that a few drops of oil be put into the suction side every so often. And in fact, the larger the refrigerator, the bigger and more capable the RU.

If one's wealth and social status were dependent upon one's ability to produce and utilize vacuums and pressure, I'd be at the top of the heap. I have five different vacuum and three pressure sources and twelve chambers in various sizes from one to fifty-five gallons that can be used for vacuum or pressure or both. I'd be living in the big house on the hill with a pool, a tennis court, a Rolls, a yacht, private jet, a trophy wife and a couple of trophy mistresses in reserve. But even with all my vast wealth and prestige, I would still see

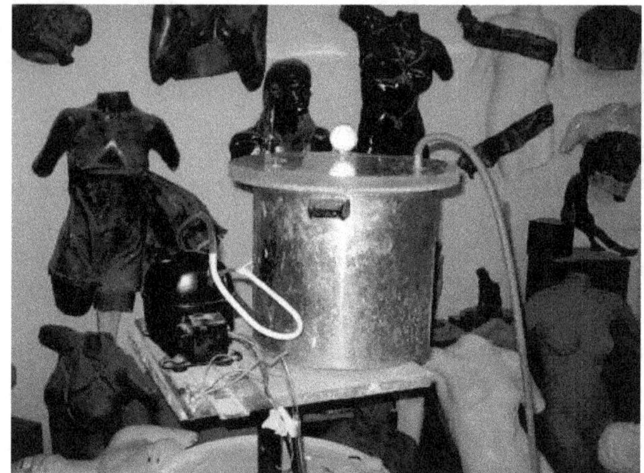
The RU attached to a vacuum chamber

two advantages to owning an RU. The first is cost which in most cases is probably going to be nothing. With minimum effort, one should be able to find an old refrigerator or freezer at little or no cost. The really slick thing is that the RU is complete in its self except for a few fittings which can be purchased at any hardware store. I have, for example, seen an automobile air conditioner compressor used for the same purpose, however it requires attaching it to an electric motor. The second is that the RU is almost completely silent. Both my vacuum pump and my compressor are very noisy. While noise in my studio is just a nuisance, it could be a serious problem for someone working in, say, an apartment.

One last thing, since I am not capable of choosing the correct fork in the road, I'm assured that I will not make the wrong decision again, I bought a frost free refrigerator.

Sculpture Journal - April 2006

Making a Pressure Chamber

By David E. Parvin, A.L.I.

This is the third in a series of four articles about constructing and using both vacuum and pressure chambers to achieve castings that are bubble free and with greater detail. The first article explained the "why" and the second told how to make a low cost yet very functional vacuum vessel. This one will describe how to assemble a similar pressure chamber. In next month's "Sculpture Journal," I will show how to use both of these to achieve some results that would be impossible without them.

In last month's article, I explained that to make a vacuum chamber one had to find a suitable container, fabricate an airtight transparent lid, attach the right fittings, and provide a vacuum source. The great news is that a pressure chamber, tank, vessel, or pot is much simpler to come by. Our friends in the painting industry have done most of the work for us by providing pressure paint tanks in all kinds of sizes that need only minor modifications plus a pressure source for our purposes.

Pressure paint tanks are available from a number of sources. For this article, I went to what is my closest source, a Harbor Freight Tools outlet. There I was able to purchase for less than $80.00 plus tax a two and half gallon paint tank Model 37515 made by Central Pneumatics. I had better explain paint tank sizes. Generally, paint tanks are designed to hold a specific size container of paint such as one, five, or fifty-five gallons. The painter puts the appropriate container of paint into the pot, seals the lid, and applies pressure to force the paint out through a hose and spray gun. This Model 37515 is different because it will hold two and half gallons poured directly into the tank. While this may make it more difficult for a painter to clean up, it is no disadvantage to us while making a bigger chamber than one designed to hold a one gallon can. (More about sizes and sources later)

While there are any number of different paint tanks available, all that I have seen are similar enough that adaptation for our use is almost identical. Notice the photograph of the paint tank assembled as intended. Attached to the lid is a regulator designed to control the volume of compressed air entering the tank. Attached to the regulator are four things, a pressure gauge, a male air intake coupling, a safety release valve, and a connector that allows air to flow into the pot. What is not visible in the photograph is a pipe (fluid tube) inside the tank that extends to the bottom of the tank as an outlet for the paint. The first step in modifying the tank into a pressure chamber is get rid of this pipe since it would only be in the way. But because this pipe was the path for the paint to escape from the tank, there remains a hole in the lid that would prevent pressurization. Threaded into this hole is an elbow on the outside of the lid that is the attaching

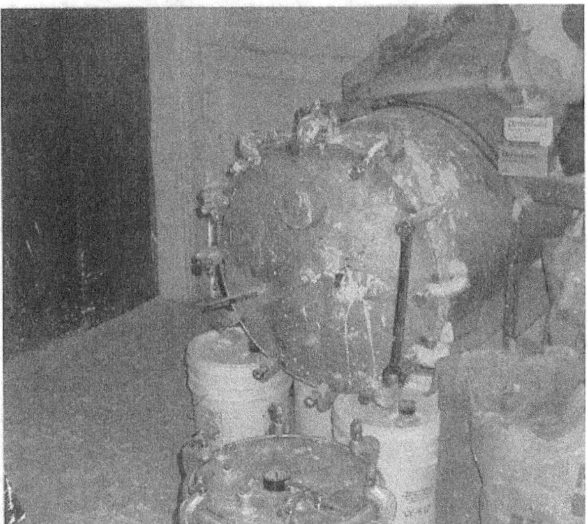

Two of the eight tanks owned by the author. The one on the floor will hold 10 gallons. The one on its side will hold 55 gallons.

the lid that would prevent pressurization. Threaded into this hole is an elbow on the outside of the lid that is the attaching point for a hose to carry the paint to the spray gun. My first thought was to remove the external elbow and install a plug. Unfortunately, the elbow was attached so *firmly* that I couldn't get it loose. I took the easy way out and screwed a plug into the outside threads plugging the hole.

At this point I had a barely functional pressure vessel. I could have connected a pressure line to the regulator and pressurized the pot and the pot would have remained pressurized as long as the pressurized input line remained connected. There are two problems with this. Let me explain the simplest one first. It would be convenient if the pressure line could be detached and the vessel would hold its pressure. All that is needed is a on/off valve between the male intake coupling and the regulator and the problem is solved. While the second problem is also easily resolved, it is a little more complicated to explain.

The regulator looks like something we need; if nothing else, it could make spouses, children and visitors respect us more for mastering what is obviously a complicated piece of machinery. But this regulator was designed to regulate the amount of paint coming out of the tank by adjusting the amount of air coming into the tank. It does not restrict the incoming air to a set pressure or it would be of more value (see below). In other words, the pressure inside the tank will eventually equal the pressure in the intake line. The regulator only allows one to regulate how quickly or slowly this

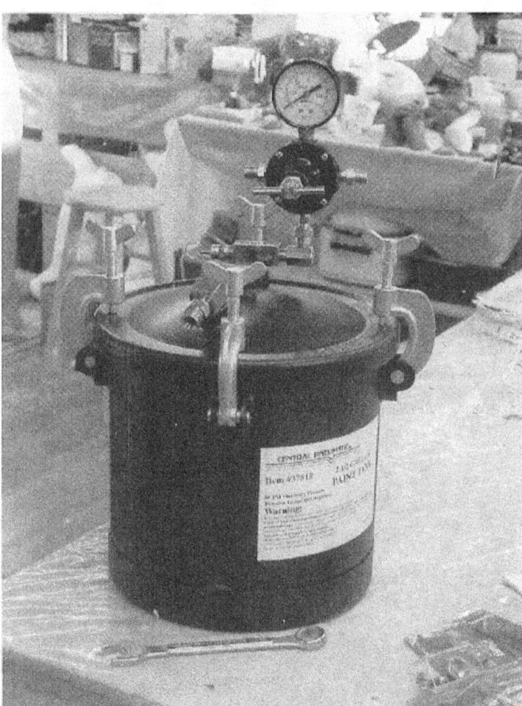

The paint tank assembled for its designed purpose

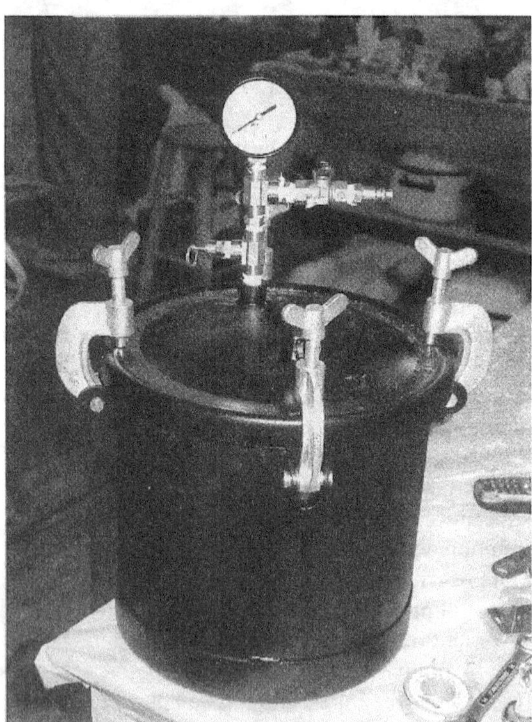

The modified tank

only allows one to regulate how quickly or slowly this happens. The same control can be had by modulating the on/off valve, the regulator is superfluous. I also found that it was just enough to interfere with the twisting of the thumb screws that secure the lid. As you can see from the photographs of the modified tank, I removed the regulator, unscrewed the attachments, and reattached them to two "T" joints. The cost of the extra fittings was about $20.00 making the total cost only around $100.00. The tank is finished.

Be aware that there is one real safety concern when using these tanks. The problem and danger is that some paint tanks probably put outs. This is especially true with the smaller

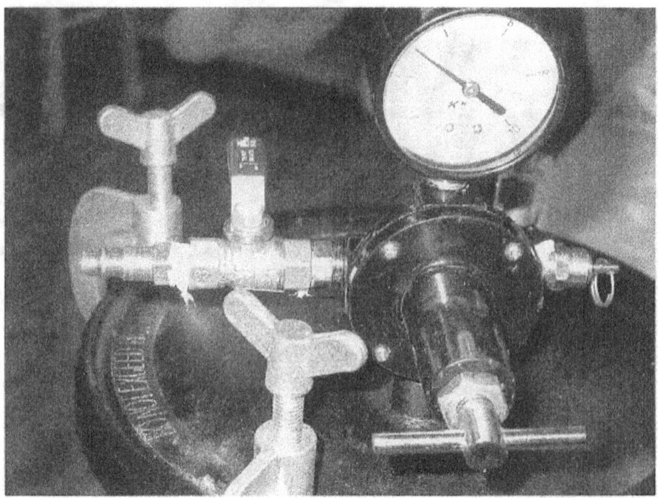

A close-up of the modified lid

probably put outs. This is especially true with the smaller tanks. The Model 37515 described in this article another small one that I own will only take 50 p.s.i. I have three larger ones that are designed for 110 p.s.i. It is, therefore, important that the safety valve be retained. Sometimes the valves leak and one might be tempted to remove a leaky one and plug the hole. But one would be smarter and safer to replace it with a new one. I am concerned enough that one of my assistants not blow him or herself up that I have installed a pressure regulator set at 50 p.s.i. branching off my compressor. This allows me to have a "safe" line on my work bench and still retain 110 p.s.i. available for tools and the higher pressure tanks at another location. Of course, I could have adjusted the outflow regulator on my compressor to 50 p.s.i. but I was concerned that switching from high to low to high, etc. was an accident waiting to happen. Another solution would be to install a pressure regulator on each pressure vessel.

Anyone living in a large metropolitan area should have no trouble finding paint tanks through the painting equipment dealers. But for those living in Left Earmuff, Montana or such can contact Grainger at www.grainger.com Granger carries a one gallon pot for $113.00 and a five gallon one for $744.00. The one I purchased for this article is available form Harbor Freight at ww.harborfreight.com. But if you keep your eyes open and be patient, I suspect that you will find any number of used but functional ones. At this time, I have eight vessels from one gallon to fifty gallons. Only three were purchased new and four were actually given to me.

Some of you may be wondering why a pressure tank can't be used as a vacuum chamber eliminating the need for two different vessels. The answer to this along with a great deal more information will be revealed in the fourth and final article next month.

The processes, methods and apparatus presented herein have not been tested or verified by Sculpture Journal magazine in anyway. Anyone using any of this information is doing so at their own risk.

Dave Parvin is a Colorado sculptor whose primary subject is the human form in a variety of materials. He may be reached at: 303-321-1074

Making a Vacuum Chamber

by David E. Parvin, A.L.I.

In the last issue of Sculpture Journal, I discussed the advantages for using a vacuum or pressure chamber or both to achieve castings that are bubble free and with better detail. But in order to reap the advantages, one has to have the equipment. In this issue, I will explain how to construct economically a very functional vacuum chamber. In next month's issue, I will do the same for a pressure vessel. The month after that, I will put it all together and describe how to achieve results that would be impossible otherwise.

All that is needed are some sort of a container, a few fittings and connectors, some pressure hose, and a vacuum source. Once you have the components, except for the time it takes for the rubber seal to cure, the assembly takes just a few minutes and costs as little as $200.00. This article is not meant to be a blueprint but does provide enough information to allow almost anyone to make a functioning system. I suspect that most of you who may live in remote areas with limited access, I have proved phone numbers and/or e-mails to make your acquisition less frustrating.

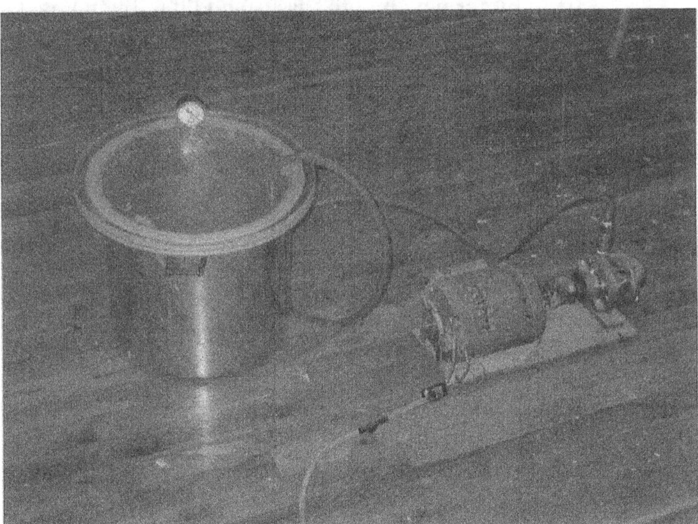

The author's home-assembled vacuum chamber

There are several possibilities for a container. The one pictured is simply a pressure cooker about 12 x 12 inches minus the lid. Since I have had this for at least 10 years, it seemed only appropriate that I check current prices. I went to my closest Target store and to my surprise, the only pressure cooker available was much smaller, too small. So I tried Sears, ditto. The same at Wal-Mart. However, Wal-Mart has a 16 quart stainless stock pot for $34.95 that looks as if it would do just fine. Sears had a similar one only the price was about $10 more. Then I hit the mother load.

I went to a restaurant supply store. I was told that larger pressure cookers are getting hard to find because too many of them blew up and nobody wants the liability of selling them. Since we are talking about creating a vacuum, the much more genteel imploding possibility doesn't seem real dangerous. But, I guess, nobody wants to bet the company's future by making a vacuum cooker ... The good news is that there is a tremendous selection of professional stock pots available in both aluminum and stainless steel. They go from way too small to large enough for two full grown people to climb into (not that they would want to). An aluminum one about 12 x 12 inches is about $50.00; stainless steel is about three times as much and no better for our purpose.

To complete the pressure chamber, you only need a strong, transparent lid that has been drilled and tapped in three places and has an air-tight seal. The lid should be 1 inch thick Plexiglas about two inches wider then your pot. (The first lid I tried was only 1/2 inch thick and noticeably bowed in under vacuum. I suspected that it would have eventually failed). As you can see in the photograph, the three attachments to the lid are the hose to the vacuum source, a vacuum gauge, and a pressure release valve. Notice that the attachments are on the outside of the lid just inside of the rim of the pot and about 120 degree apart. Holes drilled near the outside are less likely to weaken the lid than if more to the center. The hose, gauge, and release valve are probably available at your nearest Ace Hardware, Home Depot, Lowes, etc. for about $10.00, $8.00 and $2.50 respectively.

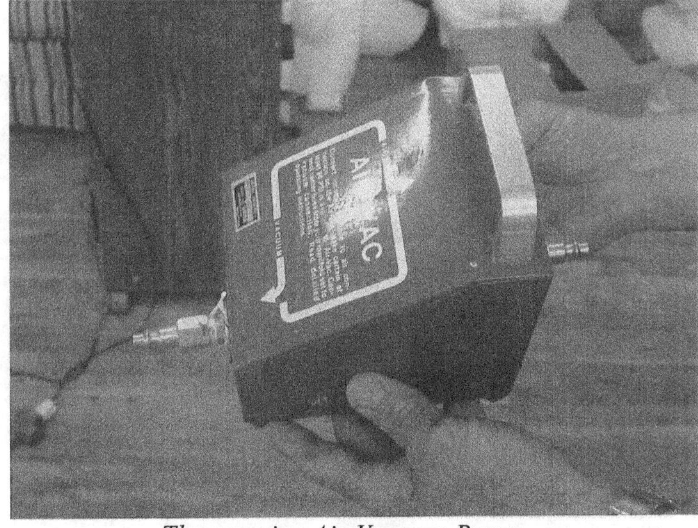

The amazing Air Vacuum Pump

The only one of these that may be hard to find is the vacuum gauge which can be ordered from Grainger at www.grainger.com.

The construction of the lid was a cinch. All I did was go to my local plexiglass/plastics store, Plasticare, and sketch out what I wanted. I had taken the vacuum gauge with me to indicate the size of the holes and the proper threads and Plasticare drilled and tapped the hoes. I had already figured out how to make a really slick, I hoped, air tight seal. It seamed to me that if Plasticare could router out a 1/4 inch deep groove around the inside of the outer edge of my spiffy new lid that was wide enough to fit over the rim of my pot, I could pour the groove about half full of rubber and have a custom made seal. Alas, I was told that this particular company did not have the capability to router out the groove. For a moment it looked as if the best laid plans of sculptors might join those of mice and men. But then I asked it the lid was made of 3/4 inch plexiglass, could a circle of 1/4 inch Plexiglas, the diameter of the inside of my intended groove be laminated to the lid. Then all that would be needed was to add a 1/4 inch thick ring that would go from the outside of the intended groove to the edge of the lid. It just so happened that they could do that and I got my groove without having to do an grooving.

Pouring the seal was no problem. All I did was mix up a little rubber and filled the groove about half full. After letting it set overnight, it was finished and works perfectly. I used a platinum cure silicone called P-15 made by Silicone, Inc. However, I am sure that any kind of rubber would work as long as it is fairly soft.

If you are confused about the lid, take a look at the photograph, and I think it will all make sense, For those of you who do not have access to a plastics fabrication company, you could contact Plasticare at 303-781-1171 and they will construct a lid to your specifications and ship it to you. As I recall, my cost was $80.00.

Up to this point you will have spent about $50.00 for a stock pot, $9.00 for a vacuum gauge, $10.00 for the hose, $2.50 for the valve, and $80.00 for the lid for a total of $150.00. All that is left is the vacuum source and you will be ready to de-air all sorts of things. You could even repeat some

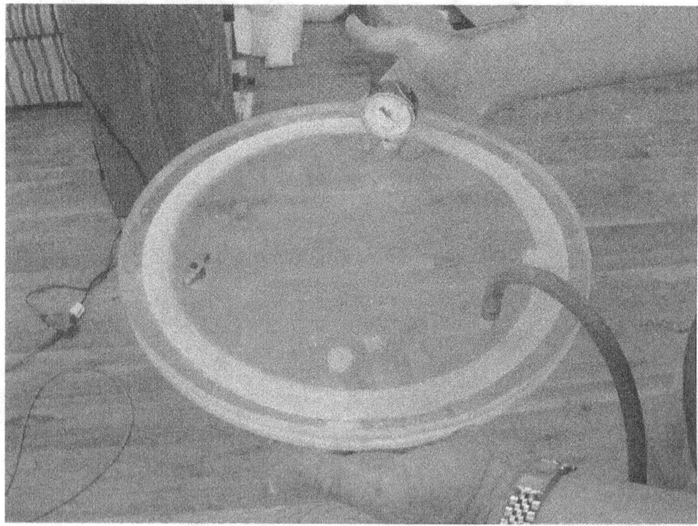

The lid with it's three fittings

sorts of things. You could even repeat some of those early nineteenth century experiments such as: can a fly fly with no air and how long do mice live in a vacuum.

The vacuum pump and motor in the photograph were purchased as a unit from Arbce Sales Co. in Chicago, IL at 312829-1468. Unfortunately, while the pump (stock number VG30, $50.00) is still available, the combination is not. But the required 1/2 horsepower, 1725 RPM electric motor and the sheaves and belt to connect hem can be ordered from Grainger for about $150.00.1 know someone who substituted an automotive air conditioner compressor (a used one at that) and had a perfectly workable vacuum source. I have been told that a refrigerator compressor also works. If you just want to purchase a combined pump and motor and aren't concerned about a few bucks, try www.gastmfg.com where you can order a 0523-101 Q-5 G588DX for $337.00 land be done with it.

But I promised that you could have a working vacuum chamber for less than $200.00 and you can as long as you already have an air compressor with at least 4.2 C.F.M. at 75 P.S. I. there is an amazing little $15.99 gadget called an Air Vacuum Pump (see the photograph) made by Central Pneumatic. It can be ordered for Harbor Freight at www.harborfreight.com. It is crated at the other end because of a venturi in-between. (You may remember that a venturi as explained by Bernoulli's principle is what allows an airplane to fly. This little box won't keep a 747 in the air, but it will pull as much vacuum as my pump. You will have to go to your local hardware store to get the correct fittings to attach it between the compressor and the chamber and you are in business.

Stand by for next month's issue and I'll tell you how to construct the companion piece of equipment, a pressure chamber. *The processes, methods and apparatus presented herein have not been tested or verified by Sculpture Journal magazine in any way. Anyone using any of this information is doing so at their own risk.*

Dave Parvin is a Colorado sculptor whose primary subject is the human form in a variety of materials. He may be reached at 303-321-1074.

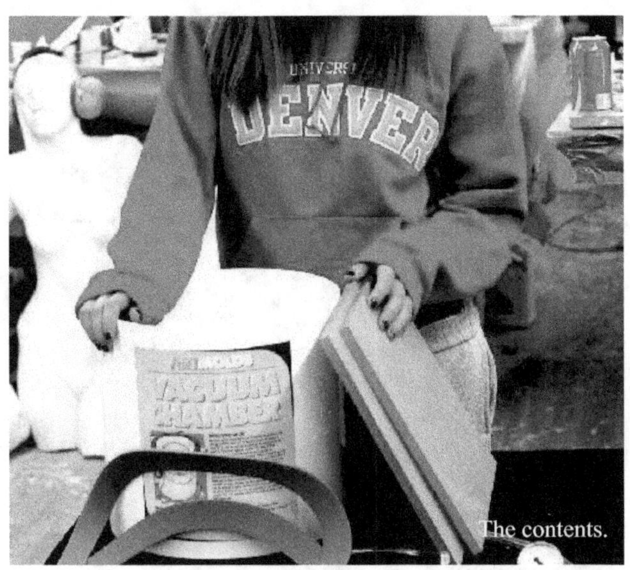

The contents.

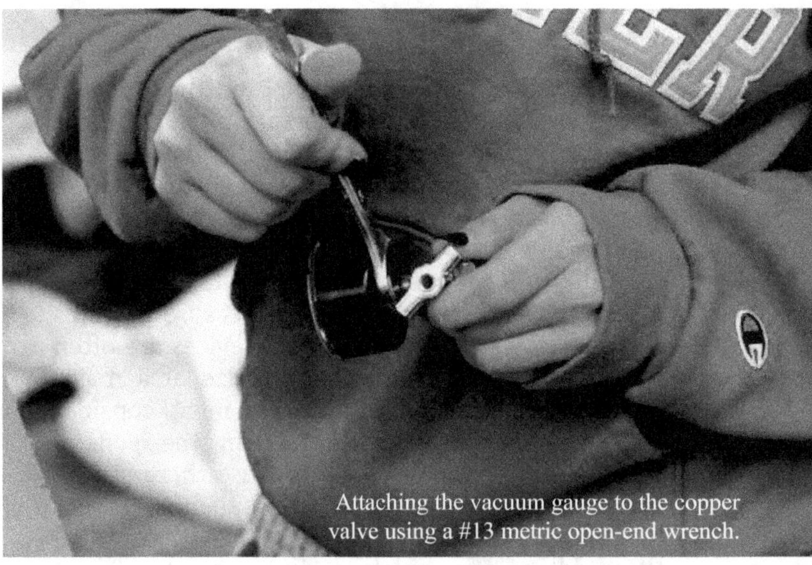
Attaching the vacuum gauge to the copper valve using a #13 metric open-end wrench.

Putting ArtMolds' New Affordable Vacuum Chamber to The Test

Mold Making and Casting Part II

This is the second in a series of four articles on vacuuming and pressurizing. The first article appeared in the previous issue, and discussed theory and advantages associated with vacuuming and pressurizing. This article describes an inexpensive, yet very capable vacuum chamber available from EnvironMolds: the ArtMolds Vacuum Chamber. In the next two issues, I will explain how to economically construct a pressure chamber and how to put both to practical use.

Years ago, I constructed a vacuum chamber by modifying a pressure cooker. It worked okay, but when I found out EnvironMolds had a functioning vacuum chamber for less money and effort than one would spend constructing his/her own, I just had to try it.

To really put it to the test, I decided to let one of my studio assistants, Stevie, do the assembly. In photograph #1, it is obvious that Stevie was just as excited as I was to see what was in the box. Don't let the Denver University sweatshirt that Stevie is wearing make you wonder if I brought in a ringer such as a fourth-year mechanical engineering student just to make the assembly look easy. At the time, Stevie was an almost-seventeen year old high school junior. So if you think you are as smart and capable as a seventeen year old, keep reading.

By David E. Parvin, A.L.I.

In photo #2, Stevie had removed the contents of the box which consisted of: Vacuum Chamber body, two rubber gaskets, two acrylic plastic lids, a vacuum gauge, an exhaust valve body assembly, a yard of plastic tubing, and a manual. The manual is only three pages long (besides the cover sheet) and the nine-step assembly instructions take less than a page. I found this encouraging because it seems that nowadays even the simplest devices are often accompanied with a manual the size of a major city's phone book. EnvironMolds must consider its customers to have more than the general population's common sense, because there are no condescendingly insulting warnings such as, "Do not feed to small children or pets," or "Do not operate in the middle of a frozen lake during spring thaw."

The only two things required for assembly that are not supplied are an adjustable wrench and a dab of petroleum jelly. I substituted 13 mm and 14 mm open-end wrenches, which worked perfectly (pliers would have sufficed as well). Stevie had no problem following each of the nine simple assembly steps with no guidance from me - except for the last one, which I will explain.

Step 1: Stevie attaches the vacuum gauge to the brass fitting (photo #3).

Step 2: The attached gauge and the fitting are connected to the vacuum chamber (photo #4).

Step 3: Stevie lubricates the hose barb fitting with a bit of petroleum jelly and presses the plastic tubing onto the hose barb (photos #5 and #6).

Step 4: Stevie removes the protective paper from the acrylic lids. The directions said to remove the paper from both sides of both lids. It is essential that you are able to view what is happening to the materials being de-aired, hence the clear lids. However, since the bottom lid would come into contact with some surface such as a counter top, and there is no reason to look through the bottom lid, my suggestion is that you leave the paper on the bottom side in order to prevent scratching of the lid surface (photo #7).

Step 5: One of the two rubber gaskets is centered on the bottom lid (photo #8).

Step 6: Stevie places the vacuum chamber in the center of the bottom gasket, making sure that the entire perimeter of the chamber is sitting evenly on the gasket (photo #9).

Step 7: Stevie centers the second gasket evenly on the top rim of the chamber (photo #10).

Step 8: The second acrylic lid is placed over the top gasket, sealing the vacuum chamber. The vacuum

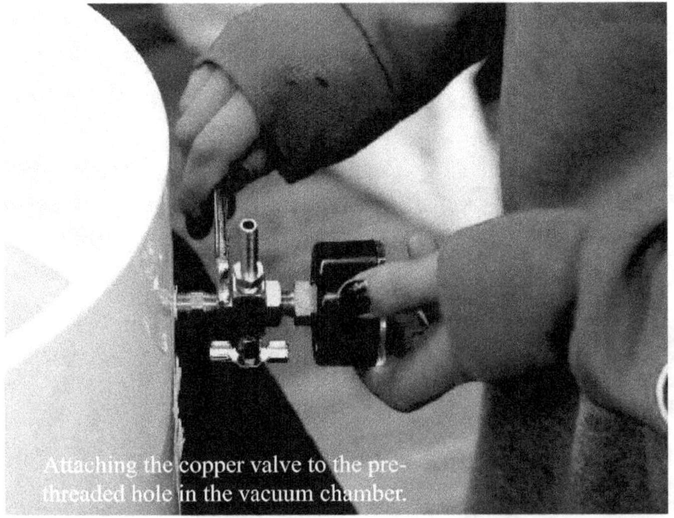
Attaching the copper valve to the pre-threaded hole in the vacuum chamber.

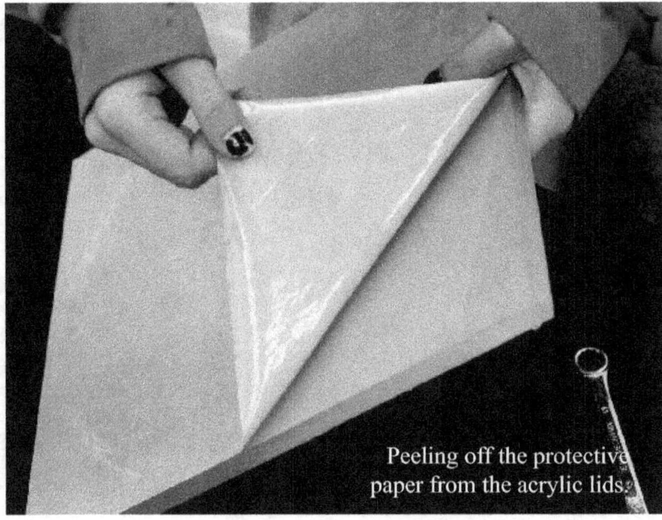
Peeling off the protective paper from the acrylic lids.

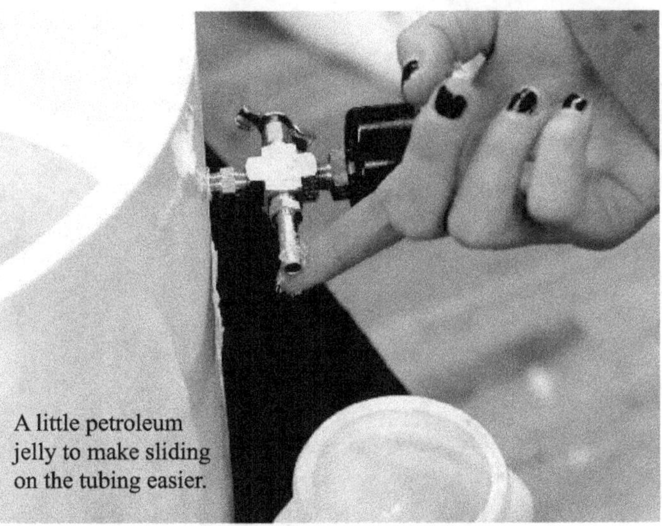
A little petroleum jelly to make sliding on the tubing easier.

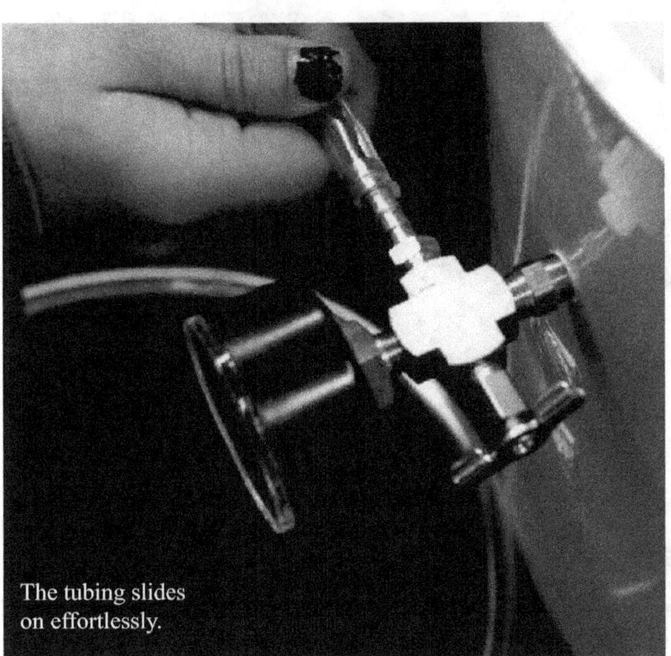
The tubing slides on effortlessly.

chamber is now completely assembled and ready for use (photo #11).

Step 9: The manual says, "Connect your plastic tube to your vacuum source. You are ready to use the vacuum chamber." Anyone with any experience with pneumatics will know how to do this; however, since Stevie had no exposure to air-driven equipment, I had to help her with this step. I showed her three different ways of doing this. In the first, I had her attach the plastic line directly to the vacuum pump with another barbed connector (photo #12). The advantage to this method is that it is the simplest and will result in the least amount of loss of vacuum due to leakage.

A second method is to attach the barbed connector to the end of a hose that is attached to the vacuum source (photo #13). If the vacuum source has other uses, connecting/disconnecting to the pressure chamber can be facilitated with a quick-release coupling (photo #14).

Notice the obvious look of satisfaction on Stevie's face in photo #15 for a job well done, when she observes what had been just moments before been a collection of miscellaneous parts has become a functioning vacuum chamber!

The vacuum chamber is large enough to contain a 2 1/2 gallon bucket as shown in photo #16. A bucket of that size is sufficient to hold a gallon of liquid and allow for expansion when evacuated. I have probably been using vacuums for at least twenty years in my studio, and do not ever recall the need to evacuate more than a gallon of liquid at one time. So as we all know, while size does matter, the ArtMolds Vacuum Chamber from EnvironMolds should be large enough to serve just about any purpose a sculptor might have.

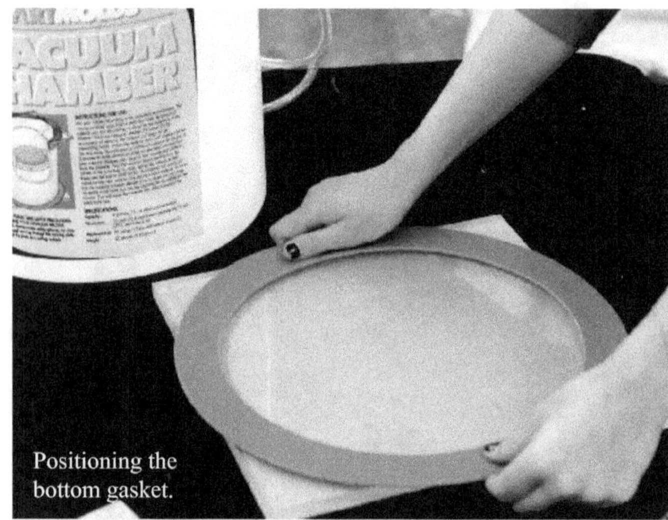

Positioning the bottom gasket.

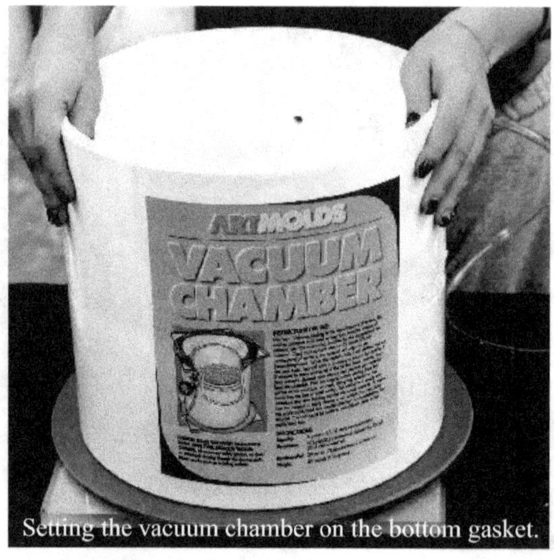

Setting the vacuum chamber on the bottom gasket.

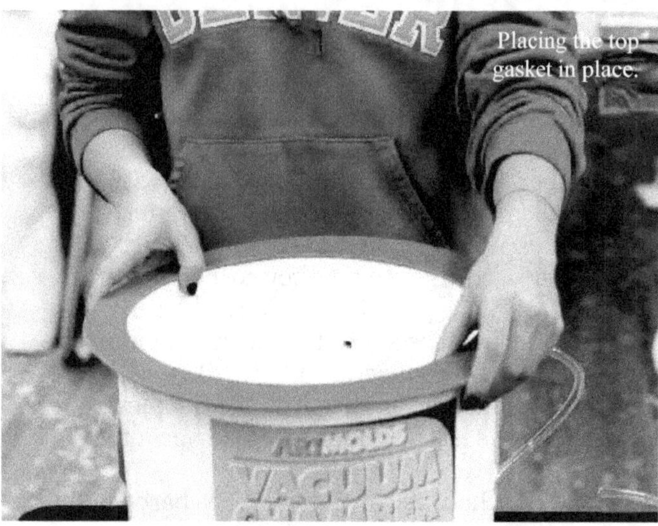

Placing the top gasket in place.

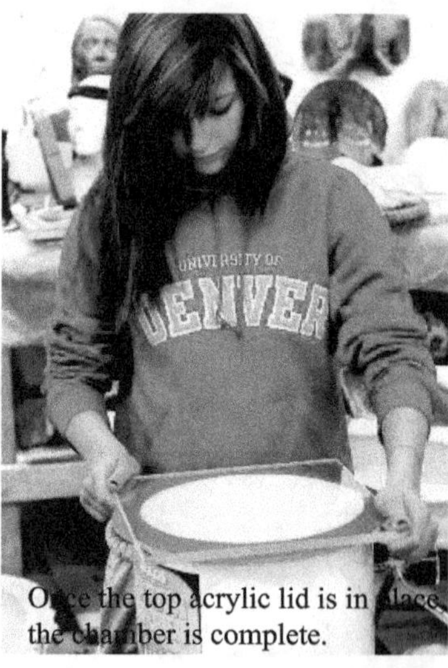

Once the top acrylic lid is in place, the chamber is complete.

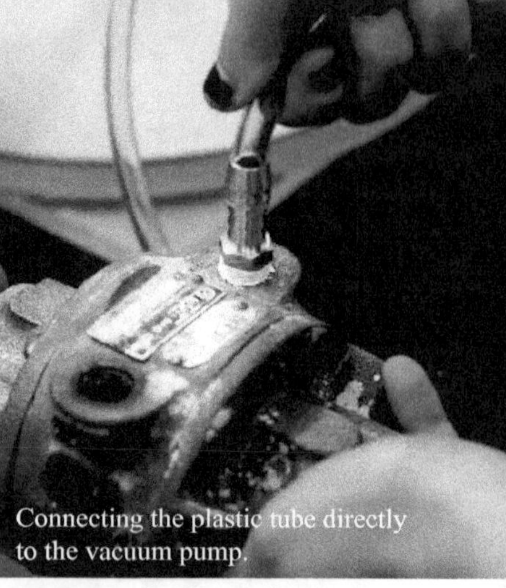
Connecting the plastic tube directly to the vacuum pump.

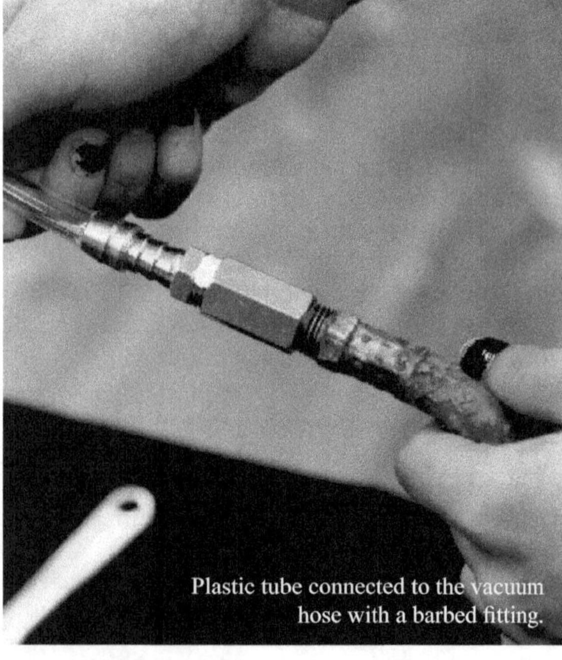
Plastic tube connected to the vacuum hose with a barbed fitting.

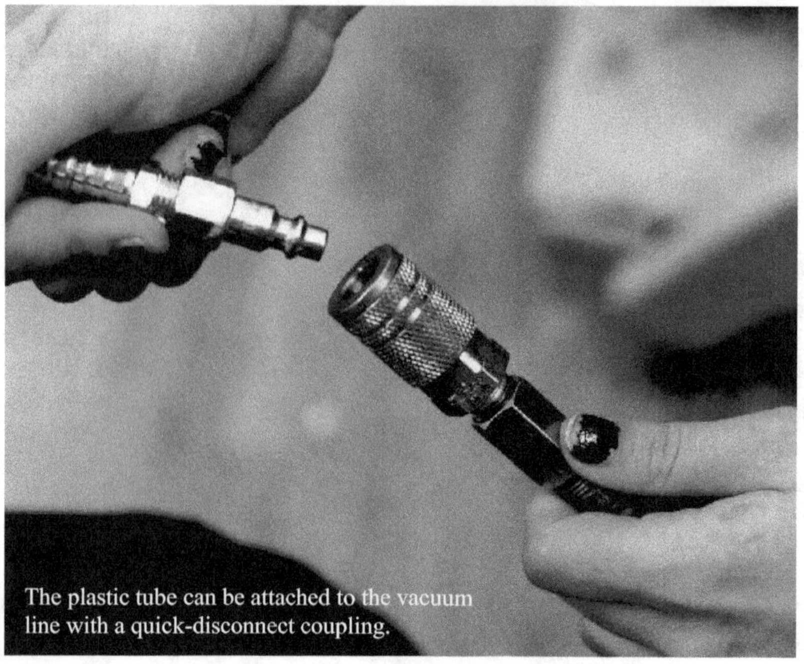
The plastic tube can be attached to the vacuum line with a quick-disconnect coupling.

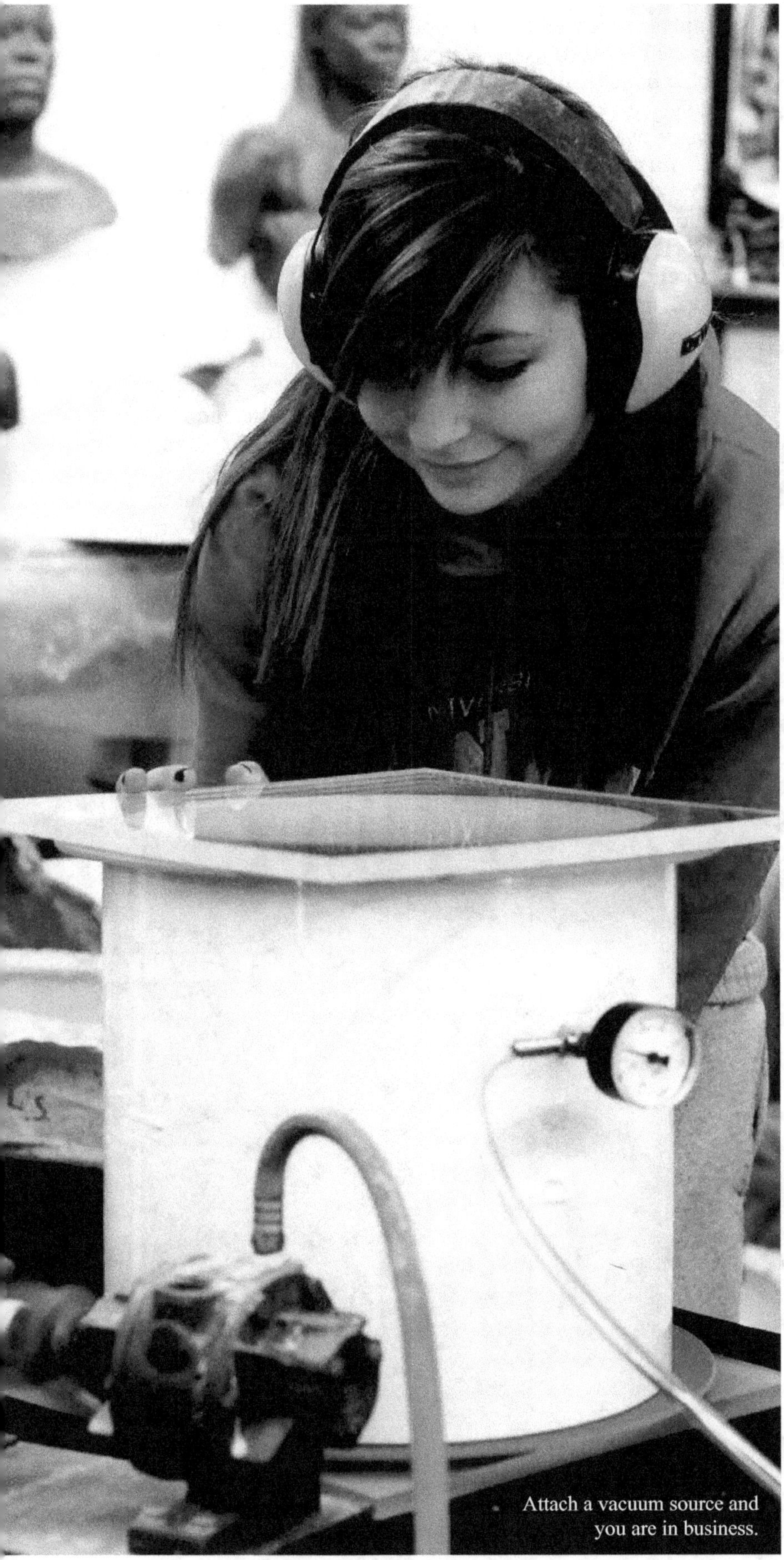

Attach a vacuum source and you are in business.

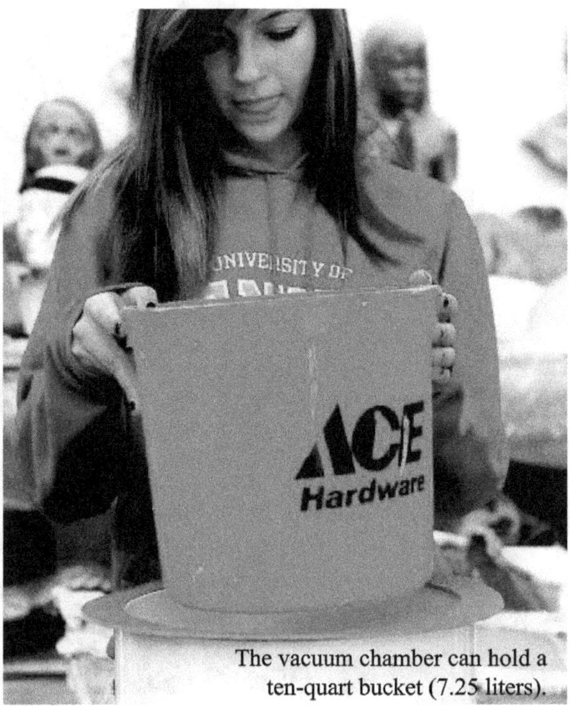

The vacuum chamber can hold a ten-quart bucket (7.25 liters).

At higher altitudes, vacuum pumps cannot pull the same twenty-nine plus inches of mercury that can be achieved at sea level, but the twenty-five inches that should be attainable in Denver is still sufficient. However, for thicker liquids it may be necessary to rock the chamber back and forth to help bring the bubbles to the surface and allow the gases to escape (photo #17). It is important that the chamber be light enough that it can be picked up for this purpose. The edges on the acrylic lid make perfectly good handles. Don't worry about the lid coming off; if you are strong enough to pull the lid loose from the chamber with an established vacuum, I suspect the US Olympic Committee and the NFL would both like to talk to you.

In summary, I am very impressed with this product and cannot think of a single negative or disadvantage to it. So how do you get one? Just go to: http://www.artmolds.com

Note: No doubt most readers are more likely to have an air compressor instead of a vacuum pump. After all, there are many tools that use compressed air, but very few that require a vacuum source. Almost any tool supply store probably has a selection of air compressors, but vacuum pumps are a little harder to find, so here are some suggestions. EnvironMolds has done the searching for you and offers two excellent choices. I have been using one of the lower cost models for about a year and a half and

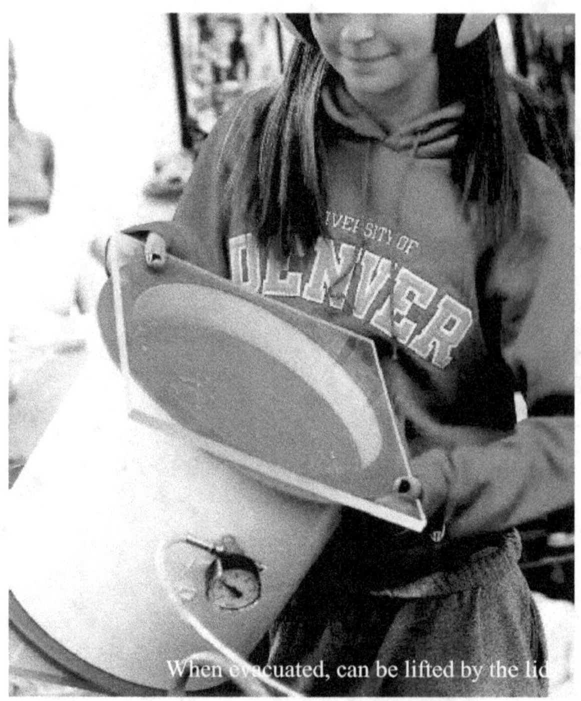
When evacuated, can be lifted by the lid

am very pleased with it. However, there are two even lower cost options that can allow you to experience just how beneficial a vacuum chamber can be. The first is a very inexpensive device called an Air Vacuum Pump made by Central Pneumatics, which works by using the Venturi effect and is also available from EnvironMolds. The other is a refrigerator compressor, which even though it provides only very low volume, does work - but is probably a last choice unless you find yourself in an end-of-civilization scenario and it is the only thing available.

Vacuum and pressure chambers can provide many advantages for sculptors, in both mold making and casting - which I thoroughly cover in my workshops. In fact, I am certain that there are things I could not have done as successfully (and in some cases not at all) without them. If you have any questions, please feel free to contact me through my "Ask Dave" column or directly at parvinstudio@comcast.net or, even better, at (720) 971-0824.

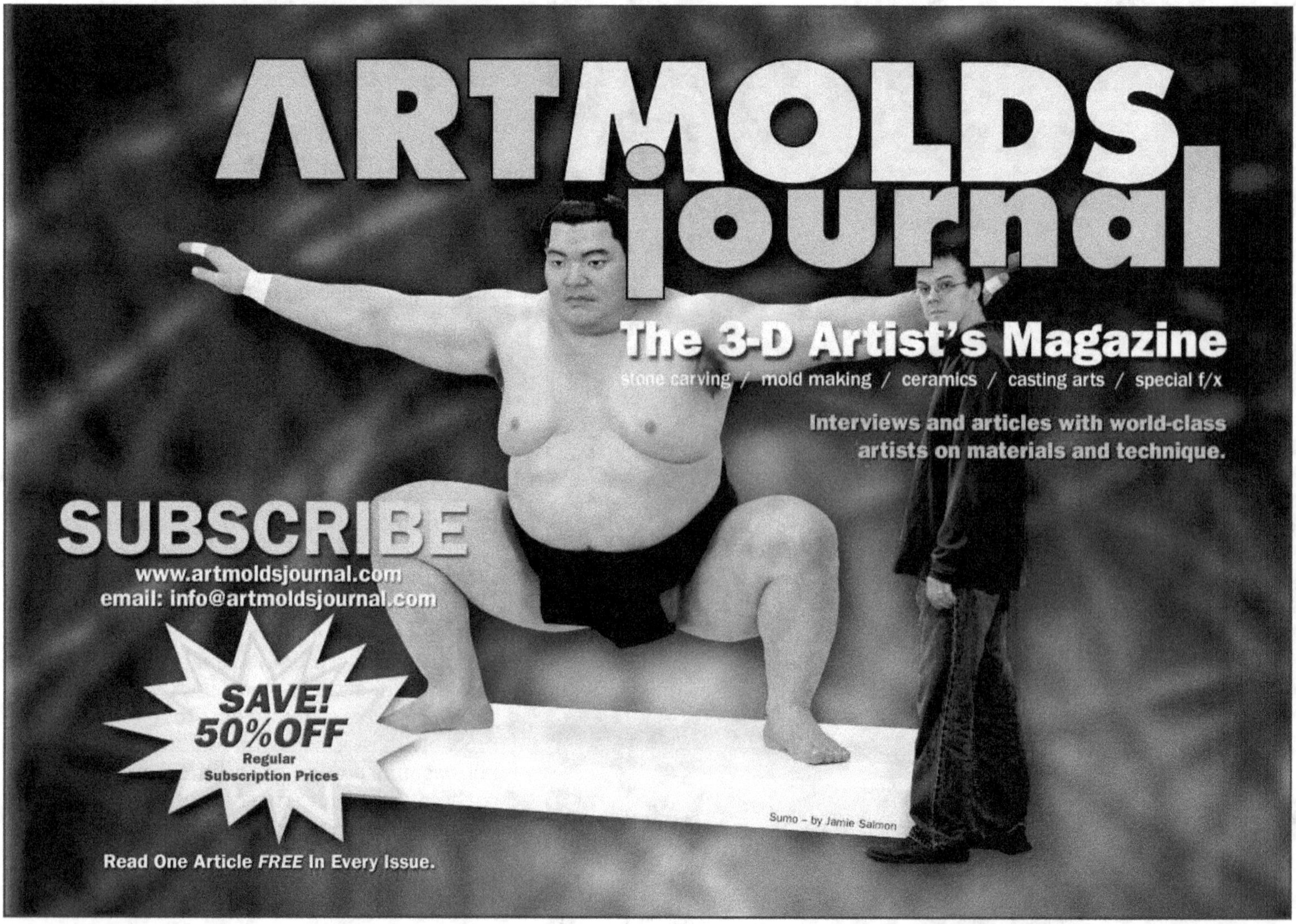

Putting Vacuum and Pressure Chambers to Practical Use

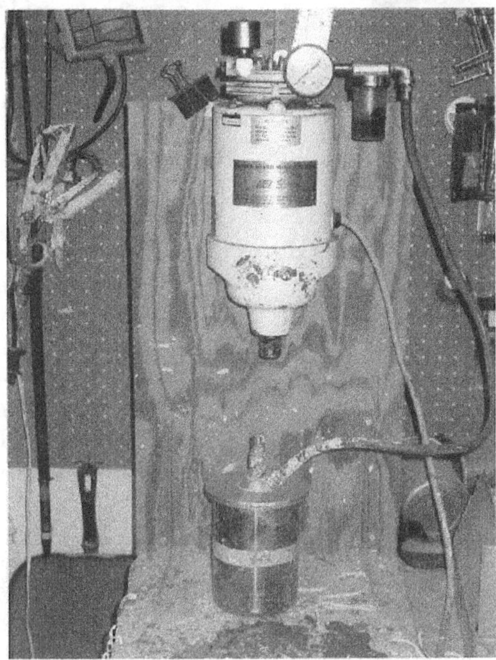

By David Parvin, A.L.I.

This is the last in a series of four articles about using vacuum and pressure chambers in casting. The first explained the "why" and second and third described how to make low cost yet very functional vacuum and pressure chambers. This last one will explain bow to put them to practical use saving time, improving quality, and even doing some things that would be impossible otherwise. So that I do not have to repeat myself and make this article so long that the whole deforestation (for the additional paper), global warming, end of civilization, extinction of mankind, and rise of giant intelligent cockroaches to rule the earth scenario happens, I would suggest that the readers review the first three articles.

While not my first application, the thing that I most often use my vacuum chamber for is de-airing rubbers. All that one has to do is mix some rubber and place the container into the vacuum chamber and suck out the air. Almost at once, looking through the clear lid you will seed the rubber increase in volume. After several minutes, the volume may be two to three times the original. Obviously, it is essential that the mixing container be large enough to contain the additional volume. If the rubber has a low viscosity, i.e. is thin and runny, the bubbles will combine and once large enough will rise to the surface and escape, sometimes with enthusiasm. If however, the rubber has a high viscosity such as those with thixotropic additives, the bubbles may not be able to rise to the surface without a little help. Just pick up the vacuum chamber and rock it slowly from side to side. This will allow the rubber to slosh up and down the sides of the mixing container exposing the bubbles and freeing the air. Once the volume has returned to its original level, de-airing is complete.

Some "store bought" vacuum systems have the chamber attached in such a way that it is impossible to lift it and agitate the rubber to assist the rise and escape the bubbles. These may work fine for low viscosity rubbers but not for high ones.

Getting the bubbles to rise is more of a problem if you live at a higher altitude such as in Denver where my studio happens to be. I can only pull a vacuum of 24 to 25 inches of mercury. At sea level one should be able to pull 28 to 29 inches. A professional mold maker once told me how she de-aired rubber. She would allow the rubber to rise to its full volume and then release the vacuum accomplishing nothing sense she was not allowing for enough time for the bubbles to escape or helping them to do so. You can tell if the de-airing is complete if when you release the vacuum, there is no change in the volume.

De-aired rubber makes better molds. This is true whether you are pouring the rubber around your sculpture to make a block mold or painting it on the surface for a skin mold. The rubber is much more likely to be bubble free both on the surface and throughout the rubber. This will result in cleaner castings which will require less chasing while the denser rubber will make the mold last longer. Molds that are bubble free inside the rubber allow you to get even better castings by casting under pressure. I'll come back to this later in the article.

This is how I made the mold of the feather in which I cast the urethane feather that I am holding in the photograph. I simply glued a feather to a thimble, glued a plastic cup around the feather and thimble and filled the cup with a low viscosity silicone rubber. There is a trick to getting the urethane to flow the feather and thimble and filled the cup with a low viscosity silicone rubber. There is a trick to getting the urethane to flow into the very narrow space

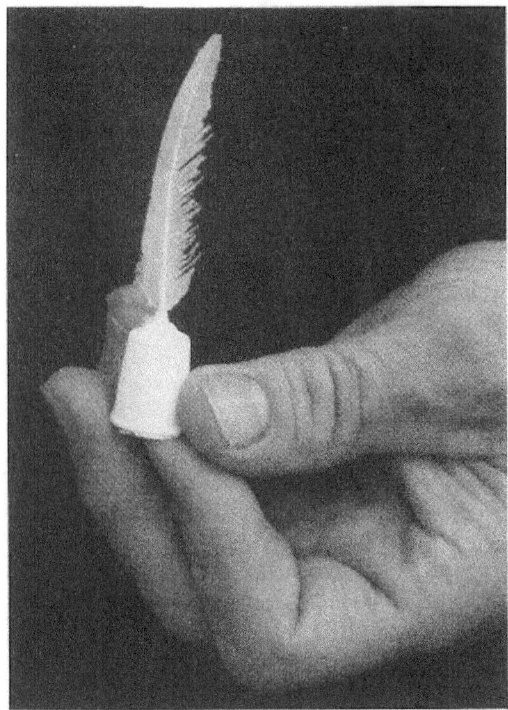

A feather cast in urethane by the author

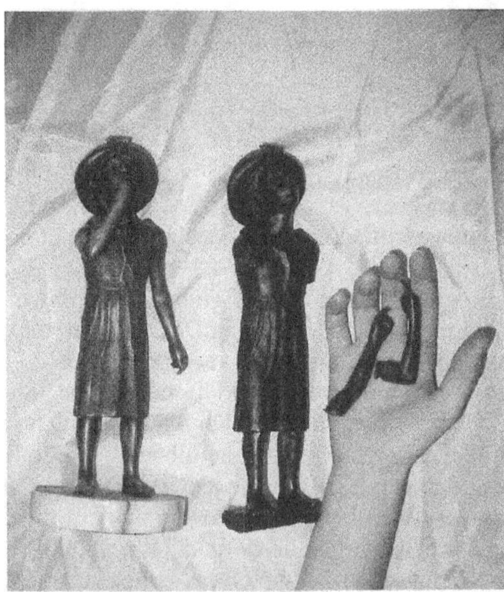

A feather cast in urethane by the author
"Fly Away Home" a small bronze by the author withl the ax

that was in the rubber after the feather was removed which I reveal above.

Let's go back to making the mold. There are two ways that can be used either separately or in conjunction to produce bubble free rubber. The first is as I have been explaining, using vacuum. Reducing the air pressure around a liquid causes air to be removed. When the liquid is brought back to atmospheric pressure, it is pressurized relative to what it was in a vacuum, just under 15 pounds per square inch at sea level. You can get the same results by curing the rubber under pressure. Let's assume that you have something that you want to mold. If you either pour rubber around it or paint a skin of rubber over it and pressurize it (50 p.s.i. is sufficient), the resultant rubber mold will be bubble free. The advantage of pressure curing the rubber over simply applying de-aired rubber is that the rubber will be forced into every nook and cranny capturing more detail. Of course, if you so desire, you can de-air the rubber first and then allow it to cure under pressure for the best possible results as long as you are mindful of the following.

Most things sculpted out of clay or wax will have some air pockets inside. Applying pressure will probably collapse the air pockets causing major flaws in the mold. What I do is place the object in a pressure chamber at 50 p.s.i. overnight and repair any collapsed places prior to applying the rubber and pressurizing. I did not want to take a chance with pressurizing the feather because I was sure that at least the stem would collapse and there would be no way to repair it. But just pouring de-aired rubber around it worked fine.

The second was that I use a vacuum chamber to de-air almost any substance that I pour into molds. These include urethane and polyester resins as well as Forton MG. Generally, the only things that I do not de-air are ones that set-up so quickly that there just isn't time. Very fast setting urethanes are a good example. But all of these including the fast setting ones I pressure cast.

I first discovered pressure casting when I was trying to figure out how to cast bubble free clear urethane. (See "It's Very Clear, One Sculptor's Experience With Urethane and Acrylics," "Sculpture Journal, January 2002"). Clear materials are especially critical because it's not just the bubbles on the surface that are a problem but those inside are also visible. Pressure worked so well with clear material that I began using it for everything that I was casting. But, unfortunately, you can not pressure cast in just any mold.

Pressure casting requires that there be no bubbles inside the rubber of the mold. If the rubber contains any bubbles, these will collapse under pressure and the casing will have a bump on the surface for each collapsed bubble. I discovered this the hard way when my casting looked as if it had chicken pox.

I was surprised to find that I could cast waxes (for lost wax) under pressure. One of the major problems that I had over the years was the time I spent chasing waxes for small bronzes. No matter how carefully or how experienced one is at pouring waxes. There were always enough small bubbles that were tedious and time consuming to repair. The fingertips of small hands were particularly bothersome. Any piece small enough to cast solid is a snap to cast perfect waxes. The only trick for casting a perfect small solid wax is for the mold to have been heated to just above the melting point of the wax so that the wax will stay liquid long enough to be subjected to pressure before solidifying. You will probably be able to use wax that is cooler than it would have to be if the mold were cold. This cooler wax will have less shrinkage than it would if the wax were hotter. A good example of what can be done is in the photograph "Fly Away Home". Both the body and the arms come out of the molds in nearly perfect condition requiring almost no chasing.

It is possible to pressure cast waxes for larger pieces that will be cast hollow, but it is a little more complicated. The normal way to prepare these waxes is to pour wax into the old and either fill it up or slosh it around so that all the surface is mold and either fill it up or slosh it around so that all the surface is covered and then dump the excess wax back into the pot. This process is repeated until the desired thickness is attained. To pressure cast, do not heat the mold as I did above, but just pour in the wax filling the mold.

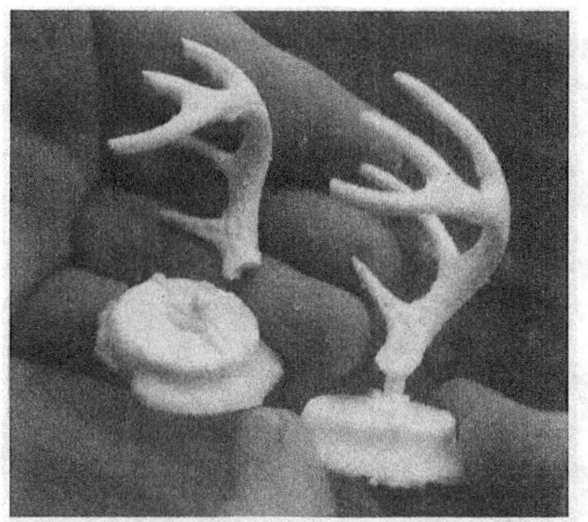

Two miniature antlers, one incomplete and the other complete

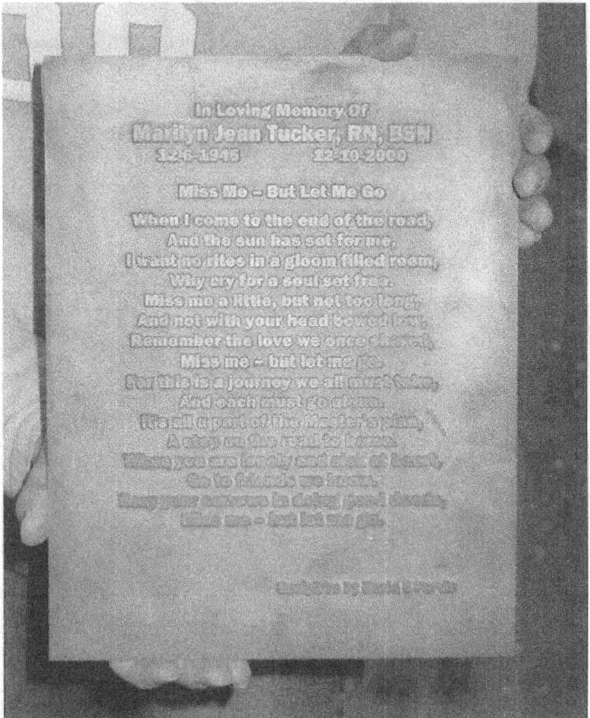

A plaque for a memorial cast in Forton MG

Pressurize the mold. Wait about five minutes, release the pressure, and dump out the excess wax. Since the mold hadn't been heated, a layer of solidified wax will have coated the inside of the mold. It may take some experimenting to discover the perfect temperature for the wax and exactly how many minutes to leave it in the pressure chamber. If necessary, additional thickness can be obtained by pouring wax in and out in the usual way. Only the first layer need be pressurized.

I have found that flawless waxes are a tremendous advantage, not only saving time and money but also assuring more consistency in quality. On those occasions when a foundry loses a casting supplying a replacement wax is not nearly as troublesome. If I expect that a particular part of a statue may be a problem for the foundry, I simply supply several waxes without having to spend a lot of time and trouble preparing them.

Notice the photograph of the plaque which is an inscription for a memorial. The good news is that with modern technology, one doesn't have to actually sculpt the letters. I simply printed what I wanted in block letters on a word processor and had an engraving company mill out the letters about 1/16" deep on a 1/8" sheet of aluminum. I made a mold under pressure, heated it to about 150 degrees F, poured in the wax, and pressure cast it. The wax was flawless and required absolutely no chasing. The final bronze was perfect. The actual plaque shown in the photograph, being held so well by my studio assistant, Morgan (lest you think that I have unusually delicate hands of an old sculptor) was cast in Forton MG with metal powder to produce a low cost example for my studio. It was also flawless.

Let's consider something a little more difficult. Notice the photograph of the small antlers. A participant in one of my life-casting workshops had a set of these in lead. She had been trying without success to duplicate them in resin. She asked if I could help. Always looking for a challenge, I replied "of course! I think I sounded more confident than I actually was. The first thing I did was make a mold in very soft silicone rubber, 10 durometer, soft enough to remove the cast antlers without breaking them. I had attached the base of the antlers to a small wad of clay so that the mold would be a reservoir to hold enough resin to fill the space needed for the antlers. As an experiment, I filled the reservoir with resin and let it set-up under atmospheric pressure. What I got is the antler in the photograph that is missing its tips and had a buckle in the stem that weakened the stem to the point that it broke.

The next time I did the same thing except that I pressurized the mold after pouring in the resin. While not shown, it was better but the tips were still not completely captured, the trapped air was preventing the resin from reaching the tips even under pressure.

Third time was the charm. Using the small pressure pot that I explained how to make in last month's article, I placed into it the mold filled with resin and attached a vacuum line. I don't normally use a pressure chamber as a vacuum chamber because you can not see into it. However, in this case I knew exactly what was happening. The vacuum drew out the air. When I released the vacuum, the atmospheric pressure forced the resin into the mold. For insurance, I attached a pressure line and pressurized the chamber to 50 p.s.i. The result was the complete antler you see in the photograph. This was the method I used to cast the feather.

There is a devise called a "Nip Mixer" that is made for dental labs and mixes material in a vacuum. It has two problems. The first is that it costs about a thousand dollars. The second is that it will only mix a small amount of material, about 200 c.c.s. While I find it useful, I will save the story for a future article.

We don't mean to imply that many things can be cast in wax, resin, Forton MG, etc. "o-natural", i.e. without using pressure and/or vacuum chambers with excellent results, however, the proper equipment can save time and frustration. I am confident, however, that you may find that what was difficult to impossible, may become routine with the proper equipment.

Dave Parvin is a Colorado sculptor whose primary subject is the human form in a variety of material. He may be reached at: 303-321-1074

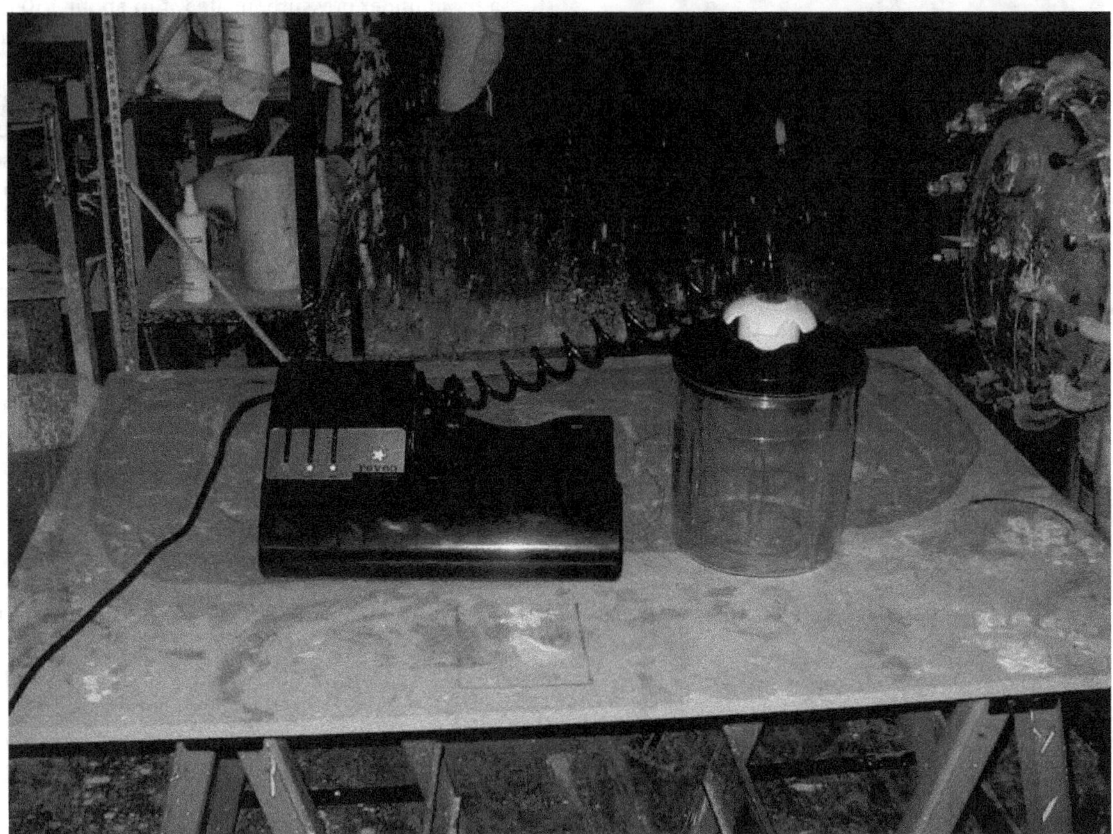

A Great New Gadget

by David E. Parvin, A.L.I.

On a wall in my studio is a framed list of "Dave's Laws" which was compiled by one of my assistants. There are thirteen starting with #1, "Dave is always right" and ending with "If Dave is wrong, refer to #1." In between are some tidbits that can help almost anyone along life's journey. One particularly useful one for surviving as an artist is #7. We are not like Robin Hood who stole from the rich, we steal from everyone!" In last month's Sculpture Journal, I wrote about the various body parts that are most likely cast for remuneration. (See "How Do I Cast Thee For Profit, Let Me Count The Ways.") After all, rather than just casting, say, babies' hands and feet, the more body parts one masters, the closer one is to being able to "rob from everyone." I said that in my next article I would explain how to go beyond pretty good and raise one's work to a higher level in order to grab a competitive advantage. My intention was to show some examples of life castings which are more creative than the usual. But I have decided to delay that article for another month and tell you about an exciting new gadget I have discovered.

There I was at 37,000 feet in an airliner headed to Ottawa, Canada with a stop in Philadelphia. I was getting pretty bored. There is no free lunch any more. The person next to me had fallen asleep in spite of my stimulating conversation. I had just finished the only book I had brought along and I had elected not to pay $5.00 to watch the obligatory "G" rated chick flick about girl gets boy after some difficulty. I had even walked back to the rear of the plane and checked the magazine rack and found only a copy of one of the racy "women's magazines' whose major article was about the 27 things any modern woman should know to do in bed besides sleep. It occurred to me that if the heroine in the in-flight movie had read that article, she could have gotten the guy a whole lot faster and had time for a couple of good motorcycle chases and I might have sprung for the $5.00 movie. After returning to my seat, I went for my last resort, the seat pocket which offered three choices: a barf bag, the airline's self promoting in-flight magazine, and the catalog of clever but expensive gadgets. I picked the most interesting of the three, but there isn't much to read on a barf bag. The gadget catalog was next. Somewhere between the solar powered nose hair clippers and the life size, radio controlled, self destructing model of the zeppelin Hindenburg, I hit pay dirt. I was so intrigued by what I discovered that as soon as we landed in Philadelphia and the flight attendant said, "You are

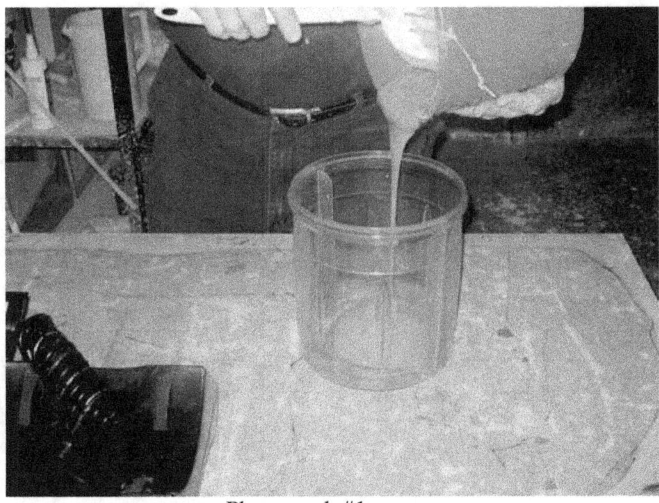
Photograph #1

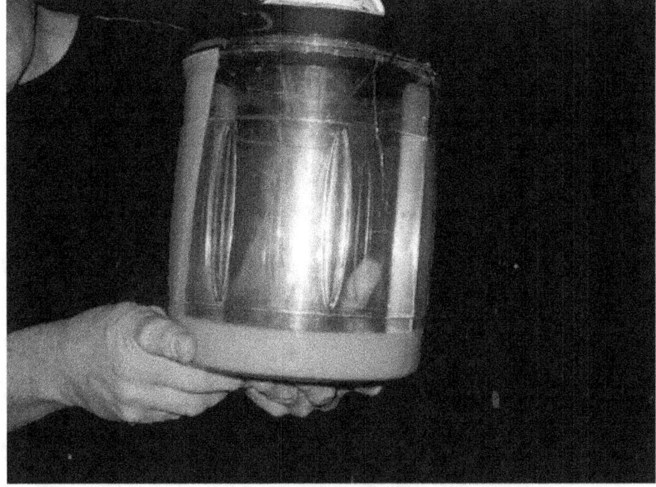
Photograph #2

"The fact that the "Reveo" is an excellent tool for de-airing rubber is reason enough to buy one. However, it can be used with other materials as well. I have used it with Forton MG, plaster and alginate and found that it is as effective as my much more expensive "Whip Mixer"

free to use your cell phones," I was calling Manila, Bombay, or wherever and placing an order.

So why did I get so excited? It appeared to me that the gadget in the advertisement might be very useful for eliminating bubbles which is one of the constant challenges in any kind of casting.

In 2003,1 wrote four articles for Sculpture Journal on this subject. The first discussed the origins of bubbles and how to eliminate them. The second and third explained how to construct economical yet very functional vacuum and pressure chambers. Their usefulness in eliminating bubbles was covered in the fourth articles. (See: "Using Vacuums and Pressure in Casting," "Making a Vacuum Chamber," "Making a Pressure Chamber," and "Putting Vacuum and Pressure Chambers to practical Use," Sculpture Journal, August, September, October and November, 2003.)

My new discovery, while developed for a completely different use, might just function as a ready made, inexpensive vacuum chamber. It's called a "Reveo" and it is the newest thing for marinating meat. What was shown and described was an air tight clear container and a base that functions both as a vacuum pump and motorized rollers. The idea is to put some meat into the container, which is large enough to hold a chicken plus some marinade. Once attached to the base with a rubber tube, the vacuum plump removes the air from the container drawing the marinade into the meat. Then the second step is to disconnect the tube and place the container on its side and allow the rollers to tumble the meat keeping it coated in marinade. Supposedly 24 hours of marinating can be accomplished in about 10 minutes. The price is $200.00 plus shipping and handling and is about the same as building your own vacuum chamber but in this case you don't have to build anything.

When my "Reveo" arrived about a week after I placed the order, I just took it out of the box and after playing with it for a few minutes, was ready to give it a try. (See photograph #1) I mixed up about a pound and a half or 700 grams of thixotropic silicone rubber and dumped it into the clear container. (Photograph #2) I closed the lid, attached the vacuum line and pressed the power button followed by the "MariVac" button. The vacuum motor ran for two minutes and then automatically shut off. The rubber had expanded to about twice its original volume. (Photographs #3 and #4) I then restarted the vacuum pump and rocked the chamber back and forth through the next two minute cycle which exposed the bubbles to the surface and caused the rubber to return to its original volume. (Photograph #5) To complete the de-airing process, I twisted the knob on the top of the lid sealing in the vacuum (or more properly, preventing air from coming into the container), disconnected the hose, placed the sealed chamber on the rollers, and pressed the third button which caused the chamber to rotate. After a couple of minutes, I removed the chamber and poured the rubber into an alginate mold of a hand and into a plastic cup. After allowing the rubber to set up, I demolded both samples. The "Reveo" had de-aired the rubber perfectly. Not only were there no visible bubbles on the surface of the samples, but slicing into the rubber in the cup showed it to be a bubble free throughout.

The fact that the "Reveo" is an excellent tool for de-airing rubber is reason enough to buy one. However, it can be used with other materials as well. I

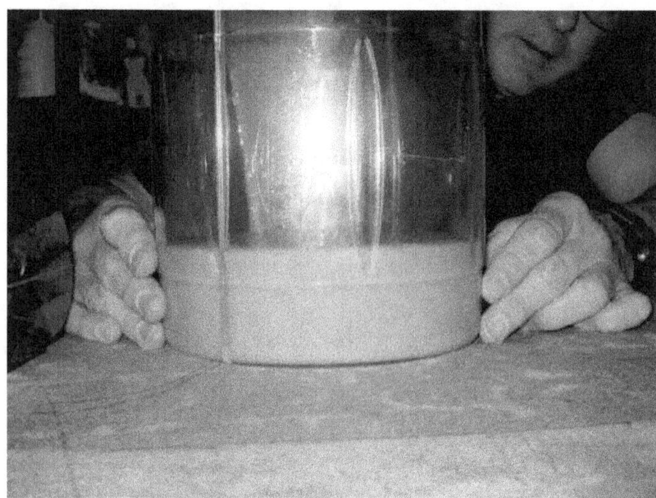
Photograph #3

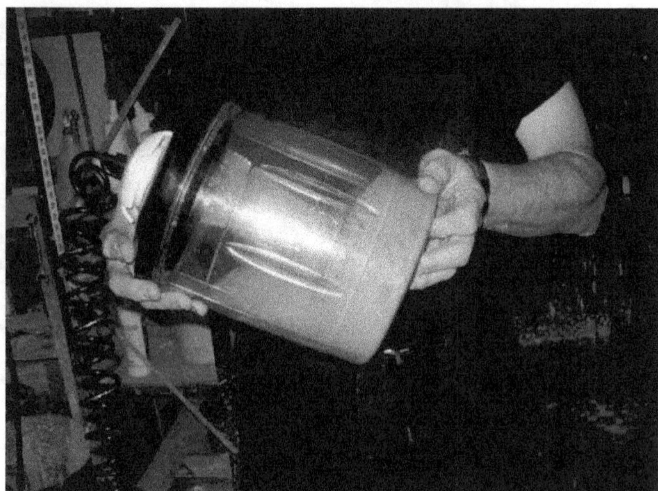
Photograph #4

have used it with Forton MG plaster and alginate and found that it is as effective as my much more expensive "Whip Mixer." While the vacuum chamber is not large, about 7 inches in diameter and eight inches tall, it can accommodate about a quart of material. In fact, the "Reveo" can de-air much larger amounts of material than can the "Whip Mixer."

One of the more useful features of the "Reveo" is that the vacuum vessel can be lifted and rocked back and forth to help the air to escape. This can be important to speed up the de-airing with fast setting materials. Also, if the material has a high viscosity such as thixotropic rubbers, reducing the air pressure will cause the air to come out of the solution and the bubbles to expand but the bubbles may not be able to rise to the surface and escape on their own. High altitudes, such as in Denver where I live and work, exacerbates the problem The turning over and over of the container on the rollers helps to get rid of the air.

As with any container, cleaning up after mixing rubber is a snap. Just let the rubber set up and pull it out. But because the vacuum vessel is not flexible, materials that harden such as plaster, Forton MG, etc. should be washed out immediately after mixing and not allowed to harden even though these materials don't seem to stick to the container. If you were concerned that a particular material might permanently stick to the vessel and damaging it, you could put a smaller container into the vacuum chamber and not turn it on its side and use the rollers. Complete vacuum chambers including lids are only $22.00 each, plus shipping. I would suggest that an extra one be ordered with the "Reveo" to keep as a spare. I ordered two just in case, but so far have had no problems.

The lid simply fits on snugly and draws down tightly as the vacuum forms. While I have been able to remove the lid after air is allowed back into it, the easiest way to do so is to blow compressed air in through the hole where the vacuum line attaches which causes the lid to pop off.

Using a vacuum gauge, I found that the built- in vacuum pump pulls just over 20 inches of mercury. While I can get several more inches with my home made vacuum chamber, which I described in one of the articles mentioned previously in the third paragraph in this article, 20 inches seems to be adequate. I suspect at sea level one would get about 5 more inches of mercury.

I am so impressed with my "Reveo" that I urge anyone who doesn't already have the capability of de-airing materials, to acquire one.

On my next flight, I plan on taking a closer look at some of the other gadgets in the catalog. I'll bet there is a use around my studio for a solar powered nose hair trimmer; I just haven't figured it out yet.

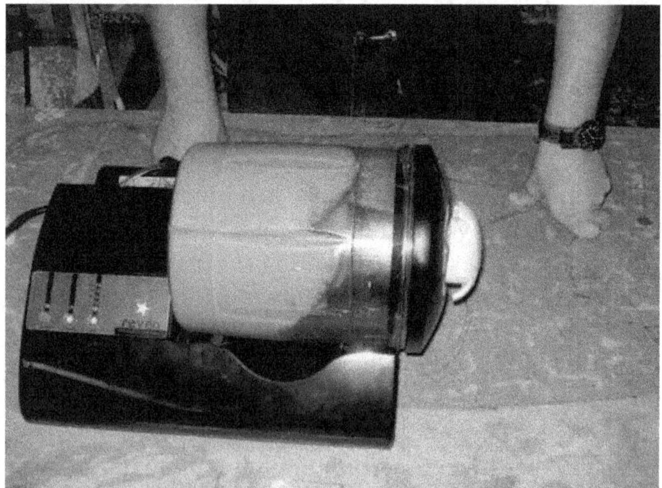
Photograph #5

The "Reveo" is manufactured by: Eastman Outdoors
PO. Box 380
Flushing, Michigan 48433 877-738-3648
www.eastmanoutdoors.com

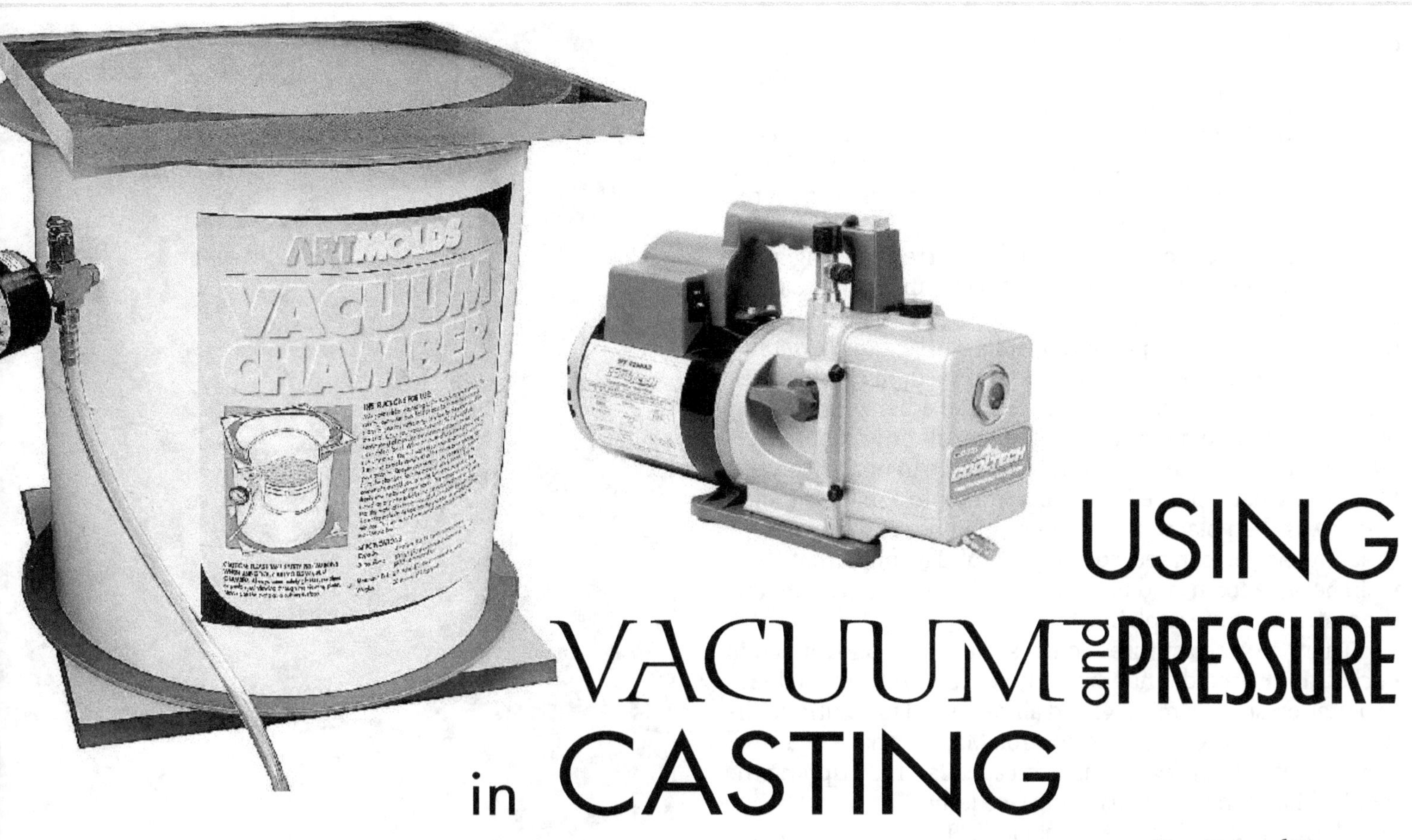

USING VACUUM and PRESSURE in CASTING

By: David E. Parvin, [A.L.I.]

This is the first in a series of articles. This one will explain just what vacuuming and pressurizing can do to improve casting quality and consistency, and also save time. Using vacuum and pressure correctly can even allow one to cast objects that would otherwise be difficult or impossible, such as the feather in Photo #1. In following issues, I will describe in detail how to acquire functional yet inexpensive vacuum and pressure chambers and how to use them.

It's all about the bubbles. Those of us who are old and lucky enough to have been to Hawaii and to have heard Don Ho sing will remember how happy and fine the tiny bubbles in wine made him feel. But for those of us who strive for casting perfection, bubbles (tiny or otherwise) are the bane of our existence. Bubbles are there in every stage of the sculpting process from sculpting the model (i.e. the "original" object sculpted and not the person whose likeness we are duplicating) to making the mold, pouring the waxes, building the shells, casting the bronze, and welding the pieces together. And if one is casting not in metal but in resin or some gypsum material, bubbles can be an even bigger problem.

Some years ago, I sculpted a figure about 12 inches tall, which convinced me at that time to avoid small pieces in the future. It was simply too time consuming to chase the waxes. The little 1-inch hands were especially troublesome; the fingertips were almost always missing and had to be reconstructed. Later, bubbles again got in my way when I began experimenting with casting in clear urethane. Clear materials present an even greater challenge since not only do surface bubbles need to be eliminated, but also those throughout the mixture. The solution was differential pressure: reducing with a vacuum, increasing with pressure, or both. Now I can easily make flawless castings in wax, resins, plaster, etc. that usually require no chasing. That benefit alone has saved me both time and money. In addition, the same technique will allow you to construct longer lasting rubber molds that more accurately capture detail with far less imperfections.

I have found that there is a general misunderstanding about what can be accomplished by casting in a vacuum. Some people think that if you surround a mold with a vacuum and then pour in the casting material while maintaining the vacuum, you will get a perfect casting because there are no pockets of air to prevent complete filling of every nook and cranny of the mold. They would be correct, as long as the only bubbles present were pockets of air trapped in the mold, and metal or wax was used as the casting material. Jewelers use vacuum casting of precious metals with exquisite detail. Also, there are a few foundries that can vacuum cast bronze with the same results. But there are three other sources of bubbles that do not affect molten medals or wax but do affect other casing materials. What you see in photo #2 was the result when I poured urethane resin into a feather mold which was then placed in a vacuum chamber and allowed to set up. As you can see, so many bubbles resulted that the resin became foam, and no resin even flowed into the shaft of the feather. Let me explain why.

There are at least three sources of bubbles: air trapped in pockets in the mold if not properly vented, air trapped due to agitation such as mixing, and air dissolved in solution. The first of these is the easiest to control. Major pockets of air can be vented to allow the air to escape. Carefully tipping the mold while filling it can also help (see Issue 2 of *ArtMolds Journal*, "A Simple Solution to Air Bubbles"). The second source, the bubbles trapped from mixing, may rise to the surface and escape if the material has a long enough working time or "pot life." Very carefully pouring into the mold will minimize additional bubbles. The final source, dissolved air, presents a greater challenge. The good news is that the solution to this final problem completely eliminates any remaining bubbles from the first two sources as well.

Liquids are capable of dissolving other materials including gasses. This takes place on a molecular level, and the gas molecules are dissolved within the liquid and are not in bubble form. The volume of gas that can be dissolved in solution increases with pressure and decreases with temperature (Charles's Law). We have all seen examples in our daily lives. Removing the tab from a can of soda and releasing the pressure causes fizzing, the bends results from nitrogen bubbles during rapid decompression as any of you who are divers know, and bubbles will appear on the sides of a glass of water as it warms up. Let's see how this affects us in molding and casting.

Imagine a container of some liquid substance that will eventually set up. It could be rubber, resin, or any number of gypsum products. Since it will set up, we can assume that at least two ingredients have been mixed together, at least one of which is liquid. There is air in this liquid from two sources: air that was in solution prior to mixing and additional bubbles that were trapped as it was mixed. If we place the liquid in a vacuum chamber and reduce the pressure, two things happen. First, the bubbles enlarge (Boyle's Law states that the volume of a gas is inversely proportional to the pressure) and some are able to rise to

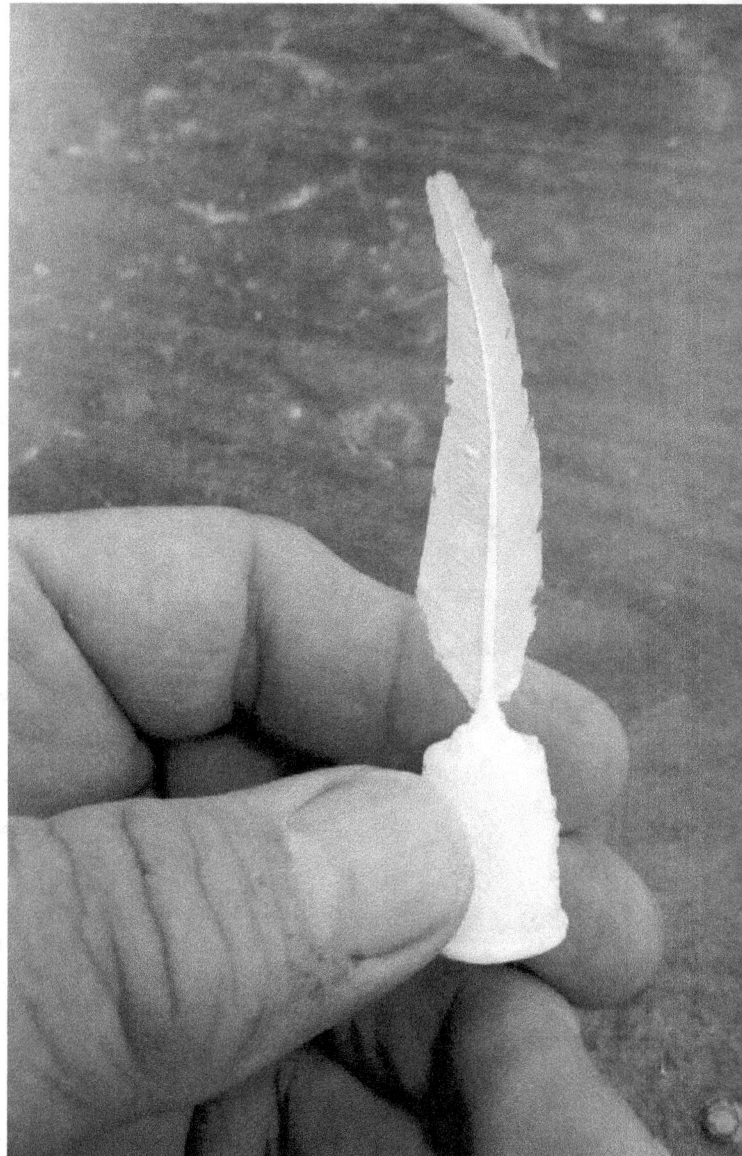

Feather cast in resin.

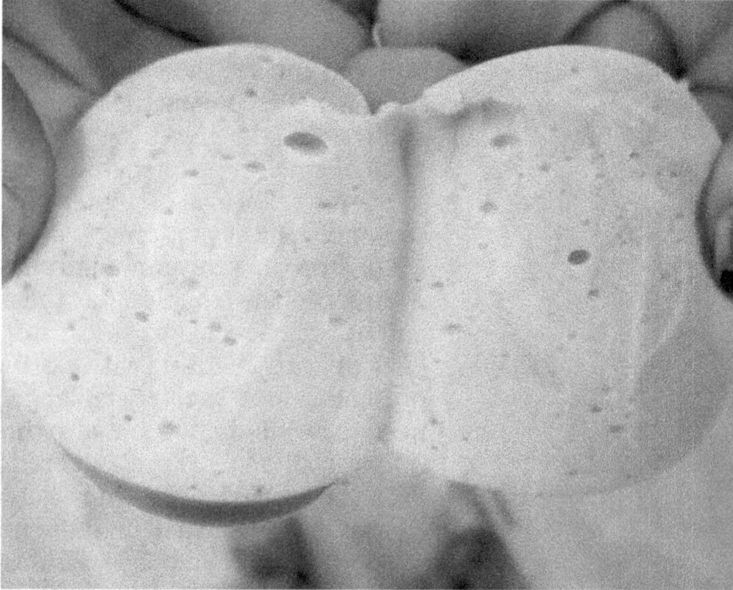

Rubber cured under atmospheric conditions. Notice the bubbles

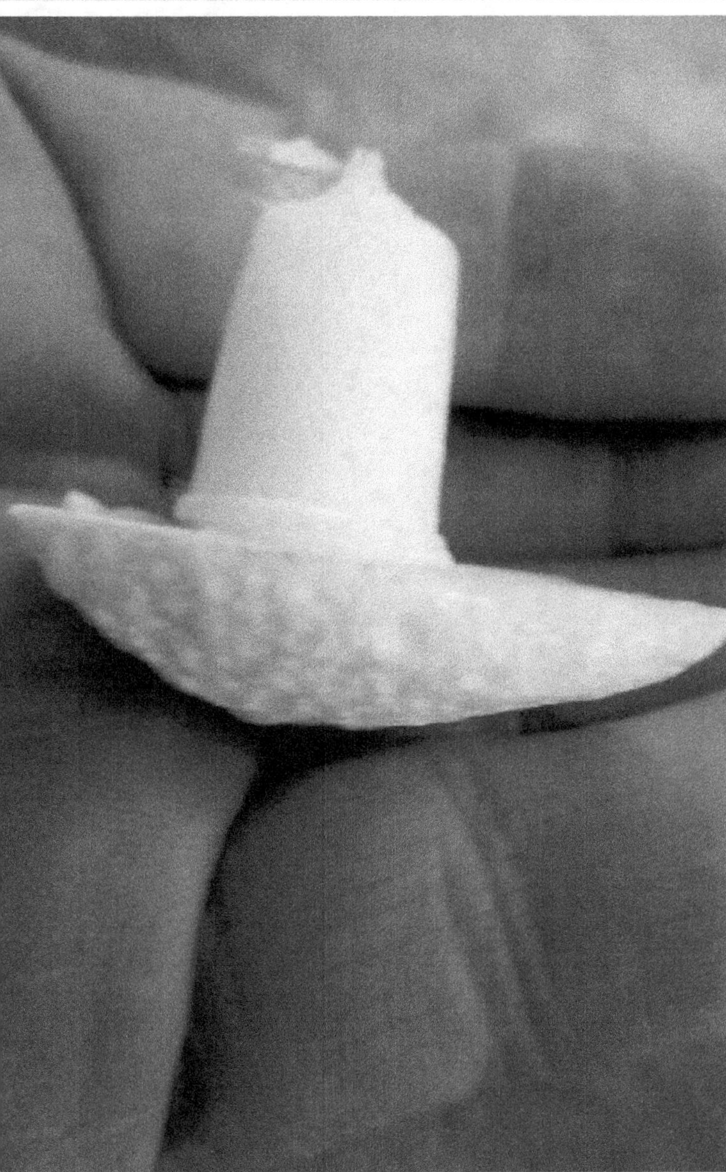

Feather cast in resin in a vacuum. Just turned to foam.

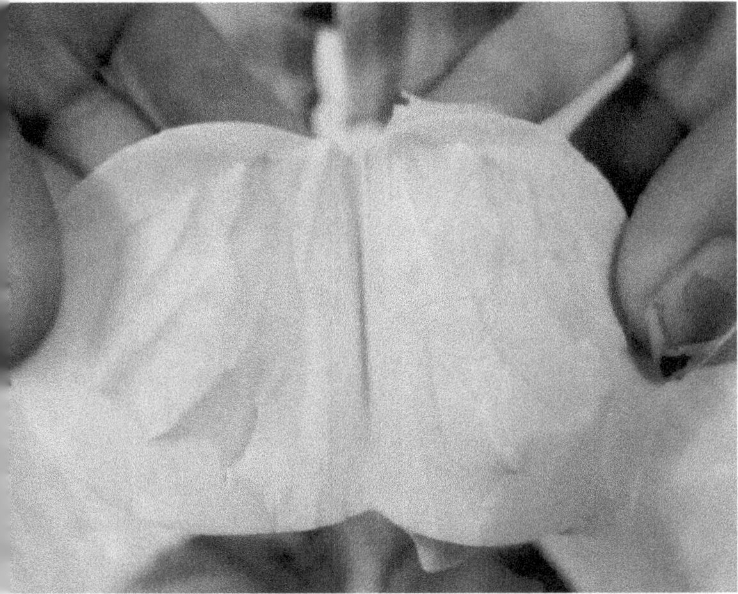

Rubber de-aired or cast under pressure will result in no bubbles.

the surface and escape. Second, air comes out of solution and forms additional bubbles which may also rise to the surface. By reducing the pressure, we will have de-aired the liquid. Here comes the good part. If we then bring the liquid back to normal, atmospheric pressure we have a mixture that has less air in solution than it previously held. Given enough time, it could reabsorb all that air and we would find ourselves back where we started. However, it will likely have set up long before that would happen. This means that when this de-aired liquid is poured into a mold, not only will those original bubbles have departed but any new bubbles trapped as the liquid is poured into the mold will be absorbed into solution along with any small amounts of air trapped in the mold and the set up material should be bubble free.

Curiously enough, pressurizing produces essentially the same results. Let's imagine the same substance prior to being de-aired. If we were to pour it into a mold, then place the mold into a pressure chamber and increase the pressure, this is what happens: There is no effect on the air already in solution. But because a liquid can hold more air in solution with increasing pressure, the air bubbles will not only reduce in size but may be absorbed into solution and disappear resulting in a bubble free casting. I have pressure chambers that will take from 50 to 110 p.s.i., but 50 is usually sufficient. Often for insurance, I will both de-air and pressurize a material. The deciding factor is usually time. Some resins in particular set up too quickly to do both.

If you'll recall, earlier I mentioned another source of bubbles: as a result of air coming out of solution as a liquid warms up. Unfortunately, setting up is an exothermic reaction with many materials, and bubbles can be an incidental by-product. The good news is that bubbles are not likely to come out of solution if the material has been de-aired or pressurized or both.

I realize that with careful handling of materials, most people can achieve excellent results without using vacuum and/or pressure and they may see no reason to make things more complicated. However, if you were to mix a sample of silicone rubber (or any other kind) and pour it into three plastic cups, you can easily see the difference if you have the equipment to run a little experiment. Allow one to cure at atmosphere pressure. De-air another and then allow it to cure at atmospheric pressure. Pressurize the third. After all three have setup, slice each in half. The first will look like a sponge (i.e. be full of bubbles). (See Photo #3) The other two will be free of bubbles.

The feather in Photo #1 was cast in an unvented mold using a very fast setting urethane. This would not have been possible to cast without both pressure and vacuum vessels. Stay tuned because in following articles, I will not only explain exactly how I did this but show you how to make your own equipment at very low cost which will save time, improve quality, and reduce frustration while you do your casting.

Modeling Instruction

Making a 3-D Faerie Portrait

By David E. Parvin, A.L.I.

In this article, I will explain how my assistants and I transformed a young lady into a three dimensional faerie portrait. The process that we used involved four steps: making a life casting of the model, enhancing the life casting, making a mold of the enhanced life casting, and casting the finished portrait. For anyone interested in learning more about the process, see the end of this article for sources of materials and information.

Often I have been asked this about the creative process, "Which comes first, the idea or the model?" Usually it's the idea and then I look for the right subject or model. But sometimes, as was in this case, the model has been the inspiration. Recently, an aspiring young ballerina, Caylie, and her mother, Sue, introduced themselves having recognized me from my involvement with Denver's dance community. I couldn't help but be impressed with how much Caylie looked like a faerie and I said so to Sue who told me I wasn't the first to say that. I invited them to come by my studio even though I had no specific idea of what we might do other than something faerie-like. But before we met again, I got to thinking that Caylie would make a great faerie portrait. Of course, with the right modifications, **anybody** can be turned into a believable faerie. It's just that Caylie's naturally occurring *faerieness* inspired me to begin this project.

I stated above that we started with a life casting, a process by which a mold is made directly from the model and if done properly captures an exact likeness in amazing detail right down to the skin texture. Life casting has been around for a very long time, at least 3000 years. Historically, the process usually involved covering a deceased subject with plaster and making a death mask. But now we now have materials that reproduce detail to a much higher degree, are approved for skin contact, and can be used on living subjects comfortably and harmlessly. The most commonly used is **alginate** which was developed for making dental impressions. Its primary ingredient is made from seaweed and getting covered with alginate is similar to getting a seaweed treatment at an exclusive spa.

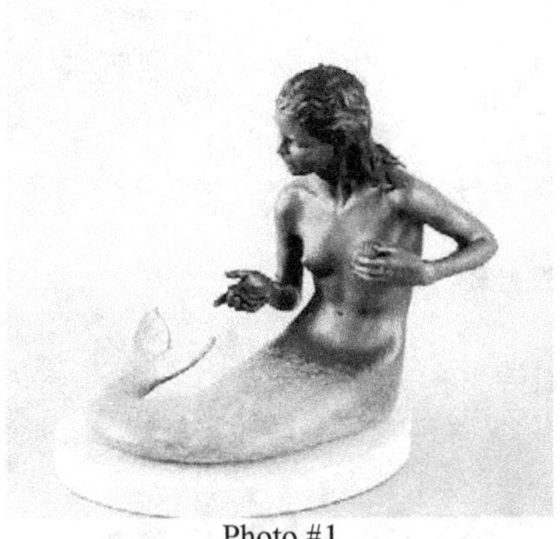

Photo #1

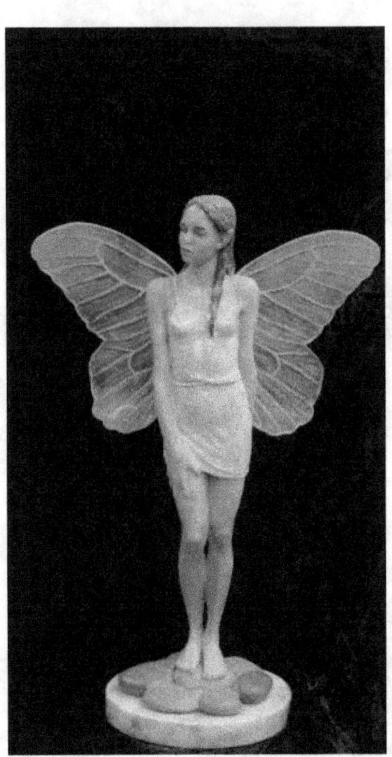

Photo #2

Of course, I could have sculpted Caylie in the more traditional method of having her sit for me while I shaped her likeness in wax or clay and then cast it in bronze or resin as in my pieces shown in photographs #1 and #2, "The Shell Game" and "Asrai." But life casting is analogous to "three dimensional photography" and just as a photograph can be more real and personal than a painting or drawing, so can a life casting be when compared to a regular sculpture. The criticism of life casting is that it is somehow "cheating." (1) But life casting is just another art form and while it may look easy, or at least easier than more traditional sculpting, doing it well does take some knowledge and practice. As in photography, anyone can take a snapshot, but not just anyone can be an Ansel Adams.

Step 1: Making a Life Casting of Caylie

I was confident that Caylie at thirteen would have no problem being cast; usually a child eight or older will endure and even enjoy the process. But to introduce her to and make her comfortable with life casting, I suggested that we first cast her foot en pointe, something all dancers are eager to do. Photo #3 shows an excited Caylie and her mom looking over her finished foot.

In photograph #4, my very able assistant, Audra Vaughn, and

I were preparing Caylie's hair with a thick conditioner to prevent her hair from becoming stuck in the alginate that would cover her. My models usually tell me that well conditioned hair was an unexpected bonus. Photograph #5 shows Audra securing a piece of cloth to cover up her Caylie's developing *assets*. The cloth was fitted tightly so as to be invisible under whatever faerie garb we later decide to add. While her left ear was completely exposed, her right ear, not shown, protruded through her hair in a very faerie-like manner.

Alginate is purchased as a powder and mixed with water to a consistency that is thin enough to spread on but thick enough to stay in place. Notice in photograph #6 that Caylie was leaning against a padded board that was tilted back about ten degrees for her comfort while Audra and I applied the alginate. While it might seem logical to have the model lie down, her hair, face, and any soft body parts such as breasts would be distorted. The alginate used here was FiberGel by Artmolds which gels to a soft rubber-like state in about five minutes.

It is necessary to reinforce the alginate so that when it is removed from the model, it will retain its shape. In photograph #7, Audra and I were applying a layer of cheese cloth and very fast setting plaster. This supporting mold is referred to as the "mother" mold. Notice that the nostrils were kept clear for her to breathe during the whole procedure which only took about twenty minutes. It is never necessary or even recommended to put straws into someone's nose, not only can they distort the nostrils but if bumped can injure the model.

In photograph #8, the mold had just been removed and an excited Caylie had soft skin and well conditioned hair. Audra and I made a plaster cast from the mold which was completed by the time Caylie emerged from the shower, photograph #9.

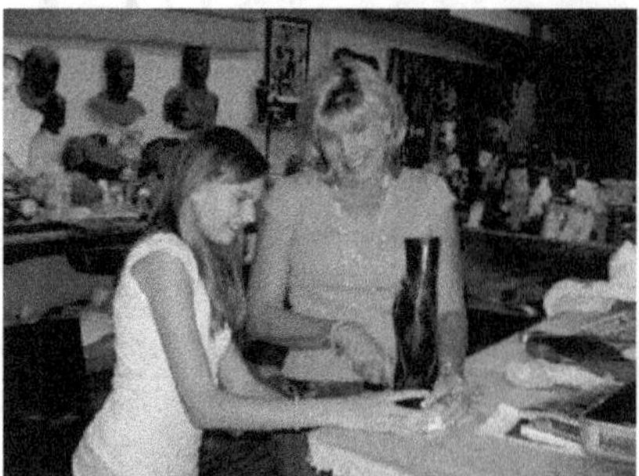
Photo #3

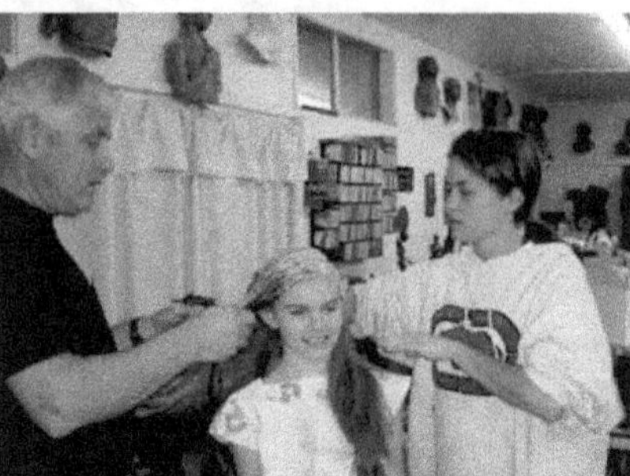
Photo #4

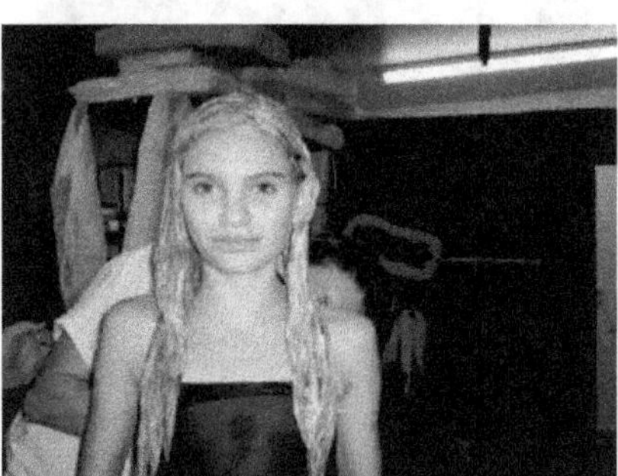
Photo #5

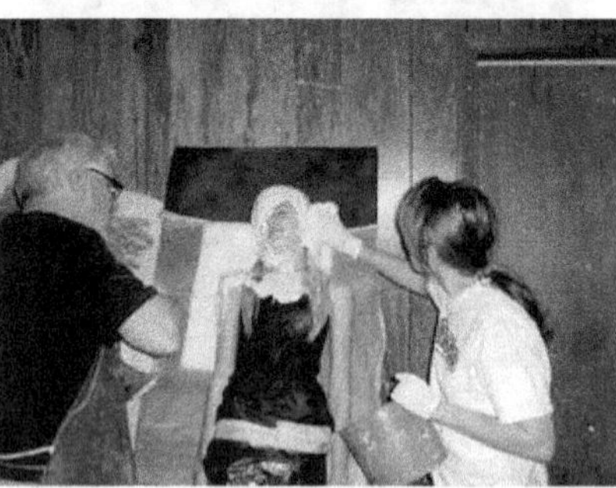
Photo #6

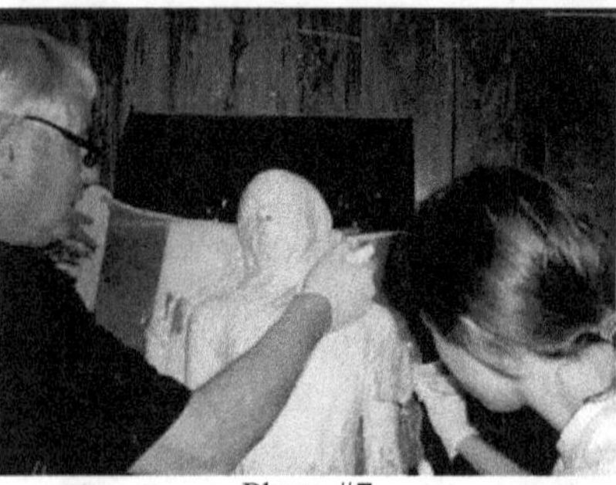
Photo #7

Step 2: Enhancing the Plaster Casting

There are always at least some repairs that need to be made to the plaster cast such as trimming the back to lie flat and fixing any small imperfections. I then had a plaster cast of the human Caylie which was too nice to waste. I went ahead and made a rubber mold of the plaster and made a cold cast bronze copy for Caylie. (Photograph #10) The process used was the same as described below for the faerie portrait. At that point, I was ready to begin the really fun part, turning Caylie into a faerie.

The first thing I did was to refresh myself on what a faerie should look like. Fortunately there is a helpful book with the encouraging title *How to Draw and Paint Fairies*. (2.) Looking through the book, I realized that all I needed to do was give her pointed ears; open her eyes; and add some faerie accessories such as flowers, leaves, and wings.

Pointing the ears was a cinch. They were shaped in sculpting wax which adheres nicely to dry plaster. The great thing about pointing the ears was that there was no right or wrong, I just experimented until the ears looked right to me. My only real concern was to be sure not to make the ears so big that she looked sinister like a werwolf.

I had Caylie return to the studio and sit for me so that I could get her eyes right. Unfortunately, opening the eyes doesn't require that you just scrape part of the eyelids off. When a person opens her eyes, the tissue surrounding the eyes changes shape somewhat. So you have to add back as well as take away. This was also done with melted wax which was added on and then shaped as necessary. I used dental tools both for the carving the plaster and shaping the wax.

For her faerie outfit, we went to a craft store and purchased an assortment of artificial leaves and flowers. We glued the leaves flat on the body to make it look as if she were wearing a dress made of leaves. A garland of flowers would be added around her head at a later stage.

Since the finished faerie portrait would be a "relief" wall hanging, we attached the plaster casting to a 24 inch round piece of 3/4 inch fiberboard that would frame the work and provide a background for constructing the wings which were made in clay. (Photograph #11.) The next step was to make a mold of the new Caylie in silicone rubber.

Step 3: Making a Mold of the Enhanced Casting.

Rubber usually consists of two liquids, a base and a catalyst, though sometimes other components are added for specific applications. Once mixed together, the components set up into what we would recognize as rubber. In photograph #12, I had just painted the first of three layers of liquid rubber into the portrait.

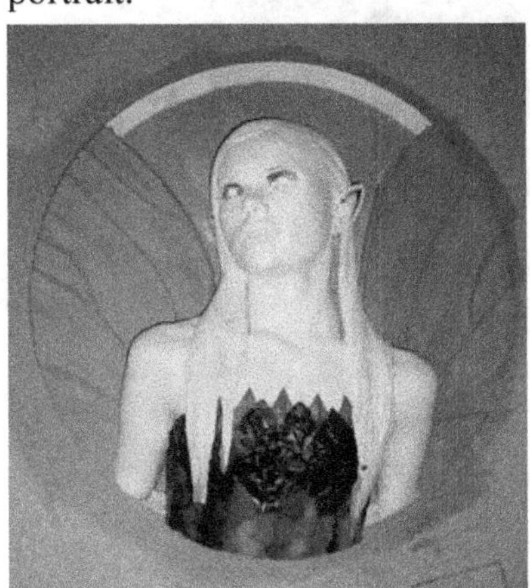

Photo #11

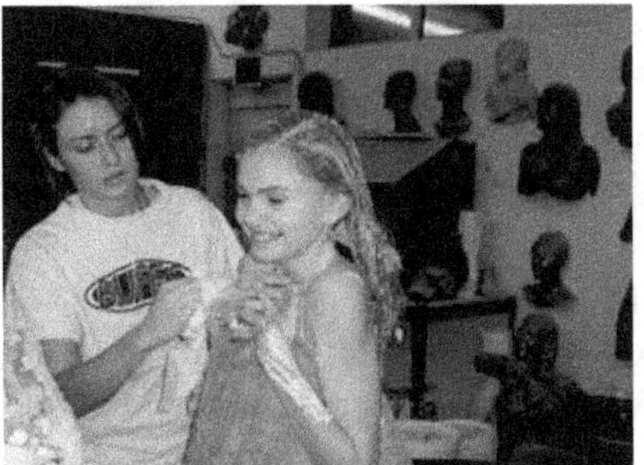

Photo #8

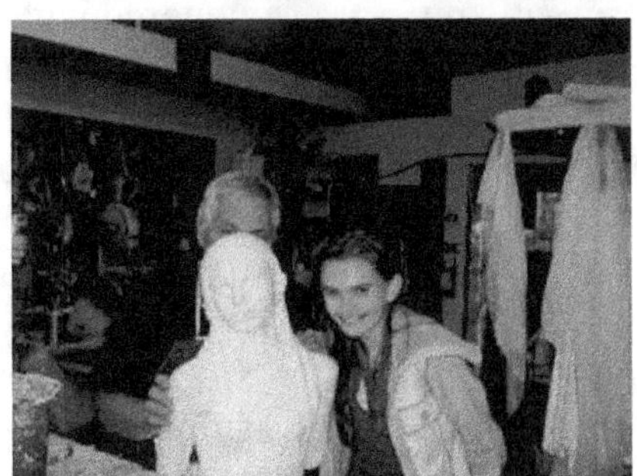

Photo #9

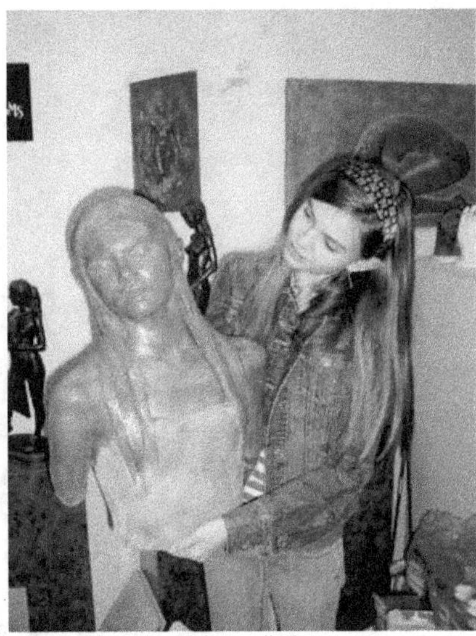

Photo #10

Just as with the alginate mold, a supporting or "mother" mold was necessary for the rubber to maintain its shape when removed from the plaster. For this purpose, I used Forton MG (3). The same Forton MG would be used below with metal and limestone powders to make the final casting. Because of the undercuts on both sides of the face and shoulders, the rigid mother mold had to be constructed in four pieces in order to separate from the rubber layer.

Step 4: Casting the Finished Portrait.

I decided to cast the skin parts and the area above her head in white by using Forton MG with powdered limestone which when buffed would simulate white marble. Her dress, wings, hair, and the molding at the top were Forton MG to which copper powder had been added producing a very credible cold cast bronze. The hair was turned black and the leaves and wings became green by using different patina solutions. The garland of flowers around her forehead was a string of artificial flowers that was coated with Forton MG with brass powder. A light blue wash was applied to the area above her so as to distinguish it from the flesh areas. Everything except the flowers was polished with soft cloth buffing wheels with either white or brown buffing compounds. The completed 3-D portrait is shown in photograph #13.

Earlier, I described life casting as "3-D photography" which begs the question as to why we didn't just get Caylie a faerie costume and take her picture, a much simpler way to go. There are two reasons. The first is that what we did, in my opinion, is far more impressive. The second is permanence. The Forton MG material that I have mentioned was developed for architectural

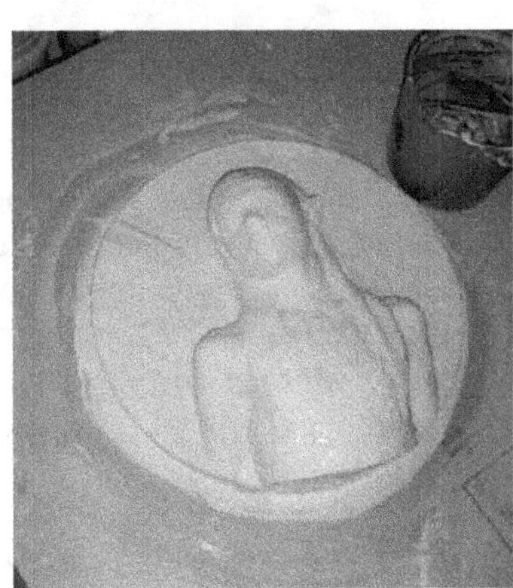

Photo #12

accouterments for the outsides of buildings and will last and last. Kept indoors, anything cast in Forton MG should last virtually forever, as in until the Sun goes supernova. Long after everything else that recorded that Caylie existed has turned to dust, this 3-D portrait should still survive. I told her to expect that in a few hundred years, it may show up on "Antiques Road Show." The art expert will probably say, "When you brought in your great, great, great, great, great, great grandmother's portrait, I got really excited because I immediately recognized it as a genuine *Parvin* (it's my fantasy!) from the early 21st century. Do you have any idea as to its worth? No. Well it should be worth a couple million dollars; but since you made a lamp out of her..."

1. I wrote an article titled "Life *Casting, Fine Art or Cheating"* in the April 2001 issue of *Sculpture Journal* which I will gladly e-mail to anyone who wants it. See below for contact information.
2. *How to Draw and Paint Fairies*, Linda Raverscroft, 2005, ISBN 08230 2383 4
3. There are any number of materials that can be utilized for mother molds and the final castings each with advantages and disadvantages in cost, weight, strength, toxicity, odor, ease of use, etc. I prefer Forton MG which has the best all around advantages and the least disadvantages of anything I know. Its components are a hydrocal, a resin, a hardener, an acrylic based liquid. Various additives will give it special characteristics such a marble or bronze appearance.
4. Fortunately for anyone interested in more information on life casting, there is a source for that has everything needed including instructional videos and all the materials used for this article. Artmolds is the only company that whose sole purpose is to meet the needs of life casters. Artmolds products are available at art supply stores world wide and may be reached at artmolds.com or by calling (866) ART-MOLDS, (866) 278-6653.

Bio

Dave Parvin was born in the Midwest, raised in the Northwest, and has lived in the Denver area for the last thirty years. The artistic path for him has taken a circuitous path. Though a beginning sculptor by the age of three, there were detours to study for the priesthood, earn a degree in biology, fly helicopters for the Marine Corps in Viet Nam, remain married to the same person for over 36 years, and raise a son to manhood to begin repeating the process with two young grandsons.

Dave's primary subject is the human form which he executes in a very realistic manner from miniature to over life size. Presently, he is lead sculptor on a veterans' tribute garden for a suburb of Denver which includes eight nine feet tall bronze statues. While best known for his traditional bronze sculptures, Dave has worked in wood, Forton MG, pewter, glass, resins, Raku, concrete, acrylic, and others. About twenty years ago, Dave began life casting and has become an innovator in this art form developing techniques and products that are commonly used throughout the life casting community. Dave was one of the first to be honored with a lifetime membership in the Association of Life Casters International. He is also one of only four persons to be given the title of "Certified Life Casting Instructor" by the same organization. Dave has written over forty published articles on sculpting and has two instructional DVDs. He feels a responsibility to pass on to others what he had learned and offers workshops several times a year on various sculpture subjects including life casting.

Always eager to discuss art, aviation, and grandchildren, he may be reached at parvinstudio@comcast.net or (303) 321-1074.

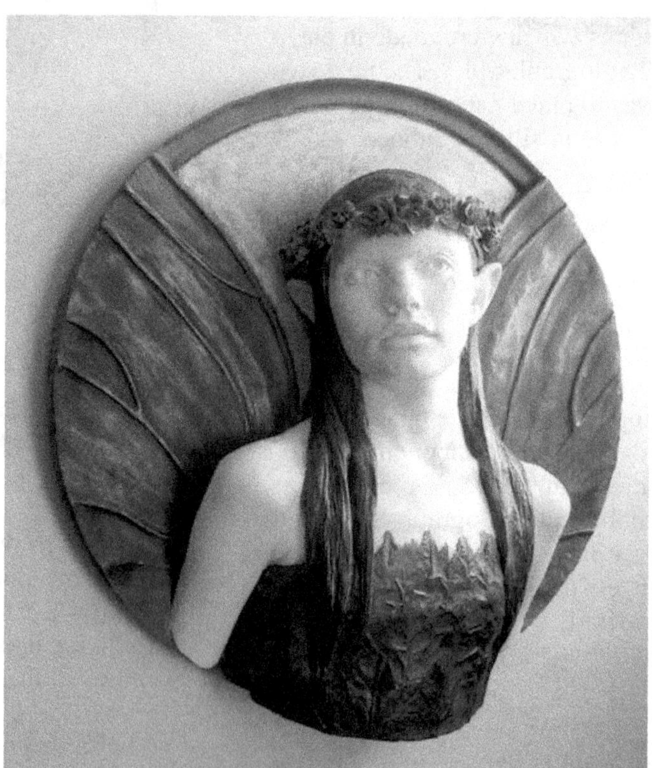

Photo #13

Faerie Magazine 2007

faerie portrait

By David E. Parvin, A.L.I.

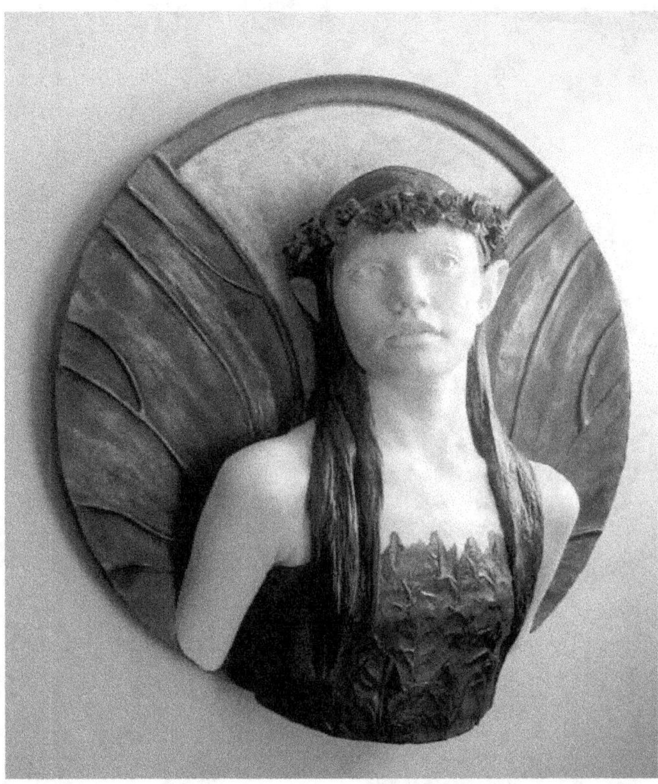

When Messier Daguerre invented the first relatively practical photographic process in the mid eighteen hundreds, many in the art world complained the it wasn't really art because the camera could only capture what was already there. In other words, there was nothing of the artist in the photograph. Though photography has long been recognized as art, the same criticism has been made of life casting. The very first article that I wrote for this magazine in April 2001 was titled "Life Casting, Fine Art or Cheating."(1) The work, "Caylie as a Faerie," is an example of how much of the artist really can come out in the art. The construction of this piece was described in an article of mine titled "Making a 3-D Faerie Portrait" that will appear in the spring issue of Faerie Magazine. If ten different artist had be told to cast Caylie and then turn her into a faerie, there would have been ten very different interpretations. Life casting is indeed alive and well as a method of individual artistic expression.

A detailed description of the construction of this piece will be in Faerie Magazine; but here is a brief summary. The original and unmodified life casting of human Caylie was made in plaster using FiberGel. Thirteen year old Caylie' s natural faerie looks helped with the transformation. The steps were to open her eyes, point the ears, sculpt in the wings, and add leaves for a dress and a flowers for a head band. After making a silicone rubber mold, the final enhanced portrait was cast in Forton MG. The white flesh parts are FMG plus powdered limestone. The light blue area around and over her head is the same but with a little blue dye. The leaves, wings, hair, and molding at the top are FMG with copper powder. "Super Antique 40" was used to turn the hair black. A green patina solution of my own making, a solution ammonium chloride and cupric chloride, was used on the leaves and wings. The garland is a string of artificial flowers dipped into FMG mixed with brass powder. All parts except the garland were buffed with either a white or a brown buffing compound.

Faerie Magazine has a circulation of almost 30,000 which means that after the spring issue comes out, a whole bunch of people,mostly new, will have been exposed to life casting.

For an email of "Life Casting, Fine Art or Cheating?" contact me at parvinstudio@comcast.net.

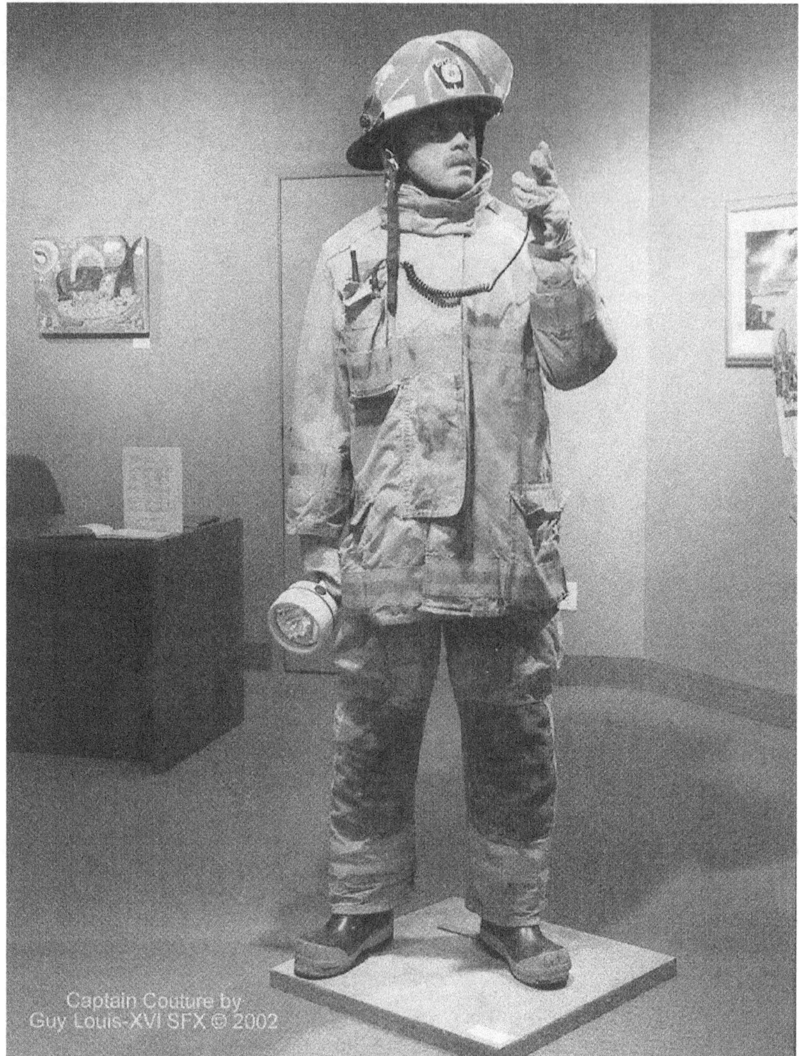

Guy Louis - XVI
Master of Ultra Realism

By David E. Parvin A.L.I.

I well remember being new to sculpting and often wondering, "How was that done?" With experience, the mysteries of sculpting, modeling, and casting became more understood. While I am always delighted to come across excellence, it had been some time since I had wondered about the process, that is, until I met Guy Louis-XVI.

His figures are so ultra realistic that I was forced to admit that I had only a very vague and partial understanding of how he does it.

I first met Guy at a convention for motion picture make-up and special effects artists in Pasadena, CA last year. He was demonstrating some of his techniques in one of the supplier's booths. He had on display a copy of the head of a Johnny Carson mannequin that he had made for a museum in Carson's hometown of Norfolk, NE. I was so impressed and intrigued that I asked if I could visit him at work in Ottawa, Ontario, Canada. I suspect that Guy probably gets that request often but almost never has the person show up on his door step. As it turned out, I had a reason to be in Ottawa a few months later and gave him a ring. He renewed his invitation.

Before going any further, let me mention a couple things about his name and his background. Guy is pronounced "Gee." Louis -XVI really is his last name. He uses the Roman numerals rather than spelling out "the Sixteenth." Guy was born in 1954 and grew up in the small town of Rockland, Ontario. Talented from the get-go, he began at 13 a career in sign writing. Over the years, he learned fiber glass lamination, mold making, casting, and welding. Fascinated by special effects, in 1988 he began experimenting in his basement with special effects techniques and dreaming of career in the motion picture industry. In 1993, he quit a job as a welder and enrolled in a professional makeup course. He became a special effects makeup artist and an expert in life casting to produce latex, silicone and gelatin prosthetics. He went to work in films and commercials. "I was the guy (or the "Gee") they'd call when they needed a throat slashed or a kidney surgery," he says. He also did make-up work over some 3000 customers for a photography studio. "That was the best thing I ever did," says Guy. "I got to look at and analyze people. I was able to look at facial features up close - the skin and the way it folds, the color of the eyes." In the mid 1990's Guy was asked by a friend to make a mannequin for a show sponsored by a company that manufactures exhibits for museums. This led to commissions from the Canadian Wax Museum and, "I was off to the races." Entering Guy's suburban house is a delight. Not only is he very friendly, but he is eager to show off examples of his work from complete figures to a gutted salmon, a severed hand, a human heart, etc. Faces are the most critical part of his work. Sometimes he begins with a life casting and other times he sculpts from scratch.

It doesn't make any difference, both look equally realistic. In my opinion, there are three things that make him one of the very best in his field. The first is that his pieces really look like the persons that they represent. The second is his attention to detail e.g. hairs are applied individually, skin texture is perfect with no visible seams. The third and most amazing to me is the translucent quality of the skin.

I know from my own experience that even a reasonably accurately sculpted face can be painted to look life-like especially if seen from a distance or in photographs. But in real life, it lacks the translucency of actual skin. Figures in wax museums are better then painted bronze or resins but still have some features painted on the outside. Guy admits that something made for a motion picture does not have to be as perfect as something to be seen close up real life. Recently Guy had several mannequins in an art show. While the press covered the event, no mention was made of his work. At first this perplexed him and then he found out that the press had him and then he found out that the press had thought his pieces were mimes!

What Guy does is paint up to seven very thin layers of pigmented silicone rubber on the inside of a mold. "You lay your colors inside the mold and build up the skin, layer by layer," explains Guy. "It gives a depth of color like human skin. A vein is painted inside the skin where it is supposed to be, not painted on the outside." Eyes are so important to Guy that he makes his own which he sells to other artists who looking for perfection.

Most of Guy's commissions are for museums. However, some of his clients want mannequins of loved ones, personal heroes, or themselves. He has produced a youthful and glamorous Hedy Lamar for a collector in Illinois and a 13 year old version of a 61 year old client in Massachusetts. While Guy can, of course, create an entire lifelike body, most collectors and museums want only the exposed parts, i.e. head and hands, to be lifelike. The body is made of a lightweight steel frame covered with foam and fabric and then clothes. A finished mannequin weighs about 29 pounds. The cost can vary from as little as $4000 and up to $35,000 depending on the complexity and detail.

I have known artists that are very stingy with sharing their "secrets" for fear that someone else will become their competition. I suspect Guy is open and

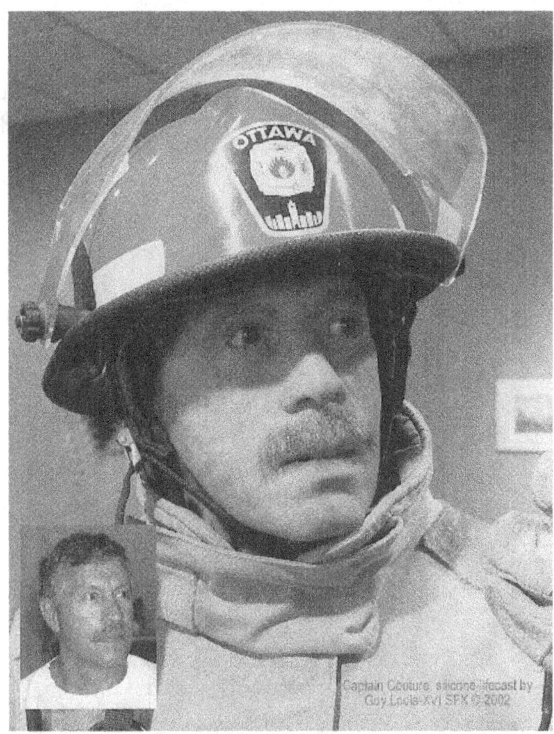

Captain Couture, Close up. Hi-tech silicone skin, life cast, private collection.

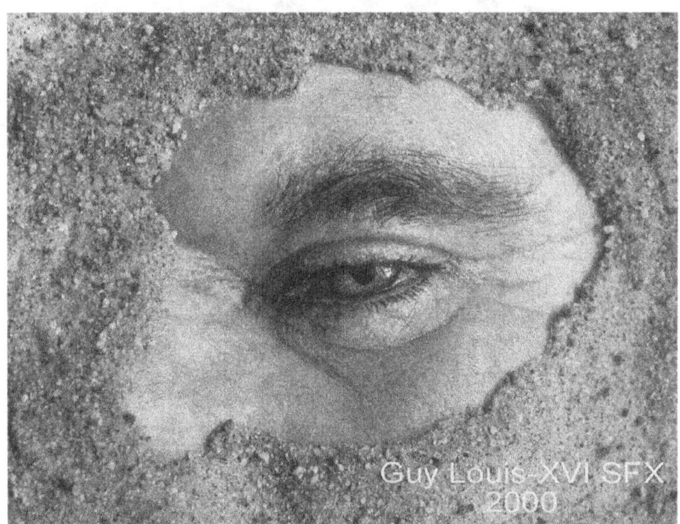

Split Char, museum prop, Cambridge Bay

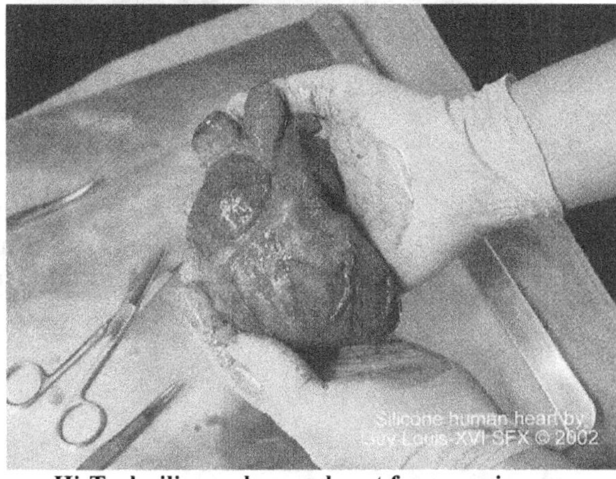

Hi-Tech silicone, human heart for a movie prop

forthcoming with the details of his methods because he well understands that knowing how something is done and doing it are entirely different. After all, Ansel Adams could have truthfully said that all he needed was an 8 x 10 camera and some very big rocks!

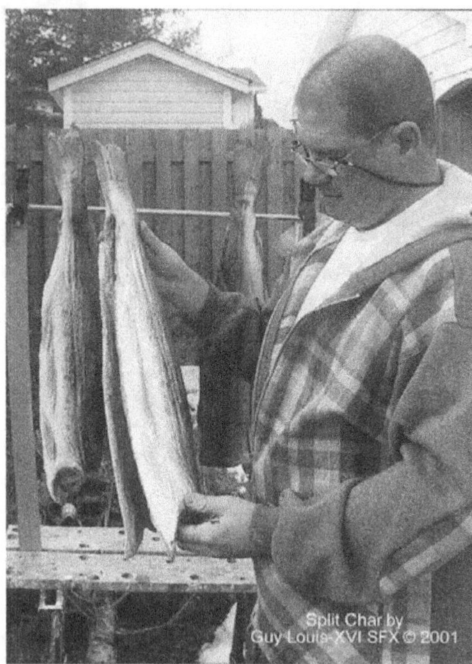

Curiosus, is a self-portrait (life cast) of myself, finished in silicone and other medium. City of Ottawa Gallery

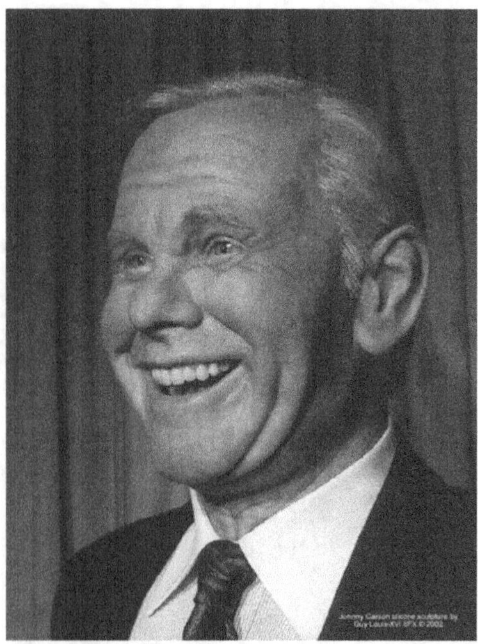

Johnny Carson, Hi-Tech silicone mannequin, sculpted from photographs, permanent exhibit, Elkhorn Museum, Norfolk, Nebraska.

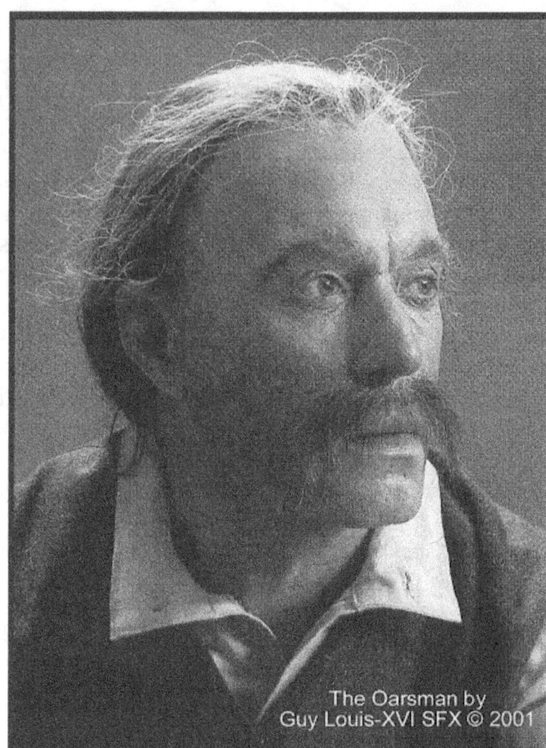

The Oarsman, Hi-Realism, Plaster/Resin composite mannequin. Life cast from live model. Founders Hall, Charlottestown, P.E.I.

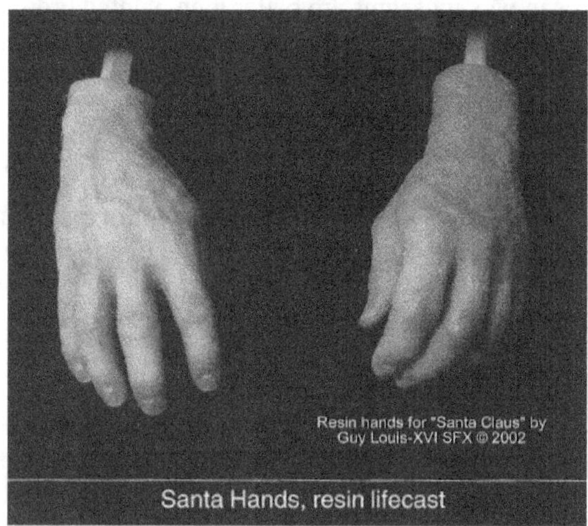

Santa Hands, resin lifecast

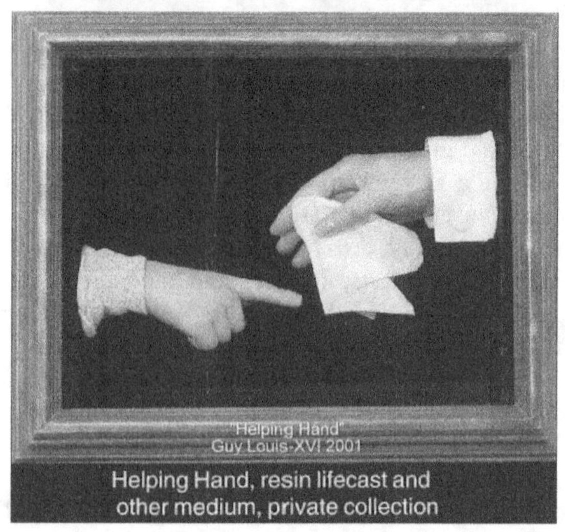

Helping Hand, resin lifecast and other medium, private collection

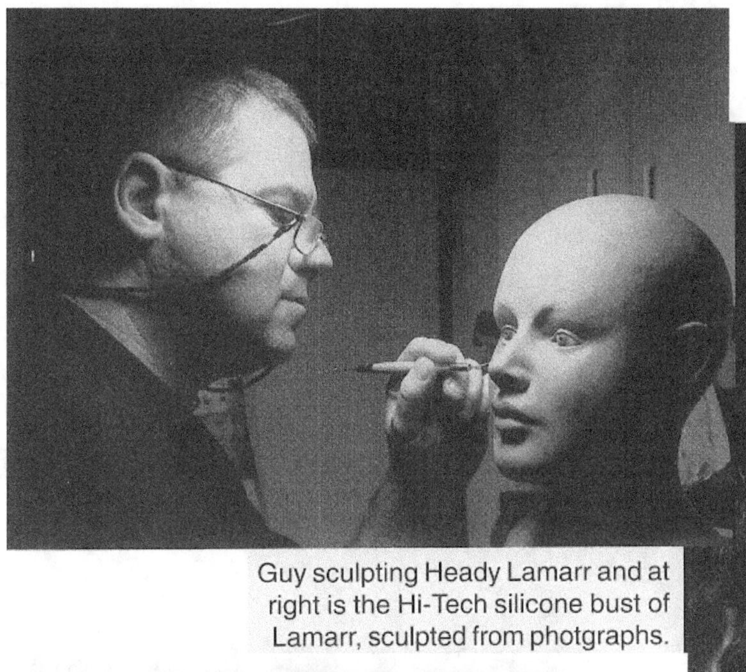

Guy sculpting Heady Lamarr and at right is the Hi-Tech silicone bust of Lamarr, sculpted from photgraphs.

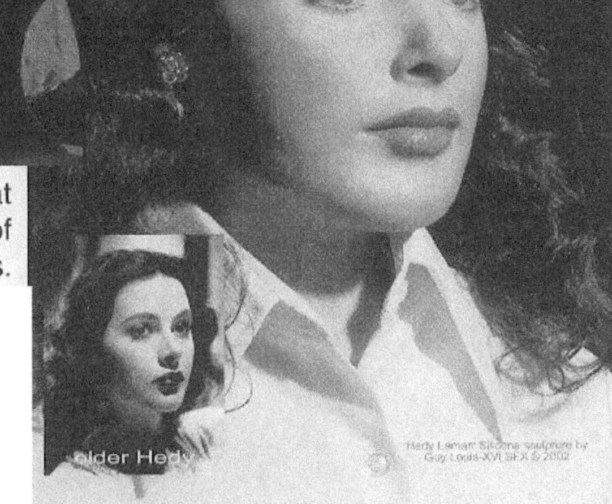

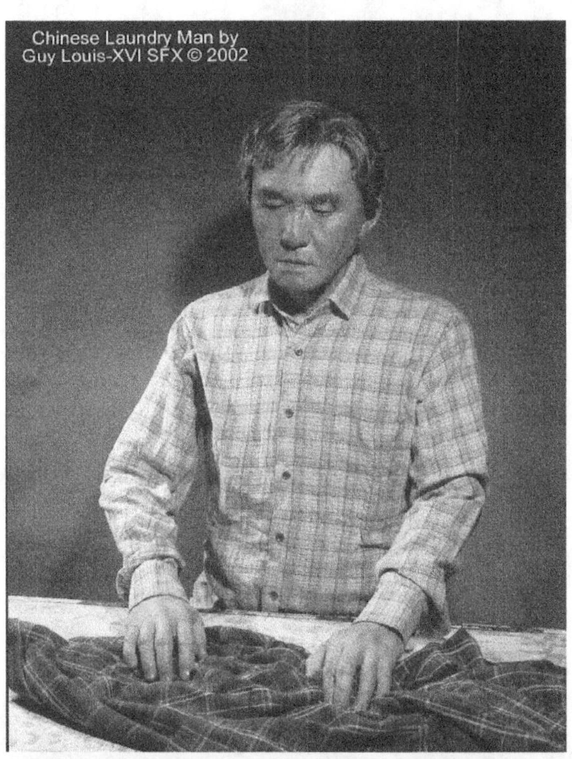

Chinese Laundry man, Hi-realism, Plaster/Resin composite mannequin depicting Chinese laundry in the early 1900's. This was done for the Canadian Museum of Civilization in Gatineau, Quebac, Canada.

For more information about Guy LouisXVI
and his work, he may be found at
www.louissvimannequins.com

Sculpture Journal April 2004

www.ingramcontent.com/pod-product-compliance
Lightning Source LLC
Chambersburg PA
CBHW080910170526
45158CB00008B/2060
* 9 7 8 0 6 9 2 4 5 4 7 3 2 *